CONTEMPORARY MORAL ISSUES

Second Edition

Wesley Cragg
Professor of Philosophy
Laurentian University

McGRAW-HILL RYERSON LIMITED

Toronto Montreal New York Auckland Bogotá
Cairo Hamburg Lisbon London Madrid Mexico Milan New Delhi Panama
Paris San Juan São Paulo Singapore
Sydney Tokyo

CONTEMPORARY MORAL ISSUES

Second Edition

ISBN: 0-07-549274-1

2 3 4 5 6 7 8 9 10   ML   6 5 4 3 2 1 0 9 8

Printed and bound in Canada.

Care has been taken to trace the ownership of copyrighted material
contained in this book. However, the publishers will welcome
information that enables them to rectify any reference or credit for
subsequent editions.

Canadian Cataloguing in Publication Data
Main entry under title:

Contemporary moral issues

Includes bibliographical references.
ISBN 0-07-549274-1

1. Social ethics. 2. Ethics. I. Cragg, Wesley.

HN110.Z9M66 1987   170   C86-094208-2

To my parents.

Contents

Preface to the Second Edition

Four years have come and gone since the first edition of *Contemporary Moral Issues*. A book of this sort needs periodic updating. It is gratifying, therefore, that *Contemporary Moral Issues* is now widely used and that as a result a second edition is justified.

Revising, I have discovered, is not an easy task. Some of the decisions have been painful. On the other hand, the increasing attention being paid to problems of applied ethics here in Canada has made the search for appropriate material a good deal easier. I have also been assisted by the cooperation and encouragement of colleagues and the editors of the journals to whom I have turned for assistance. I offer my thanks to all of these people.

Those familiar with the first edition will notice many changes. Yet much remains the same. The first three chapters required only minor alterations.

Comments by reviewers have led to the inclusion of Michael Tooley's article on *abortion* and infanticide. Since as we go to press the Supreme Court has not issued its judgement on the Morgentaler appeal against the new-trial decision of the Ontario Court of Appeal, that part of the abortion chapter has not changed.

In the chapter on *euthanasia*, one article has been deleted and one completely rewritten.

The topic of *capital punishment* remains important for Canadians, but the need to introduce new material elsewhere has led to a reduction of the number of articles in this chapter by two.

The chapter on *personal autonomy and the problem of mental illness* has been strengthened by the addition of two articles and the deletion of one.

Some changes have been made to the chapter on *censorship and the problem of pornography* to ensure that it reflects recent developments in the way this topic is discussed.

The scope of the chapter on *aboriginal rights* has been reduced to allow for a more detailed examination of the land claims issue.

The old chapter on uranium mining has been broadened into a discussion of *environmental ethics* generally.

I also made the difficult decision of dropping the chapter on moral education and substituting a new chapter on *nuclear deterrence and disarmament*.

Finally, an article has been added to the chapter on *philosophy and the resolution of moral issues*.

Throughout the process of revision, care has been taken to ensure that the positions discussed represent the wide range of views thoughtful observers of the Canadian scene would wish to examine. I hope the changes will please those who have contributed to the book, those looking for a text for instructional purposes, and students and other readers for whom the book has been prepared.

I would like to close with thanks to the editor, Rodney Rawlings, whose skillful assistance has done much to ensure a book of high quality. A special note of thanks is also due my wife Mary, who has had the difficult and time-consuming task of tracking down and corresponding with contributors, editors, and others, and who undertook to read the galleys and make corrections.

Note: In the articles I have indicated any editorial interpolations and deletions by means of brackets and ellipses in the usual manner.

Abortion

Introduction

Abortion is a complex moral issue. It affects both women who have become pregnant and women who, though not pregnant, wish to control their own fertility. Normally, it terminates the life that is aborted. It leads to questions about the status of newborn infants. The father is involved, as is the medical profession. And, finally, because procreation, the welfare of children, the family, and the rights and freedoms of individuals are affected, abortion concerns the whole community. Careful evaluation of the morality of abortion will introduce the concerns of each of these participants.

THE WOMAN

Background Considerations

With the development of reliable methods of birth control, having children has become widely viewed as a matter of choice and not a matter of necessity or obligation. But birth control is not always used; neither is it always effective. Advancements in medical science have resulted in the development of relatively safe abortion procedures. Many people now believe that if having children is really a matter of choice, the terminating of a pregnancy by abortion should, like the use of birth control, be a matter of choice.

Why might a woman seek an abortion? Sometimes the procedure is therapeutic. For example, the pregnancy might have become a threat to the life or health of the mother; it might be the result of rape or incest; or the mother may fear that she will be unable to cope with a child.

Sometimes the reason for wanting an abortion may centre on the child. It may simply be unwanted by the mother, or the parents may have concluded that there is a substantial risk the child will be born with severe handicaps — retardation, for example, or physical deformity.

Finally, abortion may be requested for what might be called reasons of convenience. Either the pregnancy or parenthood may conflict with the lifestyle of one or the other parent. Or amniocentesis may indicate that the child that has been conceived is not of the desired sex.

This list of reasons for wanting an abortion is not exhaustive. And the types of reasons set out are not mutually exclusive. For example, a doctor might well conclude that if a woman is not given an abortion, the knowledge that she is carrying and will likely give birth to a retarded child may affect her mental health. In such a situation it might also be argued that a child born to a woman who is seriously disturbed by doubts about her ability to cope with an infant will suffer. Nevertheless, this list and grouping of reasons provides a starting-point for assessing the morality of abortion.

The Current Situation

Prior to 1969, abortion was prohibited by the Criminal Code. In 1969, the Code was amended to allow for therapeutic abortions. In 1970, 11,200 therapeutic abortions were performed — three for every 100 live births. By 1979 that number had risen to 65,135, or 17.8 abortions for every 100 live births. Since 1979, increases have been very small. In fact, in 1981, and again in 1983, the total number of abortions was less than that in the preceding year. In 1983, 61,800 therapeutic abortions were performed in Canadian hospitals, or 16.5 for every 100 live births.

In 1983, 66.1 percent of women having an abortion were single, 22.4 percent married, and the remaining 11.5 percent either separated, divorced, widowed, or living common law. By comparison, in 1975, 58.4 percent of women receiving an abortion were single, 31.4 percent were married, and 10.2 percent were either separated, divorced, widowed, or of unknown status.

In 1983, 0.8 percent of women receiving an abortion were under 15 years of age, 24.1 percent were 15–19, 33.3 percent were 20–24, 20.8 percent were 25–29, 12.6 percent were 30–34, 5.9 percent were 35–39, and 2 percent were 40 or over. By comparison, in 1975, 1.2 percent receiving an abortion were under 15, 30.1 percent were 15–19, 29.1 percent were 20–24, 19.4 percent were 25–29. Ten percent were 30–34, 6.4 percent were 35–39, and 3.1 percent were 40 years of age or older.

Finally, in 1975, 88.9 percent of those receiving an abortion were doing so for the first time, while in 1983, 78.7 percent had had no previous abortion.

To obtain a legal abortion in Canada, a woman must receive the approval of a hospital committee. Any hospital may create such a committee but there is no requirement that it do so.

Requests for abortion may be granted for therapeutic reasons only. That is, the pregnancy must constitute a threat to the physical or mental health of the woman seeking the abortion. What constitutes a threat to the physical or mental health of someone is subject to varying interpretations. It would seem that some committees in large urban centres interpret this requirement so broadly that an abortion is very easily obtained; some committees interpret the rule quite narrowly; and in those areas of the country where hospitals have not established committees, legal abortions are not available.

In 1979, the number of Canadian hospitals with therapeutic abortion committees reached a peak of 270. That number had declined to 257 in 1983.

In 1983, 19 percent of hospitals with committees performed no abortions; 43 percent performed between 1 and 100 abortions and contributed only 5.2 percent of the total abortions performed in Canada in that year. Of the remaining hospitals 24 percent performed between 100 and 400 abortions each, or 22 percent of total abortions performed. Thirty-eight hospitals, less than 15 percent of the hospitals with committees, performed over 400 abortions each and accounted for 72.8 percent of all therapeutic abortions performed in that year.

The fact that women seeking abortions must have the approval of a hospital committee has been vigorously criticized by those who believe that the decision to have an abortion should be left to the woman herself in consultation with her doctor. Others have argued that abortion is not a private matter and that the law regulating access to abortion is too vague and has opened the door to abortion on demand in some areas of Canada.

A second concern is that not all women have access to an abortion committee. It has been argued that this lack of equal access is unfair and points up the need for legal reform.

The Moral Dimension

The abortion issue, like a number of the issues to be examined in later chapters, raises two distinct but related questions. First, what is the morality of abortion? Second, should we prohibit by law abortions that the community believes are not morally justified? Much of our law reflects our moral values. Yet not everything we judge to be immoral is unlawful. For example, most of us would probably agree that, as a rule, promises should not be broken. Yet the law enforces only some promises and not others. Reasons for enforcing by law some moral values and not others will be explored in later chapters. For the moment, it is important to note simply that in exploring the morality of abortion we are faced with these two questions.

Let us consider here simply whether abortion is ever morally justified. One way of approaching this question is to evaluate the types of reasons that lead to a desire for an abortion. Is abortion ever justified for therapeutic reasons? If so, when is it justified, and why? Similar questions can be asked of the second and third kinds of reasons. And as these questions are answered, a view of the morality of abortion will begin to emerge.

THE UNBORN CHILD

Background Considerations

The life and welfare of a woman seeking to terminate an unwanted pregnancy are clearly central to a discussion of the morality of abortion. But there is a second life involved. Recent advances in medical science now allow us a remarkable view of the evolution of that life from conception to birth. Pregnancy commences with the union of a human male germ cell, called a *spermatozoon*, with a human female egg in the Fallopian tubes of the female. This union creates a single cell, which carries the full genetic code of a human being whose development is thus begun. Normally, it will take a period of two weeks for this single cell, called a *zygote*, to migrate to the uterus of the female and implant itself in the uterine wall. Throughout this period of migration, growth is rapid and continuous. Implantation marks the beginning of a second remarkable stage in human development. The zygote, now an embryo, is transformed, over a period of six weeks, from a structure of cells to a being that can be seen with the naked eye, that emits brain waves, and that has all the internal organs of a child or adult. What was an embryo is now a human fetus and will continue to grow and develop until, sometime between 12 and 16 weeks, the mother will begin to notice its activity, an event that is referred to as "quickening." At some point between 20 and 28 weeks the fetus will achieve *viability*, the capacity to survive independently of its biological mother. In the normal course of events, the mother will give birth at approximately 40 weeks from the date of conception.

Normally, abortion results in the termination of the life that commences with conception. In the first two-week period following conception, terminating a pregnancy can be achieved by ensuring that the zygote does not become embedded in the uterine wall. Medical techniques designed to achieve this outcome are similar, in many respects, to those designed to prevent pregnancy. Following implantation, and through the first nine weeks of pregnancy, abortions are performed by stretching the cervix and scraping the inner walls of the uterus. This procedure is called *dilation and curettage* (D&C). A second technique, called *uterine aspiration*, draws the fetus from the uterus by means of suction. In the first nine weeks, abortions can be performed with very little risk to the physical health of the mother.

In the later stages of pregnancy, abortions are performed by injecting a saline solution through the mother's abdominal wall. The injection will normally result in the death of the fetus and will induce labour. An alternative method is a hysterotomy (a miniature Caesarean section). A child aborted in this manner does not necessarily die during the operation. In fact, the operation differs from a Caesarean section mainly in *purpose* — the hysterotomy is performed to procure an abortion, the Caesarean as an alternative to natural childbirth.

The Current Situation

Of abortions performed in 1975, 22.4 percent occurred in the first eight weeks of pregnancy, 58.9 percent occurred between nine and twelve weeks, 13.3 percent between thirteen and sixteen weeks, 5.2 percent between sixteen and twenty weeks, and 0.2 percent after the twentieth week. By comparison, in 1983, 25.9 percent of abortions occurred in the first eight weeks of pregnancy, 61 percent occurred between nine and twelve weeks, 9.7 percent between thirteen and sixteen weeks, 3.2 percent between seventeen and twenty weeks, and 0.2 percent after the twentieth week.

One final point is worth mentioning: the law, strictly applied, does not permit an abortion simply to avoid giving birth to a handicapped child. But a broad interpretation of the abortion law does allow for this possibility. It would appear that abortions are indeed performed in Canada for reasons that centre on the child.

The Moral Dimension

Rules play a central role in our lives as human beings. They govern much of what we do and how we do it. One reason for the existence of rules is to provide an environment in which individuals can grow and mature without threat to their personal existence. Hence, some of our most important rules are designed to ensure our right to life and our access to needed sources of support and assistance. An unavoidable problem in the discussion of human development concerns the point at which we become members of the human community, with all the protection its system of rules is designed to ensure. The question might, at first glance, seem a simple one. Unfortunately, in this case, first glances are deceptive. Human development from conception to birth is gradual; there are no sudden qualitative changes clearly signalling that the unborn child is now a member of the human community. Indeed, even birth, though traumatic, generates no significant, sharp, qualitative changes in a child. And so we are left with a clear dilemma. Do the rules generated by the human community to offer a social environment in which human development can continue through childhood to adulthood extend to those who are not yet born? And, perhaps more importantly, should those rules be so extended?

There is a second ethical dimension to be considered as well. As we have seen, an abortion may be requested because the parents of the unborn child have discovered that their child, if born, will be handicapped in some way, and have concluded that, from the child's own point of view, it is better that it should not be born. Approaching abortion from this point of view creates serious moral tensions, similar in many respects to those raised by euthanasia and infanticide. Those concerned with the morality of abortion are faced with the challenge of resolving those tensions.

THE NEWBORN CHILD

Once born, the child is affected by our moral outlook on abortion. To begin with, we now know that the health, strength, and intelligence of a child are shaped in significant ways by the food a mother eats, the drugs she ingests, and the life she leads during the pregnancy. Providing an environment in which a newborn child can flourish may well require that we extend protection to that same child prior to its birth. As well, the justification for abortion may well open the door to infanticide. Indeed, many of the factors that lead some women to seek abortions operate after childbirth as well as before. Hence the child, once born, continues to be a consideration in judgements concerned with the morality of abortion.

Exploring these considerations is central to the contributions of Ian Gentles and E.W. Keyserlingk in the readings that follow.

THE FATHER

Currently, the consent of the father is not legally required to obtain an abortion. Yet the father is normally assumed to have a moral obligation to support the child he has fathered. Certainly, under current Canadian legislation, he has legal responsibilities to the child. And so we can ask whether the father of a child has a moral right to participate in any decision leading to abortion or to childbirth. If the father has no moral rights in this regard, is it fair to require him to share in the responsibilities of child-rearing?

THE MEDICAL COMMUNITY

Background Considerations

To a considerable degree, abortion as we usually encounter it today is a phenomenon made possible by advances in modern medicine. There are, of course, records of abortions and attempted abortions going back to the beginning of recorded time. However, it is only in this century that medical science has developed to the point where an abortion, properly performed, poses little risk to the life or health of the person seeking the abortion.

There is another side to the story, however. The knowledge that allows for relatively safe abortions has also provided the basis for remarkable developments in the field of fetal medicine. Sophisticated techniques exist for diagnosing genetic and other disorders; blood transfusions are possible; and fetal surgery both inside and outside the womb is now a reality.

Thus modern medicine has become a means for enhancing the quality of life of a child by intervening to correct problems prior to birth. But it has also become both a means for providing information that may well lead to a request for abortion and a means for procuring that abortion with a minimum of risk.

The Current Situation

Hospitals in Canada are permitted to perform abortions under the law if they so wish. Nurses working in hospitals that perform abortions do not have a legal right to refuse to participate in an abortion procedure on moral grounds. Doctors, on the other hand, are not required by law to perform abortions or to refer women who wish abortions to a doctor who will offer assistance. The Canadian Medical Association has taken the view, however, that ''an ethical physician, when his morality or religious conscience alone prevents him from recommending some form of therapy, will so acquaint the patient.'' It defines a therapeutic abortion as:

the termination of pregnancy prior to the twenty weeks' gestation. The Association believes that abortion should be reviewed as an elective surgical procedure to be decided on by the patient and physician(s) concerned and available to all women across Canada on an equitable basis. It has recommended, that all reference to hospital therapeutic abortion committees be removed from the Criminal Code.*

The Moral Dimension

The ethical considerations faced by the medical profession are similar, in many respects, to those that have already emerged. Do doctors have moral obligations to unborn children similar in nature to their obligations to other patients? If the interests of a mother are in conflict with those of the child she is carrying, whose interests should prevail? If undertaking an abortion, does the doctor have a moral obligation to use techniques most likely to result in a live birth? Or does the mother have a moral right to decide, where a live birth is possible, that it will or will not occur?

THE COMMUNITY

Background Considerations

Previous discussion describes why abortion is an individual issue. Why is it a social issue? Let me suggest two reasons, both of which have been already introduced from another perspective. First, it is a long-held view in our society that protecting human life is a central, morally obligatory task. We do not, as a rule, leave those whose lives are in danger to fend for themselves. It is also true that extending such protection to *all* human beings, regardless of such things as race, religion, or colour, has been a difficult and frequently unsuccessful struggle for Western civilization. The abortion debate, because of the problem of determining the point in human development at which someone acquires the status of an equal member of the community with the rights and protections that confers, evokes echoes of the age-old struggle for human rights. One reason that has been given for opposing abortion is that the welfare of many ''marginal'' (handicapped or sick or rejected) individuals might well be jeopardized by widespread access to and use of abortion procedures.

Second, all societies are inevitably involved in the creation of rules concerning procreation, child nurture, and child-rearing. In our society this concern takes the form of providing medical and other facilities for the care of women who are pregnant. Further, we have laws that govern the treatment of both mother and child before and after birth. In our society, caring for children is not the sole prerogative of the biological parents. Policies regarding abortion fit into this matrix of social concerns and so become the focus for debate and evaluation.

Canadian Medical Association Journal, Vol. 133, August 15, 1985.

The Current Situation

Abortion policy in Canada has been under vigorous debate for more than 25 years. Many groups oppose easy access to abortion. The stance of the Roman Catholic Church and the existence of "right-to-life" groups that include men and women with a variety of backgrounds, religious and otherwise, testify to this fact. At the same time many groups have argued for substantially relaxed laws on abortion—for example, the Canadian Bar Association, the Canadian Medical Association, the United Church of Canada, the Anglican Church of Canada, and a variety of women's groups, including the National Advisory Council on the Status of Women.

Controversy has continued into the 1980s, fuelled in part by efforts of Dr. Henry Morgentaler to challenge the law by opening private abortion clinics in Toronto and Winnipeg. Charged with conspiring to procure a miscarriage, Dr. Morgentaler and two colleagues were subsequently found Not Guilty in a jury trial in October 1984. The case then went to the Ontario Court of Appeal, which overturned the verdict and ordered a new trial. At the time of this writing, the case is before the Supreme Court of Canada. Until the legal issues involved are resolved by the Court, the case of Dr. Henry Morgentaler v. Her Majesty the Queen (excerpts of which are included in the readings) stands as the authoritative interpretation of current Criminal Code provisions on abortion.

Those provisions were designed to permit abortions, but only in limited numbers and only when the health of the mother was in jeopardy. They permit hospitals to perform abortions subject to the recommendation of a hospital committee. As the excerpts from the Morgentaler case show, procuring an abortion except in the manner laid down in the Criminal Code is against the law and, in theory at least, subject to severe penalties.

The Moral Dimension

As we have already seen, abortion generates two closely related but distinct groups of questions. The first has to do with the morality of abortion. Is abortion ever morally justified? If so, under what conditions? The second set of issues is concerned with whether access to abortion should be regulated by law.

For the discussion of abortion, as well as for the discussion of a number of other issues raised in later chapters, it is important that these be seen as distinct groups of questions. We prize our right to form our own moral assessments and to act on those assessments. Laws created to control human behaviour circumscribe individual liberty. Thus, limiting the freedom of individuals by creating laws is a moral issue in itself. Paradoxically, failing to limit freedom of choice can also limit the freedom of individuals. This is one of the reasons the creation of laws restricting individual liberty is sometimes a moral imperative. This paradox can be illustrated by the problem of abortion. The freedom to choose for oneself to have an abortion is a very significant one to many people. But the freedom accorded to adults in this area has a direct impact on the freedom of the child, as yet unborn, to grow and mature as he or she will if the pregnancy is not terminated.

These considerations bring us full circle. Is an unborn child a person? Does (or should) he or she fall under the protection of those moral and legal rules that are so important to the welfare of each of us?

The Readings

The readings in this chapter begin with extracts from two judgements rendered by members of the Supreme Court of Canada in the case of Dr. Henry Morgentaler v. Her Majesty the Queen. This case, which is a complex one from a number of points of view, is of interest to us in our discussion of the morality of abortion for two reasons. First, in his defence of the majority view of the Court that Morgentaler was guilty of performing an illegal abortion, Mr. Justice Dickson (as he then was) sets out and explains the abortion provisions of the Canadian Criminal Code. A view contrary to that of the majority is argued by the then Chief Justice of the Supreme Court, Bora Laskin, who, alone among the nine members of the Court, concluded that Dr. Morgentaler had not performed an illegal abortion. The judgement of the Chief Justice is of particular interest because it shows that the law is subject to different interpretations and because it provides a relatively lengthy description of the situation of a woman who decided that she wanted an abortion. The Chief Justice explains the reasons for her decision and the difficulties she encountered in achieving her objective.

The third reading, from the Criminal Code, describes when, for the purposes of the Code, a child becomes a human being.

Legal attitudes toward the unborn are not defined solely by criminal law. For this reason, our fourth reading sets out a judgement of the British Columbia Supreme Court concerned with child abuse. In that judgement, Madam Justice Proudfoot concludes that child abuse can occur prior to birth. And she implies that the court is entitled to intervene in such cases with a view to protecting the unborn child. This judgement, combined with the criminal-law provisions already described, appears to generate an inconsistency in the law's view of the protection to which those who are not yet born are entitled. It is this apparent inconsistency that is the topic of discussion in the articles contributed by Ian Gentles and E.W. Keyserlingk.

The other four articles examine the morality of abortion directly. Michael Tooley argues that neither abortion nor infanticide are matters of moral concern inasmuch as neither fetuses nor very young infants have a right to life. Sheila and George Grant argue that access to abortion should be carefully limited. In their view, liberal abortion laws undermine respect for human life and our willingness to extend that respect to the very young and the old, those who are severely handicapped, and those who are in some way seriously stigmatized. L.W. Sumner attacks both the liberal and the conservative view. He argues that, early in the pregnancy, a human fetus is not a person. Hence, early abortions generate no serious moral objections. In later stages of pregnancy, however, a human fetus is a person and abortion does generate legitimate moral concerns.

In the final article, Grant Cosby argues that none of the available moral theories is capable of establishing by argument the point at which the unborn become persons. Thus, moral theory is not able to contribute to a resolution of a central issue in the debate: Is abortion infanticide?

Dr. Henry Morgentaler *v.* Her Majesty the Queen*

[A judgement of the Supreme Court of Canada]

Mr. Justice Dickson

It seems to me to be of importance, at the outset, to indicate what the Court is called upon to decide in this appeal and, equally important, what it has not been called upon to decide. It has not been called upon to decide, or even to enter, the loud and continuous public debate on abortion which has been going on in this country between, at the two extremes, (i) those who would have abortion regarded in law as an act purely personal and private, of concern only to the woman and her physician, in which the state has no legitimate right to interfere, and (ii) those who speak in terms of moral absolutes and, for religious or other reasons, regard an induced abortion and destruction of a foetus, viable or not, as destruction of a human life and tantamount to murder. The values we must accept for the purposes of this appeal are those expressed by Parliament, which holds the view that the desire of a woman to be relieved of her pregnancy is not, of itself, justification for performing an abortion.

The jurisdiction of the Court is limited by s. 618(2) of the *Criminal Code*, pursuant to which this appeal has been brought, to questions of law. The legal question now before us is whether, in answer to the charge of unlawfully procuring the miscarriage of a female person, the appellant can raise as defences (i) s. 45 of the *Criminal Code*; (ii) necessity. The trial judge held that both of these defences were available and charged the jury to that effect. The jury returned a verdict of not guilty. The Crown appealed to the Court of Appeal of the Province of Quebec and five judges of that Court were unanimous in holding that neither defence should have been left to the jury. Accordingly the Court of Appeal acted under s. 613(4) of the *Code* which empowers it, where the appeal is from an acquittal, to enter a verdict of guilty with respect to the offence of which, in its opinion, the accused should have been found guilty but for the error in law. The position, therefore, in the

---

By permission of the Minister of Supply and Services Canada.

*Editor's Note: Technical and legal argument has been edited out of this extract. The points at which material has been edited out are indicated here and throughout this volume by ellipses.

present appeal is simply this: If the Court of Appeal is correct and neither of the two defences is open to the appellant, the guilty verdict must stand; if one of the two defences is open, the appellant in my opinion is entitled to a new trial; if both defences are open, the jury's verdict of acquittal should be reinstated.

Before considering possible defences it may be appropriate to observe that since Confederation, and indeed before, the law of Canada has regarded as criminal, interference with pregnancy, however early it may take place; in 1969, the law was to some extent modified to exclude from criminal sanction abortions for therapeutic reasons carried out in compliance with prescribed conditions. It should also be noted that the appellant admits having done the act with which he stands charged, procuring the abortion of Verona Parkinson. His response to that charge simply is that he had two defences, a statutory defence of s. 45 and a common-law defence of necessity, which the jury was entitled to consider. . . .

Section 251 of the *Criminal Code*, so far as relevant in these proceedings, reads:

> 251. (1) Every one who, with intent to procure the miscarriage of a female person, whether or not she is pregnant, uses any means for the purpose of carrying out his intention is guilty of an indictable offence and is liable to imprisonment for life.
>
> (2) Every female person who, being pregnant, with intent to procure her own miscarriage, uses any means or permits any means to be used for the purpose of carrying out her intention is guilty of an indictable offence and is liable to imprisonment for two years.
>
> (3) In this section, "means" includes
> > (a) the administration of a drug or other noxious thing,
> > (b) the use of an instrument, and
> > (c) manipulation of any kind.
>
> (4) Subsections (1) and (2) do not apply to
> > (a) a qualified medical practitioner, other than a member of a therapeutic abortion committee for any hospital, who in good faith uses in an accredited or approved hospital any means for the purpose of carrying out his intention to procure the miscarriage of a female person, . . . if, before the use of those means, the therapeutic abortion committee for that accredited or approved hospital, by a majority of the members of the committee and at a meeting of the committee at which the case of such female person has been reviewed, . . .
> > (c) has by certificate in writing stated that in its opinion the continuation of the pregnancy of such female person would or would be likely to endanger her life or health, and
> > (d) has caused a copy of such certificate to be given to the qualified medical practitioner. . . .
>
> (6) For the purposes of subsections (4) and (5) and this subsection . . . "therapeutic abortion committee" for any hospital means a

committee, comprised of not less than three members each of whom is a qualified medical practitioner, appointed by the board of that hospital for the purpose of considering and determining questions relating to terminations of pregnancy within that hospital.

Subs. (1) defines the offence. The offence is committed when a person uses any means for the purpose of carrying out his intention of procuring the miscarriage of a female person. The means adopted may include the administration of a drug or other noxious thing, or the use of an instrument or manipulation of any kind. The appellant openly admits using an instrument for the purpose of procuring the miscarriage of Verona Parkinson. Subs. (2) provides that a pregnant female person who uses any means or permits any means to be used for the purpose of procuring her miscarriage is guilty of an indictable offence. Subs. (4) is of the utmost importance to any medical practitioner contemplating the use of any means to procure the miscarriage of a female person. This subsection is intended to afford, and does afford, a complete answer and defence to those who respect its terms. The subsection requires: (1) That the person procuring the miscarriage be a qualified medical practitioner; (2) The medical practitioner must not be a member of a therapeutic-abortion committee for any hospital; (3) The medical practitioner must act in good faith; (4) The means used to procure the miscarriage must be used in a hospital accredited by the Canadian Council on Hospital Accreditation or approved by the provincial Minister of Health; (5) The hospital must have a therapeutic-abortion committee comprised of not less than three members, each of whom is a qualified medical practitioner, appointed by the board of that hospital for the purpose of considering and determining questions relating to terminations of pregnancy within that hospital; (6) The committee at a meeting must review the case of the female person; (7) The committee, by a majority of the members, must have agreed to the issuance of a certificate; (8) The certificate must be in writing and must state that in the opinion of the committee *the continuation of the pregnancy of such female person would or would be likely to endanger her life or health*; (9) The committee must cause a copy of the certificate to be given to the medical practitioner who intends to procure the miscarriage. It is only too obvious, on reading s. 251, that, first, Parliament regards procuring abortion as a grave crime which carries with it the same maximum penalty as non-capital murder; second, Parliament has recognized that continuation of pregnancy may endanger the life or health of a pregnant woman, and has, therefore, made provision whereby pregnancy may be terminated by a qualified medical practitioner in an accredited or approved hospital; third, and for the purposes of the present case, of paramount importance, the decision whether or not to terminate the pregnancy is not that of the doctor who intends to perform the operation but of at least three of his peers, specially appointed to consider and determine questions relating to terminations of pregnancy; fourth, Parliament has not embodied in s. 251 a section similar to s. 1(4) of the English *Abortion Act* which relieves the medical practitioner of the need for independent medical opinions and a hospital setting prior to terminating a pregnancy in

> . . . a case where he is of the opinion, formed in good faith, that the termination is immediately necessary to save the life or to prevent grave

permanent injury to the physical or mental health of the pregnant woman.

Counsel for the appellant would have us write into s. 251 a like dispensing provision, though Parliament has not chosen to legislate it. Whether one agrees with the Canadian legislation or not is quite beside the point. Parliament has spoken unmistakably in clear and unambiguous language. The starting point for proper judicial analysis of the legal position of appellant is the statute. Justice must be done within the framework of, and according to, the rules set out in the *Criminal Code*.

. . . in answer to the question: "Was there any legal way out?" I think one must say that evidence from which a jury could conclude it was impossible for the appellant to comply with the law is wholly wanting. The plain fact is that the appellant made no attempt to bring himself within the bounds of legality in deciding to perform this abortion. . . .

I would dismiss the appeal.

Dr. Henry Morgentaler *v.* Her Majesty the Queen*

[A dissenting opinion of the Supreme Court of Canada]

Chief Justice Bora Laskin

. . . I turn now to the facts of the present case and to the legal issues raised by those facts under the Criminal Code. The appellant was charged with performing an illegal abortion on August 15, 1973 upon a twenty-six-year-old unmarried female who had come to Canada from a foreign country in 1972 on a student visa. She was without family or close friends in Canada, ineligible to take employment and also ineligible for Medicare benefits. On becoming apprehensive of possible pregnancy in July, 1973, she consulted a physician in general practice who referred her to a gynecologist. He confirmed that she was pregnant, but refused assistance to procure an abortion. On her own initiative she canvassed five Montreal hospitals by telephone and learned that if an abortion was to be performed she would have to bear the fees of a surgeon and an anaesthetist, and could envisage two or three days' hospitalization at $140.00 per day. This was far beyond her means.

Throughout the period following her apprehension and the confirmation of her pregnancy and until the abortion performed by the appellant, she was anxious, unable to eat or sleep properly, prone to vomiting and quite depressed. Her condition had an adverse effect upon her studies and it was aggravated by her being told that the longer she delayed in having an abortion the more dangerous it would be.

By permission of the Minister of Supply and Services Canada.

Editor's Note: What follows also does not include technical and legal argument.

One hospital offered her an appointment (which would result in her case coming before the therapeutic-abortion committee) at the end of August, 1973 when she would be eight to ten weeks pregnant. She got in touch with the appellant at the suggestion of a hospital or hospitals that she had contacted. There is some discrepancy between her evidence and that of the appellant as to the scope and nature of the conversation between them when she visited his clinic where the abortion was performed. In this appeal I think it proper to accept the evidence of the appellant who testified that his discussion with her went beyond asking whether she had previously had an abortion, when she realized she was pregnant and what his fee would be. He asserted that the conversation also encompassed reference to her country of origin, her vocation, her marital status and why an abortion was necessary. During the conversation the appellant said that he assessed the necessity of an abortion by reference to her state of anxiety, her inability to eat or sleep properly and the consequent adverse effect on her physical health. He also considered that her determination to have an abortion might lead her to do something foolish. The appellant was aware that his patient had approached a number of hospitals without success, but did not know that she had been offered an appointment at the end of August, 1973.

The appellant's competence to perform the abortion was unquestioned. I do not think that the fact that he has performed numerous abortions should have any adverse bearing on any defence that was open to him in this case. As a competent surgeon, the fact of his specialization should make it more likely than not that he would be in a better position than a non-specialist to determine, relative to a patient's state of pregnancy and to her state of physical and mental health, whether abortional surgery should be carried out at the particular time. The trial Judge stated in imposing sentence upon the appellant (as directed by the Quebec Court of Appeal when it set aside the jury's acquittal and entered a conviction) that there was substantial evidence at the trial that had this woman gone to an accredited hospital, she would have received the approval of a therapeutic-abortion committee to have an abortion performed, but, of course, it was merely speculation whether she would in fact have received such approval. In short, according to the trial Judge, there was evidence upon which the therapeutic-abortion committee could conclude that the continuation of her pregnancy would or would be likely to endanger her life or her health, but that did not mean that it would so conclude. Since she would have been eight to ten weeks pregnant when her case might have come before the therapeutic-abortion committee at the end of August, 1973, and since the decision might not have been made promptly or might have been adverse, the question of likely danger to health if not also to life would not be an idle one. . . .

In my opinion, there was . . . evidence of the accused that he feared that the pregnant woman would do something foolish unless she was given immediate professional medical attention to relieve her condition and her anxiety. The jury was entitled, if it so chose, to consider this evidence as raising an emergency situation in the light of the fact that the woman was a friendless stranger in this country, adrift more or less in an unfamiliar urban locality. It was for the jury to say whether in such circumstances the harm sought to be avoided by performing the abortion was an immediate and physical one . . . and whether there was enough of an emergency in this respect facing the accused as to make it certain that there could be no effective resort to the machinery of s. 251(4) to cope with the emergency.

I need hardly say that the sufficiency of evidence on any issue is a matter for the jury, which alone is charged to accept what it chooses and to weigh what it accepts in the light of the law given to it by the trial Judge. The jury discharged this function in this case; and once it is decided, as in my opinion is the case here, that there was evidence to go to the jury on the two defences which, again in my opinion, were properly left to the jury, the jury's verdict is not one which can be lightly interfered with by an appellate court.

In the result, I would allow the appeal, set aside the conviction registered by the Quebec Court of Appeal and restore the jury's verdict of acquittal.

Questions

1. In your view, was Dr. Morgentaler justified in performing an abortion in this case?
2. Is a law that allows women in some parts of Canada easier access to abortion than women in other parts of Canada morally equitable?
3. Does Canada's abortion law allow for abortion on eugenic grounds?

Section 206 of the Criminal Code

206. (1) A child becomes a human being within the meaning of this Act when it has completely proceeded, in a living state, from the body of its mother whether or not
  (a) it has breathed,
  (b) it has an independent circulation, or
  (c) the navel string is severed.
(2) A person commits homicide when he causes injury to a child before or during its birth as a result of which the child dies after becoming a human being.

Judgment Respecting Female Infant "D.J."

[A finding of the Supreme Court of British Columbia]

Madam Justice Proudfoot

The facts are as follows: On December 10th, 1981 a female infant known as "D.J." was born to Barbara McDonald. Barbara McDonald is now 25 years of age. Since the age of 12 she has been addicted to heroin. The evidence is in the last two years she has been on and off methadone as a replacement for heroin. According to the evidence she has not been an exemplary methadone-maintenance person because she has taken other drugs besides methadone according to Dr. Sydney Segal.

In August, 1981, when the mother was halfway through her pregnancy (with the baby known as "D.J.") she consulted Dr. Sydney Segal as her pediatrician for the first time. He had seen her for a previous pregnancy and actually had been treating her since 1977. Dr. Segal's evidence given at the initial hearing and in the Affidavits filed March 8th, 1982 goes on to say that regrettably her consultation with him commenced too late in the pregnancy. She was unable to go off methadone completely without injury to the baby she was carrying.

The evidence is that after the first trimester of pregnancy, complete withdrawal from methadone can cause stresses to the fetus. Such stresses can cause damage and can even cause death of the fetus. It seems it was necessary to maintain the methadone dosage through the remainder of the pregnancy. Dr. Segal referred Barbara McDonald to Dr. Bernard Whitman, an obstetrician at the Vancouver General Hospital. Seemingly after the dosage of methadone had been decided upon by him Barbara McDonald was turned over to Dr. J.J. Lederman for obstetrical care. Dr. Lederman was in charge of the whole case at that point and ultimately referred the case to Dr. Joe Bensimon. Dr. Joe Bensimon had the case from December 10th, 1981 to January 6th, 1982. On December 10th, 1981 "D.J." was born drug-addicted. "D.J." was given opium on December 14th, 1981 to assist in the withdrawal process. The opium was increased gradually then decreased. On January 3rd, 1982 the administering of opium was stopped. On January 6th, 1982 Dr. Segal states he was consulted because of his experience with drug-withdrawal babies and he took over the case again on January 6th, 1982. Dr. Segal is considered an authority on "neonatal withdrawal syndrome" and I accept him as an expert in that field. I might say his expertise was not challenged. Dr. Segal immediately started the baby again on the opium because the child was still showing strong signs of withdrawal and the baby received regular doses of opiates until January 27th, 1982.

The baby demonstrated the effects of withdrawal with the following severe physical symptoms: Incessant, inconsolable crying, vomiting, inability to sleep, twitching, reluctance to feed, poor sucking performance, irritability, resistance to being held, explosive diarrhea, profuse sweating, jittery limbs, barking cough, physical tension and squirming. The diarrhea was of special concern, because if not corrected the resultant water loss could lead to shock and death. In addition, the baby developed severe anemia, which continues to be a danger.

The evidence goes on to say that the baby now at approximately 4 months is still withdrawing from addiction as methadone stays in the tissues, particularly in the brain, for about 6–7 months. In his Affidavit Dr. Segal deposes that the infant goes through the same withdrawal syndrome as an adult and experiences extreme spasms in the stomach, excruciating pain and vomiting. The baby requires, because of the drug addiction and the subsequent withdrawal process, very careful treatment and monitoring as an "at-risk" infant.

The evidence is the baby requires careful nutritional maintenance as drug-addicted babies require twice the calories of a normal child for brain and organ growth. The severe anemia requires close observation by experienced personnel for symptoms of further withdrawal or infection. The baby requires daily weighing and skilled personnel to assess the conduct of the withdrawal process and to determine whether the level of stress in the home is such that a child is in danger of abuse or neglect.

Counsel for the Superintendent puts before me two issues:

1. Whether an unborn child can be abused—can there be abuse during the gestation period?
2. Can there be anticipatory abuse or neglect? Is there evidence of a clear and imminent danger to this child "D.J."?

From the evidence before me of the physical problems that a baby born drug-addicted has to endure it would be incredible to come to any other conclusion than that a drug-addicted baby is born abused. That abuse has occurred during the gestation period. While the Provincial Court seems to have dwelled on para. (c) as the basis for the refusal of the order, and I have said earlier that para. (a) was probably the more appropriate section, to me it makes very little difference on this application. "D.J." was born abused. Since immediately after birth, she has undergone severe physical pain during the withdrawal process. She continues to suffer from pain and, in addition, is susceptible to a myriad of life-threatening health problems. Her safety and well being has been and continues to be endangered.

"D.J." falls within the definition under s. 1 as "a child in need of protection" as would any other child born drug-addicted. The Provincial Court Judge seemed to relate the "is" in that section to the necessity of the child actually living in the home and events which might occur thereafter. There is no such necessity required; the child is born having been abused.

I find some support for my conclusion and the concept of abuse of the unborn child in the recent Ontario decision of *In the Matter of: The Children's Aid Society District of Kenora AND In the Matter of: Janis L.* wherein Bradley, P.C.J. in September of 1981 dealt with a baby suffering from "fetal alcohol syndrome." In that Judgment I note that there was evidence of some similar symptoms suffered by Janis L. as was suffered by "D.J." in the case before me. At p. 4 Bradley, P.C.J. says the following:

> He noted that, at birth, the baby was jittery, restless, had alcohol withdrawal symptoms, and alcohol in the blood while in the nursery. He treated the baby, Janis L., for the fetal alcohol syndrome.
>
> Doctor Beveridge stated that a fetal alcohol-damaged infant would most likely occur during the first trimester of pregnancy but that this could occur at any time during pregnancy.
>
> The evidence of Doctors Beveridge and Harlund establish that, on the balance of probabilities, Janis L., at birth, was suffering from the alcohol syndrome, which required medical treatment.
>
> In determining that the child was a child in need of protection prior to birth, I have considered the opinion of His Honour Judge David M. Steinberg in his text entitled *Family Law in the Family Courts* (Carswell, 1981, Vol. 1, 2nd ed.). At page 112, he states that the Child Welfare

Act does not preclude a finding that a child *"en ventre sa mère"* is in fact a child for the purpose of the Act. In reaching that opinion, he considered the definition of a child [as given in] s. 19(1)(a) and s. 6(2)(g) of the Child Welfare Act, which sets out the objects of each society.

The Unborn Child in Civil and Criminal Law

Ian Gentles

There exists today a grotesque contradiction at the heart of our legal system as it touches the unborn child. On the one hand, the unborn child enjoys the right to inherit property; she* can sue for injuries inflicted while in the womb; and she has the right to be protected from abuse or neglect by her mother. On the other hand, she no longer enjoys that right which is the indispensable precondition of the exercise of all her other rights — the right not to be killed. How has this contradiction come about? Is there any way it can be resolved?

To begin answering these questions we shall review briefly the status of the unborn child in the legal traditions of Western civilization. An interesting fact is that from the earliest times, protection of the unborn has never been a merely Judeo-Christian idiosyncrasy. Many centuries before Christ, the Sumerians, the Assyrians, and the Hittites protected prenatal human life in their legal codes.[1] The oath framed for physicians by the Greek doctor Hippocrates in the fourth century BC was well-known for its pledge "not to give a deadly drug to anyone if asked for it, nor to suggest it. Similarly, I will not give to a woman an abortifacient pessary. In purity and holiness I will guard my life and my art." The authorities on the English common law, from Bracton in the thirteenth century through Coke in the seventeenth century to Blackstone in the eighteenth, all treated abortion as a crime.[2] Blackstone summed up the law's position in the second half of the eighteenth century in the following words:

> Life is the immediate gift of God, a right inherent by nature in every individual; and it begins in contemplation of law as soon as an infant is able to stir in the mother's womb. For if a woman is quick with the child, and by a potion or otherwise killeth it in her womb; or if any one beat her, whereby the child dieth in her body and she is delivered of a dead child, this, though not murder, was by the ancient law homi-

This paper appeared in an earlier version in Eugene Fairweather and Ian Gentles, eds., *The Right to Birth* (Toronto: Anglican Book Centre, 1976).

*I have referred to the unborn child as "she" and "her" throughout this essay, as a reminder that at least half the victims of abortion are female.

cide or manslaughter. But the modern law doth not look upon this offence in quite so atrocious a light, but merely as a heinous misdemeanour.[3]

There is a vivid illustration of the law's concern for the unborn child in the Salem witch trials. In the summer of 1692 six people were found guilty of witchcraft and promptly sentenced to death. On August 19 of that year all but one—a certain Elizabeth Proctor—were hanged. Taking refuge in a custom honoured by the common law, goodwife Proctor pleaded pregnancy. Her execution was accordingly stayed until such time as her child should have been born, on the ground, as the historian of these events has put it, "that the child she was carrying was an innocent person." Happily, even after her child was born, the sentence against Elizabeth Proctor was allowed to lapse and she lived out her natural life.[4]

With their primitive medical knowledge, the jurists of the pre-modern period did not believe that it was possible to speak of an abortion before the time of quickening (i.e., the time when the mother feels the child move in her womb). Since human life did not evidently come into existence before quickening, there could not be a law against destroying it before that time. However, this anomaly was abruptly eliminated in 1803, when a law was passed making abortion a felony at any time during pregnancy.[5] This law was inherited by Canada and remained unaltered until 1969. In that year the law was amended to make an abortion permissible in cases when a three-member hospital abortion committee deemed that continuation of the pregnancy would endanger the life or health of the mother. Four years later, the United States Supreme Court swept away all criminal legislation against abortion in that country in the historical decision in *Roe v. Wade* (January 22, 1973).

The trend throughout the world in the past fifteen years towards eliminating legal hindrances against abortion is in striking contrast to the growing recognition of the civil rights of the unborn child. As recently as the end of the last century, Chief Justice Holmes in the United States had declared that the unborn child had no rights in a court of law, since he was merely a part of his mother, and not, legally speaking, a person.

This statement disregarded the fact that the unborn child's right to inherit had already been established in English common law as early as 1798, at which time it was declared that whenever it would be for his benefit, the child in the womb "shall be considered as absolutely born."[6] The first Canadian case to overturn the prevalent view expressed by Holmes was *In Re Charlton Estate* (1919). A certain Charlton had left a sum of money to be divided among "all the living children" of his brother. A child who was born three and a half months after Charlton died subsequently sued for a share of the estate, asserting that he was living at the time of his uncle's death. The Manitoba Court of King's Bench upheld the suit on the ground that a gift to "all living children" included the child who was in his mother's womb ("*en ventre sa mère*") at the time.[7]

The same principle was upheld in another case the following year. A certain Mrs. Giddings successfully sued the Canadian Northern Railway for negligence in the death of her husband, a locomotive fireman. In addition to the damages she won for herself, the court also awarded her child $6,000, even though he was unborn at the time of his father's death. The fact that he was unborn was judged to be "immaterial so long as the action is for the benefit of the child."[8]

These two cases influenced many other decisions, with the result that the unborn child's right to inherit and own property is now clearly recognized.

The much more difficult question of the unborn child's right to compensation for injuries suffered in the womb has also been decisively settled in this century in the child's favour. The Supreme Court of Canada seems to have set the standard for the rest of the English-speaking world by its momentous decision in the case of *Montreal Tramways v. Léveillé* (1933).[9] The court recognized that in 1933 "the great weight of judicial opinion in the common-law courts denies the right of a child when born to maintain an action for prenatal injuries." Nevertheless, it boldly reversed judicial precedent by declaring that a child who suffers injury while in its mother's womb as the result of a wrongful act or default of another has the right, after birth, to maintain an action for damages for its prenatal injury. Judge Lamont justified the rejection of precedent in this case on the basis of the following principle:

> If a child after birth has no right of action for prenatal injuries, we have a wrong inflicted for which there is no remedy. . . . If a right of action be denied to the child it will be compelled, without any fault on its part, to go through life carrying the seal of another's fault and bearing a very heavy burden of infirmity and inconvenience without any compensation therefor.

The principle laid down by Judge Lamont was confirmed in 1972 in *Duval et al. v. Séguin et al.*[10] The child of Thérèse Duval was permanently handicapped, both physically and mentally, as a direct result of a car accident which occurred while she was *en ventre sa mère*. In deciding in favour of the child, the judge quoted Lord Atkin's dictum: "The rule that you are to love your neighbour becomes, in law, you must not injure your neighbour." Although the unborn child was to be regarded as the "neighbour" of the negligent driver, the judge declined to state whether the child was a person in law, or at which stage she became a person.

In the case of *Watt v. Rama* in the Supreme Court of Victoria in the same year, there was no such reluctance to recognize the unborn child as a legal person.[11] The plaintiff, Sylvia Watt, had suffered brain damage and epilepsy as a result of a car accident involving her mother when the mother was two months pregnant. The defence argued that a two-month-old fetus was merely part of her mother and therefore not entitled to legal protection. The judge rejected the plea, observing that there was no essential difference between a newborn child and a child not yet born.

> As its property, real or personal, is protected, so should its physical substance be similarly protected by deeming it to be a person in being and imposing a duty of care on any other person not to commit any act of carelessness which as a reasonable man he should anticipate would injure the physical substance of the unborn child.

The judge concluded by affirming that, for the purpose of protecting her interests, Sylvia Watt was deemed to be a person at the time of the collision — two months after conception — and was thus entitled to compensation for the injuries she had suffered at that time.

The progress of the civil law in recognizing the personhood of the unborn child is trenchantly summarized by William L. Prosser, the dean of American tort law. Before 1946, he points out, most American authorities were agreed that the child could not sue for prenatal injuries. However, the situation was transformed so rapidly in the next quarter of a century that "it is now apparently literally true that there is no authority left still supporting the older rule." Furthermore, "all writers who have discussed the problem have joined in condemning the old rule, in maintaining that the *unborn child in the path of an automobile is as much a person in the street as the mother*, and in urging that recovery should be allowed upon proper proof" (emphasis added).[12]

One problem has not yet been resolved: whether the child has to be born alive in order for a suit to be entered on her behalf. Prosser believes that the trend is in the direction of holding that the child does not have to be born alive.[13] This would seem to be a logical conclusion, since it is hard to see why one should be less liable for destroying a child's life than for merely causing her to be injured. Indeed, a large number of recent cases in American courts have ruled not only that the unborn child is a person, but that an action for the wrongful death of an unborn child is maintainable even when she is stillborn.[14]

In North America, then, it is clear that no one has the right to kill the unborn child, or injure her, or deprive her of her property. No one, that is, except her mother. And after the decision in *Roe v. Wade*, the mother has, in the United States, the unrestricted right to take the child's life. Moreover, given the abortion-on-demand situation that prevails in most large Canadian cities, the mother has practically the same right in this country. This has created a profound conflict between the civil and the criminal law. Take the hypothetical example of a woman who is pregnant with her first child at the time of her husband's death. In his will he has divided his estate between his wife and all his living children. The law has established that the child in the womb can rightfully inherit a share of his father's estate. Canadian criminal law, as it is interpreted in many parts of the country, also permits the woman to destroy her child at will, right up to the moment before it is born. Legally speaking, therefore, the woman would be at liberty to have an abortion in order to keep all of her husband's estate to herself.

We can think of another instance where the interests of the unborn child may clash with those of the mother or father. Since 1963, thanks to the work of the New Zealand fetologist Dr. Albert Liley, it has been possible to make life-saving transfusions of blood to fetuses that have developed acute anemia in the womb. In one such instance where a blood transfusion had been diagnosed as medically necessary to save the unborn child's life, the mother refused the transfusion for religious reasons. Nonetheless, the New Jersey Supreme Court ordered the transfusion to be administered, stating that

> We are satisfied that the unborn child is entitled to the law's protection and that an appropriate order should be made to insure such transfusions to the mother in the event that they are necessary in the opinion of the physician in charge at the time.[15]

In 1981 the first reported successful out-of-the-womb surgery was carried out on a five-month-old unborn baby. Performed in San Francisco, the critical thirty-minute operation now points the way to the correction of a whole series of birth defects in the future.[16] The irony of this particular medical breakthrough is that, during the half hour she spends outside the womb during the operation, the child enjoys the status of a legal person, with her life fully protected. Once back in the womb, however, she resumes the status of a non-person, having, in effect, re-entered a free-fire zone where she could be killed with impunity.

The contradiction between the unborn child's status under the civil law and her status under the criminal law has led to schizophrenic behaviour in the courts. In 1972, for example, an Ottawa woman was approved for a legal abortion by a hospital therapeutic-abortion committee, but her husband objected to the abortion, was able to have himself recognized as the guardian of the unborn child, and secured a temporary injunction against the abortion. Before his application for a permanent injunction could be heard, he and his wife were reconciled and she abandoned her attempts to abort the child.[17]

In 1981, the boyfriend of a girl in Thunder Bay who had been pressured into having an abortion by her parents won an injunction against the abortion on behalf of himself and the unborn child. This injunction, the first to be granted involving an unmarried couple, confirmed that an unborn child can, in effect, act as co-plaintiff to defend her own life.[18] More interesting still was the decision of a Halifax Family Court judge not only to stop an abortion at the request of the woman's estranged husband, but to appoint a private citizen, unrelated to the family, as the unborn child's legal guardian. While the court may have exceeded its jurisdiction, it seems to have established the first instance where a child in the womb has had a guardian appointed on her behalf.[19]

To compound the confusion further, two recent cases, one Canadian, one British, have recognized the personhood of the unborn child in criminal suits. The British judge ruled that a Belfast child wounded by a bullet fired into her mother's abdomen was a legal person, with the right to sue for damages for criminal injury, and awarded her $8,800.[20] In the Canadian case, which involved a charge of criminal negligence, a British Columbia judge ruled that a fetus in the process of birth is a person under the Criminal Code. The baby in question was stillborn, allegedly because of the criminal negligence of the midwife in attendance. The defence lawyer had argued that there could be no charge of criminal negligence, since the fetus was not a person. Prior to the judge's decision, a child was not, in fact, considered to be a person under the Criminal Code until she had emerged in a living state from the body of her mother.[21]

So far, we can see that the unborn child's rights have been won *vis-à-vis* the outside world. It could be maintained that there is nothing inconsistent or irrational in allowing the child's mother to kill her through abortion, while at the same time denying to everyone else the right to injure her or deprive her of her property. The mother, after all, is the only one who has to surrender her body for the nine months of possible discomfort, embarrassment, or even physical hazard that a pregnancy can entail. Her relationship with her unborn child is clearly unique, and qualitatively different from anyone else's relationship with the child. Given that her body is being occupied by a fetus who may not be welcome in her eyes, should the mother not at least have the right to dispose of it as she pleases?

Just recently, this argument, which is condensed in the popular phrase "a woman's right to control her own body," has had to face an unexpected and awkward challenge. Since about 1970, in Canada and elsewhere, there has been much concern about child abuse, together with a determination to reduce its prevalence. In addition, there is now a much sharper awareness of how crucial are the nine months before birth in shaping the individual's whole future physical and psychological wellbeing. Many proponents of child welfare therefore urge that protection against abuse should extend into the prenatal period, and that mothers should be accountable for the welfare of their unborn children. Furthermore, they should, like anyone else, be liable for prosecution if they are guilty through negligence or abuse, of causing injury to their unborn child.

In 1981 the Ontario Family Court in Kenora recognized a fetus as "a child in need of protection" under the terms of the Child Welfare Act because of the physical abuse she suffered through her mother's excessive consumption of alcohol and the mother's failure to obtain proper treatment. The implication was clear that the fetus is protected from abuse by her mother during the full nine months of pregnancy, starting from conception. In fact, it was noted that fetal damage from alcohol is most likely to occur during the first three months of pregnancy.[22]

The Supreme Court of British Columbia came to a similar conclusion in 1982, in the case of a heroin-addicted mother whose newborn baby suffered violent symptoms of withdrawal and possible long-term damage to her health. After about seven weeks, when the baby was taken off opium, she

> demonstrated the effects of withdrawal with the following severe physical symptoms: Incessant, inconsolable crying, vomiting, inability to sleep, twitching, reluctance to feed, poor sucking performance, irritability, resistance to being held, explosive diarrhea, profuse sweating, jittery limbs, barking cough, physical tension and squirming. The diarrhea was of special concern, because if not corrected the resultant water loss could lead to shock and death. In addition, the baby developed severe anemia, which continues to be a danger.

At four months of age the baby was still withdrawing from addiction, according to the attending physician.

> . . . the infant goes through the same withdrawal syndrome as an adult and experiences extreme spasms in the stomach, excruciating pain and vomiting.

Moreover, the baby required very careful attention to her nutrition, since drug-addicted babies need twice the calories of a normal child for brain and organ growth.

In light of this harrowing description of the consequences of the mother's heroin addiction, the court ruled that the fetus whose mother is drug-addicted is "a child in need of protection," and that such a child "is born *having been abused*" (emphasis added). There was therefore no need to wait until the mother abused the child after birth before requiring that she submit to involuntary supervision.[23]

The Ontario and British Columbia decisions find support in David M. Steinberg's *Family Law in Family Courts*, where it is stated that a child in the womb may be considered a child in order to secure protection from abuse by her mother.[24]

So a mother may not neglect or abuse her unborn child. But she may still legally kill her. Aware of the pressing need to remedy this state of affairs, the director of the Canadian Law Reform Commission advocates that the unborn child's rights already established by judicial decision should be enshrined in a statute. According to Edward Keyserlingk, "there should be no contest at all between a mother's desire to smoke or consume drugs excessively and the unborn's right to be legally protected against the serious risk of resulting disability." The provision of adequate nutrition, adequate prenatal checkups, the avoidance of excessive smoking, drinking, or drug-taking should be made into a legal obligation involving potential liability for parents, doctors, and others. ". . . The law must conclude more coherently and explicitly than it has to date that the unborn has it own juridical [legal] personality and rights."[25] Yet he goes on to say that the unborn's rights would end when the mother decides to have an abortion.

Does this make sense? Would *you* rather have the right to "adequate prenatal checkups" than the right not to be killed through abortion? The stark absurdity of this position grows out of the irreducible reality that all the rights the unborn has won in the course of this century depend, as their indispensable precondition, on the right to live. Since I possess the right to inherit, to own property, and not to be injured, neglected, or abused before I am born, then logically I must also possess the right to life, since without it none of my other rights can be exercised.[26]

This terrible contradiction at the heart of our legal system cannot endure. Either we shall have to eliminate the civil rights that have been so painfully won for the unborn child, or we shall have to recognize her most fundamental right, the right not to be killed, even by her parents. We cannot have it both ways. Moreover, whatever we do, a morality will have been imposed. To think that the neutral, liberal, and value-free policy is to remove abortion from the law is to be misled. To accept the argument from pluralism is to turn a blind eye to the silent victim of every abortion—the child in the womb. It would be hardly less logical to advocate removing murder from the criminal code on the ground that, in a pluralistic society, we do not have any right to impose our moral views upon those who wish to murder.

The argument from pluralism also ignores the fact that societies that do eliminate abortion from their legal codes do not thereby give people a free choice in the matter. Instead, an "abortion climate" takes over, and overwhelming pressure is exerted on women to resort to abortion as the way out of any distressful or inconvenient pregnancy. This pressure is exerted by husbands, boyfriends, parents, peers, social workers, doctors, and governments. Governments find abortion an easy way of avoiding hard social problems like the shortage of reasonably priced family housing.

There is yet another defect in the argument from pluralism. It is said that, since there is disagreement about whether the fetus is a human being, we should allow those who believe that abortion is morally permissible to act on their beliefs. Some people certainly *wish* that there were disagreement about the humanity of the fetus. Virtually all medical authorities, however, agree that the life of the human individual begins at the moment of conception.[27] But even if there were disagreement, would it not be both prudent and humane to give the fetus the benefit of the doubt, to accept its humanity and therefore its right to legal protection? What would we say if people were arguing that blacks instead of fetuses were not human, and that people should have the right to kill them? This, after all, is the position that some people took in the United States of America just more than a century ago. Would we not argue that blacks should have the benefit of the doubt and be included within the human family, with appropriate legal protection? Is not the best rule of thumb to frame our definition of who is human broadly enough to avoid excluding particular classes of people who may happen to be out of public favour at a given moment?

At this point some people will raise a pragmatic argument. It is all very well to talk of protecting the unborn child, they say, but women have always had abortions, and they always will. No law can stop them. The only question is whether they should have abortions that are legal and safe, or should be condemned to seek back-alley "butchers," criminal abortionists who endanger their life and health.

This argument has a particle of truth to it, but only a particle. There are some women in every society and in every age who will seek abortions no matter what the law says. But the number is far smaller than is usually alleged by advocates of legalized abortion.[28] But there is little doubt that a strong law protecting the unborn child, especially if it is combined with life-promoting social policies, will reduce the incidence of abortion. This conclusion is borne out by studies, conducted in several countries, of women who were refused legal abortions. In every study it was found that only a small proportion of the women resorted to criminal abortions, although many of them had threatened to do so. Even more surprising, it was discovered in a Danish study that four-fifths of the women later said they were satisfied to have borne their children. Moreover, a Czech study revealed that these children fared just as well as children whose mothers had not tried to abort them.[29] No law is ever completely effective, but laws do have an educative function. They express the commonly accepted standards of behavior of a society, and many people consciously model their behavior according to what the law informs them is acceptable. The fact that a law is frequently broken is no reason in itself for doing away with that law. The laws against child abuse, theft, tax evasion, and assault are broken far more often than the laws against abortion. But they are still useful, both because they express our public moral standards, and because they undoubtedly prevent an even greater incidence of the offences they prohibit.

If the argument of this essay is correct, the most enlightened social policy would be to legislate solid protection of the unborn child. Such protection means that abortion would only be permissible when continuation of the pregnancy would result in the death of the mother. To adhere to this position is not to adopt a censorious moralism. It is simply to recognize that the protection of innocent human life is the most basic duty of any civilized community. Our community will be neither healthy nor civilized so long as we fail in that duty.

Notes

1. James B. Pritchard, *Ancient Near Eastern Texts Relating to the Old Testament*, 2nd ed. (Princeton: 1955), pp. 175, 181, 184ff., 190.
2. Dennis J. Horan *et al.*, "The Legal Case for the Unborn Child," in T.W. Hilgers and D.J. Horan, eds., *Abortion and Social Justice* (New York: 1972), pp. 122–124.
3. *Blackstone's Commentaries*, 15th ed., vol. I, p. 129.
4. Edward Synan, "Law and the Sin of the Mothers," in E.A. Synan and E.J. Kremer, eds., *Death before Birth: Canadian Essays on Abortion* (Toronto, 1974), pp. 146f.
5. Proclaimed by George III in 1803.
6. Thellusson v. Woodford (1798–1799), *English Reports*, vol. 3, p. 163.
7. *Western Weekly Reports* (1919), vol. I, p. 134.
8. Giddings v. Canadian Northern Railway Company, *Dominion Law Reports* (1920), vol. 53.
9. *Supreme Court Reports* (1933), p. 456.
10. *Ontario Reports* (1972), vol. II.
11. *Victoria Reports* (Australia), 1972, p. 353.
12. William L. Prosser, *Handbook of the Law of Torts*, 4th ed. (St. Paul, 1974), pp. 335–336. The other eminent authority on tort law, the Australian John G. Fleming, agrees that courts in Britain and the Commonwealth are now willing to entertain suits for prenatal injuries. *The Law of Torts*, 5th ed. (Sydney, 1977), p. 159.
13. Prosser, p. 338. Fleming, on the other hand, holds that the child must still be born alive in order to be a plaintiff (p. 161).
14. Horan *et al.*, *art. cit.*, p. 113 and references cited in n. 35.
15. *Ibid.*, p. 115.
16. *Globe and Mail*, 16 November 1981.
17. *Ibid.*, 28 January 1972.
18. *Ibid.*, 6 February 1981.
19. *Ibid.*, 25 September 1979.
20. *Ibid.*, 3 November 1979.
21. *Ibid.*, 8 November 1979.
22. *Re Children's Aid Society of Kenora and Janis L.*, 14 September 1981, Ontario Provincial Court of the District of Kenora (not reported).*
23. *Re In the Matter of Judicial Review of a Decision of Judge P. d'A. Collings Respecting Female Infant Born Dec. 11th, 1981*, Supreme Court of British Columbia, 13 April 1982.
24. Carswell, 1981, vol. 1, 2nd ed., p. 112.
25. *Globe and Mail*, 2 April 1982.
26. E.-H.W. Kluge, "The Right to Life of Potential Persons," *Dalhousie Law Journal*, vol. 3, 1977, pp. 846–847.
27. See, for example, a standard textbook, Leslie B. Arey, *Developmental Anatomy*, rev. 7th ed. (Philadelphia, 1974), p. 55.
28. See the *Report of the Committee on the Operation of the Abortion Law* [The Badgley Report] (Ottawa, 1977), pp. 71–72, and C.B. Goodhart, "On the Incidence of Illegal Abortion," *Population Studies*, vol. XXVII (1973), pp. 207–233.
29. Cf. Hans Forssman and Inga Thuwe, "One Hundred and Twenty Children Born after Application for Therapeutic Abortion Refused," *Acta Psychiatrica Scandinavica*, 42 (1966), 71–74; Henrik Hoffmeyer, "Medical Aspects of the Danish Legislation on Abortion," in David T. Smith, ed., *Abortion and the Law* (Cleveland, 1967), p. 201; V. Schuller and E. Stupkova, "The Unwanted Child in the Family," *International Mental Health Research Newsletter*, 14 (3) (Fall, 1972), 7f.

Editor's note: See the judgement of Madam Justice Proudfoot in this chapter.

Balancing Prenatal Care and Abortion

E.W. Keyserlingk

> The child, by reason of his physical and mental immaturity, needs special safeguards and care, including appropriate legal protection, before as well as after birth.
>
> Declaration of the Rights of the Child, United Nations

Medical research and experience are increasingly able to establish that some serious birth defects and complications are caused already in the prenatal stage by the pregnant woman's excessive drug-taking, smoking, or consumption of alcohol, or by such factors as her inadequate diet or not attending to her contagious diseases. Many of these prenatal abuses or omissions may result in life-long disabilities and handicaps. Many of these abuses or omissions are known by others (doctors, for instance) to be taking place, are done wilfully and negligently against medical advice and are therefore preventable by a voluntary change in conduct on the part of the pregnant woman. But what of legal intervention to protect the health of the unborn child when all else fails?

The unborn child is in the most vulnerable stage of human life; its health and protection needs are essentially the same and continuous with those it will have after birth; the effects of harm done to it in the prenatal stage by act or omission will often continue through life; it is almost totally dependent upon health choices and habits of the woman carrying it for its own health and safety.

Yet legal mechanisms and intervention to protect unborn health do not (yet) exist. To this point the legal response as regards the unborn child (in both common and civil law) has been to recognize the unborn's right of action once born for *some* prenatal injuries, and prenatal protective mechanisms to safeguard its *property* until birth. But the prenatal injuries for which the unborn child may sue once born have thus far been quite narrowly defined and have involved injuries it suffered as a result of physical negligence inflicted upon the pregnant woman by others, not as a result of abuse or neglect by the pregnant woman herself against her unborn child. More importantly, from a preventative point of view, the law has provided for no protective intervention at all for the unborn in an attempt to stop further known or suspected abuse or neglect.[1]

In our view, both the growing medical evidence as to the health needs of the unborn and the experience of doctors and hospitals that too many children are in fact born with serious and preventable problems as a result of prenatal maternal neglect, suggest that it is now imperative that the law be further evolved to meet that need. That need would be essentially met both by considering pregnant women (and others—doctors for example) to have a duty to provide adequate prenatal care to their unborn children, the failure of which would give rise to legal action for

By permission of the author. Altered and shortened version of ''The Unborn Child's Right to Prenatal Care'' in *Health Law in Canada*, Fall 1982.

damages once born, but (more importantly) the actual or reasonably suspected failure of which could give rise to protective legal intervention even before birth.

Obviously a number of components in that case need to be argued and established if the case itself is to be compelling. Four of these major components should be briefly sketched here, though given the subject of this paper only the last of them will be discussed in any detail.

The first has to do with a "right to prenatal care" itself. On the one hand it should not be made to mean the equivalent of "a right to be born healthy"[2] or a "right to be well born."[3] That would be to spread the net too widely, to attempt to include too much. In claiming for the unborn a right to be born healthy, more would be claimed than is recognized even for the already born. Statutes and duties of care make claims to the right to health *care* supportable, but not necessarily the right to health care according to objective standards, but to "adequate" health care, care which meets at least acceptable minimum levels. But on the other hand a right to adequate prenatal care should *widen* the already existing "right to non-negligent acts." As already indicated, this right should now include a far wider range of injuries, acts, omissions and right-owers than those acknowledged in judgments to date.

A second point which must be explored and established is that legal mechanisms for protective intervention can in fact be devised, mechanisms which will be adapted to the unique situation of the unborn child, both invisible to the naked eye and inseparable from the pregnant woman. Devising legal interventions which are both realistic and effective and yet not unduly onerous or intrusive upon the pregnant woman is of course no small task. In our view, devising such legal mechanisms is not, however, impossible. Inasmuch as the unborn child's vulnerability and needs are analogous to and continuous with those of the born child, a reasonable legislative starting point is that of existing child-welfare legislation. Protective legislation for the unborn could to some extent at least be analogous to that now available for children, both as to reasons justifying intervention and the particular interventions themselves. They could include for example the appointment of guardians, granting of injunctions, provision of supervision orders, assigning of homemakers and so forth. Obviously adaptations and creations would be necessary, but analogies and precedents do exist in what is now available for children.

A third component and point to be established if our case is to be compelling is that the unborn child has legal personality and right already in the prenatal stage. It is obvious that the major legal reason for the unborn child's present lack of legal protection is because it is not really acknowledged to have legal personality and rights to life and health in the prenatal stage at the time prenatal negligence can occur and protection is necessary. The full acquisition and exercise of legal personality and the rights to life, inviolability and health care await the suspensive condition or condition precedent of live and viable birth. Once born alive and viable and a prenatal injury discovered, the judgments awarding damages have "pretended" for purposes of damages that the injury really happened since birth and not before birth. Typical of this analysis was the judgment in *Duval v. Seguin*:

> While it was the foetus or child *en ventre sa mère* who was injured, the damages sued for are the damages suffered by the plaintiff Ann since birth and what she will continue to suffer as a result of that injury.[4]

That traditional analysis has presented no major problem (at least in practice if not in theory) as long as the legal interest was only in the right of action for damages. Since one would normally and certainly know of injuries to the foetus only once it is born, it did not particularly matter in practice that legal personality was "dated" from the time of viable birth. But if we are to add affirmative and protective legal duties and interventions as well, which will come into play *before* birth, they will not be assured and secure unless based upon corresponding *rights* of the unborn, rights to life, inviolability and adequate health care which must exist before birth if they are to have effect before birth. As long as the unborn is seen to have only (health and development) *needs* and not also *rights*, the basic health requirements will continue to look like weaker claims than for example the pregnant mother's habits and wishes to smoke, drink or take drugs excessively even if this proves to be seriously health-threatening for the child.

If the societal and legal interest in protecting the health and development of children and adults is to begin before birth, then so too should the relevant rights and duties, which cannot be such unless anchored in legal personality. From the point of view of legal analysis the solution would appear to lie in considering the unborn a legal person with rights to life, inviolability and adequate prenatal care on the condition *subsequent* or the resolutory condition of *not* being born alive and viable. In other words the relevant rights and duties will exist already before birth until and unless the child is *not* born alive and viable. As we shall conclude below in dealing with our fifth point a further qualification is imposed as well in view of the pregnant woman's "right" to abortion.

A fourth point to be established has to do with the imposition of a legal duty to provide adequate prenatal care, and potential liability for not doing so, upon the *pregnant woman*. This too is no easy case to make—the traditional legal stance is against imposing upon the pregnant woman herself such a duty and liability.[5] But given that it is the pregnant woman herself who has the most power to do good or ill to her unborn child, it would be impossible in our view to establish a realistic and effective right to prenatal care for the unborn (including the right of the State to intervene for protective reasons), unless the pregnant mother were to be acknowledged as one of those having corresponding duties and liability. The objections to same cannot be lightly dismissed, but are not necessarily compelling.

One typical objection is to the effect that such a duty would be excessively onerous on the pregnant woman. But as already indicated, she should not be held to a "best possible" standard, including for example knowledge of yesterday's research results on prenatal diets, but to the provision of "adequate" treatment. The right in question is not, after all, a "right to be born healthy." Other arguments as well against maternal duty and liability lose much of their force to the extent that one acknowledges a basic equality in status and rights between the unborn child and parents. Put in that perspective, arguments pointing to burdens and cruelty imposed on pregnant women in the event of such duties and liability would have to be balanced by considerations of burdens and cruelty imposed on the unborn if abused or neglected because not provided with legal protections and recourse.

A fifth and major point to be established is that the pregnant woman's right to abortion does not necessarily negate the unborn child's right to prenatal care.

It could be argued that in view of the pregnant mother's right to abortion accorded by the *Criminal Code* in s. 251(4), the right to prenatal care and the fundamental rights to life and inviolability are rendered meaningless. But not so. Our response to such a claim is in two parts. In the first place the mother's right to abortion is itself very narrowly defined and qualified in the *Criminal Code*, and the *Code* itself betrays a clear and predominant intent to protect the unborn. Secondly, the possibility of abortion need by no means render meaningless the unborn child's rights to life, inviolability and prenatal care—it would only impose a particular condition upon them.

Although according to s. 206(1) the full protection of the *Criminal Code* is available to the unborn only when it "becomes a human being" at the moment of live birth, that is not to say that before birth the unborn is accorded no protection at all, or that the interests of the conceived but unborn are granted no recognition at all. Quite the contrary. In effect the *Criminal Code* emphasis is clearly on the side of continuing legal protection from conception to birth. Section 251 makes abortion itself a crime, and since no distinction is made as to stages of gestation, abortion is presumably equally a crime at all stages of gestation. In that this section makes no distinction between stages of gestation one may also conclude that all stages are equal before the (criminal) law—from earliest embryo to fully formed foetus. Section 221(1) makes the killing of an unborn child in the act of birth an indictable offence (though not homicide), punishable by life imprisonment. Finally, according to s. 226, a pregnant woman about to give birth who does not seek necessary assistance because she wishes her child to die, commits an indictable offence, whether her child dies immediately before or during birth.

The single and exceptional justification of abortion in the *Criminal Code* is that found in s. 251(4), namely on condition that it is done by a qualified medical practitioner after approval by a therapeutic-abortion committee if that committee feels that " . . . the continuation of the pregnancy . . . could or would be likely to endanger her life or health"—s. 251(4)(c).[6] Similarly though (apparently) more restrictively, s. 221(2) permits an intervention during the act of birth by one ". . . who by means that, in good faith, he considers necessary to preserve the life of the mother of a child, causes the death of such child."

Clearly then the mother's right to life and health has legal precedence and priority over the unborn child's right to life and health when those rights of mother and unborn directly compete and require balancing. For this reason, Weiler and Catton[7] are essentially correct when they note that ". . . the law is extending its protection to the potentiality of human life, but when the potentiality of life conflicts with the rights of those actually living, the rights of the latter will prevail." The Weiler/Catton citation above may suggest that *whenever* there is a conflict between (any of) the rights of unborn human life and born human life the rights of the latter will prevail. A more accurate phrasing, however, would be that in a conflict between the life or health of both, then, but only then, *that* right of the mother *may* (not necessarily will) prevail. It remains the mother's choice as to whether or not she will choose to avail herself of what the law permits (abortion) or on the contrary accept a degree of risk to her own life and health by choosing in favour of the unborn child's right to life and health rather than undergo an abortion.

Having acknowledged the exceptional condition in which the law permits abortion, it becomes important to first of all recognize that the exception *is* in fact an exception, and therefore is to be restrictively interpreted. As Somerville has noted:

> Such approval constitutes an exception from the provision prohibiting the procural of a miscarriage and hence protecting the foetus. As section 251(4) is an exception it is to be restrictively interpreted. That is, section 251(4) must be interpreted in such a way that, consistently with acknowledging the lawfulness of a procedure to procure a miscarriage which falls within its terms, it least distracts from the provision in the general section for the protection of the foetus.[8]

Secondly, the exception allowing abortion, precisely because it is to be restrictively interpreted may well be limited only to the evacuation of the woman's uterus, and not as well to destruction of the foetus when the latter is avoidable. Somerville has compellingly established that:

> Such evacuation may or may not unavoidably involve the death of the foetus. But where it does not, the decriminalizing of the procural of the miscarriage does not in itself carry with it a right to kill the foetus unnecessarily.[9]

A third and related arguable restriction upon the scope of the exception to the essential criminality of abortion concerns the status and rights of the foetus who is born alive and viable as a result of a therapeutic abortion, no matter what method was used.[10] Whether or not the intention was to abort the foetus, and whether or not the abortion was legal, once the unborn child is born live and viable, it would appear to fall within the "definition" of "human being" in s. 206(1) and thus be entitled to the *full* range of protections available to all (other) human beings including the right to post-natal care and support.[11]

   This would mean for example that not only should the physician have a duty to choose the least-harmful-to-the-unborn means possible (consistent with the mother's "higher" right to life and health), but also that if the unborn is potentially viable he may well also have a duty to have available for immediate use after the abortion, the medical support and technology usually available to wanted but premature newborns in case of likely complications. Failing such availability a physician might be liable to a charge of homicide, for causing ". . . injury to a child before or during its birth as a result of which the child dies after becoming a human being" (section 206[2]).[12]

   Having acknowledged that the unborn child's rights to life and inviolability, and consequently to prenatal care, must give way to what present criminal law in Canada considers to be a more important (though very restricted) interest in the mother's life and health, it remains to formulate explicitly the condition thus imposed on the unborn's right to prenatal care which we are proposing. It is not rendered meaningless or non-existent. But neither can it be un-affected in the light of the present *Criminal Code.*

In our view the only justifiable result and (compromise) solution is that the unborn's rights to life, inviolability and prenatal care would arise at the time the parents (or mother) know of the pregnancy and would continue to have effect from then to viable birth *until or unless the mother decides*, for the exceptional reason allowed in s. 251(4) and s. 221(2), to undergo a therapeutic abortion. At that point and for that reason, the mother's interest in life and health may prevail over that of the unborn.

A somewhat different condition and formulation was initially attractive to us. It was suggested by the Report of the British Columbia Royal Commission on Family and Children's Law. In that Report, the Commission made this proposal:

> We have no jurisdiction to deal with abortion, because it is a federal matter. However, once a woman has decided to bear the future infant, the laws of the province should emphasize individual responsibility to provide the infant with the kind of prenatal care that will prevent unnecessary jeopardy to the child.[13]

In our view that proposal has one important flaw. It could leave uncovered by any legal duty or liability a very long period in the unborn child's gestational life. In other words, as worded above there would be no duty to provide adequate prenatal care as long as the pregnant mother has *not yet made a decision* to bear the child. In the first place many very serious and permanent injuries and disabilities may be inflicted on the unborn already in the earliest period of gestation. Assuming the pregnant mother makes a decision to bear the child, let us say in the twentieth week of gestation, by virtue of the above formulation the unborn would not have enjoyed statutory legal protections for that entire twenty-week period, nor the right of action for prenatal injuries inflicted during that same period.

Another difficulty with the above British Columbia formulation is that it seems to assume that women always make a conscious and explicit decision to bear or not bear their child. One doubts that such an assumption is justified. It is at least likely that many women make no clear decision one way or the other but are more or less passive or fatalistic about it. Should that count as a "decision," and when could "it" be considered to have been made with sufficient intent or consent to initiate a (legal) duty to provide adequate prenatal care? According to the formulation we have proposed that problem would not seem to arise.

It should be noted that we have selected the time the pregnancy is known of rather than the moment of *conception* as the point in time at which the unborn child's rights arise. The difficulty with the moment of conception as the starting point of the rights in questions is that until the pregnancy is *known* one cannot yet posit duties upon others to actually provide the needs and protections.[14]

Our own formulation as proposed above appears more in line with the thrust of this paper's argumentation, particularly in two respects. The first has to do with the medical/biological evidence that the unborn is vulnerable to injury and in need of care, and hence of legal protection, from conception onwards. The second has to do with the proposal earlier in the paper that live birth and viability should be a condition subsequent or resolutory condition of legal personality and rights, rather than a condition precedent. As such, the unborn child would be presumed to have the right to prenatal care from the time the pregnancy is realized, and would normally only lose that (and other rights) if it is *not* born alive and viable. According to the condition just proposed, the unborn would also, and by exception lose those rights if and when the pregnant mother decides to undergo an abortion to protect her life or health (which decision is then approved by a therapeutic-abortion committee).

That said we should repeat by way of conclusion that the unborn child's right to prenatal care, though not absolute, should not have to give way to maternal rights, interests, wishes or habits other than and lesser than her life or health. For example, there should be no contest at all between a mother's desire to smoke, drink or consume drugs excessively, and the unborn's right to be (legally) protected against the serious risk of resulting disability to it.

Notes

1. Though two recent Canadian judgments have at least indicated that unborn children can be "abused" within the meaning of child-welfare legislation, and that they can be in need of legal protection even before birth. In the first of these recent judgments (*In the Matter of Janis L.*, Provincial Court Family Division, District of Kenora, Ontario, September 14, 1981, unreported) Judge William Bradley said:

   > Accordingly the child was a child in need of protection prior to birth, at birth, and on the twenty-fourth day of May, 1981, being the time of apprehension, pursuant to sections 19(1)(b)(xi) and (ix) of the Child Welfare Act, by reason of the physical abuse of the child by the mother in her excessive consumption of alcohol during pregnancy, which conduct endangered the health of Janis L. . . . (p. 5).

   In a second judgment (*In the Matter of D.J.*, Supreme Court, British Columbia, March 29, 1982) Judge Proudfoot said:

   > "D.J." falls within the definition under s. 1[of the Family and Child Service Act] as "a child in need of protection" as would any other child born drug-addicted . . . (p. 9).

2. This was the wording of the right advocated as one of the basic rights of a child in the Ontario case of *Re Brown* (1975), 21 *Reports of Family Law* 315 at 323 (Ont.).
3. This is the wording of the right as advocated by Marc Ament in his "The Right to Be Well Born" (1974), November/December, *The Journal of Legal Medicine*, pp. 25–30.
4. *Duval v. Seguin* (1972), 26 *Dominion Law Reports* (3d) 418.
5. For a relatively recent expression of this traditional stance, see for example the United Kingdom Law Commission, *Report on Injuries to Unborn Children*, Her Majesty's Stationary Office, London, 1974.
6. It should be noted that the Supreme Court decision in the Morgentaler case somewhat broadened the application (though not the principle) of this exception when it held that the common-law defence of necessity could make an abortion legal though it had not been approved by a therapeutic-abortion committee. But for this defence to apply, the abortion would still have to be necessary to save the mother's life or health as specified in s. 251(4), and it must have been impossible to follow the normal procedure of prior abortion-committee approval as also specified in s.251(4). See *Morgentaler v. R.* [1976], 1 S.C.R. 616; [1974] C.A. 129; 42 D.L.R. (3d) 444.
7. Weiler, Karen M. and Catton, Katherine, "The Unborn in Canadian Law" (1976), 14, *Osgoode Hall Law Journal*, p. 647.
8. Somerville, M., "Reflections on Canadian Abortion Law: Evacuation and Destruction —Two Separate Issues" (1981), 31, *University of Toronto Law Journal*, 1, p. 15.

9. *Ibid.* Accordingly, Somerville recommends, in part, that ". . . the physician should have an obligation to take all reasonable measures to preserve the life of the fetus in so far as these are consistent with carrying out the abortion. To this end, when there is a reasonable possibility that a viable fetus is involved, the least mutilating means of abortion which are reasonably available should be used. This requirement would be subject to the proviso that such means need not be used if they constitute an undue added risk to the woman's life or health. . . . Thus section 221 could be amended or interpreted in such a way that, consistently with recognizing a woman's right to abortion under section 251(4), it will protect the fetus against being unnecessarily and intentionally killed. Further . . . two new sections, sections 203a and 204a, should be added to the code. These would legislate, respectively, the offences of negligently killing and wounding a potentially viable fetus." *Ibid.*, pp. 25–26.

10. See the *Report of the Committee on the Operation of the Abortion Law* (known as the "Badgley Report"), Ottawa, 1977, pp. 214, 310. This report indicates that live and viable foetuses (often unexpectedly) surviving therapeutic abortions are not rare. By roughly the twentieth week of gestation an unborn child is considered at present to be potentially viable, that is, capable of living outside the womb, though usually with some degree of available "artificial" assistance. In 1974 there were apparently 174 legal abortions performed after more than twenty weeks of gestation.

11. See also M. Ament, "The Right to Be Well Born" (*supra*, note 3), p. 29, who correctly observes in support of the right of such newborns to post-natal care, "Would-be aborted children who survive the birth process must be accorded full human rights. The humanity of a born child cannot depend on so frail a threat as the intention of the mother, the person performing the abortion, or the medical researcher."

12. See on this point B. Dickens, *Medico-Legal Aspects of Family Law* (Toronto: Butterworths, 1979), p. 58.

13. British Columbia Royal Commission on Family and Children's Law, Fifth Report, Part V, *The Protection of Children* (Child Care), Vancouver, 1975, p. 65.

14. It must be acknowledged, however, that our (or any other) proposed formulation cannot resolve in advance all possible conflicts between the rights of the mother-to-be and her unborn child. For example, what if the pregnant mother wishes to commit suicide or asks that her life-saving or life-prolonging treatment be stopped? These (and other) questions and conflicts will require careful attention both on the levels of ethical and legal principles, and with respect to the particular circumstances of each case.

Questions

1. Are we morally entitled to create laws that allow child-welfare authorities to take an unborn child "into custody" when that means controlling and directing the behaviour of a woman while she is pregnant?

2. If an unborn child is not a person, as some claim, do we have any obligations to it?

3. Does it make sense to say that an unborn child has the right to adequate treatment by its mother while denying that it has a right to life?

4. If we hold a woman liable for harming a child as a result of her lifestyle while pregnant, are we protecting children or providing an additional incentive for having an abortion?

In Defense of Abortion and Infanticide

Michael Tooley

This essay deals with the question of the morality of abortion and infanticide. The fundamental ethical objection traditionally advanced against these practices rests on the contention that human fetuses and infants have a right to life. It is this claim which will be the focus of attention here. The basic issue to be discussed, then, is what properties a thing must possess in order to have a right to life. My approach will be to set out and defend a basic moral principle specifying a condition an organism must satisfy if it is to have a right to life. It will be seen that this condition is not satisfied by human fetuses and infants, and thus that they do not have a right to life. So unless there are other objections to abortion and infanticide which are sound, one is forced to conclude that these practices are morally acceptable ones.[1] In contrast, it may turn out that our treatment of adult members of some other species is morally indefensible. For it is quite possible that some nonhuman animals do possess properties that endow them with a right to life.

I. Abortion and Infanticide

What reason is there for raising the question of the morality of infanticide? One reason is that it seems very difficult to formulate a completely satisfactory pro-abortion position without coming to grips with the infanticide issue. For the problem that the liberal on abortion encounters here is that of specifying a cutoff point which is not arbitrary: at what stage in the development of a human being does it cease to be morally permissible to destroy it, and why?

It is important to be clear about the difficulty here. The problem is not, as some have thought, that since there is a continuous line of development from a zygote to a newborn baby, one cannot hold that it is seriously wrong to destroy a newborn baby without also holding that it is seriously wrong to destroy a zygote, or any intermediate stage in the development of a human being. The problem is rather that if one says that it is wrong to destroy a newborn baby but not a zygote or some intermediate stage, one should be prepared to point to a *morally relevant* difference between a newborn baby and the earlier stage in the development of a human being.

Precisely the same difficulty can, of course, be raised for a person who holds that infanticide is morally permissible, since one can ask what morally relevant difference there is between an adult human being and a newborn baby. What makes it morally permissible to destroy a baby, but wrong to kill an adult? So the challenge remains. But I shall argue that in the latter case there is an extremely plausible answer.

Reflecting on the morality of infanticide forces one to face up to this challenge. In the case of abortion a number of events—quickening or viability, for instance—

From *Philosophy & Public Affairs*, Vol. 2, No. 1 (Fall 1972). © 1972 by Princeton University Press. Reprinted with permission of Princeton University Press.

might be taken as cutoff points, and it is easy to overlook the fact that none of these events involves any morally significant change in the developing human. In contrast, if one is going to defend infanticide, one has to get very clear about what it is that gives something a right to life.

One of the interesting ways in which the abortion issue differs from most other moral issues is that the plausible positions on abortion appear to be extreme ones. For if a human fetus has a right to life, one is inclined to say that, in general, one would be justified in killing it only to save the life of the mother, and perhaps not even in that case.[2] Such is the extreme anti-abortion position. On the other hand, if the fetus does not have a right to life, why should it be seriously wrong to destroy it? Why would one need to point to special circumstances—such as the presence of genetic disease, or a threat to the woman's health—in order to justify such action? The upshot is that there does not appear to be any room for a moderate position on abortion such as one finds, for example, in the Model Penal Code recommendations.[3]

Aside from the light it may shed on the abortion question, the issue of infanticide is both interesting and important in its own right. The theoretical interest has been mentioned above: it forces one to face up to the question of what it is that gives something a right to life. The practical importance need not be labored. Most people would prefer to raise children who do not suffer from gross deformities or from severe physical, emotional, or intellectual handicaps. If it could be shown that there is no moral objection to infanticide, the happiness of society could be significantly and justifiably increased.

The suggestion that infanticide may be morally permissible is not an idea that many people are able to consider dispassionately. Even philosophers tend to react in a way which seems primarily visceral—offering no arguments, and dismissing infanticide out of hand.

Some philosophers have argued, however, that such a reaction is not inappropriate, on the ground that, first, moral principles must, in the final analysis, be justified by reference to our moral feelings, or intuitions, and secondly, infanticide is one practice that is judged wrong by virtually everyone's moral intuition. I believe, however, that this line of thought is unsound, and I have argued elsewhere that even if one grants, at least for the sake of argument, that moral intuitions are the final court of appeal regarding the acceptability of moral principles, the question of the morality of infanticide is not one that can be settled by an appeal to our intuitions concerning it.[4] If infanticide is to be rejected, an argument is needed, and I believe that the considerations advanced in this essay show that it is unlikely that such an argument is forthcoming.

II. What Sort of Being Can Possess a Right to Life?

The issues of the morality of abortion and of infanticide seem to turn primarily upon the answers to the following four questions:

1. What properties, other than potentialities, give something a right to life?
2. Do the corresponding potentialities also endow something with a right to life?
3. If not, do they at least make it seriously wrong to destroy it?

4. At what point in its development does a member of the biologically defined species *Homo sapiens* first possess those nonpotential properties that give something a right to life?

The argument to be developed in the present section bears upon the answers to the first two questions.

How can one determine what properties endow a being with a right to life? An approach that I believe is very promising starts out from the observation that there appear to be two radically different sorts of reasons why an entity may lack a certain right. Compare, for example, the following two claims:

1. A child does not have a right to smoke;
2. A newspaper does not have a right not to be torn up.

The first claim raises a substantive moral issue. People might well disagree about it, and support their conflicting views by appealing to different moral theories. The second dispute, in contrast, seems an unlikely candidate for moral dispute. It is natural to say that newspapers just are not the sort of thing that can have any rights at all, including a right not to be torn up. So there is no need to appeal to a substantive moral theory to resolve the question whether a newspaper has a right not to be torn up.

One way of characterizing this difference . . . is to say that the second claim, unlike the first, is true in virtue of a certain *conceptual* connection, and that is why no moral theory is needed in order to see that it is true. The explanation, then, of why it is that a newspaper does not have a right not to be torn up, is that there is some property *P* such that, first, newspapers lack property *P*, and secondly, it is a conceptual truth that only things with property *P* can be possessors of rights.

What might property *P* be? A plausible answer, I believe, is set out and defended by Joel Feinberg in his paper, "The Rights of Animals and Unborn Generations."[5] It takes the form of what Feinberg refers to as the *interest principle*: ". . . the sorts of beings who *can* have rights are precisely those who have (or can have) interests."[6] And then, since "interests must be compounded somehow out of conations,"[7] it follows that things devoid of desires, such as newspapers, can have neither interests nor rights. Here, then, is one account of the difference in status between judgments such as (1) and (2) above.

Let us now consider the right to life. The interest principle tells us that an entity cannot have any rights at all, and *a fortiori*, cannot have a right to life, unless it is capable of having interests. This in itself may be a conclusion of considerable importance. Consider, for example, a fertilized human egg cell. Someday it will come to have desires and interests. As a zygote, however, it does not have desires, nor even the *capacity* for having desires. What about interests? This depends upon the account one offers of the relationship between desires and interests. It seems to me that a zygote cannot properly be spoken of as a subject of interests. My reason is roughly this. What is in a thing's interest is a function of its present and future desires, both those it will actually have and those it could have. In the case of an entity that is not presently capable of any desires, its interest must be based entirely upon the satisfaction of future desires. Then, since the satisfaction of future desires presupposes the continued existence of the entity in question, anything which has an interest which is based upon the satisfaction of future desires must also have an interest in its own continued existence. Therefore something which is not presently capable of having any desires at all—like a zygote—cannot have any interests at all unless it has an interest in its own continued existence. I shall argue shortly, however, that a zygote cannot have such any interest. From this it will follow that it cannot have any interests at all, and this conclusion, together with the interest principle, entails that not all members of the species *Homo sapiens* have a right to life.

The interest principle involves, then, a thesis concerning a necessary condition which something must satisfy if it is to have a right to life, and it is a thesis which has important moral implications. It implies, for example, that abortions, if performed sufficiently early, do not involve any violation of a right to life. . . .

It is possible, however, that the interest principle does not exhaust the conceptual connections between rights and interests. It formulates only a very general connection: a thing cannot have any rights at all unless it is capable of having at least some interest. May there not be more specific connections, between particular rights and particular sorts of interests? . . .

. . . These . . . can be summed up, albeit somewhat vaguely, by the following, *particular-interests principle*:

> It is a conceptual truth that an entity cannot have a particular right, *R*, unless it is at least capable of having some interest, *I*, which is furthered by its having right *R*.

Given this particular-interests principle, certain familiar facts, whose importance has not often been appreciated, become comprehensible. Compare an act of killing a normal adult human being with an act of torturing one for five minutes. Though both acts are seriously wrong, they are not equally so. Here, as in most cases, to violate an individual's right to life is more seriously wrong than to violate his right not to have pain inflicted upon him. Consider, however, the corresponding actions in the case of a newborn kitten. Most people feel that it is seriously wrong to torture a kitten for five minutes, but not to kill it painlessly. How is this difference in the moral ordering of the two types of acts, between the human case and the kitten case, to be explained? One answer is that while normal adult human beings have both a right to life and a right not to be tortured, a kitten has only the latter. But why should this be so? The particular-interests principle suggests a possible explanation. Though kittens have some interests, including, in particular, an interest in not being tortured, which derives from their capacity to feel pain, they do not have an interest in their own continued existence, and hence do not have a right not to be destroyed. This answer contains, of course, a large promissory element. One needs a defense of the view that kittens have no interest in continued existence. But the point here is simply that there is an important question about the rationale underlying the moral ordering of certain sorts of acts, and that the particular-interests principle points to a possible answer. . . .

It would be widely agreed, I believe, both that rights impose obligations, and that the obligations they impose upon others are *conditional* upon certain factors. . . .

. . . The account which I now prefer, and which I have defended elsewhere,[8] is this:

> A has a right to X

means the same as

> A is such that it can be in A's interest to have X, and *either* (i) A is not capable of making an informed and rational choice whether to grant others permission to deprive him of X, in which case, if it is in A's interest not to be deprived of X, then, by that fact alone, others are under a *prima facie* obligation not to deprive A of X, or (ii) A is capable of making an informed and rational choice whether to grant others permission to deprive him of X, in which case others are under a *prima facie* obligation not to deprive A of X if and only if A has not granted them permission to do so.

And if this account, or something rather similar, is correct, then so is the particular-interests principle.

What I now want to do is to apply the particular-interests principle to the case of the right to life. First, however, one needs to notice that the expression, "right to life," is not entirely happy, since it suggests that the right in question concerns the continued existence of a biological organism. That this is incorrect can be brought out by considering possible ways of violating an individual's right to life. Suppose, for example, that future technological developments make it possible to change completely the neural networks in a brain, and that the brain of some normal adult human being is thus completely reprogrammed, so that the organism in question winds up with memories (or rather, apparent memories), beliefs, attitudes, and personality traits totally different from those associated with it before it was subjected to reprogramming. (The pope is reprogrammed, say, on the model of Bertrand Russell.) In such a case, however beneficial the change might be, one would surely want to say that *someone* had been destroyed, that an adult human being's right to life had been violated, even though no biological organism had been killed. This shows that the expression, "right to life," is misleading, since what one is concerned about is not just the continued existence of a biological organism.

How, then, might the right in question be more accurately described? A natural suggestion is that the expression, "right to life," refers to the right of a subject of experiences and other mental states to continue to exist. It might be contended, however, that this interpretation begs the question against certain possible views. For somone might hold—and surely some people in fact do—that while continuing subjects of experiences and other mental states certainly have a right to life, so do some other organisms that are only potentially such continuing subjects, such as human fetuses. A right to life, on this view, is *either* the right of a subject of experiences to continue to exist, *or* the right of something that is only potentially a continuing subject of experiences to become such an entity.

This view is, I believe, to be rejected, for at least two reasons. In the first place, this view appears to be clearly incompatible with the interest principle, as well as with the particular-interests principle. Secondly, this position entails that the destruction of potential persons is, in general, *prima facie* seriously wrong, and I shall argue, in the next section, that the latter view is incorrect.

Let us consider, then, the right of a subject of experiences and other mental states to continue to exist. The particular-interests principle implies that something cannot possibly have such a right unless its continued existence can be in its interest. We need to ask, then, what must be the case if the continued existence of something is to be in its interest.

. . . The picture that emerges . . . is this. In the first place, nothing at all can be in an entity's interest unless it has desires at some time or other. But more than this is required if the continued existence of the entity is to be in its own interest. One possibility, which will generally be sufficient, is that the individual have, at the time in question, a desire for its own continued existence. Yet it also seems clear that an individual's continued existence can be in its own interest even when such a desire is not present. What is needed, apparently, is that the continued existence of the individual will make possible the satisfaction of some desires existing at other times. But not just any desires existing at other times will do. . . . It is crucial that they be desires that belong to one and the same subject of consciousness.

The critical question, then, concerns the conditions under which desires existing at different times can be correctly attributed to a single, continuing subject of consciousness. This question raises a number of difficult issues which cannot be considered here. Part of the rationale underlying the view I wish to advance will be clear, however, if one considers the role played by memory in the psychological unity of an individual over time. When I remember a past experience, what I know is not merely that there was a certain experience which someone or other had, but that there was an experience that belonged to the *same* individual as the present memory beliefs, and it seems clear that this feature of one's memories is, in general, a crucial part of what it is that makes one a continuing subject of experiences, rather than merely a series of psychologically isolated, momentary subjects of consciousness. This suggests something like the following principle:

> Desires existing at different times can belong to a single, continuing
> subject of consciousness only if that subject of consciousness possesses,
> at some time, the concept of a continuing self or mental substance.[9]

Given this principle, together with the particular-rights principle, one can set out the following argument in support of a claim concerning a necessary condition which an entity must satisfy if it is to have a right to life:

1. The concept of a right is such that an individual cannot have a right at time T to continued existence unless the individual is such that it can be in its interest at time T that it continue to exist.

2. The continued existence of a given subject of consciousness cannot be in that individual's interest at time T unless *either* that individual has a desire, at

time T, to continue to exist as a subject of consciousness, *or* that individual can have desires at other times.
3. An individual cannot have a desire to continue to exist as a subject of consciousness unless it possesses the concept of a continuing self or mental substance.
4. An individual existing at one time cannot have desires at other times unless there is at least one time at which it possesses the concept of a continuing self or mental substance.

Therefore:

5. An individual cannot have a right to continued existence unless there is at least one time at which it possesses the concept of a continuing self or mental substance.

This conclusion is obviously significant. But precisely what implications does it have with respect to the morality of abortion and infanticide? The answer will depend upon what relationship there is between, on the one hand, the behavioral and neurophysiological development of a human being, and, on the other, the development of that individual's mind. . . .

If one [adopts] the view that there is a close relation between the behavioral and neurophysiological development of a human being, and the development of its mind, then the above conclusion has a very important, and possibly decisive implication with respect to the morality of abortion and infanticide. For when human development, both behavioral and neurophysiological, is closely examined, it is seen to be most unlikely that human fetuses, or even newborn babies, possess any concept of a continuing self.[10] And in the light of the above conclusion, this means that such individuals do not possess a right to life. . . .

III. Is It Morally Wrong to Destroy Potential Persons?

In this section I shall consider the question of whether it can be seriously wrong to destroy an entity, not because of the nonpotential properties it presently possesses, but because of the properties it will later come to have, if it is not interfered with. First, however, we need to be clear why this is such a crucial question. We can do this by considering a line of thought that has led some people to feel that the anti-abortionist position is more defensible than that of the pro-abortionist. The argument in question rests upon the gradual and continuous development of an organism as it changes from a zygote into an adult human being. The anti-abortionist can point to this development, and argue that it is morally arbitrary for a pro-abortionist to draw a line at some point in this continuous process—such as at birth, or viability— and to say that killing is permissible before, but not after, that particular point.

The pro-abortionist reply would be, I think, that the emphasis upon the continuity of the process is misleading. What the anti-abortionist is really doing is simply challenging the pro-abortionist to specify what properties a thing must have in order to have a right to life, and to show that the developing organism does acquire those properties at the point in question. The pro-abortionist may then be tempted to argue that the difficulty he has in meeting this challenge should not be taken as grounds for rejecting his position. For the anti-abortionist cannot meet this challenge either; he is equally unable to say what properties something must have if it is to have a right to life.

Although this rejoinder does not dispose of the anti-abortionist argument, it is not without bite. For defenders of the view that abortion is almost always wrong have failed to face up to the question of the *basic* moral principles on which their position rests—where a basic moral principle is one whose acceptability does not rest upon the truth of any factual claim of a nonmoral sort.[11] They have been content to assert the wrongness of killing any organism, from a zygote on, if that organism is a member of the biologically defined species *Homo sapiens*. But they have overlooked the point that this cannot be an acceptable *basic* moral principle, since difference in species is not *in itself* a morally relevant difference.[12]

The anti-abortionist can reply, however, that it is possible to defend his position, but not a pro-abortion position, *without* getting clear about the properties a thing must possess if it is to have a right to life. For one can appeal to the following two claims. First, that there is a property, even if one is unable to specify what it is, that (i) is possessed by normal adult humans, and (ii) endows any being possessing it with a right to life. Secondly, that if there are properties which satisfy (i) and (ii), at least one of those properties will be such that any organism potentially possessing that property has a right to life even now, simply in virtue of that potentiality—where an organism possesses a property potentially if it will come to have it in the normal course of its development.

The second claim—which I shall refer to as the potentiality principle—is crucial to the anti-abortionist's defense of his position. Given that principle, the anti-abortionist can defend his position without grappling with the very difficult question of what nonpotential properties an entity must possess in order to have a right to life. It is enough to know that adult members of *Homo sapiens* do have such a right. For then one can employ the potentiality principle to conclude that any organism which belongs to the species *Homo sapiens*, from a zygote on—with the possible exception of those that suffer from certain gross neurophysiological abnormalities—must also have a right to life.

The pro-abortionist, in contrast, cannot mount a comparable argument. He cannot defend his position without offering at least a partial answer to the question of what properties a thing must possess in order to have a right to life.

The importance of the potentiality principle, however, goes beyond the fact that it provides support for an anti-abortion position. For it seems that if the potentiality principle is unsound, then there is no acceptable defense of an extreme conservative view on abortion.

The reason is this. Suppose that the claim that an organism's having certain potentialities is sufficient grounds for its having a right to life cannot be sustained. The claim that a fetus which is a member of *Homo sapiens* has a right to life can then be attacked as follows. The reason an adult member of *Homo sapiens* has a right to life, but an infant ape, say, does not, is that there are certain psychological properties which the former possesses and the latter does not. Now even if one is unsure exactly what the relevant psychological characteristics are, it seems clear than an organism in the early stages of development from a zygote into an adult member of *Homo sapiens* does not possess those properties. One need merely compare a human fetus with an ape fetus. In early stages of development, neither will have any mental life at all. (Does a zygote have a mental life? Does it have experiences? Or beliefs? Or desires?) In later stages of fetal development some mental events presumably occur, but these will be of a very rudimentary sort. The crucial point, however, is that given what we know through comparative studies of, on the one hand, brain development, and, on the other, behavior after birth, it is surely reasonable to hold that there are no significant differences in the respective mental lives of a human fetus and an ape fetus. There are, of course, physiological differences, but these are not in themselves morally significant. If one held that potentialities were relevant to the ascription of a right to life, one could argue that the physiological differences, though not morally relevant in themselves, are morally relevant in virtue of their causal consequences: they will lead to later psychological differences that are morally relevant, and for this reason the physiological differences are themselves morally significant. But if the potentiality principle is not available, this line of argument cannot be used, and there will then be no differences between a human fetus and an ape fetus that the anti-abortionist can use as grounds for ascribing a right to life to the former but not to the later. . . .

The conclusion seems to be, then, that the anti-abortionist position is defensible only if the potentiality principle is sound. Let us now consider what can be said against that principle. One way of attacking it is by appealing to the conclusion advanced in the previous section, to the effect that an individual cannot have a right to continued existence unless there is at least one time at which it possesses the concept of a continuing self or mental substance. This principle entails the denial of the potentiality principle. Or more precisely, it does so in conjunction with the presumably uncontroversial empirical claim that a fertilized human egg cell, which does possess the relevant potentialities, does not possess the concept of a continuing self or mental substance.

Alternatively, one could appeal to the more modest claim involved in the interest principle, and use it to argue that since a fertilized human egg cell cannot have any interests at all, it cannot have any rights, and a fortiori cannot have a right to life. So potentialities alone cannot endow something with a right to life.

Given these lines of argument, is there any reason not to rest the case at this point? I want to suggest that there are at least two reasons why one needs to take a closer look at the potentiality principle. The first is that some people who are anti-abortionists may wish to reject not only the particular-interests principle, but also the more modest interest principle, and although I believe that this response to the above arguments is unsound, I think it is important to see whether there aren't other arguments that are untouched by this reply.

A second, and more important, reason why it is unwise to base one's case against the anti-abortionist entirely upon an appeal to principles such as the interest principle is this. The anti-abortionist can modify his position slightly, and avoid the arguments in question. Specifically, he can abandon his claim that a human fetus has a right to life, but contend that it is nevertheless seriously wrong to kill it. Some philosophers would feel that such a modification cannot possibly be acceptable, on the ground that no action can be seriously wrong unless it violates someone's right to something. It seems to me, however, that this latter view is in fact mistaken.[13] In any case, let us consider the position that results from this modification. An anti-abortionist who is willing to adopt this position can then appeal, not to the potentiality principle, but to the following *modified potentiality principle:*

> If there are properties possessed by normal adult human beings that endow any organism possessing them with a right to life, then at least one of those properties is such that it is seriously wrong to kill any organism that potentially possesses that property, simply in virtue of that potentiality.

Since this modified potentiality principle is not concerned with the attribution of rights to organisms, it cannot be attacked by appealing to the interest principle, or to the particular-interests principle, or to some analysis of the concept of a right.

Let us now consider how the case against the anti-abortionist position can be strengthened. I shall advance three arguments which are objections to both the original and the modified potentiality principles. Since the original potentiality principle cannot be correct unless the modified one is, it will suffice to consider only the modified principle. The basic issue, then, is this. Is there any property J which satisfies the following three conditions:

1. There is a property, K, such that any individual possessing property K has a right to life, and there is a scientific law, L, to the effect that any organism possessing property J will, in the normal course of events, come to possess property K at some later time;
2. Given the relationship just described between property J and property K, it is seriously wrong to kill anything possessing property J;
3. If property J were not related to property K in the way indicated, the fact that an organism possessed property J would not make it seriously wrong to kill it.

In short, the question is whether there is a property, J, that makes it seriously wrong to kill something *only because* J stands in a certain causal relation to a second property, K, which is such that anything possessing that property *ipso facto* has a right to life.

My first objection turns upon the claim that if one accepts the modified potentiality principle, one ought also to accept the following, *generalized potentiality principle:*

> If there are any properties possessed by normal adult human beings that endow any organism possessing them with a right to life, then at least one of those properties is such that it is seriously wrong to perform any action that will prevent some system, which otherwise would have developed the property, from doing so.

This generalized potentiality principle differs from the original and the modified potentiality principles in two respects. First, it applies to *systems* of objects, and not merely to organisms. I think that this first generalization is one that ought to be accepted by anyone who accepts either the original or the modified principle. For why should it make any difference whether the potentiality resides in a single organism, or in a system of organisms that are so interrelated that they will in the normal course of affairs, due to the operation of natural laws, causally give rise to something that possesses the property in question? Surely it is only the potentiality for a certain outcome that matters, and not whether there are one or more objects interacting and developing in a predetermined way to produce that outcome.

In thinking about this issue, it is important not to confuse *potentialities* with mere *possibilities*. The generalized potentiality principle does not deal with collections of objects that merely have the capacity to interact in certain ways. The objects must already be interrelated in such a way that in the absence of external interference the laws governing their future interaction and development will bring it about that the system will develop the property in question.

The second difference is that the original and modified potentiality principles deal only with the *destruction* of organisms, while the generalized principle deals with any action that prevents an organism, or a system, from developing the relevant property. I think that the anti-abortionist will certainly want to accept this generalization. . . .

Suppose, now, that artificial wombs have been perfected. A healthy, unfertilized human egg cell has been placed in one, along with a large number of spermatozoa. If the device is turned on, the spermatozoa will be carried, via a conveyor belt, to the unfertilized egg cell, where, we can assume, fertilization will take place. The device is such, moreover, that no outside assistance will be needed at any future stage, and nine months later a normal human baby will emerge from the artificial womb. Given these assumptions—all of which are certainly empirically possible—once such a device has been turned on, there will exist an active potentiality that will, if not interfered with, give rise to something that will become an adult human being, and so will have a right to life. But would it be seriously wrong to destroy that potentiality— as might be done, for example, by turning off the machine, or by cutting the conveyor belt, so that fertilization does not place? Most people, I believe, would certainly not think that such actions were seriously wrong. If that view is correct, the generalized potentiality principle must be rejected as unsound.

In short, the first argument against the modified potentiality principle, and hence against the original potentiality principle, is as follows. It is reasonable to accept the modified principle only if it is also reasonable to accept the generalized potentiality principle, because whether the potentialities reside in a single organism or in a system does not seem to be a morally significant difference. But to accept the generalized potentiality principle is to commit oneself to the view that interference with an artificial womb so as to prevent fertilization from taking place is just as seriously wrong as abortion, and for precisely the same reason. If, as seems plausible, this is not an acceptable view, then one cannot reasonably accept either the original or the modified potentiality principle.

Let us now turn to my second argument against the modified potentiality principle. This argument turns upon the following crucial claim:

Let C be any type of causal process where there is some type of occurrence, E, such that processes of type C would possess no intrinsic moral significance were it not for the fact they result in occurrences of type E.

Then:

The characteristic of being an act of intervening in a process of type C which prevents the occurrence of an outcome of type E makes an action intrinsically wrong to precisely the same degree as does the characteristic of being an act of ensuring that a causal process of type C, which it was in one's power to initiate, does not get initiated.

This principle, which I shall refer to as the moral symmetry principle with respect to action, would be rejected by some philosophers. They would argue that there is an important distinction to be drawn between "what we owe people in the form of aid and what we owe them in the way of noninterference,"[14] and that the latter, "negative duties," are duties that it is more serious to neglect than the former, "positive" ones. This view arises from an intuitive response to examples such as the following. Even if it is wrong not to send food to starving people in other parts of the world, it is more wrong still to kill someone. And isn't the conclusion, then, that one's obligation to refrain from killing someone is a more serious obligation than one's obligation to save lives?

I want to argue that this is not the correct conclusion. . . . It is probably true, for example, that most cases of killing are morally worse than most cases of merely letting die. This, however, is not an objection to the moral symmetry principle, since that principle does not imply that, all things considered, acts of killing are, in general, morally on a par with cases of allowing someone to die. What the moral symmetry principle implies is rather that, *other things being equal*, it is just as wrong to fail to save someone as it is to kill someone. If one wants to test this principle against one's moral intuitions, one has to be careful to select pairs of situations in which all other morally relevant factors—such as motivation, and risk to the agent—are equivalent. And I have suggested that when this is done, the moral symmetry principle is by no means counterintuitive.[15]

My argument against the modified potentiality principle can now be stated. Suppose at some future time a chemical were to be discovered which when injected into the brain of a kitten would cause the kitten to develop into a cat possessing a brain of the sort possessed by humans, and consequently into a cat having all the psychological capabilities characteristic of normal adult humans. Such cats would be able to think, to use language, and so on. Now it would surely be morally indefensible in such a situation to hold that it is seriously wrong to kill an adult member of the species *Homo sapiens* without also holding that it is wrong to kill any cat that has undergone such a process of development: there would be no morally significant differences.

Secondly, imagine that one has two kittens, one of which has been injected with the special chemical, but which has not yet developed those properties that in themselves endow something with a right to life, and the other of which has not been injected with the special chemical. It follows from the moral symmetry principle that the action of injecting the former with a "neutralizing" chemical that will interfere with the transformation process and prevent the kitten from developing those properties that in themselves would give it a right to life is *prima facie* no more seriously wrong than the action of intentionally refraining from injecting the second kitten with the special chemical.

It perhaps needs to be emphasized here that the moral symmetry principle does not imply that neither action is morally wrong. Perhaps both actions are wrong, even seriously so. The moral symmetry principle implies only that if they are wrong, they are so to precisely the same degree.

Thirdly, compare a kitten that has been injected with the special chemical and then had it neutralized, with a kitten that has never been injected with the chemical. It is clear that it is no more seriously wrong to kill the former than to kill the latter. For although their bodies have undergone different processes in the past, there is no reason why the kittens need differ in any way with respect to either their present properties or their potentialities.

Fourthly, again consider two kittens, one of which has been injected with the special chemical, but which has not yet developed those properties that in themselves would give it a right to life, and the other of which has not been injected with the chemical. It follows from the previous two steps in the argument that the combined action of injecting the first kitten with a neutralizing chemical and then killing it is no more seriously wrong than the combined action of intentionally refraining from injecting the second kitten with the special chemical and then killing it.

Fifthly, one way of neutralizing the action of the special chemical is simply to kill the kitten. And since there is surely no reason to hold that it is more seriously wrong to neutralize the chemical and to kill the kitten in a single step than in two successive steps, it must be the case that it is no more seriously wrong to kill a kitten that has been injected with the special chemical, but which has not developed those properties that in themselves would give it a right to life, than it is to inject such a kitten with a neutralizing chemical and then to kill it.

Next, compare a member of *Homo sapiens* that has not developed far enough to have those properties that in themselves give something a right to life, but which later will come to have them, with a kitten that has been injected with the special chemical but which has not yet had the chance to develop the relevant properties. It is clear that it cannot be any more seriously wrong to kill the human than to kill the kitten. The potentialities are the same in both cases. The only difference is that in the case of a human fetus the potentialities have been present from the beginning of the organism's development, while in the case of the kitten they have been present only from the time it was injected with the special chemical. This difference in the time at which the potentialities were acquired is not a morally relevant one.

It follows from the previous three steps in the argument that it is no more seriously wrong to kill a human being that lacks properties that in themselves, and irrespective of their causal consequences, endow something with a right to life, but which will naturally develop those properties, than it would be to intentionally refrain from injecting a kitten with the special chemical, and to kill it. But if it is the case that normal adult humans do possess properties that in themselves give them a right to life, it follows in virtue of the modified potentiality principle that it is seriously wrong to kill any human organism that will naturally develop the properties in question. Thus, if the modified potentiality principle is sound, we are forced by the above line of argument to conclude that if there were a chemical that would transform kittens into animals having the psychological capabilities possessed by adult humans, it would be seriously wrong to intentionally refrain from injecting kittens with the chemical, and to kill them instead.

But is it clear that this final conclusion is unacceptable? I believe that it is. It turns out, however, that this issue is *much* more complex than most people take it to be.[16] Here, however, it will have to suffice to note that the vast majority of people would certainly view this conclusion as unacceptable. For while there are at present no special chemicals that will transform kittens in the required way, there are other biological organisms, namely unfertilized human egg cells, and special chemicals, namely human spermatozoa, that will transform those organisms in the required way. So if one were to hold that it was seriously wrong to intentionally refrain from injecting kittens with the special chemical, and instead to kill them, one would also have to maintain that it was *prima facie* seriously wrong to refrain from injecting human egg cells with spermatozoa, and instead to kill them. So unless the anti-abortionist is prepared to hold that any woman, married or unmarried, does something seriously wrong every month that she intentionally refrains from getting pregnant, he cannot maintain that it would be seriously wrong to refrain from injecting the kitten with the special chemical, and instead to kill it.

In short, the above argument shows that anyone who wants to defend the original or the modified potentiality principle must either argue against the moral symmetry principle, or hold that in a world in which kittens could be transformed into "rational animals," it would be seriously wrong to kill newborn kittens. But we have just seen that if one accepts the latter claim, one must also hold that it is seriously wrong to intentionally refrain from fertilizing a human egg cell, and to kill it instead. Consequently, it seems very likely that any anti-abortionist rejoinder to the present argument will be directed against the moral symmetry principle. In the present essay I have not attempted to offer a thorough defense of that principle, although I have tried to show that what is perhaps the most important objection to it—the one that appeals to a distinction between positive and negative duties—rests upon a superficial analysis of our moral intuitions. Elsewhere, however, I have argued that a thorough examination of the moral symmetry principle sustains the conclusion that that principle is in fact correct. . . .

To sum up, what I have argued in the present section is this. The anti-abortionist position is defensible only if some version of the potentiality principle is sound. The original version of that principle is incompatible, however, both with the particular-interests principle and with the interest principle, and also with the account of the concept of a right offered above. The modified potentiality principle avoids these problems. There are, however, at least three other serious objections which tell against both the original potentiality principle and the modified one. It would seem, therefore, that there are excellent reasons for rejecting the potentiality principle, and with it, the anti-abortionist position.

IV. Summary and Conclusions

In this paper I have advanced three main philosophical contentions:

1. An entity cannot have a right to life unless it is capable of having an interest in its own continued existence;
2. An entity is not capable of having an interest in its own continued existence unless it possesses, at some time, the concept of a continuing self, or subject of experiences and other mental states;
3. The fact that an entity will, if not destroyed, come to have properties that would give it a right to life does not in itself make it seriously wrong to destroy it.

If these philosophical contentions are correct, the crucial question is a factual one: At what point does a developing human being acquire the concept of a continuing self, and at what point is it capable of having an interest in its own continued existence? I have not examined this issue in detail here, but I have suggested that careful scientific studies of human development, both behavioral and neurophysiological, strongly support the view that even newborn humans do not have the capacities in question. If this is right, then it would seem that infanticide during a time interval shortly after birth must be viewed as morally acceptable.

But where is the line to be drawn? What is the precise cutoff point? If one maintained, as some philosophers do, that an individual can possess a concept only if it is capable of expressing that concept linguistically, then it would be a relatively simply matter to determine whether a given organism possessed the concept of a continuing subject of experiences and other mental states. It is far from clear, however, that this claim about the necessary connection between the possession of concepts and the having of linguistic capabilities is correct. I would argue, for example, that one wants to ascribe mental states of a conceptual sort—such as beliefs and desires—to animals that are incapable of learning a language, and that an individual cannot have beliefs and desires unless it possesses the concepts involved in those beliefs and desires. And if that view is right—if an organism can acquire concepts without thereby acquiring a way of expressing those concepts linguistically — then the question of whether an individual possesses the concept of a continuing self may be one that requires quite subtle experimental techniques to answer.

If this view of the matter is roughly correct, there are two worries that one is left with at the level of practical moral decisions, one of which may turn out to be deeply disturbing. The lesser worry is the question just raised: Where is the line to be drawn in the case of infanticide? This is not really a troubling question since there is no serious need to know the exact point at which a human infant acquires a right to life. For in the vast majority of cases in which infanticide is desirable due to serious defects from which the baby suffers, its desirability will be apparent at birth or within a very short time thereafter. Since it seems clear that an infant at this point in its development is not capable of possessing the concept of a continuing subject of experiences and other mental states, and so is incapable of having an interest in its own continued existence, infanticide will be morally permissible in the vast majority of cases in which it is, for one reason or another, desirable. The practical moral problem can thus be satisfactorily handled by choosing some short period of time, such as a week after birth, as the interval during which infanticide will be permitted.

The troubling issue which arises out of the above reflections concerns whether adult animals belonging to species other than *Homo sapiens* may not also possess a right to life. For once one allows that an individual can possess concepts, and have beliefs and desires, without being able to express those concepts, or those beliefs and desires, linguistically, then it becomes very much an open question whether animals belonging to other species do not possess properties that give them a right to life. Indeed, I am strongly inclined to think that adult members of at least some nonhuman species do have a right to life. My reason is that, first, I believe that some nonhuman animals are capable of envisaging a future for themselves, and of having desires about future states of themselves. Secondly, that anything which exercises these capacities has an interest in its own continued existence. And thirdly, that having an interest in one's own continued existence is not merely a necessary, but also a sufficient condition, for having a right to life.

The suggestion that at least some nonhuman animals have a right to life is not unfamiliar, but it is one that most of us are accustomed to dismissing very casually. The line of thought advanced here suggests that this attitude may very well turn out to be tragically mistaken. Once one reflects upon the question of the *basic* moral principles involved in the ascription of a right to life to organisms, one may find oneself driven to the conclusion that our everyday treatment of members of other species is morally indefensible, and that we are in fact murdering innocent persons.

Notes

1. My forthcoming book, *Abortion and Infanticide*, contains a detailed examination of other important objections.
2. Judith Jarvis Thomson, in her article "A Defense of Abortion," *Philosophy & Public Affairs* 1, no. 1 (1971), 47–66, argues very forcefully for the view that this conclusion is incorrect. For a critical discussion of her argument, see Chapter 3 of *Abortion and Infanticide*.
3. Section 230.3 of the American Law Institute's *Model Penal Code* (Philadelphia, 1962).
4. *Abortion and Infanticide*, Chapter 10.
5. In William T. Blackstone, ed., *Philosophy and Environmental Crisis* (Athens, GA., 1974), 43–68.
6. *Op. cit.*, 51.
7. *Ibid.*, 49–50.
8. *Op. cit.*, sect. 5.2.
9. For a fuller discussion and defense of this principle, see *op. cit.*, sect. 5.3.
10. For a detailed survey of the scientific evidence concerning human development, see *op. cit.*, sect. 11.5.
11. Consider the belief that it is *prima facie* wrong to pull cats' tails. Here is a belief that is almost universally accepted, but very few people, if any, would regard it as a basic moral belief. For this belief rests upon a nonmoral belief, to the effect that pulling cats' tails causes them pain. If one came to believe that cats actually enjoy this, one would abandon the moral belief in question. So the belief, though widely and firmly accepted, is a derived moral belief, rather than a basic one.
12. For a much more extended discussion of this point, see, for example, Peter Singer's essay, "Animals and the Value of Life," in Tom Regan, ed., *Matters of Life and Death* (Philadelphia, 1980), or my own discussion in sect. 4.2 of *Abortion and Infanticide*.

13. *Op. cit.*, sect. 7.33.

14. Philippa Foot, "The Problem of Abortion and the Doctrine of the Double Effect," *The Oxford Review* 5 (1967), 5–15. See the discussion on pp. 11ff.

15. For a much more detailed defense of this view, see sect. 6.5 of *Abortion and Infanticide*.

16. A discussion of why this is so can be found in Chapter 7 of *Abortion and Infanticide*.

Questions

1. In Tooley's view, what properties must a thing possess in order to have a right to life?

2. Has Tooley selected the right properties?

3. Are there other objections to abortion and infanticide that suggest one or the other or both practices are not morally acceptable?

Abortion and Rights

Sheila and George Grant

We are often told these days that the rights of women require the freedom to obtain abortions as part of the liberty and privacy proper to every individual. When the argument for easy abortion is made on the basis of rights, it clearly rests on the weighing of the rights of some against the rights of others. The right of a woman to have an abortion can only be made law by denying to another member of our species the right to exist. The right of women to freedom, privacy, and other good things is put higher than the right of the foetus to continued existence.

Behind this conflict of rights, there is unveiled in the debate about abortion an even more fundamental question about rights themselves. What is it about human beings that makes it proper that we should have any rights all? Because of this the abortion issue involves all modern societies (Canadian included) in basic questions of political principle.

These questions of principle were brought out into the open for Americans in 1973, when the Supreme Court of that country made it law that no legislation can be passed which prevents women from receiving abortions during the first six months of pregnancy. In laying down the reasons for that decision, the judges spoke as if they were basing it on the supremacy of rights in a democratic society. But to settle the case in terms of rights, the judges said that the mother has all the rights, and that the foetus has none. Because they make this distinction, the very principle of rights is made dubious in the following way: In negating all rights to the foetuses, the

By permission of Sheila and George Grant.

court says something negative about what they are, namely that they are such as to warrant no right to continued existence. The foetus is of the same species as the mother, and unless violent action is taken, will be a citizen in a few months. We are inevitably turned back onto the fundamental question of principle: What is it about the mother (or any human being) that makes it proper that she should have rights? Because in the laws about abortion one is forced back to the stark comparison between the rights of members of the same species (our own), the foundations of the principles behind rights are unveiled inescapably. What is it about our species that gives us rights beyond those of dogs or cattle? In discussing our laws about abortion, these fundamental issues can no longer be avoided.

The legal and political system, which was the noblest achievement of the English-speaking societies, came forth from our long tradition of free institutions and Common Law, which was itself produced and sustained by centuries of Christian belief. Ruthlessness in law and politics was limited by a system of legal and political rights which guarded the individual from the abuses of arbitrary power, by both the state and other individuals. The building of this system has depended on the struggle and courage of many, and was fundamentally founded on the Biblical assumption that human beings are more than accidental conglomerations of matter. For this reason, everybody should be properly protected by carefully defined rights. Those who advocate easy abortion in the name of women's rights are at the same time unwittingly undermining the very basis of rights. The view of human beings they are implying destroys any reason why any of us should have rights. This does not portend well for the continuing health of our freedoms.

In the modern era we have seen our basic political assumptions radically denied by Nazi and Communist regimes. Terrible programs of persecution have been carried out by these regimes, not only against their political opponents, but against whole races and against whole classes of people, such as the aged and unprotected young. Where the doctrine of rights has been denied (above all the right to existence) whole groups of individuals have been left completely unprotected. The first stage in the establishment of all modern totalitarianisms has been the explicit destruction of religion in the name of some pseudo-scientific ideology. And with the destruction of Western religion has always gone the undermining of political and legal rights.

The talk about rights by those who work for abortion on demand has a sinister tone to it. What will be demanded next: the denial of the rights of the less economically privileged who cannot defend themselves? Our system of legal and political rights is the crown of our heritage, and it is being undermined. The denial of any right to existence for the foetus has already been declared officially in the United States. There is no mention of it in our Charter. Are we going to let it happen in Canada, and open the gates to all the consequences of tyranny which will follow?

The validity of this argument must stand or fall primarily on the assertion that the foetus is a living member of our own species. It is a fact, accepted by all scientists, that the individual has his or her unique genetic code from conception onwards. He or she is therefore not simply part of the mother's body. Even the blood type may be different. After 18 days a heart beats; at three and a half weeks there are already the beginnings of eyes, spinal cord, nervous system, thyroid gland, lungs, stomach, liver, kidney, and intestines; at six weeks brain waves can be detected. It is not necessary to elaborate on the further development. It can be found in any textbook of embryology.

It would be difficult to find anyone who would deny that a foetus is a member of our species. Why is this not a possible basis for some agreement between those who differ so much as to the nature of the foetus? There is no disagreement until we try to give a name to our species. The usual one is "human beings." At these words the chasm suddenly opens between those favouring easy abortion and those against it. Immediate polarization takes place, with one side insisting that the unborn are not really human, and the others that there is nothing else they can be. The reason for this total disagreement is the fact that the word "human" has two meanings. To understand this ambiguity is the first step to any clear thinking about the abortion controversy.

In the Oxford dictionary the adjective "human" is first defined in the generic sense: "of or belonging to a man," the name of our species, covering all of its members. Then a secondary meaning is given: "having the qualities or attributes proper to a man."[1] With the word "proper" evaluation has crept in. This meaning is retained in the word "humane" (the older spelling of human), which now means "characterized by such behaviour or disposition towards others as befits a man." The generic sense of human, which applies to all our species, is specialized into meanings which are qualitative, and only apply to members of our species at their best. Words do not hold their meanings in water-tight compartments. We often use "human" in such contexts as "human values," "inhuman cruelty," "what properly befits a human being," or even "a very human person," where the word means much more than belonging to the human race, and suggests the characteristics of men and women at their maturest and noblest. Obviously such a meaning is as inappropriate for the foetus as for the infant.

Further definitions of the word are practically a free-for-all. Joseph Fletcher, a well-known proponent of abortion and euthanasia, gives a whole list of the characteristics by which life may be recognized as "human."[2] Included is "self-awareness," "a sense of time," "self-control," "capability of relating to others," "the ability to communicate," "a concern for others," "control over existence," and "a balance of rationality and feeling." (A bit unnerving when one looks at oneself!) This is an example of the word "human" being used qualitatively, and then identified with the generic sense. This is not just confusion, but a deadly double-talk, for Fletcher makes no secret of what can be done to those who fail to meet his criteria. Astonishingly, Fletcher is still taught to student doctors in bioethics classes. It is no accident that he is a member of the board of directors of the Euthanasia Education Council. The criteria for humanity work equally destructively at the beginning or at the end of life.

Similarly, the word "person" can mean an individual of our species; but can also connote a mature man or woman, capable of "personal relationships," "personal integrity," and so on. In these contexts it is almost identical with the specialized uses of "human."[3] So if, with these associations of quality in mind, we return to the naming of ourselves as "human beings," we are able to exclude the foetus from being thought of as human. We may also have no difficulty in excluding other categories of mankind that do not measure up to our view of what is "truly human" in the fullest and most meaningful sense.

A confusion is also found in the use of the word "life." "The foetus may be alive in a biological sense," we are told, "but human, no." It is implied that to talk of our species in terms of biological life is to talk on a very low level indeed. In fact, "biological life" is a misleading tautology. There is no such thing in nature as a living organism that has merely "biological life." It must belong to some species, even if it is only an amoeba. If the foetus is alive, yet is not human, what is it? No woman has yet given birth to a cat.[4]

There is another kind of double-talk about life that has a place in a United States Supreme Court decision.[5] After viability (a date varying according to the sophistication of our current supportive techniques), a foetus becomes legally recognizable as "potential life." Presumably "potential" must mean "capable of, but not yet possessing." By this vague phrase, do they mean that the foetus is not alive? If not alive, do they mean it is dead? Even the United States Supreme Court must know the difference between a living foetus and a dead one. There is no halfway. Beings with only "potential" life do not suck their thumbs in the womb in preparation for sucking the breast. It makes perfect sense to say that we all have potential not yet fulfilled, or even that we are all potentially dead, but it does not make sense to say the foetus is "potential life."

It is best to be suspicious of such phrases as "potential life," "person in the whole sense," "human in the full sense of the word." They are used to confuse what is being done in abortion. The primary, or generic, sense of "human" cannot be denied to the foetus. What a dog begets is canine; what we beget is human. Nor do we need the word "person" to defend the right of the foetus to continue developing. We do not tell the fireman not to bother rescuing the infant trapped in the burning house because that infant is not yet "a person in the fullest sense of the word."

In our day, the struggle for rights has often been effective. It now runs counter to the temper of our society to challenge the claims of personal freedom. In our society, men and women are grasping toward an understanding that would preclude violence against one another. The noble attempt to eliminate capital punishment is a good example. The fight for civil rights in the United States has won great victories, however incomplete. Women are struggling courageously for their proper equality. What of children? In the preamble to the United Nations Declaration of the Rights of a Child (November 29, 1959), it is stated that the Declaration is necessary "because the child, by reason of his physical and mental immaturity, needs special safeguards and care, including legal protection before as well as after birth." There is pressure now for this sentence to be omitted from the declaration. It is ironic that at the time of many compassionate victories there has arisen a new category of the unprotected. Despite the tradition of rights in which we were nurtured, the unborn child in the United States has been deprived of the right to exist, and the pressure to deny this right to unborn children in Canada is mounting. Strangely enough, the unborn still have some rights: they can inherit under a will, they can even be recognized as plaintiffs in a lawsuit. Recently it has been suggested that they have a right not to be born with alcoholic syndrome. But for the individuals who can be put to death at the will of the very person who brought them into existence, such rights as these are rather a bad joke.

Some distinctions must be made here between the legal situation in Canada and in the States. In January 1973, the United States Supreme Court made its declaration in *Roe v. Wade*. It affirmed a new right, nowhere mentioned in their constitution but "felt" to be "intended."[6] No legislation can infringe the right of a woman to procure the termination of her pregnancy. For the first six months of pregnancy, no reason at all need be given for the killing of the developing child. After that time, though still declared not to be a "person in the whole sense," the unborn child is recognized as "potential life." A little red tape is required, after six months, to abort the foetus; namely, one doctor must declare it necessary for the mother's health, "health" in the widest possible sense of the word, that of "well-being."

Canada's position is different. The law grants no "right to abortion." Abortion is still on the Criminal Code as a punishable offence; but an exception is made to the general prohibition in the case of danger to the life or health of the mother. An abortion may be performed, anytime during pregnancy, on the recommendation of one doctor, ratified by a hospital committee of three doctors. The committee does not need to see the woman. The numbers of ratifications done in a short time are very large. A disinclination toward bearing a child is usually interpreted as a danger to mental health. In 1980, according to Statistics Canada, 65,751 legal abortions were performed, and the number increases each year, although the medical necessity of abortion decreases. It is obvious that convenience, rather than danger, is already the usual criterion. Yet there is mounting pressure today for still easier laws. The only possible extension would be abortion on demand, which already *de facto* exists in many parts of Canada, for example Ontario and British Columbia.

What has happened to our belief in rights that, in the name of a lesser right, the primary one—the right to life—can be denied to members of our own species? Not only is the woman's own right to life affirmed, but it includes her right to freedom and privacy, and well-being, and all sorts of other good things. Yet she herself, her own unique, unrepeatable self, was once growing in her mother's womb. What magic has occurred with the passage of time that gives her all these rights, and denies any to her unborn child?

Light can be thrown on this denial of rights by looking at a familiar quotation: "We hold these truths to be self-evident; that all men are created equal, that they are endowed by their Creator with inalienable rights, that among these rights are life. . . . that to secure these rights, governments are instituted among men." Fine, ringing words, but no longer self-evident. Our world has changed. Many believe that we are accidental beings in a world that came into being through chance. In such a situation the very foundations of the doctrine of rights have been eroded. All men are not created equal; they are not created at all. But in that case, why are they equal? Justice can become a privilege society grants to some of its people, if they are the right age, and sufficiently like most other people. One can foresee a time when before one can qualify for rights, a kind of means test may be used: "Are you human in the fullest sense of the word?" "Are you still enjoying quality of life?" And here is the crunch: as the foetus loses out, so will the weak, the aged, the infirm, the unproductive. If we come to believe that we are nothing but accidents, rights will no longer be given in the very nature of our legal system. The most powerful among us will then decide who is to have rights and who is not.

The effect of this undermining of our political tradition is often sugar-coated by talk about "quality of life." The phrase "quality of life" has a high-minded ring about it. Like the slogan "every child a wanted child" it is impossible to be against it. Of course it is better for children to be wanted rather than rejected, and for lives to have a high quality rather than a low one. But let us remember for what purpose these slogans are now mainly used. They are used negatively, and with terrible, destructive implications. Every child should be a wanted child, so destroy those that do not seem to be wanted. Only quality of life deserves our respect, not life itself. So we deny rights to those who do not measure up.

When "quality of life" is urged for constructive purposes, it is indeed a compassionate approach to human suffering; but when it is used to downgrade some lives as expendable, because of their absence of quality, its proper use is perverted. It can then justify "selective abortion," or getting rid of the defective. Although our law makes no provision for "selective abortion," it is already widely practised in Canada, and is the purpose of the well-known test, amniocentesis, that identifies certain defects in the foetus. It is wonderful when medicine can eliminate certain diseases, but it is not at all the same thing to eliminate the patients suffering from them. Once we take the cost-benefit approach, and start grading the right to life in terms of quality, our criteria exclude more and more groups from human status. What will we be willing to do to these groups?

The most pressing warning of how far the destruction of rights could go in the Western world took place in Nazi Germany. We in the English-speaking world would like to think of this as a monstrous happening that was defeated, and stopped, and that has no relation to ourselves. But if we look at some of the basic programs carried out by the Nazis against their own people, we may find that, whatever our revulsions, our society seems to be moving away from the clear principles that would condemn these practices.

We are not referring to abortion, but to the Nazi program of euthanasia of the insane and the incurable that was extended, in 1943, to include children orphaned by the war. These children were put to death in the gas chambers along with the incurable and the insane. The country was thus relieved of the burden of those who could not care for themselves. The techniques of the gas chambers and the crematoria were used first for such people, then extended to the Jews, the Gypsies, and political opponents. Hitler had to keep these programs as secret as possible. Largely through the courage of Bishop Galen, the programs became known to the public, and evoked great horror among the German people, even though they were living in a totalitarian state.

We, of course, do not live in a totalitarian regime, and we do not yet kill our mentally ill. Nevertheless we are moving toward ways of thought that could be used to justify such actions. We are starting to arrogate to ourselves the power to decide not only who should live, but who really wants to live. Despite all the evidence that retarded people, or the very old, are frequently as happy and as unhappy as other people, we are coming to know better. They may seem happy, but if they were normal, they would agree that as defective or old they are really better off dead.

If this sounds unjustifiably alarmist, it is well to remember the figures of abortions since the law was amended in 1969. In 1970, according to Statistics Canada, there were 11,152 legal abortions in Canada; in 1980 there were 65,751. Certainly the rare medical necessities have not increased, for medical techniques have improved. The situation is clearly self-accelerating. If women know they never need bear children they have conceived, they are less and less likely to face the initial inconveniences. We have moved fast in a few years toward the point where, in the name of convenience, we say that a woman has an absolute right to an abortion and an unborn child has no right to existence. Such an absolute denial of rights to unborn children has moved Canada down the road to a society where the sanctity of the individual is openly denied, and where the idea of rights may gradually disappear. The end of this road is tyranny — a tyranny in which legal protection will be based upon power. This erosion of rights will be smooth, for when tyranny comes in North America, it will come cosily and on cats' feet. It will come in the name of the cost-benefit analysis of human life, sugared over with liberal rhetoric about quality of life.

Notes

1. The word "man" is used here to include both men and women. This old way of speech now seems discriminatory and should be avoided.
2. Fletcher, Joseph, "Indicators of Humanhood: A Tentative Profile of Man," *Hastings Centre Report*, 1972, pp. 1–4.
3. The Dred Scott Decision in 1856 by the American Supreme Court ruled that although negroes were human beings, they were not "persons" in the eyes of the law. The Fourteenth Amendment to their constitution was enacted specifically to overturn this, and interpreted "person" as including all living human beings.
4. The National Council of Women are evidently not quite sure about this. In 1967 they presented a resolution to a Parliamentary Committee in which abortion was defined as the "premature expulsion of the mammalian foetus." It is impossible to meet a mammal pure and simple—one meets a mouse, dog, human being, and so on.
5. *Roe v. Wade*, p. 48.
6. Justice Blackmun spoke for the majority: "We feel the Right is located in the Fourteenth Amendment's concept of personal liberty." *Roe v. Wade*, pp. 37–38.

Questions

1. Does the liberalizing of abortion laws lead to the liberalizing of laws that prohibit euthanasia?
2. If we deny to unborn children the right to life, are we undermining the right to life of other members of the human race?
3. Have the Grants provided convincing arguments for the view that a human being is a person from the moment of conception forward?

Toward a Credible View of Abortion

L.W. Sumner

As little as a decade ago most moral philosophers still believed that the exercise of their craft did not include defending positions on actual moral problems. More recently they have come to their senses, one happy result being a spate of articles in the last few years on the subject of abortion.[1] These discussions have contributed much toward an understanding of the abortion issue, but for the most part they have not attempted a full analysis of the morality of abortion.[2] Such an analysis is too large a task for a single paper, but a sketch of it will be undertaken here, the details to be filled in elsewhere.[3]

The moral problem which abortion poses results from some familiar biological and social contingencies. Because *homo sapiens* is a mammal the young of the species are carried by the female during the period of initial development. The weight of reproduction itself is therefore divided unequally between the sexes. Social practice ordinarily enhances this unequal division of labour by arranging that the woman will rear the children as well as bearing them. Her fertility is therefore no small matter for a woman, affecting as it does her opportunity to plan the course of her own life. Thus in the first instance she seeks to control whether (or when) she will conceive. But once conception has occurred its normal outcome is avoidable only by terminating the pregnancy, that is to say by killing the developing fetus. Such an intentional interruption of the gestation process is an abortion. And so the issues are drawn. Were one or another of these contingencies otherwise abortion might create no moral problem. But as matters now stand the liberty of the woman may conflict directly with the life of the fetus. Such is the stuff of the abortion issue.

The temporal boundaries of abortion are conception and birth: abortion is necessarily post-conceptive and prenatal. Therein lies its ambiguous moral status. Contraception functions by preventing pregnancy rather than interrupting it. For this reason it does not destroy life and only a small minority persists in objecting to it (or to some particular contraceptive method) on moral grounds. At the other extreme, infanticide involves killing the newborn child. Only an even smaller minority is able to accept infanticide on moral grounds, except perhaps in some extreme cases. Contraception and infanticide are relatively clear moral cases precisely because they are located on either side of pregnancy. Abortion is a difficult case precisely because it occupies this uncertain middle ground. Pro-abortionists tend to assimilate it to contraception while anti-abortionists tend to assimilate it to infanticide. An analysis of the morality of abortion must properly locate it on this continuum between the clear cases.

To speak of the morality of abortion may obscure the fact that there are at least two distinct moral problems concerning abortion. The first requires developing and defending a moral evaluation of abortion itself. We may assume that it will answer the question: When is an abortion morally permissible and when is it not? The

Reprinted by permission from *Canadian Journal of Philosophy*, Volume 4, No. 1, September 1974.

second problem requires developing and defending a state policy on abortion. We may assume that it will answer the question: When should an abortion be legally permissible and when should it not? These questions are both moral ones, since they both ask for evaluations from the moral point of view, but they are different moral questions, since evaluating abortion is not the same as evaluating abortion policies. Once we have decided on the moral status of abortion, it is a further issue how it should be treated by the law.[4]

To be complete, positions on the morality of abortion must speak to both problems and most have done so. Two such positions are worth outlining as material for discussion. The first, which may be called the liberal position, is a defense of abortion and of a woman's right to have an abortion if she so chooses. It has at its heart the contention that abortion is a matter private to the woman because it does not substantially affect the welfare of any other person. As such, it raises no moral issues whatsoever, although it may, because of its potential hazards, raise prudential ones. As in the case of other medical procedures, we need to ensure only that the operation is carried out safely, efficiently, and with consent. Any further legal regulation of abortion is incompatible with the principle that the state has no right to interfere in the private activities of the individual. Laws which prohibit or restrict abortion constitute an illegitimate tampering with individual liberties. A woman has the right to decide for herself whether to bear children, a right which is already recognized when the state refrains from regulating contraception. The availability of abortion is simply a further guarantee of this right for cases in which an unwanted pregnancy has already occurred. Furthermore, prohibitive or restrictive abortion policies have the defect of enforcing the moral views of some (anti-abortionists) against the rest. Indeed, in the light of the traditional Catholic position on abortion, such policies establish the moral beliefs of a particular religious sect, thus undermining the separation of church and state. A permissive policy, or no policy at all, leaves each woman free to decide the matter for herself.

What may by contrast be called the conservative position rests upon the view that abortion is not a private matter because it involves the killing of the fetus. It is generally agreed that the taking of human life is in most circumstances wrong. But the fetus is a human life and so abortion is always homicide. As such, it is morally justifiable only in very special circumstances, such as when the continuation of pregnancy would endanger the life of the woman. The welfare or liberty of one person is not in general sufficient to justify the killing of another. It is also usually agreed that protection of human life is one of the legitimate functions of the law. Prohibitive or restrictive laws are therefore not to be seen as the enforcement of private morals or as the establishment of a church but rather as a proper extension of laws forbidding homicide. While it may be true that more permissive laws would produce benefits for women, and perhaps for others as well, these benefits must always be balanced against the toll in human life which abortion necessarily exacts.

These two positions are the ones most commonly heard in discussions of the morality of abortion. Each is internally coherent, each has a venerable tradition behind it, and each is now promoted by vocal and organized pressure groups. The two positions are also diametrically opposed and between them they define the opposite poles in the abortion debate. Nevertheless, it is likely that each position commands the allegiance only of a minority among persons aware of the abortion problem. Many, perhaps most, find themselves somewhere in the middle ground between the two sides. To such persons neither position as it stands seems very credible, because each represents an extreme among available possibilities. The one focusses entirely on the rights of the woman and ignores the fate of the fetus; the other just as resolutely fastens on the welfare of the fetus and subordinates the problem of the woman. The one entirely assimilates abortion to contraception, while the other simply identifies it with infanticide. Each position attaches itself too thoroughly to one of the two ingredients whose conjunction creates the moral issue in the first place. Surely abortion is not just a private matter but is also not always a fullblown case of homicide. Surely there are less crude and less simplistic alternatives available than either of these.

So goes the view from the middle. This paper is an attempt to vindicate this view. It will argue that neither of the standard positions is acceptable because each is too extreme. It will also outline a more credible, because more moderate, alternative. The first step involves a closer look at the two given positions. Out of each can be distilled the basic argument around which the position as a whole is built.

Privacy Argument

P1   Actions which cause no harm are never morally wrong
P2   The law may not legitimately prohibit actions which cause no harm
P3   The fetus is not a human individual

P4   Abortion is never morally wrong
P5   The law may not legitimately prohibit abortion

Homicide Argument

H1   It is always morally wrong to kill a human individual
H2   The law may legitimately prohibit the killing of human individuals
H3   The fetus is a human individual

H4   Abortion is always morally wrong
H5   The law may legitimately prohibit abortion

Neither of these arguments is here formulated so as to be logically tight, although the missing steps could be easily supplied, and each argument is presented in a particularly strong and unqualified form. The arguments are therefore more extreme even than the positions from which they were extracted, and it may be that few would defend them in their present form. As stated, however, they will serve as excellent reference points for discussion. Ultimately it will be clearer to what extent, and in what manner, they must be weakened in order to be acceptable.

The arguments plainly have a common structure. Each contains two conclusions which speak to the two moral questions about abortion. Analogous conclusions in the two arguments (P4 and H4, P5 and H5) are mutually incompatible. Each argument derives its conclusions from three premises, of which the first two (P1 and P2, H1 and H2) are moral principles. The third premise in each case (P3 and H3) seems

to be a statement of fact about the fetus which serves as the hinge between principles and conclusions. Further, the real difference between the arguments, in virtue
of which they yield incompatible conclusions, do not seem to lie in the moral principles to which they appeal. These principles form a mutually compatible set and
when put in a somewhat more qualified manner might all have considerable appeal.
The point of departure would appear to lie in the third premise. There the homicide
argument seems to flatly affirm what the privacy argument just as flatly denies,
namely that the fetus is human.

The question about "the status of the fetus" is obviously in one way or another
at the heart of the abortion debate.[5] It cannot be true that abortion is homicide
unless the fetus is to be accounted a human person, and it cannot be true that
abortion is a private matter unless the fetus is not to be so accounted. Doubts about
abortion are above all doubts about how to classify, and therefore treat, the fetus.
Sooner or later this question must be confronted. The larger part of this paper will
be spent confronting it.

It will be convenient to organize the discussion as a commentary on the privacy
and homicide arguments, but particularly on the latter. It is natural to begin by
examining the contention that the fetus is human. The structure of the argument
suggests that this is the crucial fact about the fetus whose acceptance will pave the
way to acceptance of the argument's conservative conclusions. If this is so then one
implication follows immediately. It cannot be that the humanity of the fetus is a
matter of theological tenet or religious dogma. It is sometimes argued that an
individual is human in virtue of possession of a soul, or perhaps a distinctively human
soul, and thus that the fetus is human from the moment that it acquires such a
soul. The history of controversy about abortion within the Catholic Church consists
largely of disagreement over when to locate this moment of "ensoulment."[6]
Whereas Aquinas seems to have believed that the event occurred sometime during
the gestation period, the weight of official opinion now is that it accompanies
conception. The role of this opinion within the homicide argument will be obvious.

Whatever the merits of contrary positions within this theological debate, its
outcome cannot affect our evaluation of the homicide argument or of abortion.
The one characteristic of the event of ensoulment which seems to be universally
accepted is that, whenever it occurs, it is not observable or open to any sort of
empirical test. There exists no empirical method of confirming that, or when, an
individual is ensouled. But if the premise concerning the fetus is to play its role
within the homicide argument it must be open to confirmation or disconfirmation.
Otherwise the argument as a whole is undecidable and will carry no weight whatever
for anyone who rejects the theology on which it rests. Sectarian dogmas based
upon faith, revelation, or scriptural authority can have no place in public moral
discussion of abortion. They may of course be used to reinforce the consciences of
the faithful, but the homicide argument, if it is to carry any weight whatever for
the unfaithful, must be able to stand free of theological props.

However, once we have agreed that whether an individual is human is an empirical
fact about that individual, we encounter an intractable problem. The argument
cannot just stipulate what it will mean by this word "human" for that again
would be to abandon its aim of widespread acceptance. It must show that in some

common and ordinary sense of the word the fetus is clearly human. But therein lies the problem: there are too many such common and ordinary senses. Like all predicates the word "human" is a tool of classification; when we use it we distinguish the category of things human from things not human. But different categories suit different purposes and different contexts, and so the word comes to be used in different senses. For example, in saying that a person is human we may mean that he is particularly warm, or gentle, or loving (as opposed to inhuman, i.e., cold, callous, unfeeling), or we may mean that he is fallible or imperfect (as opposed to superhuman or divine). As a classificatory term "human" in this respect some-what resembles the word "real," which can be opposed to any of "artificial," "counterfeit," "fake," "forged," "synthetic," "imitation," "illusory," and so on, depending on the sort of object being described and on the context. Like "real," "human" admits of a variety of meanings. No doubt there are some common threads running through these meanings, but the fact remains that deciding whether the fetus is human is rather like deciding whether the wax apple is real. It may or may not be, depending on the categories one has in mind.

The nature of the term "human" makes things at once easy and difficult for the proponent of the homicide argument. It is easy to show that in some ordinary sense the fetus is human, but it is difficult to show either that it is human in all such senses or that one particular sense is privileged. The nature of the problem will be clearer if we restrict our attention, as proponents of the homicide argument tend to do, to senses of "human" which are biological in nature. It is sometimes claimed that advances in biology (and especially in genetics and embryology) in the past two centuries or so have shown beyond any doubt that the fetus is human from conception.[7] Biologists and other professionals have agreed that the fetus is human, and there's an end to it. We must be wary of arguments of the form "the professionals all agree. . . ." For one thing the professionals seldom do all agree, and the existence of many prominent pro-abortionist biologists and obstetricians would seem to indicate that they do not all agree in this instance. But even if they did, it is surely not a matter for them to decide. They will of course be expert in a number of facts which are relevant to deciding whether a fetus is human, but these may not be the only relevant facts and anyway scientific professionals have no license to tell us how to construct our categories. It will be apparent presently how deciding that a fetus is human is not making a simple statement of fact about it but rather drawing a particular conclusion from accepted facts or organizing these facts in a certain manner. Professionals are not notably better qualified than the rest of us to draw such conclusions or to decide how the facts are best organized.

If we explore what biology can tell us that is relevant to classifying individuals as human we find again more possible categories than we want. There are at least three distinct senses of the word "human," each of which is derived from and there-fore consonant with the biological facts. The first and simplest of these may be called the *specific* sense, because it pertains to the distinction of animal species. Certainly one thing we can mean by saying that an individual is human is that it is not a baboon or a tuna or a woodpecker. The category of human individuals which is generated by this sense of the word has the undoubted virtue of being quite sharp at the edges: it includes all and only members of the species _homo sapiens_. We would be uncertain only of hybrids or mutations, and these are rare.

This specific sense of "human" can be used as the basis of two other, still biological, senses of the term. Each of these further senses generates a narrower category of human individuals, since it includes only a subset of the members of the species. When biologists do animal classification (taxonomy) they tend to describe the characteristics of a given species in terms of a model individual of the species which satisfies two conditions: it is structurally and functionally normal and it is mature. This procedure is a simplifying device which involves describing the model individual first and then allowing for variations displayed by members of the species which are either abnormal (runts and albinos, for example) or immature and not fully developed. Species are compared primarily in terms of the properties of their standard or model members. Thus _homo sapiens_ is identified, and differentiated from other primate species, in terms of the height range, weight range, posture, skeletal and muscular structure, brain size, and so on, of the normal and mature individual.[8] What is interesting for our purpose is that normality and maturity can themselves serve as criteria which generate quite different, though overlapping, categories of human individuals.

Consider first normality. If a member of our species is abnormal enough in physiology then he is liable to be described as a freak, or a monster, or a vegetable, or an animal. Even staid medical science continues to use the term "monster" to describe a specified set of gross abnormalities or anomalies.[9] Since fetal growth proceeds so rapidly from such a small beginning, even minor deviations from normal development early in pregnancy can produce gross malformations in the later fetus. No part of the human physiology is immune. The most extreme fetal malformations affect the central nervous system: total absence or extreme underdevelopment of the brain, non-closure of the spinal column, and so on. Other major organ systems are however also susceptible to gross malformations. When we refer to such malformed individuals as monsters it certainly seems that we are denying that they are completely or fully human, despite the fact that they may be genetically quite normal and that they are unquestionably members of our species. They fail of being fully human because they are so abnormal, because they fall so short of the paradigm or model member of the species. It is only at the margin, only in extreme cases, that we are likely to describe members of the species, on physiological grounds, as monsters or to say that they are less than human. But to the extent that we do so we are employing a sense of the word "human" other than the specific one. It is appropriate to call it the _normic_ sense.

Finally, a member of the species can fail to exhibit the characteristics of the model individual not because it is abnormal but because it is immature. Thus if we follow the adult backward through the developmental process we sooner or later reach a stage when the individual is so undeveloped or immature that we begin to speak of its potential, or what it will become, rather than what it is. Thus the chicken is at the earliest stage an egg, the oak an acorn, the plant a seed. It is proper to say that the egg, acorn, or seed will grow into, develop into, or become the chicken, oak, or plant and also that they are not yet these things. Likewise, in our species, at the earliest stage of development the individual is a single cell (zygote), the result of the union of sperm and ovum. It is common and natural to say that this cell is a potential human individual, or that it will grow into, develop into, or become a human individual but that it is not yet a human individual. Again we tend to use this classification only at the margin; the child or infant is a human individual, but the zygote will become one. And again the operative consideration seems to be the degree to which the individual fails to exhibit the properties of the model member of the species. The zygote is microscopic in size, spherical in shape, and contains no organ systems whatsoever. When we react to this difference in degree by saying that the zygote is not yet a human individual we are once more employing a sense of the term other than the specific sense. Since level of development is now central it seems suitable to call this third sense of the word "human" the *developmental* sense.

There may well be other ways in which categories of human individuals are constructed out of raw biological data, but these three will suffice for the present discussion. It seems that even the hard facts of biology generate no unique and privileged category of human individuals. In the specific sense all members of the species are human, however abnormal or undeveloped. In the normic sense only those members of the species are human who display, or will come to display, to a sufficient degree the physiological characteristics of the normal individual. In the developmental sense only those members of the species are human who have reached some minimal stage of development. It should be stressed that each of these senses of the word is quite legitimate. Each is grounded in the biological data, though each organizes these data differently. Each picks out one of the strands of meaning in the ordinary word "human," and each of the resulting categories appears in common speech. Each is internally coherent and each enables us to distinguish tolerably well between what is human and what is not. Finally, each corresponds to analogous distinctions for other animal species.

If we bring these categories to bear on the fetus we derive divergent answers to the question whether the fetus is human. We must remember that "the fetus" is a developmental stage in the history of the individual. Technically, the fetal stage does not occupy even all of the individual's prenatal history, since it is preceded by the zygotal stage (first five weeks) and embryonic stage (next four weeks). If we use the term "fetus" loosely to cover all developmental stages prior to birth, then it is clear that the class of fetuses contains individuals very different in many important ways. A newly fertilized ovum or zygote is a tiny dot barely visible to the naked eye, while the full-term fetus is usually eighteen to twenty-two inches long and five to ten pounds in weight, with almost all major bodily systems in working order. Given the sheer quantity of development in the first nine months of life, the fetal category *must* contain very different sorts of individuals. We should of course be wary of attributing to all fetuses characteristics pertaining only to a particular stage of development.

In the specific sense of the word all fetuses conceived of human parents are human, regardless of normality or developmental stage. In the normic sense most fetuses are human, gross abnormalities being rare. In the developmental sense the zygote is clearly not yet human and the full-term fetus is just as clearly human, while the fetus at some stages in between will not be easily classifiable. We will return later, from a slightly different perspective, to both the extreme and the middle cases. For the present we need only note that in the developmental sense of the word some fetuses are human while others are not and that the difference between them lies only in their level of development.

We are now back where we started. The deceptively simple question "Is the fetus a human individual?" has no unique answer, even when only biological data are admitted. We can perhaps now see why many biologists shy away from this category of humanity. It is not itself a ground-floor biological category, but rather a way of organizing ground-floor data. Unfortunately, there are a number of alternative ways of organizing and presenting these data, none of which is privileged *so long as we consider only the facts themselves*. Even though our question certainly looks like a factual one, there seems no way to answer it satisfactorily by appeal even to a limited range of facts. The substance of premise H3 of the homicide argument is that all fetuses conceived of human parents are human. This contention is true of the specific sense of the term "human" and only of that sense. Thus the homicide argument requires this sense of the word, but there is no way of showing that this sense is privileged or that it should be preferred. The status of the homicide argument is thus far undecidable. The privacy argument, however, fares less well. The substance of its premise P3 is that no fetus, regardless of stage of development, is human. We have located no common biological sense of the word "human" in which this claim is true. Unless some viable candidate has been overlooked, which is certainly possible, we are entitled to suspect that the privacy argument rests its conclusions on a highly implausible premise.

It is an attractive strategy to consider the homicide argument piecemeal, and to begin with that premise which looks like a straightforwardly empirical one. It can now be seen why the strategy must fail. In the absence of a specific context the question of the humanity of the fetus is undecidable. But the homicide argument itself, through its first two premises, provides just such a context. Once these premises are given (and it should be remembered that each of them appears a familiar and attractive moral principle) then only one step remains to generate the argument's conclusions. In this context to concede that the fetus is human is to concede that it is to be included within the scope of the two moral principles and therefore to concede the conclusions. Conversely, if the conclusions are to be avoided, given the principles, then the humanity of the fetus must be denied. This surely is why debates about whether the fetus is human are so heated: each side knows the moral issue at stake, namely when it is morally permissible for the fetus to be killed. The assumption common to both sides is that if the fetus is human it is wrong to kill it. Against this assumption the question of the humanity of the fetus is no longer a neutral and empirical one, which is how it has so far been treated in this discussion. Suddenly all of the moral passion which is part of the abortion debate is infused into this supposed question of fact, and a decision on it, one way or the other, becomes itself a moral decision. It ought to be obvious that some basic and hard moral decisions must somewhere be involved in either accepting or rejecting the homicide argument. This fact is concealed when we are first asked to accept some moral principles which appear quite reasonable and then, because of the "facts" of the matter, shown that we are thereby committed to some strong conclusions about abortion. The facts will simply not bear this weight and the underlying moral disagreement will show itself as a preference for one or another interpretation of the word "human." Our assessment of the homicide argument will be much more clear-headed if the moral decisions involved are clearly located and carefully identified.

The homicide argument must be evaluated as a whole and not piecemeal. It is a requirement of logic that in order for the argument to be sound it must not equivocate on this word "human": the sense of the term which is employed in one part of the argument must be employed throughout. We have seen already that H3 requires the specific sense of the term; this sense must therefore be employed as well in the two moral principles H1 and H2. When interpreted in this manner the principles include in their scope all members of the species, including the fetus. To assent to the principles is to agree that the fetus, regardless of its level of development, is to be treated from the moral point of view in just the same manner as the child or the adult. It is now obvious just how much is being conceded in making even the first two moves in the argument, and how short the distance is from there to its conclusions. If H3 is rendered uncontroversially true by use of the specific sense of "human" the moral issue simply shifts to the two principles. In no way can this issue be evaded: Does the fetus belong within the scope of H1 and H2? Can we devise moral principles concerning homicide which are plausible for both the fetus and the adult? Should the fetus be accorded the same treatment, and therefore the same protection of life, as the adult? This surely is the moral crux in the abortion debate: not whether the fetus is human but how it is to be treated.

The homicide argument makes the moral claim that the fetus is to be treated in the same way as the adult and it does this by including the fetus within the scope of its principles concerning homicide. These principles state that it is wrong to take human life and that human life should have legal protection. In this somewhat stark form they are probably too strong for most moral tastes; surely killing is sometimes morally justifiable and should be sometimes legally justifiable. Still, if the argument is to yield suitably conservative conclusions about abortion, such as that abortion is justifiable only to save the life of the mother, the principles must be given a strong formulation. Proponents of the homicide argument speak sometimes of human life as possessing a uniquely high or absolute value, where this seems to mean that nothing but the preservation of life can compensate the loss of life. If we incorporate this valuation into the two principles we derive the result that it is wrong to kill except to preserve life and that in all cases save this one killing must be prohibited by law. Even in this somewhat weakened form these principles are not easy to live by. They suffice to condemn killing in almost every instance, since it is only rarely that killing is necessary to preserve life. Virtually all warfare and political terrorism, along with such practices of the state as the death penalty and firing upon criminal suspects, would be unjustifiable. We would also need to question such technological advances as the automobile where we trade annually many thousands of lives for an increase in convenience. It is a fairly safe guess that few among us are really willing to carry such principles to their inevitable conclusions. But if not, then we cannot pretend to accept the principles. This burden weighs heavy upon proponents of the homicide argument.

It is generally their purpose to show that abortion is permissible only to save the life of the mother and that in all other circumstances it should be proscribed by law. In order to generate these conclusions they require principles of the sort now under consideration. Once adopted, these principles must be applied to all cases and not just to that of abortion. The view that life can be sacrificed only for life is perhaps an admirable one, but it is a high ideal with radical implications. The acceptance of these implications, all of them, is the test of the anti-abortionist's sincerity.

Let us suppose, as the argument requires, that these are acceptable moral principles concerning human life. They are formulated for, and commonly applied to, post-natal life—infants, children, and adults. The question remains: Is the fetus to be included within their scope? In asking this question we place a severe strain on our moral principles. How far back in the life-history of the individual are we to take them to apply? To birth only? To conception? How different from the child or adult must the individual be before we will place him in a separate category? The point of the homicide argument is to extend these principles back to conception. To decide whether this extension is plausible we should look at the extreme case: the zygote, the individual at the point of conception, at the earliest stage in his life-history. If it is plausible to extend the principles to the zygote then it is plausible to extend them to all fetal stages; if it is not then the homicide argument must be rejected.

We must remember that at conception the zygote is a single cell, a tiny and barely visible entity. Consider now the following situation. Some experimental work has been done on a so-called "morning-after" pill, which is sometimes loosely referred to as a contraceptive but is in fact an abortifacient, since it causes the expulsion of the zygote should the woman conceive. What are we to think of a woman who regularly uses such a pill? She does so not knowing whether she will conceive, but knowing that if she does then the pill will cause the death of the zygote. Is she committing homicide? Her behavior is structurally similar to that of someone who regularly leaves time bombs in randomly selected locations, set to explode at randomly selected times, not knowing whether anyone will be in the proximity when the bomb explodes, but knowing that if someone is then he will die. Is our moral attitude toward the two cases the same? Are we likely to condemn the woman, on moral grounds, as a probable killer? Would we consider her using the morning-after pill to fall into a different category from using an oral contraceptive? Would we insist that the pill be taken off the market, that all testing of it be curtailed? Would we support a law which made the use of the pill punishable with the severity usual to homicide statutes? The homicide argument requires affirmative answers to all of these questions.

There is as yet no morning-after pill in general use. But many woman do now use the intrauterine device (IUD) which probably also works to expel the fertilized ovum by preventing its implantation in the wall of the uterus.[10] If so, it too is an abortifacient and all of the foregoing questions can be raised concerning it. Again the homicide argument requires that we regard women on the IUD as presumptively guilty of multiple homicide. Are we really ready to do so? Should we pass a law forbidding use of the IUD and begin arresting women who are using it? Is every such woman a public menace comparable to the setter of time bombs? If the homicide argument is correct then human life on a grand scale is at stake and innocent victims are dying every hour. But can we really accept this view of the matter?

Some laboratory experiments have united sperm and ovum in an artificial extrauterine environment. The resulting zygote does not long survive because of the absence of the sustaining uterine wall. Are experimenters who permit such conceptions murderers? Are their experiments comparable, morally speaking, to those Nazi medical experiments which cost the lives of their victims? Or consider the matter this way. Suppose that one experiment involves killing the sperm and ovum just before union while a second kills the resulting zygote immediately after union. Should we regard the two as radically different in their moral implications because conception occurred in the second but not in the first? The homicide argument requires that we do so. Finally, a large number of pregnancies end in spontaneous abortions. If the homicide argument is correct every such case costs a human life. Should we not take care that the abortion, while certainly accidental and unintended, was not in any way the result of negligence on the part of the woman? After all, we do take just such care to ensure that accidental death resulting from a highway accident was not the result of negligence on the part of the driver. A genuine desire to protect human life in the womb, however early its development, would surely require such steps. But are we really prepared to accept them?

The argument so far is simply an attempt to identify commonly shared moral intuitions. The homicide argument has certain unavoidable implications for the case of the zygote. If these implications are unacceptable then the argument must be rejected. I believe that most persons who reflect carefully on the situations described will be unable to accept these implications. I know that I cannot. Most persons, I suspect, regard the developmental stage of the individual as relevant to the morality of killing that individual. Killing the zygote does not strike us as homicide because developmentally the zygote is too primitive, too unlike the adult, child, or even the fetus in its later stages. It is precisely level of development which the homicide argument rules out as relevant. It tries to draw a firm and inflexible line at conception. Before that point no questions about homicide occur, while immediately after it the individual is to be regarded morally as the equal of a child or adult. Few will accept this hard-and-fast division of cases. The zygote for most will not seem to fall in a different moral category from the sperm or ovum, despite the fact that the zygote is, and the sperm and ovum are not, a genetically complete member of the species. Abortion at the earliest stage, through the agency of the morning-after pill or IUD, will be regarded by most as morally identical to contraception. At this extreme abortion is indeed assimilable to contraception for the purposes of morality.

Consider now the opposite extreme case, the full-term fetus. At term the fetus differs from the newborn (neonate) principally in its occupation of a quite different environment. Because this environment is both confined and fluid, the fetus is unable to breathe or to ingest food. Both oxygen and nourishment are received from the maternal blood supply through the medium of the placenta. All other organ systems which will be functioning just after birth are functioning just before it. The birth process transfers the individual to a new environment and severs the direct physical link between mother and child: the neonate must breathe and eat. In no other important respect does birth alter the individual. The process occupies only a few minutes and the individual is the same size, weight, and shape directly after it as before. Most of his bodily systems are unaffected by the process. In the light of these facts it seems difficult to accept the view that birth is of crucial importance from the point of view of the morality of killing. Assuming that it is wrong to kill the infant directly after birth, it would seem equally wrong, and for the same reasons, to kill it directly before birth. The differences between full-term fetus and neonate do not seem morally relevant, especially when we consider that the temporal point at which birth occurs varies widely and therefore that many full-term fetuses are older and more developed than many newborn infants. It would seem natural then to extend our moral principles concerning killing beyond the neonate to embrace the full-term fetus. At this extreme abortion is morally assimilable to infanticide. If this view of the matter is taken then the privacy argument as well cannot be accepted, since it implies that abortion at no stage of pregnancy, however late, is to be considered as an instance of homicide.

If I am right then upon reflection most persons would be willing to include the full-term fetus, but not the zygote, within the scope of moral principles concerning homicide. They will therefore reject both the homicide argument and the privacy argument. Since attention has here been focussed especially on the homicide argument, its fate should be described in detail. Its three premises must all employ the same sense of the word "human." The appeal to moral intuition implies that if the specific sense is chosen, so as to render H3 true, then H1 and H2 are both false. Conversely, if the developmental sense is chosen so as to render H1 and H2 true, H3 is false. There is no possible formulation of the homicide argument which preserves the truth of all three premises. In order to be acceptable, the homicide argument must be amended. There are two alternatives open:

Amended Homicide Argument (1)

H1   It is always morally wrong to kill a human individual
H2   The law may legitimately prohibit the killing of human individuals
H3*   Some fetuses are human individuals and some are not

H4*   Some instances of abortion are morally wrong and some are not
H5*   The law may sometimes legitimately prohibit abortion and sometimes not

Amended Homicide Argument (2)

H1*   It is sometimes morally wrong to kill a human individual and sometimes not
H2*   The law may sometimes legitimately prohibit the killing of human individuals and sometimes not
H3   The fetus is a human individual

H4*   Some instances of abortion are morally wrong and some are not
H5*   The law may sometimes legitimately prohibit abortion and sometimes not.

Formulation (1) employs the developmental sense of "human" and therefore preserves H1 and H2 from the homicide argument, but not H3. Formulation (2) employs the specific sense of "human" and so preserves H3 from the homicide argument, but not H1 and H2. It is now clear that the question of whether the fetus is human is not in itself crucial to the argument, since the same conclusions are derivable in either case. The considerations which would lead us to classify the fetus at different stages as human or not, in the developmental sense, are of course relevant since the developmental level of the fetus plays a large part in our moral decisions concerning abortion. But the ultimate questions at stake are moral ones.

The liberal and conservative positions, and the arguments on which they rest, are unacceptable because they entail conclusions which are too extreme. The case against these positions has been made entirely by appeal to commonly shared moral intuitions. It would be strengthened if these intuitions could be shown to cohere well with our considered views on moral issues other than, but related to, abortion.

It does not seem wrong to kill a zygote, even if the reason for doing so is simply that the woman does not wish to be pregnant, while it does seem wrong to kill a full-term fetus for this reason. The difference between the two cases seems to lie principally in the level of development of the fetus. This suggests a developmental approach to abortion in which the justifying conditions for an abortion will contract as the fetus develops. On this conception the fetus comes gradually to be treated as a moral person in the full sense.[11]

The question is why fetal development should be considered morally relevant in this way. As the fetus grows it changes in two main aspects: globally (increase in size, alteration of shape) and systemically (acquisition of major body systems). Of these the latter seems the more important from the moral point of view. We should probably treat as moral persons individuals who were systemically identical to us, especially in the functioning of their central nervous systems, but who differed, even radically, in size, shape, or both. Even among organ systems many seem only marginally relevant. There is nothing distinctive about much of our bodies: other animals are swifter, stronger, better shielded, and keener of sense than we. In one respect alone are we pre-eminent, our brains having evolved to a point where we have the capacity for thought and the expression of thought (language). Emphasis on the development of the central nervous system is the physiological correlate of the ancient view that man is distinguished from other creatures by his rationality.

It seems plausible to suppose that we are willing to treat a fetus as a moral person only when it has come to possess a central nervous system developed at least to some minimal extent. Once this developmental view of abortion is taken it can be connected to views on cognate moral issues. A zygote and an embryo are distinguished by their relative lack of a central nervous system. A similar lack is rare, though possible, among other members of the species. An anencephalic is an individual in which the higher levels of the brain remain underdeveloped or totally absent. Such individuals rarely survive until birth and never long thereafter. In such cases abortion, or for that matter infanticide, does not seem morally objectionable. The condition is also approximated in those victims of disease or accident who have permanently lost the functioning of the higher levels of the brain but continue to live. In such cases euthanasia does not seem morally objectionable. An early abortion is therefore similar, from the moral point of view, to some cases of eugenic abortion (early or late) and to some cases of euthanasia, in that the individual who is killed lacks at the time a central nervous system functioning in more than a rudimentary manner. The cases are of course distinguished by the fact that the early fetus has not yet developed such a system while the anencephalic will never develop one and the accident victim has lost the functioning of a developed system. Thus in the former case but in neither of the latter one is preventing the evolution of an individual who otherwise would come to possess not only a highly developed central nervous system but also all of the characteristics typical of adult members of the species. But there seems nothing wrong with preventing the development of a human person (thus the moral innocuousness of contraception) while there seems much wrong with terminating the life of one which has already developed to a considerable degree. This single difference in the case of early abortion does not appear therefore to be morally relevant.

Somewhat further afield we encounter the treatment of other species. This issue is too complex to be discussed thoroughly but some broad features should be noted. Our attitudes toward other species are complicated by our need for a reliable food supply, by our love of killing for its own sake, and by our habit of keeping certain species of animals as pets. In general the protection of life we offer to other species is largely determined by our own needs: thus we may hunt mountain lions to extinction while supporting a burgeoning population of household cats and we may eliminate wolves while protecting poodles. But we do make a pervasive distinction between the value of human life and the value of the life of all other animal species, once again on the basis of what is considered distinctive in us. Thus through all the complicating factors we display a marked preference for the more intelligent and highly evolved species. The differences are, as always, most apparent at the extremes. We destroy insects when they are merely inconvenient for us while feeling a much closer kinship to those species of great apes who are our nearest living relatives. Here too we construct our moral categories in part around this most crucial of all human characteristics.

To mould these still scattered attitudes and practices into a single coherent system would require a thoroughgoing analysis of life and death and above all an account of when and why killing is wrong. This undertaking is too ambitious for the present but until it has been completed no view of abortion can be taken as firmly established. Once such an analysis is available, however, it is very likely that only a developmental view of abortion will be compatible with it.

It has thus far been left unspecified how abortion should be regarded between the extreme cases of the zygote and the full-term fetus. I will simply state my view of the matter with little supporting argument.[12] The major factors relevant to evaluating abortion are the situation and needs of the mother and the level of development of the fetus. The gradual and continuous nature of the latter renders the drawing of sharp lines out of the question. The attempt to draw such a line (whether at conception or both) is precisely the mistake common to the liberal and conservative positions. Any such line must make an arbitrary distinction between adjacent and similar cases. The developmental view must allow for the gradual acquisition by the fetus of the status of a moral person and the accompanying right to protection of life. It is customary to divide pregnancy (calculated at forty weeks) into trimesters of approximately thirteen weeks. Even by the end of the first trimester the fetus is well advanced in the development of its central nervous system, as well as other bodily systems. It has entered a transitional or threshold stage between its early undeveloped state and its later developed state. Likewise, the end of that trimester is the latest point at which the safest abortion procedures (dilatation and curettage, vacuum aspiration) can be employed, and by that time every woman has had an adequate opportunity to decide whether she wishes to continue her pregnancy. For all these reasons, during the early weeks of pregnancy an abortion is morally permissible whatever the woman's reason for wishing it, while during the final four or five months it is permissible only in very special circumstances analogous to those which justify killing in the case of post-natal persons. Between these relatively clear cases lies the borderline threshold period occupying a few weeks around the end of the first trimester. During this stage the morality of abortion is simply unclear.

This is so far only a sketch of a position, but when it is fully elaborated and properly defended we have a developmental view of abortion which is far more plausible than either the liberal or conservative position. While it lacks the elegant simplicity of the extreme views it makes up this lack by taking into account factors which they simply ignore. The morality of abortion is a difficult question in part because the fetus itself is so different at various stages of pregnancy. Only the developmental view allows us to attend to these differences in adopting a moral stance on abortion. It is for this reason that it both matches more closely our intuitions about abortion and coheres better with our views on related moral issues than does either of the more prominent positions.

The abortion policy appropriate to this view would permit abortion at the request of the woman before some fixed time limit, and would carefully screen abortions after that limit. Since the law must operate a workable policy, it cannot tolerate borderline cases and therefore must establish a clear and definite time limit. It is reasonable to set this limit around the end of the third month of pregnancy. Such a limit lies within the threshold period, coincides with the latest stage at which the safest abortion methods can be used, allows every woman sufficient time to discover that she is pregnant and decide whether to terminate the pregnancy, and captures the majority of abortions actually performed even where there is no time limit. After the third month the law will consider abortion as homicide and will specify the grounds on which it will be permitted. We may assume that these grounds will be narrow and strictly medical in nature and that some screening apparatus will be established. Again the details of the policy and of its justification cannot be considered here.

Notes

1. R.B. Brandt, "The Morality of Abortion," *The Monist*, LVI, No. 4 (October 1972); B.A. Brody, "Abortion and the Law," *Journal of Philosophy*, LXVIII, No. 12 (June 17, 1971), and "Thomson on Abortion," *Philosophy and Public Affairs*, I, No. 3 (Spring

1972); R.J. Gerber, "Abortion: Parameters for Decision," *Ethics*, LXXXII, No. 2 (January 1972); Judith Jarvis Thomson, "A Defense of Abortion," *Philosophy and Public Affairs*, I, No. 1 (Fall 1971); Michael Tooley, "Abortion and Infanticide," *Philosophy and Public Affairs*, II, No. 1 (Fall 1972); Mary Anne Warren, "On the Moral and Legal Status of Abortion," *The Monist*, LVII, No. 1 (January 1973); Roger Wertheimer, "Understanding the Abortion Argument," *Philosophy and Public Affairs*, I, No. 1 (Fall 1971); B.A. Brody, "Abortion and the Sanctity of Human Life," *American Philosophical Quarterly*, X, No. 2 (April 1973).

2. The exceptions are the articles by Tooley and Warren (see note 1), each of which attempts to justify what I have classified as a liberal position on abortion. The present paper was completed before I encountered these articles and thus I have not commented on their arguments. Two of my purposes, however, are to discard this liberal view and to argue for an alternative to it.

3. A more thorough treatment of the matters discussed in this paper, and others pertinent to the abortion issue, is included in *Abortion and Moral Theory* (Princeton, N.J.: Princeton University Press, 1981).

4. An answer to the first question is, however, an important step toward answering the second. The close connection between a particular view of the morality of abortion and a particular sort of abortion law is stressed by Brody (*op. cit.*).

5. The unavoidability of this issue is the main point of the discussions by Brody.

6. For an account of this history see John T. Noonan, Jr., "An Almost Absolute Value in History," in *The Morality of Abortion: Legal and Historical Perspectives*, ed. John T. Noonan, Jr. (Cambridge: Harvard University Press, 1970).

7. Catholic law professor Sergio Cotta, speaking for the Vatican against the 1973 United States supreme court decision on abortion: "By investigating the basic genetic structure of life, science has determined with unquestionable certainty that since the moment of conception the embryo is a living human being, entirely distinct from the parents." Reported in the Toronto *Star*, January 24, 1973.

8. For a typical taxonomical profile of our species see E.L. Cockrum *et al.*, *Biology* (Philadelphia: W.B. Saunders Company, 1966).

9. For a standard classification and description of fetal abnormalities see Edith L. Potter, *Pathology of the Fetus and Infant* (second edition: Chicago: Year Book Medical Publishers, 1961).

10. See the discussion of the intrauterine device in Germain Grisez, *Abortion: The Myths, the Realities, and the Arguments* (New York and Cleveland: Corpus Books, 1970), pp. 106–109.

11. For the purpose of this discussion, an individual is being treated as a full moral person when the conditions generally accepted as justifying the killing of that individual are those and only those that are generally accepted as justifying killing members of the species in general. In the language of the earlier discussion, the individual must be included within the scope of general moral principles concerning homicide.

12. A full defense of this view is made in the book referred to in note 3.

Questions

1. Does Sumner provide convincing moral arguments in support of the view that an unborn child is *not* a person from the moment of conception?

2. Does Sumner provide convincing moral arguments for the view that an unborn child becomes a person sometime prior to birth?

3. Assuming that the unborn child becomes a person at some point after conception and prior to birth, does it follow that aborting the pregnancy after that point would be immoral in all cases? If not, under what conditions would abortion late in pregnancy be justified?
4. How should the Criminal Code be amended, assuming that Sumner's view of abortion is the correct one?

Abortion: An Unresolved Moral Problem

Grant Cosby

Voluntary abortion involves the preventable destruction of an unformed or partly formed human organism. It is disagreement about the moral significance of this fact which sustains the controversy over abortion. This disagreement derives from a dispute about the sanctity, or morally protected position, of the destroyed organism, which in turn results from conflicting opinions about the basis or criterion of sanctity rather than any uncertainty over how they may apply. The thesis of this paper is that this last disagreement about the criterion of moral sanctity cannot be settled by rational, i.e. non-circular, argument; and hence, that there is no rational method of resolving the controversy over the morality of abortion.[1]

Concern with abortion springs from the practical need to ascertain whether or not voluntary abortion (involving the preventable destruction of an unborn human) is morally wrong. It is a mistake, therefore, to deal with this problem by asking whether the unborn embryo, fetus or zygote has a right to life, since by answering the question whether the fetus has a right to live, we do not necessarily answer the prior question, whether it is wrong to destroy it.[2] It is also a mistake to treat the problem as one that turns on whether the unborn organism is a human being or not. Obviously it is. All agree to be referring to the species *homo sapiens*, not *homo habilis* or some other primate species. But "difference of species is not *per se* a morally relevant difference."[3] The humanity of the fetus is relevant to the morality of abortion only to the extent that a property characteristic of human beings is also a ground for the sanctity of any living entity. The question of primary importance, then, is what property must a living entity have if it is to be wrong to destroy it. It is of secondary interest to know whether this is a distinctive property of all, or only, human beings.

The Capacity for Future Valued States

If moral sanctity is to be based on certain properties belonging to human beings rather than their relationship to others, if it is a protected status with which they

Reprinted by permission from *Dialogue*, Vol. XVII (1978), No. 1.

are endowed rather than one that must be earned, then it is plausible to maintain that it is the capacity for valued states of consciousness that is the basis of moral sanctity. At least this appears to be the common denominator of both pro- and anti-abortion arguments.

At the conservative end of the spectrum of views regarding abortion we are said to be human in a normally significant sense at the moment of conception. As Noonan puts it:

> . . . at conception the new being receives the genetic code. It is this genetic information which determines his characteristics, which is the biological carrier of the possibility of human wisdom, which makes him a self-evolving being.[4]

If true, it would follow that abortion was wrong at any time except on grounds which justify the taking of an adult's life. This has the advantage, so galling to proponents of abortion, of including moral protection for every stage of human life which anyone thinks should be protected. If it errs, it errs on the side of safety and respect for life; it risks being too inclusive rather than too exclusive. His position has the additional advantage, rare in moral philosophy, of providing a relatively precise measure of sanctity.

The question which such a view raises is whether this conception of humanity accounts for the alleged sanctity of human life. Genetic properties may be reliable for the purpose of species-identification, but are they plausible for the purpose of status-justification? The one fact that might justify a morally protected position for the newly formed zygote is that it is "the biological carrier of the possibility of human wisdom," or, in other words, it has the "genetic" capacity to develop into a rational adult.[5] As a result of conception, the human embryo is self-sufficient in genetic material. New sets of genes will be formed mitotically from the original infusion during fertilization, and under normal conditions, the newly formed embryo will develop into an adult human. The position is not implausible. Perhaps to paraphrase Rousseau, man is not conceived free, but conceived to be free.

At the liberal end of the spectrum, proponents of abortion commonly claim that we are not fully "human," not really a "person," unless we are sentient or conscious beings. According to one writer, "only that which is rational, self-conscious and embodied in an animal organism counts as a human person."[6] According to another, "in order to be a person, i.e. to have a serious right to life," a being must have "the capacity to envisage a future for oneself, and to have desires about one's future states."[7] And finally, another bases respect for persons on their "capacity for entertaining ends and goal-oriented action, and appraising events and states of affairs in the light of such ends."[8] All these versions stress the significance of one or more mental capacity requiring some degree of sentience or consciousness. On any of them abortion will pose no problem since the prized capacity presupposes a mental life which the unborn are presumed not to have. Indeed, they often require a degree of cognitive development not found until late infancy, if then. As a consequence, the defence of abortion may be accompanied by an acceptance of infanticide, which is morally distasteful to many still uncertain about the morality of feticide.

Though such theories sometimes lead to the sanctioning of infanticide, and are unavoidably vague in establishing the time at which the stated condition of sanctity is reached, they at least accord value to living beings on the basis of properties probably everyone would endorse as morally relevant. Their principal strength and source of legitimate appeal stem from the ostensibly relevant nature of mental attributes. Insentient beings like stones, plants and insects, which lack feelings, cannot experience pain, fear death, or wish for life, do not elicit independent moral consideration.

But the concept of a sentient or conscious being is importantly ambiguous. We may have in mind a being who is in a conscious state, or a being who, although not necessarily conscious at the time, has the capacity for conscious states. If we are concerned with the morality of destroying a sentient or conscious being it makes a difference whether we base its sanctity upon an occurrent or dispositional property of sentience. Although it is possible to deny that an unborn human is a conscious or sentient being in either sense, only the latter can be used as a reason for denying its sanctity. Otherwise protection would be denied to everyone whenever they temporarily ceased to be in the requisite conscious state. The moral difference, if any, between killing a fetus, or infant, and killing an adult must be that the former cannot, rather than does not, feel, think, or experience while the latter can.

But if it is the possibility of future states of consciousness that is alleged to account for the sanctity of living beings, it is far from obvious when that living being is entitled to be protected by moral rules; for "can" has many senses. There are different kinds of capacity, from the undeveloped, "genetic" capacity of the newly formed zygote, to the fully developed "mental" capacity of the completely formed adult of the species. Hence, if it is a capacity for consciousness that is the basis of sanctity, then the morality of abortion must be decided on the basis of the kind of capacity which is pertinent to being protected by moral rules.

This brief examination of both conservative and liberal positions indicates that for many writers it is the organism's capacity for certain valued states of consciousness which is the basis of moral sanctity. They disagree about what type of capacity is required: an undeveloped or fully developed capability for these valued end-states. Before turning to this outstanding issue, it is worth asking whether, insofar as valued conscious states are relevant, it is the possibility of such conscious states existing in the future that is sufficient for sanctity. Or is the present or prior existence of consciousness necessary?

That the possibility of future states of consciousness is an important part of sanctity can be seen in cases not involving abortion. If a patient is comatose due to a kidney malfunction, no one would question the obligation to put them on a kidney machine if they can thereby recover consciousness. But if during an extended kidney failure irreparable brain damage had occurred such that recovery is no longer physically possible, the obligation to put them on the kidney machine would be moot at best, since it would no longer serve any point.

The contentious issue, however, is whether the possibility of future consciousness is sufficient to warrant keeping a patient alive, insofar as states of consciousness are relevant at all. Certainly the existence of present valued states of consciousness is not a necessary condition of sanctity; otherwise it would never be wrong to kill someone in their sleep or whenever they were not experiencing that valued conscious state. It cannot be right to destroy a living entity only because it would be painless, or because it was not consciously desiring to live or was not engaged in reasoning, appraising or a valued kind of thinking, because then it would not be wrong to strike while someone is unconscious, or to drug, or anesthetize them first and kill them afterwards, or simply to destroy them while they were distracted from the mental activity alleged to be valuable. The remaining question, then, is whether a prior state of consciousness is necessary for sanctity. If it were, then abortion could be justified and the debate about different kinds of capacity would be academic.

On the face of it, holding that a prior state of consciousness is a necessary condition of moral sanctity is not very plausible. The fact that it was a newborn infant who was comatose because of a diabetic mother would not be grounds for denying it insulin treatment while administering it to the mother. Nevertheless, it has been argued by Michael Tooley that the existence of consciousness must predate the existence of a right to life. We are asked to suppose that we could perform the technical feat of constructing a complete adult human in the laboratory at a temperature where the organism is frozen. Suppose further, he asks, that we have the technology to thaw him out without putrefaction to become a "conscious, adult human with beliefs, desires, and a distinct personality."[9] Would grinding our frozen organism up for hamburger be open to moral criticism? Tooley thinks not, because:

> Until the organism has been brought to consciousness, and until it envisages a future for itself, and has hopes and desires about such a future, one does not violate anyone's right to life by destroying the organism.[10]

If persuasive, this example would have the interesting implication that even the possession of fully developed human faculties would not normally suffice to make it wrong to destroy an organism. But the example does not show what Tooley intends. Let us suppose, in addition to what has been asked, that before its destruction, a temporary laboratory malfunction has led to its being unwittingly thawed out one night, and that during an interval of awareness our monster glimpsed a bright object which he wanted to reach out and touch, just before being returned to a frozen state. Would the telltale EEG signs the following morning convince us that the monster we contemplated destroying was now a person endowed with the right to life? Clearly not; that moment of minor passion does not make a moral difference the morning after. It may be that we felt no obligation to the frozen adult, but this is attributable to the fact that it has been portrayed as a question of personal rights, rather than moral wrong, or because it is not clearly alive, or possibly because it is a monstrosity. Our indifference need not have anything to do with the absence of any pre-existing state of consciousness, as the morality of his destruction remains unchanged, should consciousness have been present.

So it would appear that, insofar as the mental life of a living entity is the reason that it is wrong to destroy it, the possibility of future sentient states is normally a sufficient reason for its sanctity. It may be that not every state of awareness is of sufficient value to warrant the protection of life forms capable of that awareness, and that only so-called "higher forms of consciousness," whatever they be, warrant protection for sentient beings endowed with such capacities. The conclusion, however, will be the same: that it is the capacity for future states of such awareness which is the condition for the sanctity of life. Again, it may be the case that states of awareness are not the only source of values. Most discussions seem to presuppose that the locus of end-values resides exclusively in our mental life; this presupposition may not be valid. Still, whatever mental or physical activity is thought to be of value, it can be argued that it is the capacity to carry out that activity, not the present nor the prior occurrence of that activity, which is a sufficient condition for protecting organisms which exhibit it. Thus, if it is laughter which is held to be the sole end of life, then it is some sense of "the capacity to laugh" which is a tenable ground for the sanctity of *homo ludens* since we cannot be laughing all the time.

That the capacity for end-values is the basis of moral sanctity is further borne out by reflecting on the function of moral rules, many of which — like the prohibition of killing — serve to limit our liability to avoidable harms. To the extent that our moral concern is future-oriented we are enjoined to treat one another in ways which are at least compatible with the realization of whatever is thought to be an end-value. This explains why possessing the capacity for those valued end-states makes it wrong to destroy a living entity, since it is a property which is causally relevant to their realization. For the like reason that the undeveloped or unused capacity to realize valued states is not worth having, it is also wrong to prevent or impair their development.

The Capacity to Develop vs. the Developed Capacity

Given that the property which makes it morally wrong to destroy a living entity is its capacity for future valued states, the problem of moral sanctity resolves into the question: "In what sense is 'the capacity for future valued states' a property the possession of which by a living organism justifies the prohibition of its destruction?" Although there are a number of discernible stages of development from conception to maturation, it will not prove necessary to examine each growth-stage with its concomitant capacity in order to determine whether the abortion issue is resolvable. It is enough to compare the undeveloped, genetic capacity which constitutes the basis of sanctity for many opponents of abortion, with the range of developed capacities which can serve as the bases of sanctity for proponents of abortion.

Nor is it necessary to specify the allegedly valuable qualities the capacity for which is held to be a ground of sanctity. The issue can be stated simply in terms of the existence of the capacity to develop *vs.* the existence of developed capacities. What it is a capacity for is irrelevant to this remaining moral issue. For example, it may be thought morally wrong to kill any sentient creature which can apprehend its own death and fear for its own safety. The question, then, will be whether it is the genetic capacity for developing the emotion of fear, or the developed emotional capacity itself, that makes it wrong. Or it may be thought morally wrong to destroy any being who can rationally distinguish between right and wrong. The question then would be whether it is the capacity to develop moral insight or the developed moral capacity itself that makes it wrong. In short, there is nothing to choose between anti- or pro-abortionist stands as far as valuable activities, or states of awareness, are concerned. Whatever culminating activities or states of consciousness are held to be worthwhile, the disagreement about the significance of different kinds of capacity remains.

It might be maintained, at this point, that tenable positions based upon distinct capacities cannot be found, because there are only differences of degree between the existence of an undeveloped capacity for thought and a fully developed capacity. If true, clear-cut criteria of sanctity are out of the question. But there are discontinuities in growth which can serve as the basis of a properly articulated position. For example, if it is a "genetic" capacity then there will be a definite time when the fertilized egg will have the full complement of genes. Before conception has occurred, the human reproductive cells will be incapable, without an infusion of chromosomes, of independent mitotic development. After conception has occurred, the human zygote will be genetically self-sufficient and capable, without any additional chromosomes, of developing by mitosis. Before conception occurs, the incomplete reproductive cells would lack moral sanctity. With conception the genetically complete embryo would gain moral sanctity. Similarly, it is possible to distinguish when the embryo or infant has developed the "brain" capacity, or later the "learned" capacity, although the time may be more indeterminate.

Attempts at refuting an anti-abortion position based on the fetus' potentiality for conscious thought by a reduction to an extreme anti-contraception position have failed to appreciate the tenability of a properly articulated position on the sanctity of human life. The same can also be said for attempts to refute a pro-abortion position based upon more developed potentialities. Their tenability can be argued by analogy to contractual obligations like that of promising. It does not follow from the claim that it is wrong to destroy an already formed fetus having the capacity to become conscious, that it is also wrong to prevent or refrain from the formation of an organism with the same capacity. Otherwise, from the fact that it was wrong to break a promise which has already been made, it would follow by the same reasoning, that it was also wrong to prevent someone from making a promise or to refrain from making a promise one contemplated making. Though promises are unlike pregnancies in some respects, they are similar in the relevant ones. Any obligation arising from the creation of a human fetus may not be so readily overridden as an obligation arising from the creation of a verbal undertaking. Still, in both cases, anyone who believes that a promise or a pregnancy generates a moral obligation to respect what has come to exist, is not forced to concede a further obligation to bring about the conditions which generated the obligation. Otherwise, moral commitments would lead to further moral commitments indefinitely. Of course, an obligation to conceive may be claimed, but only on the basis of an independent rule.[11] In the case of abortion, a human organism having attained a capacity alleged to be grounds for moral sanctity, it follows that one is under an obligation as a result that one was not under before it occurred. And this will be the case whether the capacity alleged to be morally significant is the genetic capacity to develop acquired at conception or a developed capacity acquired on the way to maturation.

Given the possibility of tenable positions based upon the presence of putatively significant kinds of capacity, the major task for both conservatives and liberals must be to demonstrate a morally relevant difference between the kind of capacity each endorses as a ground for sanctity, and the kind endorsed by those of a different persuasion. If there is any danger of a slippery slope, it stems from the failure to rationally defend one kind of capacity for consciousness or any other valued state, over against another kind as the ground of moral sanctity.

The Futility of Moral Arguments

The task of demonstrating a moral difference between different kinds of capacity to realize a valued state of consciousness can only be carried out by moral argument. This simply follows from what was argued earlier; namely, that, properly understood, the abortion controversy gives rise to the question whether it is morally wrong or not to destroy an unborn human organism at any state of gestation. What is needed, then, are moral considerations which are logically sufficient to warrant asserting or denying that it is wrong to destroy an unborn living entity which is genetically capable of developing whatever qualities are to be valued in human beings, or in any species where they are to be found. The conflict between those who dispute the wrongness of destroying an embryo, fetus or even an infant can only be resolved rationally by appealing to logically adequate general principles of right and wrong.

Such a principle is to be found in some form of utilitarianism, which is commonly appealed to in order to resolve specific conflicts of moral opinion. Essentially, we are faced with a disagreement about the adoption or extension of certain moral rules. The pro-abortionist position here might be that we ought to adopt the rule that it is seriously wrong to kill a living being if and only if it is neurologically capable of consciousness, i.e. if it is sentient. The anti-abortionist position might be that we ought to adopt the rule that it is seriously wrong to kill a living being if and only if it is genetically capable of becoming conscious. Can we resolve this disagreement about what rule against killing to adopt by means of a principle of utility? Brandt thinks that we can. If we were to be governed by the principle of adopting moral rules which will "maximize expectable average utility," then, he thinks, there would not even be a *prima facie* prohibition of abortion, except in the special circumstance of a labour shortage. "For, in general, the prohibition of abortion will detract from the expected average utility."[12] More people being born will mean fewer resources available and hence a lowering of the average utility for those already born. We could dispute the purely economic measures of utility which Brandt employs, but the main problem with his principle of utility is that using it here begs the question. If we are to be governed by the general principle of following those rules the adoption of which will maximize average expectable utility for those who are already born or already sentient, then abortion will not be wrong since it will not adversely affect the average expectable utility of those who are sentient. On the other hand, if we were to be governed by the general principle of following those rules the adoption of which will maximize average expectable utility for all who are genetically capable of becoming sentient as well as those already sentient, then abortion will adversely affect the maximization of average expectable utility by discriminating against the production of average expectable utility for the class of the unborn.

The difficulty encountered with Brandt's principle of utility will be encountered with other forms as well. A necessary condition of the unequivocal application of any principle of utility is the specification of the class of beings whose utility (benefits and harms) is to count. We must be able to answer the question, "Maximum utility for whom?" Insufficient attention has been paid to this problem in the past; it was thought enough to answer, "for all concerned." But whose good or harm is of moral concern or relevance is precisely what is in dispute when we are faced with conflicting opinions about the moral status of the embryo and fetus. If we decide to count only future goods or harms of those already born, sentient or having any property which is not also a property of the embryo or fetus, then the corresponding principle of utility will tend to favour abortion. If we decide to count the future goods or harms of those not yet born or sentient but having the capacity to become so, then the corresponding principle of abortion will not favour abortion. But we cannot adopt one principle of utility or the other without first deciding on the moral significance of being genetically capable of sentience, as opposed to being, say, neurologically capable of sentience. Hence we cannot appeal to any principle of utility to resolve disagreements of opinion about the latter without begging the very question at issue; unless, of course, there is some sort of an independent method for deciding what form of general moral principle to adopt. I shall consider this possibility in a moment.

The second kind of general principle which might be found persuasive in settling conflicts about what kind of living being it is wrong to destroy would be a general principle of justice, providing we could find one that would be regarded as valid. For example, it might be argued that abortion is wrong on grounds of fairness since it denies the fetus or embryo an equal opportunity to enjoy life.[13] The general principle of justice underlying the argument might go as follows. We ought always to support those rules, policies or practices the adoption of which will bring about an equal opportunity to realize what is good and avoid what is harmful. Life, obviously, is something to be enjoyed, not suffered. Hence we should follow rules which guarantee to all the equal chance to enjoy life. However, what seems to be a general consideration unfavourable to abortion is, like the general considerations of utility, dependent on how we specify who is entitled to an equal opportunity. In order to know how the general principle applies, we must specify who qualifies to enjoy life. If fairness requires an equal opportunity for all living beings having at least the genetic capacity to enjoy life, then abortion will be *prima facie* unfair; if fairness requires an equal opportunity for all living beings having a developed capacity to enjoy life, then abortion will not be *prima facie* unfair. We cannot in this case, nor in any other, know what is fair or unfair without a prior knowledge of what kinds of capacities for enjoyment qualify a being for equal treatment. Hence, we cannot appeal to considerations of fairness to justify the inclusion or exclusion of living beings characterized in terms of one kind of capacity or another without once again begging the very question at issue.

General principles of justice, like general principles of utility, are not independent means of arbitrating disputes about whether our moral concern should extend equally to all living beings with certain genetic capacities or equally to all living beings with the corresponding developed capacities; this is so because the applicability of these principles depends upon first resolving the dispute about the correctness of including in their formulation concern for either or both classes of beings. Nor can we hope to uncover any other moral rule or principle which will provide what the principles of justice and utility cannot. A few minutes' reflection will reveal why searching for a moral principle to resolve the undoubtedly moral question of the limits of our justified concern is fruitless. What is at issue is a question about the scope and limits of application of any and all our moral rules; it is a question of whether those who have certain developed capacities or those who have the capacity to develop those same capacities warrant moral concern, as expressed in rules which define, specifically or generally, what is right and wrong. Hence, the question of whether it is the zygote's genetic capacity for "human wisdom," etc., or the child's brain-capacity for human wisdom, etc., which is morally relevant to the wrongness of killing a living entity, is at the same time a question about the scope of application of all those moral rules and distinctions which set limits to our liability to harm. In short, the problem of interpreting the commandment "Thou shalt not kill" is a general problem of the interpretation of moral rules.[14] Does it apply to humans, or to persons or to all creatures? If to humans, on what definition of humanity? Etc. The same question will arise for any other moral rule indeterminate as to its proper scope. Hence, we cannot resolve differences of opinion about what class of beings should count when applying moral rules by appealing to any of those rules whose applicability is being questioned.

It might be hoped, however, that we can turn to the rational decision-making procedures which are currently employed to validate general moral principles in order to resolve any dispute about the scope of such principles. Presumably, if we have a rational method of showing why the principle of maximizing average expectable utility should be accepted, we may be able to adapt that rational method in order to establish the scope of such a principle. Indeed, success in the former project would seem to require success in the latter, since no principle is applicable as a guide to action until and unless its scope has been determined.

On one theory, employed by some of the contributors to the present controversy, we can and should determine whether abortion is wrong according to a valid rule of morality by considering whether the rule forbidding abortion will be preferred by all persons who:

a. expected to be subject to the rule
b. were rational in being guided by all relevant information
c. were impartial in not being influenced by information about how they will be affected by application of the rule.[15]

In order to be able to derive a decision on this sort of procedure we have to know, in addition to what information will be supplied and what withheld, how a rational impartial person will be motivated to use this information. According to current versions of this rational method, all persons are expected to be self-interested, but we could equally postulate that everyone will be guided by fellow feelings. The particular motive will make no appreciable difference in the present case. We can simply ask whether a rule protecting the life of any being having the genetic capacity to develop any valued capacity or a rule protecting only the life of any being having the developed capacity, would be preferred by any hypothetical being who was (a) subject to that rule, (b) rational as defined, and (c) impartial as defined.

The virtue of such an approach is that it is allegedly fair. As Green puts it, by "stripping" participants in this choice procedure of any information except that which is necessary to their rationality they can "come to substantial agreement upon rules which do not unfairly favor one party or another."[16] Following this method, Green goes on to argue that fetuses and infants have no basic rights, only those conferred upon them according to the interests of the more developed rational agents. In contrast, James Childress contends that "it is arbitrary to restrict the span of life that agents consider."[17] Apparently, then, not everyone who uses the procedure agrees what moral rules should be followed. On the one hand, we have the view that a fair and impartial situation for deciding on the proper rule can include the information that one is not a fetus or infant; on the other, we have the view that a fair and impartial situation for decision-making cannot include this information. Which is correct?

This disagreement does not show that one of the self-appointed participants in this moral referendum must be mistaken. The critical factor in this case is information about what stage of one's whole existence from conception to the death-bed one is at. If such information is relevant to knowing what rules to subject yourself to, then its knowledge is a condition of (b) being rational; if the information is not relevant to knowing what rules to subject yourself to, then ignorance of it is a condition of (c) being impartial. If participants are allowed to know that they have already developed certain rational or moral capacities when considering which rule to follow, they can disregard the fate of fetuses, etc. and "rationally" prefer a rule which protects only their own existence and that of those with similar developed capacities. But if the participants are not allowed to know whether they have already developed certain capacities or whether they would exist only as a zygote with the genetic capacity to develop those capacities, they will prefer a rule which protects their existence, should they still exist only in the womb. The outcome of the vote, then, will depend upon whether the person must know that he is sentient in order to be rational or must be ignorant of whether he is sentient in order to be impartial.

However, the solution to this dilemma about what knowledge (or ignorance) is necessary to properly meet the stated conditions of the decision-making procedure depends in turn upon whether moral rules are supposed to protect living beings with human genetic capacities or only those with developed human capacities. On the decision-making procedure in question, if it is *prima facie* wrong to destroy any living being with human genetic capacities, then it will be relevant to be aware of the general fact that abortion after conception destroys such a being, and it will be important to be ignorant of the particular possibility that one is not a zygote with only genetic capacities. Likewise, if it is only *prima facie* wrong to destroy a living being with developed human capacities, then the general fact that a living being has certain genetic capacities will not be relevant, and ignorance of the particular fact that one is not a zygote with only genetic capacities will no longer be important. In short, the decision-making procedure is indeterminate with regard to the matter at hand, i.e. the proper scope of moral concern. How it will be made determinate will depend upon who is thought to fall within the proper area of moral concern. Hence we cannot make this procedure for demonstrating the validity of conflicting moral rules effective without at the same time deciding on the proper scope of moral rules. Accordingly, the procedure is either powerless to resolve the question of whether genetic or developed human capacities are sanctity-making properties of living entities, or it begs the question by building one opinion or its contrary into the choice procedure which is supposed to arbitrate independently between those opinions.

Moral democracy may be a fine device for assuring non-coercive solutions to problems of human conflict among those who are given the vote. But they can also serve to cloak a coercive solution to a problem of conflict between humans and those whose humanity is denied. Democratic methods cannot tell us the proper subjects of moral concern because they operate primarily to guarantee impartial consideration for all subjects of moral concern whose propriety they presuppose.

The attempts thus far made to provide a rational basis for abortion have failed. This does not imply that abortion is morally wrong; rather, these failures suggest that the property whose possession allegedly endows an organism with moral sanctity cannot be determined by rational argument as it has been supposed. After all has been argued, we are left to make what we will of the acknowledged facts of the stages of human growth from conception to maturation. Here the dogged defender of a rational solution might appeal as a last resort to a conception of morality in order to determine whether an unformed human being is entitled to equal and independent moral consideration. According to a familiar conception, "morality is an expression of human rationality and represents the application of reason to the conflicts that arise in the course of social life."[18] As a description of morality the conflict-resolution theory is false, since moral rules have also served the goals of individual perfection and the establishing of man's relationship with a deity. It is highly doubtful that there is any unitary, non-vacuous goal or function common to all moral rules. But as a prescriptive model of what is of moral concern, the conflict-resolution theory merely raises the question encountered all along: What property must human organisms have if they are to warrant moral protection in the event that their existence conflicts with the interests of others?

What seems clear is this: There is a class of moral rules, like the prohibition against killing, which function to set moral limits to an individual's liability to preventable harms. What is singular about the problem of abortion is that it raises the question of the valid scope of all moral rules having this function, whatever additional purposes they may serve as well. In seeking to determine the conditions of moral sanctity we are attempting to establish the conditions that a living entity must satisfy in order to enjoy equal protection under these moral laws. At what point a growing human organism falls within these protective limitations is neither obvious nor, apparently, decidable by argument. Nevertheless, this must be established if we are to know how to apply rules of this class, so it will have to be included as a basic assumption of any system of protective moral rules or any method validating such a system.

Notes

1. This conclusion is not drawn from a general position of moral scepticism but is based upon features specific to the issue of abortion.
2. S.I. Benn makes a similar point in "Abortion, Infanticide, and Respect for Persons," when he suggests that "there may be morally relevant reasons" against abortion which do not take the form of ascribing a right to the unborn fetus. See *The Problem of Abortion*, edited by Joel Feinberg (Belmont, California: Wadsworth Publishing Company, 1973). . . .
3. Michael Tooley, "A Defence of Abortion and Infanticide," in *The Problem of Abortion*, edited by Joel Feinberg, p. 74.
4. John T. Noonan, "An Almost Absolute Value in History," in *The Problem of Abortion*, edited by Joel Feinberg, p. 15.
5. In a recent article Hare makes the same point. "The single, or at least the main, thing about the fetus that raises the moral question," he says, "is that, if not terminated, the pregnancy is highly likely to result in the birth and growth to maturity of a person just like the rest of us." See R.M. Hare, "Abortion and the Golden Rule," *Philosophy and Public Affairs* 4 (1975), p. 207.
6. H.T. Engelhardt, "The Ontology of Abortion," *Ethics*, 84 (1974), p. 229.
7. Tooley, "A Defence of Abortion and Infanticide," in *The Problem of Abortion*, edited by Joel Feinberg, p. 59.
8. Benn, "Abortion, Infanticide, and Respect for Persons," in *The Problem of Abortion*, edited by Joel Feinberg, p. 100.
9. Tooley, "A Defence of Abortion and Infanticide," p. 63.
10. Tooley, "A Defence of Abortion and Infanticide," p. 64.
11. A formidable attempt to demonstrate by means of an alleged formal "generalized potentiality principle" that anyone opposed to abortion must also be opposed to contraception, has been made by Tooley. If his argument were to succeed, it could also be used against liberal positions which make sanctity conditional upon a more developed potentiality. However, the argument does not succeed because it fails to differentiate between the physical possibility of growth which is attributable to reproductive cells prior to fertilization, and even to non-reproductive cells (e.g. cloning), and the genetic capacity for growth which is only attributable to a genetically complete fertilized ovum. As a result, Tooley goes beyond the generalization of the conservative's principle to introduce substantive considerations a conservative need not accept.
12. Richard Brandt, "The Morality of Abortion," *The Monist* (1972), p. 517.
13. This is an argument which Tooley suggests that conservatives might use to oppose abortion even in the case where the mother's life is endangered. "Two moral principles lend support to the view that it is the fetus which should live," he claims. "First . . . should not one give something to a person who has had less rather than to a person who has had more? The mother has had a chance to live, while the fetus has not. The choice is thus between giving the mother more of an opportunity to live while giving the fetus none at all, and giving the fetus an opportunity to enjoy life while not giving the mother a further opportunity to do so. Surely fairness requires the latter." (Tooley, "A Defence of Abortion and Infanticide," p. 53). The argument is hypothetical, however, since it

rests on the presumption that the fetus is a person, which Tooley goes on to dispute.
14. Another example would be the Golden Rule, which Hare in an ingenious re-formulation brings to bear on the problem of abortion. According to Hare, "we should do to others what we are glad was done to us." The need for a re-formulation is indicative of the fact that the rule was not devised with abortion in mind. In order to know whether the rule remains as good as gold after re-formulating it, we have to know whether fetuses are included among "others" or not. This we can never find out from the rule itself, since it needs interpretation in the respect which is in question.
15. This is one of the versions of a Rawls-type validation-procedure which Brandt employs in his attempt to settle the abortion issue; although he prefers a different formulation of (c), according to which partiality is to be avoided not by keeping the moral voter in the dark about his personal fate, but by having him keep in mind that whatever he advocates must be acceptable to all, i.e. a rule of unanimous assent.
16. Ronald Green, "Conferred Rights and the Fetus," *Journal of Religious Ethics*, 2(1974), p. 60.
17. James Childress, "Response to Ronald Green," *Journal of Religious Ethics*, 2(1974), p. 81.
18. Green, "Conferred Rights and the Fetus," p. 59.

Questions

1. Is Cosby right in thinking that there is no rational way of determining whether the unborn child is a person?
2. If the moral status of the unborn child cannot be settled by moral argument, how should it be settled?
3. If we cannot decide through rational moral argument whether the unborn child is a person, how should we decide whether the unborn child should be protected by rules designed to protect human life — for example, rules that prohibit murder?

Suggestions for Further Reading

- R.F. Bagley, *Report of the Committee on the Operation of the Abortion Law*. This report was prepared for the Minister of Justice and the Attorney General of Canada in 1977. It is a descriptive study of the operation of the Canadian therapeutic abortion law from 1969 to the the date of the report.
- Lorenne Clark, "Reply to Professor Sumner," *Canadian Journal of Philosophy*, Vol. 4 No. 1 (September 1974). This article is a reply to the Sumner selection included in this chapter. Clark argues *contra* Sumner that abortion should be freely available on request throughout pregnancy.
- Jane English, "Abortion and the Concept of a Person," *Canadian Journal of Philosophy*, Vol. 5, No. 2 (October 1975). This article begins from the

view that philosophical analysis cannot resolve the problem of whether a fetus is a person. If the problem of abortion is to be resolved, therefore, it will have to be by reference to other considerations. The article concludes by arguing that ''abortion is justifiable early in pregnancy to avoid modest harms and seldom justifiable late in pregnancy except to avoid significant injury or death.''

- Edward W. Keyserlingk, ''The Unborn Child's Right to Prenatal Care,'' *Health Law in Canada*, Fall 1982. This is an extensive study of the problem taken up in the second section of this chapter.

- John T. Noonan, Jr., ''An Almost Absolute Value in Human History,'' in *The Morality of Abortion: Legal and Historical Perspectives* (Cambridge, Mass.: Harvard University Press, 1970). This article is a defence of the view that abortion is almost always immoral. The article has been reprinted in numerous anthologies.

- Paul Sachdev, *Abortion, Readings and Research* (Toronto: Butterworths, 1981). This book is a collection of articles whose focus is the Canadian abortion law. Part I is particularly useful in providing background information, as it includes articles on the period leading to the 1969 amendments, an analysis of the Canadian law by Bernard Dickens, a perspective on the role of the psychiatrist under the current law, and a study of the Canadian experience under the law from 1969 to about 1979.

- Margaret A. Somerville, ''Reflections on Canadian Abortion Law: Evacuation and Destruction—Two Separate Issues,'' *University of Toronto Law Journal,* Vol. 31 (1981). The author argues that the current law may encourage a physician performing an abortion to ensure that the fetus is not born alive. This effect is morally undesirable and requires that the Criminal Code be amended to ensure that where there is a reasonable possibility of a live birth, ''the least mutilating means of abortion which are reasonably available should be used.''

- L.W. Sumner, *Abortion and Moral Theory* (Princeton, N.J.: Princeton University Press, 1981). In his book, Sumner develops the position he sets out in the article included in this chapter.

- Judith Jarvis Thompson, ''A Defence of Abortion,'' *Philosophy and Public Affairs,* Vol. 1, No. 1 (1971). The author grants that an unborn child is a person from conception but argues that, nevertheless, under certain conditions, abortion is morally acceptable.

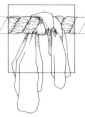

Euthanasia

Introduction

The comments that introduced Chapter 1 examined the issue of abortion from a number of points of view. But underlying the discussion was a concern to establish points of reference against which the morality of abortion could be assessed. We saw, for example, that it is widely believed that a number of the basic rules of law and morality are designed to protect individuals from the threat of death. Moral rules and laws prohibiting murder are one example.

Not surprisingly, the concern with the protection of life also plays a central role in discussions of the morality of euthanasia. But protection of life is not the only concern at stake. Two others are of particular relevance. First, suffering is a common feature of the human condition and one that human beings almost invariably try to avoid. Many people think that, both collectively and as individuals, we have an obligation to help each other alleviate suffering wherever we can, and offer relief if it is available. Second, as moral agents we are assumed capable of thinking through moral problems and deciding how we ought to act. It is sometimes argued that the special significance of being human lies in just this capability. Does it follow that, as autonomous moral agents, we ought to be allowed the freedom to act on our own assessments of what, morally speaking, is required of us in any given situation? The answer here is no. If there were no restrictions on my freedom to act on my assessment of what is required, the result might well be that your freedom to act as you think right would be seriously reduced or eliminated. This limitation is sometimes expressed by saying that respect for persons as moral agents requires that each person be given as much freedom to act on his or her moral beliefs (or lack of them) as is compatible with others having an equal degree of freedom to do the same.

We now have three principles to consider: the *protection-of-life principle*, the *avoidance-of-suffering principle*, and the *moral-autonomy principle*. If the first of these principles were the only one that inspired our respect, euthanasia would not generate any moral problems: it would simply be wrong in all cases. If the avoidance-of-suffering principle were the only one of the three principles worthy of respect, again euthanasia would generate no moral problems. Euthanasia would be morally acceptable if ending someone's life were the only effective way of ending that person's suffering. Finally, if the moral-autonomy principle were the only one operative, we might well conclude that it was morally acceptable to respect someone's request that his life be terminated if we believed that in arriving at his request, he was acting as an autonomous moral agent.

In fact, all three principles are widely regarded as worthy of respect. Situations do arise, however, in which it would appear that all three cannot be applied. Should that happen, we are faced with a decision. Which of these principles should have priority?

Background Considerations

Societies rooted in the Judeo-Christian tradition have, in the past, thought euthanasia immoral. This attitude reflects the view that human life is sacred and that rules protecting human life should override all other considerations. Thus, euthanasia has never been sanctioned in law in the Western world. But should this traditional view continue to command respect? Have medical advances in the twentieth century rendered the traditional view obsolete?

The Current Situation

In recent years, the morality of euthanasia has been subjected to increasing scrutiny, largely because of remarkable developments in medical science. Many life-threatening diseases have been conquered, smallpox being but one example. Many people can now be rescued from serious illness where death would once have been inevitable. Accidents that might once have caused death are no longer fatal. At the same time, our society has made funds available for creating social and medical services that allow most of us to benefit from these medical advances.

Paradoxically, however, there is another side to this picture. Modern medicine can rescue seriously ill or injured persons from death. But it is not always capable of restoring the capacity to enjoy the life that has been prolonged. Thus, the elderly can frequently be cured of illness, disease, or injury (pneumonia, for example) which in the past might well have resulted in death. But should the cure be effected if the person in question is senile? Children born with serious handicaps which once would have hastened death can be saved using modern medical techniques. But should they be saved if the alternative to death is a life plagued with pain, or one handicapped by mental retardation or serious physical disability?

Faced with situations of these kinds, some people now argue that the traditional view of euthanasia is no longer adequate. In their view, where continued existence has become intolerable through suffering or has lost its meaning because of mental degeneration or retardation, euthanasia is not immoral. Some would go even further. They would argue that members of the medical profession have an obligation to take the life of those whose suffering has become intolerable or whose capacity to enjoy life has ended.

The view that euthanasia is sometimes justified is frequently defended by appealing to the avoidance of suffering principle. However, the moral autonomy principle has also found a place in current debates. There is a deeply entrenched view in our society that each person should be left free to act on his or her own assessment of what is required in particular situations unless there are strong reasons to the contrary. Applied to the euthanasia debate, this view would seem to imply that both individually and collectively we should respect a person's decision should he decide that he wishes his life to be ended, unless ending his life will cause harm to others.

The Moral Dimension

There are three types of situations in which the problem of euthanasia arises. First, a person may decide that his life has become intolerable and request that it be ended as an act of mercy. The request may be direct. Or it may be communicated in a "living will," a document in which a person indicates that treatment is not to be attempted if, for example, he has suffered serious brain damage or serious and irreversible physical disability. Euthanasia which is performed in response to a "direct" request is said to be voluntary.

The problem of euthanasia can also arise in situations where someone is believed to be suffering in an intolerable or pointless way but, because of his condition, cannot direct how he is to be treated. If euthanasia is administered under these conditions it is non-voluntary. The assumption is that it is not contrary to the presumed wishes of the person in question. Nevertheless, it is not voluntary because it has not been explicitly requested.

Finally, it is sometimes argued that euthanasia is justified, on occasion, even when the "victim" does not concur, or might not concur, or might reasonably be expected not to concur. We might describe this third possibility as coercive euthanasia. Infanticide in cases where a child is seriously deformed or retarded (thalidomide babies, for example) *may* be an example of coercive euthanasia depending on why the action is taken. The Nazi practice of putting mentally defective, ill, old, and other "socially useless" persons to death is another example of coercive euthanasia.

Discussions of euthanasia, then, give rise to three questions. Is voluntary euthanasia ever justified? Is non-voluntary euthanasia ever justified? Is coercive euthanasia ever justified?

A final distinction should be noted. Some participants in the debate argue that it is important to differentiate between active and passive euthanasia, a

distinction that is intended to mark the difference between actively intervening to end a person's life (by administering an injection, for example) and simply not treating a person who has been injured or is ill, knowing that without
treatment the person will likely die. Assessing the merits of this distinction is
also an essential step in evaluating the morality of euthanasia.

The Readings

In the readings which follow, many aspects of euthanasia are examined.
Colin P. Harrison, a practising west-coast physician, argues that euthanasia
has no place in the practice of medicine; the doctor's task is to protect and
preserve life. Patrick Nowell-Smith emphasizes the relief-from-suffering and
the moral-autonomy principles, and argues that euthanasia should be legalized.
Joseph Fletcher argues that we do not have an overriding moral obligation to
protect and preserve life; sometimes moral considerations ought to lead us,
for example, to the view that an infant's life should be terminated.

E.W. Keyserlingk takes the view that there is no inevitable conflict between
what he calls the "sanctity-of-life" principle and the "quality-of-life" principle.
He argues that committment to the sanctity of life requires a deep concern for
the quality of life. He concludes that passive euthanasia may well be justified
in some situations, but that active euthanasia is always morally wrong.

The final reading in the chapter is the text of a bill that was presented for
first reading to the Ontario legislature in 1977, but was withdrawn before a
final vote was taken. The bill is included to provide you with a concrete proposal
for change, a proposal designed to give expression to the principle that
individuals should be free to specify the conditions under which they wish
not to be treated.

Finally, readers should also note the special relevance of the last four articles in the previous chapter to this topic.

Euthanasia, Medicine and the Law

Colin P. Harrison

It should be no surprise that the legalization of abortion was followed rapidly
by a growing interest in euthanasia. The devaluation of humanity at one end of the
life span has enabled us already to dispose of a large number of problem humans,
albeit with no foreseeable end in sight at the moment. It promises to be equally
fruitful at the other end of the span. But the debate often illuminates the great
confusion that exists between euthanasia and sound medical practice. Between mercy
killing, on the one hand, and the inexcusable prolongation of death and suffering, on the other, lies the sound medical care of the dying patient. Though this is

By permission of the author.

part of the normal practice of medicine, it is separated off because the prudential judgments involved are altered by the loss of hope and failure of the therapeutic process. To it, Ramsay[1] has applied the term "agathanasia," which means good death without the implication of killing. This enables the physician to escape between the horns of the apparent dilemma "euthanasia or not." This service requires great courage, a courage that must be based on a clear understanding of the issues involved — a courage to discontinue treatment that no longer affects the patient's disease, and to use pain-relieving measures in adequate amount. These are matters of sound medical practice, not of positive and negative euthanasia. Without that courage on the part of the physician, the patient will suffer inordinately, and the situation may well arise in which the physician who is afraid to use drugs in adequate amount lest his dying patient die will use an overdose to ensure his death. That would be folly, but in this day of confusion not an unlikely folly.

By virtue of the content of medical education, the expertise of the physician relates to health and disease, not to life and death, however much these may become entwined. The physician is obliged to recognize realistically the limits of his expertise and to treat the patient *secundum artem*, whatever effect that might have on the length of life of the dying patient. It is not the physician's right to decide when the patients should die and the law must not be allowed to make it otherwise. Both "life" and "death" are indefinable realities, and while we can identify what is positively alive and what is positively dead, we cannot identify the point at which the one merges into the other. The physician is not obliged to keep the patient alive (or preserve him from decomposition) or to kill him, but to treat his terminal illness as best he can. He must not presume to be able to weigh the value of continued life against death for the practical reason that he has not the faintest idea of what it means to be dead and because, from the philosophic point of view, there is no element common to being and non-being by which the one can be valued against the other. If the physician pushes the patient through death's door he does so without knowing what is on the other side. That is a denial of responsibility.

During the last decades we have resolutely denied the reality of death, and the word "death" has been considered obscene—as was the word "sex" in Victorian times. We are recovering from this delusion, but its effect has been that the care of the dying patient has not kept pace with the rest of medical care. There is now growing interest in the care of the dying, but there is a great deal to be learned and many changes to be made. That knowledge and those changes will not eventuate if medicine embarks on euthanasia, for then it will be infinitely simpler to kill the patient than to care for him. The earlier he is killed, the more pain he is spared, the easier it is on the physician and relatives, and the less the cost of hospitalization. Why keep the patient alive when there are so many advantages in killing him? Surely that is a philosophical question and there is now no unifying philosophy of medicine.

As the emphasis of medical care has changed from the sick to the healthy, it has changed from the personal to the impersonal, from the concrete and real to the putative, from a holistic to a fragmented discipline. At the same time, the ratio of academics to practising physicians has increased and there have been changes in medical practice and medical ethics that have subverted the traditional philosophy of medicine. In addition, there is a covert tension between the academic and the practising physician who, because their points of view are basically opposed, compete with each other for the authorship of the philosophy of modern medicine. It is a competition that goes badly for the practising physician and for the patient. If this philosophy is elaborated by the practising physician it will embody the values he sees in medicine and it has some hope of being concrete, real, holistic and people-oriented. Medicine might then remain the servant—and medicine can be free only so long as it is the servant, for the state will not cast covetous eyes on its position of servitude. But if this philosophy is elaborated by the academic it will become health-centred and medicine will grow in power and become a tyrant, then be rapidly deposed by the state. The World Health Organization has defined "health" as a *petitio principii*, susceptible of almost any interpretation. Health is more than health; it is a pristine order of well-being such as might have existed only in the Garden of Eden before the Fall. This mutual well-being is a mystery of faith, known only to the élite. It is not man without disease, it is man without sin; and man who was once said to have been created in the image and likeness of God is to be recreated in the current idiom of well-being. The logical extension of this idea of health is unlimited and there is nothing that cannot be imposed in its name. So it is that in the name of the same health, we assault the unborn child of one woman because she does not want it and at the same time we assault the pregnant, anemic Jehovah's Witness with a blood transfusion for the sake of her child. There is no logical nexus between the two but it does not really matter, for we are not practising medicine, we are exercising power. If health is to be measured in terms of mutual well-being, what more certain and efficient mechanism can be found than the killing of those who are interfering with that well-being?

In theory, the killing of the fetus was legalized for the sake of health but, practically, it can be used for any end that might be subsumed under the title of "happiness." It is not, however, the happiness of the one aborted, but of everybody else. So it is likely to be with mercy killing if that be legalized, and this despite the fact that there is a great deal of human sympathy in the euthanasia movement. It is the killing and not the mercy that appeals as the answer to our social problems. For there are real social advantages in killing:

1. It terminates the patient's suffering.
2. It reduces the strain on the family and the physician.
3. It makes the death convenient: if the physician is to kill the patient, he must do it at some specific time.
4. It speeds up the turnover of beds for patients with terminal illnesses.
5. It has a benevolent effect on the statistics of human morbidity.
6. It reduces the cost of terminal illness.

The suffering patient may well ask for death, but it is relief from suffering, mental and physical, that he seeks. He does not know what death is; how, then, can he desire it? As Kübler-Ross[2] has pointed out, the patient can come to terms with his own death and become resigned to it, and in the resignation overcome the fear. But he can only desire surcease from suffering. That surcease the physician should try to give from all that is available to him. It is possible that some physicians, out of sympathy, sometimes practise mercy killing, but it is no easy matter to disentangle the motive of mercy from the practical considerations already listed. Granted that it is mercy killing, all of the effects mentioned above still occur, so that the sympathy of the physician at the personal level becomes transformed into the benefits of killing at the social level. That is the real danger of legal euthanasia.

It is important to recognize the part played by emotion in the ethical equation. It explains why an act occurred and it absolves the agent from ethical condemnation. But it does not make the act ethical. Emotion is a psychological force that tends to bring the act about; it is not a rational judgment. Finally, the human sympathy of the physician is personal and not transformable into a social mechanism such that it can be represented in law. The fact is that the law can legalize the killing but it cannot possibly ensure the mercy. But perhaps what is really wanted is the right to kill off our elderly and ailing human burdens as we presently kill off our prenatal ones. That at least would be consistent, but it would open a floodgate that would be impossible to close.

Notes

1. Ramsay, P., quoted in Byrne, P.M. and Stogre, M.J. "Agathanasia and the Care of the Dying," *Can Med Assoc J.* 112: 1396 (1975).
2. Kübler-Ross, E., *On Death and Dying* (New York: Macmillan, 1969).

Questions

1. Harrison argues that abortion leads to euthanasia. What reasons does he give for this view? Are those reasons sound?
2. Harrison lists six "real social advantages" in legalizing euthanasia. Which, if any, of these advantages provide morally acceptable grounds for euthanasia?
3. Identify what Harrison considers to be "the real danger of legal euthanasia" and evaluate the seriousness of that danger from a moral point of view.
4. Evaluate Harrison's view of the medical alternative to euthanasia.

The Right to Die

Patrick Nowell-Smith

Do we have a right to die at a time and in a manner of own choice? That this question is being more and more urgently asked is due to two changes, one technological and one social, that have occurred in our lifetime. Modern medical technology has virtually eliminated the main killer diseases of the past; in particular the introduction of antibiotics has made possible the prevention and cure of pneumonia, a disease that used to be called "the dying man's friend." Human beings can be kept biologically alive, though unconscious, almost indefinitely.

As for the social change, before the First World War there could hardly have been an adult who had never watched over a parent, baby, child, neighbour, or friend and seen him die. In short, death was familiar. And *accepted*. Sad, to be sure; often very sad indeed. But it was nonetheless accepted as part of the natural order of things, talked about openly, and frequently dealt with in literature. All that has changed. Apart from those professionally concerned, few of us have ever seen a corpse unless it was laid out for viewing. Most of us will die in an institution. Death has replaced sex as the unmentionable topic.

Euthanasia is commonly divided into "active" (killing) and "passive" (letting die), a distinction that will be challenged later. It is also divided into "voluntary" (at the request or with the consent of the person) and "involuntary" (without such consent). The legal position in the United Kingdom is simple. Before 1961 suicide had always been a common law crime, and aiding suicide was therefore automatically a crime as well. But when, in 1961, the crime of suicide was abolished, a new statutory offence of *aiding* suicide was introduced, except in Scotland. Active euthanasia was always treated as murder, and still is. So much for the law on paper, which is pretty much the same in all common law jurisdictions.

However, this severity toward mercy killing and aiding suicide is in practice greatly mitigated by the wide powers of sentencing which our legal system accords to judges, especially when the issue is one of passive rather than active euthanasia. If a doctor allows a grossly deformed baby to die, he will be discharged if he can show that his decision not to treat the baby was standard medical practice; and there are many cases which are not even prosecuted. In cases of active euthanasia judges almost always impose a very light sentence or no sentence at all, when the motive was clearly compassion.

Since the methods most of us would choose to commit suicide require the illegal cooperation of others, it is clear that we have at best a very restricted *legal* right to die at a time and in a manner of our own choice. Whether or not we have a *moral* right which ought to be reflected in the law depends on the type of moral theory we take as a starting-point. On a theory which starts from the concept of individual rights, we have a right to do anything we like provided there are no good reasons for prohibiting what we want to do—for example that it infringes on the equal right of another. The countervailing reasons can be divided into the religious, the moral, and the practical.

Of the religious reasons little need be said. It is argued that we are not the absolute owners of our own lives, but hold them in trust from a God who gave them to us, so that the times of our dying should be chosen, not by us, but by God. But whatever the theoretical merits of this argument, it would be wrong to base any prohibition solely on the grounds that others have a religious objection to what someone proposes to do.

The main categories of moral theories are the *rights-based* and the *utilitarian*. For a rights theorist, the right to life, the right not to be killed, is the most fundamental of all rights. When rights are listed, it always comes first, for the very good reason that to deprive someone of life is to deprive him at one blow of all his rights, of all possibility of earthly enjoyment. But if we grant, as no doubt we all do, that everyone has a right to life, it follows at once that we have a right to choose to die. For it is a feature of all rights that they can be invoked or not *at the option of the right-holder*. If you owe me ten dollars, I have a right to demand and get ten dollars from you. But I have no *duty* to demand repayment; I may, if I choose, waive my right—in this example forgive the debt. Similarly, the correlative of my right to life is your duty not to kill me; but I can release you from this duty by requesting you to kill me or giving my consent. To deny this is to confuse the right to life with the duty, if there is one, to go on living.

In special circumstances there may be such a duty. For example, if a person is the only breadwinner of a family and has no life insurance, it may well be his duty to struggle on against his desire to die. For some few of us, perhaps, some larger loyalty, even the national interest, might require us to forego our right to die. But such considerations are rare and not likely to figure in the type of case that leads people to advocate a more liberal law on euthanasia. Their concern is for people who, either from incurable disease or from extreme old age, are unlikely to be able to contribute substantially to the good of others.

A large majority of the people who join voluntary euthanasia societies are people in their sixties and seventies who are still enjoying life but do not like what they see in front of them in a society in which more than three-quarters of us will die in institutions. They ask for the various guides to self-deliverance issued by some of these societies not because they want to use the information now, but because they want the security of knowing that, in the words of John Donne, the keys of their prison house are in their own hands. The following letter sent to the Canadian society Dying with Dignity is typical.

> I am seventy-nine years of age, in relatively vigorous health and constantly amused with life while it lasts. But I saw my mother and my father, years apart, in the same chronic care hospital suffering helplessly for months when they might have been quietly released; and this makes me dread a similar fate unless the law is changed so that one can choose, if still able, to slip away in dignity from the inhuman methods many hospitals employ today to keep one from dying a natural death.

Inevitably some people will be sad when a person dies; but that sadness will come to them anyway, and it should be lessened rather than increased by the thought that the person they loved died as he wished to die.

But what if no one is willing to kill me or to help me die? What then becomes of my right to choose death? This objection can be met by pointing out that the right to life and its corollary, the right to die, are only *negative* rights. My right to life imposes on you a duty not to kill me without my consent, but it imposes on you no duty to keep me alive (though, for other reasons, you may have such a duty). The same is true of the right to die. Supporters of voluntary euthanasia are not asking for "death on demand." They are not asking that anyone be saddled with a duty to kill a person who asks for death. They assert only that neither a person who asks for help in dying nor a person who gives that help is committing a moral wrong, and they claim that this moral position should be reflected in our criminal law.

If we look at the question from the point of view of utilitarianism, we get the same result. The utilitarian judges the morality of an action by assessing the good and the evil consequences, for the agent and all others concerned, of either doing something or not doing it. Obviously such calculations are not easy; but they are not always impossible. *Ex hypothesi*, a person who asks for death has come to the conclusion that, for him, dying is better than staying alive. He may be mistaken; but often this is very unlikely, and in any case he is the best judge of his own interests. As for the interests of others, his choice of death will be morally right so long as the benefit for them of his remaining alive is less than the burden on them and on him.

Let us now turn to the practical arguments, according to which, even if the moral admissibility of voluntary euthanasia were conceded, proposals to change the law would run into insuperable difficulties. First, it is argued that no proposal to change the law has any chance of success unless it has the support of the medical profession, which, it is said, it will never have. "Doctors vary in their approach to passive euthanasia but the profession condemns legalised active voluntary euthanasia."[1] Nevertheless, there are some British physicians who practise active voluntary euthanasia, but it is difficult to find out just how many there are. Since such an admission would, under present British law, be a confession of murder, it is understandable that they do not openly admit it.

On the other hand, voluntary active euthanasia is now practised openly in Holland, where there are between 5000 and 6000 cases a year.[2] The procedure starts with an application by the patient. A team is then formed consisting of a doctor and a nurse, a pastor if the patient asks for one, and others as appropriate.[3] The team discusses the application with the patient, and then either grants or refuses it. Some years ago, Dr. Pieter Admiraal, a leading proponent of the practice, was convicted of aiding suicide, but was discharged on the grounds that his actions had been medically necessary. "What made Dr. Admiraal's actions acceptable were (1) the patient's voluntary and spontaneous requests, (2) the rational and 'durable' nature of the requests, (3) the presence of unacceptable and 'endless' suffering, and (4) Dr. Admiraal's consultation with his colleagues."[4] If the consensus of medical opinion could change in the course of a few years in Holland, it could change in other countries too.

The second type of practical objection comes from lawyers, who, like doctors, are on the whole opposed to active euthanasia and the assistance of suicide. In 1984 the Law Reform Commission of Canada's report *Euthanasia, Suicide, and Cessation of Treatment* recommended that the law on active euthanasia and aiding suicide should not be changed. One of its arguments for this conservative stance was that the law in action is much less severe than the law on paper:

> Our legal system has internal mechanisms which offset the apparent harshness of the law. It is *possible* that in *some* circumstances the accused would be allowed to plead guilty to a lesser charge. . . . Finally in *truly exceptional circumstances*, the authorities already have it within their discretion to decide not to prosecute.[5]

But this is cold comfort indeed, since the circumstances in which people wish to die are, even now, not "truly exceptional"; and as the population ages and the power of medical technology increases such circumstances are likely to become even more common.

Many doctors and paramedics would like to put an end to suffering they know to be hopeless; but they are law-abiding people, and they have a special need to be careful of their reputations. That they are less inclined than they used to be to follow their humane inclinations is due to fear of possible prosecution and of malpractice suits if they do not pull out all the stops to keep a patient alive. It is not fair to say to them, as the Commission in effect does, "What you are doing is against the law, but we *may* turn a blind eye."

The Commission's second argument was that any relaxation of the law could lead to mistakes and to serious abuses. This is a weighty argument, and it will be considered later; but it is surprising that the Commission did not consider the possibility of building safeguards against abuse into a more liberal law. Perhaps the reason for this omission was that it relied most heavily on its third argument: that relaxation of the law would be "morally unacceptable to the majority of the Canadian people."[6] This, however, is not a moral question, but a question of empirical fact, and the Commission should surely have produced some evidence to support its view. But not only did it cite no evidence; it ignored such evidence as there was. In 1968, the Canadian Institute for Public Opinion (the Gallup Poll) had asked the following narrowly worded question:

> When a person has an incurable disease that causes great suffering, do you or do you not think that competent doctors should be allowed by law to end the patient's life through mercy-killing, if the patient has made a formal request in writing?

Forty-five percent of the firm answers were yes, 43 no. In 1974 the proportion was 55 to 35 percent. By 1978 the favourable replies outnumbered the unfavourable by more than two to one, and this result was repeated in 1984. In Britain a similar 1969 survey showed 51 percent in favour of active voluntary euthanasia. By 1976 the fraction had increased to 69 percent; in 1985 it was 72 percent. In the United States, though the proportion of favourable replies was lower, the trend was similar. In 1973 the Harris Poll showed only 37 percent in favour; by 1985 the figure had reached 61 percent.[7]

This disparity between legal and popular thinking is also shown by the many cases in which even newspapers of a generally conservative complexion have criticized a court decision. One example must suffice. In December 1984 an 84-year-old lady who had many reasons for ending her life tried to commit suicide by taking a lethal drug. She had a legal right to do so; but, fearful that the attempt might not succeed, she asked a friend, Mrs. Charlotte Hough, to sit with her and to place a plastic bag over her head after she had lost consciousness. Mrs. Hough did so and reported her action to the police. Initially she was charged with murder, but because of the uncertainty as to whether the death was due to the drug or to the plastic bag, the charge was reduced to attempted murder. She pleaded guilty, and was sentenced to nine months' imprisonment, a sentence upheld on appeal.[8] The judge said that although he had the greatest sympathy for Mrs. Hough, a prison sentence was necessary to uphold the law. On this *The Sunday Times* commented:

> What is often morally right in this sensitive area remains legally incorrect because, as a nation, we tend to sweep discussion of death under the carpet. In 1976 Baroness Wootton introduced a bill into the House of Lords which would have brought a modicum of good sense and regulation to the subject of euthanasia. But it was not supported. As a result, uncounted numbers of people kept alive by medical science, often die without dignity. . . . Mrs. Hough's crime was compassion and it served to underline once more the need for better legislation governing voluntary euthanasia and the dangers of being without it. People should be allowed to die on their own terms and, as Barbara Wootton once wrote, "not those of nature's cruelty or doctors' ingenuity."[9]

The third type of objection arises from the possibility that mistakes will be made and abuses will occur. It would be a pity, it is said, if someone were to choose death when a cure for his condition was just around the corner. As it stands, this objection is based on a misunderstanding of the nature of biomedical research. The time that elapses between someone's thinking of a new drug or a new application of a known drug and its actual availability is to be measured, not in weeks or months, but in years. So, if there is really a new treatment likely to be available soon, that fact will be known. The patient should be told what the treatment can do for him now or in the near future and left to choose whether or not to hang on and hope for the best. New cures apart, it is true that people whose case seemed hopeless have recovered to lead meaningful lives; so it may well be true that some of those who chose to die would also have recovered. But, from the nature of the case, we can never know whether a person who chose to die would have recovered, and since cases of unexpected recovery are rare, it must be presumed that in most cases they would not.

The possibility that a more liberal law might be abused is a much more serious objection. How can we be sure that when a patient chooses death the choice is *fully voluntary*? Obviously this opens one of the most notorious cans of worms in the history of philosophy. Aristotle defined a voluntary action as one not taken under compulsion or due to ignorance,[10] and no one has been able to improve significantly on that definition. But this raises the problem of what counts as compulsion. Subtle pressures which would not amount to coercion in law might be put on old people to sign their own death warrants, for example by greedy heirs who want to inherit sooner rather than later; and even if there is little to inherit, family members might want to get the old person off their backs. Senility, even without the aid of high technology, can last quite a time and people who need constant care can be a great nuisance. It is also tempting for family members to insinuate that the old person really has a duty to get out of the way.

A more liberal law to mitigate the uncertainties and inhumanity of our current laws is urgently needed; but the problem of devising adequate safeguards is one, not for philosophers, but for lawyers. For the law has great experience of dealing with problems of coercion and constraint in other areas. The validity of a contract may depend on whether the parties freely consented to its terms; and in many crimes the guilt of the accused depends on whether or not he intended of his own free will to commit the crime. So we might insist that possible sources of coercion be fully investigated, that the would-be suicide has been fully informed of the options, and that his will has been expressed several times over a stipulated period. Under the Dutch system the most serious abuses—coercion and fraud—are all but eliminated since active voluntary euthanasia is practised openly, only in hospitals, and after consultations so wide that there can be no reasonable doubt that the patient's request is uncoerced, considered, and durable.

Passive euthanasia (letting die), whether voluntary or not, is now generally accepted except by the more fervent right-to-life groups. But, while most religious leaders, doctors, and lawyers consider it morally acceptable, they still regard *active* euthanasia as morally wrong. Their morality can be summed up in Clough's often-quoted words "Thou shalt not kill, but needst not strive/Officiously to keep alive." But what, if any, is the difference?

There is certainly a conceptual difference between killing and letting die. A lifeguard who holds a child's head under water till he drowns certainly kills the child; a lifeguard who sits on the bank watching the child drown as certainly does not. He lets the child die. But is there any *morally relevant* difference between these two cases? Is not the lifeguard in the second case just as culpable, just as responsible for the death of the child as the lifeguard in the first? The law has long accepted the principle that acts of omission can be just as criminal as acts of commission, and popular morality accepts that they can be just as reprehensible.

If a baby is born with Tay-Sachs disease or anencephalic, it is routine practice to prescribe "nursing care only" and when the baby dies this is thought of as a merciful dispensation of Providence. But in this sort of case the physician intentionally causes death, for all that he causes it, not by action but by refraining from taking action. So there is no moral superiority of passive over active euthanasia here, and if the fomer is allowed to be morally permissible (as it generally is), the latter is also permissible. In fact, if there is any moral superiority here at all, it lies with active euthanasia, since, assuming the baby to be conscious, its suffering will be shorter. On this point the conventional moral position seems to be simply confused.

The fundamental principle of medical ethics has always been that a physician should act in the best interests of his patient, and this principle has been reaffirmed by two eminent bodies, the World Medical Assembly[11] and the United States President's Commission for the Study of Ethical Problems in Medicine and Biomedical and Behavioral Research.[12] Both of these bodies advocate passive euthanasia as often preferable to the use of "extraordinary" measures to keep a person alive. What neither of them asks, however, is whether letting someone die, even with the best possible care while dying, is really better for that person than giving him a quicker release.

The question of what is in a person's best interests is not an easy one to answer and the World Medical Assembly did not try to answer it. But the President's Commission did.

In its report *Deciding to Forego Life-sustaining Treatment* the Commission says that all patients have an interest in well-being and that, in addition to this, normal adult or competent patients also have an interest in self-determination. . . . In other words, seriously disabled infants should, according to the Commission, not have their lives sustained if their lives are likely to contain more suffering and frustrated desires than happiness and satisfactions.[13]

In line with the Commission's thinking, the United States Surgeon General recommended that an infant who cannot be nourished orally "should not be put on hyperalimentation for a year and a half . . . but should be provided with a bed and food by mouth knowing that it was not going to be nutritious" and thus allowed to die.[14] But once it has been decided that it is better for the baby to die than to be kept alive by extraordinary means, would it not be in his best interests to die quickly rather than slowly and perhaps painfully?

In one recently publicized case, an 85-year-old patient starved himself to death over a 47-day period. But who would seriously want to suggest that it is in the patient's best interests to be dehydrated and starved to death? It appears that the World Medical Assembly and the American President's Commission would.[15]

If there is no moral difference between passive and active euthanasia, it is illogical to accept the former and reject the latter; and if there is a moral difference *in favour of* active euthanasia, current medical practice is immoral as well.

In the case, not of an infant, but of a competent patient who, in addition to an interest in general well-being, has an interest in self-determination, the inconsistency of the Commission's position is even more glaring, since it says that a competent person's interest in and right to self-determination is paramount.

Competent patients should be allowed to die when, from their point of view, life in a distressing or seriously debilitating condition is no longer worth while. Different patients will decide differently under similar circumstances. These goals and values ought to be respected. Hence, the Commission says, "no uniform, objective determination can be adequate—whether defined by society or by health care professionals."

No objective determination can be adequate, the Commission states, because normal adult persons have an overriding interest in self-determination, that is, in the exercise of their "capacity to form, revise, and pursue his or her own plans for life." It is self-determination, the Commission suggests, which gives persons an element of worth and dignity.[16]

But if the right to self-determination really has the paramount status which the Commission accords to it, it must surely extend to include a right to die at a time and in a manner of one's own choice.

Postscript

I have argued that changes in the law of common law jurisdictions are urgent, that such changes will not occur without the support of the medical profession, and that, to judge from the polls, public opinion is more liberal on these issues. But opinion polls are notoriously unreliable, because the respondents are often unaware of the complexities of the issues underlying the questions put. Other evidence suggests that the public is, on the whole, indifferent. For example, though it is growing fast, the total membership of the 27 right-to-die societies that exist in 17 countries remains very small.

What we need to bring about is a change in our whole society's attitude toward death and dying. Instead of sweeping it under the carpet, we must learn again to accept it as our forefathers did, as not only the inevitable, but the natural end to earthly life. My own ideal death is that of Socrates who took poison and died discussing the immortality of the soul with his friends. To be sure, his reason for choosing to die was that he had been condemned to death by the law of his country, which he felt bound to obey. But change that story a little: Socrates is growing old; he can no longer handle his stonemason's tools with his old skill, and worst of all, he can no longer match his friends in philosophic discussion. Life has no more that he values to offer him. So he accepts death, not knowing what is to come, having enjoyed life to the end.

Notes

1. *Handbook of Medical Ethics* (British Medical Association, 1980), p. 31.
2. John Dawson, "An open and gentle death," *News Review* (British Medical Association), Vol. 12, No. 1 (January 1986), p. 22.
3. Pieter V. Admiraal, "Active voluntary euthanasia," *Newsletter* (Voluntary Euthanasia Society, London), No. 24 (May 1985).
4. Dawson, *op. cit.*, p. 23.
5. Law Reform Commission of Canada, *Euthanasia, Suicide, and Cessation of Treatment* (Ottawa, 1984). Emphasis added.
6. *Ibid.*
7. *Newsletter* (Voluntary Euthanasia Society, London), No. 24 (May 1985), p. 5.
8. *Ibid.*, No. 23, pp. 1–2.
9. *The Sunday Times* (London), December 16, 1984.
10. Aristotle, *Nicomachean Ethics*, III, 1110a.
11. "Statement on terminal illness and boxing, October 1983," *Medical Journal of Australia*, Vol. 141 (1984), p. 549. I am indebted for this and the following references to Dr. Helga Kuhse of the Centre for Human Bioethics, Monash University, Australia.
12. *Deciding to Forego Life-sustaining Treatment* (Washington: U.S. Government Printing Office, 1983).
13. Helga Kuhse, "Euthanasia—again," *Medical Journal of Australia*, Vol. 142 (1985), p. 612.
14. Quoted by Peter Singer and Helga Kuhse, "The future of Baby Doe," *New York Review of Books*, No. 31 (1984), pp. 17–22.
15. Kuhse, *op. cit.*, p. 611.
16. *Ibid.*, p. 612.

Questions

1. Does the commitment of our society to religious freedom imply, as Nowell-Smith suggests, that religious objections to euthanasia should not be allowed to influence the debate on the legalization of euthanasia?
2. Let us grant that all human beings have a right to life. Does it follow, as Nowell-Smith suggests, that everyone has a right to waive his or her right to go on living and ask that his or her life be ended?
3. A recurring theme in the discussion of euthanasia is the problem of preventing the abuse of legislation allowing euthanasia under specified conditions. Are the concerns of Colin P. Harrison in this regard adequately dealt with by Nowell-Smith?

Infanticide and the Ethics of Loving Concern

Joseph Fletcher

The question whether infanticide is ever justifiable, and if so when, can be approached more appreciatively if we begin by locating infanticide on the total map of induced death, that is to say, of death humanly intended and contrived. Therefore, I shall first look at the moral variants in a spectrum of the different ways we might take to induce death, and then focus on infanticide in particular.

In what follows we will be looking primarily at dying when it is chosen or elected in the sick room, which might be called medical euthanasia; I will prescind from such practices as vendetta, military life-taking, capital punishment, mortal risk-benefit choices, and other ways of assuming control over life and death — other kinds of human decisions not to leave death to "natural" causes. *The Oxford English Dictionary* defines euthanasia (literally "good death" or what medieval philosophers called *bene mori*) this way: "In recent use: the action of inducing a gentle and easy death." Several variables arise between medical and nonmedical situations, even though the constants are equally important. In our present society, however, the problem is more commonly posed in the context of medical care and treatment.

The moral problems of suicide and allocide are, of course, not new. Nevertheless, they are taking a new shape recently because of advances in medical capabilities, especially in resuscitation and life-support technologies. Once upon a time the typical problem in serious life-threatening illnesses was to find a way to prolong life, but often now the problem is how long and how much to do so, particularly

---

From *Infanticide and the Value of Life*, © 1978 Marvin Kohl, ed., with permission of Prometheus Books, Buffalo, New York.

when we find we are prolonging dying rather than living, "saving" biological life at the expense of human life.

Locating Infanticide

My premise will be that induced death, as such, may not be condemned categorically, and that truly rational ethical issues only arise when responsible moral agents set about determining answers to operational questions—who, why, what, when, and how. It is unreasonable ethically to say that all acts of euthanasia are wrong, just as it would be to say that none are.

Another premise is that what is good and right for a person when he does it for himself, e.g., suicide, is just as good and right, and for the same reasons, when it is done for him by proxy (i.e., allocide). Thus the English law which decriminalizes self-administered euthanasia but continues to outlaw it when it is carried out by others, such as physicians, nurses, paramedics, or a member of the family, at the subject's request or with his agreement, is logically untenable.

The most significant ethical discrimination we make when we evaluate intended and induced dying ("elective death") is between voluntary and involuntary cases. This would, at least, be true for those with whom freedom of choice is a highly important element of personal integrity—a first-order value. The "right to die" is therefore taken ordinarily to mean one's right to choose one's own death, rather than any right (at least ordinarily) to choose death for somebody else.

Voluntary dying is chosen consciously by the subject, whether in the event or prior to it. An example would be fulfilling the wishes of patients that treatment be stopped when to do anything more would be fatuous. Their wishes might be expressed either at that time or recorded earlier in a living will. Involuntary dying would be exemplified by an accident victim's death on the operating table, or when a comatose patient's treatment is stopped because to continue would be pointless and cruel—the decision being made without the patient's consent and without any knowledge of his preference, past or present. The difference hangs on the factor of consent.

Euthanasia, however, poses not one but four critical distinctions. Its form may vary not only as to (1) consent (voluntary or involuntary) but also as to: (2) whether the method used to end the patient's life is by a positive act or by omitting life-preserving treatment (direct or indirect); (3) whether the agent of the action is the subject himself or somebody else (active or passive); (4) whether the patient's condition is terminal or non-terminal—i.e., whether or not death has been determined to be imminent.

Direct euthanasia is death induced by doing something that entails the patient's death as an immediate consequence. Instances would be the patient taking a highly toxic drug such as potassium cyanide, or the physician's administering it, or somebody removing an endotracheal tube from a patient with pulmonary arrest. Euthanasia is indirect when something is done that foreseeably results in death as a "subsequence" but not the direct consequence. Such would be a patient's refusal to eat, or if he (or another) disconnected intravenous inserts for hyperalimentation (i.e., starving the patient to death). This direct-indirect distinction has to do, in short, with whether the relation between cause and effect is immediate or not, i.e., whether the foreseeable result of the action follows at once from the act or only after a series of effects set in train by the primary action.

A pathetic case illustrating the direct-indirect phase of infanticide occurred some years ago at the Johns Hopkins Hospital in Baltimore; it has had a wide follow-up discussion, based on a film about it circulated for teaching purposes. A newborn had all the stigmata of Down's syndrome and the parents therefore refused consent to the corrective surgery needed to remove a duodenal atresia and thus open up the infant's food tract and save it from death.

The physicians in charge believed that direct euthanasia is wrong but that doing it indirectly, though undesirable, was morally tolerable. Hoping that it would die of dehydration and starvation in three or four days, they wheeled it off into a corner where it lay dying for fifteen days, not three or four. Some form of direct termination would have been far more merciful as far as the infant, nurses, parents, and some of the physicians were concerned. In that case indirect was morally worse than direct — if, as I and most of us would contend, the good and the right are determined by human well-being. Indirect euthanasia did no good at all in that case, but lots of evil.

The third distinction, between active and passive, has to do with whether an act of euthanasia is done by the patient or by somebody else. It is active when the subject (patient) does it, for example, by taking an overdose of a barbiturate or opiate. It is passive when another person does it for the subject, whether directly (e.g., closing down a patient's lungs with a specific for pulmonary paralysis) or indirectly (e.g., removing the support provided by a respirator). We have already suggested that there is no ethical difference between active and passive ways of inducing death. The only difference is in the agent, which makes it suicide or allocide, but this is instrumental, not intentional. Either way the patient's death is the end being sought, whether the patient or some other person brings it about. If the patient's release from an irreversibly painful and hopeless existence is contrived for him instead of by him, no onus lies on the agent unless it lies on the patient too.

By the same reasoning, direct and indirect euthanasia are morally alike, on a par. As I have put it elsewhere, "It is morally evasive and disingenuous to suppose that we can condemn or disapprove positive acts of care and compassion but in spite of that approve negative strategies to achieve exactly the same purpose."[1] Kant was on sound ground to insist that if we will the end, we will the means. Purposive acts of commission are morally no different from acts of omission that have the same goal. A decision not to open an imperforate anus in a trisomy-18 newborn is "mercy killing" as surely as if they used a poison pellet. Not eating is suicide as surely as jumping off the Eiffel Tower; it just takes longer.

Our fourth and last distinction is between terminal and non-terminal cases. A patient is terminal if he is going to die of his present condition no matter what treatment is given; an example would be the man with amyotrophic lateral sclerosis in Dr. I.S. Cooper's novel, *It's Hard to Leave When the Music's Playing*.[2] A non-terminal case would be one in which death would not be expected from any present pathology; e.g., a man who hangs himself because his life, as such, does not seem worth living.

In short, euthanasia has significantly different forms. It may be voluntary or involuntary, direct or indirect, active or passive, a response to terminal illness or to some other condition. A number of combinations and permutations of these variances is to be met with every day in the realities of dying, as human beings strive to control dying for human or humane reasons. Some of these differences, however, are without much, if any, ethical weight.

Infanticide

Infanticide is the induced death (euthanasia) of infants. Because of their various deficits, when death comes to infants it is necessarily involuntary. Whether it comes naturally or by human design it happens without the subject's knowledge or consent. Knowledge and consent are impossible—as impossible for neonates as for fetuses when abortion is considered. It is reasonable, indeed, to describe infanticide as postnatal abortion, which is what it obviously was in the South Pacific when Robert Louis Stevenson visited the atolls and found that the Polynesians practised infanticide with newborns showing disabling birth diseases and defects. (Theirs was a situation of radically scarce resources, both economic and medical, and Stevenson's initial revulsion was set aside after a period of observation.)

Furthermore, infanticide is passive. An infant cannot put an end to its own life. This makes it allocide, not suicide. Its variables are only (1) with respect to the euthanasiast's choice of direct or indirect means; and (2) whether it is done within the context of terminal illness or some other adverse state.

Some writers have argued that a fetus is a person as truly as an infant is, and that therefore both abortion and infanticide are unjust killing (murder). This argument has as its premise the rule that persons (human beings) ought never to elect or be elected to die by human initiatives. This universal negative or prohibition implies that death must always be imposed non-humanly by God or nature or some other cosmic arbiter. It is a position with which we are familiar in classical Catholic moral theology and Protestant ethics (although not all theologians defend it), and in "pro-life" propaganda. Paul Ramsey has defended this view.[3] I have contended for the opposite position, i.e., that both abortion and infanticide can be justified if and when the good to be gained outweighs the evil—that neither abortion nor infanticide is as such immoral.[4] John Fletcher has tried to establish a middle position, arguing for the liceity of abortion but against infanticide.[5] He gives three reasons why infants are different from fetuses and should be differently treated: (1) a neonate has a separate existence, (2) tends to arouse parental feelings of attachment, and (3) is treatable. (Each of these things, however, is true of fetuses too.)

Another ground for opposing infanticide has been chosen by E.-H.W. Kluge.[6] His major premise is his belief or metaphysical assertion that an infant is a person, which he defines as any individual with not only an actual but a *potential* capacity for human self-awareness. His contention is that persons *qua* persons have a right to live—and that ethically this right may not be abridged. Because in his opinion a "structural potential" exists in fetuses (he fails to discriminate those cases in which the potential is not present), he assigns personal status to both fetuses and infants. He concludes: "Therefore infanticide is—to say the least—morally reprehensible. In fact, it is murder." (This appears to be an instance of the fallacy of the potential, i.e., arguing by prolepsis that the potential is the actual. Henry David Aiken calls this fallacy in this context "fetishism."[7])

Here we come to the crucial issue. Do persons, however defined, have an absolute or unqualified right to live? The courts have never found one, nor has jurisprudence. So-called human rights, as a term much employed in political rhetoric, are certain moral claims (e.g., to privacy, to property, liberty, and the like) that are ordinarily or commonly conceded. Street talk about "rights" ("I have a right to" such things as relief checks, free parking, health care, education, old-age benefits, or whatever) means nothing more than an expression of belief, well or ill founded that people *ought* to have certain things. However, all these claims are only relatively valid, whether they are or are not constitutionally formulated. At best they are only "prima facie." They are relative and not absolute for the sufficient reason that they can and often do cut across each other. Ethical problems are, when thoroughly examined, problems of relative choice among competing values or "goods," and to posit values at all entails priorities for making risk-benefit and gain-loss judgments. Hence the relativity of rights.

Kluge's real sting is in his tail. Not until the very last sentence of his discussion of infanticide does he come out of the closet and declare openly, "And if it is argued that this [condemnation of infanticide] depends on the further assumption that there are absolute values, I must unabashedly admit that this is something I hold to be the case."[8]

This means, if it means anything, that the life of persons, which he believes infants and fetuses to be, has an absolute value that cannot be relatively weighed by any moral scales to other competing values and dysvalues. It means that life, as such, is sacrosanct and taboo, no matter how much suffering and tragedy and deprivation might be the price.[9] Given this as his "bottom line," he (Kluge) could not cope with the decision-making for an infant with 94.5 per cent full-thickness, 92 per cent total-body burns and irreversible lung damage from smoke inhalation. Or, again, how could he make a judgment ethically about an infant with spina bifida cystica, plus a meningomyelocele and meningeal infection already widespread? Or about an infant born with retinoblastoma after slipping through the antenatal screen, when post-operative diagnosis shows that the surgical removal of its eyes has not stopped the spread of cancer?

If the life of these infants, such as it is, is sacrosanct as far as human initiatives are concerned, they would have to suffer — according to the taboo ethic — until they died "naturally" or until "God called them" out of life. If life is absolutely good, unconditionally good, we cannot talk about quality of life, since in common use the phrase requires us to be open to judging the quality of life itself, as well as making quality judgments on things within the ambiance of life. As the Jesuit theologian R.A. McCormick once put it, ethical reasoning collapses when anybody says, "There's no such thing as a life not worth living."[10]

The rejoinder to Kluge and others like him is that they have misplaced the debate. Careful and candid analysis will show that deciding whether and when an infant is a person is not the determinative question.[11] The right one is, "Can a person's life ever be ended ethically?" (Kluge compromises his taboo by allowing one exception—killing in self-defence.) It all turns on the issue of whether the value of a human life is absolute or relative.[12] It is this "metaethical" question which lies at the heart of the disagreement about infanticide. We could accept Kluge's thesis that fetuses are persons and still justify abortion and infanticide in some cases, because, in a given case, to prolong life would be to engender more evil than good. This tragic situation occurs frequently in perinatal medicine, even though its frequency is not great statistically. It is Kluge's second premise (that we may not take a person's life) that is rejectable, whether or not we accept his firm premise (that fetuses and infants are persons.)[13]

Pediatricians or others who would sometimes justify letting a newborn die, or even helping a newborn die, would do so on value grounds. Life itself would be only one value among values, even though a high-order one, and therefore some infants' lives (like some lives in any other age group) might properly be sacrificed on the principle of proportionate good. No undeclared premises are hiding behind the discussion in this essay. It is based on ethical relativism—i.e., situational or contextual relativism, not cultural relativism. This is my mode of approach to the ethics of induced death in general and infanticide in particular.

To contend that there are cases in which it is good, and therefore right, to induce the end of a person's life obviously assigns the first-order value to human well-being, by either maximizing happiness or minimizing suffering; it assigns value to human life rather than to merely being alive. On this view it is better to be dead than to suffer too much or to endure too many deficits of human function. In this mode of ethical reasoning the criterion of obligation is caring or kindness or loving concern—various terms have been used to denote it.[14] Its basic value stance is that we ought to do whatever promotes well-being and reduces suffering, and therefore, it ending a life is judged to do so, so be it.

William Frankena has classified my ethics as "modified act agapism," which simply means that loving concern for human beings comes first, before rules of conduct.[15] As Frankena shows, it is a form of utilitarianism and consequentialist ethical decision-making. The only "rule" it follows consistently is to do whatever offers the most human benefit, and on this basis we would sometimes save lives, sometimes end them (directly or indirectly, actively or passively.)

In another place citing various philosophical discussions, Frankena rashly and arbitrarily says that Henry Sidgwick, William Temple, and I all assume that belief in the "sanctity of life" means holding life to be absolute and inviolable, but, in fact, all three of us accept the distinction Frankena draws between *absolute* respect for life (not, however, sanctifying it) and "*qualified* respect for human life" —which last Frankena and the rest of us endorse, all alike.[16]

Loving concern ("agape") is a standard of good and evil that could be validated in either a theistic or a humanistic belief system. A theist might, of course, believe that God forbids infanticide by a rule, perhaps along with other things such as adultery or baking bread on Sundays. On the other hand, he might believe that the divine will or command is only that we do the most loving thing possible in a given situation, leaving it to the moral agent to decide what that is. Likewise, a humanist might decide that ending infants' lives is in general inhumane and therefore ought never to be done (as with some rule utilitarians),[17] or he might hold instead that we should seek to optimize human well-being in every case, thus allowing for infanticide sometimes (as in act utilitarianism).

If one's standard of the good is human well-being, and one's duty or obligation is to seek to increase it wherever possible, with a consequent willingness to save lives sometimes and end them sometimes, then it will follow that infanticide is acceptable (sometimes). If one's standard is a divine will or other cosmic authority (e.g., Natural Law), one could still accept infanticide, depending on whether the divine will is believed to be expressed in universal and absolute rules (such as we can find in revealed codes), or in a general command to be loving (beneficent, kind, humane, et cetera) with flexibility as to the variables in particular cases.

In fact, the differences between religious ethics and ethnical autonomy do not determine the issue of the ethics of infanticide. The only real issue is whether concern for persons in hopeless misery ranks higher or lower than taboo.

Notes

1. Joseph Fletcher, "Ethics and Euthanasia," *American Journal of Nursing* 73 (April 1973): 670–675.
2. I.S. Cooper, *It's Hard to Leave When the Music's Playing* (New York: W.W. Norton & Co., 1977).
3. Paul Ramsey, "Abortion," *The Thomist* 37 (1973): 174–226.
4. Ramsey, "Abortion," pp. 174–226.
5. John Fletcher, "Abortion, Euthanasia, and Care of Defective Newborns," *The New England Journal of Medicine* 292 (January 9, 1975): 75–78.
6. Eike-Henner W. Kluge, *The Practice of Death* (New Haven, Conn.: Yale University Press, 1975), pp. 207–209.
7. Henry David Aiken, "Life and the Right to Life," in *Ethical Issues in Human Genetics*, ed. Bruce Hilton et al. (New York: Plenum Press, 1973), p. 182.
8. Later on Kluge says that although there are absolute rules, nobody has yet identified them, and this he promises to do some day. Kluge, *Practice of Death*, pp. 242–244.
9. As Barbara Kellum and others have shown, even in the religious era of medieval England, infanticide, like abortion, was regarded as only a venial sin, not mortal. Thomas of Cobham's penitential said that if an infant was disposed of by its mother's own hand, it was a venial sin on a par with overlaying, and a refusal to nurse an infant was also. For a summary account, see Cyril Means, "The Phoenix of Abortional Freedom," *New York Law Forum* 17 (1971): 335.
10. R.A. McCormick, "To Save or Let Die: the Dilemma of Modern Medicine," *Journal of the American Medical Association* 299 (July 8, 1974): 172–176.
11. Michael Tooley also focusses on the problem of *when* a neonate acquires "a serious right to life," which he concludes is decisive for both fetuses and infants. But the right question is something else: Is this right absolute, no matter how the right itself is established? See Tooley's "Abortion and Infanticide," *Philosophy and Public Affairs* 2 (1972): 37–65.
12. Aiken, "Life and the Right to Life," shows why the right to life is "not only conditional but contingent."
13. He cannot justify an absolute taboo on humane or humanistic grounds. It must presumably be supported by a cosmic authority, God or Mother Nature, established by revelation or metaphysics, but whatever it is, he keeps it secret and undeclared.
14. Bentham and Mill called it utility. Marvin Kohl calls it "reasonable kindness" in his *The Morality of Killing* (New York: Humanities Press, and London: Peter Owen, 1974). In my own language it is called loving concern (Joseph Fletcher, *Situation Ethics* [Philadelphia: Westminster Press, 1966]).

15. See William Frankena, *Ethics*, 2nd ed. (Englewood Cliffs, N.J.: Prentice-Hall, 1973), pp. 36, 55–57.

16. William Frankena, "The Ethics of Respect for Life," *Respect for Life in Medicine, Philosophy and Law*, ed. O. Tempkin, W.K. Frankena, and S.H. Kadish (Baltimore: Johns Hopkins University Press, 1976), pp. 32–33.

17. Rule utilitarianism could theoretically set up an opposite norm or rule, that it is right to practise infanticide in certain kinds or classes of situations.

Questions

1. How would Harrison and Nowell-Smith respond to the case at the Johns Hopkins Hospital in which a child with Down's syndrome was left to die of dehydration and starvation? How does Fletcher respond to this case? In your view, which of these responses offers the most sound approach, looking at the case from a moral perspective?

2. Is Fletcher correct in his view that, with regard to the right to life, the determinative question is "Can a person's life ever be ended ethically?" and not "Is an infant a person? And when did he or she become one?"

3. Is Fletcher right in thinking that we "ought to do whatever promotes well-being and reduces suffering" including, if necessary, ending a life? Can you think of examples which might provide reasons for thinking Fletcher wrong on this point? How would Fletcher respond to those examples?

Sanctity of Life and Quality of Life—Are They Compatible?

E.W. Keyserlingk

Especially in the context of discussion and debates about euthanasia, the expression "quality of life" tends to incur either enthusiastic support or total rejection. Consideration of a patient's quality of life (hereafter QOL) as a criterion for decision-making in a life-and-death context tends to evoke from both its supporters and its opponents general agreement on two counts:

   i. QOL considerations inevitably and essentially involve entirely subjective (not objective) judgments, and the assigning of only relative (not absolute) value to the lives of others. For QOL supporters that is to be applauded; for others, it makes QOL considerations at best highly suspect.

By permission of the author.

ii. Since (both sides claim) the sanctity-of-life principle (hereafter SOL) obliges the conviction that all lives are of equal and absolute value, based upon their inherent sacredness as opposed to their state of health, therefore QOL and SOL must be mutually exclusive. Much said and written on the subject states or implies that there are only these two irreconcilable sides, and no middles ground between them. To espouse SOL is to reject QOL and vice versa, and never the twain shall meet.

Consider, for example, the following not untypical approval by a proponent of QOL:

> The traditional Western ethic has always placed great emphasis on the intrinsic worth and equal value of every human life regardless of its stage or condition. . . . This traditional ethic is still clearly dominant, but there is much to suggest that it is being eroded at its core and may eventually be abandoned . . . there is a quite new emphasis on something which is beginning to be called the quality of life. . . . It will become necessary and acceptable to place relative rather than absolute values on such things as human lives, the use of scarce resources and the various elements that are to make up the quality of life or of living that is to be sought.[1]

Or consider the following and equally typical disapproval by an opponent of QOL:

> The quality-of-life ethic puts the emphasis on the type of life being lived not upon the fact of life. . . . What the life means to someone is what is important. Keeping this in mind, it is not inappropriate to say that some lives are of *greater value than others*, that the condition or meaning of life does have much to do with the justification for terminating that life. The sanctity of life ethic defends two propositions: 1. That human life is sacred by the very fact of its existence; its value does not depend upon a certain condition or perfection of that life. 2. That, therefore, all human lives are of *equal value*; all have the same right to life. The quality-of-life ethic finds neither of these two propositions acceptable.[2]

But must the "quality-of-life" ethic necessarily find those two propositions unacceptable? Must we, in fact, choose between the "traditional Western ethic" (SOL) and a "quite new emphasis" (QOL)? Are SOL and QOL as incompatible, opposed, and mutually exclusive as both spokespersons just cited assume? Have the meanings, context, and implications for medical decision-making been sufficiently explored and articulated to justify the sort of polarization indicated? Our own answer to all these questions is in the negative, and it will be the task of this paper to argue that case.

The double-barrelled thesis we will sketch and define is, first of all, that the sanctity-of-life principle is not as absolute and rigid in its maintenance of life as is often claimed or assumed. At the same time, the quality-of-life concept need not involve attaching only relative or subjective value to human life. Briefly stated, SOL and QOL may, and even should, be seen and used as compatible and complementary standards and, in a very real sense, respect for the sanctity of life includes attending to the quality of life.

At issue is more than just semantics and subjective interpretations of the terms in question. Obviously, one could peremptorily assign to both SOL and QOL meanings that would *make* them compatible and complementary, whatever violence is thereby done to roots, traditions, or common usage. But apart from the dishonesty and pretension inherent in such a semantic fiat, why create when discovery will do? In other words, on careful examination of the roots and tradition behind the SOL principle, in philosophy and theology and reflected in sound medical practice, one discovers that there are no grounds for the view that that principle demands that human life must always be "aggressively" maintained, no matter what the damage or prospects for recovery. As for those quality-of-life factors, the manner in which they influence sound medical decision-making in actual practice establishes that QOL need not essentially mean anything different from what is meant by more readily acceptable terminology, such as "ordinary-extraordinary treatment."

At issue here as well is more than just an interesting academic debate. It would be no great accomplishment simply to establish the compatability and complementarity of SOL and QOL if the outcome did not have important and practical implications for medical decision-making and attitudes toward human lives. But it is arguable that there are indeed such implications for decisions to support or not support life. Let us suggest two at this point. On the one hand, a respect for the sanctity of human life that includes concern for the quality of that life escapes the sort of simplistic medical decisions that pretend that complex, multi-dimensional, and difficult cases can be solved by the application of one simplistic, rigid, and unqualified standard. While comforting, easier, and righteousness-inducing for the one or ones making the decision or policy, black-and-white standards applied to mostly gray problems can be detrimental to the particular benefits, rights, and needs of the patient in question. To that extent, simplistic interpretations and applications of the SOL principle can be decision-avoiding rather than decision-making tools.

But on the other hand, decisions to support or not support life based on the particular patient's conditions and prognosis (that is, on that patient's quality of life) are less likely to be reduced to another party's subjective values and biases if they are tested by and restrained by the more general principle of the sanctity of life. More on this below.

We should note that the sort of decision-making we have in mind is that involving decisions made *by others* (doctors, families, agents, courts, etc.) for patients who, because of age and/or disability, are unable to make them for themselves. These second- or third-party decisions, made without knowing the wishes and preferences of the patient (or defective newborn) are the ones that always risk the imposition of someone else's wishes and values, and hence the ones that require some limiting and guiding principles and policies. Decisions made by *competent* patients for them-selves are another matter. Ethical, legal, and medical stances should, and increasingly do, affirm that competent patients should have the right to make their own judgments about their remaining quality of life, and accept or refuse further treatment whether death results and whether others consider that decision foolish and disrespectful of the sanctity of that person's life.

Let us consider first the SOL principle itself. It is often assumed that it is more or less equivalent to "vitalism." "Vitalism" is the view that maintains that, where there is human life, even mere metabolism and vital processes, whether fetal, deformed, suffering, brain-dead, or dying life, and no matter how damaged it is, it would be wrong not to preserve it by any means possible and for as long as possible. If this is the meaning chosen for SOL, then of course SOL and QOL would be incompatible, opposed, and mutually exclusive.

But a careful study of both the Biblical/theological roots and more recent philosophical analyses of the SOL principle suggest another and better meaning and choice. Those Biblical/theological roots of the principle clearly emphasize, on the one hand, that human life is to be respected, and never to be taken, altered, or left unprotected without justifying reasons, because only God has full dominion over it, and not humans. But on the other hand, those same traditions, as well as more recent theologies, insist that God has "deputized" to and shared with humans some of this dominion, some of this control over life, extending even to responsible decision-making in matters of life and death.[3] To accept that God-given responsibility is not "playing God" but "*being* human." In effect, from the theological perspective, responsible decision-making even in life-and-death contexts finds its basis and starting point in Genesis 1:28: ". . . Fulfill the earth and subdue it; and have dominion over the fish of the sea and over the birds of the air and over every living thing that moves upon the earth." It would be a form of cowardice and abdication of responsibility to hide behind a vitalistic understanding of a principle that (like all general principles) is too vague and indeterminate to solve complex ethical problems all by itself. One physician put it this way:

> When it comes to many of the social problems of medicine . . . doctors retreat behind the cliché that they won't play God. This type of intellectual cowardice, this mental retreat, is irrational. It lacks logic completely, because through the nature of his work, a doctor is constantly intruding himself into the work of the Deity. Does he wait for God to show His decision by making some outward manifestation before he undertakes a Caesarean section, orders a transfusion, or per-forms a risk-fraught open-heart operation?[4]

Many recent analyses from the perspective of moral philosophy emphasize essentially the same points about the SOL principle, leaving out, of course, the element of divine creation and dominion. On the one hand, human life is worthy of respect, wonder, and protection. A philosopher posited a "secular" interpretation and affirmation of the SOL principle:

The chief feature of the proto-religious "natural metaphysic" is the affirmation that life is sacred. It is believed to be sacred not because it is a manifestation of a transcendent creator from whom life comes: it is believed to be sacred because it is life. The idea of sacredness is generated by the primordial experience of being alive, or experiencing the elemental sensations of vitality and the elemental fear of its extinction. Man stands in awe before his own vitality, the vitality of his lineage and his species. The sense of awe is the attribution and therefore the acknowledgment of sanctity . . . if the sanctity of life goes then nothing else would be sacred.[5]

But on the other hand, it cannot be made to answer all questions in advance about *how* life is to be best respected in all circumstances; it cannot carry by itself the whole moral load of ethical decisions. Largely for that reason, some philosophers conclude that the SOL principle is at best meaningless.[6] We do not agree. Its value and role emerge only if we remind ourselves of the role of principles— that of testing moral rules.[7]

Two kinds of evaluation are involved at the "ought" level of life. One involves *facts* (what is), the other involves *rules* (what ought to be done or not done). Sometimes (and increasingly in our times) in the light of new facts, such as evolving perceptions and new scientific knowledge or possibilities, a rule becomes open to reconsideration. But how shall that rule or a new rule be tested, evaluated? What parameters and limits should it respect? It is precisely the role of general principles like SOL to answer those questions. It is *not* its function to prohibit new rules, or to preclude the difficult and sensitive task of weighing competing needs, rights, and benefits, or to insist that we should not attempt to evolve and rephrase our old rules in the light of new facts.

To questions such as, "Would it be a good rule that abortions be performed in certain circumstances?" or, "Would it be a good rule that life-supporting treatment be ceased in certain circumstances?" the SOL principle replies, "Would the proposed rule respect and protect the human life in question and indirectly all human life, or would it degrade and threaten the life in question and indirectly all human life?"

Thus the sanctity-of-life principle itself leads us inescapably to face such questions as: What *is* human life? What are its normative signs? What are the qualities or properties of human life that demand our respect for and preservations of that life? In other words, the SOL principle itself leads us inescapably to QOL concerns. One can emphatically agree that human life is "sacred" but what is human life? What makes this a question at all, and an increasingly urgent and difficult one, are precisely the new facts we cannot ignore in the form of both new knowledge about how life does begin, continue, and end, as well as availability of new medical technology to control how life *could* begin, continue, and end. In the biomedical context, as in any other, knowledge and technology are not value-neutral. Depending upon how human life and human benefit are defined, they can be used beneficially or harmfully.

Because our increasingly sophisticated technology can now arrest and prolong the dying process at any level of life from near fullness to merely biological, "quality" choices related to that technology cannot be avoided as they may have been in a simpler age. Now, in more and more cases not to choose is to choose. Not to make choices on reasoned and moral bases is to risk that those choices will be made by bureaucrats or technicians, and to the detriment of both the individual patient under consideration and, ultimately, all patients. If decision-making norms are not anchored in careful ethical analyses and choices about what we mean by and value about human life, then those norms will focus on the sort of quality-of-life criteria such as usefulness or burden to others, and social worth.

It is precisely at this point that the sanctity-of-life principle performs its limiting and testing function. It urges us to exclude from life-and-death decision-making (about factually or legally incompetent patients) all considerations of social worth and usefulness to others, and insists that the only valid norm is benefit to the patient in question, not burden or benefit to others.

This norm, in turn, makes it arguable that in decisions to initiate, continue, or cease "aggressive" medical treatment for patients who are incompetent and seriously or terminally ill or for seriously defective newborns, those are two justifiable *quality-of-life* concerns: the patients' (or newborns') actual and potential capacity to experience or relate; and the intensity, protraction, and susceptibility to control of their pain and suffering. The first concern would appear to matter if one grants that the capacity to experience and relate to the world around us is the essence of human life. The second concern assumes what is, in fact, medical experience, namely that there are still some cases of excruciating and intractable pain, despite the existence of sophisticated palliative and painkilling techniques.

One could therefore formulate, as a quality-of-life rule, perfectly consistent with the sanctity of life, the following: if, despite aggressive treatment, there is not and cannot be restored a minimal capacity to experience or relate, or if the level of pain and suffering will be prolonged, excruciating, and intractable, then a decision to cease or not initiate treatment is justified and perhaps even imposed. In other words, for irreversibly comatose adults, for example, or for some defective newborns with severe spina bifida and a host of complications for whom the prognosis is a life of excruciating suffering, the most beneficial decision (for them), the one most respectful of the sanctity of their lives, may well be ceasing to support those lives.

What then of the "equal-lives" argument? Does not the use of quality-of-life language imply that there is an *inequality* between lives and the degree of protection they therefore merit? Some think so, as the following indicates:

> Can one really use a condition-of-life criterion and still insist that every life is of equal value regardless of condition? . . . does not one statement cancel out the other in the actual ethical climate in which today's debate is taking place?[8]

But surely it depends upon what is meant by and should be meant by human life. Increasingly, in a medical context it appears necessary to distinguish between what could be called "human biological life" and "human personal life" if one is to determine the human life the support of which the sanctity-of-life principle has in mind. Clearly there can be no human personal life, a life capable of enjoying, relating, communicating, and so forth, unless there is also human biological life. But increasingly, thanks in large part to new medical techniques and life-support systems, there can be human *biological* life without any significant human *personal* life. Both sorts of life are "human" — after all, even anencephalic new-borns or irreversibly brain-dead adults were born of humans, but the human life the support of which the sanctity-of-life principle promotes is surely human personal life.

Insofar as humans are essentially relating, communicating, experiencing beings, mere human biological or metabolic life is not a good in itself, but a condition for the capacities of the human person. If human life essentially means "personal life," then there is no inconsistency or inequality in deciding that not all lives should be supported. All persons are of equal value no matter what their condition. But not all lives in the biological sense are equally of value to the individual person concerned. We want life for what can be done with it, because it is at least minimally bearable, enjoyable, and worthwhile, not for what it is in itself. As has been rightly observed:

> It always seems to be assumed that life, of whatever quality, is the most priceless of possessions. Physicians often assume that patients would always prefer life, no matter how handicapped, to death. The opposite is often the case.[9]

All lives are not equal if "equal" means that all lives are to be treated and supported identically no matter how different their condition. What is to be avoided is unjust discrimination in treatment and support. But inequality of treatment need not be unjust. Injustice and inequality are avoided if decisions focus on what is of benefit to the particular patient's quality of life.

Respect for both the sanctity of life and the condition or quality of that life could guard against either of two extremes—on the one hand considering all human lives as good in themselves, equally meaningful and equally to be supported no matter what, and on the other hand, ascribing *no* meaning, value, or support to lives that are handicapped or burdensome.

One can only be enormously impressed by the compassionate and heroic care extended to seriously defective newborns and infants, as well as irreversibly comatose or terminally ill adults by parents, families, and staff of institutions. Undoubtedly such experiences and the people they care for are extremely meaningful to those who provide the care, and they are provided with unique opportunities for extending and learning compassion, love, and fidelity. Those who care find meaning and purpose:

> Someone in the institution was capable of relating closely to every child, and at every bedside as we made rounds there would be a staff

member who could tell us the child's history. . . . Severe hydro-cephalics and markedly obtunded neurologically damaged children were called by name and regarded as individuals. Their disease and related irascibility was understood, explained away, and assuaged by acts of comfort.[10]

That observation leads us to add an important qualification to what has been said thus far about QOL. It is this: a newborn's or adult patient's quality of life or condition is not always a static reality and can sometimes be considerably improved not only by strictly medical treatment but by the love, compassion, and persistence of those who surround that newborn or adult. For that reason, quality-of-life rules or criteria indicated earlier should be expanded in this manner: if and when a reliable diagnosis and prognosis can be made, including a reliable assessment of how *both* loving care as well as (presently or likely to be available) medical techniques and treatments may improve the patient's condition, ability to function, or level of pain, then and only then are we in a position to make ethical decisions to allow or not allow others to die.

Yet such rounds in such institutions can also raise two nagging suspicions. One is that in *some* of these cases (no doubt a minority), if decisions had been made soon after birth or later not to treat or support life aggressively, decisions based on the sorts of quality-of-life criteria indicated above, they may well have been decisions for the benefit of those children. The second suspicion is that *sometimes* we do not make such decisions partially at least because we, the healthy, derive meaning, purpose, and satisfaction from experiences that can have no such positive features for those children. To a certain extent, we may be deriving *our* satisfaction and meaning at *their* expense.

But the other extreme is just as, if not more, worrying: the tendency to ascribe no meaning or value to those who are handicapped and to cherish and support people not for what they are but for what they can do or make and only if they are not very burdensome to us. Such a stance is encouraged by proposals of what could be called criteria for "optimal" human life, standards and tests that give higher marks and more attention (including life support) to those who are brighter, have more self-control, need less help. One finds this tendency reflected not only in the context of life-and-death decision-making, but also, for example, in those who ask sperm banks for the product of donors with high IQs. In both cases there is a distasteful and distorted exaggeration of rationality and a disdain for human "imperfections."

Typical of this stance is the moral philosopher Joseph Fletcher, who proposed fifteen criteria as indicators of "human" or "person," with particular stress on rationality. He is both arbitrary and demanding when he decrees, for example, that, "Any individual of the species homo sapiens who falls below the IQ 40 mark in a Standford-Binet test . . . is questionably a person; below the 20 mark not a person."[11]

Should such a criterion ever become normative, many of the mentally retarded and senile now receiving care and able to function, albeit at a minimal level, would be excluded from care and support. There is a flavour of reductionism and elitism to such proposals that makes them inconsistent with respect for the sanctity of life.

The attempt by the Judeo-Christian tradition to seek a balance between two unacceptable extremes has been well described:

> In the past the Judeo-Christian tradition has attempted to walk a balanced middle path between medical vitalism (that preserves life at any cost) and medical pessimism (that kills when life seems frustrating, burdensome, "useless"). Both of these extremes root in an identical idolatry of life—an attitude that, at least by inference, views death as an unmitigated, absolute evil, and life as the absolute good. The middle course that has structured Judeo-Christian attitudes is that life is indeed a basic and precious good, but a good to be preserved precisely as the condition of other values. It is these other values and possibilities that found the duty to preserve physical life and also dictate the limits of this duty. In other words, life is a relative good, and the duty to preserve it a limited one.[12]

It is sometimes argued that the more traditional "ordinary-extraordinary-means" tradition and language is a better alternative to the use of quality-of-life criteria because the former is more likely to focus on objective considerations. Leonard Weber, for example, claims that, "The focus on means is a constant reminder that we should not decide who should live or die on the basis of the worth of someone's life." Paul Ramsey notes that:

> The terms "ordinary/extraordinary," however cumbersome, opaque and unilluminating, directed the attention . . . to *objective* considerations in the patient's condition and in the armamentarium of medicine's remedies.[13]

But arguments that QOL criteria are necessarily more likely to result in subjective decisions about the "worth" of the lives of others than the means criteria are not convincing. The ordinary-extraordinary-means distinction is notoriously ambiguous, and in any case cannot really escape consideration of the quality or condition of the patient in question. Does it mean that "usual" treatments are morally obligatory, while "unusual" treatments are not? Hardly—if so, no change in medical policy or practice would ever occur. Does it mean that "useful" treatments are morally obligatory, while "useless" treatments are not? This would seem the more reasonable and justified meaning of the distinction, but useful in what respect? Useful to save life? But if so, at what level of function? Useful to provide comfort rather than prolong life? And is "usefulness" the only justifiable consideration? What about questions of costs, indignity, and so forth involved in the medical means being considered?

For all these reasons, various alternatives to the ordinary-extraordinary-treatment distinction have been proposed, some of which focus much more directly on quality-of-life considerations yet attempt to guard against the imposition of someone else's subjective values. An example is the "reasonable/unreasonable-treatment" distinction proposed by Robert Veatch:

> A reasonable person would find a refusal unreasonable (and treatment thus morally required) if the treatment is useful in *treating a patient's condition* (though not necessarily lifesaving) and at the same time does not give rise to any significant *patient-centred* objections based on physical or mental burden; familial, social, or economic concern; or religious belief [emphasis added].[14]

One may conclude that, in the final analysis what matters most is where the lines are drawn, not what particular terminology is used. In our view, behind the "ordinary-extraordinary-means" language inescapably lie judgments about burdens, handicaps, damage, prognoses, and degrees of same—in other words, quality-of-life considerations. What will ultimately provide the needed protection and objectivity for a patient unable to make a decision is not the particular language and terminology used, but that the decision is tested in the light of the sanctity of that person's life and made for that person's benefit, not the benefit of others.

Two final points merit brief consideration. The first has to do with active euthanasia, the second with the care of the dying.

If it is sometimes justifiable for quality-of-life reasons and consistent with the sanctity-of-life principle not to initiate or continue supporting life, does the not-continuing extend beyond allowing-to-die to active euthanasia or killing? Moral 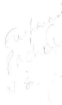 arguments in favor of active euthanasia generally fall within one of two lines of reasoning. The first is that, because the motive can be benevolent in both cases, there is no moral difference between allowing to die (or passive euthanasia) and active euthanasia; if the former is sometimes justified, so is the latter. The second is that, even if there are moral and other differences between them, it is nevertheless sometimes justifiable to kill. We disagree on both counts.

Regarding the first line of argument, one may agree that the motives in both cases may be the same — that the patient, friend, or relative in question will die as soon as possible so that, for example, his or her intense and intractable suffering will cease. But motives alone do not determine morality. There are other considerations as well, among them the methods used and the nature of duties owed. For example, a physician may not always have a duty to provide life-saving treatment. In fact, a physician may have a duty *not* to provide it faced with a patient's refusal, or faced with the knowledge that it would impose too heavy a burden on the patient. In such cases the cause of death is the illness that it is no longer reasonable or merciful to fight. In our view it is misleading to label such decisions "passive" or "negative" euthanasia — they are not euthanasia and not the "cause" of anything, but rather good medical decisions based on evidence that curing is no longer possible. But a physician may, and we think does, have a duty not to kill, not to be the cause of death. In practice, physicians understand and insist upon the difference. This moral difference between acting (killing) and not-acting (allowing to die) has been well expressed:

> Acting seems to start with a presumption against it: e.g. killing is *prima facie* wrong. Not-acting starts without any such presumption, and it is only by establishing a duty to act that we show that not-acting is wrong. Killing needs to be justified; not saving life does not.[16]

What then of the second line of argument? Even if there is a moral difference, is active euthanasia in fact sometimes justifiable? We think not. What makes the morality of active euthanasia attractive is, of course, that there are indeed individual cases in which it would indeed appear to be more humane not simply to allow to die but to actively hasten death. But it should not be necessary to argue or prove that this is not so to establish that a general policy against active (even voluntary) euthanasia, one allowing no exceptions, is nevertheless the policy most consistent with the sanctity of human life. Not to kill in some instances is tragic for those individual cases, there is no point in denying that.

But the greater tragedy may well be that of following our natural sympathies and actually killing. Apart from religious arguments against it, there are a number of others that merit attention. One is the argument from medical fallibility. At least sometimes, to kill would preclude the chance for life in the event of prognostic error. Another is the serious harm such a change in moral and legal policy would do to the trust required in patient-physician relationships. A third is the wedge argument — to allow killing, even by exception, may well prove to be the thin edge of the wedge, sooner or later putting all life in a more precarious position. After all, rules against killing are not isolated from other rules and attitudes promoting respect for life. To disturb and qualify the rules against killing would seem inevitably to weaken the whole web of rules and attitudes that foster that respect.

What, finally, of allowing to die itself? If it is sometimes justified, once that decision has been made do we have no further duties toward the person concerned? By no means. There remains the continuing obligation to provide for the newborn's or patient's care and comfort. The obligation to aggressively prolong life may well cease, but allowing to die with care never does. The duty to provide care and comfort applies whether life-prolonging treatment continues or not, no matter how damaged the patient's condition or quality of life. The SOL principle surely calls for at least the same respect and consideration for dying human life as for healthy human life. And if greater need should elicit greater care and concern, then those who are irreversibly and seriously ill or dying deserve most care of all. In this regard the growing skills in pain control and palliative care reflect the growing awareness of medicine: that while it is *sometimes* about curing, it is *always* about caring; though the former goal sometimes becomes unrealizable, the latter always is. The art of medicine is, in large part, the art of knowing when to stop trying to cure and how to continue caring.

Notes

1. Editorial, *California Medicine*, September, 1970, pp. 67–68.
2. Weber, Leonard J., *Who Shall Live?* (New York: Paulist Press, 1976), pp. 41–42.
3. Among these theologians are, for example, Dietrick Bonhoeffer, Karl Rahner, Johannes Metz, Harvey Cox, Rudolf Bultmann, Teilhard de Chardin and many others. See for example Johannes Metz, *Theology of the World* (New York: The Seabury Press, 1972).
4. Guttmacher, Alan F., "The United States Medical Profession and Family Planning," in Bernard Berelson (ed.), *Family Planning and Population Problems* (Chicago: University of Chicago Press, 1966), p. 458.
5. Shils, Edward, "The Sanctity of Life," in Edward H. Labby (ed.), *Life or Death: Ethics and Options* (Seattle: University of Washington Press, 1968), pp. 12–13.
6. For example K. Danner Clouser, "The Sanctity of Life: An Analysis of a Concept," (1973)78 *Annals of Internal Medicine*, pp. 120–121.
7. On the role of abstract principles see Henry David Aiken, *Reason and Conduct* (New York: Alfred A. Knopf, 1962). See especially ch. 4, "Levels of Moral Discourse."
8. Weber, Leonard J., *Who Shall Live?* (New York: Paulist Press, 1976), p. 83.
9. Gellman, Derek, (1975)52 *Dimensions in Health Services*, p. 23.
10. Diamond, Eugene F., M.D., "Quality vs. Sanctity of Life in the Nursery," (1976)135 *America*, p. 397.
11. Fletcher, Joseph, "Indicators of Humanhood: A Tentative Profile of Man," (1972) 2 *Hastings Center Report*, p. 1.
12. McCormick, Richard, "To Save or Let Die," (1974)229 *Journal of the American Medical Association*, p. 174.
13. Weber, Leonard, op. cit. supra (note 8), p. 85.
14. Ramsey, Paul, "Euthanasia and Dying Well Enough," (1977)44 *Linacre Quarterly*, p. 44.
15. Veatch, Robert, *Death, Dying and the Biological Revolution* (New Haven: Yale University Press, 1976), p. 112.
16. Fitzgerald, P.J., "Acting and Refraining," (1967)27 *Analysis*, p. 136. See also T.L. Beauchamp, "A Reply to Rachels on Active and Passive Euthanasia," *Social Ethics* (McGraw-Hill, 1977), pp. 67–74. For the opposite view see James Rachels, "Active and Passive Euthanasia," (1975)292 *The New England Journal of Medicine*, pp. 78–80.

Questions

1. Is Keyserlingk right in thinking that the sanctity-of-life principle and the quality-of-life principle are compatible?
2. Are the arguments Keyserlingk advances for distinguishing between active and passive euthanasia sound?
3. Based on his distinction between curing and caring, how would Keyserlingk deal with the child with Down's syndrome at the Johns Hopkins Hospital described by Fletcher? Is the method implied by Keyserlingk's approach morally preferable to that implied by Fletcher's approach? Why or why not?

An Act Respecting the Withholding or Withdrawal of Treatment Where Death Is Inevitable

[First Reading, Ontario Legislature, 1977]

Explanatory Note

The purpose of this bill is to provide a means whereby an individual may limit the effect of a general or implied consent to medical treatment to prevent the use of life-sustaining procedures while in a terminal condition.

The bill is designed to achieve this purpose by permitting an individual to execute a direction limiting [his or her] consent. Once a physician or hospital employee has notice of this direction, there is no defence of consent as a basis to avoid civil liability if the patient is treated with life-sustaining procedures during a period of terminal condition.

Her Majesty, by and with the advice and consent of the Legislative Assembly of the Province of Ontario, enacts as follows:

1. In this Act,   *Interpretation*

   (a) "attending physician" means a physician selected by or assigned to a patient and who has responsibility for the treatment and care of the patient;

   (b) "life-sustaining procedure" means a medical procedure or intervention that utilizes mechanical or artificial means to sustain, restore or supplant a vital function to postpone the moment of death, but does not include a medical procedure or intervention for the purpose of alleviating pain;

   (c) "physician" means a person licensed under Part III   *1974, c. 47* of *The Health Disciplines Act, 1974*;

   (d) "terminal condition" means an incurable condition caused by injury or disease by reason of which, in reasonable medical opinion, death is imminent and only postponed without improvement of the condition during the application of life-sustaining procedures.

2. (1) Any person who has attained the age of majority, is   *Direction limiting* mentally competent to consent, is able to make a free and   *consent* informed decision and has, or is deemed to have, consented to medical treatment may, in writing in Form 1 signed by him, direct that the consent does not extend to the application of life-sustaining procedures during a terminal condition.

   (2) A direction under subsection 1 is not valid unless   *Witnesses* the signature is witnessed by two persons neither of whom is a   *of direction*

relative or an attending physician or other person engaged in the health care of the person giving the direction.

(3) No person who witnesses a direction under subsection 2 is entitled to any benefit from the estate of the person who gives the direction, except charges or directions for payments of debts. Beneficiary of estate as witness

(4) A direction is valid for five years from the date of its signing unless revoked under section 3. Duration

3. (1) A direction under section 2 does not take effect unless it is given to the attending physician of the person giving the direction, or where the person is a patient in a health facility, is given to the attending physician or a person on the medical staff of or employed by the health facility. When direction effective

(2) Upon a direction being given to one of the persons mentioned in subsection 1, the direction or a copy of it shall be included in the medical records of the person giving the direction. Direction included in medical records

(3) Where the person signing a direction in any manner and without regard to mental competency indicates to one of the persons mentioned in subsection 1 an intention to revoke the direction or is pregnant, the direction is revoked and shall be removed immediately from the medical records and destroyed. Revocation

(4) Notwithstanding subsection 1, a direction given thereunder by a person who had not attained the age of majority, was not mentally competent to consent, or was not able to make a free and informed decision, is valid for the purposes of this Act if the person who acted upon it had no reason to believe that the person who gave it had not attained the age of majority, was not mentally competent to consent, or was not able to make a free and informed decision, as the case may be. Direction deemed valid

4. Where doubt exists as to whether or not a terminal condition exists for the purposes of a direction, Terminal condition

(a) a terminal condition shall be deemed to exist where in the opinion of two physicians, each of whom has made a separate diagnosis in respect of the person giving the direction and neither of whom has any medical responsibility for that person, the terminal condition exists; and

(b) a terminal condition shall be deemed not to exist where in the opinion of one physician whose opinion is sought for the purposes of clause *a* a terminal condition does not exist.

5. No action or other proceeding for damages lies against any person for any act done or omission made in good faith and without negligence in the observance or intended observance of a direction purporting to be given under this Act. Civil liability

6. Nothing in this Act shall be construed to impose an obli- Other obligations not affected gation to provide or perform a life-sustaining procedure where the obligation does not otherwise exist at law.

7. (1) A death that occurs subsequent to the withholding Insurance or withdrawal of life-sustaining procedures pursuant to a direction signed under this Act shall not be deemed to be a suicide or self-induced death under any policy of insurance.

(2) A requirement that a person sign a direction as a Idem condition for being insured for or receiving health care services is void.

8. Subject to subsection 3 of section 3, every person who Offence wilfully conceals, cancels, defaces or destroys the direction of another without that person's consent is guilty of an offence and on summary conviction is liable to a fine of not more than $1,000 or to imprisonment for not more than thirty days, or to both.

9. This Act comes into force on the day it receives Royal Commencement Assent.

10. This Act may be cited as *The Natural Death Act, 1977.* Short title

---

Form 1

(The Natural Death Act, 1977)
Direction to Attending Physician and Medical Staff

I, ... , being of sound mind, wilfully and voluntarily, direct that all life-sustaining procedures be withheld or withdrawn if at any time I should be in a terminal condition and where the application of life-sustaining procedures would serve only to artificially prolong the moment of death.

It is my intention that this direction be honoured by my family, physicians and medical staff as the final expression of my legal right to refuse medical or surgical treatment and to die naturally.

Made this . . . . day of . . . . (month, year).

. . . .
(Signature)

The person signing this directive is personally known to me and I believe him/her to be of sound mind.

. . . .
(Witness)

. . . .
(Witness)

Questions

1. Evaluate the act critically from the points of view of the authors who have contributed to this chapter.
2. In your view, is an act of this kind morally acceptable? Could it be improved? Are the safeguards it provides enough to prevent abuse?

Suggestions for Further Reading

On Euthanasia and Abortion

- E-H.W. Kluge, *The Practice of Death* (New Haven: Yale University Press, 1975). This book examines the morality of abortion, infanticide, and euthanasia. The author comes to the view that abortion in the early months of pregnancy is morally acceptable. But, following the development of "the constitutional capabilities for rational symbolic thought and self-awareness, a person exists." This occurs between the fourth and sixth months of pregnancy, after which time abortion is murder. It follows that infanticide, too, is the killing of a person and therefore murder. Euthanasia is, however, acceptable in certain specified situations. Michael Tooley offers a sustained critical evaluation of Kluge's thesis in "The Practice of Death," *Canadian Journal of Philosophy*, Vol. 6, No. 2, June 1976.
- John Ladd, ed., *Ethical Issues Relating to Life and Death* (Oxford: Oxford University Press, 1979). This volume includes articles by a number of notable authors and takes up many of the issues touched on in the first two chapters of this book.
- John Woods, *Engineered Death: Abortion, Suicide, Euthanasia and Senecide* (Ottawa: University of Ottawa Press, 1978). Adopting a secular, liberal perspective, the author finds himself directed (to his own surprise, given current liberal views on these subjects) toward the conclusion that abortion is rarely permissible but euthanasia frequently is.
- See also Chapter 1 above.

On Euthanasia and Infanticide

- E.W. Keyserlingk, *Sanctity of Life or Quality of Life in the Context of Ethics, Medicine and Law*. This is a report prepared as a background study for the Law Reform Commission of Canada. The report studies the notions of "sanctity of life" and "quality of life" in depth and goes on to make a series of proposals. Although the focus of the Commission work is law reform, this report is primarily ethical in nature.
- Marvin Kohl, ed., *Beneficent Euthanasia* (Buffalo: Prometheus Books, 1975). This book contains an excellent collection of articles on the

subject of euthanasia viewed from many perspectives — religious and secular, pro and con.
- Marvin Kohl, ed., *Infanticide and the Value of Life* (Buffalo: Prometheus Books, 1978). Again, an excellent collection of articles representing a variety of perspectives on the subject of infanticide.
- See also Chapter 1 above.

On the Distinction between Active and Passive Euthanasia

- R.C.A. Hunter, "Euthanasia, A Paper for Discussion by Psychiatrists," *Canadian Journal of Psychiatry*, Vol. 25, No. 5 (August, 1980). Hunter asks, "What are the problems posed for psychiatry by euthanasia?" Tentative answers are offered, and the author concludes by suggesting that there is no case in his experience for active euthanasia. However, judicious (conservative) use of passive euthanasia is in some cases warranted.
- James Rachels, "Active and Passive Euthanasia," *New England Journal of Medicine*, Vol. 292, No. 2 (9 January 1975), pp. 78–80. In this influential article, reprinted in an expanded version in *Ethical Issues Relating to Life and Death*, ed., John Ladd (Oxford University Press, 1979). The distinction between active and passive euthanasia is examined and rejected as not morally relevant. Rachels argues that under certain conditions euthanasia is morally acceptable and ought to be legalized.
- Douglas Walton, "Splitting the Difference: Killing and Letting Die," *Dialogue*, Vol. 20, No. 1, 1981. Is there a morally relevant distinction between killing and letting die? Some have argued that there is and some have argued equally strongly that there is not. In this article, Walton explores the distinction. In particular, he examines the position of James Rachels, an American author who has written extensively in defence of euthanasia and concludes that there is no distinction to be made between active and passive euthanasia which is morally relevant.

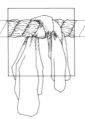

Capital Punishment

Introduction

Background Considerations

Capital punishment is thought of today as a punishment inflicted on persons who have been found guilty of murder. But the idea that capital punishment should be reserved only for murderers has gained wide acceptance only in this century. At one time in English history, for example, the penalty of death might be imposed for the theft of anything worth more than 12 pence. Blackstone, an influential eighteenth-century commentator on the law, discovered 166 crimes punishable by death in English law. By 1810, there were 300 offences, including forgery, for which the death penalty could be imposed in England.

The view that capital punishment should be reserved for murder is the product of more than one hundred years of law reform, the result of which has been increasing moderation in the use of capital punishment in many countries in the Western world.

Execution by hanging for murder has been a feature of Canadian law throughout our history. Until the 1950s murder was rather broadly defined as the unlawful killing of a human being by someone who intended to bring about his victim's death or who intended to inflict bodily harm on his victim, and where the harm inflicted resulted in his victim's death. For such a crime the mandatory sentence was death by hanging. A judge had no discretion in the matter and only the Governor General, acting on the advice of the Canadian government, could intervene to prevent the execution from taking place. Such interventions were relatively rare.

Toward the end of the 1950s support for moderation in the use of capital punishment began to grow. It resulted first in a decision that no one under the age of 18 was to be executed. A second step was taken in 1960: the law was altered to differentiate between murder and capital murder. Capital murder, for which capital punishment was the mandatory sentence, comprised those murders which were planned and deliberate. The change was not intended to be a step in the direction of the abolition of capital punishment. Nevertheless, from 1957 to 1963, the Conservative government commuted 80 percent of all death sentences. And from 1963 to 1967, the Liberal government commuted one hundred percent of all death sentences. Thus, by 1967 abolition of capital punishment had in fact come about, though in law capital punishment continued to exist.

By 1967, substantial pressure for the formal abolition of capital punishment was being felt by the government. The result was a bill restricting capital murder to situations where the victim was a police officer or a prison guard. All other acts of murder were to result in a sentence of life imprisonment. The bill was to remain in force for an experimental period of five years. After a stormy debate, the bill was adopted in a vote in which members were free of party discipline and could vote according to what they believed to be right. In 1973, the same bill was renewed for a further five-year period by a vote of 119 in favour, 106 opposed. At the same time, public-opinion polls suggested that a majority of Canadians wished to return to a wider definition of capital murder.

Between 1967 and 1977 all death sentences were commuted to life imprisonment by the Governor General on the advice of the government.

The final step toward the abolition of capital punishment was taken in 1978 when capital punishment was eliminated. Murder is now classified as first-degree murder or second-degree murder. If a murder is planned or deliberate, carried out for pay, or committed in the course of an actual or attempted hijacking of an aircraft, kidnapping, sexual assault with or without a weapon, or aggravated sexual assault, or if the victim is a police officer or prison employee or the murderer has been convicted of murder before, it is first-degree murder. Most other acts of murder are second-degree. Both are punishable by a mandatory sentence of life imprisonment. However, persons convicted of first-degree murder must serve a minimum sentence of 25 years before they are eligible for parole. A conviction for second-degree murder now results in a minimum of ten years in jail before becoming eligible for parole.

The Current Situation

In Canada, although capital punishment has been abolished, there is considerable pressure for its reinstatement. At the time of the abolition debate, public-opinion polls indicated that two-thirds of Canadians wished capital punishment retained. More recent polls indicate that a majority of Canadians continue to favour a return to capital punishment, a position which police associations across the country advocate strongly.

In England, abolition was brought about in 1965 by a free vote in spite of the fact that a public-opinion poll taken at the time showed that 79 percent of the British people were opposed. In 1969, abolition was reaffirmed, a situation which has continued to the present.

The current situation in the United States is somewhat different. There, criminal law is established by each state; hence the situation varies from one part of the country to another. In those states which have retained capital punishment, executions are increasingly common.

The Moral Dimension

Any form of punishment inflicts suffering on the offender being punished. For that reason, punishment needs to be justified. The death penalty is a particularly severe form of punishment because it inflicts suffering on an offender by taking his life. How then can a society that claims to be committed to the view that human life is sacred tolerate capital punishment?

Those who endorse the death penalty tend to justify their position by appealing to one of two views. The first view is that, because the protection of human life is a fundamental obligation which the community has toward its members, it must do everything it legitimately can do to deter those who might otherwise commit murder. Capital punishment is the most effective deterrent available and so is justified. In short, capital punishment is a means to securing respect for the principle that both individually and collectively we have an obligation to preserve and respect human life.

Evaluating the merits of the view that capital punishment is justified as a deterrent requires that we address two questions. First, does the threat of capital punishment deter people from committing murder? Some have argued that it does not. They point to a host of studies undertaken in several countries over the past several decades which have failed to provide any evidence for the view that capital punishment is a deterrent to murder. Others have argued that the studies which have been done are inconclusive; further, the suggestion that capital punishment is not a deterrent conflicts with practical experience and common sense. Assessing the merits of these conflicting points of view is a theme which runs through several of the readings.

There is a second question to be considered. Let us assume for the moment that the death penalty is a deterrent. Does it follow that capital punishment is justified? Many people are prepared to accept that it does. But for others, harming some individuals as a way of securing benefits for others is not acceptable, particularly where taking human life is involved.

Let us turn now to a second view — namely, that justice requires that those who break the law should be punished. On this view justice requires that offenders receive the punishment they deserve for the crime which they have committed. That is, the punishment should fit the crime. The punishment which those who commit murder deserve, that is the punishment which fits the crime of murder, is death.

Assessing the merits of this view requires, once again, that we address two questions. First, does justice require that those who break the law be punished? A complex variety of arguments have been advanced by those who reject a "just deserts" view of punishment. Some have suggested that those who commit serious crimes like murder are not autonomous moral agents responsible for their actions; rather they are mentally ill; or they are victims of their upbringing or their environment. The findings of the social sciences are frequently cited in support of these arguments. Others argue that we are never justified in imposing suffering in the form of punishment unless we can establish that punishment will serve to reform or rehabilitate the offender, or that it will result in benefits to the community. Obviously, reform or rehabilitation of the offender is not the point of capital punishment. And empirical research has failed to establish that capital punishment reduces the volume of crime in general or murder in particular. Hence, they conclude that capital punishment is immoral.

Those who advocate capital punishment on the grounds that execution is the fitting punishment for those who commit murder must address a second question. Let us assume that justice requires that those who break the law be punished. Does it follow that execution is a just punishment for those who commit murder? This question requires serious consideration. Murder is frequently committed in a moment of uncontrollable anger or while the offender is heavily intoxicated. Frequently the victim is closely related to the murderer, a husband or wife, a parent, or a son or daughter. Of course, not all cases of murder fall into this category. But here, too, there are objections. For example, courts have been known to make mistakes. Innocent people have been found guilty in the past. This has led some to argue that the death penalty is simply too final a punishment to be inflicted by fallible human institutions. Those who commit very serious crimes like murder should be given very long prison sentences, to leave open the possibility for errors to be corrected.

The Readings

The readings in this chapter reflect a variety of positions on the morality of capital punishment.

The first three readings will provide you with an opportunity to evaluate the arguments of some of the key participants in the debate which led to a decision by Parliament to abolish capital punishment. The position of the Canadian Chiefs of Police was presented in the first instance to the Justice Committee of the House of Commons when it was considering the abolition of capital punishment. Police forces in Canada continue to call for capital punishment for particularly serious offences. The bill abolishing capital punishment was presented to the House of Commons by Warren Allmand. His contribution to the readings comprises a part of his response to the arguments of the police. Ezzat A. Fattah was commissioned by the government to undertake a study of the deterrent effect of capital punishment. The resulting report was used extensively in the abolition debate. In the article included in this chapter, Fattah reviews and compares his original findings to the results of more recent research.

The next group of essays focusses on the view that justice requires the use of the death penalty for particularly serious crimes. Walter Berns defends capital punishment as an appropriate and necessary penalty. Hugo Adam Bedau argues that offenders should receive their just deserts; nevertheless, the death penalty is not a morally acceptable punishment. The final reading in this group is contributed by Alan Brudner. He undertakes an evaluation of the view that punishment should only be inflicted if it will lead to a rehabilitation or reform of the offender or benefit the community at large. Having rejected this utilitarian approach to punishment, he then defends the view that justice requires that offenders be punished and that their punishment should fit their crime. He concludes that putting to death those who have committed serious crimes is consistent with, but not required by, the view that punishment should fit the crime. A society which is secure in its values will not need to resort to capital punishment to communicate its commitment to protecting human life.

Capital Punishment*

Canadian Association of Chiefs of Police

Introduction

The Canadian Association of Chiefs of Police, representing Chief Administrators of police and security forces across Canada and therefore responsible directly or indirectly for over 50,000 law-enforcement officers, wishes to set before the authorities of the federal government their views on the matter of the death penalty.

We recognize that representing peace officers whose duty it is to see that society respects the laws which have been democratically enacted by governments at all levels, many might colour our representations and label them as biased and unobjective.

In this view of this, and in our sincere desire to be just fair to all, the Association has made an exhaustive study of the *problem* in order that our recommendations may precisely be as objective as possible and for the good of society as a whole.

It is unfortunate that in the five-year mortorium little research or study was done to find an alternative to the death penalty if only to ensure that there is not an alternative that would satisfy those who claim that the death peanlty has no place in today's society. Federal authorities might well have used the moratorium, not only as a waiting period after which an evaluation of a *trial legislation* would be made, but also a period of time during which specific groups having made representations in the past would have been charged with the compilation of specific information according to their views for presentation at the end of the moratorium.

From a brief submitted to the federal government by the Canadian Association of Chiefs of Police, Ottawa, Jan. 1973.

Editor's Note: The above article has been slightly edited for this edition.

While this may still happen as in the case of this Association, we feel that a directed and cooperative effort should have been made, not to enhance or secure the views of one particular group or aspect, but rather with a view of solving the *problem*.

That there is a problem is best illustrated by the booklet on capital punishment produced by the then Honourable Minister of Justice, Guy Favreau in June 1965. This booklet gathers "material relating to the purpose and value of capital punishment and the initial paragraph in the summing up of the comments collected identifies the *problem*." It states that "some persons approach the issue of the death penalty from a straightforward moral viewpoint, the abolitionists among them believing that it is wicked and unwarranted for the State to take a human life in any circumstances and the retentionists believing that the crime of murder is so heinous that death is the only punishment that is consonant with a sound moral sense in the community. Neither of these groups is likely to change camp upon considerations of deterrent effect; the conclusions are deeply and subjectively rooted in background, training, philosophy and religion."

We would like to add that in more precise terminology the soft sciences of sociology, criminology, psychology, corrections and any other science based on theory and on what *could* and *should* happen are by very nature prone to be opposite and do not often concur with what actually *is*. We certainly do not condemn or categorize the soft scientist as a dreamer or a resident of the proverbial ivory tower, but his realm is one of debate, argument and possibly conjecture as opposed to the hard statistics of life encountered by the police, which represent the facts as they are. . . .

Analysis of Crime and Principles of Punishment

What Is Society?

Society is not the State. When one refers to the State the only significance according to Fustel de Coulange in *Cité Antique*, Thomas More in *Utopia*, Machiavelli in *The Prince* and many other classics, is the all-powerful Government acting solely in the interest of the State much as if it were a corporate being without regard to the individual or the definition of Society as we would understand its makeup according to the fathers of democracy.

The fathers of democracy were the Greeks and to them Society, as for the Romans, consisted of the members of a family as its cell with many families making up the city-state which was governed by them and for them. The famous quote of Lincoln of a democratic government being of the people, for the people and by the people was not original even in his time and in this study of capital punishment, since so many quotes refer to "the State," we submit that a differentiation must be made between the State and Society.

This differentiation must be taken into consideration in order that no mistake be made that the State should not take precedence over the individual. Similarly, the rights of the individual must not be considered as sacred to the point where the rights of society are subjugated thereto.

What Is Crime?

Without going into the dictionary definitions or the sociological aspects, crime may be defined as the commission or omission of something which has an adverse effect on the enjoyment by society of not only its natural rights, but those given to it by its government. Even the natural rights added to those given by Government must be limited to a certain extent in order to ascertain that Society, not the State, can enjoy every freedom possible with the minimum of risk. Otherwise, it would be a question of each individual establishing his *right* onto himself. With every human being thinking in a different manner, it would not take long before the interpretation of the rights of one individual came into conflict with the interpretation of the rights of another and chaos would reign. There must be an order established and we like to think that this order is the establishment of rules and regulations called laws which hopefully represent the minimum required to ensure the maximum freedom by society. We consider under this aspect the creation of traffic rules which, on the one hand, restrict the activities of the individual, but on the other hand create protection for society in general.

As activities and freedoms enjoyed by the individual and Society as a whole are graduated in importance to both the individual and Society, anything done to impede, stop or hinder the enjoyment of those things is also graduated and qualifies the act of the person committing that hindrance. In one sense everybody who contravenes the laws of the government is a criminal by definition. But the graduation of the scale is such, however, that the use of the word *criminal* hardly applies in all circumstances, as for example the traffic offence of passing through a red light as compared to robbery with violence.

Crime therefore is the rejection of the laws of the land or an obstruction to an individual's freedom. But there is more to crime than simply the external act mentioned above. There is also the willingness or unwillingness to commit an offence coupled with the degree of care or negligence that accompanied the act.

We feel, therefore, that based on sound logic, acts which involve the most serious crime or deprivation of freedom, which is undoubtedly loss of life should be examined to the fullest in the light of the components that have just been listed. Under Federal Bill C-92 (1960), an attempt was made at drawing guidelines for the determination of capital and non-capital murder as distinct from manslaughter. We submit that the nature of crime today, as would entail the death penalty, should be reviewed in the light of what society considers injurious to its freedoms, the value it places on these freedoms and the bases for components constituting the crime.

Insofar as crime and its nature is concerned, therefore, we submit that for the purpose of the study of the death penalty, three elements should be considered and these are: the act of commission or omission; the desire to pose the act or omit doing it; and thirdly, the consciousness of one's action.

From these factors follow three types of homicide which we would type as: capital murder, embodying the three elements; non-capital murder, which embodies the commission of the act and the willingness but not the consciousness; and thirdly, manslaughter, which would have simply the commission of the act accompanied by a varying degree of consciousness. In the order of importance, we would suggest capital murder in the first instance, followed by manslaughter because of its varying degree of consciousness, and thirdly non-capital murder, which would fall into the category of temporary insanity, crime passionel or justifiable homicide.

Climate of Today's Society

With the ever-increasing knowledge of the motivation of an individual with today's facilities of probing the mind, it is essential that a proper evaluation of the offender must be made. Today's society considers itself as being enlightened but one wonders at times if the light has not blinded as well as enlightened. It should be noted that many forms of punishment which today are considered as barbaric were introduced or resulted from modifications of yet more grisly punishment at the time of the Renaissance when the world emerged from the Dark Ages. Today we find that the code of Hammurabi exacting "an eye for an eye and a tooth for a tooth" no longer applies according to the thinking of many experts in the field today, and there is little doubt that such a code is harsh when an offender can justifiably claim purely accidental circumstances. A true and accurate evaluation of the climate of today's society is difficult and would tend to be unobjective because society itself is considered as being attacked.

The report of June 1965 prepared by the late Honourable Guy Favreau is an excellent catalogue of comments by the United Nations, the Joint Committee of the Senate and House of Commons on Capital Punishment, the Royal Commission on Capital Punishment as well as other reports presenting logical, understandable, acceptable arguments both for and against the death penalty. But judging from surveys made in the public at large, there is no doubt that the majority favour the retention of the death penalty.

Insofar as surveys involving the public at large are concerned, we are somewhat concerned by the type of article such as that written by Doctor Jayewardene, part of which, such as at page 375, dealing with public opinion, takes to task and criticizes these surveys. What is forgotten are the letters to the editors from a great number of people as well as editorials in all Canadian newspapers, which themselves have polled public opinion along with the now-popular "hot lines." An example of the probably involuntary bias of the soft sciences is that the article itself is titled "Canadian Movement Against the Death Penalty" without stating till deep in the article that it refers to a specific group. In such general terms, it would have been more accurate to say that there was a movement in Canada favouring the abolishment of the death penalty.

We, the police, as private citizens, are also of the society we protect. In order to form an objective view, we feel that it is better to divorce ourselves from this society and to analyze as a group of law enforcers, the situation that exists to create this climate.

With the freer laws that are being enacted, there is also an increase in crime of all kinds. Statistics will show in spite of arguments to the contrary, that murders are on the increase. If somehow it could be argued that there are fewer murders even in relation to the increase in population (which is not the case), there is certainly a rise in attempted murder and violent crime in the nature of armed holdups and robberies. It could be argued, therefore, that if there are less murders it may well be that the publicity campaign of "Don't Resist a Criminal" has been heeded and there are less dead heroes today than there were yesterday.

It is also interesting to note that the silent majority at times has not been so silent. In the surveys mentioned above, there was no doubt as to the wishes of this silent majority and it is reasonable to wonder why in certain circumstances the legislator, to justify the enactment of a law, states that "this is the wish of the people" and yet when the people express themselves on the question of capital punishment, the people are ignored.

Type of Individual Constituting Today's Criminal Population

If one is to look back in history one cannot contest the assertion that "no man with money or influence is ever hanged." Similarly, it is all too often true the meagrest of punishment is meted out to these individuals if at all. This, however, only serves to show that there is a breakdown in social administration and that crime is committed by everybody regardless of class. Today's criminal population is no exception. In fact, where it was more common some two hundred years ago to consider the criminal as being the exclusive product of the poor society, it was probably because the rich was able to cover up his tracks or that communications were not what they are today. Certainly, in the twentieth century, we find the poor, the rich, the uneducated and the university graduate side by side in the criminal ranks. What happens by way of punishment particularly when a death is involved leaves much to be desired. We feel that society in a manner of speaking has failed the individual and itself in not ensuring uniform facilities, service and punishment for the types of crime involved. The peace officer is in a particularly well-suited situation to observe the above-noted phenomenon and furthermore being in daily contact with the offender probably knows him better than anybody else. No amount of theory can equal the factual experience of daily meetings with the inoffensive "wino," the habitual traffic violator, the first offender in breaking and entering, the drug trafficker, the armed robber, the confidence artist, the cold-blooded killer, the frightened accused of manslaughter and the bewildered non-capital murderer. We know them all.

The peace officer can also recognize those criminals who are starting off and will be graduating to more serious crime in subsequent years. The question of graduating to more serious crime opens the door to another category other than wealth and education or lack thereof but also the question of age and environmental formation.

Yet another facet concerns the activity that occupies the majority of the time of the offender. For lack of better terminology we are considering the behavorial factor which is of great concern to the soft scientists and here we find the category of the hard-core political activist blinded to anything but his own tenets, the repeating offender, the high-placed carrion of society to name but a few, and the consequence of their acts.

We therefore feel that in evaluating the future of the death penalty in the light of modern thinking, a study should be made of who now commits murder and other crimes that may be deemed worthy of the death penalty or its alternative, why he commits crimes and how. We also feel that this is another reason why the categories of crime involving the loss of life should be determined.

Purpose of Remedial and Corrective Measures

One of the main concerns in considering the problem of abolishing or retaining capital punishment is whether or not the crime demands the penalty or whether the penalty is suitable to the crime.

There is no doubt that in graduating the offences, as noted above, the punishment is also graduated proportionately on a reasonably equitable basis. However, the more serious the crime becomes, the more difficult it is to evaluate the punishment inasmuch as more criteria for the evaluation of the commission of the crime enter into the picture.

In reviewing many sociological texts, history books, philosophy, there is no doubt that the principle of punishment for an offence has never been questioned. However, there are many diverging and varying views on the nature of the punishment and the intention of the punishment.

Today's permissive elements consider punishment as revenge or the paying of a debt in proportional amount to the offence committed and feel that it is wrong. Rather, according to the soft sciences, society should try to reshape an individual, or to understand the commission of the crime, and to take constructive measures to rehabilitate.

The above philosophy is a laudable one which may work in some instances, but practical experience has shown beyond the shadow of a doubt that some people who choose to ignore the laws of society simply cannot, will not and do not want to be *rehabilitated*, and the only alternative which society has openly demanded time and again is the absolute assurance that the crime will not be repeated.

In any social organization, the member must abide by the rules and any infraction thereof is met with proportionate punishment and usually after repeated offences, he is dropped from the membership. The same principle applied in the Napoleonic Code as well as the Civil Code of the Province of Quebec insofar as criminals were concerned, in that they were shorn of their civil rights. Amendments to the Civil Code of Quebec removed this proviso inasmuch as it was too general in application.

As a basic principle an individual who will not abide by the laws of society should be removed from that society and dealt with in the proper manner. The proper manner might well vary according to the individual and to the crime committed, graduating to the severest punishment for the worst offence. There is no doubt that the taking of a life is indeed the worst offence that can be committed. The severest punishment has traditionally been death. If one is to consider the purpose of remedial and corrective measures from the rehabilitation point of view, then death as a penalty is of little value. On this premise some question the value of the death penalty; identify it to revenge; and that it is hardly a "corrective" measure because of its finality. But the death penalty and punishment is not of its nature vengeful. Does a father spank a child out of revenge? Punishment is more related to a forceful remedial action, one that will have a marked "corrective" effect and be so shocking to the recipient or others that the act which merited the punishment will not be repeated if only because it attacks the self-preservation instinct and the natural desire to freedom of the offender.

Inasmuch as rehabilitation has its place where there is an assured chance of success, society has nevertheless unequivocally rejected the experimental attitude and has expressed the unqualified desire that the principle of maximum punishment as opposed to the principle of rehabilitation be retained so that, where applicable, the severest penalty as a penalty will be applied.

Value of Actual and Contemplated Corrective Measures in Rehabilitation and Punishment

The value of rehabilitation and punishment as separate ideas and methods in the field of corrections has long been debated. Some quarters feel that the idea of punishment as being vengeful is not proper but we submit that in this instance they have erred in removing punishment and substituting rehabilitation. Both have their value but they are dependent upon the nature of the individual as well as the nature of the crime and what society expects by way of protection for itself as a whole as well as protection of its individuals.

In establishing the value of the present programs being promoted and those that are contemplated by the *soft scientists*, we must look at their origins. From the many writings to which considerable authority is lent there would appear to be little doubt that the term and the idea of punishment would no longer be entertained as having any value in relation to today's crime. It is equally apparent that rehabilitation is given prime consideration.

As mentioned at the outset of this brief, we do not feel that the issue of death as a form of punishment is cut and dried. Not only do we refer to the arguments for and against as contained in the capital punishment booklet of June 1965 but we reiterate the importance of establishing the types of crime in order to better gauge the suitable punishment. We submit as a formula that for the ultimate crime of taking a life there should be the ultimate punishment. We feel that the ultimate punishment would be the banishment from society and if capital punishment is the answer, then this Association stands categorically in favour of capital punishment and demands its enforcement. It has been advocated by some that the "removal from society" might take the form of banishment to a penal colony or again the imposition of a true and meaningful life sentence that would not include any rehabilitation program but rather a sentence which would be befitting the animal status of which the offender has made himself worthy. The Canadian Association of Chiefs of Police has already witnessed too many arguments referring to the cost of maintaining criminals in prison; other arguments in favour of rehabilitation; statements that such life imprisonment without hope may be even worse than death itself, to label any of these suggestions as anything else but wishful thinking. Though the arguments are not cut and dried, the only alternatives are either the abolishment of the death penalty or its retention.

The Police are not insensitive to any undesirable aspect of capital punishment but they are not insensitive, either, to the feelings of their own families and the society which they serve.

This brings in the next facet in the evaluation of actual and contemplated corrective measures in rehabilitation and punishment. In either case it is stated without argument from any quarter that the object is the prevention of crime and that the exercise or measure taken must have a deterrent quality. The quality of deterrents can be looked upon from two aspects, the first being repetition and the second being prevention. Following up on this premise, which is tenable even using the arguments of the abolitionists, the only penalty that can achieve the maximum deterrence of both repetition and prevention is death. The principles of rehabilitation, so-called life imprisonment or other measures, in the eyes of society if not in the eyes of sociologists and others, have not proven adequate.

In considering the value of actual and contemplated corrective measures in rehabilitation and punishment, we have deliberately avoided the method of carrying out a death penalty inasmuch as we felt that this item was in itself controversial and was not related to the principle of capital punishment and we also felt that along with the cataloging or listing the crimes to which the death penalty would apply, such an operation should follow the establishment of the principle rather than precede it or cloud the issue by accompanying it.

Inasmuch as we feel that the principle should be established first, we reiterate unequivocally that society should not be vengeful but certainly the animal killer should be dealt with at the animal level. In this respect, whatever legislation is presently on the books should not be treated lightly and should be invoked to the full.

Questions

1. The Chiefs of Police suggest that ''it is reasonable to wonder why in certain circumstances the legislator, to justify the enactment of a law, states that 'this is the wish of the people' and yet when the people express themselves on the question of capital punishment, the people are ignored.'' How would you respond to this observation? (Note that this issue is addressed at length in the last reading of the chapter by William Conklin. You may want to read his contribution to the discussion before developing your own position on this issue.)
2. On issues like capital punishment, does experience provide a better foundation for making moral judgements than theory or research?
3. The Chiefs of Police reject the view that inflicting capital punishment is just a way of getting revenge. How then do they think the death penalty in particular and punishment in general should be justified?
4. Consider the statement that ''the animal killer should be dealt with at the animal level.'' What view of punishment does this imply? Does it imply that those who commit murder place themselves outside the moral community and therefore outside of the ambit of rules aimed at protecting and preserving human life? Do you agree with this view?

The Prevention and Control of Crime in Canada

Warren Allmand

The Causes and Circumstances Associated with Violent Crime and the Deterrent Value of Capital Punishment

Restoration of capital punishment is prompted by the fear that murders, particularly murders where police officers have been the victims, are increasing due to a failure to provide a sufficiently strong deterrent. It is evident that capital punishment may satisfy the strong sense of moral and emotional outrage that many of us experience when a murder is committed, and there is no doubt that the threat a particular individual has posed to society is terminated absolutely. There are, however, other crucial issues involved.

The paramount issue is one of morality. Are we justified in taking a human life through capital punishment? Execution does not erase the crime of murder. It takes away another life. The commandment, *"Thou shalt not kill"* is part of our Judaeo-Christian heritage. It emphasizes the value of human life and should make us ponder whether we should take yet another life in retribution. Personally, I believe it is wrong to take the life of another person except as a last resort in self defence. Before we had statistical evidence on the effectiveness of capital punishment, it was indeed considered as a last resort in the defence of society. However, evidence now available shows this is not the case.

This evidence bears directly upon the argument of deterrence. We now know that most types of violent crime are not deliberate or rationally planned. One or more of the following factors are usually present: quarrels or a history of quarrels between friends and family members; situations where alcohol or drugs are present; situations where immediate access to firearms exists; situations where the eventual offender feels threatened by the others present in the situation; and cases of mental or emotional instability and derangement. Given the sudden, unplanned nature of most homicides it appears unlikely that most individuals who commit murder take into account the existence or non-existence of capital punishment before carrying out the act.

Another factor in discussing this problem, is that there exists a certain group of people who might be classed as "adventurers" for whom the danger of death has little or no effect. Mercenary soldiers, auto racers, parachute jumpers and citizens who volunteered to fight in Viet Nam and other foreign wars are examples. In the criminal field, there are examples of people for whom the penalty of death is no deterrent. Criminals know full well that the police carry weapons and that many criminals are shot by the police during the commission of a crime. Despite this threat against their lives, these criminals still commit armed robbery and other offences knowing that they could be shot by the police. The danger of "on-the-spot" capital punishment does not seem to serve as a deterrent for this type of criminal.

Reprinted from *Crime and Justice*, May 1976.

Before and since becoming Solicitor General, I have examined the available evidence on the question of the deterrent effect of capital punishment. The more I have studied this question, the more I have become convinced that capital punishment is not the solution to murder. An examination of the evidence, statistics and research in Canada, the United States and Europe, indeed indicates that capital punishment does not effectively lower the murder rate. As a matter of fact, the lowest murder rates in the world are found in those countries and those states where capital punishment has been abolished for a long time. For example, Sweden, Minnesota, Wisconsin, Rhode Island and Maine. On the other hand, some of the highest murder rates are found in countries and states where capital punishment has applied for a long time, for example in France, Spain, Florida, South Carolina, Louisiana and Georgia. Insofar as the United States are concerned, the recent article published in *Crime and Delinquency* (October 1974) by Daniel Glaser and Max S. Zeigler shows that the states which have historically used executions most are the same ones which have the highest murder rates.

In saying that there is no evidence to show that capital punishment effectively lowers the murder rate, the evidence I have seen reaches the same conclusion as that of a *1968 United Nations* document assessing international data on capital punishment.

> With respect to the influence of the abolition of capital punishment upon the incidence of murder, all the available data suggests that where the murder rate is increasing, abolition does not appear to hasten the increase; where the murder rate is decreasing, abolition does not appear to interrupt that decrease; where the rate is stable, the presence or absence of capital punishment does not appear to affect it.

It is my view that the burden of proving that capital punishment is a good deterrent against murder is on those who want to retain capital punishment. On the basis of the facts and data available, I do not believe that this is a burden that they can discharge.

The Questions of Commutation of Death Penalty and Whether Parole Should Be Granted to Those Convicted of Murder

The final issue I wish to deal with is that of the commutation of death sentences, parole and temporary absence of persons convicted of murder.

In every case where the death sentence must be passed, the jury is required by the Criminal Code to consider whether they recommend for or against clemency, although they may also decide that they will not make any recommendation either way. This provision of the Code is designed to ensure that the Cabinet will have before it the opinion of the jury as to whether it wished to make a recommendation for or against clemency. On the question of the commutation of death sentences by the Federal Cabinet it is sometimes thought that, because the trial judge has no option but to pass the sentence of death, executions must follow if the law is to be observed faithfully. Some think that because all five cases considered since December, 1967, were commuted, when the Criminal Code was first amended to restrict the circumstances in which the death sentence applies, there has been some kind of miscarriage of justice. This is simply not so. The Criminal Code provides that the Governor in Council may commute a sentence of death. Indeed, the Criminal Code requires that the trial judge, in fixing a date for the execution, must set that date at a time far enough in the future so that the Governor in Council may first determine whether the sentence should be carried out. I must make it clear, however, that the decision to commute in a specific instance does not establish a precedent in any way whatsoever.

Statistics published by the National Parole Service show that between January 1920 and September 1974 a total of 182 persons who had a death sentence commuted were granted parole. Only 14 had their parole revoked by reason of their not adhering to parole conditions, and only 9 persons forfeited their parole upon conviction for an indictable offence. Between 1867 and 1974 only one person who had his death sentence commuted has committed a second murder. He was executed for this crime in 1944. We do not have complete data for other murderers, that is those who were sentenced to life imprisonment by the court, but the indications are that the rate of recidivism in these cases is extremely low.

Some argue that the time served by individuals who had their death sentences commuted is minimal and bears no relation with the seriousness of the offence committed. The 28 individuals serving death-commuted sentences, who were paroled between January 1, 1961 and January 3, 1968 served an average of 12 years in a penitentiary prior to release. For the 42 persons serving death-commuted sentences, who were paroled between January 4, 1968 and September 30, 1974, the average time served rose to 13.35 years. This does not cover those who have not been paroled. This average time served is of course longer than the average time served for any other type of offence.

We also have recent data on the Temporary Absence program in our penitentiaries. During 1974, 1,019 temporary absence permits were issued to some carefully selected inmates convicted of capital murder. In only one instance did an inmate fail to return on time. During the same period, 2,106 temporary absence permits were granted to inmates serving life sentences for non-capital murder. In six instances, inmates failed to return on time.

I think it is also important to remember that the authority to release an inmate convicted of murder rests with the Cabinet who acts on the advice and recommendation of the National Parole Board. Before placing a case before Cabinet, an in-depth study of the case is made by the National Parole Board. Psychiatric reports are obtained in all cases of murder. A judge's report is required, and in most cases minutes of the Court Proceedings are obtained. Progress reports from the correctional institution are obtained as well as a comprehensive report on the inmate's release plan.

In concluding, I feel it is important to present an accurate view of the extent to which violent crime is prevalent in our society and what its causes and its consequences are. Our chief concern is to find the most effective answers to these questions. Current debate seems to have focussed on the question of the capital punishment and left it at that. I think that the evidence I have put forward shows that this is not an effective means of combatting violent crime.

What, then, do I suggest in place of this? Some of the measures that I propose to prevent and reduce crime are the following: better trained, better deployed and better equipped policemen; effective gun control; proactive rather than reactive police work; more effective correctional programs for juveniles and adults; more effective social and economic programs to remove the causes of crime; improved treatment for alcoholics and drug addicts; improved education and recreation programs; possible restrictions on the showing of violence on television and through other media; measures to promote respect for legitimate authority in the home, the school, the church, community associations and government. If these and other measures were pursued with more vigor, we would do much more to lower our crime rate than we would if we merely emphasized the application of harsh penalties after the fact.

In the recent article published in *Crime and Delinquency*, to which I referred above, Daniel Glaser and Max S. Zeigler have examined possible explanations for the fact that the states (U.S.) which have historically used executions most are the same ones which have the highest murder rates.

Their concluding paragraph is worthy of careful consideration:

> Demands that capital punishment be restored are raised whenever the public is outraged at a particularly heinous and highly publicized killing, but the geographic and historic facts presented here suggest that this "gut response" is counterproductive as means of reducing the prevalence of murder. The evidence shows that where use of the death penalty is most frequent there is less long-run outrage against killers than prevails in states that forbid any murder, whether by private parties or by the government. The alternatives to violence are, in addition to a respect for the sacredness of life, the many civilized procedures and practices of analyzing, negotiating, legally adjudicating, or simply tolerating disagreements. All of these alternatives are impaired or impeded rather than nurtured when the government resorts to the murderer's methods.

Questions

1. Allmand seems to imply that if capital punishment did deter the commission of murder, it would be justified. Do you agree?
2. What should weigh more heavily in deciding whether capital punishment is a deterrent, the views of police officers and others who are in frequent contact with those who break the law, or statistical research?
3. Allmand suggests, as an alternative to capital punishment, a course of action which the Chiefs of Police appear to reject as inadequate. Compare the arguments developed by the Chiefs of Police against a rehabilitation/social-action/education-oriented approach with those

presented by Allmand in favour of such an approach. Is it possible to determine which set of arguments is stronger?

4.   What do Glaser and Zeigler mean when they say that capital punishment is counter-productive? Are they right about this?

Is Capital Punishment a Unique Deterrent?

Ezzat A. Fattah

The Deterrence Argument: Why Is It Popular?

Retributive, religious and philosophical arguments in support of the death penalty have lost favour with many of its advocates. The radical change in penal philosophy that took place in the second half of the twentieth century was bound to bring about a change in retentionists' rhetoric and strategy. At a time when correctional philosophy was dominated by the rehabilitative ideal and when correctional efforts were geared towards treatment and change, it was no longer fashionable to advocate the principles of Talion Law and to claim a life for a life, an eye for an eye and a tooth for a tooth. Advocates of the death penalty chose to focus instead on its presumed preventive effects and protective functions. Gradually, the deterrent effect of capital punishment became the focal point in arguments to support its retention or its reintroduction and continues to be presented by its supporters as the indisputable justification for the State's deliberate taking of human life. This change in focus that characterized death penalty debates of recent years is understandable. The deterrence argument is, in many respects, an attractive one:

Firstly, deterrence makes sense. It is common knowledge that people are afraid of death and will do everything they can to avoid it. The threat of execution is, therefore, likely to deter them from committing the criminal offences carrying the death penalty. In fact, the logic of the deterrence argument is impeccable. After all, what can be more obvious than the assumption that people cherish life above everything else and will not willingly and deliberately put it in peril? Common sensical views, however, are not always correct. And if we are to justify the retention of the death penalty solely, or mainly, on grounds of its preventive effects, it supporters will have to come up with a more solid and convincing proof than mere conventional wisdom.

Secondly, the deterrence argument is more civilized than arguments based on revenge and retribution. Retaliation and expiation are no longer acceptable as the ultimate goals of criminal sanctions. Changes in philosophy are not always accompanied by changes in people's sentiments. Since vindictive, retributive feelings continue to exist it is only appropriate to cloak them in rational arguments such as deterrence

From *Canadian Journal of Criminology*, Vol. 23, No. 3 (July 1981). By permission of the Canadian Criminal Justice Association.

and protection of society. The deterrence argument thus serves to disguise the primitive desire to see the murderer pay for his crime with his life. As Hanz Zeisel puts it:

> It is the belief in retributive justice that makes the death penalty attractive, especially when clothed in a functional rationalization.[52]

Thirdly, the deterrence argument provides a utilitarian rationale for the shedding of blood since this is supposedly indispensable for saving innocent lives.

The superiority of the deterrence argument to others advanced in support of the death penalty was reaffirmed by the Subcommittee on Moral Arguments For and Against the Death Penalty. The Subcommittee stated that:

> The only moral ground on which the State could conceivably possess the right to destroy human life would be if this were indispensable for the protection or preservation of other lives. This places the burden of proof on those who believe that capital punishment exercises a deterrent effect on the potential criminal. Unless they can establish that the death penalty does, in fact, protect other lives, at the expense of one, there is no moral justification for the State to take life.[48]

Not only did the Subcommittee proclaim deterrence as the only legitimate justification for the death penalty, but it also squarely placed the burden of proof on the shoulders of the retentionists.

Is Capital Punishment a Unique Deterrent?

Discussions around the deterrent effect of capital punishment usually center on a wrong question. The question to be asked is not whether the death penalty deters would-be murderers, but whether it deters them more than the prospect of life imprisonment. The question is not whether the death penalty has a deterrent effect but whether it provides a unique and supreme deterrent, whether it is the most powerful and most effective of all deterrents. It seems obvious that the death penalty cannot be justified on grounds of its deterring function alone unless and until it has been proved beyond a reasonable doubt that it supplies an additional increment of deterrence above and beyond the alternative which, in most jurisdictions, is life imprisonment. Has such a unique deterrent effect been unequivocally proven? The answer to this question is no.

Early deterrence research failed to show any relationship between the abolition or reinstatement of the death penalty and homicide rates. Despite the fact that several different studies reached the same conclusion, namely that the death penalty has no noticeable effect on the rates of homicide, these studies were dismissed by retentionists as "extremely primitive statistically" and as having been done by "not very good statisticians." Retentionists, on the other hand, were quick to hail the one study that reached an opposite conclusion, namely the now famous Ehrlich study.[14] They either failed to detect the flaws in Ehrlich's data and methodology or simply decided to ignore whatever defects the study suffered from.

Empirical Tests of the Deterrence Hypothesis

Scholars who tried to assess the preventive functions of the death penalty used various methods to test the deterrence hypothesis. And proponents and opponents of the death penalty used various types of evidence to support or to challenge its unique deterrent effect. This evidence may be divided into two main categories: anecdotal stories and statistical findings.

Anecdotal Stories

Proponents of the death penalty usually argue that almost every prisoner under sentence of death seeks a reprieve and welcomes it when it comes. This is seen as evidence that men fear death more than anything else and far more than life imprisonment. It seems fallacious to assume from the terror of death experienced and manifested by an individual on death row that the same fear was operative in his mind at the time of the crime. This argument overlooks one indisputable fact: the difference between a potential and remote danger and one that is imminent and seemingly inevitable. In Sellin's words:

> Surely a murderer for whom a possible death penalty had proved to be
> no deterrent, would be considered abnormal were he not to make every
> effort to escape death after being discovered and sentenced to die.[41]

Another fact this argument overlooks is that the murderer on death row who is showing extreme fear and terror in face of execution has not been deterred by the threat of death in the first place. It seems illogical to use the words or the psychological state of those who were not deterred by the death penalty to prove this penalty's unique deterrent effect!

Proponents of the death penalty also cite real-life stories of criminals who have told the police that they refrained from killing the victim or from shooting at the pursuing police officer to avoid being put to death. For example, the Los Angeles Police Department reported to a California Senate Committee considering the abolition of the death penalty[47] that during the course of one year, 13 robbery suspects had told the police that they used unloaded or simulated guns "rather than take a chance on killing someone and getting the gas chamber." The unreliability of such anecdotal evidence is too obvious and for every story alleging that the fear of the death penalty has acted as a deterrent there are ten others alleging that it has not. Clinton Duffy, former warden of San Quentin prison, asked thousands of prisoners convicted of homicide or armed robbery whether they had thought of the death penalty before their act. Not one had!

Among the most frequently quoted stories to deny the deterrent effect of capital punishment are those of the English pickpockets who actively plied their trade in the shadow of the gallows from which their fellow knaves were strung. Another often cited story is the one of an Ohio convict named Charlie Justice who devised the clamps that held the condemned man in the electric chair. After his release, he was convicted of murder and electrocuted. A similar fate befell Alfred Wells, who helped install San Quentin's gas chamber in 1938. It was his conversational cachet around the prison yard, usually with the moral: "That's the closest I ever want to come. . . ." Four years later, back at San Quentin for a triple killing, he was sealed in the chamber to die.

Needless to say that arguments and claims based on this kind of anecdotal evidence tend to neutralize each other and are of little help in settling the basic factual question whether or not the death penalty is a unique deterrent.

Statistical Evidence

Earlier studies on the preventive functions of the death penalty tried to ascertain its deterrent effect in five different ways:

a. examining the effect of a declining rate of executions on criminal homicide rates;
b. comparing homicide rates within countries and/or states before and after they abolished or restored the death penalty;
c. comparing homicide rates between adjacent and apparently congruent states with and without the death penalty;
d. ascertaining whether law-enforcement officers and prison guards were safer from murderous attacks in states with the death penalty than in those without it; and
e. examining homicide trends in cities where executions were carried out and were presumed to have been widely publicized.

The Effect of a Declining Rate of Executions on Homicide Rates.   If capital punishment is as its supporters claim, a unique deterrent to murder, then a declining use of it reflected in a decreasing rate of executions (which necessarily means an improved chance of escaping it) should be accompanied or followed by an increase in the murder rate. Yet statistics available from many countries, and particularly from the United States, tend to show that this is not the case. These statistics indicate, in fact, that murder rates have either remained constant or declined despite trends away from the use of capital punishment.

Chambliss[12] compared the number of prisoners executed under civil authority and murder rate from 1951 to 1966 in the United States and found that the substantial decline in executions has not been accompanied by any significant change in the murder rate.

Another study carried out in Ohio[49] tested the relationship between execution rates and homicide rates. Both rates for the entire state for a half-century (1909–1959) were computed. The statistical correlation did not indicate that homicides have increased as executions have decreased, or the reverse. Any correlation between the two rates seemed to be direct rather than inverse, indicating only that homicide rates and execution rates have risen and fallen together. The researchers concluded that the statistical analysis of Ohio execution and homicide rates over the fifty-year period revealed no evidence that executions have any discernible effect on homicide rates.

A third study conducted in Australia by Barber and Wilson[5] similarly revealed that the relationship between execution and murder rates tends to be a positive rather than a negative one. It was found that the State of Queensland has had a higher execution rate than the other Australian states over a longer period of time (1860–1915) and that the murder rate in that state during the pre-abeyance period (1901–1914) was also considerably greater than in New South Wales and South Australia. Barber and Wilson concluded that:

> The apparently disproportionately high frequency of executions in Queensland during this period would not, then, seem to have had a very great deterrent effect on potential murderers in Queensland. Indeed the evidence is more supportive of Sir Samuel Romilly's contention that brutal punishments accustom people to brutality, and tend to create attitudes conducive to the commission of violent crimes.

The Effect of Repeal and Reintroduction of Capital Punishment on Homicide Rates.   The experience of those European countries which abolished the death penalty in the nineteenth or early twentieth century and for whom statistics are available shows that the abolition was followed by a decrease rather than an increase in homicide rates. But it is the experience of those countries which more recently repealed capital punishment statutes that is really worth mentioning.

Morris and Blom-Cooper evaluated the British experience and reported their findings in an article published by the *Observer*, in 1979. The authors analyzed murder statistics in England and Wales since 1957 when hanging was partially abolished and concluded that the abolition has had no visible effect on the murder rate in Britain:

> One aspect stands out starkly. The penalty of the crime of murder has no discernible influence on the rate at which murder is committed.[26]

Following the suspension of the death penalty in Canada in 1967 for a trial period of five years I conducted a study[15] in which I attempted to assess the impact this suspension has had on homicide rates. The study clearly showed that the statistical increase in criminal homicide in Canada could in no way be attributed to the suspension of the death penalty. The large differences in homicide rates among the Canadian provinces suggested that the rates are conditioned by factors other than the death penalty. They confirmed what criminologists have held for a long time namely that the causes of criminal homicide are not related to any single factor but to a total social situation in which a special law or a particular punishment can have little or no effect.

The effect of reinstating capital punishment on criminal homicide rates has been thoroughly researched by Professor Sellin. He examined and analyzed statistics for eleven American states that experimented with abolition for periods of time varying in duration. Here is the conclusion he reached:

> If any conclusion can be drawn from all the above data, it is that there is no evidence that the abolition of the death penalty generally causes an increase in criminal homicides or that its reintroduction is followed

by a decline. The explanation of changes in homicide rates must be sought elsewhere.[37]

Professor Sellin's conclusion is almost identical to the one reached by the British Royal Commission on Capital Punishment (1949–1953):

> The general conclusion which we have reached is that there is no clear evidence in any of the figures we have examined that the abolition of capital punishment had led to an increase in the homicide rate or that its reintroduction has led to a fall.[46]

Comparisons of Homicide Rates in States With and Without Death Penalty.   Professor Sellin[35,40] compared homicide rates for states with similar outlook in the United States. He selected five sets of three states each and compared their crude homicide death rates. The comparisons covered a 43-year span for each set of states, extending from 1920 to 1963. In each set, at least one of the three states did not provide the death penalty for all or a part of the period while the others did provide it. Each of the three states in each set borders one or both of the other two. The figures showed clearly that homicide death rates in all the states have followed the same trends, whether or not the death penalty was provided. In all of the 15 states covered by the comparisons, homicide death rates reached peaks in the 1920s and early 1930s, then followed a general downward trend, leveled out in the 1940s and continued through 1960 at about that level. Comparison of trends and rates revealed no differences among adjacent states with and without the death penalty which can be ascribed to either its presence or absence. Professor Sellin found that:

- the level of rates is not the same in all regions;
- within each group of contiguous states it would be impossible to identify the abolitionist state, were it not designated as such; and
- the trends of the rates of the states compared are similar.

The inevitable conclusion, therefore, is that the presence of the death penalty, either in law or practice, does not influence homicide death rates. As Professor Sellin puts it:

> The important thing to be noticed is that, whether the death penalty is used or not, or whether executions are frequent or not, both death penalty States and abolition States show rates which suggest that these rates are conditioned by other factors than the death penalty.

Comparisons of Risks to Law Enforcement Officers in States With and Without the Death Penalty.   Proponents of the death penalty claim that it provides superior protection to law-enforcement officers and prison guards whose job, it is argued, would become more difficult and more hazardous if it were abolished. Since the 1950s the truth of this assumption has been subjected to several tests.

   In 1956 Father Donald Campion published a study of 24 American police forces, 18 of which represented death-penalty states and six of which represented abolition states. The study covered a fifty-year period from 1905 to 1954 and took many factors into account, such as the varying size of the police forces and the populations they served. Father Campion concluded that the data

> do not lend empirical support to the claim that the existence of the death penalty in the statutes of a State provides a greater protection to the police than exists in States where the penalty has been abolished."[10]

Professor Sellin[36,38] did an extensive study of police homicide rates over a 25-year period. He examined the rates for 183 cities in eleven capital-punishment states and for eighty-two cities in six abolition states. The general results of the study demonstrated that between the years 1919 and 1954 the cities in death-penalty states had a police homicide rate of 1.3 per 100,000 population, while the cities in abolition states had a police homicide rate of only 1.2 per 100,000 population. Commenting on his findings Professor Sellin writes:

> It is obvious from an inspection of the data that it is impossible to conclude that the States which had no death penalty had thereby made the policeman's lot more hazardous. It is also obvious that the same differences observable in the general homicide rates of the various States were reflected in the rates of police killings.

Sellin concluded further that:

> The claim that if data could be secured they would show that more police are killed in abolition States than in capital punishment States is unfounded. On the whole, the abolition States, as is apparent from the findings of this particular investigation, seem to have fewer police killings but the differences are small. If this, then, is the argument upon which the police are willing to rest their opposition to the abolition of capital punishment, it must be concluded that it lacks any factual basis.

Some years later, Professor Sellin[38], using statistics of policemen killed in the U.S.A. by offenders or suspects during 1961–1963 (140 policemen) and using as a base the number of police in the 15 states where the killing occurred according to the 1960 census, found that the annual average risk for the three years was 1.312 per 10,000 police in abolition states and 1.328 in the bordering states. There was, then, no significant difference.

Cardarelli[11], analyzing the same data (police killed by criminal action from 1961–1963) came to the conclusion that data "lend no weight to the argument that the death penalty states afford more protection."

Robin[30,31] found that in any given year the policemen in the U.S.A. are approximately six times more likely to kill than to be killed in the course of their duty; at the same time the probability of either event occurring is very small.

More recently, Professor Sellin[41] did yet another study of police killings in abolitionist and retentionist states based on data published in 1975 in the FBI annual report. His conclusion did not differ from his earlier ones:

Not only did the police in retentionist States run a greater risk of being feloniously killed, but so did the slayers and suspects involved in these homicides. . . .

The data presented in these pages permit only one conclusion, namely that the belief of the police that in order to be safer in their occupation they need laws that threaten potential murders with death has no factual basis. Indeed, it is evident that the police are more efficient executioners than the public hangman and should inspire more fear than any capital law could do if deterrence were operative.

Studies by Morris,[25] Sellin,[29] Akman[4] and Buffum[8] clearly show that the hazards involved in prison life are not increased by the abolition of the death penalty. Neither does such abolition result in an increase in homicidal or assaultive behaviour in those penal institutions where convicted murderers are detained. Moreover, it is obvious that those who present the greatest danger are insane murderers. Yet, these murderers are by definition excluded from the possible infliction of the death penalty and nobody is calling for their execution as a way of protecting the staff or the patients in the psychiatric institutions in which they are usually held.

Examining Homicide Trends Following Widely Publicized Executions.   In 1935 Dann[13] conducted a study to assess the impact of publicity of executions on deterrence. He hypothesized that if the death penalty is a deterrent, its greatest effect should be shown through executions which are well publicized. Furthermore, the effect should be more noticeable in the community where the offence occurred, where the trial aroused wide publicity and the offender lived and had relatives, friends and acquaintances. To test the hypothesis, Dann compiled the dates of executions of Philadelphia residents for a period of several years and was able to find five cases that met the study's specifications. Three of the five cases were of great notoriety. The study found no significant difference in homicide rates for equal periods before and after the execution. There was a total of 105 days free from homicides during the 60-day periods before the executions and 74 in the periods after the executions. There were a total of 91 homicides in the "before the execution" periods and 113 in the "after" periods. Of the 204 homicides included in the study, 19 resulted in sentences for murder in the first degree. Nine of them had occurred during the 60-day periods preceding and ten in the corresponding periods following the executions. During the ten days just before the executions there were two, and during the ten days immediately following there were three such first-degree murders in Philadelphia.

Another study was undertaken, also in Philadelphia, by Savitz.[32] After examining homicide trends before and after four widely publicized trials during the 1940s, Savitz concluded that no pattern emerges that would indicate deterrence and that the assumption that the deterrent effect of the imposition of the death penalty might be felt shortly after the date of sentencing is not borne out by the data. He further concluded that on the basis of the data "there was no significant decrease or increase in the murder rate following the imposition of the death penalty on four separate occasions."

Recently, Phillips[19] examined weekly murder statistics for the city of London, England for the period 1858–1921 and came to the conclusion that the homicide rate drops during the week of a highly publicized execution and during the following week then it begins rising again.

> Within five or six weeks of a publicized execution, the drop in homicides is cancelled by an equally large rise in homicides.

Phillips' results were in contrast to those of Bowers and Pierce[7] who used monthly rather than weekly murder rates. They found an increase of two murders during the month following a highly publicized execution.

Isaac Ehrlich's Study and Its Replications

Until 1975, researchers analyzing murder or criminal homicide statistics were unanimous in their conclusion: they found no empirical evidence to support the presumed unique deterrent effect of the death penalty and could discern no visible effect this penalty has on the rates of homicide. But in 1975 a study reporting an opposite conclusion was published.[14] The study was done by I. Ehrlich, an economist at the University of Chicago. Ehrlich used a set of assumptions to construct an econometric model, employed aggregate data and claimed to have found evidence that a capital execution would indeed deter some potential killers and perhaps save as many as eight lives:

> Empirical analysis suggests that on average the trade-off between the execution of an offender and the lives of potential victims it might have saved was of the order of magnitude of one for eight for the period 1933–1967 in the U.S.A.

Not only was Ehrlich's claim at odds with the findings of all studies done in the U.S. and elsewhere but it was the first time ever a researcher has claimed to have been able to estimate the number of murders prevented by each execution. Ehrlich's findings received a great deal of publicity and were circulated widely by many police forces in the U.S.A. and Canada. More important still was their presentation as evidence in support of the death penalty before U.S. courts. Until then the deterrence debate was largely an academic one and was rarely used in the courtroom. But in 1976 statistical evidence in support of the deterrence hypothesis was submitted to the U.S. Supreme Court in Fowler vs. North Carolina (428 U.S. 904, 1976). It was in this case that the Solicitor-General submitted to the court an *amicus curiae* brief citing Ehrlich's conclusion that capital punishment deters murder. And in another case, Gregg vs. Georgia (428 U.S. 153, 169, 1976), the Supreme Court ruled that "the punishment of death does not invariably violate the constitution" and added that for many murderers "the death penalty undoubtedly is a significant deterrent." One would have expected the Court to substantiate such claim with empirical evidence but the Court did not although such evidence was not totally ignored. The Court stated that although some of the studies suggest that the death penalty may not function as a significantly greater deterrent than less penalties, there is no convincing empirical evidence either supporting or refuting this view.[17] Zeisel[52] took issue with the Court's statement arguing that the evidence about the deterrent effect is, indeed, "quite sufficient" and that the request for more proof is but "the expression of an unwillingness to abandon an ancient prejudice."

Because of the nature of Erhlich's claim and the publicity they received there were several replications of his study. The replications revealed fundamental weaknesses in his assumptions, his model and his analysis. His detractors claimed that his evidence of deterrence depends upon a restrictive assumption about the mathematical relationship between homicides and executions,[6,18,28] the inclusion of a particular set of observations, the use of a limited set of control variables and a peculiar construction of the execution rate, the key variable.

One important criticism of Ehrlich's study is his use of time-series data for 1933–1969 in which homicides and executions were aggregated for the entire U.S. The Panel of the National Academy of Science[50] pointed out that Ehrlich's findings were particularly sensitive to the time period included. This sensitivity was largely due to the fact that during 1962–1969, executions in the U.S. ceased while homicides increased though not more than did other crimes. When Bowers and Pierce[6] reproduced Ehrlich's analysis using data from slightly different periods, all beginning in 1935 but each ending in a different year in the 1960s, their findings were entirely different from those of Ehrlich. They concluded that:

> It becomes evident that the so-called deterrent effect of execution risk altogether disappears when the effective time period is foreshortened by dropping recent data points.

Another researcher, Passell,[27] used cross-sectional data in various states in the U.S. from the period 1950 and 1960. He also concluded that there was no reasonable way of interpreting the cross-sectional data that would lend support to the deterrence hypothesis.

A third researcher, Forst,[17] replicated Ehrlich's analysis while avoiding some of the major flaws that were identified in Ehrlich's research. For instance, he focused on a unique decade during which the homicide rate increased by over 50% and the use of the death penalty ceased. He examined, as well, changes in homicides and executions over time and across states. His findings did not support Ehrlich's claim that capital punishment deters homicides. His final conclusion:

> The results of this analysis suggest . . . that it is erroneous to view capital punishment as a means of reducing the homicide rate.

Probably the most detailed critique of Ehrlich's research was published in Canada.[21] Hahn is very conscious of the serious policy implications defective studies might have and is particularly perturbed by the great publicity Ehrlich's study received. His final comments contain both a warning and an advice:

The techniques introduced by the economists may represent significant advances over those used in the past. These techniques and the behavioural models used by economists are, however, useless unless they are combined with sufficient, accurate and relevant data. Unfortunately, it will be many years before data of sufficient quality and quantity is available for undertaking research which is adequate for supporting deterrence policy.

Until that time, uncritical publicity of the earlier economic findings, publicity that has in the past bordered on the irresponsible, should cease. Economists like Ehrlich should also exercise more professional responsibility in undertaking and reporting what amounts to circumstantial results.

How Effective Is the Death Penalty as a Means of Prevention and Societal Protection?

The nature of the death penalty, its irrevocability, together with the safeguards necessary to avoid errors in its application are such that it can never become an effective means of crime prevention or of societal protection. This point will be illustrated through a discussion of three aspects related to the application of the death penalty.

Capital Punishment Is the Least Certain of All Punishments

More than two hundred years ago Beccaria noted that severity and certainty of punishment are hard to reconcile. In this he was referring to the inverse relationship that often exists between the two variables: the more severe the punishment, the less certain it is. The same point was well stated in what is known as the "Rejected Preamble" of Sir Samuel Romilly's Bill of 1808:

> Whereas the extreme severity of penal laws has not been found effectual for the prevention of crimes; but, on the contrary, by increasing the difficulty of convicting offenders, in some cases affords them immunity and in most cases renders their punishment extremely uncertain.

This rule applies to capital punishment more than to any other. In my study of the deterrent effect of capital punishment[15] I compiled data on charges and sentences for murder, manslaughter and for other violent offences in Canada during the period 1881–1967. The average yearly conviction rate for murder proved to be the lowest among all crimes of violence.

Capital Punishment Endangers Society by Preventing Convictions

Capital punishment is known to exercise an inhibitory effect on juries and judges in capital cases. Those who are familiar with the administration of justice know that retaining the death penalty, especially if it is made mandatory, reduces the likelihood that indicted offenders will be convicted. In this way, the menace of the death penalty tends more to protect the accused through intimidation of the jury than to protect society through the conviction of the murderer. In a democratic, fair system of justice it is doubtful that the death penalty can ever reach the certainty level necessary for it to operate effectively as a deterrent. This difficulty was outlined in the introduction to the British criminal statistics furnished by the Home Office.

> In consequences of the strong proof of guilt necessary for conviction of crimes punishable by death, the proportion of acquittals for murder is higher than for most other crimes, and an acquittal in such a case does not necessarily imply failure to detect the perpetrator of the crime.[44]

One of the paradoxes of the death penalty is that if it is made mandatory it results in a high acquittal rate and leads to many murderers being let free. If, on the other hand, it is made discretionary then its application becomes arbitrary, discriminatory and erratic.

The Paradoxical Nature of the Death Penalty

If capital punishment is really a unique deterrent then a scarce and sporadic use of it would undoubtedly weaken its deterrent value by reducing the possibility and the threat of execution. It is in this fact that the real paradox of capital punishment lies. If it is used lavishly it loses its horror, people become accustomed to it and are no longer affected or deterred by it; if it is rarely applied, then the probability of incurring it sinks to insignificance in the minds of potential offenders.[33] This led him to declare that "the death penalty probably can never be a deterrent. Its very life seems to depend on its rarity and therefore on its ineffectiveness as a deterrent."

Another paradox of the death penalty relates to the nature of the crimes for which it is provided. Where it is wanted and used, that is for crimes of violence and sex, it is not likely to be effective. Where it might be effective (such as for rational economic crimes) it is not wanted.

Why Capital Punishment Fails as a Deterrent

The belief, shared by many, in the effectiveness of the death penalty as a deterrent and in its uniqueness as a means of dissuasion can usually be traced to a lack of knowledge as to the penalty's applications, to an inadequate understanding of the nature of criminal homicide, to psychology of the killer and to a failure to realize that deterrence has its limits.

The Odds Against Incurring the Death Penalty

In his study of the death penalty in Canada, Topping made the following statement:

> It seems clear that there is an inverse relationship between severity of punishment and certainty of punishment, and that Canadians are suffering under a delusion when they assert that they know how to hang. The net result of the administration of justice in Canada as it relates to capital offences is that murder has become the least risky of any or all the offences which a citizen might choose to commit.[43]

In an attempt to assess the level of certainty of the death penalty in Canada and the odds against incurring it, I compiled statistics for the 80-year period from 1881 to 1960.[16] The 80 years were then divided into periods of five years each. The highest percentage of death sentences to charges (45.9%) was recorded in the period from 1931 to 1935 when a person charged with murder had approximately an even chance of being sentenced to death. The last period, 1956 to 1960, revealed a low percentage of death sentences (33%), the highest percentage of commutations (73%) and the lowest percentage of executions (23.8%). In other words, during that period, although capital punishment was still the mandatory penalty for murder, a person charged with murder had only one chance in three of being sentenced to death. Once sentenced to death, he had more than three chances out of four of escaping the death penalty. The chances of being executed during that period for a person accused with the capital offence of murder was eight in a hundred, a very low probability indeed. If the period is examined as a whole, we find that out of a total of 3,249 persons charged with murder, only 634 were actually executed. The percentage of executions to charges was 19.5 meaning that only one charge in five led to an execution, again a very weak probability.

Those who feel that the death penalty, despite the very low probability of incurring it, still provides an effective means of societal protection simply forget that the other risks the potential killer takes are far greater than the risk of legal execution. Comparisons between the rates of legal executions and the rates of offenders killed by the police, the intended victim or by some bystander during or after the crime, show that this latter risk is much higher than the former. If the potential killer is not deterred by the greater threat of being killed on the spot while committing his crime or while escaping could it be claimed that he would be deterred by the minor and remote threat of being legally executed? The fact is, the potential killer rarely contemplates the consequences of his acts, calculates the risk involved or makes a rational consideration of gain or loss.

To illustrate the differential risks to which the potential killer is exposed, Sellin[34,35] made the following calculations:

> During the period 1934–1954, in Chicago, for instance, policemen killed 69 and private citizens 261 criminals or suspects involved in homicide, or a total of 330. During the same period there were 45 persons executed for murder in the Cook County jail. In other words, there were nearly 8 times as many homicidal offenders killed unofficially, so to speak, as were those electrocuted. There were 5,132 murders and non-negligent manslaughters known to the police during those years. In connection with 6.45% of these homicides, a criminal or suspect met his death at the hands of police or citizens, while 0.88% were put to death in the electric chair.

The Impulsive and Pathological Character of Many Homicides

Paradoxically the crime for which the death penalty is most often provided and applied, namely murder, is one of the offences least likely to be deterred. It is universally recognized that homicide is most frequently an emotional and impulsive crime, rarely subject to control by reason or fear of consequences. In the majority of cases the crime is the result of a sudden impulse or a violent over-mastering passion. The high emotions and strong motivations involved are likely to preclude a careful consideration of consequences or to outweigh the threat of any punishment be it life imprisonment or even death. Quite often the victim is closely associated with the offender.

A large number of homicides are committed under the influence of alcohol, drugs, sexual stimulation or provocation with the thought of punishment hardly crossing the mind of the killer. Only a small percentage of all criminal homicides are truly thought out and premeditated. This small percentage is usually perpetrated by persons [so] convinced of their ability to escape detection as to rule out all thought of consequences. As Calvert[9] pointed out, one of the most common characteristics exhibited by the murderer who commits an apparently cold-blooded crime is an exaggerated sense of confidence in his ability to escape detection.

The Undeterrability of Many Potential Killers

The act of killing is quite commonly committed by mentally deranged or psychologically abnormal individuals under the spell of an obsession, an irresistible impulse or under the pressure of some unusual circumstances. Abnormal offenders, offenders suffering from mental illness, those reacting to provocation and those acting under the influence of alcohol or drugs commit their crimes while in a state of mind that does not enable them to foresee or to consider the consequences of their actions. The more savage, heinous and atrocious the crime is, the greater is the likelihood that the criminal will be declared not guilty by reason of insanity. Many of the cases cited in support of the death penalty or to justify its retention are cases to which the death penalty does not apply because of the insanity of the offender.

Another category of murderers comprises individuals who are actually attracted by the prospect of death. And still another type is attracted by the notoriety the principal actor in a murder trial gets. In such cases the death penalty is likely to act as an incentive rather than a deterrent. It might even exercise a morbid fascination.

Professional killers, or "hired guns" as they are sometimes called, often mentioned in discussions advocating the death penalty, consider punishment, be it death or otherwise, a professional risk in the same way a physician considers the risk of contamination or a race-driver the risk of a car crash. The great majority of these killers are adventurers who are not afraid of death; they are rather attracted by it in the same way mercenaries are attracted to the dangers of war.

As to terrorists and other political criminals, often singled out as a group to whom the death penalty should be applied, their fanaticism and dedication to their cause counteract and neutralize whatever legal threat is meant to deter them. Moreover, many of them do seek through their actions their own self-destruction, destruction which they view as the easiest and quickest way to the state of martyrdom [to which] they aspire.

Murderers' Indifference to Death

The death penalty cannot be an effective deterrent to those who are indifferent to death, are not afraid of it or those who have a conscious or unconscious desire to die. The large percentage of murderers who commit or attempt suicide fall into this category. Figures from some European countries show that one quarter to one half of murder cases are followed by the suspects' suicide.

According to West[51] something like half of the murders in England are followed by the suicide or attempted suicide of the aggressor.

Home Office researchers Gibson and Klein[19,20] report in their study of murder in England and Wales in the years 1952–1960 that about one third of all suspects in cases finally recorded as murder committed suicide. In over half of the murders known to have been committed by females, suicide followed the crime.

A Danish study by Siciliano[42] covering all homicides in Denmark over a period of 28 years reported that 42.2% of the Danish killers subsequently killed themselves and a further 9.6% made a serious suicidal attempt. The incidence of suicide was particularly high among female offenders with 63.9% killing themselves and 16.1% making serious suicidal attempts. Obviously none of these murders would have been prevented had the death penalty been in effect in Denmark during that period.

Another category of potential killers unlikely to be deterred by the prospect and threat of the death penalty are those who see the ultimate sentence as a way of achieving a death wish. In such cases capital punishment acts as a direct incentive to murder.

Abrahamsen[2,3] and Hurwitz[23] cite the epidemic of indirect suicides that took place in Norway and Denmark in the seventeenth and eighteenth centuries when depressed people committed murder in order to be put to death since they would not commit suicide for religious reasons. These cases were so frequent that a special law had to be passed excluding such individuals from the death penalty to stop this particular type of homicide. Several recent cases reported in the literature confirm that this form of indirect suicide by means of the death penalty still exists.

Man's Inability to Conceive of His Own Death

Two important factors that weaken to a considerable extent whatever deterrent effect the death penalty may have are the time dimension and man's inability to conceive of his own death. This latter phenomenon has been discussed and documented by many psychiatrists.

Modern life is full of hazards. But the dangers in every-day life do not stop people from going about their daily activities oblivious to the risks involved. This is made possible by this peculiar aspect of human psychology: the inability of man to conceive of his own death. It is this inability that explains why the risk of accidental death does not prevent people from driving or flying, auto-racers or bull-fighters from competing, etc. It explains why the risk of death from lung cancer or from liver cirrhosis does not prevent people from smoking or drinking.

The British Select Committee on Capital Punishment noted that

> The mass of mankind put death in the far distance and push it into the doubtful future. Men peril it for trifling aims. Some are reckless of others, reckless of life itself. Be its consequences what they may, they will take them. Some dodge death and think they can evade all its

penalties; and flatter themselves that, whatever the penalty, they will never be found out.[45]

The Remoteness of the Threat

For punishment to elicit the desired behavioural response from the potential killer it has to pose an immediate threat of unavoidable dire consequences. The threat the death penalty poses is both remote and improbable. It is well known that the threat of the most dire consequences can have little effect if the prospect is uncertain and distant in time. The threat of hell and damnation has not been effective in deterring people from sin and it would be too naive and too optimistic to expect the death penalty to deter them from crime. In both cases the effectiveness of the threat is greatly weakened by its remoteness and uncertainty. Even if potential killers were rational and careful calculators of gain and loss, as some assume they are, the remoteness of the threat would always tip the scale against the death penalty. As Honderich puts it

> . . . it is a truism that people do not choose between possible courses of action in a prudential way if the possible consequences of one course are distant in time and the consequences of the other immediate. A penalty is a distant possibility, the gain from an offence is usually immediate.[22]

Summary

1. If the death penalty is a unique deterrent to murder, then a declining use of it should be followed by an increase in murder rates. Yet statistics from many countries and particularly from the United States show that murder rates have remained constant or declined despite trends away from the use of the death penalty.

2. The experience of European countries that abolished the death penalty in the nineteenth or early twentieth century shows that abolition was followed by a decrease rather than an increase in criminal homicides. Moreover, countries that recently abolished the death penalty (U.K., Canada) report that abolition has had no discernible influence on the rate at which murder is committed.

3. The reintroduction of the death penalty after it has been abolished for some or many years does not lead to a decline in homicide rates.

4. Comparisons of homicide rates in adjacent, congruent states with or without the death penalty clearly show that the presence or absence of capital punishment has no visible influence on homicide rates.

5. Comparisons of homicide rates in Canadian provinces suggest that such rates are not related to the penalty provided by law but to a total social situation in which a particular punishment can have little or no effect.

6. Comparisons of police killing in abolitionist and retentionist states in the U.S.A. do not lend empirical support to the assumption that law-enforcement officers are better protected when the death penalty is retained or that their occupational risks are increased by its abolition.

7. The abolition of the death penalty does not increase the hazards involved in

prison life and does not result in an increase in homicidal or assaultive behaviour in those penal institutions where convicted murderers are detained.

8. Capital punishment tends to defeat its own purpose, that is protection of society, by increasing the number of acquittals in capital cases. Its presence especially when it is made mandatory, reduces the likelihood that indicated offenders will be convicted.

9. Comparisons of execution rates and rates of offenders killed by the police, the intended victim or others, during or immediately after the crime, reveal that this latter risk is much greater than the former. If death is a deterrent, potential killers should be more deterred by the risk of being killed than by the threat of legal execution.

10. In a system of a fair and democratic justice, the application of the death penalty can probably never attain the certainty and expediency levels necessary for it to operate as a deterrent.

11. If the death penalty is used lavishly it loses its horror, people become accustomed to it and are no longer affected or deterred by it. Conversely, if it is rarely applied, then the probability of incurring it sinks to insignificance in the minds of potential offenders.

12. The alleged deterrent effect of the death penalty is based on the assumption of free and rational choice. Yet the crime for which the death penalty is most frequently prescribed, that is criminal homicide, is mostly committed in circumstances that preclude the existence of free will or a rational consideration of the consequences.

13. The death penalty is not likely to be an effective deterrent for those who are unafraid of death, those seeking martyrdom, or those who have a conscious or unconscious wish to die.

14. For certain categories of potential offenders the death penalty may act as an incentive to murder and for certain personalities it has a morbid fascination and a pathological attraction.

15. The deterrent effect of the death penalty is considerably weakened by the remoteness and uncertainty of the threat it presents and by man's inability to conceive of his own death.

Notes

1. Revised version of a paper presented at the VI UN Congress on the Prevention of Crime and the Treatment of Offenders—Session on Capital Punishment Organized by Amnesty International, Tuesday, August 26, 1980.
2. Abrahamsen, D. *Crime and the Human Mind.* New York: Columbia University Press, 1944.
3. Abrahamsen, D. "The Dynamic Connection between Personality and Crime, and the Detection of the Potential Criminal, Illustrated by Different Types of Murder." *Journal of Criminal Psychology.* 5:481–488. 1944.
4. Akman, D.P. "Homicides and Assaults in Canadian Penitentiaries." *Canadian J. of Corrections.* Pp. 284–299. 1966.
5. Barber, R.N. and Wilson, P.R. "Deterrent Aspect of Capital Punishment and Its Effect on Conviction Rates: The Queensland Experience." *Australian and New Zealand Journal of Criminology.* 1:2, 100–108. 1968.
6. Bowers, W. and Pierce, G. "The Illusion of Deterrence in Isaac Ehrlich's Research on Capital Punishment." *Yale Law Journal*, 85, pp. 187–208, 1975.

7. Bowers, W. and Pierce, G. Research on Publicity of Executions and Homicide Rates. Reported by Associated Press, Monday, October 6, 1980.

8. Buffum, P.C., "Prison Killings and Death Penalty Legislation." *Prison Journal.* Pp. 49–57. 1976.

9. Calvert, R. *Capital Punishment in the Twentieth Century.* London and New York: G.P. Putnam's Sons. 1927.

10. Campion, D. "The State Police and the Death Penalty." *Congressional Record.* March 6, 1956, A2076–2080. Also in Appendix F of *Minutes of the Proceedings and Evidence.* No. 22. Joint Committee of the Senate and the House of Commons on Capital Punishment. Ottawa: Queen's Printer.

11. Cardarelli, A.P. "An Analysis of Police Killed by Criminal Action: 1961–1963." *Journal of Criminal Law, Criminology and Police Science.* 59:3, pp. 447–453. 1968.

12. Chambliss, W.J. "The Deterrent Influence of Punishment." *Crime and Delinquency.* 12:1, 70–75. 1966.

13. Dann. R.H. "The Deterrent Effect of Capital Punishment." *Friend's Social Service Series Bulletin.* 29, March. 1935.

14. Ehrlich, I. "The Deterrent Effect of Capital Punishment: A Question of Life and Death." *American Economic Review.* 65, pp. 397–417. 1975.

15. Fattah, E.A. *A Study of the Deterrent Effect of Capital Punishment with Particular Reference to the Canadian Situation.* Ottawa: Information Canada. 1972.

16. Fattah, E.A. "Sentencing to Death: The Inherent Problem." In B. Grosman (ed.). *New Directions in Sentencing.* Pp. 157–193. Toronto: Butterworths. 1980.

17. Forst, B.E. "The Deterrent Effect of Capital Punishment: A Cross-state Analysis of the 1960's." *Minnesota Law Review.* 61, p. 764. 1977.

18. Forst, B., Filatov, V. and Klein, L.R. "The Deterrent Effect of Capital Punishment: An Assessment of the Estimates." In A. Blumstein, J. Cohen and D. Nagin (eds.). *Deterrence and Incapacitation: Estimating the Effects of Criminal Sanctions on Crime Rates.* Pp. 336–360. Washington, D.C.: National Academy of Sciences. 1978.

19. Gibson, E. and Klein, S. *Murder: A Home Office Research Unit Report.* London: H.M.S.O. 1961.

20. Gibson, E. and Klein, S. *Murder 1957 to 1968: A Home Office Statistical Division Report on Murder in England and Wales.* London: H.M.S.O. 1969.

21. Hahn, R.G. *Deterrence and the Death Penalty: A critical Review of the Research of Isaac Ehrlich.* Ottawa: Ministry of Supply and Services. 1977.

22. Honderich, T. *Punishment: The Supposed Justifications.* London: Pelican Books. 1971.

23. Hurwitz, S. *Criminology.* London: George Allen and Unwin Ltd. 1952.

24. Mattick, H.W. *Unexamined Death: An Analysis of Capital Punishment.* Centre for Studies in Criminal Justice. University of Chicago Law School. Chicago: John Howard Association. 46 pp. 1966.

25. Morris, A. *Homicide: An Approach to the Problem of Crime.* Boston: Boston University Press. 1955.

26. Morris, T. and Blom-Cooper, L. "Research on the Effect of Abolition of the Death Penalty on Homicide Rates in England and Wales." Reported in the *Observer* of London. 1979.

27. Passell, P. "The Deterrent Effect of the Death Penalty: A Statistical Test." *Standford Law Review.* 28, pp. 61–80. 1975.

28. Passell, P. and Taylor, J.B. "The Deterrence Controversy: A Reconsideration of the Time Series Evidence." In H.A. Bedau and G. Pierce (eds.). *Capital Punishment.* New York: AMS Press. Pp. 359–371. 1976.

29. Phillips, David P. "The Deterrent Effect of Capital Punishment: New Evidence on an Old Controversy." *American J. of Sociology.* 86: 1 (July), 139–148. 1980.

30. Robin, G.D. "Justifiable Homicide by Police Officers." *J. of Criminal Law, Criminology and Police Science.* 54:2, 225–231. 1963.

31. Robin, G.D. "Justifiable Homicide by Police Officers." In M.E. Wolfgang (ed.). *Studies in Homicide.* New York: Harper and Row, 88–100. 1967.

32. Savitz, L.D. "Study in Capital Punishment." *Journal of Criminal Law, Criminology and Police Science.* 49:338–341. 1958.
33. Sellin, Th. "Common Sense and the Death Penalty." *Prison Journal.* 12:4 (Oct. 1932).
34. Sellin, Th. *The Death Penalty: A Report for the Model Penal Code Project of the American Law Institute.* Philadelphia Executive Office of the American Law Institute. 1959.
35. Sellin, Th. "Capital Punishment." *Federal Probation.* 25:3, 3–11. 1961.
36. Sellin, Th. "The Death Penalty Relative to Deterrence and Police Safety." In N. Johnson et al. (eds.). *The Sociology of Punishment and Corrections.* New York: John Wiley and Sons. 1962.
37. Sellin, Th. "Effect of Repeal and Reintroduction of the Death Penalty on Homicide Rates." In H.A. Bedeau (ed.). *The Death Penalty in America.* Chicago: Aldine. Pp. 339–343. 1966.
38. Sellin, Th. *Capital Punishment.* New York: Harper and Row. 1967.
39. Sellin, Th. "Prison Homicides." In Sellin, T. (ed.). *Capital Punishment.* New York: Harper and Row. 1967.
40. Sellin, Th. "Homicides in Retentionist and Abolitionist States." In Sellin, T. (ed.). *Capital Punishment.* New York: Harper and Row. 1967.
41. Sellin, Th. *The Penalty of Death.* California: Sage Publications. 1980.
42. Siciliano, S. "Risultati Preliminari di Un'indagine sull Homicidio in Danimarca." *La Scuola Positiva.* 3: 4, 718–729. 1965.
43. Topping, C.W. "The Death Penalty in Canada." *The Annals of the American Academy of Political and Social Science.* 284 (Nov.): 147–157. 1952.
44. U.K. Home Office. *British Criminal Statistics.* London: HMSO. 1924.
45. U.K. *British Select Committee on Capital Punishment—Report.* London: HMSO. 1930.
46. U.K. *Royal Commission on Capital Punishment 1949–1953—Report.* London: HMSO. 1953.
47. U.S.A. California, *Senate Committee's Report on the Death Penalty.* California. Pp. 16–17. Quoted in H.A. Bedeau (1976). *The Death Penalty in America.* New York: Anchor Books. 1960.
48. U.S.A. Massachusetts, *Report*, Sub-committee on Moral Arguments For and Against the Death Penalty. 1958.
49. U.S.A. Ohio, Ohio Legislative Service Commission. *Capital Punishment: Report.* Columbus, Ohio. 1961.
50. U.S.A. The Panel of the National Academy of Sciences. *Deterrence and Incapacitation: Estimating the Effects of Criminal Sanctions on Crime Rates*, by A. Blumstein, J. Cohen and D. Nagin. Washington, D.C.: National Academy of Sciences. 1978.
51. West, D.J. *Murder Followed by Suicide.* London: Heneman. 1965.
52. Zeisel, H. "The Deterrent Effect of the Death Penalty: Facts v. Faith." In P.B. Kurland (ed.). *The Supreme Court Review, 1976.* Chicago: University of Chicago Press. 1976.

Questions

1. Is the deterrence argument more civilized than arguments based on revenge and retribution as Fattah implies?
2. Should the burden of proving that capital punishment is a deterrent be placed on the retentionists?
3. Is Fattah right in saying: "The question is not whether the death penalty has a deterrent effect but whether it provides a unique and supreme deterrent"?
4. Is capital punishment a unique deterrent? If not, does it follow that capital punishment should be abolished?

Defending the Death Penalty

Walter Berns

For Capital Punishment is, so far as I know, the first book-length defense of the death penalty written by someone other than a professional law-enforcement officer.[1] As its author, I expected to be denounced in the liberal press, and I was. The best I could have hoped for was that the book would not be reviewed in certain journals. Unfortunately, the *New York Review of Books* did review it,[2] in a manner of speaking (the reviewer suggested that its author ought to be psychoanalyzed). Surprisingly, the *New York Times*, at least in its daily edition, gave it a good review, one I could have written myself;[3] Garry Wills, on the other hand, devoted an entire column to the book, during the course of which he told several outright lies about me and the book.[4] Then when I appeared on a live television show in Washington debating the death penalty with a man who has devoted his entire professional life to the effort to abolish it, my wife, at home, began to receive threatening telephone calls, many of them saying that her husband was the only person who deserved to be executed (or, as one persistent caller put it, "to sizzle"); these calls continued until we were forced to change our telephone number, which is now unlisted.

I recite these events only to make the point that capital punishment is a subject that arouses the angriest of passions. I suspect that opponents of the death penalty also receive threatening telephone calls, but somehow I doubt that theirs could match mine in nastiness. To the opponents of the death penalty, nothing can be said in its favor, and anyone who tries is a scoundrel or a fool. "Hang-hards" (Arthur Koestler's term) might defend it, the Ayatollah Khomeini might defend it, and police officers might be forgiven for defending it, but no rational person can defend it. That was Garry Wills's opinion, and that appears to be the opinion of the liberal world in general.

In one respect, at least, I have no quarrel with my hostile critics. The history of capital punishment is surely one that should give everyone pause: too many fanatics, too much ruthlessness, and too many disgusting public spectacles. On the other hand, there is also a history of the argument concerning capital punishment, and that history reveals something that ought to give pause to its opponents and arouse some doubts regarding the opinion prevailing in today's intellectual circles. Long before the current debate, political philosophers addressed themselves to the question of justice and, therefore, of crime and punishment; none of them, with the qualified exception of Jeremy Bentham, opposed the death penalty.[5] Opposition to capital punishment is in fact a modern phenomenon, a product of modern sentiment and modern thought. Except to unreconstructed progressives—I mean persons who believe that every area of thought is characterized by progress—this fact is one that ought to cause us at least to hesitate before, so to speak, picking up the telephone.

Reprinted, with permission of the National Council on Crime and Delinquency, from Walter Berns, "Defending the Death Penalty," *Crime & Delinquency*, October 1980, pp. 503–527.

Do we really know more about crime and punishment than did the ancients? Are we better qualified to speak on these subjects than Sir Thomas More? Are we more concerned with human rights than were the founders of the school of human rights—say, John Locke? Than the founders of the first country—our own—established specifically to secure these rights? In matters of morality are we the superiors of Kant? Are we more humane than Tocqueville? Than John Stuart Mill? Thomas Jefferson? George Washington? Abraham Lincoln?

Or, alternatively, have we become so morally ambivalent, and in some cases, so guilt ridden, that we cannot in good conscience punish anyone and certainly not to the extent of putting him to death? In this connection, it is relevant to point out that, contrary to the public statements of some modern churchmen, the Bible cannot be read to support the cause of abolition of capital punishment—not when its texts are read fairly.[6] Furthermore, it is not insignificant that in the past, when the souls of men and women were shaped by the Bible and the regimes that ruled in the West were those that derived their principles from the Bible, death was a customary penalty. Some of these regimes were the most sanguinary known to history, which suggests that piety and harsh punishment go together.

I am not contending that there might not be moral objections to capital punishment (there certainly are when it cannot be imposed fairly, or in a nondiscriminatory fashion), but only that neither political philosophy nor the Bible lends support to these objections. The abolition movement stems, instead, from what can fairly be described as an amoral, and surely an anti-religious, work: Cesare Beccaria's unusually influential *On Crimes and Punishments*, first published in 1764.[7] Beccaria, whose teacher was Thomas Hobbes, set out to accomplish more than a few changes in the criminal codes of Western European countries: his revisions required the establishment of the modern liberal state, a state from which the Church's influence would be excluded. Like Hobbes, Beccaria argued that there is no morality outside the positive law.[8] Here is the source of that moral ambivalence to which I referred and which has gradually come to characterize the so-called enlightened opinion respecting punishment; the public opinion lags behind somewhat. A Norwegian judge (quoted by the well-known criminologist Johannes Andenaes) remarked this when he said that "our grandfathers punished, and they did so with a clear conscience [and] we punish too, but we do it with a bad conscience."[9]

Why, indeed, do we punish criminals? Some of us try to ease our uneasy consciences by saying that the purpose of punishment is the rehabilitation of the criminal. But we ought to know by now that we cannot in fact rehabilitate criminals. An occasional criminal, yes, but not criminals as a class or in significant numbers. We cannot rehabilitate them any more successfully than our penitentiaries can cause them to repent, or to become penitent. One reason for this is that too many of us, and especially those of us in the rehabilitation business, are of the opinion that criminals are not wicked. Who are we to ask them to repent when, essentially, we think they have nothing to repent of? How can we in good conscience ask them to be rehabilitated when, in effect, we deny that there is a moral order to which they should be restored? We look upon the criminal as disturbed, yes; sick, perhaps; underprivileged, surely; but wicked, no. Karl Menninger, a leading criminal psychologist, accuses us in *The Crime of Punishment* of being criminals because we damn "some of our fellow citizens with the label criminal."[10] We who do this are, he says, the only criminals. The others are sick and deserve to be treated, not punished. The immorality of this position, whose premise is that no one is reponsible for his acts, requires no elaboration.

Or we punish criminals in order to deter others from becoming criminals. Punishment for this purpose is utilitarian, and, like Beccaria, we can justify something if it is truly useful. But again, to inflict pain on one person merely to affect the behavior of others is surely immoral, as our criminology texts have not hesitated to tell us.

Perhaps we can be persuaded of the necessity to punish criminals in order to incapacitate them, thereby preventing them from committing their crimes among us (but not, of course, against their fellow prisoners). I must point out, however, that unless we concede, as I do, that even incarcerated criminals are no less worthy of our concern than are law-abiding persons, this policy is also immoral.

What we have not been able to do (although there are signs here and there that this is changing[11]) is to admit that we punish, in part at least, to pay back the criminal for what he had done to us, not as individuals but as a moral community. We exact retribution, and we do not like to admit this. Retribution smacks of harshness and moral indignation, and our Hobbesian-Beccarian principles forbid the public expression of moral indignation. In the 1972 death penalty cases, Justice Marshall went so far as to say that the eighth amendment, forbidding cruel and unusual punishment, forbids "punishment for the sake of retribution."[12] In the words of Marshall's closest colleague, Justice Brennan, to execute a person in order to exact retribution is to deprive him of his human dignity, and "even the vilest criminal [is] possessed of common human dignity."[13]

In the past, when men reflected seriously on the differences between human and other beings, human dignity was understood to consist of the capacity to be a moral being, a being capable of choosing between right and wrong and, with this freedom, capable of governing himself.[14] Unlike other animals, a human being was understood to be a responsible moral creature. The "vilest criminal" was not being deprived of his human dignity when he was punished, not even when he was punished by being put to death; he had lost his dignity when he freely chose to commit his vile crimes. Retribution means to pay back, or to give people what they deserve to get, and it implies that different people deserve to get different things. But if human dignity is the standard according to which we determine who deserves to get what, and if everyone, no matter what he does, possesses human dignity, as Brennan would have it, then no one deserves to be treated differently and, unless everyone deserves to be punished, no one deserves to be punished.

I agree that a world built on Brennan's idea of human dignity may not exact retribution. It has lost all confidence in its opinions of right and wrong, good and evil, righteous and wicked, deserving and undeserving, and human and inhuman. It is, as the most eloquent opponent of the death penalty put it—I refer to the late Albert Camus—a world without God. As he said so well in his brilliant novel, *L'Etranger*, this is a world of hypocrites affecting the language of justice and moral outrage. Of course it is entitled to execute no one; such a world may punish no one. And that, he said, is our world. He did not act as if he believed it—he was a very brave enemy of both Hitler and Stalin—but he did most emphatically say it.[15]

The issue of capital punishment can be said to turn on the kind of world we live in (or the world we want to live in): a moral world or a morally indifferent world.

Contrary to Justices Marshall and Brennan, we in the United States have always recognized the legitimacy of retribution. We have schedules of punishment in every criminal code according to which punishments are designed to fit the crime, and not simply to fit what social science tells us about deterrence and rehabilitation: the worse the crime, the more severe the punishment. Justice requires criminals (as well as the rest of us) to get what they (and we) deserve, and what criminals deserve depends on what they have done to us.

To pay back criminals is not only just but, as Andenaes allows us to see, useful as well. For years he has been speaking of what he calls "general prevention," by which he means the capacity of the criminal law to promote obedience to law, not by instilling fear of punishment (the way of deterrence), but by inculcating law-abiding habits. I think the criminal law has this capacity, although Andenaes has never been able to explain the mechanism by which it works. To do so requires me to adopt an old and by now familiar manner of speaking of the law.

The law, and especially the criminal law, works by praising as well as by blaming. It attaches blame to the act of murder, for example, by making it a crime and threatening to punish anyone convicted of having committed it. This function of the law is familiar to us. What is unfamiliar is the way in which the law, by punishing the guilty and thereby blaming them for deeds they commit, also praises those persons who do not commit those deeds. The mechanism involved here is the satisfaction of the law-abiding person's anger, the anger that person ought to feel at the sight of crime. This anger has to be controlled, of course, and we rightly condemn persons who, at the sight of crime, take it upon themselves to punish its perpetrators. But we ought not condemn the anger such persons feel; indeed, that anger is a condition of a decent community. When no one, whether out of indifference or out of cowardice, responds to a Kitty Genovese's screams and plaintive calls for help, we have reason really to be concerned. A *citizen* ought to be angry when witnessing a crime, and, of course, that anger takes the form of wanting to hurt the cause of the anger—for example, whoever it was who mugged and murdered Kitty Genovese. The law must control or calm that anger, and one way it can do that is by promising to punish the criminal. When it punishes the criminal it satisfies that anger, and by doing so, it rewards the law-abiding persons who feel it. This is one purpose of punishment: to reward the law-abiding by satisfying the anger that they feel, or ought to feel, at the sight of crime. It rewards, and by rewarding praises, and therefore teaches, law-abidingness.

Anger, Aristotle teaches us,[16] is the pain caused by him who is the object of anger. It is also the pleasure arising from the hope of revenge. It has to be controlled or tamed, but it is not in itself reprehensible; it can be selfish, but, contrary to Freud, it need not be selfish. In fact, it is one of the passions that reaches out to other persons—unlike greed, for example, which is purely selfish—and, in doing so, can serve to unite us with others, or strengthen the bonds that tie us to others. It can be an expression of our caring for others, and society needs people who care for each other, people who, as Aristotle puts it, share their pleasures and their pains, and do so for the sake of others. Anger, again unlike greed or jealousy, is a passion that can cause us to act for reasons having nothing to do with selfish or mean calculation; indeed, when tamed and educated, it can become a most generous passion, the passion that protects the community by demanding punishment for its enemies (and criminals are enemies). It is the stuff from which both heroes and law-abiding citizens are made; and when it is aroused for the right reasons (and it is the job of the law to define those reasons), it deserves to be rewarded.

Criminals are properly the object of anger, and the perpetrators of great crimes (James Earl Ray and Richard Speck, for example) are properly the objects of great anger. They have done more than inflict injury on isolated individuals (and this is especially evident in the case of Ray). They have violated the foundations of trust and friendship, the necessary elements of a moral community. A moral community, unlike a hive of bees or hill of ants, is one whose members (responsible moral creatures) are expected *freely* to obey the laws; and, unlike a tyranny, are *trusted* to obey the laws. The criminal has violated that trust, and in doing so, has injured not merely his immediate victim but also the community as such. It was for this reason that God said to the Jewish community, "Ye shall take no satisfaction [or ransom] for the life of a murderer, which is guilty of death: but he shall be surely put to death."[17] The criminal has called into question the very possibility of that community by suggesting that human beings cannot be trusted freely to respect the property, the person, and the dignity of those with whom they are associated. Crime is an offense against the public, which is why the public prosecutes it.

If, then, persons are not angry when someone else is robbed, raped, or murdered, the implication is that there is no moral community because these persons do not care for anyone other than themselves. When they are angry, that is a sign of their caring; and that anger, that caring, should be rewarded. We reward it when we satisfy it, and we satisfy it when we punish its objects, criminals.

So the question becomes, how do we pay back those who are the objects of great anger because they have committed terrible crimes against us? We can derive some instruction in this subject from the Book of Genesis, where we find an account of the first murder and of the first disagreement as to the appropriate punishment of a murderer. Cain killed Abel, and, we are told, God forbade anyone to kill Cain in turn: Vengeance, said the Lord, is mine, and he exacted that vengeance by banishing Cain "from the presence of the Lord."[18] The appropriate punishment would appear to be death or banishment; in either case, the murderer is deprived of life in the community of moral persons. As Justice Frankfurter put it in a dissent in one of the expatriation cases, certain criminals are "unfit to remain in the communion of our citizens."[19]

To elaborate this point, in my book I discussed two famous literary works dealing with murders: Shakespeare's *Macbeth* and Camus' *L'Etranger* (variously translated as *The Stranger* or *The Outsider*).[20] I pointed out that in *Macbeth* the murderer was killed, and I argued that the dramatic necessity of that death derived from its moral necessity. That is how Shakespeare saw it.

As I indicated above, Camus' novel treats murder in an entirely different context. A moral community is not possible without anger and the moral indignation that accompanies it; and it is for this reason that in this novel Camus shows us a world without anger. He denies the legitimacy of it, and specifically of an anger that is aimed at the criminal. Such an anger, he says, is nothing but hypocrisy. The hero—or antihero—of this novel is a stranger or outsider not because he is a murderer, not because he refuses to cry at his mother's funeral, not because he shows and feels no remorse for having murdered (and murdered for no reason whatever); he is a stranger because, in his unwillingness to express what he does not feel—remorse, sadness, regret—he alone is not a hypocrite. The universe, he says at the end of the novel, is "benignly indifferent" to how we live. Such a universe, or such a world, cannot justify the taking of a life—even the life of a murderer. Only a moral community may do that, and a moral community is impossible in our time; which means there is no basis for friendship or for the ties that bind us and make us responsible for each other and to each other. The only thing we share, Camus says in his essay on the death penalty, is our "solidarity against death," and an execution "upsets" that solidarity.[21]

Strangely, when some of the abolitionists speak of the death penalty as a denial of human dignity, this is what they mean. Abe Fortas, writing after he left the supreme court, said that the "essential value," the value that constitutes the "basis of our civilization," is the "pervasive, *unqualified* respect for life."[22] This is what passes for a moral argument for him (and I have no doubt that he speaks for many others). In contrast, Lincoln (who, incidentally, greatly admired Shakespeare's *Macbeth*[23]), who respected life and grieved when it was taken, authorized the execution of 267 men. His respect for life was not "unqualified." He believed, as did the founders of our country, that there were some things for which people should be expected to give up their lives. For example, as he said at Gettysburg, Americans should be expected to give up their lives in order that this nation "shall have a new birth of freedom."

There are vast differences between Camus, a man of deep perception and elegance of expression, and Fortas, but they shared a single vision of our world. Camus, however, gave it a label appropriate to the vision: a world without dignity, without morality, and indifferent to how we treat each other. There are statutes in this world forbidding crimes, but there is no basis in the order of things for those statutes. It is a world that may not rightly impose the sentence of death on anyone—or for that matter punish anyone in any manner—or ask any patriot to risk his or her life for it.

Shakespeare's dramatic poetry serves to remind us of another world, of the majesty of the moral order and of the terrible consequences of breaching it through the act of murder (the worst offense against that order). Capital punishment, like banishment in other times and places, serves a similar purpose: it reminds us, or can remind us, of the reign of the moral order, and enhances, or can enhance, its dignity. The law must not be understood to be merely statutes that we enact or repeal at our pleasure and obey or disobey at our convenience, especially not the criminal law. Whenever law is regarded as *merely* statutory, by which I mean arbitrary or enacted out of no moral necessity or reflecting no law beyond itself, people will soon enough disobey it, and the clever ones will learn to do so with impunity. The purpose of the criminal law is not merely to control behavior—a tyrant can do that—but also to promote respect for that which should be respected, especially the lives, the moral integrity, and even the property of others. In a country whose principles forbid it to preach, the criminal law is one of the few available institutions through which it can make a moral statement and, thereby, hope to promote this respect. To be successful, what it says—and it makes this moral statement when it punishes—must be appropriate to the offense and, therefore, to what has been offended. If human life is to be held in awe, the law forbidding the taking of it must be held in awe; and the only way it can be made to be awful or awe-inspiring is to entitle it to inflict the penalty of death.

Death is the most awful punishment available to the law of our time and place. Banishment (even if it were still a legal punishment under the constitution[24]) is not dreaded, not in our time; in fact, to judge by some of the expatriated Vietnam war resisters I used to see in Toronto, it is not always regarded as a punishment. And, despite the example of Gary Gilmore, the typical offender does not prefer death to imprisonment, even life imprisonment. In prison the offender still enjoys some of the pleasures available outside and some of the rights of citizens, and is not utterly outside the protection of the laws. Most of all, a prisoner has not been deprived of hope—hope of escape, of pardon, or of being able to do some of the things that can be done even by someone who has lost freedom of movement. A convicted murderer in prison (Ray) has retained more of life than has the victim (Martin Luther King). A maximum-security prison may be a brutal place, and the prospect of spending one's life there is surely dreadful, but the prospect of being executed is more dreadful. And for the worst of crimes, the punishment must be most dreadful and awful—not most painful (for the purpose of punishment is not simply to inflict pain on the guilty offender), but awful in the sense of "commanding profound respect or reverential fear."

Whether the United States, or any of them, should be permitted to carry out execution is a question that is not answered simply by what I have written here. The answer depends on our ability to restrict its use to the worst of our criminals and to impose it in a nondiscriminatory fashion. We do not yet know whether that can be done.

Notes

1. Walter Berns, *For Capital Punishment: Crime and the Morality of the Death Penalty* (New York: Basic Books, 1979).
2. June 28, 1979, pp. 22–25.
3. July 16, 1979, III, p. 14.
4. Garry Wills, "Capital Punishment and a Non Sequitur," *Washington Star*, Apr. 16, 1979, A-11. Wills's column was actually devoted to an excerpt from the book which was published in *Harper's* (April 1979). My reply to Wills was published in the *Washington Star*, Apr. 21, 1979, A-9.
5. See Berns, *For Capital Punishment*, pp. 21–22.
6. Ibid., pp. 11–18.
7. Cesare Beccaria, *On Crimes and Punishments*, trans. Henry Paolucci (Indianapolis: Bobbs-Merill, Library of Liberal Arts, 1963).
8. Ibid., p. 41.
9. Joannes Andenaes, *Punishment and Deterrence*, with a foreword by Norval Morris (Ann Arbor, Mich.: University of Michigan Press, 1974), p. 133.

10. Karl Menninger, *The Crime of Punishment* (New York: Viking Press, 1969), p. 9. At the twenty-second National Institute on Crime and Delinquency, Menninger was given the Roscoe Pound Award for his outstanding work in "the field of criminal justice"; see *American Journal of Corrections*, July–August 1975, p. 32.
11. See, for example, Norval Morris, "The Future of Imprisonment: Toward a Punitive Philosophy," *Michigan Law Review*, May 1974, pp. 1161–1180; and Andrew von Hirsch, *Doing Justice: The Choice of Punishments*, Report of the Committee for the Study of Incarceration (New York: Hill & Wang, 1976).
12. *Furman v. Georgia*, 408 U.S. 238, 343–344 (1972).
13. Ibid., pp. 272–273.
14. Pico Della Mirandola, *Oration on the Dignity of Man*, trans. A. Robert Caponigri (Chicago: Henry Regnery, Gateway Editions, 1956).
15. See comments below.
16. Aristotle, *Rhetoric* 1378b1–5.
17. Numbers 35:31.
18. Genesis 4:15–16.
19. *Trop v. Dulles*, 356 U.S. 86, 122 (1958). Dissenting opinion.
20. Camus was the most powerful and eloquent opponent of capital punishment. See Albert Camus, "Reflections on the Guillotine," in *Resistance, Rebellion and Death*, trans. Justin O'Brien (New York: Knopf, 1961).
21. Ibid., p. 222.
22. Abe Fortas, "The Case against Capital Punishment," *New York Times Magazine*, Jan. 23, 1977, p. 29. Italics added.
23. In a letter from Lincoln to James H. Hackett written on August 17, 1863, Lincoln says, "Some of Shakespeare's Plays I have never read, whilst others I have gone over perhaps as frequently as an unprofessional reader. Among the latter are *Lear, Richard Third, Henry Eighth, Hamlet*, and especially *Macbeth*. I think nothing equals *Macbeth*. It is wonderful." *The Collected Works of Abraham Lincoln*, vol. 6, Roy P. Basler, ed. (New Brunswick, N.J.: Rutgers University Press, 1953), p. 393.
24. Banishment, insofar as it would be comprehended by expatriation, has been declared an unconstitutionally cruel and unusual punishment. *Affroyim v. Rusk*, 387 U.S. 253 (1967).

Questions

1. Capital punishment has served Western societies, until recently, as an acceptable response to some crimes. Is that fact an argument for continuing the use of capital punishment today? If so, why? If not, what weight should it carry in current debates on the subject?
2. Do we know more about crime and punishment than was known in the past?
3. How would you go about assessing the view that criminals (particularly those found guilty of first-degree murder) are sick rather than evil or immoral?
4. Is punishing offenders a morally acceptable way of rewarding those who do not break the law?
5. Do you think that respect for the laws which protect life has diminished with the abolition of capital punishment? What facts would lead you to change your mind?

Capital Punishment and Retributive Justice

Hugo Adam Bedau

There are two leading principles of retributive justice relevant to the capital-punishment controversy. One is the principle that crimes should be punished. The other is the principle that the severity of a punishment should be proportional to the gravity of the offense. (A corollary to the latter principle is the judgment that nothing so fits the crime of murder as the punishment of death.) Although these principles do not seem to stem from any concern over the worth, value, dignity, or rights of persons, they are moral principles of recognized weight and no discussion of the morality of capital punishment would be complete without them. Leaving aside all questions of social defense, how strong a case for capital punishment can be made on the basis of these principles? How reliable and persuasive are these principles themselves?

Crime Must Be Punished

Given [a general rationale for punishment], there cannot be any dispute over this principle. In embracing it, of course, we are not automatically making a fetish of "law and order," in the sense that we would be if we thought that the most important single thing society can do with its resources is to punish crimes. In addition, this principle is not likely to be in dispute between proponents and opponents of the death penalty. Only those who completely oppose punishment for murder and other erstwhile capital crimes would appear to disregard this principle. Even defenders of the death penalty must admit that putting a convicted murderer in prison for years is a punishment of that criminal. The principle that crime must be punished is neutral to our controversy, because both sides acknowledge it and comply with it.

It is the other principle of retributive justice that seems to be a decisive one. Under the principle of retaliation, *lex talionis*, it must always have seemed that murderers ought to be put to death. Proponents of the death penalty, with rare exceptions, have insisted on this point, and it seems that even opponents of the death penalty must give it grudging assent. The strategy for opponents of the death penalty is to show either (a) that this principle is not really a principle of justice after all, or (b) that although it is, other principles outweigh or cancel its dictates. As we shall see, both these objections have merit.

Is Murder Alone to Be Punished by Death?

Let us recall, first, that not even the Biblical world limited the death penalty to the punishment of murder. Many other nonhomicidal crimes also carried this penalty (e.g., kidnapping, witchcraft, cursing one's parents). In our own recent history, persons have been executed for aggravated assault, rape, kidnapping, armed robbery, sabotage, and espionage. It is not possible to defend any of these executions (not to

From *Matters of Life and Death: New Introductory Essays in Moral Philosophy*, edited by Tom Regan, © 1980 by Random House, Inc. Reprinted by permission of the publisher.

mention some of the more bizarre capital statutes, like the one in Georgia that used to provide an optional death penalty for desecration of a grave) on grounds of just retribution. This entails that either such executions are not justified or that they are justified on some ground other than retribution. In actual practice, few if any defenders of the death penalty have ever been willing to rest their case entirely on the moral principle of just retribution as formulated in terms of "a life for a life." Kant seems to have been a conspicuous exception. Most defenders of the death penalty have implied by their willingness to use executions to defend limb and property, as well as life that they did not place much value on the lives of criminals when compared to the value of both lives and things belonging to innocent citizens.

Are All Murders to Be Punished by Death?

Our society for several centuries has endeavored to confine the death penalty to some criminal homicides. Even Kant took a casual attitude toward a mother's killing of her illegitimate child. ("A child born into the world outside marriage is outside the law . . ., and consequently it is also outside the protection of the law.")[1] In our society, the development nearly 200 years ago of the distinction between first- and second-degree murder was an attempt to narrow the class of criminal homicides deserving of the death penalty. Yet those dead owing to manslaughter, or to any kind of unintentional, accidental, unpremeditated, unavoidable, unmalicious killing are just as dead as the victims of the most ghastly murder. Both the law in practice and moral reflection show how difficult it is to identify all and only the criminal homicides that are appropriately punished by death (assuming that any are). Individual judges and juries differ in the conclusions they reach. The history of capital punishment for homicides reveals continual efforts, uniformly unsuccessful, to identify before the fact those homicides for which the slayer should die. Benjamin Cardozo, a justice of the United States supreme court fifty years ago, said of the distinction between degrees of murder that it was

> . . . so obscure that no jury hearing it for the first time can fairly be expected to assimilate and understand it. I am not at all sure that I understand it myself after trying to apply it for many years and after diligent study of what has been written in the books. Upon the basis of this fine distinction with its obscure and mystifying psychology, scores of men have gone to their death.[2]

Similar skepticism has been registered on the reliability and rationality of death-penalty statutes that give the trial court the discretion to sentence to prison or to death. As Justice John Marshall Harlan of the supreme court observed a decade ago,

> Those who have come to grips with the hard task of actually attempting to draft means of channeling capital sentencing discretion have confirmed the lesson taught by history . . . . To identify before the fact those characteristics of criminal homicide and their perpetrators which call for the death penalty, and to express these characteristics in language

which can be fairly understood and applied by the sentencing authority, appear to be tasks which are beyond present human ability.[3.]

The abstract principle that the punishment of death best fits the crime of murder turns out to be extremely difficult to interpret and apply.

If we look at the matter from the standpoint of the actual practice of criminal justice, we can only conclude that "a life for a life" plays little or no role whatever. Plea bargaining (by means of which one of the persons involved in a crime agrees to accept a lesser sentence in exchange for testifying against the others to enable the prosecutor to get them all convicted), even where murder is concerned, is widespread. Studies of criminal justice reveal that what the courts (trial or appellate) decide on a given day is first-degree murder suitably punished by death in a given jurisdiction could just as well be decided in a neighboring jurisdiction on another day either as second-degree murder or as first-degree murder but without the death penalty. The factors that influence prosecutors in determining the charge under which they will prosecute go far beyond the simple principle of "a life for a life." Nor can it be objected that these facts show that our society does not care about justice. To put it succinctly, either justice in punishment does not consist of retribution, because there are other principles of justice; or there are other moral considerations besides justice that must be honored; or retributive justice is not adequately expressed in the idea of "a life for a life."

Is Death Sufficiently Retributive?

Given the reality of horrible and vicious crimes, one must consider whether there is not a quality of unthinking arbitrariness in advocating capital punishment for murder as the retributively just punishment. Why does death in the electric chair or the gas chamber or before a firing squad or on gallows meet the requirements of retributive justice? When one thinks of the savage, brutal, wanton character of so many murders, how can retributive justice be served by anything less than equally savage methods of execution for the murderer? From a retributive point of view, the oft-heard exclamation, "Death is too good for him!" has a certain truth. Yet few defenders of the death penalty are willing to embrace this consequence of their own doctrine.

The reason they do not and should not is that, if they did, they would be stooping to the methods and thus to the squalor of the murderer. Where criminals set the limits of just methods of punishment, as they will do if we attempt to give exact and literal implementation to *lex talionis*, society will find itself descending to the cruelties and savagery that criminals employ. But society would be deliberately authorizing such acts, in the cool light of reason, and not (as is often true of vicious criminals) impulsively or in hatred and anger or with an insane or unbalanced mind. Moral restrains, in short, prohibit us from trying to make executions perfectly retributive. Once we grant the role of these restraints, the principle of "a life for a life" itself has been qualified and no longer suffices to justify the execution of murderers.

Other considerations take us in a different direction. Few murders, outside television and movie scripts, involve anything like an execution. An execution, after all, begins with a solemn pronouncement of the death sentence from a judge, is followed by long detention in maximum security awaiting the date of execution, various appeals, perhaps a final sanity hearing, and then "the last mile" to the execution chamber itself. As the French writer Albert Camus remarked,

> For there to be an equivalence, the death penalty would have to punish a criminal who had warned his victim of the date at which he would inflict a horrible death on him and who, from that moment onward, had confined him at his mercy for months. Such a monster is not encountered in private life.[4]

Differential Severity Does Not Require Executions

What, then, emerges from our examination of retributive justice and the death penalty? If retributive justice is thought to consist in *lex talionis*, all one can say is that this principle has never exercised more than a crude and indirect effect on the actual punishments meted out. Other principles interfere with a literal and single-minded application of this one. Some murders seem improperly punished by death at all; other murders would require methods of execution too horrible to inflict; in still other cases any possible execution is too deliberate and monstrous given the nature of the motivation culminating in the murder. Proponents of the death penalty rarely confine themselves to reliance on this principle of just retribution and nothing else, since they rarely confine themselves to supporting the death penalty only for all murders.

But retributive justice need not be thought to consist of *lex talionis*. One may reject that principle as too crude and still embrace the retributive principle that the severity of punishments should be graded according to the gravity of the offense. Even though one need not claim that life imprisonment (or any kind of punishment other than death) "fits" the crime of murder, one can claim that this punishment is the proper one for murder. To do this, the schedule of punishments accepted by society must be arranged so that this mode of imprisonment is the most severe penalty used. Opponents of the death penalty need not reject this principle of retributive justice, even though they must reject a literal *lex talionis*.

Notes

1. Immanuel Kant, *The Metaphysical Elements of Justice* (1797), tr. John Ladd, p. 106.
2. Benjamin Cardozo, "What Medicine Can Do for Law" (1928), reprinted in Margaret E. Hall, ed., *Selected Writings of Benjamin Nathan Cardozo* (1947), p. 204.
3. *McGautha v. California*, 402 V.S. 183 (1971), at p. 204.
4. Albert Camus, *Resistance, Rebellion, and Death* (1961), p. 199.

Questions

1. Is Bedau correct in thinking that one can be a retributivist yet oppose capital punishment without inconsistency?

2. Does capital punishment enhance respect for human life, as Walter
    Berns suggests? Or does it cheapen human life as Bedau argues?

Retributivism and the Death Penalty

Alan Brudner

A reasoned approach to the death penalty presupposes a comprehensive theory of punishment. A comprehensive theory of punishment is an account of punishment which distinguishes it from arbitrary and unjust violence and which, in doing so, provides a criterion for the legitimate deprivation of rights. Whether or not the death penalty is just, whether it should or should not be retained or restored can be decided only with reference to the criterion of justice generated by a true account of punishment.

Since Beccaria, the argument for the abolition of the death penalty has customarily been advanced from within the framework of a utilitarian theory of punishment. According to this theory, punishment is an expression of the impulse for self-defence moralized by the feeling of sympathy.[1] Whereas the former is rooted in the self-regarding desire for pleasure and aversion to pain, the latter allows us to transcend the narrow bounds of self and identify our own with collective pleasures and pains. Thus punishment is collective self-defence. Since the aim of collective defence is what constitutes punishment as a moral phenomenon in contradistinction to private revenge, it alone can provide grounds for the legitimate pursuit of the aim. For punishment is an evil that can be justified only as a means of avoiding greater evil; that is, only if its social benefits exceed its social costs.[2] That punishment is an evil follows from the hedonistic psychology and ethics of utilitarian thought. For Bentham the good at which all human beings aim is happiness, understood as the excess of pleasure over pain. Therefore the good at which all just policy must aim is the maximization of pleasure in the social aggregate. Now punishment inflicts suffering and so belongs in the debit column of the social utility ledger. It is acceptable, therefore, only if it yields a return of pleasure greater than its cost in pain. The benefits to be derived from punishment are: deterrence of potential offenders, the protection of society against actual offenders, and the rehabilitation of the criminal. Accordingly, the decision as to whether a particular instance of punishment is moral or immoral is basically an accounting decision. If the punishment works more harm than good, or if the same benefits can be obtained at less cost in suffering, then the punishment is unjust in the only sense intelligible to a utilitarian. It is especially the latter criterion that has provided the major focus for policy research on the death penalty and that has structured whatever rational debate one can find on the subject. Once the utilitarian premises are granted, it remains to determine by means of empirical

Reprinted from *University of Toronto Law Journal*, Vol. XXX, No. 4, 1980, by permission of University of Toronto Press.

studies whether, as compared with long-term imprisonment, the death penalty is either a uniquely effective deterrent to murder or a uniquely effective protection against those convicted of murder. Of its rehabilitative effects nothing need be said.

From a utilitarian standpoint the death penalty is difficult to justify. The statistical evidence fails to confirm (though neither does it decisively refute) the common intuition that capital punishment deters potential murderers and protects society from actual ones more effectively than incarceration for life.[3] It is true that no study of the deterrent effect of capital punishment can be conclusive, since it is impossible to compare the effects of retention and abolition within the same jurisdiction over the same time period. But since the burden of justification rests with those who would take a life, inconclusive data ought properly to weigh in favor of abolition. Ernest van den Haag has, to be sure, formulated a retentionist case that takes into account the lack of firm proof for the marginal deterrent value of the death penalty.[4] He argues that, given our uncertainty about deterrence, capital punishment should be retained in order to minimize the costs of our being wrong. The risk of causing unnecessary suffering to the criminal is preferable to that of exposing innocent people to murderers who might have been deterred. Though ingenious, this argument can, I think, be countered on utilitarian grounds. One could point out that, in retaining capital punishment, we choose the alternative that carries a risk of injustice over the one which carries none. For if we abolish the death penalty and people murder who would have been deterred, we have committed no injustice because we could not have known they would be deterred. But if we retain it and execute someone in vain, then we have done wrong in killing someone without sufficient reason. A more plausible justification of capital punishment from a utilitarian perspective is that of John Stuart Mill, who simply challenged the commonplace assumption that life imprisonment inflicts less suffering on the criminal than death.[5] Yet even this point argues less in favor of capital punishment than for granting the convict the right to choose, and so merely shifts the moral dilemma from capital punishment to suicide or euthanasia.

Were the utilitarian account of punishment the true one, therefore, we should have no doubt but that the movement toward abolition in the western world is securely grounded in reason, and that opposition to this movement, however broadly based, can be justly disregarded. However, a number of legal philosophers have insistently called attention to shocking inadequacies in the theory, and the result of their efforts is that the classic or pure utilitarian position outlined above now stands discredited even among philosophers whom one could still class as utilitarians.[6] As yet little has been done to assess the implications of this development for the moral status of the death penalty.[7] Such an assessment is, however, an urgent necessity, because the downfall of utilitarianism directs our attention once again to retributivism, a theory of punishment that has traditionally furnished arguments in favor of the death penalty.[8] Accordingly, the next section of this paper recapitulates the main objections to the utilitarian position and argues that recent efforts to rescue it by retreating to a qualified utilitarianism are in vain. The succeeding sections attempt both to vindicate retributivism as the only morally defensible account of punishment and to explore its implications for the death penalty. I intend to show that, far from specifically enjoining capital punishment for first-degree murder, retributivism provides grounds for favouring abolition as an ideal, though also for opposing it in circumstances which make the realization of the ideal imprudent.

The test of an adequate theory of punishment is whether it can save, provide an explicit ground for, and so confirm the prephilosophic distinction between punishment and arbitrary violence. Sense-perception alone cannot distinguish between murder and judicial killing, or between abduction and judicial detention. Our common-sense conviction that a difference nonetheless exists must therefore remain a prejudice vulnerable to skeptical questioning unless a philosophy of punishment can disclose the real basis of the distinction and so confirm it to rational insight. Now there are two levels at which thought can seek to clarify punishment. At one level it attempts merely to analyse the concept of punishment, to isolate the various elements implicit in its definition that distinguish it from wrongful injury. Although this approach yields important results, it can never produce a ''justification'' of punishment, for it deals only with a conventional object, with what we mean by punishment, without ever showing that what we mean has a foundation in reality. Thus analysis merely describes—it cannot confirm—the content of moral opinion.

The second level is that of theory. Here thought aims at a scientific account of the phenomenon of punishment. Rather than analysing an abstract concept, it seeks to disclose the real nature of the thing. The effect of such a theory may well be to debunk the common opinion regarding the essential distinction between judicial and criminal force, or it may be to confirm that opinion—that is, to provide a justification of punishment. But although only theory can justify punishment, the analytic approach is a necessary preliminary, because it alone can provide standards for the verification of theory. By specifying the conceptual elements of the distinction between punishment and violence, analysis furnishes the criteria by which we can assess the validity of justificatory theories of punishment.

There are at least three factors which distinguish punishment from violence for common sense. One of these is purpose. Punishment differs from unjust violence in that it is directed towards a good that is genuinely common—that is, common both to those who punish and to him that is punished—while unjust violence aims at some particular or exclusive interest. It is this factor of aim that distinguishes punishment not only from criminal aggression but also from that form of violence with which it is in all other essential respects identical, namely, revenge. Second, punishment differs from unjust violence in that it is intrinsically related to desert. Punishment, we may say, is the deserved infringement of a right. That it is connected with desert further implies that punishment can only be (a) a reaction to wrongdoing, and (b) a measured reaction—measured, that is, to the gravity of the wrong. The question as to the meaning and criterion of an appropriate measure is of course the crucial one in a discussion of the death penalty, and I shall return to it presently. For now let us simply say that implicit in the notion of punishment (as connected with desert) is a relation of fitness between punishment and crime. This means that penalties must be measured not only to the seriousness of the objective but also to the degree of subjective responsibility, since it is responsibility alone that constitutes wrongdoing. Thus civilized criminal codes recognize various degrees of culpable homicide ranging from manslaughter to first-degree murder, the degrees of guilt or desert corresponding to degrees of intent (or what is called *mens rea*), and they prescribe penalties which vary in severity according to the degree of intent. The converse of this principle of proportionality is that of strict liability, according to which the intention of the individual is irrelevant to the determination either of guilt or of the appropriate statutory penalty. Accordingly, a morally sound theory of punishment must (a) justify punishment with reference to a good that is genuinely universal, (b) save the connection between punishment and wrongdoing, and (c) save the rule of proportionality as between punishment and crime.

As has been frequently argued, the utilitarian theory fails on all three counts. In the first place, it views punishment as an evil inflicted on one individual for the benefit of others. The criminal is sacrificed, or used as a means, to the welfare of the majority, so that punishment becomes indistinguishable from the criminal use of force. Secondly, the utilitarian theory can countenance "punishment" of the innocent. This is because it defines just punishment in terms of aims that are only contingently related to desert. If punishment is justified by its deterrent effect, then in circumstances which made the risks of disclosure worth bearing, the state could legitimately fabricate evidence against an innocent man in order to make an example of him. Moreover, collective or vicarious punishment could, in extreme cases, also be socially expedient, and where expedient, just. And if punishment is justified by the protection it affords society, then justified in certain cases are preventive detention and the indeterminate sentence—that is, punishment related not to actual wrongdoing but to expected wrongdoing. From the standpoint of self-defence, waiting for a known psychopath to strike is absurd.

What of the requirement that punishment be proportioned to the offence? At first sight the utilitarian theory seems to preserve this relation, at least with respect to the nature of the objective act. Deterrence requires that the punishment be severe enough to make the crime a bad risk to the potential offender; utilitarian justice demands that it be no more severe than what is needed to deter the crime, and no more socially injurious than the crime unpunished. Furthermore, penalties must be so graded that anyone embarking on a criminal course will be encouraged to commit the less rather than the most harmful offence. However, we must recall that deterrence is only one of three aims contemplated by utilitarian punishment, and that of these three only deterrence looks to the crime. The goals of self-protection and reform have regard not to the offence but to the offender. They consider the criminal in terms of psychological rather than legal categories: not as the responsible author of a particular offence but as a dangerous or deviant personality, the subject of unique characterological attributes and propensities of which the crime is but a particular manifestation. Accordingly, since a penal practice which aimed exclusively at minimum deterrence would accomplish these other goals only accidentally, utilitarianism must fix penalties which leave sufficient room for judicial discretion in imposing individualized sentences. In doing so, however, it defines the moral degree of punishment by reference to something other than the offence, hence in a way that subverts the rule of natural justice requiring that punishments be proportioned to crimes. On utilitarian principles the pathological petty offender may warrant more severe punishment than the "normal" armed robber.

It is questionable, moreover, whether utilitarianism preserves the rule of proportionality respecting punishment and responsibility. Bentham, to be sure, claimed that it did. He argued that the circumstances recognized in the common law as excusing or extenuating wrongdoing—namely, accident, insanity, coercion, and provocation—are all confirmed by utilitarian theory as factors which render punishment "inefficacious."[9] Punishment of the insane, for example, would serve no useful deterrent purpose; and punishing a provoked crime with the same severity as a premeditated one would mean paying more than is necessary for the deterrence purchased, since a man provoked is not the rational maximizer of utilities envisaged by Benthamite psychology. Bentham, however, was wrong on two counts. He was wrong, first of all, in supposing that because the threat of punishment in cases where intent is absent is useless for deterrence, it is also useless for other utilitarian goals. From the standpoint of self-protection, for example, doing away with excusing conditions might conceivably be socially beneficial, for it would eliminate the opportunities that criminals now have for deceiving juries. He was wrong, secondly, in supposing that because the threat of punishment in such cases is useless for particular deterrence, it is also useless for general deterrence. As H.L.A. Hart has pointed out, punishing the insane will not deter them from striking again, but it may effectively deter others, especially if they know that a defence of insanity will do them no good.[10] From the standpoint of deterrence, in other words, excusing conditions are just so many loopholes in the law which the unscrupulous may be encouraged to exploit. Furthermore, persons engaged in an activity governed by a statute of strict liability are likely to exercise added caution, knowing that a plea of accident or of reasonable mistake will not excuse them; indeed they may be discouraged from undertaking the activity altogether. For all these reasons it can be said that any conduct which society wants to prevent is more effectively prevented by a statute of strict liability than by one which recognizes excusing or extenuating conditions. Hence the requirement of natural justice that responsibility be a condition of criminal liability finds in utilitarianism only contingent support. No doubt the question of responsibility would still be relevant for a utilitarian at the sentencing stage, where it would serve to indicate the kind of reformative or protective measures that need to be taken.[11] But adapting measures of social hygiene to the mental condition of the offender is a far different thing from proportioning punishments to legal responsibility. And it would be a sheer accident if their results were congruent. A crime of passion deserves less punishment than a calculated one; but the offender may require a more prolonged period of "treatment."

There have been several recent attempts to rescue the utilitarian position from the moral anomalies to which it leads. The weakest consist in definitionally limiting punishment to mean infliction of pain on the deserving, as if by calling "punishment" of the innocent by some other name utilitarians could stop worrying about sanctioning it.[12] Others have held that punishing innocents is condemned by a utilitarianism rightly interpreted, one that judges the morality of acts by their utility not in isolated circumstances but when generalized as a rule.[13] If sacrificing innocent persons for the sake of deterrence were standard policy, it is argued, the costs in terms of public anxiety would far outweigh the benefits of a reduced crime rate. Yet surely it is quite consistent with "rule-utilitarianism" for governments to empower themselves to use all expedient means (including collective punishment) for coping with emergencies, provided that the type of emergency is specified in law and is sufficiently grave to warrant such extraordinary powers. Because, in other words, it is possible to formulate rules not only for the general case but also for exceptional circumstances of a given type, rule-utilitarianism cannot, any more than act-utilitarianism, absolutely exclude punishing innocents under the colour of right. A third defence is in the nature of a strategic retreat. Professor Hart has acknowledged the pitfalls of a thoroughly consistent utilitarianism yet sees no need to discard it once it is suitably qualified. Deterrence and self-protection continue to justify punishment in general but cannot alone guide us in determining whom and how much to punish. For these questions principles (e.g., that punishment be only for an offence) must be applied that limit the extent to which the individual can be sacrificed for social ends—principles that guarantee a calculable world in which choices have a bearing on one's fate.[14] This solution is similar to that of John Rawls, in that it consists in splitting up the phenomenon of punishment into the general institution and the particular applications and in applying different moral criteria to each—a salutary eclecticism.[15] Whereas social utility justifies the former, principles associated with (but, according to Hart, not exclusive to) retributive punishment must guide us in the latter.

A number of rejoinders can be made to this argument. First, the splitting up of punishment in this way denies the organic link between the universal and its particularization. Just as a law is properly a law only if it is regularly enforced, so a set of penalties affixed to rules is a system of punishment only in so far as the penalties are imposed for violations of the rules. Conversely, a specific imposition of a sanction is an instance of punishment only in so far as it is carried out under the system of rules and procedures defining the legal use of force. While distinct, therefore, the institution of punishment and its particular applications are united in essence; neither *is* apart from the other. Consequently, one cannot coherently adopt one set of principles to govern the institution of punishment and another set to govern its concrete applications. Taking a utilitarian position on the universal commits one to taking it on the particular as well, because the latter is the realization of the former. Of course one may wish to limit the application of deterrence and security considerations by other values, but either these values are likewise grounded in social utility or they are not. If they are not, then we must abandon utilitarianism as a general justifying theory. If they are, then they lie at the mercy of the utilitarian calculus and so cannot serve as an unconditional stop to the encroachments of society. Secondly, the mixed theory of punishment is designed to extricate utilitarianism only from the charge that it justifies punishment of the innocent. It is no answer to the objection that utilitarianism fails to provide a morally acceptable justification for punishing the guilty. On the mixed theory, law-breakers are still harmed to satisfy the particular interests of others. Finally, the solution of Hart and Rawls involves a refusal to submit to rigorous standards of theoretical adequacy. The test of a theory of a natural phenomenon is the empirical one of whether it is confirmed by the observed facts. The test of a theory of a moral phenomenon is the dialectical one employed by Socrates. If an account of the phenomenon (e.g., courage, justice, punishment) logically entails, or is consistent with, consequences that involve the collapsing of the phenomenon into its opposite (e.g., punishment into arbitrary violence), then the account must be abandoned as a resting point, because it has failed to grasp the thing's specific essence. Certainly one cannot think to have rescued it by holding it aloof from its contradictions. Had Cephalus replied to Socrates in *Republic I*, "While I grant that in certain circumstances paying one's debts may work injustice, and that in those cases difference principles would have to guide us, nevertheless I maintain that justice in general is paying one's debts," he would have responded in the manner of Hart and Rawls. It might be objected, however, that the utilitarian theory of punishment offers not an account of punishment in this explanatory sense but only as a set of justifying conditions, and so is not rigorously committed to all its logical implications. But this is not the case. The utilitarian position is ultimately an answer to the question, What is punishment? It offers criteria and conditions for distinguishing authentic punishment from arbitrary violence. Explanation and justification are thus inextricably meshed: what justifies punishment is also what constitutes its essence and vice-versa. The utilitarian position is thus a full-fledged "account" of punishment, which, to be tenable, must offer non-collapsible criteria for distinguishing it from criminal force.

Given the very serious deficiencies of the utilitarian account of punishment, the impressive array of statistics adduced to question the superior deterrent force of the death penalty suddenly becomes irrelevant. Whether or not capital punishment is a uniquely effective deterrent to murder or the only sure-fire means of self-protection is beside the point if these criteria are not the ones we should be using to determine the justice of capital punishment. But not only are these questions theoretically irrelevant. Inasmuch as they orient research that determines our policy, they implicate us in immorality, because they suppose the criteria of an immoral view of punishment.

Let us then consider the chief rival to the utilitarian account of punishment and inquire as to the implications it bears for the death penalty. I refer to the retributivist account, the classic formulations of which are by Immanuel Kant and G.W.F. Hegel.[16] In contrast to utilitarianism, the retributive theory views punishment as a moral good rather than as an evil requiring justification in terms of extrinsic advantages. Whether or not punishment yields these advantages is irrelevant to its justification, because the principal end of punishment is neither to deter, nor to protect, nor to reform, but to annul wrong and thereby vindicate right. This is not to say that the retributivist is indifferent to these other goals or regards them as improper objects of policy. The criteria of reform, deterrence, and protection do have their place, but it is a very subordinate one. Specifically, they are relevant only to the secondary question of how we shall punish and not to the primary question of whether we have the right to punish. Furthermore, even within the limits of the secondary question (with which we are here concerned) they have relevance only *after* the moral issue has been settled and what remains is merely the choice, judicial or administrative, beween various morally acceptable types and measures of punishment. For the retributivist the sole criterion of just punishment as well as of a just measure of punishment is whether it annuls the wrong.

But precisely how, we may ask, does punishment annul wrong? "Can the shrieks of a wretch recall from time, which never reverses its course, deeds already accomplished?" thundered Beccaria. Obviously punishment cannot undo the deed, for the past is irrevocable. And yet by "annulment" of the wrong retributivists must mean something more than mere restitution, for restitution is not punishment. According to Hegel, punishment annuls wrong by demonstrating the non-being of the criminal principle, which might otherwise have seemed to possess validity.[17] The principle of crime is the claim to a right of the arbitrary and unrestrained freedom of the will. Seen in this way, crime is more than, as Plato thought, a sickness in the individual soul; it is a challenge to the natural moral order underpinning civilized society. This is because it denies the validity of natural law and gives this denial itself a show of validity. Punishment, then, is the denial of the denial and so the vindication or reaffirmation of natural law. It is, in other words, the objective demonstration that the criminal claim is without natural support or sanction, without reality.

Because it looks backward to a crime over and done with rather than forward to its social effects, retributive punishment has always seemed to utilitarians a relic of more barbarous times, a mere rationalization of the lust for revenge. In part this judgment reflects the utilitarian's rationalist suspicion of popular sentiment, in which he is wont to see only vulgar prejudice and blind emotionalism. Beccaria saw in the penal law of his time only "the accumulated errors of centuries," and this attitude finds its modern counterpart in the demand to keep separate the questions, Why do men punish? and What justifies punishment?[18] On the other hand, because of his commitment to natural law, the retributivist is more inclined to see in public opinion a dim perception of moral truth. And he is thus also inclined to see his task as one of providing a rational account of action already in itself moral rather than one of excogitating a criterion of morality to which society may be indifferent. To his utilitarian critic, therefore, the retributivists would reply that his punishment is not a form of revenge, but that revenge and punishment are both forms of natural retribution, punishment being alone the adequate form because emancipated from subjective interest. He would, moreover, counter with the charge that whereas utilitarianism plays havoc with our common-sense notions of penal justice, retributivism confirms them.

First of all, retributivism justifies punishment by reference to a good that is genuinely common. Punishment vindicates human rights. It thus affirms and makes objective the real rights of the criminal himself, who, in asserting a right to unlimited freedom, had undermined right as such, his own no less than others'. In receiving punishment, therefore, the criminal is subjected not to someone else's good, but to his own true good, hence to his own rational will. His autonomy and dignity are thus respected.

Secondly, retributivism accounts for the connection between punishment and desert. If punishment is the vindication of right against wrong or the denial of a denial, then it logically presupposes wrongdoing. Thus retributivism condemns punishment of the innocent. Furthermore, if what requires annulment is not the criminal deed itself but rather its claim to validity, then clearly intent or *mens rea* is saved as a determinant of wrongdoing and hence of criminal desert. Retributivism thus condemns strict liability.

Thirdly, retributivism saves the rule of proportionality respecting the relation between punishment and crime. The punishment must annul the wrong. This it does by demonstrating the self-contradictoriness—that is, the inherent nullity—of the criminal act. If I steal, I deny the existence of property even for me. My act recoils upon itself and so destroys itself. Now punishment simply brings home this contradiction, or is this contradiction objectively manifest. I assert a right to unbridled freedom; I thereby deny the existence of right, which denial punishment brings home to me by depriving me of mine. I am the author of my punishment, inasmuch as the latter is simply the inner consequence of my deed. "The Eumenides sleep," says Hegel, "but crime awakens them, and hence it is the very act of crime itself which vindicates itself."[19] Now this account of punishment explains the demand that the punishment fit the crime. Punishment must be related to the gravity of the wrong because it must signify nothing but the recoiling of the criminal's own act against itself. Only as such is punishment natural retribution and not another act of violence. It is in this sense that Hegel speaks of the criminal's "right" to punishment— that is, to be subjected only to the consequences immanent in his act and never to the alien exigencies of society.[20] To punish the offender in accordance with the principle laid down by his deeds is to honour his human subjectivity, his essential self-determination, while to fix penalties according to the requirements of deterrence or correction is to degrade him to an object and a tool. Moreover, only if the measure of punishment is derived from the deed itself does the punishment logically annul the wrong. Were a fine the penalty for murder, we would feel that murder had not been sufficiently repaid, hence not decisively invalidated. The Biblical *lex talionis* as well as the common opinion that the criminal incurs a debt that can be discharged only by suffering the appropriate punishment are prephilosophic apprehensions of punishment as nemesis.

Before considering the implications of retributivism for the death penalty, I should briefly mention a third view of punishment often linked with retributivism but in reality quite distinct from it. Variously referred to as the denunciatory, the reprobative, or the expressive view of punishment, this theory holds that punishment is the emphatic denunciation of crime by society, an authoritative expression of disapproval that both vents popular indignation towards the criminal and reaffirms the positive morality of a people. The most frequently quoted exponent of this view is Sir James Fitzjames Stephen, a Victorian judge and the author of *Liberty, Equality, Fraternity*, a contemporary attack on Mill's *On Liberty*. "It is highly desirable," wrote Stephen in 1883, "that criminals should be hated, that punishments inflicted upon them should be so contrived as to give expression to that hatred, and to justify it so far as the public provision of means for expressing and gratifying a healthy natural sentiment can justify and encourage it."[21] A somewhat more temperate version of this position was expressed by Lord Justice Denning in hearings before the Royal Commission on Capital Punishment. "The punishment inflicted for grave crimes," said Denning, "should adequately reflect the revulsion felt by the great majority of citizens for them. It is a mistake to consider the objects of punishment as being deterrent or reformative or preventive and nothing else. . . . The ultimate justification of any punishment is not that it is a deterrent, but that it is the emphatic denunciation by the community of a crime."[22] Denning thus opposed the denunciatory view of punishment to the deterrence school and saw it as implying a retentionist position on the death penalty. The vilest of crimes demanded the most emphatic of all denunciations. Nevertheless, the two positions are not as incompatible as they may seem, nor does the denunciatory theory necessarily entail retention of capital punishment. If the public condemnation of crime is held to be desirable as a salutary outlet for moral indignation and as a vindication of social norms, then the denunciatory theory is a species of utilitarianism, and the rivalry between it and the deterrence school is a rivalry between siblings. It has thus been quite a simple matter in practice for utilitarian policy-makers to assimilate the criterion of reprobative power to their own theoretical framework and to formulate alternatives to the death penalty which take into account this desideratum.

On the other hand, if the apparent opposition between the denunciatory and the deterrence schools conceals a fundamental agreement, the affinity between the former and the retributivists masks a real opposition. There is, to be sure, an element of denunciation in retributive punishment, but the author of this condemnation is nature rather than society. Punishment expresses the objective nemesis of crime, not the revulsion of men. Of course feelings of revenge, revulsion, and moral indignation enter into punishment, but they have nothing to do with its essence or justification. In retributive punishment, furthermore, denunciation is linked to a principle of fitness in the light of which one can distinguish between natural retribution and human violence. By itself the denunciatory theory contains no such principle; it sets a minimum limit to punishment but not a maximum. In short, the question as to whether a particular punishment is sufficient to denounce a crime is indeed relevant to the issue of a just measure, but it has to be developed out of a morally acceptable theory of punishment in general. The denunciatory theory is not such a one. Either it justifies punishment by reference to the social benefits of denouncing crime, in which case it is a disguised utilitarianism; or it justifies punishment as an expression, good in itself, of moral indignation, without bothering to explain why this feeling should lend moral weight to violence. We do not allow anger as an excuse, let alone a moral justification, for assault or homicide; why then should we admit it just because it is also self-righteous?

What guidance does the classic retributivist theory offer in the matter of capital punishment? It is usually assumed that retributivism logically entails retention of the death penalty for first-degree murder because of its apparent confirmation of the *lex talionis*. Certainly this connection was maintained by Kant, for whom fitness meant, quite simply, equality. The murderer must die, insists Kant, because "there is no sameness of kind between death and remaining alive even under the most miserable conditions, and consequently there is also no equality between the crime and the retribution unless the criminal is judicially condemned and put to death."[23] Theorists of punishment have had little difficulty in demolishing this conception of justice, thinking in having done so to have dealt a death-blow to retributivism. If by equality is meant equality in kind, then we must repay theft with theft, adultery with adultery, forgery with forgery, and so on. If equal value is meant, then we must punish mass murderers on a scale repugnant to our moral sense. Moreover, even if it were possible to compare qualitatively different injuries in terms of their painfulness according to an average preference scale, the commensurability of crimes and punishment would be destroyed as soon as we added considerations of *mens rea* to the balance. For although suffering can be compared with suffering, how can suffering be compared with wickedness?[24] All these and other arguments are useful and valid against the *lex talionis*, but against retributivism itself they are quite harmless. For the demand that, as the criminal has done, so shall it be done to him is merely a sensuous representation or image of the inner identity of crime and its nemesis. The conceptual likeness is represented by the popular imagination as a qualitative (or quantitative) one, and, as in the allegory of the cave, the representation is taken for the thing represented. That retributive justice has nothing to do with crude conceptions of equality was emphasized by Hegel. While agreeing that equivalence is the criterion of justice in the distribution of punishment, he pointed out that "in crime, as that which is characterized at bottom by the infinite aspect of the deed, the purely external, specific character vanishes."[25] In other words, the injury to be annulled by punishment is not the determinate injury done to the victim but the noumenal injury done to the moral order. Hence the measure of punishment is properly derived not from the qualitative or quantitative aspects of the crime (as in revenge) but from its moral significance. The seriousness of the criminal's infringement of Right must be matched by an infringement of his right of "equal" weight. Since, however, the first of these variables eludes measurement in quantitative terms, "equal weight" cannot mean more than "proportionate severity." That is to say, the principle of equivalence properly understood translates into the rather vague demand for a graded proportionality, whereby more serious crimes are punished with severer penalties. Thus retributivism does not specifically enjoin the death penalty for first-degree murder, but neither of course does it absolutely condemn it. This result is not as unenlightening as it may seem, for that capital punishment is neither a moral imperative nor a moral wrong is no trivial conclusion.

Can we, however, go further? Can retributivism offer any guide as to how to go about matching punishments to crimes? Let us immediately grant the argument that, given the impossibility of assigning values to degrees of "seriousness" or wickedness," we cannot fit penalties to offences according to the principle of proportionality literally construed. We may regard murder as a more serious crime than robbery, but as we have no way of assigning a numerical ratio to this comparison, we cannot achieve proportional equality between the relative severity of punishments and the relative seriousness of crimes. But although there is no principle of fitness by which we could establish natural correspondences between specific penalties and specific crimes, we can at least seek considerations relevant to determing the overall severity of the punishment scale taken by itself. And I want now to suggest that such considerations may be supplied by the retributivist understanding of mercy.

The charge is often heard that retributivism leaves no room for mercy, that it establishes not only the right to punish but also the positive duty to do so, so that any waiving of the right appears, on this theory, to be itself an injustice.[26] I shall argue, however, that it is not retributivism as such which leads to this conclusion so much as Kant's metaphysical assumptions, and that Hegel offers a metaphysical context for retributivism significantly different from Kant's, one that saves mercy. Furthermore, the difference between the two accounts of mercy will suggest a criterion for determining whether and for what crimes death is an appropriate punishment.

Let us first notice what Kant says about the right to pardon. In *The Metaphysical Elements of Justice* he writes:

> The right to pardon a criminal . . . is certainly the most slippery of all the rights of the sovereign. By exercising it he can demonstrate the splendor of his majesty and yet thereby wreak injustice to a high degree. With respect to crime of one subject against another, he absolutely cannot exercise this right, for in such cases exemption from punishment constitutes the greatest injustice toward his subjects. Consequently he can make use of this right to pardon only in connection with an injury committed against himself.[27]

Kant is clearly uneasy about the right to pardon; indeed, he is totally at a loss to account for it and would restrict its application to the crime of treason. This is precisely what one would expect from a philosopher who regards punishment as a categorical imperative, an unconditional duty to be performed for its own sake and irrespective of its consequences. Kant would have the whole human race perish rather than exempt a criminal from punishment, for "if legal justice perishes, then it is no longer worthwhile for men to remain alive on this earth."[28]

Now consider what Hegel says about the right to pardon.

> The right to pardon criminals arises from the sovereignty of the monarch since it is this alone which is empowered to actualize Spirit's power of making undone what has been done and wiping out a crime by forgiving and forgetting it.
>
> Pardon is the remission of punishment, but it does not annul the law. On the contrary, the law stands and the pardoned man remains a criminal as before. This annulment of punishment may take place through religion, since something done may by Spirit be made undone in Spirit. But the power to accomplish this on earth resides in the king's majesty alone and must belong solely to his self-determined decision.[29]

Here there is no uneasiness. The right of pardon exhibits the majesty, the supreme self-confidence of Spirit in its cosmic authority, and Hegel places no limitations on its exercise. How can we account for this difference within retributivism between the Kantian and Hegelian attitudes towards mercy?

The answer lies, I believe, in their different understandings of the basis of human dignity. For Kant, the individual's dignity, and thus his title to rights, rests on his sharing the common personality of the human species. This common personality—Kant's pure ego—is a human essence abstracted from the empirical personality, which is ruled by self-love and which remains as a fixed reality opposed to the rational self. Now the fixed reality or naturalness of the self-seeking person poses an ever-present challenge to the objective reality of human dignity. For Kant this dignity is inherently insecure, because it is nothing more than a subjective claim asserted over against a hostile nature, a claim that must therefore be continually vindicated through the external conquest of its antithesis. From this perspective, therefore, to grant mercy to a criminal would be to leave standing the claim of selfishness to validity and thus to leave justice unsatisfied.

For Hegel, by contrast, the basis of human dignity is not solely a human essence of personality. It is a transcendent or divine Personality of which human selfhood is a subordinate though essential element. And this divine Person is no mere abstraction which leaves evil as a fixed reality outside it. Rather it is a Spirit which itself submits to negation by evil in order that, by the annulment of evil's claim to positive reality, its sovereignty might be objectively manifest. Stated otherwise, the natural (self-centred) will is for Hegel not primary and absolute, but is rather posited within the divine ground as an appearance of something independent, in order that, by the demonstration of its independence as appearance, the divine ground of being might be vindicated as such.[30] This means that the naturalness of egoism is inherently a show, a passing phase in the self-reintegration of Spirit. Punishment is just the practical demonstration that the right of egoism is a mere show, and this constitutes its justification. But now mercy is a more perfect demonstration of this truth. For Kant, mercy was opposed to justice because it meant leaving unrefuted the claim of egoism to reality. For Hegel, mercy is a form of justice because it is itself the refutation of that claim. The passage quoted above suggests a distinction as well as a relation between divine and human forgiveness. Divine forgiveness flows from the divine nature as that which incorporates as a constituent element of itself the individual's alienation from, and return to, the divine ground. From the divine standpoint, therefore, mercy is reconciled with justice because, far from leaving the natural will in its otherness, it is the very process of positing and conquering it. Human forgiveness flows from the recognition that divine mercy robs evil of its power of being and so establishes man's dignity beyond threat of subversion.[31] Thus, not even from the human standpoint is mercy opposed to justice, for it too attests to the nullity of evil. Like punishment, mercy presupposes wrongdoing; but it affirms that the wrong is insignificant, that its claim to validity is a mock claim, that it is powerless to prevail against right. This, then, is how mercy can have a place within a retributive theory of punishment. Mercy, no less than punishment, "wipes out" the wrong, not by repaying it but by forgetting it.

Now the relevance of all this to the death penalty is simply this. If the purpose of punishment is to vindicate human rights against the pretended validity of the criminal act, it seems consequent to suppose that the severity of punishment in any epoch will depend on the perceived magnitude of the threat that crime poses to the reality of human dignity. A claim of human worth resting on the supposed sovereignty of individual personhood finds its sole objective confirmation in outward possessions. It will therefore see in any offence against property an infinite challenge to itself and punish it accordingly. Since, moreover, the absolutization of the isolated person brings the state of nature into political society, the penal system will take upon itself the enforcement of the law of private revenge, centralizing without reconstituting it. Retribution will thus take the form of the qualitative and quantitative redress of personal injury, and torture, the giving back of pain for pain, will be the paradigmatic form of punishment.[32] On the other hand, a claim of dignity resting, like Kant's, on the assumed sovereignty of a common humanity (and hence of law) will view this dignity as established independently of external things, though still challenged by a natural will now regarded as evil. Since the state of nature is here abrogated as a normative principle, the law of retaliation will be reinterpreted as the impersonal vengeance of the general will, and minutely differentiated corporal punishments will give way to the uniform abstraction of imprisonment, corresponding to the abstraction of crime as an offence against right in general. Moreover, since it is now the principle of the criminal will and not the criminal act itself that challenges the objective reality of human worth, punishments will be adjusted more subtly to the evil quality of the will, and, in particular, the death penalty will be reserved for the only crime which, by destroying the body, also destroys the person. Finally, a people confident that human dignity is no mere subjective claim pitted against an indifferent nature but an objective fact rooted in a divinely governed cosmos; a people confident, in short, that the human personality cannot be destroyed will be inclined to temper punishment with mercy. We may imagine, therefore, that there exists an ideal penal code corresponding to the highest strength of the human spirit and in which the death penalty perhaps plays no part. But like representative government, this simply best penal code is not suited to all peoples at all stages of their moral development. At any stage, the strength of the basis of self-definition will determine the scale of punishments needed to preserve and reinforce the positive morality (understood as a particular perception of natural morality) on which the social order is founded. And any attempt to impose a higher, less severe code on a people unprepared for it risks undermining the belief in a natural moral order on which depends the conviction of personal worth as well as the habit of self-restraint.

Somewhat surprisingly, therefore, retributivism issues in a counsel of pragmatism with respect to the use of the death penalty. It leads to the Montesquieuian conclusion that that penal code is best which suits the "spirit" of a people, by which is here understood the system of life-organizing beliefs regarding the foundation of human value. Not to be confused with this result is the conclusion of Beccaria, who thought that the scale of punishments ought to be relative to the level of civility of a people, the more savage requiring stronger deterrents. The question legislators must ask is not how much punishment is needed to deter potential criminals in the present state of society, but how much is needed to reassure decent men in the present state of their self-knowledge. Obviously these questions lead to different oracles. The first directs us to data on differential crime rates, the second to public opinion.

Notes

1. Mill, "Utilitarianism," in Lerner (ed.), *Essential Works of John Stuart Mill* (1961), 236.
2. Bentham, *The Principles of Morals and Legislation* (Darien, Hafner 1970), 170.
3. Sellin, "Death and Imprisonment as Deterrents to Murder," in Bedau (ed.), *The Death Penalty in America* (1964) 274–284; Sellin, "Does the Death Penalty Protect Municipal Police?" in Bedau, 284–301; Sellin, "Effect of Repeal and Reintroduction of the Death Penalty on Homicide Rates," in Bedau, 339–343. Stronger, though still not conclusive, evidence for the uniquely effective deterrent force of the death penalty is offered by Ehrlich, "The Deterrent Effect of Capital Punishment," 65 *American Economic Review* (1975), 397–417.
4. Van den Haag, "On Deterrence and the Death Penalty," 78 *Ethics* (1968), 280–287. See also Goldberg, "On Capital Punishment," 85 *Ethics* (1974) 67–74.
5. Mill, "Speech in Favor of Capital Punishment," 1868 in Ezorsky (ed.), *Philosophical Perspectives on Punishment* (1972), 271–278.
6. See, e.g., Mabbott, "Punishment," 48 *Mind* (1939); McCloskey, "A Non-utilitarian

Approach to Punishment," 8 *Inquiry* (1965); Armstrong, "The Retributivist Hits Back," 70 *Mind* (1961).

7. See, however, Hart, "Murder and the Principles of Punishment," in Hart, *Punishment and Responsibility* (1968), 54–89. My disagreements with Hart will be spelled out below.
8. For a recent retributivist argument in favor of retention see Berns, *For Capital Punishment* (1979).
9. Bentham, supra note 2, 172–175.
10. Hart, *Punishment and Responsibility*, supra note 7, 77 and passim.
11. See Wootton, *Social Science and Social Pathology* (1959), ch. 8, and *Crime and the Criminal Law* (1963) 47–57.
12. Quinton, "On Punishment," in Acton (ed.), *The Philosophy of Punishment* (1969), 55–64.
13. Rawls, "Two Concepts of Rules," in Acton, supra note 12, 105–114.
14. Hart, *Punishment and Responsibility*, supra note 2, 22–24, 44–49, 80–81, 181–183.
15. Rawls, supra note 13.
16. Kant, *The Metaphysical Elements of Justice* (trans. Ladd, 1965), 99–108; Hegel, *Hegel's Philosophy of Right* (trans. Knox, 1952), paras. 90–103.
17. *Philosophy of Right*, supra note 16, paras. 97, 99.
18. Beccaria, *On Crimes and Punishments* (trans. Paolucci, 1963), 9; Hart, *Punishment and Responsibility*, supra note 2, 74.
19. *Philosophy of Right*, supra note 16, addition to para. 101.
20. Ibid. para. 100.
21. Stephen, *A History of the Criminal Law of England* (1883), Volume 2, 81.
22. Quoted in Ezorsky, supra note 5, 250.
23. Kant, supra note 16, 102.
24. The problems in matching punishments to crimes are discussed in two recent articles. See Wertheimer, "Should the Punishment Fit the Crime?" 3 *Social Theory and Practice* (1975) 403–423; Goldman, "The Paradox of Punishment," 9 *Philosophy and Public Affairs* (1979), 42–58.
25. Hegel, supra note 16, para. 101.
26. This accusation has been repeated by Honderich, *Punishment: The Supposed Justifications* (1969), 12–13. Here we may note that it is really utilitarianism that abolishes mercy. The latter presupposes the right to punish; it is a forgoing of the right. Now if the circumstances of utility give us the right to punish, then we must do so, since to forgo the right is to satisfy the criminal's interest at the expense of the general welfare, which is to commit an injustice. On the other hand, if considerations of utility lead us to forgo punishment, this is not to show mercy, for we had no right to punish.
27. Kant, supra note 16, 107–108.
28. Ibid., 100.
29. Hegel, supra note 16, para. 282 and addition.
30. Hegel, *The Phenomenology of Mind* (trans. Baillie, 1931), 93–94, 96–99, 789–790, 806–807.
31. Hegel, *Early Theological Writings* (trans. Knox, 1971), 224–244; *Phenomenology of Mind*, supra note 30, 668–679.
32. See Foucault, *Discipline and Punish* (trans. Sheridan, 1977), 32–69.

Questions

1. In his contribution, "Is Capital Punishment a Unique Deterrent?", Ezzat Fattah provides three reasons for thinking that a utilitarian justification of capital punishment is superior to a retributivist justification. How would Brudner respond to each of these reasons?

2. Brudner argues that retributivism is the only morally defensible account of punishment. Are his arguments for this view sound?
3. What do you think Brudner's position implies for the capital punishment debate in Canada in the 1980s?
4. What is Brudner's response to the charge that retributivism leaves no room for the exercise of mercy?

Suggestions for Further Reading

Books

* Hugo Adam Bedau, *Matters of Life and Death*, ed. Tom Regan (New York: Random House, 1980). In the fifth chapter, ''Capital Punishment,'' Bedau explores the various justifications for capital punishment. (Regan's book is a useful resource for exploring the issues of abortion and euthanasia as well as capital punishment.)
* Walter Berns, *For Capital Punishment* (New York: Basic Books Inc., 1979). The various arguments against capital punishment are set out and systematically examined and rejected. The author then constructs a defence of capital punishment in a manner similar to that set out in the article included in this chapter.
* David Chandler, *Capital Punishment in Canada* (Toronto: McClelland and Stewart, 1976). The author describes his book as a study in the sociology of law. It provides a background study of the history of capital punishment in Canada. Key debates in Parliament are set out; the positions of political parties and individuals are described and analyzed and conclusions with respect to the capital punishment debate are suggested.
* *Crime and Delinquency* is a journal published by the American National Council on Crime and Deliquency. Their October 1980 issue, which is devoted to the topic of capital punishment, includes the article by Walter Berns in this chapter.

The other articles are, for the most part, opposed to the use of capital punishment. The emphasis is on research designed to establish the effect of capital punishment on the occurrence of murder. One particularly interesting article argues that there is no evidence that capital punishment deters people from committing murder; and that there is empirical evidence suggesting that capital punishment has a brutalizing effect — that is to say, that capital punishment is actually a stimulant to murder.

Government Reports

These reports should be available in the public-documents section of your university library.

* *Capital Punishment: New Material 1965–1972.* This was prepared for

the Solicitor-General of Canada in 1972 as a resource document for the public and for Parliament in the 1972 abolition debate. It is an update of a similar study done in 1965. The report, though somewhat out of date, provides an interesting summation of the arguments for and against capital punishment.

- *A Study of the Deterrent Effect of Capital Punishment with Special Reference to the Canadian Situation.* This research report was prepared by E.A. Fattah for the department of the Solicitor-General as a resource document to be used in the debate of 1972. The report is a somewhat dated but highly regarded study. Much of the information it contains is still of value.

Articles

- E.A. Fattah, ''Perceptions of Violence, Concern about Crime, Fear of Victimization and Attitudes to the Death Penalty,'' *Canadian Journal of Criminology*, Vol. 21, No. 1 (January 1979). This is an empirical survey of available information and studies of attitudes in Canada and the United States with a view to discovering relationships among the factors indicated. The findings suggest that the attitude toward the death penalty is stable, resistant to change, and not ''greatly influenced by the level of general concern about crime, or by the degree of personal fear of victimization.''
- J. Feinberg, ''The Expressive Function of Punishment,'' *The Monist.* La Salle, Illinois, Vol. 49 (1965), No. 3.

Over the past two or three decades there has developed in legal and government circles the view that denunciation of crime is a central purpose of punishment. Among punishments, capital punishment is the strongest tool of denunciation available; therefore, capital punishment is appropriate where the most emphatic form of denunciation is required — namely, murder. This view is set out and defended by Feinberg in this article, which is reprinted in *Punishment*, referred to below. For a critical assessment of Feinberg's argument see ''Crime, Punishment and Emphatic Denunciation,'' an article by me printed in the special issue, Vol. 11, No. 1 (November 1981), of *The Laurentian University Review* devoted to the topic ''Law and Justice.'' It is argued here that the justification of punishment as denunciation is at root simply a variation on the deterrence justification. For such a view to support the use of capital punishment it would have to be shown that capital punishment is a unique deterrent. Adopting a view similar to that developed by Fattah in this chapter, the argument is that it is not. The article is available from me on request.

On Punishment in General

Discussion of the merits of capital punishment inevitably leads to discussions on the justification of punishment. A good deal of worthwhile material is available on this issue. For example, the Law Reform Commission of Canada has prepared a number of reports and commissioned a number of studies. Of these the following are certainly of interest:

- *The Meaning of Guilt* (Working Paper 2). In this paper the Commission argues that punishment is justified in name of fairness to those who obey the law and in the name of self-defence.
- *Imprisonment and Release* (Working Paper 11). As the title suggests, this study examines the justification of punishment and what that justification implies for sentencing and imprisonment.
- *Studies on Sentencing* (Working Paper 3). This paper includes two studies of interest. The first, by John Hogarth (then chairman of the B.C. Police Commission), examines alternatives to our adversary system of justice with their implications for the imposition of punishment. The second (by Paul Weiler, professor of law at Osgoode Law School), "The Reform of Punishment," examines a variety of theories of punishment. A deterrence justification is rejected and a retribution model advanced.
- *Fear of Punishment*. This study was published in 1976. It contains two essays. The first, by E.A. Fattah, is "Deterrence: A Review of the Literature." The second, "Deterrent Effects of Punishment for Breaking and Entering and Theft," is an empirical analysis.
- Finally, a good source of articles written from a philosophical perspective on the subject of punishment is *Punishment*, edited by Gertrude Ezorsky and published by the State University of New York Press (1972).

Audiovisual Resources

- As is the case for the topics of Abortion and Euthanasia, the Ontario Education Authority has produced two half-hour videotapes on capital punishment. The first tape is called "The Last Hangings in Canada." It is built around an account of the last days of the last two people to be executed in Canada and includes discussions with a number of academics, American prison personnel who supervised executions, and a number of men on death row in American prisons at the time of filming. The second, "Capital Punishment," is a round-table discussion. Participants include Hugo Bedau and Walter Berns, both of whose work is included in this chapter.

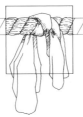

Personal Autonomy and the Problem of Mental Illness

Introduction

The freedom to act as we think is required in particular situations is central to the idea of moral autonomy. Without that freedom our capacity to make moral judgements and act on them cannot be exercised. As we have seen in earlier discussions, this principle, the autonomy principle, plays an important role in the discussion of the morality of abortion, euthanasia, and capital punishment. We have also seen that by its very nature the moral autonomy of individuals cannot be absolute. Paradoxically, the protection of individual autonomy requires placing restraints on individual autonomy.

    In this chapter we once again encounter what is sometimes described as the paradox of freedom. Normally, mental disorder is treated much as physical disorders are treated. A person who is troubled will normally seek help, perhaps of a professional nature. Sometimes, however, someone who is believed to be suffering from a serious disorder refuses all assistance. How should we respond in such cases? One response is to require that such persons be treated against their will. Coercive confinement and treatment constitute a serious threat to personal autonomy. For this reason, they generate significant moral issues.

Background Considerations

The practice of confining people who are believed to be suffering from mental disorders has a long history. What is perhaps more recent is the conviction that while forcible institutionalization may still be necessary, treatment of those with mental disorders is, in many cases, a genuine possibility. This view has been reinforced by the growth of professions and disciplines like psychiatry, psychology, sociology, and social work, which have made great strides in the treatment of mental illness. These treatments may range from counselling to psychoanalysis, from aversion therapy to the use of drugs, and from electro-convulsive therapy to brain surgery.

But the treatments available are not all equally efficacious. And some have become very controversial. That controversy has become particularly vigorous where coercive treatment is involved.

The Current Situation

Legislation which allows persons diagnosed as mentally ill to be forcibly institutionalized is commonplace, though in Canada the law varies somewhat from province to province. In Ontario, for example, under the 1978 amendments to the Mental Health Act, a person can be "hospitalized" where serious bodily harm to himself or others is anticipated. Thus, forcible confinement in mental institutions is a reality in Canada, though it is not resorted to as frequently as in some other countries—for example, the United States.

Criminal offenders, too, are sometimes subject to forcible confinement in mental institutions. There are many points in criminal proceedings where mental disorders may enter as a consideration. However, in this chapter we shall consider the problems raised by mental disorders only in the case of offenders who are serving a prison sentence.

At the present time there are provisions which allow inmates who have been diagnosed as suffering from mental disorders to be treated. Furthermore, on the advice of a committee of psychiatrists the government has proceeded to build treatment centres for dealing with such persons, a decision which has drawn a good deal of criticism.

The coercive hospitalization of prison inmates raises many of the problems which the practice of civil commitment generates. But in some respects those problems are more severe. Indeed, the very possibility of voluntary treatment in a prison setting has, in recent years, been questioned. Be that as it may, the forcible confinement and treatment of the mentally disordered inmate has also become a serious moral issue.

The Moral Dimension

When are we justified as a community in forcibly confining someone in a mental institution? Furthermore, are we ever justified in allowing persons who have been forcibly confined to be treated against their will? Answering these questions is complicated by three problems. First, recent research has thrown a good deal of doubt on the accuracy of professional diagnosis of mental illness. It is very hard to establish, for example, that diagnoses indicating dangerousness are at all reliable. These doubts have come to play a key role in the evaluation of the morality of forcible confinement and treatment.

The second problem is that normally a person who voluntarily submits to treatment for a physical disorder does so in the belief that those offering advice will be motivated by a concern for his best interests. This assumption is not always justified, of course. Both medical ethics and the law require that on occasion a doctor or a medical institution must respond to social concerns as well. Thus, certain infectious diseases must be reported whether the patient is in agreement or not. But these cases are the exception to the rule which otherwise prevails.

Where mental disorder is concerned, however, the rule just set out is often seriously compromised. This is particularly true when persons have been confined against their will. In some cases a person will be coercively institutionalized in what is thought to be his or her own interests. (The first reading in this chapter provides some good examples of situations where confinement is motivated by this kind of concern.) However, persons may also be forcibly committed because they are believed to be a serious threat to the welfare of others. Here decisions made by those involved, including medical personnel, are not motivated exclusively by a concern with the welfare of the person who is subject to confinement and treatment. Under these conditions, a person might well have grounds for being uneasy about, or suspicious of, the treatment recommended.

The final problem is that a person who has been diagnosed as mentally ill frequently encounters serious difficulty in challenging the diagnosis of his or her illness or participating in decisions relating to treatment. There are a number of reasons for this. First, it is normally assumed that one's judgement is affected by mental illness. Furthermore, resistance to institutionalization or treatment is often regarded as confirming the diagnosis. Secondly, because the interest of others frequently motivate decisions leading to forcible confinement, the wishes of the person being, or already, confined are not of paramount importance. Finally, treatment or classification procedures may require isolation. Under these conditions one's ability to communicate with others is seriously restricted.

Each of these three problems complicates assessment of the morality of the coercive confinement and treatment of the mentally ill.

The Readings

In the readings which follow we see a variety of views presented and defended. The report of the Committee on Mental Health Services in Ontario recommends procedural safeguards to protect the interests of those who face forcible commitment. Neil Boyd reviews literature which challenges both the nature and accuracy of psychiatric classification of persons designated as mentally ill, including the reliability of attempts to identify the potentially dangerous. He argues that procedures for involuntary institutionalization ought to be carefully restructured. The ethics of confining and treating the mentally disordered are examined by a council of the board of directors of the Canadian Psychiatric Association. Central to this discussion is the distinction between involuntary detention (''hospitalization'') and involuntary treatment. An extract from the Law Reform Commission report *Mental Illness and the Criminal Process* explores the purpose of sentencing and the role of compulsory treatment of offenders. Rodger Beehler examines the morality of the coercive treatment of those prone to violence, using *A Clockwork Orange* (both the novel and the film) as a catalyst for the discussion. Finally, James Woodward evaluates two conflicting approaches to justifying and limiting coercive interference with the decisions of others.

The Involuntary Patient—Civil Commitment of the Mentally Ill

Committee on Mental Health Services in Ontario

Under The Mental Health Act, Ontario in common with many other jurisdictions has adopted the following general scheme for the hospitalization of a person who is seriously ill but who will not attend hospital on a voluntary basis.

a. By order of a physician, a police officer, or a judge, the unwilling patient is compelled to *attend* a specialized psychiatric hospital for examination;
b. At the hospital an *examination* occurs, at the conclusion of which there may be a decision to commit;
c. *Internal review* of such decision occurs at those intervals when renewal certificates are required;
d. *External review* of the above steps is made by an independent board.

This scheme for commitment and review is well accepted and has operated in this province for several years. However, there has been criticism of the process of compulsory admission for assessment and of the functioning of boards of review. It has also been emphasized that commitment is equivalent to incarceration and must be resorted to only in extreme cases.

Admission to Hospital for Examination

It must be borne in mind that any legal process—and the step-by-step procedure outlined above is essentially a legal rather than a medical procedure—must be viewed as a *whole*. The keystone of the procedure under the Mental Health Act, for example, is not the initial examination; this determination is often made by a physician who is not a psychiatrist. The really important stage of the process is the comprehensive examination at the psychiatric hospital.

Thus it would be unwise to legislate protections so elaborate that it would be overly difficult to have persons taken to hospital for examination. Instead, we feel

From the 1979 report of a Legal Task Force, Ontario Council of Health, Committee on Mental Health Services in Ontario.

that the initial procedure must be sufficiently flexible so that there is a high probability that seriously ill persons will get to hospital for assessment; once they are there, the period of assessment must also be long enough to allow the job to be done.

The Mental Health Act recognizes three routes to hospital:

1. Examination by a physician and completion of a form for admission; this authorizes the conveyance of the person to hospital and his examination (s. 8).
2. Conveyance by a police officer on his own initiative to a psychiatric or health facility for examination (s. 10).
3. An order by a justice of the peace after receiving evidence; this authorizes conveyance to a psychiatric or health facility for examination (s. 9).

Examination by a Physician

In practice it will be a physician, under section 8 of the Mental Health Act, who will authorize the admission of a mentally ill person to hospital for assessment. There is no question of the appropriateness of a physician, but should para-medical personnel be given this authority as well?

There is precedent for this: In Alberta, admission can be authorized by two physicians *or* by a physician and a "therapist"; while in Great Britain, certain specifically designated social workers have the authority to refer persons to hospital for assessment. The Law Reform Commission of Manitoba has suggested the power might be given to a psychiatric nurse. It has been brought to our attention that in certain circumstances, as in remote areas, physicians are not always available, and certain other persons, such as psychiatric social workers and public health nurses, should be authorized to fulfill this function. We support this view and, therefore, recommend:

Rec. 9. THAT the section 8 application for psychiatric assessment continue to be authorized by a physician unless otherwise designated by the Mental Health Act or Regulations. This would allow a degree of flexibility which could apply to areas in which medical personnel are unavailable.

The Justice of the Peace

From the briefs submitted and the public hearings, it is clear that justice of the peace procedure (section 9) is rarely used. If it is considered necessary, however, to preserve a judicial hearing for the purpose of forcing an examination, then the procedure should be before an experienced judicial officer, such as a judge of the Provincial Court.

It is important to note that this section does not contemplate a lengthy judicial adversary proceeding with both parties represented. We feel that this intent would be clarified if it were made clear that the application could be made *ex parte*. Also, such application should be heard as a matter of urgency and *in camera*.

The Powers of the Police

It is important for police officers to have clear powers, but we do not feel that the wide discretion of a physician should be granted to a police officer; thus we would not agree that the police officer, on his own, should be given the power to intervene in any case of non-violent behaviour (e.g. a recluse). Only specific overt behaviour that would justify conveyance to a hospital for examination (such as the threat of *physical injury to self or others or physical destruction of property*) justify police intervention.

We feel that the police officer should be able to act in cases where he "has reasonable grounds to believe" such actions may occur. The present requirement that he "observe a person" would so limit a police officer that his ability to act would be restricted to those cases in which he has actually observed a person exhibiting a violent form of behaviour; it would not permit him to act in cases in which he has arrived immediately after a psychotic episode and the person has quieted down. The police officer should also be able to intervene when the person is "in a public or private place." The police have advised us that they are uncertain as to their authority if the person is in a private home.

The most difficult issue faced by the Task Force was the legal test that should be employed to support an order for examination in hospital, under section 8, 9, or 10.*

Under the 1967 Mental Health Act a patient suffering mental disorder was ordered to be hospitalized "in the interests of his own *safety* or the *safety* of others" (s. 8, 1967 Act, emphasis added).

The 1978 amendments have changed this test and now provide that a physician (or police officer or justice of the peace) may order an examination if he finds mental disorder that may result in:

a. *Serious bodily harm* to the person;
b. *Serious bodily harm* to another person; or
c. *Imminent and serious physical impairment* of the person.
(S. 8, 1978 amendments, emphasis added.)

Serious Bodily Harm.   That mentally disordered persons who are likely to seriously injure others or themselves should be taken to hospital for assessment as soon as possible is beyond debate. But what is a "serious harm"? Does a family fight that results in blows (if it resulted from mental disorder) indicate that *serious* bodily harm is likely to occur in the future?

Imminent Physical Impairment.   The 1978 amendments provide for the admission of persons who are suffering from a mental disorder that will likely result in "imminent and serious physical impairment of the person." This is meant to provide for the elderly recluse who is wasting away and may well starve. But what is "imminent" in such cases?

Harms Not Contemplated.   We are concerned that the present legislation excludes the physical destruction of property, the wasting of assets, and severe emotional

---

*The question of the criteria to be employed is not easily resolved. Ontario has followed many American states in emphasizing dangerousness; other provinces and the United Kingdom provide more flexibility in their legislation. The Manitoba Law Reform Commission (which dealt with the matter in its report February 12, 1979) was unable to reach a *unanimous* recommendation and was divided between the broad criteria of the Alberta Act (which 2 members favoured) and the new Ontario legislation (which 3 members favoured).

damage to the immediate family. The following clinical examples are a sample of cases that would not be caught by the amendments to the Mental Health Act:

1. Recently a psychiatrist committed a patient in a manic state. Within a period of 2 weeks she had bought a very expensive car, decided to remove the furniture from her home, and rented a hotel suite for herself and her two children. The largest part of the family's hard-earned savings was depleted. No rational discussion or argument would convince her that she was ill. It was only after medical treatment that she became aware that she had experienced a manic episode. During her manic phase she was not dangerous to herself or others in the usual sense.

2. A fifty-three-year-old middle-class housewife was brought to a physician by her husband. She had been a very efficient homemaker, a good wife and mother, and had had an active social life until she began to pray excessively, up to twelve, fourteen, or even sixteen hours a day. There was a dramatic change in her personality. She rarely went out to meet people but instead stayed in the house praying. Her family was tremendously concerned, watching her deteriorate for three months. She was successfully treated but, because she appeared to be completely well, she discontinued her medication. Some years later she experienced a second attack of acute schizophrenia and refused to enter the hospital again. She has not done harm to herself or others but she is harming her social life and her reputation and is causing unimaginable pain to her family. Treatment cannot be forced under the new amendment to the Mental Health Act.

3. A thirty-nine-year-old married professional man has begun to suspect his friends and his wife. He is becoming increasingly accusatory, more isolated, and is letting his home deteriorate. He is quite certain that there is a conspiracy against him. He believes that he has no alternative but to go to the United States and live there on a farm. His wife is extremely upset, and since her husband has the financial resources to go to the United States, she suspects that he in fact will leave the country. He does not appear to be physically dangerous to himself or others, but his mental condition is likely to persist if it remains untreated, and his wife and child would suffer severe emotional harm. However, he cannot be compelled under the new amendment to enter hospital and accept treatment.

The issue is described in the following terms in the reprint of the Manitoba Law Reform Commission.

> One category of patient is the patient who is causing severe emotional or mental stress, psychological harm not physical harm, to family or friends. Another is the usually "manic depressive" individual, who, by reason of his illness, has wasted and/or is continuing to waste assets to the detriment of the family. Both of these examples are major problems to which such legislation is not addressed. Examples abound of family members, especially children, friends and business associates, who suffer emotionally as a result of the strain they must endure in

day-to-day contact with the afflicted person. And, if we accept that an individual can inflict on another mental damage which is as great as physical damage, then the criteria for admission for psychiatric care should be broadened.

It is our view that admission to hospital for examination is justified in all cases in which there is mental disorder and *serious physical* or *emotional* harm may be anticipated. It must be remembered that the admission to hospital for assessment, while important in itself, is not the final decision to commit. Furthermore, with modern treatment most patients are released or become voluntary within a short time.

In addition, the legislative scheme should be relatively simple and easily understood. Section 8* seems unnecessarily complex having regard to those, usually busy, G.P.s, who will have to apply it in emergency situations.

We do not feel the present emphasis on *bodily harm* (or indeed the former emphasis on *safety*) is adequate to deal with all serious emergencies which arise from mental disorder. We feel that a simpler test that will give the practitioner greater flexibility is in the interests of the individual, the family, and society at large. In this case, we recommend a specific wording:

Rec. 12.   THAT section 8, subsection (1) of the Mental Health Act be amended to read:

"8 (1) Where a physician examines a person and the physician is of the opinion that the person is apparently suffering from a mental disorder of a nature or quality that requires immediate hospitalization in order to prevent:

a.   serious harm to the mental or physical condition of such person; or

b.   serious harm to the mental or physical condition of another person; and such person is not suitable for admission as an informal patient, the physician may make application in the prescribed form for a psychiatric assessment of the person."

---

*"8(1). Where a physician examines a person and has reasonable cause to believe that the person,

a.   has threatened or attempted or is threatening or attempting to cause bodily harm to himself;

b.   has behaved or is behaving violently towards another person or has caused or is causing another person to fear bodily harm from him; or

c.   has shown or is showing a lack of competence to care for himself; and if in addition the physician is of the opinion that the person is apparently suffering from mental disorder of a nature or quality that likely will result in,

d.   serious bodily harm to the person;

e.   serious bodily harm to another person; or

f.   imminent and serious physical impairment of the person,

the physician may make application in the prescribed form for a psychiatric assessment of the person."

Questions

1. What objections might be raised in response to the view that compulsory admission to a hospital for examination is justified "in all cases in which there is mental disorder and serious physical or emotional harm may be anticipated"?
2. How serious are those objections?
3. Does the report deal adequately with them?

Ontario's Treatment of the "Criminally Insane" and the Potentially Dangerous: The Questionable Wisdom of Procedural Reform

Neil Boyd

In the past decade the Ontario government has both proposed and enacted legislation to better protect the rights of "insane" offenders and potentially dangerous individuals.[1] Through the medium of The Mental Health Act of 1968[2] the government has set up a review process for offenders detained under warrant of the Lieutenant-Governor and set out criteria to be employed in the event of involuntary civil commitment. Newly proposed amendments to The Mental Health Act will serve to make these criteria more stringent.[3] The government, civil-rights advocates,[4] and psychiatrists[5] have all pushed in the direction of such procedural reform.

Yet such reforms may well be of little import. An analysis of criminal and civil commitment structures forms the crux of this article; this analysis suggests that procedural safeguards constitute an improper focus for the most meaningful legislative change. It is suggested that the focus of legal reform be centred upon a re-thinking of The Mental Health Act's civil commitment procedures and upon the abolition of *indeterminate* criminal commitment for "insane" offenders.

The purpose of this paper, then, is to examine critically Ontario's treatment of the "criminally insane," and as a necessary adjunct, treatment of the potentially dangerous. An initial analytic overview can be rather simply restricted to the development of two somewhat related arguments. It is first suggested that both the decisions to commit and to release the "criminally insane" are necessarily political and not medical decisions.

The initial *definition* of intolerable deviance is not a skill that falls within the psychiatrist's bag of tricks; defining dangerousness upon release similarly falls outside the realm of psychiatric "expertise." Alan Dershowitz of Harvard has noted that lawyers have virtually handed over both the civil and criminal commitment processes

---

From *Canadian Journal of Criminology*, Vol. 22. No. 2 (April 1980). By permission of the Canadian Criminal Justice Association.

to psychiatrists. He argues, "My own conversations with psychiatrists reveal wide differences in opinion over what sorts of harms justify incarceration. As one would expect, some psychiatrists are political conservatives while others are liberals; some place a greater premium on safety, others on liberty. Their opinions about which harms do . . . justify confinement probably cover the range of opinion . . . in any educated segment of the public. But they are opinions about matters which each of us is as qualified to make as they are."[6]

The second argument that will be developed is more fundamental than the first. It suggests that psychiatric distinctions between sanity and insanity fail to be either reliable or valid. The most that one can say of the "insane" is that they tend to perceive a reality that most cannot comprehend or relate to. Their perceptions of events have a tendency to show a marked deviance from societal norms. What one can say, then, is that the distinction drawn between sanity and insanity is not a particularly useful or helpful distinction.

The essentially procedural concerns of law "reformers" are consequently seen as misplaced; such concerns can serve to divert attention from careful evaluation of the wisdom of commitment and release proceedings. Psychiatric diagnoses and predictions are best understood as lacking any practical application in the legal context.[7] Ennis and Litwack argue that, ". . . there is literally no evidence that psychiatrists reliably and accurately can predict dangerous behavior. To the contrary, such predictions are wrong more often than they are right. It is inconceivable that a judgment could be considered an 'expert' judgment when it is less accurate than the flip of a coin."[8]

There is no purpose to be served in classifying individuals as "sane" and "insane" or "dangerous"—in classifying individuals as to their "treatment needs." There is no evidence to suggest that Penetang and similar facilities have any rehabilitative efficacy.[9] If the powers that be were to allow individuals convicted of serious criminal offences to *choose* their own modes of incarceration (rather than enforce a designation of "sanity" or "insanity"), the criminal system would be run a good deal less oppressively.

Penitentiary inmates who wished treatment might select institutions that offered as much; inmates who wished to do their time without the encumbrance of treatment might choose a strictly custodial setting. The lack of rehabilitative efficacy evidenced by the treatment model would demand that institutional choice not affect the length of incarceration. In the civil sphere the fact that committed individuals have not violated any criminal laws initially suggests that they should not be deprived of their liberty.

A Structural Overview: Civil vs. Criminal Commitment— The Validity of the Distinction

Federal and provincial legislation respecting the commitment of the "criminally insane" appears to be partially overlapping provincial procedures for civil commitment—and a preliminary explanation of the sense of this essentially theoretical overlap appears advisable. Where an accused person is found to have been insane during the commission of an offence, section 542(2)[10] of the Criminal Code demands that

". . . he be kept in strict custody . . . until the pleasure of the Lieutenant-Governor of the province is known."[11] At the point of the prisoner's release, or for the purposes of administrative review, Ontario's Mental Health Act[12] occupies the field. Section 31(8) of the Act provides that the advisory review board shall submit their recommendations respecting release to Cabinet; the Cabinet is ultimately responsible for release decisions. Section 31(5) of the Act provides that the case of every prisoner detained under a warrant of the Lieutenant-Governor shall be reviewed on a yearly basis.

Confusion arises when one then looks at civil commitment procedures under Ontario's Mental Health Act. The purposes of civil commitment appear to be consonant with the purposes of criminal commitment. Section 8 of the present Act provides that a patient be involuntarily hospitalized, ". . . in the interests of his own safety or the safety of others."

What empirical evidence exists shows civil commitment of this sort to be a rather unpracticable procedure. Ennis and Litwack have led empirical evidence which demonstrates that judgments that predict dangerousness are no more accurate than the flip of a coin.[13] If an individual has committed a criminal offence, the state arguably has reason for his or her confinement; if there has been no offence, the state is simply confining the innocent individual without cause.

The federal Law-Reform Commission has proposed that there is no validity in making a distinction between civil and criminal commitments.[14] More accurately perhaps, they suggest that individuals who are acquitted by reason of insanity should only be subject to civil-commitment proceedings. They argue that ". . . not guilty by reason of insanity could be made a real acquittal, subject only to a post-acquittal hearing to determine whether the individual should be civilly detained on the basis of his psychiatric dangerousness."[15] The Commission's proposal is positive in the sense that it would abolish the purposeless distinction between civil and criminal commitment but negative in the sense that it finds value in retaining essentially psychiatric distinctions between non-responsible and responsible offenders.

In any event there can be no justification for civil commitment that is not founded upon the commission of a serious criminal offence. Jackson has noted that the purposes of criminal commitment are essentially equivalent to the state interests justifying civil commitment—the protection of society and individual rehabilitation.[16] Given these purposes, civil commitment is no more than preventive detention—a practice which at least the rhetoric of the "free" North American society is generally not willing to uphold. Though the benevolent talk of psychiatric "helping" appears to make the practice palatable, the empirical evidence of the sense of such detention is very disconcerting. Rappeport and Lassen found that the intervention of psychiatric commitment did not affect patient arrest rates.[17] They concluded from their study of almost, 3,000 psychiatric patients, "Comparison of pre- and post-hospitalization arrest rates were made and revealed no differences . . . ."[18]

I think it fair to say, then, that analysis of the sense of criminal commitment must move beyond the confines of section 16 of the Criminal Code. "Insanity" at the time of the offence is not a valid commitment criterion. It is more properly the sense of *civil* commitment criteria which must be examined. It is in this context that the sense of procedural reforms are most appropriately evaluated.

Ontario's Mental Health Act: Recent Reform

In June of 1964 Ontario's Minister of Health directed that a comprehensive study of provincial mental-health legislation be undertaken. The Honourable M.B. Dymond stated that the purpose of the study was ". . . to assess the laws and practices with respect to the management of the mentally disordered as a basis for recommendations for new mental health legislation better suited to the needs of Ontario."[19]

The present Mental Hospitals Act had been largely untouched in thirty years.[20] The Act set out rather broadly stated prerequisites to involuntary civil commitment—the individual need only be found "mentally ill or mentally defective" to justify commitment.[21]

After two years of work the findings of the 1964 study project were presented to government. These findings spawned Ontario's Mental Health Act of 1968. On introducing The Mental Health Act into the Legislative Assembly M.B. Dymond outlined the principles and objectives which the new legislation sought to satisfy. He noted that the Act would ". . . place, wherever possible, the prevention, treatment and rehabilitation for mental disorder on the same basis as that for other illnesses."[22] He added later in his delivery, "Under the new act admission procedures are streamlined, and treatment of mental disorder will, wherever possible, be on a basis parallel to that for physical illness."[23] There was to be thoroughgoing transplantation of the medical model; psychiatrists were believed to have the expertise necessary to treat behavioural problems. The surgeon was to cut out the appendix; the psychiatrist was to cut out the paranoia.

The 1970 Report of the Committee on the Healing Arts in Ontario heaped praise on the provincial Mental Health Act.[24] The report noted that the Act was ". . . one of the foremost pieces of mental health legislation in the world." The Report claimed that the Act was essentially ". . . aimed at removing any stigma attached to mental illness and at providing for the care and treatment of the mentally ill on a basis that is equal to that for physical illness."[25]

The apparently benevolent rhetoric masked a rather unhappy reality. There was no need for involuntary commitment procedures to be different from medical-commitment procedures; it was seemingly more important for the "mentally sick" individual to receive the benefits of treatment. Although the standard of commitment was now more stringent (i.e., safety of the individual), section 8 of the Act allowed a single physician to involuntarily commit a patient.

And yet even the "safety" standard was not made operationally explicit—much was left to individual judgment in the criterion, ". . . in the interests of his own safety or the safety of others." As Ingber has noted, "As long as commitment is viewed as beneficial to the individual, there is limited incentive to enunciate carefully the criteria for the degree, kind and certainty of danger necessary to justify the procedure."[26] A great deal of discretionary decision-making was handed then to Ontario physicians—on the erroneous assumption of psychiatric expertise.

Opposition spokesmen of the day concerned themselves with the procedural sense of The Mental Health Act. Stephen Lewis questioned the applicability of review proceedings in the event of an involuntary committal;[27] James Renwick questioned the review procedures open to an individual detained under a warrant of the Lieutenant-

Governor.[28] There was no debate as to the sense of either civil or criminal commitment or release.

Late in December of 1977 the Honourable Dennis Timbrell introduced Bill 124, "An Act to Amend The Mental Health Act," [29] into the Legislative Assembly. The Minister of Health noted that while there had been no major changes in the given legislation in 10 years, ". . . there have been significant changes in the philosophy of the delivery of mental health services."[30] Yet a careful reading of the Minister's speech gives no discernible indication of philosophical change. It is not clear as to why there is to be a slight tightening of the criteria for civil commitment.

The Minister notes of civil commitment that a ". . . lack of legislative clarification has resulted in some confusion."[31] It does not appear that the present system of commitment has been malfunctioning or operating against the best interests of the involuntary psychiatric patient—there is simply some confusion.

Mr. Timbrell goes on to say, "It is important to note that to complete a certificate of involuntary admission a physician other than the one who completed the application must now conduct the assessment. When the certificate of involuntary admission is completed, the subject will now have an immediate right of appeal to a regional review board."[32] Implicit in these remarks is the notion that present commitment proceedings are more flexible than they ought to be. There is again no suggestion of impropriety. The remarks seem rather to simply reflect that the good will of the Ontario government is operative—here is evidence of a keen concern for the civil liberties of Ontario residents.

The legislative changes respecting civil commitment are in fact probably well understood as little more than this sort of good public relations.

The Minister noted in his introduction of Bill 124 that, ". . . the ambiguous nature of the word 'safety' gives physicians necessary latitude in judgment [respecting committal]."[33] A meeting of government hospital administrators and psychiatrists at that time expressed concern over a lack of clarity in the standards required for civil commitment. They were not clear as to what the term "safety" encompassed. In the legislature the Minister noted that the word "safety" required greater precision. But there seemed to be no fundamental change in philosophy implicit in such an admission. Physicians were still to be given great latitude in their efforts to determine whether society demands protection from the given individual—and these are efforts that empirical evidence has shown to be little more than guesswork.

The net effect of the legislative changes will be to make physicians aware that the "safety" of society is jeopardized where the given individual will cause "serious bodily harm" to himself or others.[35] The physician is asked to ensure that when he civilly commits an individual he does so only on the basis of concern for that individual's *physical* safety. One might hope that physicians are not attempting to do otherwise at the present time.

A more detailed analysis of the Bill's involuntary commitment criteria, however, reveals its more substantial weaknesses. Section 5(1)(c) of the Bill sets out the criteria for involuntary commitment. The attending physician is to involuntarily admit a patient if he or she is ". . . of the opinion both that the person is suffering from mental disorder of a nature or quality that likely will result in, (i) serious bodily harm to the person, (ii) serious bodily harm to another person, or (iii) imminent and serious physical impairment of the person, unless the person remains in the custody of a psychiatric facility and that the person is not suitable for admission as an informal patient."[36]

The physician is being asked to predict the dangerousness, be it to self or others, of the given patient. In so doing the physician is making a legal or political decision and not a medical decision. There is no universally agreed upon medical standard of "dangerousness"; The Mental Health Act allows physicians to impose their own notions about what kinds of expected or potential behaviours may be classified as "dangerous." Dershowitz has said of the physician involved in this process, "He may—in his own mind—be defining 'likely' [to assault] to mean anything from virtual certainty to slightly above chance. And his definition will not be a reflection of any expertise but again of his own personal preference for safety or liberty."[37] It is simply false to formulate the concept of dangerousness in medical terms.

Potentially more troublesome here is the fact that psychiatrists have no demonstrated skills with respect to predictions of dangerousness. Shah has noted, "The studies which are available indicate quite clearly and consistently that psychiatrists and other clinicians uniformly over-predict dangerousness, i.e., the great majority of the persons predicted to be dangerous turn out to be 'false positives' (persons predicted as likely to be dangerous but who in fact will *not* display such behavior)."[38]

Wenk et al. attempted to predict violent offenders from a sample of over 4,000 California Youth Authority wards.[39] They used elaborate case histories, measures of mental and emotional functioning and professional prognoses to make their predictions. The study was seeking ". . . to develop a classification device for estimating assaultive potential with sufficient accuracy to be useful in correctional program decisions."[40] The researchers concluded that their predictions of violence ". . . failed to yield an operationally practical prediction instrument that would warrant implementation in actual preventive or correctional practice."[41] More recent empirical work has produced similar findings.[41a]

Albert Rosen has noted a similar lack of predictive ability with respect to individuals labelled as suicidal.[42] The evidence that Rosen presents leads him to state that, ". . . very few of those patients who are severely depressed or who express suicide thoughts or threats actually commit suicide . . . data from such patients should not arbitrarily be grouped under the class term 'suicidal.' "[43]

In the Canadian context Klein has attacked "dangerous offender" legislation as being no more than "forensic folklore."[44] He argues that empirical evidence reveals predictions of dangerousness as little more than guesswork.

In a broader vein, Sawyer has noted that clinical (i.e., psychiatric) predictions of future behaviour tend to be less accurate than statistical predictions. His compilation of 45 empirical studies dealing with prediction of behaviour indirectly suggests that psychiatrists have no individual expertise to bring to the civil-commitment process.[45]

A study commissioned by the Canadian Civil Liberties Association revealed that over 70 percent of 200 Ontario involuntary civil-commitment certificates failed to satisfy the requirements of The Mental Health Act.[46] The two senior counsel who conducted the study found that over 140 of the certificates contained "serious legal defects." These certificates were ". . . virtually devoid of any suggestion that 'safety' was a factor in the commitment decision."[47] Ironically enough, though, this finding should not be surprising to those well acquainted with the empirical literature. The impossibility of the "safety" standard can make necessary its circumvention.

What should also be noted at this point is section 5(1)(iii) of the proposed amendment of The Mental Health Act. The section dictates involuntary commitment where ". . . the person is suffering from mental disorder . . . that likely will result in . . . (iii) imminent and serious physical impairment of the person." If this section was simply designed to encompass would-be dangerous offenders, it appears redundant. Sections 5(c)(i) and (ii) speak of the likelihood of "serious bodily harm" directed toward the self (5[1][c][i]), and toward others (5[1][c][ii]).

Section 5(1)(c)(iii) would appear to be rather a hangover from the habituate provisions of the forementioned Mental Hospitals Act. Section 51 of that Act provided that "A person . . . suffering from the effects of alcohol or drugs may be admitted . . . and detained . . . for a period not to exceed thirty days on the certificates of two medical practitioners. . . ." The "safety of the individual" standard in the present Mental Health Act would appear to encompass the possibility of habituate patients, and section 5(1)(c)(iii) of the proposed amendment to The Mental Health Act simply restates this old criterion of commitment, albeit in a different form.

In sum, both Bill 124 and its predecessor, The Mental Health Act, would appear to make provisions for civil proceedings that cannot be justified on any rational basis. Involuntary civil commitment need not follow any criminal offence—there can be no arguments of deterrent value. More importantly, the criteria for involuntary commitment cannot be *reliably* applied and in no way accomplish what they purport to accomplish. Shah has noted of this apparent perplexity, "Even though lay people might well continue to maintain a stereotyped and inaccurate view of the mentally ill as more likely to be dangerous, surely one would expect the *experts* to be more familiar with the relevant empirical evidence . . . given the available literature on the topic of prediction of rare events, one would expect the *experts* to be aware of the technical limitations and other evidence."[48]

What seems most likely is that the experts are actually quite familiar with the relevant theoretical and empirical literature. The psychiatrists simply find themselves placed in a role which demands of them that they ". . . assist in the labelling and social control of persons who are perceived by the community as disturbing, discomforting and threatening."[49] In this context it is worth noting the opposition that Ontario psychiatrists are expressing to the recent proposed amendments to The Mental Health Act. They are worried that they cannot meet the predictive standard that the Act sets out[50]—a likelihood of "serious bodily harm." The Ministry of Health has been trying to assure the psychiatrists that false predictions would simply be ". . . mistakes of judgment for which they could not be held responsible."[51]

Shah has noted further that the role of "skilled expert" ". . . requires (of psychiatrists) that they not jeopardize this ascribed expertise—and thus the associated status, prestige and power."[52] Finally Shah notes, "It is not surprising that psychiatrists and other experts turn to *medical* decision rules which state: When in doubt, suspect illness; When in doubt, suspect dangerousness."[53] Such cautious suspicion is the stuff of medical training.

Yet this cautious suspicion and its consequent inaccuracy is only the tip of the iceberg. What now appears troubling is that individuals criminally committed to Penetang and civilly committed elsewhere cannot be shown to have been helped in any meaningful way by "treatment." The empirical evidence suggests that the coerced rehabilitation employed at Penetang and elsewhere is little more than an empty promise.

The Mythology of Rehabilitative Efficacy and Psychiatric Diagnosis

The literature from Penetang speaks of Oak Ridge as a "therapeutic community." One particular pamphlet notes, "Every Oak Ridge resident acquired the right to live here by demonstrating insufficient adaptability to the community or, to put it another way, by demonstrating an inability to interact in ways most people would consider appropriate. With these considerations, it seemed reasonable to organize the Oak Ridge residents into communities especially geared for coping with problems in interacting or in community involvement."[54] Another paper notes that the patient at Penetang is the principal architect of recovery and that ". . . the most helpful experiences are acts of genuine communication—direct encounters."[55]

The rhetoric is appealing. Few of us would dispute the value of an empathetic, caring community; such a community is sought by both the "mentally ill" and the "mentally healthy." What is really contentious here is a claim more central to the enterprise. Barker notes, "The use of force is legitimate in treating patients for illnesses which they do not recognize, in settings where they will be incarcerated until they change."[56] It is the notion of *coerced* rehabilitation that is difficult for the reader to swallow here.

Though most Oak Ridge patients have committed criminal offences prior to admission, the sense of their involuntary commitment to *treatment* programs demands justification. If one accepts the notion that the deprivation of a convict's liberty exists for the purpose of specific and general deterrence, one should clearly question the point of coerced treatment. Such treatment would only seem to be appropriate if it can be shown to have a corrective efficacy that is superior to that of the strictly custodial setting. Treatment that demonstrates no greater corrective efficacy than would simply incapacitation of the accused is best described as costly and purposeless punishment. The imposition of such treatment is not consistent with the purposes of the criminal sanction. It is incumbent upon those who proffer coerced treatment to demonstrate its superior corrective efficacy.

The empirical evidence on the rehabilitative efficacy of Penetang is initially convincing. Justice Haines enthusiastically noted a recidivism rate of nine percent for individuals found either unfit to stand trial or detained under a warrant of the Lieutenant-Governor[57]—the rate is staggeringly low when contrasted with penitentiary recidivism.[58] But the nine percent figure is deceptive, to say the least. As the study in question states, "release" is defined not as release to the community but simply as release from Oak Ridge. Quinsey *et al.* note, "Most patients are released from Oak Ridge to other institutions and not returned directly to the 'street.' "[59] The low recidivism rate becomes less surprising.

A second factor worthy of consideration is the age of the patients upon release. Quinsey *et al.* note, ". . . the patients were relatively old when released, and the literature indicates that criminal recidivism decreases with age."[60] Finally, Quinsey *et al.* found that the population they were studying tended to be ". . . non-criminals who committed a violent offence—usually against a member of their own family."[61] In this respect the subject pool differs markedly from that of the penitentiary and again the literature would indicate substantially lower recidivism rates for the Penetang population.[62]

In sum, the low recidivism rate so enthusiastically quoted by Justice Haines is little more than misleading. The definition of "release" is suspect; the population at Oak Ridge is in few ways comparable to a penitentiary population. The data presented offers no demonstration of therapeutic efficacy. In a recent paper Quinsey and Boyd summarize the variables that have been found to predict recidivism among inmates detained under warrant of the Lieutenant-Governor—age on release, diagnosis of personality disorder and committal for offences against persons.[63] They note that these variables have been used to predict recidivism among other incarcerates and ". . . can, therefore, be used with some confidence."[64] Quinsey and Boyd fail to note that this finding speaks ill of the Oak Ridge "treatment" program. What tends to predict success are variables that are totally unrelated to the daily operations of the institution. The "treatment" program appears to have no predictive import. What appears to be of value are characteristics that inmates possessed prior to incarceration.

At this juncture then, both the therapeutic efficacy of Oak Ridge and the sense of the institution's release proceedings have been impugned. The "treatment" program has little justification; the Ontario Cabinet cannot, statutory appearances to the contrary, predict dangerousness. But what is yet to be empirically developed is the fact that even the initial civil or criminal committal is founded upon a mythology of expertise. Indeed, the fact that psychiatrists can neither reliably nor validly diagnose "mental illness" can be seen as a final blow to their badly tarnished credibility. It will be seen that the criminal-court psychiatrist has no expertise to contribute to the legal determination of individual accountability.

The psychiatrist who ventures into the criminal court is not asked to judge the ultimate issue—the sanity of the accused. He is rather to give the court some understanding of the mental state of the accused at the time of the offence. Though his status as an expert assumes that his psychiatric diagnosis is both reliable and valid, neither can be seen to be true.

Ash asked three psychiatrists whether given patients fit into one of the following categories of psychopathology—mental deficiency, character disorder, psychosis, neurosis, normal.[65] He found that the trio of psychiatrists agreed less than fifty percent of the time—that even the reliability of these very *broad* diagnostic categories was suspect. And Ennis and Litwack suggest that additional skepticism may be in order here: "Studies of reliability conducted under such controlled conditions produce higher rates of diagnostic reliability than are likely to be obtained in actual psychiatric practice. There the lack of controls means that such factors as inexperience . . . psychiatrists, particularized interviewing techniques and conditions, definitional ambiguities and biases, semantic differences, and so on all contribute to lower diagnostic reliability."[66]

The *validity* of psychiatric diagnoses of mental illness is similarly suspect. Though studies which indicate such diagnoses to be of limited reliability would strongly suggest a complementary lack of diagnostic validity, other empirical literature also prompts a similar conclusion. Ennis and Litwack noted that Frank, after an extensive review of such literature, concluded, ". . . save for perhaps the grossest kind of psychotic behavior, there were few if any correlations between diagnoses and patterns of behavior . . . these data seem to point to the lack of validity of this mode of classifying behavior, and question the usefulness of diagnosis."[67]

It is now instructive to look at the recent decision of the Ontario Court of Appeal in R. vs. Rabey[68]—the sense of the empirical evidence is confirmed. A Dr. Orchard testified that the respondent entered into a complete dissociative state—not a mental illness and not a "disease of the mind." A Dr. Rowsell testified that he believed the respondent did not go into a dissociative state—but that had he gone into such a state it would have been ". . . by definition, a subdivision of hysterical neurosis, which is definite mental illness."[69]

Yet his lack of diagnostic reliability is overshadowed by Rowsell's presumptuous treatment prescription. Given absolutely no empirical evidence that could support claims of therapeutic efficacy, Rowsell nevertheless suggested that ". . . the respondent still had a psychiatric problem for which he required treatment to help him to face up to what had occurred."[70] Rowsell suggested that ". . . the treatment would take six months to a year, and could be undertaken on an out-patient basis."[71]

The North American legal system has maintained a reliance on psychiatric testimony that is difficult to justify. Even those psychiatrists who admit that their predictions of mental illness and consequent judgments of offender dangerousness simply err on the side of societal safety cannot find any grounds for such caution. The criminally committed offender has been acquitted—he is innocent; the civilly committed individual is similarly innocent. The overly cautious detention of these individuals does great damage to a most fundamental principle of criminal law—innocent until proven guilty. As Ennis and Litwack note, ". . . even under controlled conditions, at least 60 to 70 percent of the people whom psychiatrists judge to be dangerous may, in fact, be harmless."[72] The credo that is operative in present release proceedings would appear to be most aptly stated: Better that three "guilty" men be confined than that seven "innocent" men go free. The mythology of there being a valid and reliable distinction between the insane and the non-insane offender has forced the legal system to admit to this unhappy state of affairs. One suspects that in fact considerations of retribution and general deterrence have more to do with the confinement of the mentally disordered offender than do considerations of the "innocent's" dangerousness.

The Wisdom of Procedural Concerns

Law reformers involved in the mental health field have been urging that there be better procedural safeguards afforded involuntary psychiatric patients. Toronto lawyers have noted that a lack of access to psychiatric files has effectively precluded a judicial hearing on the release of criminally committed patients.[73] Amendments to Ontario's Mental Health Act will slightly tighten civil commitment criteria.

But the sense of such procedural reforms is elusive. Though greater access to and control of psychiatric "expertise" may ultimately expose the problematic nature of commitment practices, there is an implicit approval of present procedures in such reform. There will continue to be involuntary civil commitment.

The empirical evidence that can be assembled on the effect of procedural reform suggests a number of possibilities as to the present mechanics of the civil commitment process (see Table 1).[74]

The explanation of the data that is most complementary to procedural reform views the passage of The Mental Health Act as facilitating a reduction in involuntary admissions. In 1968, the number of involuntary admissions was almost halved, falling from just over 13,000 to just over 7,000. In ten years involuntary admissions to provincial psychiatric facilities have fallen from almost 20,000 to just over 3,000. One suspects that many lawyers, civil-rights advocates and psychiatrists have knowingly or inadvertently aided and abetted the creation of this statistic. Psychiatrists have become more reluctant to admit involuntary psychiatric patients—and this reluctance is expressed in the statistics that we have.

But also of importance is the statistic that documents a rise in voluntary admissions within this ten-year period. In 1968 a drop of 6,000 in involuntary admissions was accompanied by a rise of 5,000 in voluntary admissions. A Ministry of Health official has noted that individuals who in the past might have been admitted involuntarily are now being admitted voluntarily. The official notes that in some instances psychiatrists impress upon patients the benefits of voluntary admission—the individual is given the "choice" of voluntary or involuntary admission. If this practice is widespread, it would suggest that psychiatrists are simply circumventing the standards of involuntary commitment through inappropriate coercive means. The tenfold increase in voluntary admissions is difficult to understand—the past decade has not seen such a population explosion—and one might reasonably doubt that ten times as many Ontarians are seeking *hospitalization* for psychiatric reasons.

What should also be considered in explication of these statistics is the role of the economy. The past decade has seen a tightening of the public purse and growing

Table 1

Civil Admissions to Provincial Psychiatric Facilities in Ontario (1964 to 1973)

	Criterion of Involuntary Admission	Involuntary	Voluntary
1964	Two Physicians' Certificates	19,822	1,412
1965	Two Physicians' Certificates	18,911	1,415
1966	Two Physicians' Certificates	17,931	1,480
1967	Two Physicians' Certificates	13,033	4,644
1968*	(a) Two Physicians' Certificates		
	(b) "Safety" (s.8, M.H.A.)	7,062	9,731
1969	"Safety" (s.8, M.H.A.)	5,822	10,122
1970	"Safety" (s.8, M.H.A.)	4,974	10,072
1971	"Safety" (s.8, M.H.A.)	4,949	10,294
1972	"Safety" (s.8, M.H.A.)	3,914	10,905
1973	"Safety" (s.8, M.H.A.)	3,011	11,193

*The Mental Health Act came into force June 1, 1968.

concern over perceived abuses in government spending. The reduction of the psychiatric population (both voluntary and involuntary admissions) may in some ways be a response to such conern.

In the context of the voluntary-involuntary distinction the role of economics should also be considered. The provincial psychiatric facilities receive operating grants that are contingent upon the amount of business transacted.[75] There are substantial economic pressures to keep the enterprise functioning at an acceptable level. Any large-scale reduction in services might entail institutional cut-backs and possible lay-offs. A substantial rerouting of involuntary patients into the voluntary stream would tend to at least forestall this possibility.

Whatever the explanation of the mechanics of civil commitment, what remains clear is that procedural reforms do not address the process itself. Any *actual* reduction in involuntary admission, while in many respects desirable, might have the effect of diverting attention from the proceedings themselves. The proceedings would have been revamped to meet ". . . significant changes in the philosophy of the delivery of mental health services."[76]

Ingber has noted that North American society, rather than squarely confronting the ideological problem of commitment, has passed it on to the doctors.[77] Procedural reforms to date have allowed civil commitment to remain a medical decision rather than become the legal and political decision that it properly is. Procedural reforms have also allowed the social control that Oak Ridge embodies to continue its masquerade as therapeutic efficacy. Though Oak Ridge is presently constituted as little more than a form of preventive detention and though civil commitment is essentially a form of preventive detention, the procedural reformers seem oblivious. The Canadian Civil Liberties Association, in making submissions respecting Ontario's Mental Health Act, suggested a number of procedural safeguards.[78] Though they quietly questioned the sense of civil commitment,[79] the Association opted for tighter controls on the actual proceedings. Gary Draper has urged in a recent Alberta Law Review article that ". . . certain of the legal procedures for involuntary confinement for mental disorder are in need of change."[80] Daniel Share has urged that a heavy burden of proof be placed upon the civil commitment process.[81]

The potential attraction of these procedural proposals and others takes us back to the points that were made at the outset and developed in the course of the paper. First, civil commitment is entirely a legal and political decision that has been taken over by the psychiatric profession. Second, and more important, there is no justification for civil commitment that is predicated upon a prediction of dangerousness. Involuntary civil commitment that is predicated upon a demonstrated inability to care for oneself is properly and humanely addressed by The Mental Incompetency Act of Ontario.[82] But involuntary commitment on the basis of presumed dangerousness is a form of preventive detention with an absence of predictive accuracy.

Decisions respecting criminal commitment and release are similarly legal and political decisions that can be strongly influenced by psychiatric judgment. Here again, while there is the danger that psychiatric judgment will totally usurp legal judgment in such circumstances, the danger is all the more profound when one is made aware of the lack of psychiatric expertise respecting criminal commitment.

The future of procedural reform appears bleak. This paper has attempted to demonstrate that the proposed 1977 amendment to The Mental Health Act is not necessarily understood as a meaningful "reform."

Procedural reform of the future may similarly lack meaning. It will probably centre upon a transfer of the civil commitment process from the hands of psychiatrists to the hands of the judiciary—a potentially valuable reform, but one that still fails to come to terms with the social utility of the commitment process, itself.

A restrictive judicial interpretation of civil commitment can be circumvented by a rerouting of more patients into the voluntary stream—as discussed above, a change already in progress. Second, restrictive judicial interpretation may well not materialize to the extent desired.

Virginia Hiday's empirical study of judicial commitment in North Carolina reveals that in 37 percent of *contested* cases neither judge nor counsel pressed for evidence of imminent danger.[83] Hiday also found that over 20 percent of all judicial commitment were made ". . . without a showing, by a preponderance of the evidence, that there was imminent danger due to mental illness."

Hiday's data, while also supportive of some judicial independence of psychiatric opinion, nevertheless points to an irrational reliance on psychiatric expertise.

The point being made here, then, is that reform is simply not enough. The social utility of the commitment process, itself, must be critically appraised. There is no doubt that some among us perceive reality in ways that are difficult to comprehend. Yet the civil commitment process does not seem to recognize this. It does not presuppose any attempt at mutual understanding. It is founded on control—on a hierarchy of power. It is unfortunately a kind of control—a hierarchy of power—that appears to lack social utility.

Notes

1. The Mental Health Act, *infra*, was enacted in 1968; "An Amendment to the Act," *infra*, was proposed in 1977.
2. The Mental Health Act, R.S.O. 1970, Chap. 269.
3. "An Act to Amend The Mental Health Act," Bill 124, 31st Parliament, 1st Session. Queen's Printer, Toronto, 1977 (s. 5).
4. Canadian Civil Liberties Association, *Submissions to the Honourable Dennis Timbrell re Involuntary Civil Commitment*, Toronto, March 28, 1977.
5. A meeting of government hospital administrators and psychiatrists in the fall of 1976 revealed that some Ontario psychiatrists were concerned about the lack of precision in the term "safety." (Reported by G. Sharpe, counsel with the Ministry of Health, in a telephone conversation, May, 1978.)
6. Dershowitz, A., "Psychiatry in the Legal Process: A Knife that Cuts Both Ways," *51 Judicature*, No. 10, 1968.
7. Ennis, B.J. and Litwack, T.R., "Psychiatry and the Presumption of Expertise: Flipping Coins in the Courtroom," *62 California Law Review 693*.
8. *Ibid.*, p. 737.
9. This evidence will be led under the heading, *The Mythology of Rehabilitative Efficacy and Psychiatric Diagnosis*.
10. The Criminal Code, R.S.C. 1970, Chap. C-34, s. 542.
11. *Ibid.*, s. 542(2).
12. The Mental Health Act, *supra*, note 2.
13. Ennis and Litwack, *supra*, note 7.

14. Law Reform Commission of Canada, *Report on Mental Disorder in the Criminal Process*, Ottawa.
15. *Ibid.*, p. 4.
16. Jackson, S.K., "Commitment and Release Standards and Procedures: Uniform Treatment for the Mentally Ill," *41 University of Chicago Law Review* 825 (1974).
17. Rappeport, J.R. and Lassen, G., "Dangerousness–Arrest Rate Comparisons of Discharged Patients and the General Population," *121 American Journal of Psychiatry* 766 (1965).
18. *Ibid.*, p. 780.
19. Debates, Legislative Assembly of Ontario, May 19, 1967, p. 3637.
20. The Mental Hospitals Act, R.S.O. 1960, Chap. 236.
21. *Ibid.*, s. 23(2). See also ss. 22–25.
22. Debates, *supra*, note 19, p. 3638.
23. *Ibid.*, p. 3638.
24. Report of the Committee on the Healing Arts, Ontario, Queen's Printer, Toronto, 1970.
25. *Ibid.*, Part 111, p. 141.
26. Ingber, S., "Procedure, Ceremony and Rhetoric: The Minimization of Ideological Conflict in Deviance Control," *56 Boston University Law Review* 266.
27. Debates, Legislative Assembly of Ontario, June 12, 1967, pp. 4577–4578.
28. *Ibid.*, p. 4578.
29. "An Act to Amend The Mental Health Act," *supra*, note 3.
30. Debates, Legislative Assembly of Ontario, December 13, 1977, p. 2923.
31. *Ibid.*, 2923.
32. *Ibid.*
33. *Ibid.*
34. See note 5, *supra*.
35. "An Act to Amend The Mental Health Act," *supra*, note 3, section 5.
36. *Ibid.*, section 5.
37. Dershowitz, *supra*, note 6, p. 376.
38. Shah, S.A., "Some Interactions of Law and Mental Health in the Handling of Social Deviance," *23 Catholic University Law Review* 674, p. 705.
39. Wenk, E.A. *et al.*, "Can Violence Be Predicted," *18 Crime and Delinquency* 393 (1972).
40. *Ibid.*, p. 393.
41. *Ibid.*
41a. See Schlesinger, S.E., "The Prediction of Dangerousness in Juveniles," *24 Crime and Delinquency* 40 (1978). For a most recent concise statement on clinical prediction of dangerousness see Roesch, R., "Letter to the Editor," *24 Crime and Delinquency* 486 (1978).
42. Rosen, A., "Detection of Suicidal Patients: An Example of Some Limitations in the Prediction of Infrequent Events," *18 Journal of Consulting Psychology* 397 (1954).
43. *Ibid.*, p. 397.
44. Klein, J.F., "Dangerous Offender Legislation: 'Forensic Folklore' Revisited," *18 Canadian Journal of Criminology and Corrections* 109.
45. Sawyer, J., "Measurement and Prediction, Clinical and Statistical," *66 Psychological Bulletin* 178 (1966).
46. Canadian Civil Liberties Association, *supra*, note 4.
47. *Ibid.*, p. 5.
48. Shah, S.A., *supra*, note 38, p. 706.
49. *Ibid.*, p. 710.
50. Telephone conversation with G. Sharpe, counsel with the Ministry of Health, May, 1978.
51. *Ibid.*
52. Shah, S.A. *supra*, note 38, p. 710.
53. *Ibid.*, p. 710.
54. Emond, B. *et al.*, *Systems For Decision-Making in Oak Ridge Community Organizations*, Oak Ridge, Penetanguishene, Ontario.

55. Barker, E.T. and Mason, M.H., "Buber Behind Bars," *13 Canadian Psychiatric Association Journal* 61 (1968), p. 71.
56. *Ibid.*
57. Personal conversations with Justice Haines, November, 1977.
58. Waller, I., *Men Released from Prison.* University of Toronto, University of Toronto Press, 1974.
59. Quinsey, V.L. *et al.*, "Released Oak Ridge Patients: A Follow-Up Study of Review Board Discharges," *15 British Journal of Criminology* 264 (1975), p. 264.
60. Quinsey, V.L. *et al.*, "A Follow-Up of Patients Found 'Unfit to Stand Trial' or 'Not Guilty' Because of Insanity," *20 Canadian Psychiatric Association Journal* 461 (1975), p. 466.
61. *Ibid.*
62. Waller, I., *supra*, note 58.
63. Quinsey, V.L. and Boyd, B.A., "An Assessment of the Characteristics and Dangerousness of Patients Held on Warrants of the Lieutenant-Governor," *4 Crime and Justice* 268 (1977).
64. *Ibid.*, p. 274.
65. Ash, "The Reliability of Psychiatric Diagnosis," *44 Journal of Abnormal and Social Psychology* 272 (1949).
66. Ennis and Litwack, *supra*, note 7, p. 703–704.
67. *Ibid.*, p. 711.
68. R. vs. Rabey, 17 O.R. (2d) 1, (1978).
69. *Ibid.*, p. 11.
70. *Ibid.*, p. 11.
71. *Ibid.*, p. 11.
72. Ennis and Litwack, *supra*, note 7, p. 714.
73. Personal conversations with T. O'Sullivan, *Borins, Birnbaum, Steinberg and O'Sullivan*, and R. Manes, *Torkin and Manes.*
74. This material was gathered from the *Annual Reports of the Mental Health Division*, Ministry of Health, Ontario, 1964 to 1973, Toronto, Queen's Printer.
75. Provincial psychiatric facilities are required to submit an operating budget to government. The budget is naturally dependent upon the amount of business to be transacted. (Telephone conversation with official in Psychiatric Services, Ministry of Health.)
76. *Debates*, Legislative Assembly of Ontario, December 13, 1977, p. 2923.
77. Ingber, S., *supra*, note 26.
78. Canadian Civil Liberties Association, *supra*, note 4.
79. *Ibid.*, p. 10. "To the extent that involuntary civil commitments are continued. . . ."
80. Draper, G., "Due Process and Confinement for Mental Disorder," *14 Alberta Law Review* 266 (1976), p. 288.
81. Share, D., "The Standard of Proof in Involuntary Civil Commitment Proceedings," *2 Detroit College of Law Review* 209 (1977).
82. The Mental Incompetency Act, R.S.O. 1970, c. 271.
83. Hiday, V., "Reformed Commitment Procedures: An Empirical Study in the Courtroom," *11 Law and Society Review* 651 (1977).

Questions

1. Why does Boyd think that a person should not be admitted to a hospital simply to prevent serious self-inflicted harm to himself? Are Boyd's reasons sound when assessed in the light of the three cases described on page 201?

2. Why does Boyd reject the view that the state is justified in compelling

a person to enter a hospital because that person is likely to cause serious harm to the mental or physical condition of someone else? Are his reasons sound?

3. Evaluate the assertion that in predicting dangerousness, a physician is making a "legal or political decision" and not a "medical decision."

4. Suppose we have taken the view that we are morally justified in institutionalizing people because they are perceived as a threat to themselves or others. Does it follow that we are morally justified in institutionalizing people because they are perceived as likely to commit a criminal offence?

5. Does it follow from Boyd's argument that we are never justified in using force to prevent a person from committing suicide no matter how convinced we are that the person in question is seriously disturbed? Or does it follow that we are simply not justified in forcibly detaining such a person? If the only way of preventing that person from committing suicide were short-term forcible detention, would compulsory institutionalization be justified?

6. To what extent does Boyd's argument depend on the view that the moral autonomy principle should override the protection-of-life and the avoidance-of-suffering principles where respect for the moral-autonomy principle is incompatible with respect for the other two?

The Ethics of Involuntary Treatment

[Prepared for the Professional Standards and Practice Council, chaired by Dr. N. el-Guebaly, and approved by the Board of Directors of the Canadian Psychiatric Association in May 1981]

C.H. Cahn, M.D.

This paper deals primarily with the medical treatment of the mentally ill in the absence of a valid consent given by the patient. Consideration is given to certain central issues, such as the semantics of "involuntary" and of "treatment," the attitude of concerned persons, the notion of "dangerousness," and the setting where the treatment takes place. It also deals with certain paired concepts that are frequently discussed as one opposed to the other: detention versus treatment, least intrusive versus most effective treatment, effective treatment in exchange for loss of freedom, the right to treatment versus the right to refuse treatment, emergency versus definitive treatment, the psychiatrist's obligations to the patient as against his duties to the rest of society, and "judicialization" versus "psychiatrization."

Some other issues that are related to the subject are considered beyond the scope of this paper, such as the involuntary treatment of children and of moribund patients,

Reprinted from *The Canadian Journal of Psychiatry*, Vol. 27, No. 1 (February 1982).

behavior control, the sterilization of the mentally retarded, involvement of patients in psychiatric research without their personal consent, and the involuntary treatment of political dissidents in certain other places.

Brief Historical Note

The issue of the involuntary treatment of the mentally ill has come into much sharper focus as a result of several historical trends: the patients' rights movement; the much greater availability of potent treatment methods; the changing role of psychiatric hospitals; the greater interest in the subject by the legal profession; and the increased emphasis on the quality of life in general and of handicapped persons in particular. Some would add the "anti-psychiatry" movement to this list.

During the past 200 years one may say that not a decade has gone by without major publicity having been given to alleged abuses of the mentally ill: patients being put in straitjackets, secluded for long periods of time, "put away" in "lunatic asylums," patients treated against their will for insufficient reasons, patients forgotten and rejected by their families and society in general, and patients being discriminated against because of their mental illness. Fortunately in Canada such adverse publicity occurs less often; when it does occur it is sometimes quite distorted or excessively dramatized. However, in the minds of ethicists, legislators, health professionals, lawyers, and others, there is still a rather large area of concern. That is why this paper is being presented now.

Let us return for a moment to one of the most important developments in psychiatry during the past fifty years: the introduction of active psychiatric treatments. Some of these such as insulin coma, lobotomy, and continuous narcosis at first appeared to be most promising, but because of side effects and sometimes serious complications are now seldom used. Others, such as ECT and pharmacotherapy, are still held to be controversial by some, but are very effective, have undergone many refinements and continue to be evaluated carefully.

Definitions

Ethics

The Oxford dictionary defines ethics as "the science of morals and rules of conduct," and the word "moral" is defined as "concerned with character or disposition, or with the distinction between right and wrong." The Canadian Medical Association's Code of Ethics is a guide to the ethical behavior of physicians and contains forty-nine clauses. Two of these are particularly relevant to our subject: "An ethical physician will recognize that the patient has the right to accept or reject any physician and any medical care recommended to him" and "an ethical physician will, when the patient is unable, and an agent unavailable, to give consent, render such therapy as he believes to be in the patient's interest." These two clauses, when considered together imply that the attending physician fully respects the right of the patient to accept or refuse the treatment offer, but intervenes therapeutically when the patient is unable to give or refuse consent, for whatever reason. Another position paper, on "Consent in Psychiatry,"[1] deals with the various aspects of the consent process, including the psychiatrist's role in determining whether or not the patient is capable of giving a valid consent. Whenever a physician overrules the objections of a mentally ill person to receive a certain treatment, the physician is faced with an ethical dilemma. This theme will be elaborated below.

Involuntary

Other words used to describe restrictions placed on mentally ill patients are "commitment," "formal admission," "*cure fermée*" (in Quebec), all of which are covered by the various provincial mental-health acts.[2] In addition, there are lieutenant-governor's warrants and other court orders according to which restrictions are imposed on patients under the Criminal Code of Canada. These laws are concerned primarily with involuntary admission to designated facilities, and do not usually distinguish clearly between "involuntary admission" and "involuntary treatment." In the Province of Quebec, the term "*cure fermée*" is particularly interesting from the etymological and semantic points of view. One interpretation of this expression that psychiatrists in Quebec have given is that it confers on psychiatrists the right to order treatment which in their opinion such patients need. Another interpretation is that the expression "*cure fermée*" merely means the detention in the hospital of a patient who may receive there ordinary care such as food, shelter, clothing, basic nursing care, and so forth, but not psychiatric treatment such as anti-psychotic medication. Further clarification from the legal point of view is required.

In other provinces, such as Ontario, the law makes a distinction between control of dangerous behaviour due to illness by drugs in an emergency situation (which is permitted without the patient's consent), and definitive psychiatric treatment, for which the patient's consent is required. This is so even if the chemical substance remains the same as the patient passes from the emergency to the non-emergency situation. Further provisions are made for situations in which the patient is not able to give his valid consent (as this position paper deals with the ethics rather than the legalities of involuntary treatment, the reader is referred to the relevant texts for further information).

Treatment

We are here primarily concerned with the psychiatric treatment of patients by physical or chemical means. Psychotherapy is not included in this discussion, as it is hard to conceive of "involuntary" psychotherapy[3] in the usually accepted meaning of these words. Behavior therapy and its varieties are not considered here, and as already stated above the involuntary application of behavior modification techniques are beyond the scope of this paper; it will be the subject of another paper.

Involuntary Treatment

It should be pointed out that the notions of voluntary and involuntary are not like white and black, but that there are many shades of grey. In fact there is a continuum of voluntary to involuntary, which could be described as follows: active cooperation, passive cooperation, ambivalence, silent objection, irrational opposition, rational refusal. A patient may move along this continuum in either direction during the course of his illness. Furthermore, the patient may accept some treatments but not others, or may change his mind.

Another fact to be considered is the non-psychiatric medical or surgical treatment of the mentally ill; general practitioners, surgeons, and other medical specialists to whom patients with physical problems are referred are involved in the decision-making process, and, depending on the urgency of the situation, may have to intervene without the patient having given or being able to give a valid consent.

Attitudes of Concerned Persons

The Public

There are still many misunderstandings and misperceptions as to the power of psychiatrists to take away the freedom of persons because of mental illness. The public still grossly overestimates the number and percentage of involuntary patients in psychiatric hospitals. Civil libertarians, certain lawyers, and the "anti-psychiatry movement" contribue to this negative image. Stone[4] has stated: "The rich admixture of science and humanism that diffuses the discipline and the idiom of psychiatry all too often arouses the antipathy of the skeptical, tough-minded lawyer who is trained to demand and expect precision."

Psychiatrists

Some psychiatrists are more permissive, others more authoritarian in their approach to involuntary treatment. Psychiatrists at either end of the scale are more likely to be criticized than the ones in the middle. The literature in recent times focuses more on the interventions by "over-zealous psychiatrists"[5] while, as discussed below, in the minds of the relatives of patients, psychiatrists often do not go far enough. Psychiatrists as members of the medical profession have a long tradition of being committed to placing the patient's well-being and longevity above all else and in using their own judgment in decision-making rather than that of others. Physicians have often felt that patients were too ignorant to make decisions on their own behalf and that it was better to treat the patient promptly, without inducing new fears and reinforcing unwise decisions on the part of the patient. Nowadays increasing demands are put on the physician to enter into a meaningful dialogue with the patient and to obtain from the patient a valid consent insofar as this is possible.

Patients

Relatively few patients are skillful in articulating well their stand with regard to involuntary treatment. Many who express negative opinions have delusions or impaired judgment. The majority of patients do not express any opinion at all; very few raise valid objections, but when this happens, psychiatrists and other mental health authorities are sometimes strongly criticized. "Let one paranoid patient bleat but once about mistreatment, and 15 members of the Civil Liberties Association make headlines with it for a year."[6]

Relatives

Relatives of mentally ill patients far more often wish involuntary treatment than any other group of interested pesons. In the present atmosphere, where the rights of the individual have encroached so heavily on the rights of others, relatives frequently suffer the most from threatening, frightening, and/or annoying behavior of the mentally ill. In the past, when paternalism was more acceptable it was easier to take the problems caused by patients out of the hands of relatives by having the patient hospitalized, sometimes for long periods of time. Nowadays, with paternalism often being equated with excessive authoritarianism, and with the shorter duration of stay in hospital, patients are more likely to be repeatedly troublesome to their relatives. The latter can sometimes obtain comfort and support from organizations such as the Association of Relatives and Friends of the Mentally Ill.

Dangerousness

This subject has been debated extensively and a great number of papers have been written on it. Where there is actual or obvious danger to self or to others due to a patient's mental illness, few would argue that involuntary treatment is required; the arguments start when one considers what kind of treatment is indicated, and also when the danger is less obvious. This is one of the most complex issues psychiatrists are facing today. As long as it is proved statistically that psychiatrists are no better than others in predicting dangerousnes it is likely that the law will not or will no longer permit psychiatrists to restrict the liberty of patients to refuse treatment on the basis of potential danger alone. It would seem that only in cases of patients who repeat the same pattern of dangerous behavior which responds favourably to psychiatric treatment but recurs when the patient discontinues such treatment may there be justification in treating a patient against his will on a preventive basis. However, we must not forget that criminal recidivists are not placed in preventive detention in countries where human freedoms are as highly prized as in Canada. Therefore, whenever possible, a psychiatrist should have a frank and full discussion with a patient who has recovered from an episode of mental illness with dangerous behavior, hoping that the patient will co-operate with continued psychiatric treatment on a voluntary basis.

In the case where a patient never does achieve this sort of insight and repeatedly breaks off therapy, it may be better to utilize Section 16 of the Criminal Code of Canada, that is, the patient, having been charged with an offense is acquitted by reason of insanity and is then placed under a "Lieutenant-Governor's Warrant"; if such a patient refuses treatment, the Provincial Review Board may authorize psychiatric treatment. A patient under "L.G.W.", having been hospitalized may be discharged and followed as an outpatient in the way similar to a convicted ciminal discharged from a detention centre being helped by a probation officer to keep the peace.

Detention versus Treatment

Psychiatric hospitals, whatever their previous title (lunatic asylum or mental institution) have a long history of functioning as quasi-jails for persons who have had to be admitted involuntarily ("committed") or who had been charged as criminals but found to be too mentally ill to be cared for in prisons or other detention centres. Only in recent times have other psychiatric treatment facilities been included in accepting involuntary patients. This seems eminently fair, as it tends to diminish the stigma attached to psychiatric hospitals, and fits better with modern concepts of community psychiatry. But there is still the problem of the use or perhaps abuse of psychiatric facilities for the detention of persons considered mentally ill by the public, the police, or judges as an alternative to imprisonment, even for people with personality disorders for whom psychiatrists have no adequate treatment. For such individuals the hospital serves primarily as a detention centre. Psychiatrists are reluctant to allow hospital beds to be occupied for long periods of time by such individuals, especially when there are waiting lists for psychiatric patients for whom treatment is more successful. However, the public tends to regard hospitalization as a treatment in itself; in fact, before the days of active psychiatric treatment, and even today, psychiatrists may themselves regard admission to hospital as the most important treatment for the patient. In the hospital, the patient is taken care of, that is, he receives food, clothing, shelter, nursing care, and a program of structured activities, which for many patients improves the quality of their life as compared with the life they led in the community. Whether a patient benefiting from being in the hospital under these circumstances should in addition have to undergo involuntary psychiatric treatment, because the psychiatrist has a treatment that he thinks should be given in the belief that it will further improve the patient's mental condition, remains a controversial issue. This issue is causing a good deal of friction between psychiatrists of the more traditional type and patients' rights advocates of the more activist type.

One of the most important functions of physicians is to relieve suffering; therefore, although psychiatrists may ardently wish to treat all the mentally ill who are treatable, there are certain patients such as simple or hebephrenic schizophrenics who do not appear to be suffering very much from their symptoms (judging from their facial expressions they may actually seem to be enjoying some of their symptoms). Certainly it is ethical to treat involuntarily patients who are in patent or overt distress because of the illness (such as patients with depressive or paranoid delusions). This does imply that some patients, especially certain chronic schizophrenics, will continue to have symptoms and may have to remain hospitalized or otherwise be looked after if they refuse active psychiatric treatment, even though the psychiatrist is convinced that with such treatment the patient would be greatly improved. The psychiatrist may feel perfectly justified in pursuing an objective of active treatment, in the belief that it will reduce chronicity, save money, or improve the hospital's discharge statistics. But the more ethical approach is for the psychiatrist to allow the patient to make some decisions for himself, or at least to have a continuing dialogue with the patient to try to persuade him to accept treatment on a voluntary basis.

Setting

Involuntary treatment may be given in hospitals, in detention centres, and also in some jurisdictions on an outpatient basis or even at home. The most frequent setting for involuntary psychiatric treatment is of course the hospital. It is in the hospital where the therapeutic team is working in familiar surroundings. Expert staff and up-to-date equipment are readily available, especially in emergencies. Patients can be treated involuntarily in other settings, but the desirable supportive services are less readily available there. For relatively uncomplicated treatment, such as bi-weekly fluphenazine injections, an outpatient setting or treatment in the patient's home is quite feasible.

Discharging the Uncooperative Patient

Physicians are generally the only group of professionals entitled to order the admission and discharge of patients (patients under lieutenant-governor's or judge's orders are considered separately). When a patient refuses the treatment offered, the attending physician often responds by discharging the patient from the hospital. The physician may wish to make the bed available to a more cooperative patient. The hospital may have a utilization review committee whose objective is to enusre that the duration of stay in hospital is not too long. Hopefully the patient will not be discharged prematurely by reason primarily of hostile reaction of the attending staff. Some patients wish to stay in hospital without necessarily accepting the treatment offered. More frequently, patients leave the hospital, but soon return because their mental condition becomes worse, or there may be more subtle reasons. Some patients have learned how to take advantage of their "mentally ill" status as a means to evade the law or other social responsibilities. For financial or political reasons there may be an overall policy to discharge chronic patients back into the community. If the patient is not properly prepared, there is the risk of "replacing back wards with back alleys." All these factors have to be considered carefully by the attending physician when deciding how a given patient is best managed. None of them singly seems to be sufficient to justify intrusive psychiatric treatment against the patient's will.

Least Intrusive versus Most Effective Treatment

In psychiatry, as in much of medicine and surgery, the most effective treatment is often the most intrusive. One could compare psychosurgery with the surgical removal of a brain tumour, or neuroleptic therapy for schizophrenia with insulin therapy for diabetes, or physically restraining a violent patient with the reduction of a dislocated shoulder. There are many similar examples, but the most important difference is that where there is no mental illness, a valid consent given by the patient to the intervention, no matter how drastic, can usually be readily obtained before the intervention is undertaken. Hence the vigorous search for effective psychiatric treatments with less instrusiveness and fewer side-effects. Psychosurgery has all but disappeared from the therapeutic armamentarium. ECT has been very much refined and more carefully controlled. Psychopharmacology researchers are constantly searching for new drugs with fewer side-effects. Greater effort is being made to evaluate the quality of treatment by means of medical audits and peer review.

Furthermore, the setting where the treatment takes place is constantly being improved: psychiatric hospitals have more and better staff than formerly, fewer patients are admitted involuntarily and for shorter periods of time, alternative settings for treatment such as departments of psychiatry in general hospitals, various outpatient clinics, day care, home care, and supervised community living are all being utilized much more than heretofore. The advantages of treating the patient in the least restrictive setting must be weighed against the disadvantages of not always being able to offer the most effective treatment; for example, it is more difficult to prevent the suicide of a severely depressed patient at home than in hospital.

Effective Treatment in Exchange for Loss of Freedom

The medical profession has always held that the patient has the right to receive the best available treatment. In the case of the mentally ill, physicians have above all wished to give their patients the maximum benefit of available treatments even if this meant that the patient, because of his mental illness, was not entirely free to decide for himself what should be done. This has given rise to the notion of "*quid pro quo*," which implies that the patient will receive effective and beneficial treatment in exchange for the loss of his freedom. What certainly is no longer acceptable is that patients be detained in hospitals "without more." The more the patient's freedom to move around as he pleases and to make his own decisions is restricted, the greater is the obligation on the physician and the hospital staff to provide effective and harmless tretment. It is very difficult to apply this equation with perfect fairness, but psychiatrists and other health professionals should always strive towards this ideal.

There are four possibilities which are illustrated in Table I (simplified for theoretical purposes; in reality the lines of demarcation are by no means clear cut).

Table 1

Conceptualization of the *Quid Pro Quo* Argument According to Traditional Medical Ethics

	Voluntary	Involuntary
Effective Treatment	Best	Second Best
No Treatment	Third Best	Worst

Comments

"Effective Treatment" ideally is treatment that has been proven to be effective by scientific-research methodology; but treatment may be effective in a given case without having been validated scientifically.

"No Treatment" here means that the patient does not receive effective treatment. There may be four possible reasons for this:

1. Effective treatment is not available; for instance, for Alzheimer's Disease.

2. The patient refuses treatment—patients' rights advocates sometimes claim this comes above all other considerations; in extreme cases they would accord the right to refuse treatment even to the most psychotic patient.

3. The treating physician may not yet have found the most effective treatment for the patient, or there may be a difference of opinion between one physician and another as to what is the most effective and up-to-date treatment. Whenever there are such doubts or other uncertainties the attending physician is advised to consult a colleague.

4. The facility cannot afford to provide effective treatment—this should no longer be a major problem for scientifically validated effective treatments, but still may be a

problem in the case of other less well accepted methods of treatment; for instance, certain types of psychotherapy, and certain behaviour modification techniques may be very effective in given cases, but may require extra staff, extra time, and extra expertise. Furthermore, there are psychiatric disorders with underlying physical causes which may require diagnostic services not readily available, and for which patients may have to be transferred to special treatment facilities.

The *"quid pro quo"* problem also exists in certain facilities with maximum security for dangerous patients in need of psychiatric treatment.

Value judgments will continue to have to be made and priorities assigned before budgets are approved to spend the public's tax dollars for this category of patients. Although ideally the cost of treatment should not be a factor, in reality it will continue to be especially difficult to apply the above equation fairly to all mentally ill offenders inside maximum security facilities.

The Right to Treatment versus the Right to Refuse Treatment

This is one of the most contentious issues in modern psychiatry. A paper by Redlich and Mollica in the *American Journal of Psychiatry*[7] entitled "Overview: Ethical Issues in Contemporary Psychiatry" described the historical, ethical, legal, as well as medical points of view in the United States. One of the statements these authors make is as follows: "With some shame we state that most of the changes in establishing patients' rights were not brought about primarily by psychiatrists but civil libertarians led by lawyers, and that the most important decisions were by enlightened judges." The authors of this paper discussed changing moral values at length and seemed to be rather critical of the American medical profession in general and psychiatry in particular.

In Canada so far there is not as much concern in this area; certainly far fewer legal actions have been taken against psychiatrists and psychiatric treatment facilities than south of the border. But this should not lead us to a false sense of security; on the contrary, we should keep ourselves well informed as to the involvement of our American colleagues.

Even in Great Britain where medical ethics reach further back in history than on the North American continent this matter has received increased attention—following a six-hour debate in the British House of Commons in February 1979 on the review of the Mental Health Act, the reporter for the *British Medical Journal*[8] stated: "On the question of consent to treatment there were two safeguards for the patient in circumstances where staff had to override his wishes. Firstly, treatment should be imposed against the patient's wishes only if it is necessary to save life, to prevent violence, or to prevent deterioration in the patient's condition. Secondly, the Government had proposed that except in an emergency the patient's wishes should be overridden only when a concurring second opinion had been obtained."

From the above it is evident that psychiatrists have a growing obligation to evaluate, as objectively as possible, the patient's prognosis for behaviour dangerous to self or to others before subjecting the patient to involuntary treatment. In Britain it appears that the psychiatrist may still order involuntary treatment "to prevent deterioration in the patient's condition"; in the United States, the patients' rights movement seems to make this increasingly difficult, and only behaviour imminently dangerous may justify involuntary treatment. In Canada, as is so often the case, we seem to be somewhere in between the British and the American situation.

In true emergencies, that is, where a patient's behaviour due to mental illness is obviously dangerous to self or to others, the medical profession has great leeway to intervene energetically with therapeutic and preventive motivation. In fact, society confers on the physician the obligation to treat the patient until the emergency is over. This may be a matter of minutes, hours, or days, but rarely longer than that. Of course the emergency may recur, especially if definitive treatment is not instituted.

There are also two related questions which are not always easy to answer: When is the emergency over? Who defines what is an "emergency"? The psychiatrist has to observe the patient closely for at least the period of time when he believes that the emergency still exists, and for some time afterwards, and he also has to take into account other people's opinions as to what constitutes an emergency even if he himself does not think there is one, or vice versa. In any case, the psychiatrist has to get to know the patient as quickly as possible, and dispel the uncertainties in his mind and that of those closely associated with the patient (family, friends, employers, police, hospital staff, and so on).

Once the psychiatrist has decided that emergency treatment is indicated, he has available a choice of measures including a forceful verbal approach to the patient, seclusion, manual or mechanical restraints, or various drugs administered orally or parenterally ("chemical restraint"). Fortunately, these measures are in most cases effective and relatively harmless.

The difficult ethical problem does not exist so much at the beginning of the emergency, but later on: at what point in time is the psychiatrist no longer justified in treating the patient without a valid consent? It is here that the psychiatrist's knowledge and skill have to be optimally applied; it is hoped that this paper will help the psychiatrist to weigh the various factors before proceeding with the treatment.

A comment concerning the emergency treatment given by non-psychiatric physicians to patients who have made suicidal attempts: it would appear to be more ethical for such physicians, especially those working in general hospitals with psychiatrists on the staff, to request a psychiatric consultation before sending the patient home than to omit this. This statement is not intended to question the ability of the non-psychiatric physician to handle emergencies occasioned by patients with mental disorders, but merely to point out an ethical aspect of the situation. It is suggested here that the medical staff by-laws of general hospitals with departments of psychiatry or psychiatrists on their staff include a consideration of this matter.

Psychiatrist's Duties to Patient versus Duties to Society

The psychiatrist is often called upon to "wear two hats," one as the patient's therapist, when his allegiance is with the patient, and the other, when he has to communicate with third parties such as giving explanations to the patient's family or other interested persons, when he has to make reports to the courts, or declare the patient incompetent for one reason or another. In acting thus as a "double agent," the psychiatrist must always establish his own priorities in terms of his ethics, the reality of the situation, his relationship with the patient, and his responsibility to both the patient and the public. Since so many psychiatric patients are uncooperative or lack insight, the psychiatrist in making decisions may disregard the patient's present attitude to treatment for the sake of obtaining a good result later on. Does the end justify the means? In any case, psychiatrists should inform the various parties concerned what action they are going to take.

Related to this issue is the question of the choice of therapist: does the patient have the right to choose his psychiatrist? There are many problems in the organization of psychiatric services in hospitals, and with the widespread shortage of psychiatrists patients often do not have much choice, if any. Thus one patient may find himself with an attending psychiatrist who is rather authoritative, whereas another patient has one who is much more permissive. The first type of psychiatrist is more likely to prescribe involuntary treatment than the second. This is an ethical problem insofar as in the first case the patient is more likely to complain, while in the second case the relatives are more likely to complain about the psychiatrist's attitude, with the result that society accuses psychiatrists as a group of being inconsistent.

"Judicialization" versus "Psychiatrization"

By "judicialization" is meant the excessive involvement of the legal profession in decision-making concerning the mentally ill just as the word "psychiatrization" implies the excessive involvement by psychiatrists in matters (sometimes remotely) related to mental health or mental illness. Redlich and Mollica[9] have stated that: "Psychiatrists in general opt for medical informality rather than for legal formality and for flexible medical therapeutic action rather than bureaucratic and legal surveillance. . . . The control of deviance—largely forced upon psychiatry by society—is more of a curse than a boon to our profession . . . we should be happy to leave it in the hands of the law for enforcement."

The history of the relationship between the legal and medical professions is lengthy and full of controversy, with the pendulum swinging from side to side insofar as ultimate authority is concerned. We now appear to be in a phase where the legal profession has the ascendancy, and psychiatrists, particularly in the United States, seem to be more affected by the phenomenon of "judicialization" than the legal profession is by the phenomenon of "psychiatrization." In Canada a similar tendency is discernible, but to a lesser extent. One may assume that the excesses of the one side are a reaction to the excesses of the other; our primary goal should be to avoid such excesses.

Sharing to Decision-Making

If we are to conceptualize the doctor-patient relationship as a form of partnership, we must recognize that the degree of cooperation attainable between the two depends to a large measure on the patient's mental condition: to the extent that the latter precludes cooperation, third parties may be called upon to enter this relationship. A partial list of such "third parties" would include another physician; another health professional, relatives and friends; a guardian, trustee, or curator; an ombudsman; a citizen advocate; the clergy; and members of the legal profession. With such a variety of persons who may be involved in patient management, the subjective factor is bound to enter in, mistakes may occur and the art of public relations is very important. Psychiatrists are usually well trained in the dynamics of interpersonal relationships and are in a good position to control the degree of involvement of third parties. The psychiatrist can usually decide who should be involved, when, and to what extent, but there are many uncontrollable and unforeseeable situations where this is not possible. When decisions are made to treat a patient against his will, it becomes that much more important to have the other appropriate parties well briefed, and to make frequent reviews with them of the effectiveness of the treatment plan.

Returning to the issue of who should have the ultimate authority for instituting involuntary treatment, ideally this is a decision which should be shared by the attending physician and a judge according to "due process of law." For strictly practical reasons, medical decision-making saves a lot of time, and may save lives. (For instance, it was reported that a depressed patient jumped out of a window of a courthouse while the psychiatrists had to wait for the judge's decision.) In that sense, it is more ethical *not* to rely on the conventional legal system, because it tends to be unwieldy and slow. If a judge were readily available at the treatment centre, the problem might be solved; but this is an expensive arrangement, and has not been instituted anywhere as far as we know. In the meantime it will be necessary in most instances for the attending psychiatrist or other physician, as the case may be, to decide when a patient's objection should be overruled and when not. In any doubtful case, it is advisable to obtain the opinion of a colleague. In extreme cases, judicial opinion should be sought.

Recommendations

Psychiatrists must consider carefully the semantics of "involuntary treatment" and help to explain to the public the difference between involuntary hospitalization ("commitment") and involuntary treatment. They are to evaluate carefully the equations "least intrusive versus most effective treatment" and "effective treatment in exchange for loss of freedom."

The attending psychiatrist is to attempt to have a continuing dialogue with an objecting patient to try to persuade him to accept treatment on a voluntary basis. In emergencies, the attending psychiatrist is to carry out promptly all the necessary treatments, but when the emergency is over, he should carefully review with the patient what was done and what still remains to be done.

It is therefore recommended:

1. That a patient's objection to treatment be respected when the patient is competent to give or refuse consent to treatment.
2. That psychiatrists continue to be allowed, under mental-health legislation, to overrule patients' objections to treatment when it is obvious that the treatment is urgently needed; and that treatment may be continued as necessary when it will result in great improvement of the patient's condition.
3. That when acting in the interests of both the patient and a third party (relative, judge) the attending psychiatrist inform the patient of it and establish his priorities in terms of ethics, the reality of the situation, his

relationship with the patient, and his responsibility to the patient and to the public.

4. That psychiatrists cooperate closely with general practitioners and other specialists with regard to the necessity for involuntary treatment of physical illness(es) that a mentally ill patient may have.

5. That psychiatrists continue to be allowed under mental-health legislation to exercise their right to discharge from hospital uncooperative patients, taking careful account of the patient's actual mental condition and the alternatives available to the patient for continuing care and supervision.

6. That psychiatrists respect the due process of law as it exists and strive to influence for improvement provincial mental-health legislation and regulation to ensure that their patients receive the best possible medical care.

7. That the attending psychiatrist involve an appropriate third (neutral) party or at least consult a colleague when a difficult decision has to be made to treat a patient involuntarily.

Notes

1. Consent in psychiatry. Position Paper of the Canadian Psychiatric Association. Can J Psychiatry 1980; 25: 78–85.
2. Toews J, Prabhu V, el-Guebaly N. Commitment of the mentally ill: current issues. Can J Psychiatry 1980; 25: 611–618.
3. The subject "Ethics of Psychotherapy" is thoroughly covered in an article by T.B. Karasu in the *American Journal of Psychiatry*, Volume 137, pages 1502–1512, December 1980, with 79 references.
4. Stone Alan A. Overview: the right to treatment—comments on the law and its impact. Am J Psychiatry 1975; 132: 1125–1134.
5. Reiser SJ. Refusing treatment for mental illness: historical and ethical dimensions. Am J Psychiatry 1980; 137: 329–331. Anand R. Involuntary civil commitment in Ontario: the need to curtail the abuses of psychiatry. Can Bar Review 1979; 57(2): 250–280.
6. Beck MN. Personal communication.
7. Redlich F, Mollica RF. Overview: ethical issues in contemporary psychiatry. Am J Psychiatry 1976; 133(2): 125–136.
8. Review of Mental Health Act. Br Med J 1979; 1: 695.
9. Redlich and Mollica, 125–136.

Questions

1. How effectively does the code of ethics proposed in this article deal with the objections to compulsory institutionalization raised by Neil Boyd in his article "Ontario's Treatment of the 'Criminally Insane' and the Potentially Dangerous"?

2. On the basis of Boyd's argument, how should the three cases introduced in this selection be handled?

3. How important or useful is the distinction between "involuntary commitment" and "involuntary treatment"?

Mental Disorder after Trial

[From Working Paper 14 of the Commission]

The Law Reform Commission of Canada

Trial normally results in conviction or acquittal. If acquitted the accused is free to go and the criminal law has no further interest in him or his mental health. But if convicted, the offender's mental health may be taken into account. Certainly not if he is absolutely discharged or merely fined, but if he is discharged conditionally, released on probation or imprisoned, his mental health may be considered.

A. The Principles of Sentencing and Mental Disorder

How a person's mental disorder should be considered when he is imprisoned or on probation depends on the view taken of sentencing and disposition. Our view is set out in our third Working Paper, *The Principles of Sentencing and Dispositions*. We must here consider the implications of that paper for mental disorder in sentencing.

If, as we said in our Working Paper *The Meaning of Guilt*, criminal law has to do with bringing offenders to justice, then sanctioning offenders has to do with righting of wrongs and protecting basic values as an expression of that justice. The role of sentencing is an educative one. It makes clear the responsibility of the offender for the injury caused the victim and reaffirms the importance of the values infringed. Sentencing must try to ensure that: "(1) the innocent are not harmed, (2) dispositions are not degrading, cruel or inhumane, (3) dispositions and sentences are proportional to the offence, (4) similar offences are treated more or less equally, and (5) sentencing and disposition take into account restitution or compensation for the wrong done."

Such a sentencing policy relegates rehabilitation and treatment to a secondary role; the primary concern is the determination of a sentence that is just and fair in the circumstances. Sentences therefore cannot be based on estimates of the length of time required to treat or rehabilitate offenders.

This is not to say that treatment of an offender's mental disorder has no place in sentencing policy; its place, though limited, is important nonetheless. Treatment within the framework of a just sentence is an obligation of society to the offender, which some feel he may demand as a right. Certainly a humanitarian claim can be made. Although there are serious doubts as to the effectiveness of therapeutic programs in reducing recidivism, to the extent that treatment renders punishment more humane and reduces (however marginally) the likelihood of reoccurrences, it has a place in a just sentence.

This view has two implications for psychiatric treatment of offenders. First, the perceived need for treatment may not affect the length or the form of sentence. Second, treatment administered within the context of the prescribed sentence must be consented to by the offender. In regard to the latter, we must bear in mind that

Reprinted by permission of the Law Reform Commission of Canada from Working Paper 14, Sec. 6, p. 43.

an offender who has reached the sentencing stage has been found both criminally responsible and fit to stand trial. He is considered responsible for his acts and should be entitled to make his own decision whether he wants to avail himself of existing medical support.

B. Mental Disorder and Probation

We feel that psychiatric treatment sometimes is and can properly be a condition of probation. This may include an order to follow a particular treatment program, involving periodic visits to a psychiatric out-patient facility or even part-time residence in an institution which provides some form of psychiatric supervision. For the most part, conditions of probation are unrestricted in the Criminal Code. Although this allows for flexibility and change, it can lead to abuse.

To check such abuse we recommend the same safeguards here as we have for sentencing generally: openness, reviewability, and treatment only with consent. The offender and his counsel should actively seek and suggest the appropriate treatment and try to secure the agreement and cooperation of the treatment personnel. Probation orders with conditions of psychiatric treatment should be made only where: (1) the offender understands the kind of program to be followed, (2) he consents to the program, and (3) the psychiatric or counselling services have agreed to accept the offender for treatment. If the conditions are accepted then breached, the offender may be charged with breach of a condition of probation or be returned to court for re-sentencing. So long as such conditions entail the agreement and cooperation of the offender, they are quite compatible with our suggested sentencing policy.

C. Mental Disorder and Imprisonment

It is perhaps surprising to many persons to learn that an accused may be charged, brought to trial, convicted, and sentenced to imprisonment notwithstanding that he is mentally disordered. But this only underlines what was pointed out earlier in this paper—the criminal law is concerned not with mental disorder *per se* but with its legal consequences. If the accused's mental illness does not cause him to be diverted before trial, or render him unfit or criminally irresponsible, he not only may, but should, continue in the process through to its conclusion—acquittal or conviction and sentence.

Frequently, sentencing judges realize that some offenders suffer from mental disorder, but under present law they have no power to order that the term of imprisonment be spent in whole or in part in a psychiatric facility. Judges sometimes do make recommendations for psychiatric treatment hoping that prison authorities will do something as a result. Sometimes such recommendations are followed, often they are not. Although it is theoretically possible for prison authorities to transfer mentally disordered offenders to mental hospitals, in practice such transfers are rare. Because of the sparse facilities for psychiatric treatment in prisons generally, many prisoners suffering from serious mental disorders are detained without the prospect of treatment.

This situation should not be allowed to continue. After thoroughly examining the problem of sentencing mentally disordered offenders to prison and after exposing alternative methods of providing psychiatric treatment to those offenders, we recommend that judges be given the power to order that a term of imprisonment be spent in whole or in part in a psychiatric facility. This sentencing alternative we call a hospital order. A similar approach has been used in England since 1959 and has been recommended previously in Canada by two national research bodies.

i. Hospital Orders

The essence of our proposal is this:

1. Where a person is convicted of a crime and has been sentenced to a fixed term of imprisonment, the accused or his counsel may raise the question of whether a hospital order would be appropriate.
2. Before a hospital order may be made, several criteria must be met:
   - the offender must be convicted of a criminal offence and have been sentenced to a term of imprisonment;
   - the court should, unless extensive psychiatric information is available, remand the offender under the Criminal Code to a psychiatric institution to determine whether he is suffering from a psychiatric disorder that is susceptible to treatment and whether the institution to which he has been remanded or another institution is able and willing to provide a program of treatment, if any.
3. After having considered the psychiatric report and the representations of both defence counsel and the prosecution the presiding judge may, with the consent of the accused, and the agreement of the appropriate psychiatric institution, order that the accused spend part or all of his sentence in a hospital or psychiatric institution.
4. An offender who has lawfully consented to the hospital order may request that the balance of his sentence be served in the correctional system even if he could still benefit from further treatment in the hospital. He should perhaps also have the right to apply to a review board to be transferred to another hospital if he is not receiving the anticipated treatment.
5. The hospital administration may discharge the offender back to the correctional system at any time before the expiration of the hospital order. Before such a discharge is made, however, the offender should be informed in writing of the reason for the discharge and have the right to apply to a review board for transfer to another hospital.
6. An offender sentenced to a hospital order shall be entitled to parole in the same manner as all other offenders. In addition, the hospital authorities may recommend, for psychiatric reasons, that the offender be released on parole rather than returned to prison.
7. An offender serving his sentence under a hospital order is deemed to be serving his sentence in prison for the purposes of escapes and being at large without lawful excuse. Other rights and privileges such as recreation, visiting, correspondence, or temporary absences will be governed by the rules and regulations of the psychiatric institution and such criteria of fairness and decency as may be provided for in the law.

8. The judge's decision to impose or not to impose a hospital order may be appealed in the same manner as any other sentence of the court.

ii.   The Need for Hospital Orders

Do we really need hospital orders? Could not a prisoner's psychiatric needs be adequately provided for within the prisons or through transfers to outside psychiatric hospitals? At present, psychiatric services within prisons generally, and transfer procedures, are inadequate and ineffective. But even if, as we recommend, psychiatric services and transfers are improved, there would still exist a need for hospital orders. In our view hospital orders will improve the sentencing process and provide needed psychiatric treatment for offenders without first sending them into the correctional system.

iii.   The Need for Consent

The most contentious aspect of our proposal is that the offender must consent to the hospital order. This is in contrast to the position taken in two earlier Canadian studies recommending a similar disposition and is also at odds with present practice in England. Nonetheless, we feel such a requirement is essential. Compulsory treatment conflicts with our previously stated sentencing policy that within the context of a just sentence the offender should not only have access to adequate psychiatric treatment but should also have a right to refuse such treatment. We feel that an offender who has been found responsible for his acts and capable of being tried should also be capable of consenting to or refusing medical treatment. His status as a prisoner should not deprive him of the right to make this decision any more than it does his right to decide whether he will have his tonsils removed or his wisdom teeth pulled.

We realize that there are problems in requiring hospital orders to be made by consent only, especially where the offender's refusal stems directly from his disorder. For example, a person paranoid about doctors and hospitals would always refuse treatment. Notwithstanding this possibility, we feel that there are other values at stake and that the requirement of consent is too important to waive even in these special cases. Here, it should again be noted that we are dealing with an offender who was fit to stand trial and responsible enough to be sentenced. Is it not only fair that he also be considered fit and responsible enough to make his own choice with regard to treatment? As well, we feel there is great danger in opening the door even slightly to non-consensual treatment. Exceptions might soon become the rule and could result in the imposition of hospital orders in virtually all cases on the basis that an offender who refuses help is obviously irrational and unable to exercise rational choice.

As is often the case in criminal law, this is a question of choosing between competing values. Some feel that society is justified in imposing any treatment on offenders if it will reduce the possibility of further criminality. This is an assumption, however, which is not supported by clinical evidence. Others take the view that the involuntary treatment of offenders is an unwarranted interference with basic individual rights. The position adopted by the Commission is that conviction of a criminal offence may warrant, as a last resort, the deprivation of an offender's liberty, but not deprivation or interference with other basic rights, one of which is the right not to be subjected to treatment without consent. Our position is further reinforced by the well-documented failure of many compulsory treatment programs in other jurisdictions.

iv. Conclusion on Hospital Orders

Hospital orders should improve sentencing policy and practice. It is not, however, to be regarded as a "cure-all" and may, indeed, be restricted to relatively few offenders. There will still exist a need for diversion of the mentally ill at the pre-trial stage, the traditional concept of fitness to stand trial and to consider the effects of mental disorder on criminal irresponsibility. There will also continue to be need for psychiatric services within prison themselves; this we discuss in the following paragraphs.

D. Mental Disorder in Prisons

i. Transfers to Mental Hospitals

There are currently several statutory provisions authorizing the transfer of mentally disordered prisoners to psychiatric hospitals. But these provisions have been ineffective for years. Examples of inefficiency, neglect and official indifference were first cited in official investigations in 1938, again in 1956 and, most recently, in 1969. There has been little indication that this situation has significantly improved.

Why is this the case? Although the written law could be improved the real problem here is with practice. In the jurisdictional game between departments and governments the players have lost sight of the objective—the needs of the mentally ill prisoner. It is inexcusable that such inmates are neglected while federal and provincial governments argue over who has responsibility for their custody, care and treatment, and who should foot the bill. The various governments and departments need to sort out their respective jurisdictions and cooperate to provide expeditious and efficient transfer provisions from prisons and penitentiaries to psychiatric facilities. As with hospital orders, such transfers should require the consent of the prisoner and the agreement of the psychiatric facility which is to receive him. Either the prisoners or the hospital may request his return to the correctional system subject, in the case of the hospital, to review by a review board. As well, what was said concerning hospital orders with respect to privileges, remission, parole, etc., apply equally here.

ii. Section 546 of the Criminal Code

There is one transfer provision that must go. It is section 546 of the Criminal Code which provides that a prisoner apparently suffering from mental disorder may be transferred to a psychiatric facility under a lieutenant governor's warrant. This section is redundant where there are similar provisions for transfers in the provincial and federal correctional legislation. It is also repugnant because it is of indefinite length and not subject to appeal or review. We therefore recommend, as has been recommended in other studies, that section 546 be repealed.

iii. *Psychiatric Services within Prisons*

There is a need for increased psychiatric services within penitentiaries and provincial correctional facilities. Inadequacies of present service are well documented elsewhere and need not be rehearsed here. It must be said, however, that there is also recent indication that such services are being considerably up-graded in some areas.

By recommending that present psychiatric services in prisons be improved we acknowledge that society should provide basic psychiatric treatment for those it imprisons. This obligation is part of society's wider obligation to respect basic human rights of all members of the society. It follows that prisoners should not be deprived of health services that would have been available to them had they not been in custody.

Questions

1. Is the compulsory treatment of persons who have broken the law ever justified?
2. In answering question 1, should the type of offence a person has committed be taken into consideration?

Containing Violence

Rodger Beehler

The novel and, more recently, the film, *A Clockwork Orange*, have been thought by many to raise in a compelling way the question of humane treatment of persons convicted of criminal brutality. What rights has the man who has himself violated, even to the point of death, the rights of another? Many claim to see in Anthony Burgess's fictional treatment of this question a delimitation of the kind of practices which may be followed in preventing crime. In *A Clockwork Orange* we find employed a method of prevention which, it is claimed, morality requires us to condemn, because it is destructive of the very possibility of moral choice and so of an essential feature of human personality.

I wish to examine this judgment. I shall seek to show that in a crucial respect the judgment is unwarranted. The question of the acceptability of preventive methods such as that of *A Clockwork Orange* being then reopened, I shall go on to inquire whether, and for what reasons, this or similar methods of containing violence should be ruled out.

From *Ethics* 92 (July 1982): 647–660. Published by The University of Chicago Press.

I

1. In *A Clockwork Orange* a young man, Alex, is made to observe on film acts of brutality of a sort he himself has committed. At the same time a drug is injected into his bloodstream which induces acute nausea. As a result Alex is eventually unable to strike out violently against persons without being immediately overcome by nausea to the point of suffocation. When this condition is reached he is released from prison.

Alex's own initial evaluation of his treatment is in terms of his release. The prison director at one point remarks: "[We] can use him as a trail-blazer. He's young, bold, vicious. Brodsky will deal with him tomorrow and you can sit in and watch. . . . It works all right, don't worry about that. This vicious young hoodlum will be transformed out of all recognition."[1] Alex comments: "And those hard slovos, brothers, were like the beginning of my freedom."[2]

We, however, are meant to appreciate that Alex has, by the treatment, been deprived of freedom—the freedom to choose between evil and good. In the book, after Alex has been conditioned, he is subjected to a humiliating roughing-up before a select audience of prison and government officials and is made (literally) to lick the boots of his aggressor. As the lights go on a voice is heard: " 'Choice,' rumbled a rich deep goloss. [Alex] viddied it belonged to the prison [chaplain]. 'He has no real choice, has he? Self-interest, fear of physical pain, drove him to that grotesque act of self-abasement. Its insincerity was clearly to be seen. He ceases to be a wrongdoer. He ceases also to be a creature capable of moral choice.' "[3] This verdict of the prison chaplain upon Alex's condition, and so upon the treatment which created it, proceeds from the following reasoning (the words are the chaplain's own, taken from several places in the novel).[4]

> The question is whether such a technique can really make a man good. Goodness comes from within. . . . Goodness is something chosen. When a man cannot choose he ceases to be a man.[5]

> Alex is to be made into a good boy. . . . Never again will he have the desire to commit acts of violence or to offend in any way against the State's peace.[6]

> What does God want? Does God want goodness or the choice of goodness? Is a man who chooses the bad . . . in some way . . . better than a man who has the good imposed on him? . . . And yet, in a sense, in choosing to be deprived of the ability to make an ethical choice, you have in a sense really chosen the good? So I should like to think.[7]

But the chaplain is not able to think this, despite his wish to. The conclusion which keeps forcing itself upon him is that the man who can choose, though he chooses the bad, *is* better than the man who "has the good imposed on him." Not in the sense that he is a better man, but in the sense that, morally considered, it is better that a man should be capable of choosing evil than that he should be incapable of choosing at all.

The idea which grips the chaplain is this. A man who chooses evil, at least *could* choose good. He could become a good man. But the man who has been deprived of the ability to choose evil, cannot, therefore, choose good either. He cannot become a good man. "For goodness comes from within. Goodness is something chosen."

2.   This reasoning, I shall try to show, is mistaken. But first I wish to point out that the chaplain also makes a mistake as to fact, a mistake which helps him to commit the error of reasoning I have just spoken of. It is not true that Alex will never again desire to commit acts of violence or to offend in any way against the state's peace. When, following the treatment, Alex is harassed for the benefit of the select audience, he reacts to that harassment in this way:

> Now I knew that I'd have to real skorry and get my cut-throat britva out before this horrible killing sickness whooshed up and turned the like joy of battle into feeling I was going to snuff it. But, O my brothers, as my rooker reached for the britva in my inside carman I got this like picture in my mind's glazzy of this insulting chelloveck howling for mercy with the red krovvy all streaming out of his rot, and hot after this picture the sickness and dryness and pains were rushing to overtake, and I viddied that I'd have to change the way I felt about this rotten veck. . . .[8]

Later, when he returns home, Alex would like very much to knock about the lodger who has displaced him, but he is forced, as he puts it, "to be all reasonable and smiling for my health's sake." He continues to be capable of lies and of theft. But more: it is not altogether clear that there is anything in Alex's condition to prevent his violating people by remote control, as it were. He might very well be an effective director of Murder Inc. The evidence for this is his reaction to the photograph of a woman he and his companions had (before his confinement) brutally raped. "I viddie his wife on the wall, a bolshy, blown-up photo, so I felt a malenky bit sick remembering." He felt a *little bit* sick remembering. Fine. Keep away from what makes you remember.

Alex continues, then, to desire to commit acts of violence. The difference is that now he cannot. He would like to go on as before; but he cannot. This is the man "on whom the good has been imposed."

3.   I turn now to the error of reasoning spoken of a moment ago. Burgess and the chaplain continually see the technique as making Alex no longer capable of choosing evil. "He has no real choice, has he?" And this alleged fact, that Alex can no longer *choose* evil, is, they claim, what puts the technique morally out of reach. But there is an ambiguity attaching to the expression "can no longer choose evil." Alex can (and in fact continues to) choose evil after the treatment. For he can, and does, *desire* to do what it is wrong to do. What he cannot choose is to do it.

The argument of the book, put barely, is this:

1.   Goodness comes from within; goodness is something chosen.
2.   Alex has been deprived of the ability to make an ethical choice. Therefore

3. Goodness is not possible for Alex. He has been deprived of the possibility of becoming a good man.

It is for this reason, that Alex is no longer a moral chooser, that we are to oppose the treatment.

But it is not true, what the chaplain asserts (and students with whom I have discussed these issues insist), that Alex ceases upon treatment to be capable of moral choice. What is true is that he ceases to be capable of moral choice respecting acts of violence. He ceases to be so, just in the sense that, as remarked earlier, he cannot now *choose* whether to commit, or not to commit, acts of violence. He cannot but keep from committing them. But this does not mean that he ceases to be a creature capable of moral choice *tout court*. The imprisoned man too is deliberately deprived of the opportunity to choose whether or not to keep from wrong. Yet in his case, and even more so in Alex's, there remain myriad opportunities open to each for the exercise of moral choice. The chaplain's charge that upon treatment Alex "ceases to be a man" is groundless and confused.

However, the fatal confusion in the chaplain's reasoning is his equating "goodness comes from within" with "goodness is something chosen." In the most important construction of this word relative to our inquiry, goodness is *not* something chosen. It is the good (or bad) *act* which is chosen, but not the good or bad character or disposition.[9] Because the chaplain runs together the good act, which can be chosen, and the good "will" or disposition, which does come from within, and cannot be chosen, he thinks that because Alex has been deprived of the possibility of moral choice respecting acts of violence he has been deprived of the possibility of becoming a good man.

But if goodness does "come from within," why cannot it come to Alex? All this will require is that he should come to desire not to hurt others, for their sake. Or to put it the other way about: that he should cease to desire to hurt them.

We are all, I expect, agreed that so long as Alex keeps from brutal wrongdoing only because it is imperative, for his own sake, that he keep from it, he is not a good man. He has not chosen goodness. Nor did Alex at any time see himself as choosing goodness. He was cynical about the treatment from the start. He looked to it for nothing except release from prison. And it demonstrably did not transform him into a good man.

But neither did it rule out his becoming a good man. It does not follow, because he now avoids doing wrong for self-interested reasons, while still desiring to hurt others, that he has somehow been made irredeemable. He is as redeemable, or as unredeemable, as he was before. He may in fact be a bit more redeemable, in that he may now be forced to submit to more stable and continuous relations with others of a kind which might conceivably in time give rise to disinterested concern on his part for the welfare of others. But whether this will occur or not is irrelevant. The fact is that it is as conceivable now that Alex should reform—that he should cease to want brutally to mistreat others, for their sake—as it was conceivable before. Before the treatment he was by everyone, including the chaplain, accounted capable of ethical choice. Why is he not capable of it now? All he has to be capable of is choosing the good of others: where this means only that he should sincerely desire their good; or, at least, that he should desire that they not suffer. The fact that after the treatment Alex *cannot* harm others does not matter here, so long as he can come to *desire*, out of a genuine concern for others, *not* to harm them. What is to prevent him coming to desire this? If you say "the kind of person he is," he was that kind of person before the treatment.

II

It seems, then, that any ruling out of the *Clockwork Orange* technique as a method of containing criminal violence cannot turn on the argument "it deprives the violator of moral choice, and therefore puts him or her outside the possibility of goodness." This reasoning does not convince. There is in the novel a further claim which requires to be weighed: that to accept such a technique would be to put into the hands of governments a tool which might be used to subject anyone to their will. But tools virtually as effective exist already and are not for this reason withdrawn.

Still the question remains, are we to accept the use of techniques like that of the novel to contain criminal violence? To this question I now turn.[10] (It is, of course, conceivable that the prohibition even of nonviolent actions might be executed by such means. Thus people might be kept from reading books by such a method. But I shall confine my attention to a proposal to employ the technique only against criminal violence. And I shall, unless otherwise noted, assume that the treatment is to be nonvoluntary, i.e., imposed.)

1.   Persons who wish to resist the use of such techniques may insist upon the uncertainty which attaches to our assessment of a person's being liable to violate others. They may wish to stress that we do not *know* that a man, even a man already convicted of criminal violence, will in future assault or kill persons. But the fact that we do not know is not reason enough to settle the question as these people wish it to be settled. For it will be sufficient if we have very good reason to believe that a man will violently mistreat others. And sometimes, as in the case of Alex, we have every reason to believe that he will. (No one is going to argue for a blanket use of such techniques, and everyone will want to insist that some persons found guilty of violent wrongdoing could never in justice be deserving of subjection to the treatment being discussed.)

Those who wish to stress the uncertainty factor will be joined by others who from the beginning will admit that in the case of someone like Alex transgression is virtually certain, but nevertheless wish to insist that the method of containing violence under discussion must be ruled out. Some other method, such as imprisonment, must be employed.

A man who is imprisoned cannot choose to violate others (so long as no one is vulnerable to him).[11] He cannot, if the proper precautions are taken, kill or inflict pain until such time as he is returned to the company of persons outside prison. But the imprisoned man can continue to desire to work his violence on others. He can hate. He can resent. He can be further corrupted. He can form intentions which time may give him the opportunity to fulfill. It is precisely for this reason that in respect of persons like Alex imprisonment gives rise to what has to date appeared to be an insuperable problem: for how long (and how effectively) can such persons be kept imprisoned? I do not have in mind here the economic question of public expense. I have in mind the questions: Can we risk their escaping? Can we allow them to be paroled? The evidence to date is depressing in suggesting that people who enter prison, certainly those who enter as the kind of human being Alex is, are released, or escape, from prison unchanged. If they leave changed, it is often for the worse, especially in respect of their ability to fit into, and find themselves within, the on-going life of a community from which they have for a long time been removed.

Some of those who wish to insist that imprisonment is the only humane way to deal with persons of a vicious nature propose a life term without parole as the answer to the question whether such persons ought in time to be released. This suggestion does not obviously carry great appeal. In the course of the still current discussions in Canada about whether to reintroduce the death penalty it has been suggested that at least as effective a deterrent would be a twenty-five-year sentence without parole. Fifteen convicted murderers were asked what their response was to this proposal. They replied that such a sentence would tend to turn a man into an animal; that deprived of hope of release within an endurable length of time, a man would kill to escape. He would, these men said, having nothing to lose.

2.   Suppose, however, it were possible to remove by some method the very desire to kill or inflict pain (through performance of a surgical operation of the brain, say).[12] Unlike Alex, who ceases to inflict pain because of pain which he himself is made to feel, the person treated by the surgical technique is now to experience no desire or inclination to inflict pain. This is a change, not in what he is able to do, but in him.

We are inclined, I think, to say that this method of control would be more radical than the *Clockwork Orange* technique. Are we also to say that it is more to be deplored? Under the method of the novel, desires to wreak violence are present but frustrated. With the surgical technique there is no consequent frustration or pain. Is this not a more desirable, even if more radical, method? I think the answer must be that it is (or would be) more desirable—provided it has no other effects. (Unless one is to put greater weight, not on protection and control, but on punishment and retribution. But if we are able to choose between a greater certainty of prevention, without punishment, and a lesser certainty of prevention, but with punitive incarceration or frustration of the criminal, is someone to prefer the second to the first?)

"By surgery we remove the desire of the person to inflict harm on others." But what exactly is it that we bring about? Is it simply that the person *as a matter of fact* no longer desires to inflict harm on others? Or is it that he or she *is no longer capable* of desiring to inflict harm on others? These two are different. Many persons presently do not desire to inflict harm on others. They do not take pleasure in the brutal violation of another human being. On the contrary, they wish others to go unharmed. These persons are, therefore, in a sense, incapable of inflicting brutal harm on others. But this is a psychological, not a physical, incapacity, and does not make them other than self-directed. If then what the surgical treatment did was to make the brutal man a person of this kind, it would leave him self-directed also. Objection to the surgical technique could not be mounted on the ground that it deprives one of self-direction. It would have to turn on the fact that this transformation from evil to good was not self-directed.

If, on the other hand, the person, after surgery, were to be physiologically incapable of desiring to inflict harm on others, in the sense that such actions could not "neurologically" be an object of his or her desire, here we may indeed seem to have someone who, in respect of one particular class of actions, is no longer self-directed.[13] This person who has been surgically treated no longer desires to inflict harm on others, not (as in the case of the humane person) because he desires the opposite, but because his objects of possible desire have now been confined by surgery, and this one kind of actions (brutal actions) has been ruled out. They are ruled out not by choice, or by desire, or by "character," but by surgery. Here we are, I think, inclined to say that in respect not merely of the commission of violent wrongs but of the very desire to inflict harm, this person has been interfered with in a way which leaves him not "self-" but "surgically-"directed.

But this is not, I have already established, the case with the method of the novel. Alex not only can desire to do violence after the treatment, he does desire to do it. He can even attempt to do violence. What is changed is that he cannot now successfully attempt it. Furthermore, in respect of autonomy, persons treated by the method of the novel continue to be able to respond to life in all the manifold ways which are not affected by the treatment. Their autonomy is affected only in that they are, literally, in respect of one type of actions, coerced.

3.   Some may answer that the treatment in the novel is destructive of autonomy in a different way in that it amounts to the replacement of rational engagement by brute control. And it is true that in respect of violence there is no rational engagement with the person treated. There is no appeal to reason to control his actions. But appeals to reason are only effective where there are desires of a sort that are susceptible to reasons. The fact that a gun is pointed at his head will be a reason for someone like Alex to cease or keep from violence because he desires to live. But when he is alone with a victim, what reason has he not to work his will on him? The fact that he may be caught will not always be a sufficient reason; for it is also a fact that he may not be caught. And appeals to reason which take the form "have pity on them" will (*ex hypothesi*) not have any force here. For people like Alex, therefore, there will be no foothold for any recourse to reason to keep them from harming others, unless we can give them a reason not to harm others—unless we can make it worth their while to desist. But for how long can we effectively do this?

It is, admittedly, true that persons treated by the method of the novel are themselves now more vulnerable to wrongful treatment by others. Persons who cannot violently strike out against others are at the same time unable to use violence to defend themselves—or others—against aggression. It has been suggested to me[14] that one proposal might be: let everyone be treated in this way. The force of this proposal turns, I think, on our awareness of the enormous good that would be realized in human life if violence were entirely done away with. It is the picture of this good which makes the proposal attractive as well as alarming. The alarm, unfortunately, is as well grounded as the attraction. What irrevocably rules out this proposal is, I think, the risk that it would be open to abuse. Those who had control of the processes of treatment might too easily exclude themselves and thus deliver everyone into their hands, incapable of defense. (This is not to mention the seemingly insuperable difficulties which attach to the present division of humankind into states; or the fact that the suggestion will seem to many a retreat from all that is manly and courageous.)

It is undeniable, therefore, that treatment will leave the violator at greater risk that he will be mistreated, being incapable of defense. This risk is further increased if his condition becomes widely known. And it would have to be, to some extent, publicly known, since one thing which would be a paramount importance in the event such a method of prevention were allowed is that the conviction and treatment of persons for unregenerate criminal brutality should be closely overseen by ombudsmen and the press. But this scrutiny need not involve prominent or even mass circulation of the fact. And such risk as obtains would almost certainly be no greater than that which attaches to confinement in a prison with other convicted felons. Furthermore, it needs to be remembered throughout that any loss in the form of increased risk to the violator is paralleled by the gain that all innocent persons who would be violated by him will now go unharmed.

4.   It has been proposed that one means of preventing criminal acts would be to monitor the movements, and also the conversations, of convicted persons released on probation or parole. It has been urged against this proposal—by Charles Fried—that electronic surveillance removes the possibility of relationships "which we would hardly be human if we had to do without." Fried observes:

> In the role of citizen or fellow worker [a person] need reveal himself to no greater extent than is necessary to display the attributes of competence and morality appropriate to those roles. In order to be a friend or lover one must reveal more of himself. Yet where any intimate revelation may be heard by monitoring officials, it loses the quality of exclusive intimacy required of a gesture of love or friendship. Thus monitoring, in depriving one of privacy, destroys the possibility of bestowing the gift of intimacy, and makes impossible the essential dimension of love and friendship.
>
> Monitoring similarly undermines the subject's capacity to enter into relations of trust. . . . Trust . . . require[s] the possibility of error on the part of the person trusted. The negation of trust is constant surveillance—such as monitoring—which minimizes the possibility of undetected default. The monitored parolee is denied the sense of self-respect inherent in being trusted by the government which has released him. More important, monitoring prevents the parolee from entering into true relations of trust with persons in the outside world. An employer, unaware of the monitoring, who entrusts a sum of money to the parolee, cannot thereby grant him the sense of responsibility and autonomy which an unmonitored person in the same position would have. The parolee in a real—if special and ironical—sense, cannot be trusted.[15]

Do these considerations which Fried has isolated in respect of monitoring bear as well upon the treatment of *A Clockwork Orange?*

I believe the answer to this question must be no. In the first place, what is done to

Alex does not deprive him of privacy. It is not the equivalent of monitoring. It involves nothing like observation. It is a form of incapacitating, more analogous to tying up a person's arm than following him about the streets and overhearing. It is true that some persons will know of Alex's condition. But this can hardly count as an indefensible invasion of privacy, since it has a daily parallel in the knowledge of some persons that others do not pay their bills, have been fined for traffic offenses, or convicted of petty theft—or murder—and so on.

Second, in the case of the *Clockwork Orange* treatment the person treated can obviously continue to be trusted in respect of everything except violence. He is able to enter into all manner of human activities and relationships where he can obviously be trusted to do or keep from doing all manner of things.

Third, while it is true that Alex is not trusted to keep from doing violence, this is not any change introduced by the treatment. That is partly why he was in fact treated: to keep him from doing what he could not be trusted not to do. What then has changed? "What has changed," some may say, "is that, as Fried points out, now he *cannot* be trusted, because he is unable to do what one might have trusted him not to do." But there is a sense in which Fried is wrong and Alex (and the monitored parolee) can be trusted after the treatment or release. Fried at one point in his discussion remarks: "There can be no trust where there is no possibility of error. More specifically, a man cannot know that he is trusted unless he has a right to act without constant surveillance so that he knows he can betray the trust. Privacy confers that essential right. And since, as I have argued, trust in its fullest sense is reciprocal, the man who cannot be trusted cannot himself trust or learn to trust. Without privacy and the possibility of error which it protects that aspect of his humanity is denied to him."[16] I have difficulty with each of these claims. The first claim, interpreted as Fried intends it, is, I believe, false. Fried is saying that one peson cannot trust another where it is not possible for the person trusted to do what he is trusted not to do. But what Fried ought to have said is that one person cannot trust another where the one who is to trust *knows* that the other person cannot do what he is "trusted" not to do. It is not, as Fried claims, that there cannot be trusting where there is no possibility of breaking the trust; it is rather that there cannot be trusting where there is knowledge by the one who is to trust that there is no possibility of breaking the trust. Trusting is something this person (the one who is to trust) *does*. And what is to prevent my trusting you if I do not know that, as a matter of fact, you cannot do what I am prepared to trust you will not do? I do not know that; and until some reason arises which causes me to withdraw my trust, I trust you.

And you can know that. You can know that my attitude toward you is one of trust. Fried says that a man cannot know that he is trusted if he knows that he cannot betray the trust (the suggestion being that the man cannot therefore be trusted). But Fried gives no argument here, and until he does I am unable to see why we should accept his claim. Nor why we should allow that a man who is monitored cannot himself trust others; trust them, for example, not to disclose to others that he is on probation or parole.[17]

If I am right, persons treated by the *Clockwork Orange* technique could be trusted, even in respect of violence. They could be left alone in situations where before they would have committed violations, by persons who do not know that they cannot violate. And these people who have been treated could know that they are trusted. They could appreciate that someone who is unaware of their past, or that they have been treated, does trust them. They could therefore—what Fried claims cannot occur—*feel* trusted.

This possibility could, in fact, be a foothold for these persons' coming to be someone for whom integrity, being trusted, could matter. If one of these persons saw that other people trusted him, he might find himself desiring to be worthy of that trust. He might find himself wanting not to betray it. This could be the beginning of moral redemption.

It cannot, then, be for the reason that "it deprives of privacy, and so of relationships we should scarcely be human without" that the method of *A Clockwork Orange* is to be ruled out.[18]

5. There is an objection to the method which has not yet been considered which many will, I believe, account decisive. This objection is that in employing the method of the novel against offenders we should cease to respect, and to treat, these persons, *as persons*.

Ordinarily the only way to render a person incapable of doing violence is to overpower the person or to confine him or her in isolation. The difference the treatment being discussed makes is that a person who is not overpowered or confined by other persons is yet continuously coerced. He is coerced by a psychophysiological reaction to his own desire or effort to commit violence.

Now this condition of a person will be judged by almost everyone an undesirable state—considered alone, without attention to any other considerations. But some will hold that to introduce such a condition in some persons may be justified by the good that accrues from it to others. However, those whose objection I am trying to sketch will judge that the bringing about of this condition can never be justified because it constitutes the denial of that capacity to act, or keep from acting, which is (held by them to be) one of the constitutive features of a person. Removal of this capacity, they will claim, especially in respect of actions which are deeply expressive of the individual's "personality," is reduction from a person to something nearer a thing, in relating to whom we are now able to circumvent the kind of engagement appropriate to (and required of us by) a person.

These opponents of the technique admit that placing this absolute importance upon the psychophysiological integrity of persons restricts the means we may take to decrease the possibility of evil. But whatever greater risk of evil results from this restriction of methods, and so whatever greater evil comes to be done, is accepted by them, as one of the costs of a world in which persons are to be respected as persons, no matter how brutal or terrible their acts. Many who are claimed by this view will further insist that alternative methods (the creation of a more humane social environment or changes in child upbringing) are (and always have been) available to us which promise to be at least as, if not more, effective than the kind of method being discussed. The extraordinary effort and difficulty (as compared with our present expenditure) which these options involve are a cost, and so a sacrifice, that any community genuinely moved by compassion but also by a respect for persons must, and should, be prepared to bear.

This judgment, which is impressive in its charity and humanity, has a parallel in an earlier judgment by John Stuart Mill. Mill resisted virtually every form of interference with the voluntary acts of persons except where such interference was necessary to prevent wrongdoing. One exception he made was voluntary enslavement, which he was prepared to employ the law to prevent. It is Mill's reason for opposing voluntary enslavement which affords the parallel:

> The reason for not interfering, unless for the sake of others, with a person's voluntary acts, is consideration for his liberty. His voluntary choice is evidence that what he so chooses is desirable, or at least endurable, to him, and his good is on the whole best provided for by allowing him to take his own means of pursuing it. But by selling himself for a slave, he abdicates his liberty; he foregoes any future use of it beyond that single act. He therefore defeats, in his own case, the very purpose which is the justification of allowing him to dispose of himself.[19]

Very briefly, Mill distinguishes between an act freely performed and liberty. Liberty is not an act but a condition. It is the condition of not being subject to interference, except when one should seek to harm others. This condition Mill values absolutely. So, too, in the objection being discussed, a person's being able to act is accounted a good independently of any good or evil effects of his actions. An absolute value is being placed on the integrity of a person to act, which integrity is identified as partly constitutive of what a person is and as partly constitutive of the condition appropriate to a person. In each case, to violate this capacity is to disregard, to fail to respect, the nature and entitlements of personhood.

Now Mill, as we have seen, objects to enslavement because it constitutes a continuous restriction upon a person's acts. But the technique of the novel is proposed to be used to restrict only acts which Mill himself would wish to have restricted. Does this mean that we may, after all, allow the technique of the novel, provided it is employed only against those who prove a threat to others?

Mill would, I believe, still oppose the technique, for a reason which many would wish to second. The reason Mill opposes even voluntary enslavement is because he considers it the distinctive mark of a human life that a person's acts proceed from his or her own deliberations and initiative. Slavery negates or severely diminishes the ability (and need) to deliberate and choose, because the routine of one's actions is laid down by another. There is a depreciation of the need for a critical, rational engagement with one's experience, and for the discrimination, evaluation, and adjustment of one's wants, aspirations, and practice in the flow of time. A life is lived, but its pattern is not the work of the one who lives it. There is a diminishment of what D.H. Lawrence called "the venture into consciousness," and so (therefore) a lessening of the possibility of any growth or development which is, at least in part, a self-development.

Similarly, the technique of the novel accomplishes control of a person's violent inclincations, not through a moral response on the part of the person to others, but by means of a psychophysiological incapacitation. Mill would, I believe, argue that such a control diminishes the possibility of moral engagement, and of moral development, on the part of the individual. (It is important to note that the objection is not simply that evil is prevented here other than by the voluntary refraining—for moral reasons—on the part of the person in question. For this is true even of seizure and imprisonment, which virtually all of us are at some point prepared to do.)

6. Can anything be urged in reply to this position? I think at least two things can be said. First: since the technique allows the person to be restored to the community—that is, to liberty as Mill understands it—there may in fact be a greater chance of moral redemption than when the person is confined in prison. (There is also, it might be urged, a greater respect for the violator as a person; for it is still possible for him or her to engage in that overwhelming majority of activities and relationships which are not morally prohibited.) Second, situations may arise where a violator asks to be treated in this way because he wants to be kept from violent acts but knows that this cannot be assured solely through a personal determination to reform. In Burgess's novel the chaplain at one point asks, in a passage quoted earlier: "In *choosing to be deprived* of the ability to make an ethical choice, . . . have [you] in a sense really chosen the good?" Once we see that no such deprivation attends the technique sketched in the novel we are even better able to appreciate that it might voluntarily be sought as a first step toward moral reclamation. (And notice that persons who seek out a variant of the technique in order to stop drinking or smoking are not for this reason alone judged to be bankrupt of moral will. The seeking out may be a moral advance.)[20]

However, there is a final objection which needs to be uttered against this reply. This is that the use of techniques of criminal control like that in the novel could easily have the effect of preventing—by reducing the political need for—changes in those features of our society which contribute most to the emergence of persons like Alex in the first place. Would these changes be striven for if such methods were available to neutralize the amoral and brutal offspring of our common life?

Appendix

Glossary of Terms from *A Clockwork Orange*

Bolsby Big, great	*Glazzy* Eye	*Ptitsa* Chick	*Slovo* Word
Britva Razor	*Goloss* Voice	*Rooker* Hand	*Snuff It* Die
Carman Pocket	*Krovvy* Blood	*Rot* Mouth	*Veck* (*See* Chelloveck)
Charlie Chaplain	*Malenky* Little, tiny	*Skorry* Quick	*Viddy* See
Chelloveck Person, man, fellow			

Notes

1. Anthony Burgess, *A Clockwork Orange* (Harmondsworth: Penguin Books, 1972), p. 74.
2. Ibid. (For those unfamiliar with the slang employed by Alex, a glossary is appended to the paper.)
3. Ibid., p. 99.
4. Perhaps it is worth remarking that they are also, in more than the ordinary sense, Anthony Burgess's words as well. I have twice heard Burgess in a televised interview

give precisely the judgment upon the *Clockwork Orange* technique that the chaplain gives in the novel and for the same reasons. I have also heard him declare at my own university, in a public lecture and in a seminar, that his purpose in writing the book was, in part, to resist such methods of control. (Burgess has restated this verdict in *The Clockwork Testament, Or Enderby's End* [London: Hart-Davis, MacGibbon, 1974]; see, e.g., p. 86.)

5. Burgess, *A Clockwork Orange*, p. 67.
6. Ibid.
7. Ibid., pp. 67, 76.
8. Ibid., p. 98.
9. For a rebuttal of the contrary position see Rodger Beehler, "Reasons for Being Moral," *Analysis* 33 (1972): 12–16; and *Moral Life* (Oxford: Basil Blackwell, 1978), chap. 6.
10. I had not, when I first began this essay, intended to take up this question. The need to face up to it was pressed on me by H.J.N. Horsburgh. He at least must now forgive the inadequacy of what follows.
11. In *A Clockwork Orange* a man thrust into an already overcrowded cell is brutally beaten to death.
12. This alternative was suggested to me for consideration by G.T. Monticone. I want to thank him, and Kai Nielsen, for a conversation (now a long time ago) which gave me this, and one other, suggestion for consideration.
13. I am assuming throughout that the surgery has just the effect mentioned. One reason why the chaplain and others are inclined to see the technique as removing *all* choice or self-direction may be that we find it hard not to imagine that intrusion into a person's brain to effect any change would reduce the person completely to a "robot."
14. By Kai Nielsen. (I do not wish to suggest that Kai Nielsen subscribes to this proposal.)
15. Charles Fried, *An Anatomy of Values: Problems of Personal and Social Choice* (Cambridge, Mass.: Harvard University Press, 1970), pp. 147–48. The relevant pages are reprinted under the title "Privacy" in *Philosophical Issues*, ed. James Rachels and Frank Tillman (New York: Harper & Row, 1972). pp. 220–221.
16. Ibid., p. 145.
17. There is, however, a difficulty about trust in the probation and parole cases. One possible objection to monitoring movements, though it applies still more to recording conversations, might be, not that it deprives the person of the possibility of being trusted by anyone (which it does not), but that it renders inoperative the function, certainly of probation, but also, to a certain extent, the function of parole. It removes any possibility of settling whether this or that probationer or parolee ought to be trusted. We who follow his movements or associations cannot trust him to keep from wrong. How then are we ever to be able to point to a successful probation or parole as justifying our releasing him from interdict (or police surveillance)? We have deprived ourselves of the opportunity of seeing whether he can be trusted.
18. One of the journal referees has with wonderful courtesy put to me the question whether relations of mutual trust which depend on ignorance of the treated person's condition could have the value Fried has in mind. I believe they could have the most important values identified by Fried: they could foster self-respect, so far as the treated person appreciates that he or she is being received trustingly by the other, and a sense of responsibility, so far as the treated person appreciated that this trust is given in the expectation it will not be betrayed. It is true that persons who must be treated to render them no threat to others might not be moved by these recognitions. But this is no effect of the treatment.
19. John Stuart Mill, *On Liberty*, chap. 5.
20. I was helped to recollect this fact by the comment of an anonymous member of a university audience in Victoria several years ago, where I first delivered the thoughts that have become this paper. Perhaps this is the place as well to thank the members of the departments of philosophy and political science at Dalhousie University, who later listened to a longer version of this essay and encouraged me to think it had merit.

Questions

1. In earlier contributions to this chapter, authors have made a distinction between restraining those thought to pose a danger to others and treating such persons against their will. Is the conditioning imposed on Alex described in section I of Beehler's essay an example of imposing restraint or of imposing treatment? Does Beehler's discussion suggest that the distinction is less clear and less helpful than might be thought?
2. Beehler suggests that the condition imposed on Alex is not an obstacle to his becoming a good man. Although his freedom to act in a violent way has been blocked, he is still free to choose to alter his attitude toward violence, an attitude that in fact remains in spite of the conditioning process. Do you agree?
3. Would Alex have been better off if the treatment imposed on him had also removed his desire to commit violent acts?
4. Are techniques of behaviour control similar in nature to that imposed on Alex acceptable alternatives to imprisonment?
5. How effective is Beehler's defence of the conditioning technique used on Alex (see Beehler's point 6 above) against the kind of objection to be derived from Mill's objection to slavery (discussed by Beehler in point 4)?
6. Beehler offers no response to the objection formulated in the last paragraph of his essay. What kind of response could be constructed? Is this a weighty objection to the kind of treatment imposed on Alex?

Paternalism and Justification

James Woodward

Much recent discussion in moral philosophy has focused on the contrast between those moral theories which are consequentialist in structure and those moral theories which admit independent side constraints on the means which can be used to achieve various ends. In this essay* I shall attempt to show that this contrast provides an illuminating framework against which to understand two conflicting strategies for justifying paternalistic interference. The first, consequentialist strategy takes paternalistic interference to be justified when it will protect or perhaps enhance some valued goal or end state, such as an agent's welfare or future ability to choose.

Reprinted from *New Essays in Ethics and Public Policy* (*Canadian Journal of Philosophy*, Supplementary Vol. 8, 1982), edited by Nielsen and Patten.

*I would like to thank Phillip Devine, Norman Gillespie, Hardy Jones, Martin Perlmutter, and Ken Winkler for helpful comments on earlier versions of this essay.

Gerald Dworkin's essay "Paternalism"[1] contains what is perhaps the most compelling recent development of this sort of rationale for paternalistic interference and accordingly much of my subsequent discussion will focus on this essay. The second, non-consequentialist strategy holds that the consent of the person interfered with functions as a side-constraint on the justification of paternalistic interference and that without such consent, paternalistic interference is not justified, no matter how much good it may do an agent. In this essay I shall develop the contrast between these two different ways of justifying paternalistic interference and attempt to show that the second, non-consequentialist kind of justification is to be preferred to the first.

By paternalistic interference we may understand interference with a person's liberty of action or ability or opportunity to acquire information for reasons having to do not with rights and welfare of others but rather with the good of the person so treated. It is true, of course, that when a person engages in self-damaging behavior, he often also imposes costs on others. These costs will sometimes yield very good reasons for restricting such conduct, but these reasons will not be paternalistic reasons and hence will be beyond the scope of this essay.

I

One very plausible consequentialist rationale for paternalistic interference is suggested, if not fully endorsed, by Gerald Dworkin in his essay "Paternalism." Agreeing with Mill's contention that paternalistic interference is justified in order to prevent someone from selling himself into slavery, Dworkin writes

> The main consideration for not allowing such a contract [in which a person sells himself into slavery] is the need to preserve the liberty of the person to make some future choices. This gives a principle—a very narrow one—by which to justify some paternalistic interferences. Paternalism is justified only to preserve a wider range of freedom of the individual in question.[2]

Let us call this rationale the diminishment of freedom rationale (DFR). This rationale tells us that paternalistic interference is justified only when it is necessary to prevent an agent from engaging in a course of action which will significantly diminish his freedom to make future choices.

We can think of DFR as one instance of a general family of consequentialist rationales for paternalistic interference which share the same general structure. Each such rationale will attach great moral value to an agent's being in a certain condition or end-state (where this value is at least in part independent of the agent's choosing, valuing, or consenting to being in that condition) and will then urge that paternalistic interference is justified when it will preserve or perhaps promote this value. Another member of this family, which will be attractive to many, is the diminishment of welfare rationale (DWR), which permits interference in order to prevent a serious diminishment in an agent's welfare. And, insofar as there are other kinds of bad consequences for agents (e.g. loss of moral character, religious faith, or aesthetic sensitivity) besides losses of freedom or welfare, one may imagine consequentialist principles which permit paternalistic interference in order to preserve these values as well. One may also envision consequentialist principles that permit interference to enhance as well as to prevent diminishments in the above values, and "mixed" principles which permit interference in order to protect or enhance combinations of the above values.[3] In what follows I shall argue that all of the rationales in this family share certain fundamental defects which have to do with their consequentialist structure and not with the content of the particular end-states which they take to warrant interference.

Consequentialist justifications for paternalistic treatment differ fundamentally from those justifications which make reference in some way to the consent of the person so treated. I turn now to an exploration of such justifications. As a number of writers have noted, one of the cases in which paternalistic interference seems most obviously justified is when the person interfered with actually gives his consent to such interference. Consider, to use Gerald Dworkin's example, the case of Odysseus, who "commands his men to tie him to the mast and refuse all future orders to be set free, because he knows the power of the Sirens to enchant men with their songs." Here Odysseus explicitly consents to the subsequent interference with his freedom of action by his men.[4] Their interference does not frustrate Odysseus' attempt to attain those aims he judges most important but rather represents the way which Odysseus chooses to attain his ends. According to a consent-based theory, it is Odysseus' consent and not the fact that in interfering the sailors will preserve something thought to be good for Odysseus (e.g. his freedom or welfare) which justifies interference.

In other cases in which paternalistic interference seems obviously justified, the person interfered with (call her Alice) fails to consent to interference prior to the time at which it occurs but (a) it seems reasonable to attribute this failure to the fact that Alice lacks certain capacities or opportunities to gather information which are necessary for informed consent and (b) it seems reasonable to suppose that Alice will possess such opportunities or capacities in the future and that when she does so, she will restrospectively consent to the interference with no serious prospect of a change of mind. A variety of cases fit this pattern. Imagine, to use an example of Mill's, that Alice is unknowingly about to try to cross a washed-out bridge. If there is not time to warn her it seems justifiable to restrain her at least until the condition of the bridge can be described to her. A consent-based theory will see the considerations which justify interference in such a case as natural extensions of the considerations which justify interference in the Odysseus case. In the Odysseus case, the sailors choose, in interfering, as Odysseus himself has explicitly chosen. In the present case we have no explicit expression of choice to act on before interference, but we can rely on (can, in choosing, be guided by) the next best thing: the requirement that we choose as we may reasonably expect the person interfered with would choose, had she the capacities and opportunities necessary for informed choice. Thus, according to a consent-based theory, interference is justifiable in the above case because there is every reason to suppose that Alice will retrospectively consent to being restrained once she is informed of our assessment of the condition of the bridge.[5]

In another kind of case in which it is reasonable to expect retrospective consent the person interfered with fails to consent to interference at the time it occurs not because he lacks certain relevant information, but because he temporarily lacks the volitional and deliberative capacities which are necessary for informed consent. If, for example, a highly inebriated friend announces at a party that he can jump without injury from a fifth story window and makes preparations to do so, one is surely justified in restraining him against his will. According to a consent-based theory of paternalistic interference, it is justifiable to restrain him because at the time of interference there is good reason to suppose that, because of his drunkenness, he lacks the capacity for informed choice and consent, and because we may reasonably suppose that he will consent to having been restrained the following morning. (Indeed if he jumps and survives he might justifiably reproach us for having failed to restrain him, on the grounds that we ought to have expected that he would wish to be restrained.)

There are other cases in which a person bent on self-harming behavior may lack the capacity for informed consent and may be unlikely to acquire that capacity in the future. In such cases we may sometimes give a justification for interference which resembles that appealed to in the Odysseus case by invoking the notion of hypothetical consent. We may argue that interference is justified on the grounds that if the person interfered with were to re-acquire the capacity for informed consent, he would consent to the interference. We are, I think, justified in preventing a person who has become permanently deranged from harming himself in certain ways even if it is unlikely he will regain full use of his faculties and consent to our interference as long as it is likely that if he were to regain his capacity for informed consent, he would consent to our having interfered with him.

In the cases considered so far, the person interfered with has either consented to our present interference or fails to consent to the interference at the time at which it occurs because he lacks the capacity to consent or because he lacks certain relevant knowledge. Is paternalistic treatment ever justified when a person has not consented to being so treated, and does not lack either the capacity to consent or relevant information regarding the consequences of his actions? It seems to me that it is consistent with the spirit of a consent-based rationale to hold that in cases of this kind paternalistic treatment may be justified if there is good reason to believe that the agent's refusal to consent is temporary and that he will come to consent to having been interfered with in the future. Cases in which a person acts while in the grip of a mood or emotion which is incongruent with his most long term and deeply held values and projects may fall into this category. Imagine a man who is plunged into deep grief and depression by the death of his wife and resolves to kill himself. Such a man may not lack the capacity for informed choice and consent in the way that a seriously mentally ill person or a small child does, but there may nonetheless be good reason to think that his inclination toward suicide is temporary and that when he recovers from his grief and depression he will consent to having been restrained (and indeed be grateful for this).

A consent-based theory seems to me to give a plausible rationale for interference in such cases. There is no reason, within the framework of a consent-based theory, to give a pre-eminent status to a person's present choices and desires no matter how transitory or unreflective of his underlying personality and values these may be. A person, at any moment, is more than the time-slice of his desires and emotions at that moment.

A plausible consent-based criterion for paternalistic treatment thus might claim that such treatment is justified when and only when it has either (a) actually been consented to in a free and informed way, or (b) there is failure to consent to such treatment only because the person affected acts out of ignorance or temporary incapacity in his deliberative or decision-making abilities and it seems reasonable to suppose he will consent to the interference once this ignorance or incapacity has been removed, or (c) the person affected fails to consent to the treatment only because of an incapacity which is not temporary, but nonetheless it seems reasonable to suppose that he would consent to the interference if he were to regain this capacity, or (d) while the person interfered with does not consent to the treatment at present and does not lack the capacity for rational deliberation and decision-making, it is nonetheless reasonable to suppose that because of his most deeply held projects and values he will come to consent to the treatment in the future.

My interest, however, is not so much in arguing for this specific version of a consent-based theory as in exploring the contrast between those rationales which make reference to the consent of the person interfered with and those rationales which attempt to justify interference by reference to the preservation or enhancement of some good for the agent. It is important to see that when we restrain a would-be suicide on the grounds that he may change his mind about the desirability of suicide, we appeal to a rationale for interference which is quite different from a rationale which makes reference to the preservation of his welfare or freedom of action. The former consent-based rationale would permit restraint of a normally optimistic man who resolves on suicide during a period of deep depression following the loss of his job; it would not permit restraint of a man who gradually develops, over a period of time, a desire to end his life, a desire which is the natural outcome of his most persistent beliefs and values. On the other hand, a diminishment of freedom or diminishment of welfare criterion would presumably permit interference in both of these cases.

Before we turn to a more detailed exploration of the differences between consent-based and consequentialist rationales for paternalistic treatment, it may be useful to remove some possible misunderstandings. Note to begin with that on a consent-based theory there must be (actual, expected, or hypothetical) *consent* to the specific kind of interference contemplated and not just a general recognition on the part of the subject of the desirability of the good which the interference is designed to protect. This point is often not appreciated. Gerald Dworkin, for example, seems to assume that even on a consent-based theory, interference becomes unproblematic once a person comes to see the relevant portions of his conduct as undesirable. Thus, in the case of a smoker, who recognizes the desirability of not smoking but who suffers from "weakness of will" and continues to smoke, Dworkin writes "[in this case] there is no theoretical problem. We are not imposing a good on a person who rejects it. We are simply using coercion to enable people to carry out their own goals."[6]

From the perspective of a consent-based theory this conclusion is too quick, for there are several different cases here which must be distinguished. A person may view certain portions of his conduct as irrational or undesirable and yet consistently refuse to consent to being prevented by another from engaging in that conduct. He may regard smoking as a dangerous habit, fervently wish that he had the will-power to stop smoking and yet consistently and indignantly resist any attempt to coerce him into not smoking. He may attach sufficient importance to other people not having control over this portion of his life that he would prefer not to stop smoking at all if this could be accomplished only through such coercion. When this is the case, and there are no grounds for thinking that he will change his mind and no grounds for attributing his failure to consent to interference to incapacity or ignorance, paternalistic interference will not be justifiable according to a consent-based rationale, even if the subject sees the good for the sake of which interference is taken as desirable. On the other hand, a person may not only suffer from weakness of will in the sense that he wishes to stop smoking and does not, but he may be quite willing that others step in to make him stop smoking. In this sort of case paternalistic interference will be justified according to a consent-based theory.

Secondly, it is important to recognize that the kind of hypothetical consent which may appropriately be appealed to by a consent-based theory is hypothetical consent of a rather special kind. If we are to take seriously the idea of justifying interference by considerations continuous with those at work in the Odysseus case and the correlative idea of choosing as the subject herself would choose had she the capacity to do so, we must, in employing the notion of hypothetical consent in clause (c) above, hold the agent's actual plans, values, and desires as nearly intact as is consistent with imagining her to possess the capacity for rational consent and choice and then ask how she would choose if she possessed such capacities. When the notion of hypothetical consent is employed in his way, I shall speak of hypothetical$_1$ consent.

If, in applying the test of hypothetical consent, we are allowed to imagine a person's projects, values, and desires as however different we wish (consistent with some minimal condition of rationality) from her actual projects, values, and desires and if we can justify interference by what a person would "consent" to if she possessed this novel set of projects, values, and desires, then we have moved away from the idea of choosing as the person interfered with would choose and from the kinds of considerations we used to justify interference in the cases described above. If Beatrice is in a coma from which unaided recovery seems unlikely and we are wondering whether it would be justifiable to perform an operation which would allow her to recover, the appropriate notion of hypothetical consent to employ if we wish to construct a consent-based justification for interference is one according to which it makes a difference, in determining what Beatrice would consent to, whether or not Beatrice is a Christian Scientist who has often said that she would not undergo surgery under any circumstances. If Beatrice is such a Christian Scientist, we cannot claim to be appealing to her hypothetical$_1$ consent, in the sense of that expression which is appropriate to a consent-based theory, if we argue that the operation is justified on the grounds that if Beatrice was an Episcopalian or someone who valued her health above all else, she would consent to the interference. If we think that it would be justifiable to perform the operation in this case, we must appeal to considerations which cannot be seen as continuous with the considerations which justified interference in the Odysseus case.

For similar reasons we must be careful to distinguish hypothetical$_1$ consent from the kind of hypothetical consent which is appealed to in a "rational will" argument for paternalistic interference.[7] By a "rational will" argument, I mean an argument that proceeds in the following way: It is contended that a fully rational agent will always wish to maximize (or at least preserve a minimal level of) certain goods such as welfare or future ability to choose and that if a person fails to do this, interference to preserve those goods is justified on the grounds that he is not rational (since he does not act to preserve the goods in question) and that if he were rational he would consent to the interference (since he would wish to preserve the goods in question).

Obviously if arguments of this kind are thought of as yet another legitimate way of appealing to the consent of the person interfered with, the contrast I have attempted to draw between consent-related and consequentialist justifications of paternalistic treatment will collapse. Given any consequentialist theory according to which it is justifiable to interfere in order to preserve or enhance an agent's possession of G, it can always be argued that any agent who fails to preserve or enhance G is not fully rational, and hence that, by virtue of a rational will argument, interference is justified. While a full discussion of this argument must be beyond the scope of this essay, it should be clear that the sort of hypothetical consent to which a rational will argument appeals is not hypothetical$_1$ consent. Rational will arguments abstract from the specific plans, values, and beliefs of agents in the way in which the appeal contemplated above to what Beatrice would consent to if she were an Episcopalian abstracts from her specific plans, values, and beliefs. The notions of choice and consent appealed to in consent-based theories only have application in those contexts in which individual plans and values are held to matter, in contexts in which it is allowed that two persons can be "rational" in the sense that they both meet the preconditions for morally effective choice and yet, because of individual differences, choose differently. If we think, as the rational will argument does, entirely in terms of agents who are abstract and interchangeable and who, insofar as they are rational, will always "choose" the same thing, then we have really abandoned the notions of choice and consent, in the sense in which they are employed in a consent-based theory. At least in the case of persons with the general capacities for informed consent, rational will arguments should not be regarded as legitimate appeals to their consent.[8]

One final point: It is sometimes suggested that it is only appropriate to use the word "consent" where there has been actual consent, and that it is always confused or misleading to speak of hypothetical$_1$ consent. If this suggestion is to amount to anything more than a verbal quibble, it must involve the claim that hypothetical$_1$ consent either plays no natural justificatory role in moral argument or at least no role that very closely resembles the role played by actual consent. But in fact there are many very ordinary cases, having nothing to do with paternalistic treatment, in which it seems natural and appropriate to appeal to hypothetical$_1$ consent in the sense indicated above. Suppose that you wish to use something that Charles owns. Putting aside special cases (in which, e.g., using Charles' property is necessary to prevent serious harm to someone), it seems that the justification for using the property must make reference in some way to Charles' consent. The simplest, most paradigmatic case is one in which you may use Charles' property because he has actually consented to your doing so. But if Charles is not available to consent or is unable to do so, there are many circumstances in which you might naturally and appropriately justify your use of Charles' property by showing that he will or would consent to your use when he has the opportunity or ability to do so. ("I borrowed your rake, Charles. You weren't at home but I was sure you wouldn't mind," may be a perfectly cogent justification, even if it is sometimes abused. And such a justification remains cogent even if the situation is one in which it is likely that Charles will never have the opportunity or ability to actually consent to my use of the rake.) These justifications for using Charles' property, which make reference to his expected or hypothetical$_1$ consent, stand in sharp contrast to those justifications which appeal to the good consequences of such use for me, or society at large (or, for that matter, Charles); in their focus instead on Charles' values, desires, and projects they seem to have a moral force like the moral force of actual consent.

II

I want now to explore in more detail some of the differences between consent-based rationales for paternalistic treatment and consequentialist rationales like DFR and DWR and to introduce some of the considerations which seem to me to favor the former set of rationales. Let us note to begin with that if (as I believe) we can give sense to the idea that a person with the full capacity for informed consent may refuse to consent (and may be such that there is no prospect of his coming to consent) to interference with some freedom-diminishing course or welfare-diminishing course of action which he is about to adopt, it will follow that DFR and DWR will justify a much wider range of paternalistic interference than a consent-based rationale. For example, it seems reasonable to suppose (and Dworkin seems to agree) that DFR would support legislation requiring automobile passengers to wear seat belts and restricting cigarette smoking (driving without seat belts and heavy smoking are, after all, activities that significantly increase the chances of one's freedom of action being severely limited in the future). DFR also (although Dworkin does not explicitly suggest this) seems to provide prima facie support for legislation limiting the consumption of fried foods and legislation requiring people to have regular medical checkups. DWR and the various enhancement rationales mentioned above would presumably support even more extensive paternalistic interference. By contrast, if it is possible for a person to possess the capacity for informed consent and yet refuse to consent, with no prospects of his coming to consent, to being required to wear seat belts, stop smoking, limit his consumption of fried foods, or have regular medical checkups, a consent-based rationale will not justify legislation requiring people to do these things.

In addition to the quite different judgements they seem to yield regarding particular cases, a consent-based theory and the consequentialist theories like DFR and DWR are associated with two quite different ways of understanding paternalistic interference. On a consent-based criterion we think of the person interfered with as an independent subject with whose actual, expected or hypothetical$_1$ permission we assist in achieving his aims. We "interfere" with this person's activities not to frustrate or alter his aims, or to promote some other value (his freedom or welfare) which he may not wish to see promoted at the expense of his other aims, but rather to better help him achieve his aims. Even as we interfere with the agent's activities we interfere in a way that acknowledges or evinces our respect for his status as an agent whose choices are deserving of respect because they are his choices. By contrast, on a diminishment of freedom or diminishment of welfare criterion, we do not evince respect for the agent's choices because they are his choices, but rather evince respect for some other value—the agent's future welfare or ability to choose—which the agent may not share.

One reason why reliance on a consent-based criterion for paternalistic interference rather than DFR may seem paradoxical is this: Underlying the consent criterion is, of course, the idea that an agent's autonomous and informed choices agent are of great moral value and significance. But how can the respect to be accorded to such choices ever require that we allow someone to choose in such a way that his choice diminishes his ability to choose in an informed and autonomous way? If the ability of an agent to choose freely is of great moral significance or value, shouldn't we, other things being equal, always take steps to maximize the value, or at least to prevent its serious diminishment, wherever we can? It is this line of thought which leads Dworkin to DFR and Mill to the conclusion that paternalistic interference is justified in order to prevent someone from selling himself into slavery. To retain some form of the consent criterion we must hold that the rationale for paternalistic interference is not to be understood solely in consequentialist terms. One can quite consistently hold, to use Bernard Williams' example,[9] that a world in which two people keep their promises is, other things being equal, morally preferable to a world in which only one person keeps his promise, and yet deny that one ought to break his promise if that is the only way one can get two other people to keep theirs. In a similar way, one can agree that a world in which Alice retains her ability to choose autonomously is morally preferable to a world in which that ability is significantly diminished, and yet deny that it is right to interfere with Alice's autonomous choices in order to promote or preserve the achievement of this more desirable world. On this sort of view, which is embodied in a consent-based criterion, Alice's consent (actual, expected, or hypothetical$_1$) to our interference constitutes a "side-constraint" on the goal of preventing diminishment in Alice's ability to choose freely. Just as certain "routes" (namely, those that involve my breaking my promise) to the desirable state of affairs in which Beatrice and Charles keep their promises are not permissible, so certain routes (namely, those that involve interference with her conduct without her actual or hypothetical$_1$ consent) to the desirable state of affairs in which Alice's ability to choose is preserved are also not permissible. The idea is that sometimes respect for a person's free choices requires that she be allowed to choose in a way that may diminish her ability to choose freely in the future. We can thus think of both DFR and a consent-based rationale for paternalistic interference as theories which attempt to assign a fundamental importance to a person's free and autonomous choices, but nonetheless have quite different structures, structures which reflect the general difference between consequentialist and non-consequentialist moral theories.

We may develop this theme further by noting that a consent-based theory of paternalistic interference, like non-consequentialist theories generally, attaches a great deal of significance to *who* makes a certain choice or brings about a certain result.

(Thus on a non-consequentialist, but not on a consequentialist theory, it will make a great deal of difference, in many cases, whether I commit a murder or simply fail to do something which has the consequence that someone else commits a murder.) DFR, like other consequentialist theories, focuses instead on the end result of an action, being indifferent to who (whether the person whose freedom or welfare is in danger or someone else) chooses or brings about that result, except insofar as this affects the value of the end result. On a theory like DFR or DWR, the person interfered with is thought of as a repository of certain values which are to be protected and anyone who can may (and perhaps ought) to take appropriate steps to protect this value. By contrast, the whole point of a consent-based theory is that who chooses some end which is good for an agent—whether it is the agent or someone else—is morally crucial.

We can further remove the appearance of paradox from a consent-based rationale for paternalistic interference by noting its close connection with the notion of privacy. It is commonly recognized that certain kinds of surveillance may constitute a wrongful infringement of a person's privacy even if this surveillance does not actually result in the diminishment of his welfare or freedom of action. This reflects the fact that a person has a concern with controlling certain aspects of his life that goes beyond his interest in preserving his own welfare or freedom of action. When a hidden camera is used to monitor a person's sex life, he is wronged even if this information is never used to his detriment, and he remains unaware of the surveillance. He is wronged because it is no longer up to him who shall observe (and in one sense, participate in) certain activities which are of fundamental importance to him, and because in consequence he no longer has full control over the character and significance of those activities. In violating a person's privacy, we thus wrong him by showing a kind of disrespect for his status as a person which is at least in part distinct from any wrong we may do him by unjustifiably diminishing his welfare or restricting his freedom. To respect another's status as a person we must, among other things, respect his status as a chooser, and this involves respecting the integrity of certain of his aims and projects, and his control over certain portions of his life.

We can use a natural extension of this line of thought to provide support for a consent-based criterion for paternalistic interference. Once we recognize that a person's interest in controlling certain portions of his life is, at least in part, independent of his interest in preserving his freedom and welfare and that we can wrong a person by showing a disrespect for his status as a chooser, even if we do not diminish his freedom or welfare, it becomes easy to see how it can be wrong to frustrate an agent's purposes, to remove certain portions of his life from his control, even if in doing so we preserve or enhance his freedom or welfare. Just as the right to privacy seems to derive, at least in part, from a more general right which persons possess to control certain portions of their life, to carry out certain projects as they see fit, so we may plausibly maintain that a person's right to be free of the sort of paternalistic interference which would be justified by DFR or DWR derives from a similar basis.

III

There are a number of additional respects in which consent-based theories seem to me to be superior to consequentialist theories like DFR. To begin with, these two kinds of theories assign a very different significance to individual differences among persons. Consequentialist theories are concerned with the protection and enhancement of some end state (freedom, welfare, etc.) which is thought of as valuable for all persons. Whether paternalistic interference is permissible is thought of as a question which can be settled without any direct reliance on information having to do with the particular desires, plans, goals, or values of the person interfered with. By contrast such information will be of crucial importance in a consent-based theory, for it will in large measure determine what an agent can be expected to consent to.

Consider a concert pianist, Dora, whose hand has become seriously infected in such a way that there is a high probability that she will die of blood poisoning unless the hand is amputated. Suppose, that because of her commitment to her career, she strenuously insists that the operation not be performed—she prefers instead to take the relatively small chance that she will survive with her hand intact.

It seems to me that if potential losses and gains in Dora's welfare or ability to choose can be objectively assessed at all, DFR and DWR yield a very good case for proceeding with the operation against Dora's wishes. It seems reasonable to suppose that the loss in welfare or future ability to choose represented by the loss of Dora's life, discounted by the rather high probability of its occurrence without the operation, will outweigh whatever gain in these values would be produced by Dora's survival with her hand intact, discounted by the small probability of its occurrence. Certainly there is nothing in DFR or DWR which suggests that, in deciding whether interference would be justifiable, one should take into account Dora's distinctive wishes and projects, except insofar as these are (one piece of) evidence for the course of action which is most likely to preserve Dora's freedom or welfare. Except for this last qualification (about which I shall say more below), both DFR and DWR presumably instruct us to treat Dora exactly like Frank, who faces the same situation as Dora but does not attach any greater than average significance to the use of his hands and who enthusiastically consents to the operation.

By contrast, for a consent-based rationale for paternalistic interference these differences between Dora and Frank will matter in a direct and crucial way in determining what should be done. Given that Dora is competent, and that her refusal to consent to the operation derives from her most deeply held plans and values, so that there is no reasonable prospect of a change of heart, there will be no justification for performing the operation on Dora, while performing the operation on Frank will of course be unproblematic.

Cases of this sort can be multiplied endlessly. Consider persons who wish to strenuously pursue religious, intellectual, aesthetic, or political projects when doing so will gravely undermine their physical or mental health or even hasten their deaths. DFR and DWR would presumably provide a rationale for interference in many such cases, while a consent-based rationale would not. Or consider the fact that persons facing unavoidable risks may have different preferences regarding how those risks are distributed over their lives. Suppose that Gus must choose between a high risk operation which if successful will guarantee his survival over the next ten years and a series of treatments which spread the risks he faces out evenly over the ten-year period. Here again it looks as though for DWR and DFR the issue of which alternative Gus should be required to undergo can be settled simply by calculating the probabilistically discounted value (whether this is a matter of welfare or freedom) associated with each alternative—presumably if one of these alternatives is seriously inferior to the other Gus must be required to take the other, regardless of his preferences.

From the perspective of a consent-based theory, consequentialist theories like DFR and DWR treat persons as abstract and interchangeable, as mere repositories or loci of certain goods or values which it is desirable to protect or enhance, regardless of whether these goods figure in the plans or projects of the persons interfered with. By contrast, according to the moral vision which underlies a consent-based theory, persons are not to be thought of in this way. On this view it is central to the very idea of a person that a person will have a distinctive set of goals, values, plans, and projects which he has formed and which are constitutive of his individuality. Respect for another's status as a person requires that when we attempt to aid him we do not treat him in a way which abstracts entirely from such considerations. It is, so to speak, not the bare, abstract idea of a rational chooser (and still less the abstract idea of an experiencer of pleasure or a possessor of welfare) which is to be respected, but rather this particular choosing person. When we seek to protect certain values (even those that are "good" for an agent) in a way that fails to take into account his particular plans and projects, we treat him as a thing or means which can legitimately be used for purposes other than his own, just as surely as when we ignore his own purposes in order to use him as a means to further some other agent's interest.

At least in the case of DWR it might be responded, however, that this line of criticism is unfair.[10] It may be argued that since whether or not a course of action will preserve a person's welfare depends in part on his particular desires, values, and projects, DWR in sensitive in an appropriate way to the differences among persons. Thus it may be contended that if it is indeed wrong to force the pianist to undergo the amputation of her hand in the example above, this is because it is likely, in view of the depth of her commitment to playing the piano, that she will be so miserable without her hand, that her welfare will fall to a level which will be significantly below the level associated with her survival with her hand intact, even discounted by the small probability of its occurrence. Similarly it might be argued that if it is wrong to require a Christian Scientist to undergo an operation necessary to save her life, that is because, given the unhappiness she would feel at the violation of her religious convictions, this course of action is not likely to yield significantly more welfare for her than the alternative of allowing her to die.

There are several points worth noticing about his line of argument. Note first that if DWR is not to collapse into a consent-based justification for interference, what a person consents to cannot always be taken as decisive in determining whether a course of action will best preserve her welfare. If the mere fact that Dora refuses to consent to a course of action shows that there are no significant welfare values which can be protected by requiring that course of action, then in fact we have abandoned DWR in favor of a consent-based justification of paternalistic interference. If DWR and similar principles are to retain their distinctively consequentialist features, it must be possible for a person to object strenuously to interference and to be convinced that interference will significantly decrease her welfare—and yet for interference to have just the opposite consequence.

Quite apart from this, it seems to me that to the extent a principle like DWR (or any other consequentialist principle) focuses on individual differences, it will focus on them in the wrong way. On the interpretation of DWR we are considering, what is presumably crucial is how unhappy, miserable, and devastated a person will feel in the long run when his choices are overridden. Suppose, in the example above, that there is good reason to think that if her hand is amputated Dora will not be thoroughly miserable for the rest of her life—she is a cheerful and resourceful sort of person who will probably "adjust" to the loss of her hand and adopt a new set of concerns and make the best of a bad situation although she may be counted on to object strenuously to having been forced to undergo the operation for the rest of her life. DWR seems to suggest that to the extent this outcome may be expected, imposition of the operation becomes more justifiable, while to the extent that Dora will be plunged into permanent misery or despair by the amputation, imposition of the operation will not be justified. It seems to me that it is simply a mistake to think that these considerations—these features of Dora's individuality—are morally crucial in determining whether paternalistic treatment is justified. To the extent that the character of Dora's subsequent life matters in determining whether it is justifiable to impose the operation on her, it seems to me that it matters in the way a consent-based theory would suggest—that is, that the crucial consideration is whether Dora can subsequently be expected to consent to the operation.

From the perspective of a consent-based rationale for paternalistic treatment, a rationale like DFR or DWR misconstrues the sort of role that Dora's concern about her music plays in her life. On DFR or DWR this concern is taken to be of significance only insofar as it bears on some other value—Dora's happiness or freedom to choose. But this need not (and presumably is not) the way Dora thinks about her piano playing ability—she does not value it only insofar as it contributes to (or is part of) her happiness or freedom to choose. It is presumably because she attaches a value to her music which is independent of the contribution it makes to other values in her life—because she does not think of her music primarily as a way of making herself happy or well or free—that she is prepared to sacrifice (or run the risk of sacrificing) her welfare or freedom in order to have a chance to continue her music. Similarly in the case of a scientist who pursues her research even though in doing so she knows she will very seriously undermine her health, it is typically not the case that she thinks of the research simply as the most effective way of preserving her happiness or welfare (or anything else). Presumably the scientist values both her welfare and research in their own right, as ends, and thinks of these ends as in genuine conflict—she elects to pursue her research *at the cost* of her welfare.

In DWR and DFR, individual differences matter only insofar as they bear on a value (welfare, freedom to choose) which is taken to be of uniformly paramount importance for everyone. The superior sensitivity of a consent-based theory to individual differences consists in the fact that on such a theory a person's values and choices are valued in their own right, and not just in virtue of the contribution they make to other values. A consent-based theory recognizes, in a way that DWR and DFR do not, that individuals differ not only with regard to what is likely to make them well or free, but with regard to the importance they attach to their welfare or freedom or welfare vis-à-vis other values.

I turn now to another respect in which a consent-based theory seems to be superior to consequentialist theories like DFR and DWR. Consider the fact that we are, as a general rule, far more likely to think that paternalistic interference is justifiable when factual rather than (fundamental) evaluative differences are at issue.[11] If a person refuses to undergo an operation which is necessary to preserve his health or life, it seems to many people to matter a great deal, in determining whether it would be justifiable to require him to undergo the operation, whether he refuses because he has not had the opportunity to acquire or reflect on certain information and is in consequence seriously misinformed about crucial factual matters (e.g. about the seriousness of his condition, or the after-effects of the operation), or whether he refuses because, although he appreciates the facts of his situation perfectly well, he objects to the operation on religious grounds. It seems to me that, at least in a situation in which the operation cannot be delayed without great danger, our pre-theoretic judgement is that the case for paternalistic interference is much stronger in the former case than in the latter. Similarly, the case for paternalistic interference seems, preanalytically, to be much stronger in the case of Henry, who attempts to cross a bridge in a dangerously deteriorated condition because he is ignorant of its condition, than in the case of Jack, who fully appreciates the facts concerning the bridge's condition but wishes to take the risk of crossing it because of the value he attaches to the completion of some other important project.

This difference is, I think, difficult to satisfactorily account for on consequentialist theories. Such theories permit interference whenever a person is about to do something which is seriously damaging to some favored value—the *reason* why this person is about to embark on this damaging course of action is not seen as affecting the justifiability of the interference in any fundamental way. Refusing to undergo the operation or attempting to cross the bridge carry with them the same objective probability of loss whether they are prompted by a "non-standard" value or by a "non-standard" factual assessment of one's situation.

By contrast, a consent-based theory is able to account in a natural way for our (usual) greater willingness to interfere when a person's factual assessment differs from ours. According to a consent-based theory, this differential treatment of factual and evaluative differences is justified by two considerations. First, it is, as a general rule, much more likely that those whose factual assessment of their situations differ from our own "standard" factual assessment can be brought into agreement with this standard assessment (and hence can be brought to retrospectively consent to our interference) than it is that those whose evaluative assessments differ from our "standard" evaluative assessments can be brought into agreement with our evaluative assessments (and hence to retrospectively consent to our interference). Secondly, the amount of change a person with an unusual factual assessment of his situation must undergo before he comes to agree with our "standard" factual assessment is usually smaller than the amount of change required to bring a person with unusual values into evaluative agreement with us.

In the case of Henry, who is simply ignorant of the condition of the bridge, we (justifiably) feel confident that when we have communicated our assessment of the condition of the bridge, he will adopt that assessment and (probably) consent to our having interfered with him. But in the case of Jack, who attempts to cross the bridge because his values differ from our own (because unlike us, he is willing to risk his life to complete a certain project) there are no grounds for the corresponding expectation

—no reason to think that when we acquaint him with our evaluative assessment of his situation, he will come to share it, and consent to our interference. Related to this is the fact that the change which Henry must undergo before he will come to consent to an interference seems less deep and fundamental than the change which Jack must undergo. No doubt some factual beliefs a person holds play a fundamental role in his sense of who he is and what matters to him. But the factual beliefs held in the examples above do not deem to be of this sort, while the evaluative beliefs do. The non-standard evaluative beliefs held in the examples above seem to be constitutive of the individual personalities who hold them in a much deeper way than the non-standard factual beliefs held in the above examples. So interfering with the choices of those holding the non-standard evaluative beliefs, especially given the small likelihood of their ever coming to consent to the interference, seems a much more fundamental intrusion into their personalities than interference with the choices of those holding the non-standard factual beliefs.

There is yet another kind of case in which consent-based theory seems to yield results which are intuitively more satisfactory than the results yielded by consequentialist theories like DFR or DWR. Consider cases in which a person is about to do something, either because he is ignorant or temporarily incompetent, which will have results he will find quite undesirable, but which are not such that they will significantly undermine his welfare or ability to choose. Imagine, to use an example which John Hodson uses to make a similar point,[12] that Jane is about to drink some very foul-tasting but harmless liquid, having mistaken it for water. If there is no opportunity to warn her, and if she can be restrained without significant interference, many people would think it justifiable to temporarily restrain her, at least until we have had an opportunity to explain the situation. Yet since there is no question here of a serious diminishment in Jane's welfare or ability to choose, DFR and DWR seem to provide no justification for interference. Nor does it seem an acceptable strategy to deal with such cases by modifying DFR or DWR to permit interference in order to prevent small or harmless unpleasantries—this would permit a degree of interference with persons' lives that even the most ardent paternalist would surely wish to avoid. By contrast, a consent-based theory provides a natural explanation of why interference is justified in the above case, for it is clear that Jane acts out of ignorance and, in the absence of any evidence to the contrary, it is reasonable to assume that Jane wishes to avoid the foul-tasting liquid and will retrospectively consent to our (minimal) interference once the situation is explained. This sort of case also seems to suggest that it is not, as the consequentialist supposes, the kind or degree of the harm threatened which justifies paternalistic interference, but rather the attitude of the person interfered with toward the harm and the contemplated interference.

IV

There is one final point I wish to make. In my discussion above I have urged that individual differences among persons must be taken into account in determining the justifiability of paternalistic interference. In a number of cases—perhaps most commonly when a private citizen is contemplating paternalistic interference with a friend, relative, or obviously endangered stranger or when a professional is contemplating paternalistic treatment of a client—it may not be unduly difficult to take whatever information of this kind is available into account, in a way that satisfies the requirement that the interferer be guided by the prospects of actual, expected, or hypothetical$_1$ consent. But, in many cases in which governments or other large organizations contemplate paternalistic measures, it may be very difficult or very undesirable for them to make (and to act on the basis of) the fine discrimination among individuals that a consent-based theory demands. It may be that the legal system or conceivable administrative agencies lack the (conceptual and material) resources to make such discriminations or to make them accurately. To empower the legal system or other agencies to make such discriminations may have the consequence of entrusting too much to the individual discretion of judges or administrators. It may have the consequence that people find it impossible to anticipate whether their behavior will invite interference. It may simply be that it is thought by most people to be undesirable that the state, or certain other organizations, become implicated in certain kinds of decision-making. It is thus quite likely that situations will arise in which some of those affected by paternalistic legislation can be thought of as giving their (actual, expected, or hypothetical$_1$) consent to such legislation and others cannot and in which it is also difficult or undesirable for the state to attempt to distinguish between these two groups. For these and other reasons, paternalistic measures adopted by the state or other large organizations seem to raise distinctive issues which may not be raised by paternalism in other contexts.

While a thorough examination of these issues would require another paper, I might remark that the argument made in this paper does not seem to me to yield the conclusion that legislation restricting self-harming behavior described above is necessarily unjustified if it does not gain the actual, expected, or hypothetical$_1$ consent of all of those affected. What my argument does suggest is that there is no acceptable *paternalistic* justification for imposing such legislation on those who do not consent to it. If the legislation in question is justifiable, the justification will not be that the legislation is for the good of the non-consenting group, but rather must be that the consenting group has a right to make use of the legal system to realize their purpose of self-protection, even if in doing so they restrict the choices of the non-consenting group in certain ways. Since I do not think it at all plausible to hold that only the consent of those affected justifies imposing non-paternalistic restrictions on conduct, the possibility remains open that legislation to prevent people from harming themselves will sometimes be justifiable (although not on paternalistic grounds) even if only a portion of those affected consent to it. As in other cases of non-consensual restrictions on conduct, the justifiability of such restrictions will depend on such matters as the nature, extent, and distribution of the harms prevented or the benefits conferred by the restrictions, on whether the restrictions burden fundamental rights, and on the character of the procedures used to arrive at the restriction.

Select Bibliography

Carter, Rosemary, "Justifying Paternalism," *Canadian Journal of Philosophy*, 7 (1977) 133–145.
Dworkin, Gerald, "Paternalism," in *Morality and the Law*, ed. Richard Wasserstrom (Belmont, CA: Wadsworth 1971) 107–126.

Feinberg, Joel, "Legal Paternalism," *Canadian Journal of Philosophy*, 1 (1971–1972) 105–124.

Gert, Bernard and Culver, Charles, "The Justification of Paternalism," *Ethics*, 89 (1979) 199–210.

Hodson, John, "The Principle of Paternalism," *American Philosophical Quarterly*, 14 (1975) 61–71.

Husak, Douglas, "Paternalism and Autonomy," *Philosophy and Public Affairs*, 10 (1980–1981) 27–46.

Ten, C.L., "Paternalism and Morality," *Ratio*, 13 (1971) 55–66.

VanDeVeer, Donald, "Paternalism and Subsequent Consent," *Canadian Journal of Philosophy*, 9 (1979) 631–642.

VanDeVeer, Donald, "Autonomy-Respecting Paternalism," *Social Theory and Practice*, 6 (1980) 187–207.

VanDeVeer, Donald, "The Contractual Argument for Withholding Medical Information," *Philosophy and Public Affairs*, 9 (1979–1980) 198—205.

Williams, Bernard, "A Critique of Utilitarianism," in Smart, J.J.C. and Williams, Bernard, *Utilitarianism: For and Against* (Cambridge: Cambridge University Press 1973).

Notes

1. Gerald Dworkin, "Paternalism" in *Morality and the Law*, ed. Richard Wasserstrom (Belmont, CA: Wadsworth 1971) 107–126.

2. Dworkin, 118. I think that the context makes it clear that Dworkin thinks of DFR as a condition which is sometimes sufficient as well as necessary for paternalistic interference. I might also remark that I follow Dworkin in using "freedom to choose" and "ability to choose" interchangeably.

3. A rationale for paternalistic interference resembling DWR is endorsed, for example, by C.L. Ten in his "Paternalism and Morality." Ten would permit paternalistic interference when (but not only when) "the harm inflicted on the agent is of a severe and permanent type" (C.L. Ten, "Paternalism and Morality," *Ratio*, 13 [1971] 56–66). Bernard Gert and Charles Culver base their justification of paternalistic treatment on a mixed consequentialist principle in part: they hold that paternalistic treatment is only justified "if we are preventing significantly more evil to (the person interfered with) . . . than we are causing" (Bernard Gert and Charles M. Culver, "The Justification of Paternalism," *Ethics*, 89 [1979] 199–210). Because Gert and Culver hold that paternalistic treatment will always involve violating a moral rule with regard to the person so treated, they also require for the justification of such treatment that one be able to publicly advocate such violations.

4. Some may wish to say that because Odysseus consents to the sailors' treatment, they do not really "interfere" with him at all (e.g., see Donald VanDeVeer in "The Contractual Argument for Withholding Medical Information," in *Philosophy and Public Affairs* 9 [1979–1980] 198—205). If I am correct in contending below that justifications of paternalism which appeal to retrospective and hypothetical$_1$ consent are a natural extension of those that appeal to actual consent, such persons also *ought* to say, as VanDeVeer does not, that paternalism which is justified by such appeals also does not involve "interference." And if they use "paternalistic" in such a way that paternalistic treatment must involve interference, they will find it more perspicuous to express the conclusions of this essay by saying that paternalistic treatment is never justified, that what can be justified is treatment that appears paternalistic, but is revealed by analysis not to be paternalistic at all, since it does not involve interference. I have no quarrel with this way of

putting matters; it seems to me that nothing turns on whether my conclusions are expressed this way or in the way I have chosen.

5. It is important to understand that in my view, what justifies interference in this case is not the actual occurrence of Alice's subsequent consent, but the fact that it is reasonable to expect that Alice will subsequently consent. Making the justifiability of interference depend on Alice's actual subsequent consent would, as Donald VanDeVeer notes, have the bizarre consequence that whether or not interference is justified would depend upon, e.g., whether Alice is killed by a bolt of lightning before she is able to consent (cf. Donald VanDeVeer, "Paternalism and Subsequent Consent," *Canadian Journal of Philosophy*, 9 [1979] 631–642).

6. Dworkin, 124.

7. The characterization of arguments of this sort as "rational will" arguments is taken from John Hodson's "The Principle of Paternalism," *American Philosophical Quarterly*, 14 (1975) 61–71. An apparent willingness to regard such a "rational will" argument as a natural extension of a consent-based justification of paternalistic interference can be found in Dworkin's "Paternalism." A distinction similar to the distinction I have drawn here between hypothetical$_1$ consent and the sort of hypothetical consent appealed to in a "rational will" argument is also made by Donald VanDeVeer in his "Autonomy-Respecting Paternalism," *Social Theory and Practice*, 6 (1980) 187–207.

8. See my "The Rational-Will Argument for Paternalism," in preparation. I might also remark in this connection that a consent-based theory will draw a sharp distinction between those who have had a general capacity for informed consent in the past and have thus had an opportunity to form a distinctive set of values and projects and those (such as small children, persons who have been severely retarded since birth) who have never had this capacity and thus have not formed a distinctive set of values and projects. In the latter sort of case we cannot appropriately invoke the notions of retrospective and hypothetical$_1$ consent and must fall back on something like a "rational will" argument in determining whether paternalistic interference would be appropriate. It is only in this latter sort of case that a concern with consent collapses a concern with the sort of consequentialist considerations represented by DFR and DWR. (Even here, of course, one should not ask "What would be best for any rational agent?", but rather "What would be best for this kind of child or retarded person?" Thus in the case of normal children, paternalistic treatment should be undertaken with an eye toward, among other things, developing their capacities for informed choice, while this sort of purpose may be inappropriate, because incapable of fulfillment, in the case of the severely retarded.) I might also note in this connection that once this last point is recognized, the worries of writers like Rosemary Carter ("Justifying Paternalism," *Canadian Journal of Philosophy*, 7 [1977] 133–145) that a consent-based theory like that described above will permit parents to "distort" their children's values or stunt their capacities in such a way that their upbringing itself manufactures subsequent consent to having been brought up in that way can be seen to be misguided.

9. Bernard Williams, "A Critique of Utilitarianism," in J.J.C. Smart and Bernard Williams, *Utilitarianism: For and Against* (Cambridge: Cambridge University Press, 1973).

10. While it is true that whether or not a certain course of action will preserve a person's welfare depends in part on his particular desires, values, and projects, a parallel claim in the case of DFR seems to have little plausibility. Although it is sometimes suggested that if someone who does not plan or desire to do X, is deprived of the freedom to do X, his freedom is not diminished, this surely is a mistake. In the relevant sense the extent of an agent's freedom has to do with whether he will have the ability and opportunity to make certain choices or take up certain options if he wishes to do so. Whether he will in fact wish to do so is (at least largely) irrelevant to the question of how free he is.

11. This fact is noted by Dworkin, 122, but no explanation is offered.

12. John Hodson, "The Principle of Paternalism."

Questions

1. In the report of the Committee on Mental Health Services in Ontario three cases are outlined. In which of the three cases, if any, would interference be justified given a consent-based rationale? In which, if any, would interference be justified given a consequentialist rationale?
2. Do the answers arrived at in question 1 help to decide whether a consent-based or a consequentialist approach to paternalistic interference is to be preferred?
3. Could the treatment imposed on Alex as described in *A Clockwork Orange* and discussed in ''Containing Violence'' above be justified on a ''side-constraint,'' non-consequentialist model? Could it be justified on a ''diminishment of freedom'' (or ''diminishment of welfare'') theory?

Suggestions for Further Reading

Books

- Judi Chamberlin, *On Our Own, Patient-Controlled Alternatives to the Mental Health System* (Toronto: McGraw-Hill Ryerson, 1978). Rejecting conventional approaches to the treatment of mental illness, the author explores radical, patient-controlled treatment alternatives. The final chapter is called ''Coercion and Co-operation.''
- Nicholas N. Kittrie, *The Right to be Different: Deviance and Enforced Therapy* (Pelican Books, 1973). This book provides an excellent look at the legal, moral, and medical aspects of enforced therapy as practised in the United States. The author provides a sustained critical evaluation of existing practices and calls for reforms in law and in the practice of medicine.
- John Marshall, *Madness: An Indictment of the Mental Health Care System in Ontario* (Toronto: Ontario Public Services Union, 1982). Marshall evaluates current practices in the treatment of the mentally ill in Ontario institutions. The study is based on a public inquiry commissioned by the Ontario Public Service Employees Union.
- Thomas Szasz, *Law, Liberty and Psychiatry* (New York: Macmillan, 1973). Szasz is a psychiatrist who has been offering sustained criticism of the use of enforced therapy in dealing with mental illness since the 1950s. This book is a statement of his views.

Government Studies and Reports

- Law Reform Commission of Canada, *The Criminal Process and Mental Disorder* (Working Paper 14). The Commission sets out proposals designed to ensure that persons who are thought to be in need of treatment but who are also enmeshed in the criminal-law system are fairly dealt with. The Commission bases its proposals on the underlying principle that the purpose of imprisonment is punishment, not treatment. However, where treatment is indicated it should be made available to those in prisons who wish it and may benefit from it.

- *Hospital Orders*, a study paper prepared for the Law Reform Commission and published in 1974, provides detailed support for a number of the positions taken by the Commission in Working Paper 14.
- *The General Program for the Development of Psychiatric Services in Federal Correctional Services in Canada*. This report was prepared for the Solicitor-General of Canada in 1972 by an advisory board of psychiatrists. It makes a number of detailed recommendations on the role of psychiatry in federal prisons. Many of those recommendations have been implemented. The report has generated a good deal of critical appraisal. See, for example, my own "Psychiatry, the Inmate and the Law" in *The Dalhousie Law Journal,* Vol. 3, No. 2 (October 1976), and Fred Desrochier's "Regional Psychiatric Centres—A Myopic View" in *The Canadian Journal of Criminology*, Vol. 15, No. 2.

Articles

- J. Arboleda-Flores, "Some Ethical Issues in the Treatment of Offenders at the Regional Psychiatric Centre (Abbotsford)," *Canadian Journal of Criminology*, Vol. 20 (1978), No. 3. The author, who practised forensic psychiatry at Abbotsford, discusses the moral dilemmas he encountered. Dr. F.C.R. Chalke, author of the advisory committee report to the Solicitor-General (1972) referred to above, replies to this article in a letter to the editor of the Journal (see Vol. 21 (1979), No. 2 at page 149).
- Prablu el-Guebaly Towes, "Commitment of the Mentally Ill," *Canadian Journal of Psychiatry*, December 1980. The authors review trends in commitment procedures in North America.
- Michael McDonald, "Autarchy and Interests," *The Australasian Journal of Philosophy*, Vol. 56 (1978), August. In this essay, McDonald defines autonomy as rational self-sufficiency. Rejecting an individualistic analysis, he argues that rational self-sufficiency grows out of relational or group activities. (See also section III of "Ideology and Morality in Hard Times" in Chapter 9.)

Censorship and the Problem of Pornography

Introduction

The concept of moral autonomy explored in previous chapters also plays a central role in discussions of the morality of censorship, particularly the censorship of pornographic materials. How do we assess the limits beyond which the exercise of freedom on the part of some becomes an unacceptable threat to the freedom or well-being of others? This question provides a focus for the discussions of this chapter.

Background Considerations

The Criminal Code of Canada has contained provisions restricting the circulation of obscene material from its earliest formulations. The 1892 Code prohibited the sale or display of anything which tended to "corrupt public morals" or was "disgusting" or "immoral." It also banned the use of the mails for the transmission of anything which was "immoral," "obscene," or "indecent." The law did provide, however, that serving the public good was an adequate defence to an obscenity charge.

The Code was expanded in 1927 to include the sale, public display, circulation, distribution, and possession of "obscene" materials or "materials tending to corrupt public morals." No further major change was made until shortly after the Second World War, when the Code was expanded once more to include crime comics—material which through the use of pictures depicted the commission of real or fictitious crimes. The Code was also revised to remove any reference to "the tendency to corrupt public morals."

The 1950s were a period of social change. Increasing wealth and sophisticated printing and distribution techniques led to dramatic increases in the circulation of pornographic materials. Concern with this trend resulted in the creation of a Senate Committee on Salacious and Indecent Literature. The committee hearings provided a public forum for debate, and individuals and groups used the occasion to set out their views. Those who advocated stricter control argued that the Criminal Code should be strengthened. There was clear concern about the involvement of children.

Those who opposed further regulation did so on two grounds. Some argued that current provisions provided adequate control. Others argued that any control limited freedom of speech, interfered with the right of adults to choose to read what they wished, and was objectionable except where needed to protect people from serious harm.

In 1958, a series of changes were proposed to Parliament by the Minister of Justice, Davie Fulton, who presented his amendments with two objectives in mind. To begin with, there was no statutory definition of obscenity. Prior to 1958, material was judged obscene by the courts if it had a "tendency to deprave and corrupt those whose minds were open to such immoral influences and into whose hands a publication of the sort in question might fall." This test, laid down by a British judge, Chief Justice Cockburn, in the case of R. vs. Hicklin in 1868, was known as the Hicklin test. And it had come under severe criticism as being subjective and open to uneven application. Davie Fulton proposed in his amendments to supplement this test with a more objective standard. The courts were to regard as obscene "any publication a dominant characteristic of which was the undue exploitation of sex or of sex and crime, horror, cruelty, and violence." Fulton was also concerned to stem the circulation of what he described in the House of Commons as "the kind of muck on the newsstands against which our main efforts in this definition are directed." The aim, therefore, was to strengthen control of pornographic materials.

The proposed amendments were adopted and have remained unchanged to the present time.

It is perhaps ironic that legislation designed to reduce the amount of objectionable material in circulation had the opposite effect. The key to this development was the case of Queen vs. Brodie, which was finally decided in the Supreme Court and in which the court was asked to determine whether the unexpurgated text of *Lady Chatterley's Lover* was an obscene publication under the 1958 provisions of the Criminal Code. The Court decided, five votes to four, that it was not. Although the Supreme Court was divided on a number of issues, its decision had a decisive impact on Canadian law and its treatment of obscene materials. To begin with, the Hicklin test ceased to be used. This in itself had a liberalizing impact. Secondly, a book could be judged obscene only if undue exploitation of sex was a dominant theme of the whole publication. Judgement could no longer be based on passages taken out of context.

Further, artistic merit could now be considered, with the result that today it is unlikely that works of serious literary merit could be judged obscene under the Code no matter how explicit their treatment of subjects defined by the law as obscene. Finally, the notion of "community standards" was introduced. A publication could be judged obscene only if it exceeded community standards of tolerance.

Each of these factors finds a place in the judgement of Judge Loukidelis in "The Queen versus Sudbury News Service," one of the readings included in this chapter.

The 1970s saw a strong renewal of public concern with pornography in response to a flood of increasingly explicit, widely circulated, pornographic publications. Relaxation of legal controls was criticized. By 1977 a number of private-members' bills dealing with pornography had been proposed. The government of the day felt itself under increasing pressure to tighten legislative controls. The result was a decision to examine all the proposed amendments to the Criminal Code through public hearings to be conducted by the Justice and Legal Affairs Committee of the House of Commons.

The pattern followed in the hearings was similar, in many respects, to that of the Senate inquiry which had taken place two decades previously. Those who advocated stricter controls called for an objective test of obscenity. There was a sharply focussed desire to eliminate child pornography. And the theme of violence played a significant role in the discussions. These opposed to increased control argued that current provisions were adequate if properly applied, and pointed to the undesirable aspects of censorship in any form.

The committee reported in 1978 and indicated that it was concerned with the depiction and advocacy "in clear and explicit terms" of such activities as "sodomy, cunnilingus, fellatio, incest, masturbation, bestiality, necrophilia, sadism, and masochism." It argued that "the effect of this type of material is to reinforce male-female stereotypes to the detriment of both sexes," and went on to say that "such literature attempts to make degradation, humiliation, victimization and violence in human relationships appear normal and acceptable." The committee concluded that Canadians were justified in controlling the circulation of this kind of material and proposed a series of amendments. However, the report was not acted on as of 1982, and the 1958 provisions remain intact.

Concern with pornography has not been an exclusively Canadian phenomenon. Over the past decade studies have been commissioned in both the United States and Great Britain. The resulting reports (mentioned in the bibliography at the end of the chapter) have concluded that, in spite of obvious public concern, research has not established that exposure to pornography stimulates an increase in sexual crimes such as rape or indecent exposure. On the basis of these findings the committees have recommended that, because controls limit freedom of choice and expression, and because no direct harm in the form of criminal activity seems to result from exposure to such materials, legislative control of pornographic material should be reduced or eliminated.

The Current Situation

Pornography today is big business. Moreover, if the report of the Justice and Legal Affairs Committee is to be believed, a substantial portion of the business is controlled by organized crime in the United States. Of course, not all pornography is illegal, as a visit to the magazine shelf of the corner store would quickly reveal. Of the ten best-selling magazines in Canada today, six are explicitly sexual in content. Two examples are *Playboy* and *Penthouse*.

The public attitude toward pornography is not easy to gauge. Over the past ten years the courts have accepted a wider and wider range of materials as not exceeding community standards of tolerance. At the same time, Parliament has been under constant political pressure since the mid-1970s to strengthen the law. And in 1982, government-supported legislation, whose focus was the elimination of child pornography, was presented. At the close of the 1982 sitting, this legislation remained unadopted.

In summary, the nature and availability of pornography poses vexing questions for Canadians both as individuals and as a community.

The Moral Dimension

Some people believe that pornography is beneficial, in part because it provides an outlet for sexual fantasies which might otherwise find expression in violent or coercive behaviour. None of the readings in this chapter adopts this stance, though some of the readings examine it. Others have argued that pornography is a form of sexual expression which is simply a matter of personal preference, and, as such, morally neutral if participation is voluntary and those participating are adults capable of deciding their own lifestyle. This view, too, is examined in the readings. Much more common is the view that pornography is objectionable either because of the way it depicts human sexuality and because of the sexual morality it appears to advocate, or because of specific and common ingredients such as violence or the way it represents women or children or a combination of these.

However, the debate does not end here, for two reasons. First, those who feel quite strongly that pornography is seriously objectionable face a further question. Should pornography be censored in general or only in certain cases? For those who do not feel strongly on the subject, a slightly different question is raised. When is a majority entitled to override the moral autonomy of individuals and impose, by law, a standard of conduct?

We have already examined one possible answer to this question. We have seen it argued that communities are justified in creating legal constraints on individual autonomy in order to protect human life. Clearly this answer would not justify the censorship of pornography.

Is there another principle available to help answer these two questions? It is widely argued that there is such a principle. People should be allowed to pursue their own lifestyle and determine their own behaviour up to the point at which the behaviour begins to harm themselves or others.

We have already had an opportunity to evaluate the principle that the community ought to intervene to protect individuals from self-inflicted harm in our examination of euthanasia and the problems generated by mental illness. In this chapter problems associated with self-inflicted harm are perhaps secondary. The question around which the pornography debate usually revolves is whether the voluntary use of pornography by some is harmful to non-users or the community at large.

The suggestion that the basic issue in assessing the justifiability of censorship is its harmfulness for non-users carries with it a deceptive air of simplicity. In its most basic form, harm is associated with physical abuse resulting in injury or illness. But there are more complex dimensions to the concept. We can cause psychological harm through insults or misrepresentations or bad faith. Furthermore, at a social level each of us is dependent on others in a wide variety of ways. That dependence results in cooperation. But cooperation is possible only if there are shared rules and patterns of behaviour. If confidence in those rules and patterns of behaviour is undermined, the consequences can be damaging. For example, yelling "Fire!" in a crowded theatre may well cause panic. Panic is a state of mind in which confidence in normal rules or patterns of behaviour has collapsed. The result is invariably harmful for many of those caught in such a situation.

It is also the case that the kinds of events or things the term "harm" applies to will vary according to the values of the person assessing those events and the context in which those events occur. What is cheerful hubbub to party-goers may be harmful irritation to a student preparing for examinations. A decision not to build a concert hall will be seen as of no significance for those who see classicial music as valueless. For those who think otherwise, the decision implies cultural impoverishment.

Once we recognize the complexity of the notion of harm, we are faced with yet another dimension to our first problem. Are all types of harm to be given equal weight? Or do some kinds of harm have a higher priority than others? If so, how are the priorities to be determined? That is, by reference to whose system of values are decisions to be made?

There is a second type of difficulty which complicates the debate. Given that we agree on what we are looking for, how do we trace the impact of pornography on its users and on the community generally? The answer might be thought to be relatively straightforward. We can set up research studies designed to provide us with the facts. The simplicity of the suggestion hides the complexity of the situation. The tools available to social scientists in analyzing and explaining human conduct are not precision instruments. In addition, there are serious moral limitations on the kinds of studies which are allowed.

A further and more serious difficulty is frequently obscured by the emphasis on empirical research. It may be that the most important characteristic of pornography is its impact on how people think about the world in which they live. Some people are opposed to anti-Semitic literature not because research shows it leads directly to harm to Jews. In fact, it is unlikely that any direct cause/effect relationship could be demonstrated. Rather, the concern is with the way in which such literature affects how its users and members of society generally think about or see themselves and others. The harmful impact of pornography may as a consequence be at the level of ideas or concepts and not (except perhaps indirectly) at the level of behaviour.

We have, then, two difficulties which lie in the way of ready agreement on the consequences of exposure to pornography. There is a third difficulty to be considered. Where does the onus of proof lie? Should we take the view that obscenity legislation is justified only if substantial harm can be demonstrated to flow from free and uncontrolled circulation of pornography? Or should we take the view that until pornography is shown to be harmless, legislative control is justified? Furthermore, should we resolve this issue in the case of pornography differently than we would in the case of pollution or safety standards? The question is important, at least in part because available research about the effect of pornography on users and on the community is inconclusive.

The Readings

It can be seen that there are three distinct types of difficulty which lie in the way of agreement on the nature and impact of pornography. Each is encountered in the readings which follow. The first two items in this chapter include the relevant provisions of the Criminal Code and a recent judgement which illustrates how the courts have come to interpret it. The case against censorship is then set out in the extracts taken from the Law Reform Commission report on obscenity. In their report, the Law Reform Commissioners accept that pornography is socially harmful. They then examine whether use of the Criminal Code is morally legitimate in countering the harm caused. After an extended consideration of the alternatives, they conclude that censorship is legitimate where its aim is to protect those who do not wish to be exposed to pornography. Further, society is entitled to use the law to shield children. But private consumption should not be prohibited. L.W. Conolly provides a brief but accurate account of the type of research which has led many to the conclusion that pornography is not harmful. He argues further that the onus of proof is on those who favour censorship. It does not follow, however, that pornography is either benign or beneficial. Since it is, in fact, a pervasive form of literature, if pornography has no impact on attitudes and values then neither does literature in general. This view he cannot accept. Conolly concludes that pornography does have an effect on our perception of the nature of human sexuality, an effect which is not subject to empirical measurement. Nevertheless, censorship is not an acceptable way of dealing with this problem. Thus the focus of his analysis is the second and third problem: How do we trace the harm caused by pornography and where does the onus of proof lie?

Margaret Atwood looks at various characterizations of pornography, identifies *violent* pornography as the problem, and suggests that it be considered hate literature, from the point of view of its impact on sex education and as an addictive substance.

Lorenne Clark agrees with Heintzman that the liberal philosophical assumptions which imply that pornography is harmless are mistaken. What the debate lacks is an adequate concept of harm. She then proceeds to offer a view based on alternative presuppositions and concludes that legislative control is both justified and morally imperative. In the process, Clark argues that the onus of proving that pornography is not harmful must rest with those who are opposed to legislative controls.

Finally, Raymond D. Gastil suggests it is plausible to argue that pornography is socially harmful. Thus, the majority, who regard pornography as morally objectionable, have grounds for controlling and limiting its use.

Offences Tending to Corrupt Morals

[Canadian Criminal Code, Section 159]

159.(1) Every one commits an offence who   Corrupting morals
  (a) makes, prints, publishes, distributes, circulates, or has in his possession for the purpose of publication, distribution, or circulation any obscene written matter, picture, model, phonograph record, or other thing whatsoever, or
  (b) makes, prints, publishes, distributes, sells, or has in his possession for the purpose of publication, distribution, or circulation, a crime comic.

(2) Every one commits an offence who knowingly, without lawful   Idem
justification or excuse,
  (a) sells, exposes to public view, or has in his possession for such a purpose any obscene written matter, picture, model, phonograph record, or other thing whatsoever.
  (b) publicly exhibits a disgusting object or an indecent show,
  (c) offers to sell, advertises, publishes an advertisement of, or has for sale or disposal any means, instructions, medicine, drug, or article intended or represented as a method of causing abortion or miscarriage, or
  (d) advertises or publishes an advertisement of any means, instructions, medicine, drug, or article intended or represented as a method for restoring sexual virility or curing venereal diseases or diseases of the generative organs.

(3) No person shall be convicted of an offence under this section   Defence of public
if he establishes that the public good was served by the acts that are   good
alleged to constitute the offence and that the acts alleged did not extend
beyond what served the public good.

(4) For the purposes of this section it is a question of law whether   Question of law and
an act served the public good and whether there is evidence that the   question of fact

act alleged went beyond what served the public good, but it is a question of fact whether the acts did or did not extend beyond what served the public good.

(5) For the purposes of this section the motives of an accused are irrelevant. — *Motives irrelevant*

(6) Where an accused is charged with an offence under subsection (1) the fact that the accused was ignorant of the nature or presence of the matter, picture, model, phonograph record, crime comic, or other thing by means of or in relation to which the offence was committed is not a defence to the charge. — *Ignorance of nature no defence*

(7) In this section, "crime comic" means a magazine, periodical, or book that exclusively or substantially comprises matter depicting pictorially. — *"Crime comic"*

(a) the commission of crimes, real or fictitious, or

(b) events connected with the commission of crimes, real or fictitious, whether occurring before or after the commission of the crime.

(8) For the purposes of this Act, any publication a dominant characteristic of which is the undue exploitation of sex, or of sex and any one or more of the following subjects, namely, crime, horror, cruelty, and violence, shall be deemed to be obscene. — *"Obscene"*

160.(1) A judge who is satisfied by information upon oath that there are reasonable grounds for believing that any publication, copies of which are kept for sale or distribution in premises within the jursidiction of the court, is obscene or a crime comic, shall issue a warrant under his hand authorizing seizure of the copies. — *Warrant of seizure*

(2) With seven days of the issue of the warrant, the judge shall issue a summons to the occupier of the premises requiring him to appear before the court and show cause why the matter seized should not be *forfeited* to Her Majesty. — *Summons to occupier*

(3) The owner and the author of the matter seized and alleged to be obscene or a crime comic may appear and be represented in the proceedings in order to oppose the making of an order for the forfeiture of the said matter. — *Owner and author may appear*

(4) If the court is satisfied that the publication is obscene or a crime comic, it shall make an order declaring the matter forfeited to Her Majesty in right of the province in which the proceedings take place, for disposal as the Attorney General may direct. — *Order of forfeiture*

(5) If the court is not satisfied that the publication is obscene or a crime comic, it shall order that the matter be restored to the person from whom it was seized forthwith after the time for final appeal has expired. — *Disposal of matter*

(6) An appeal lies from an order made under subsection 4 or 5 by any person who appeared in the proceedings — *Appeal*

(a) on any ground of appeal that involves a question of law alone,
(b) on any ground of appeal that involves a question of fact alone, or
(c) on any ground of appeal that involves a question of mixed law and fact,

as if it were an appeal against conviction or against a judgment or verdict of acquittal, as the case may be, on a question of law alone under Part XVIII and sections 601 to 624 apply *mutatis mutandis*.

(7) Where an order has been made under this section by a judge in a province with respect to one or more copies of a publication, no proceedings shall be instituted or continued in that province under section 159 with respect to those or other copies of the same publication without the consent of the Attorney General. Consent

(8) In this section Definitions

"court" means a country or district court or, in the Province of Quebec, the provincial court, the court of sessions of the peace, the municipal court of Montreal, and the municipal court of Quebec; "Court"

"crime comic" has the same meaning as it has in section 159; "Crime comic"

"judge" means a judge of a court. "Judge"

161. Every one commits an offence who refuses to sell or supply to any other person copies of any publication for the reason only that such other person refuses to purchase or acquire from him copies of any other publication that such other person is apprehensive may be obscene or a crime comic. Tied sale

162.(1) A proprietor, editor, master printer, or publisher commits an offence who prints or publishes Restriction on publication of reports of judicial proceedings
(a) in relation to any judicial proceedings any indecent matter or indecent medical, surgical, or physiological details, being matter or details that, if published, are calculated to injure public morals;
(b) in relation to any judicial proceedings for dissolution of marriage, nullity of marriage, judicial separation or restitution of conjugal rights, any particulars other than
  (i) the names, addresses, and occupations of the parties and witnesses,
  (ii) a concise statement of the charges, defences, and countercharges in support of which evidence has been given.
  (iii) submissions on a point of law arising in the course of the proceedings, and the decision of the court in connection therewith, and

(iv)   the summing up of the judge, the finding of the jury, and the judgment of the court and the observations that are made by the judge in giving judgment.

(2)   Nothing in paragraph 1(b) affects the operation of paragraph 1(a).   Saving

(3)   No proceedings for an offence under this section shall be commenced without the consent of the Attorney General.   Consent of Attorney General

(4)   This section does not apply to a person who   Exceptions

(a)   prints or publishes any matter for use in connection with any judicial proceedings or communicates it to persons who are concerned in the proceedings;

(b)   prints or publishes a notice or report pursuant to directions of a court; or

(c)   prints or publishes any matter

(i)   in a volume or part of a *bona fide* series of law reports that does not form part of any other publication and consists solely of reports of proceedings in courts of law, or

(ii)   in a publication of a technical character that is *bona fide* intended for circulation among members of the legal or medical professions.

163.(1)   Every one commits an offence who, being the lessee, manager, agent, or person in charge of a theatre, presents or gives or allows to be presented or given therein an immoral, indecent, or obscene performance, entertainment, or representation.   Immoral theatrical performance

(2)   Every one commits an offence who takes part or appears as an actor, performer, or assistant in any capacity, in an immoral, indecent, or obscene performance, entertainment, or representation in a theatre.   Person taking part

164.   Every one commits an offence who makes use of the mails for the purpose of transmitting or delivering anything that is obscene, indecent, immoral, or scurrilous, but this section does not apply to a person who makes use of the mails for the purpose of transmitting or delivering anything mentioned in subsection 162(4).   Mailing obscene matter

165.   Every one who commits an offence under section 159, 161, 162, 163, or 164 is guilty of   Punishment

(a)   an indictable offence and is liable to imprisonment for two years, or

(b)   an offence punishable on summary conviction.

Sudbury News Services Limited and Her Majesty the Queen

[A court judgement]

Judge Loukidelis

This is an appeal from the conviction entered and sentence imposed by His Honour Judge G.R. Matte on March 31st, 1978 on an information "that Sudbury News Service Limited . . . and William Paden did between March 9, 1976 and March 17, 1976 at the City of Sudbury in the District of Sudbury unlawfully distribute obscene publications to wit:

> *Cinema X*, Vol. #7, No. 7; *Blade*, Vol. #1, No. 1; *Modern Man*, March 1976; *Debonair*, May, 1976; *Topper*, April, 1976; *Man's Magazine*, April, 1976; *Men*, April, 1976; *Ace*, April, 1976; *Genesis*, April, 1976; *Carnival*, Vol. #1, No. 9; *Man's Pleasure*, Winter Quarterly; *American Swinger*, Vol. #4, No. 1; *Penthouse*, April, 1976; *Stag*, April, 1976; *Gallery*, April, 1976; *Adam*, Vol. #1, No. 20; *Man's Pleasure*, April 1976; *New Q.T.*, Vol. #2, No. 4; *Swank*, April, 1976; *Knave*, Vol. #7, No. 12; *Oui*, March, 1976.

While the company and Mr. Paden were both charged with the offence, the Crown withdrew the charge against the accused individual after plea.

An earlier decision in this matter by Judge Matte was appealed by way of stated case and that appeal was heard by R.E. Holland J. and reported at (1978) 17 O.R. (2d) 186. In his decision, he answered two questions in the affirmative of the six questions propounded by Judge Matte and did not answer the remaining four. He allowed the appeal and set the conviction aside.

Subsequently, the matter was heard by the Court of Appeal, by leave, and the decision of the court was given by Howland C.J.O. and reported at (1978) 18 O.R. 428. In the result, the court allowed the appeal by setting aside the order of R.E. Holland J. and the conviction of Judge G.R. Matte and remitted the matter to the learned provincial court judge for determination in accordance with the opinion expressed in that judgment.

On March 31st, 1978, the matter having been argued, the court entered a conviction and fined the corporate accused.

On or about the 15th day of March 1976 Sergeants R. Cowley and R. Weston visited five confectionery stores and smoke shops in the City of Sudbury and seized a number of books. Subsequently, these books were reviewed by these police officers and charges were laid.

While some time and effort were expended on the issue of distribution, it appears from the transcript that counsel for the accused admitted distribution by the corporate accused.

The magazine *Cinema X* (Vol. #7, No. 7) (Exhibit 5), included a series of twelve photographs entitled "Erotic Inferno." This depicts male and female partners as well as female and female partners in various states of undress involved in a variety of forms of sex play. Acts of sex or simulated sex are shown on succeeding pages as well as some acts of sex in which there are more than two participants. Included is a commentary on what is sometimes called "Blue Movies." In the words of the witness Cowley (page 19—Vol. #1) *Cinema X* can be described as being concerned with:

> The predominant characteristic is the pictorial displays of the female and male bodies in various acts of sexual activity.

In the magazine *Blade* (Vol. #1, No. 1) (Exhibit 6), the first part of the magazine includes letters to the editor, photographs of female models and includes photographs and a feature article on Xaviera Hollander. In the book as well is found a photograph depicting acts or simulated acts of anal sex.

The magazine *Modern Man* (March 1976 issue) included colour displays of female models displaying the complete vaginal area of the female body. There were advertisements for sex-aids and an article at page 14 entitled "Confessions of a Cheerleader." The last was a story of the sex exploits of a young teen-aged American female.

In the magazine *Debonair* (May 1976 issue) there were numerous photographs displaying the vaginal area of the female and articles or stories that are wholly concerned with sex. In this and the previous three magazines the opinion of Sergeant Cowley was that their dominant characteristic concerned sex and its undue exploitation.

Similarly, *Topper* magazine (1976 April issue) was concerned in its photographs and its stories of sexual acts, sexual activity by models and advertisements dealing with sexual aids. There was very little content concerned with non-sexual matters.

In the April 1976 issue of *Man's Magazine* there were numerous photographs of the female vaginal area, stories including ones entitled "Sex Slaves" and "The Kinkiest Orgy of Them All." The stories generally concern sexual activities and one article dealt with masochism. Very little of the magazine was devoted to matters of a non-sexual nature.

The book *Carnival* (Vol. #1, No. 9) has a similar theme. *American Swingers* (Exhibit 13) consists of a number of advertisements accompanied by photographs in most cases of which individuals seek out partners for sex. This also includes female physical statistics and their sexual preferences.

In a somewhat different category is the April issue of *Penthouse* in 1976 which includes not only photographs and articles of a sexual nature but other matters as well. While the magazine is not predominantly sexual, there is a substantial content that is sex-oriented.

The magazine *Knave* (Vol. #7, No. 12) (Exhibit 15) includes numerous photographs of the vaginal areas of various models and stories of a sexual nature. While this magazine, like *Penthouse*, was not predominantly sex-oriented, many of the articles and photographs in the magazine concerned sexual activities. The magazine *Oui* (Exhibit 16) has various coloured photographs of various sex acts or simulated sex acts by female and female and male and female. There are pictorial displays of vaginal areas and the book closes with a cartoon in full colour which shows various positions for sexual intercourse.

These magazines were found in five stores, three of which were termed neighbourhood confectioneries while the remaining two were smoke shops in the inner city core. As to the neighbourhood confectioneries (Legace, Presley's and Fox) people of all ages including children came there to shop. These stories carried sundries, grocery items and magazines.

In relation to the magazines introduced through Sergeant Cowley, there was an admission by that witness that two of the magazines, namely *Penthouse* and *Oui*, had other written material of a general literary interest. In the former there was a work of fiction and in both, there were articles of general interest. For example, there was one story that dealt with the problems of the Vietnam veteran and another concerning the destruction involved in the bombing of Dresden in the Second Great War.

Detective Weston gave evidence in relation to *Ace* magazine (April 1976 issue) (Exhibit 20). This magazine contained numerous photographs showing nude females with the vaginal area exposed in some cases. There were written articles entitled "Three for Me" and "How Moral is Oral?" The copy of *Genesis* magazine carried similar photographs and similar stories. The winter quarterly of the magazine entitled *Man's Pleasure* included articles of various forms of sex.

In all of these, Sergeant Weston gave as his opinion that the dominant characteristic was the undue exploitation of sex. Similar evidence was given in relation to all of the magazines that were put in through him.

In relation to the corner store known as Presley's, Mrs. Ann Yurkovich, the proprietor, gave evidence that she received magazines of the kind entered as exhibits from the accused corporation. Some of the magazines she refused to display after perusing them and placed them in the return box so that she could receive credit from the accused. Her evidence was that in her view some of the magazines weren't "quite right for my store." The reason she carried the magazines was mainly because of competition as other stores in the area carried magazines of the same description. She acknowledged that the traffic through her store included persons of all age groups and described her business as a family business. On cross-examination her evidence was that it was her decision whether to display the books or not and how to display them and she was not obliged to carry any of the books.

Mrs. St. Jean, the owner of Fox's Confectionery, also gave evidence that competition required her to carry the magazines and that their sale was profitable as well as bringing traffic into the store. Her evidence was that her store attracted customers of all ages. Her evidence too confirmed that the accused did not dictate how the magazines were to be displayed and that, had she wanted, she could have placed these magazines out of reach of children.

The evidence called by the defence included not only academics and distinguished critics but, as well, employees of some of the publishing companies that produced the magazines listed in the information. The evidence of Mr. Nils Shapiro, the editor and publisher of *Gallery Magazine*, satisfies me that his magazine has a substantial circulation in Canada of 65,900 copies of which 39% are sold in Ontario.

He further indicates that there is an average pass-along of about three. This means that the magazine is loaned out or read by three other people besides the purchaser.

Gerard Vanderleun, the senior editor of *Penthouse*, was called as was Richard Fogel, the circulation manager of the magazine. His evidence is that the April 1976 edition of *Penthouse* had a total circulation in Canada of 418,146 copies which included 13,212 subscribers. Its total circulation throughout the world was 4½ million copies.

It might be added at this point that all of these magazines are produced outside of Canada and must pass through customs. The evidence of Mr. Shapiro is that his company has never had any difficulty in bringing *Gallery* magazines into Canada.

Arnold Edinborough, a distinguished writer, teacher, editor and television personality, gave evidence in relation to the April issue of *Penthouse* 1976 and the March 1976 issue of *Oui*. His evidence concerned the great changes that have taken place in the past fifteen years in the reading habits of people, which he has deduced in part from the large circulation enjoyed by magazines like *Penthouse* and *Playboy*. He concludes that they have general acceptance and that they are not considered beyond those standards by a great many people nor indeed by the authorities in the jurisdictions in which they are sold. While concluding that the pictorial display in *Penthouse* magazine is remarkably explicit, it is no more explicit than many of the movies that are shown in the movie houses in this city and throughout the country. While some of the material in the magazines were personally offensive to him he did not believe that they were offensive to "the generality of the people of this country."

In relation to the movie *Last Tango in Paris*, Mr. Edinborough gave evidence for the prosecution. In the movie, there was an act of buggery, several acts of intercourse and masturbation. He referred to many movies that are now shown in Toronto that have had long and successful runs there.

In relation to literature, he referred to best-selling books written in Canada. In one entitled *Bear*, a librarian finds a tame bear in the house which she has inherited and makes various advances to the bear and eventually tries to copulate with it. His view is that this is highly symbolic within the framework of the novel and that the novel is not sexually oriented. In live theatre, language taboos changed considerably and in the last few years there has been nudity on the stage.

The evidence of Mr. Edinborough is that magazines such as he has examined have general acceptance in the community as witnessed by the large circulation figures attained by magazines like *Penthouse* and *Playboy* and this general availability and acceptability is a factor in determining community standards. This is so because if people were outraged they would not buy.

Dr. Hank Davis, a professor of psychology at the University of Guelph, gave evidence. His particular expertise within his discipline includes human sexuality and sexual oppression. He examined exhibits 5 to 28. He concluded that he found nothing in those magazines which, in any way, "outsteps or exceeds what I would consider to be the mode of sexual experience which occurs in any other magazines, papers or media in this community." In addition, he concludes that the range of contemporary cinema available includes degrees of sexual expression which equal and in some cases exceed the degree of sexual explicitness found in the magazines. The movies he refers to are those shown in movie houses like *Taxi Driver* which concerns a twelve-year-old prostitute in which are portrayed simulated sex scenes. Other movies referred to by him include *The Exorcist, Charlotte* and *Last Tango in Paris*. From this he concludes that the range of what is popular and what is demanded in films appears to include the same type of selection as that found in the magazines introduced by the Crown. He also refers to some live theatre where similar standards may be found.

In the field of popular music he refers to the highly explicit nature of the words which are directed to a younger audience. The sexual emphasis of certain forms of modern music have been commented upon by magazines such as *Time* (December 29, 1975 issue).

Referring to certain psychological studies, Dr. Davis indicates that there is a body of research that indicates that this type of material has not produced illegal or deviant behaviour but rather it "might in fact serve as a safety valve and keep one from performing such acts." Referring to studies by Veniste and Kutchinsky the legalization of pornography in Denmark in the late 1960s showed documented decreases in sex crimes.

Betty Lee, a journalist, compared the magazines to movies shown in Toronto and not including those shown in "porno movie houses." There have been scenes, according to her, of necrophilia, oral sex, anal sex, masturbation, incest, all of which are shown on a scale, in some cases, more explicit than those in the magazines. She pointed out that some of the movies have been financed by the taxpayers of Canada and that the Canadian Film Development Corporation has made money on such movies. One, in particular, called "Les Deux Femmes," is a story of two wives who invited in the iceman, newspaper man and coalman into their homes, to have sex, while their husbands were away. Her evidence was that she also accompanied Xaviera Hollander to Sheridan College where she spoke to an overflow audience of students and some staff about matters of a sexual nature including graphic descriptions of how to achieve oral sex. She points out that Miss Hollander was a prostitute in New York who left the United States for a time because of difficulties with the taxation authorities there and made her home in Canada.

Professor Stanley Mullins, professor in the department of English at Laurentian University, sometime head of the English department at Laval University and president of Laurentian University, gave evidence which referred to the changing standards in modern Canadian literature. In particular, he refers to a number of books written in Canada which have achieved best-seller status including *Bear*, *The Candy Factory* and *The Stud Horseman*. To him changing standards over the past decade can be seen in newspapers, literature and psychological and sociological studies which report a continuing swing towards liberalization. In relation to some of the literary works to which he has referred, he is of the opinion that they had a literary value and were symbolically oriented. On the other hand the magazines entered as exhibits in this case had "very little literary value."

Approaching the matter from another side, he concludes that the printed word found in novels, poems, plays and newspapers are more suggestive than the pictorial display. A pictorial display leaves little to the imagination and the imagination is not called to dwell upon them. The printed word and imagery that it creates can be expanded, deepened or emphasized by the imagination of the reader.

In relation to the judgment on literary merit made by Professor Mullins, Mrs. Aviva Layton, a professor of English at York University, concluded that there was absolutely no literary merit to the magazines in that they were poorly and sloppily written for the most part and that the photographs are "poor, sloppy, vulgar pictures." She was unwilling, however, to deal with these magazines on their literary merit. She has compared the magazines to *Bear* on the basis that both deal with sexual acts and that they both fall within community accepted standards.

In relation to the photographs in the magazines she concluded that there was no reason for the photographs to be in the magazines except to stimulate sexuality. "It has no reason whatsoever except sexual stimulation. I can't say that it has any other reason because it obviously doesn't."

The offence charged here is found in section 159(1)(a) which reads as follows:

> Everyone commits an offence who . . . distributes . . . any obscene written matter, picture, model, phonograph record or other thing whatsoever.
>
> (8) For the purposes of this act, any publication a dominant characteristic of which is the undue exploitation of sex, or of sex and any one or more of the following subjects, namely, crime, horror, cruelty and violence, shall be deemed to be obscene.

The offence here is one of distribution which the accused, through its counsel, has admitted. Apart from the admission, I would be prepared to hold that the evidence of the two merchants satisfies me that this ingredient has in fact been proven. . . .

Dealing with the ingredient of obscenity, I find that the Parliament of Canada has provided a definition of that word in section 159(8). The decision of the Supreme Court of Canada in *Dechow v. The Queen* (1977), 35 C.C.C. (2d) 222, 76 D.L.R. (3d) 1, and 40 C.R.N.S. 129, has concluded that the definition of obscenity in that sub-section is exhaustive. Summarizing the substance of the Dechow case, Howland C.J.R. at p. 433 concludes:

> Under s. 159(8) of the code for a publication to be deemed to be obscene it is not sufficient that a dominant characteristic of it has been the exploitation of sex. There must have been an "undue" exploitation of sex. In determining what is undue exploitation within s. 159(8) the test to be applied is whether the accepted standards of tolerance in the contemporary Canadian community have been exceeded.

What are the standards and how are they to be determined? It would appear that the Supreme Court of Canada in R.V. Brodie (1962) adopted the standards of the community as a test of undueness which was later defined in Freedman J.A. in *Dominion News and Gifts (1962) Limited v. The Queen* (1964) as being:

> . . . not set by those of lowest taste or interest. Nor are they set exclusively, by those of rigid, austere, conservative, or puritan taste

and habit of mind. Something approaching a general average of community thinking and feeling has to be discovered.

This determination of the general average of community thinking obviously is a changing one as times and ideas change.

At page 434, the court has summarized these principles as including:

1. It is the standards of the community as a whole which must be considered and not the standards of a small segment of that community.
2. The standard to be applied is a national one.
3. The decision whether the publication is tolerable according to Canadian community standards rests with the court.

In this case we have heard evidence from professors of English and psychology whose evidence was introduced to assist the court in determining community standards. That decision, however, is not the decision of the experts to make but rather that of the judge. One of the arguments advanced by the defence before the provincial judge was that the failure of the Crown to call such expert evidence meant that the Crown had failed to prove the Canadian community standard. While advancing the view that Courts have sometimes come to the position that such expert evidence is not required, it would be so only in the clearest of cases where the nature of the material under scrutiny clearly departed from any standards. In that case, expert evidence would not be required. However, at page 435, the Court of Appeal in this case concluded that expert evidence is admissible as to community standards but is not essential.

> The trier of fact, Judge or jury as the case may be, will no doubt rely on the best evidence available and will draw on a lifetime experience in the Canadian community. The task is to determine in an objective way what is tolerable in accordance with the contemporary standards of the Canadian community, and not merely to project one's own personal ideas of what is tolerable. Expert evidence has to be considered in determining the weight to be given to it, but it can be rejected in its entirety if the conclusion is reached that no finding can be based on it. Expert evidence may be of considerable assistance, particularly in areas where the Judge or jury making the determination has no expertise, such as the understanding and appreciation of art.

The next question is whether there is an interaction in the determination of the issue of obscenity or determination of the Canadian community standards by the constitutency which will have access to their purchase or use. One one side of the spectrum, there are some photographs or publications that could be termed indecent as not being tolerable by the Canadian community under any circumstance. There are some where the conclusion of indecency would depend largely on the persons who would have access to such material. At page 435 the court found,

Some pictures are offensive to the majority of people to the point that the Canadian community would not tolerate them on a billboard or on the cover of a magazine, or on a television screen where persons of all ages and sensibilities would be exposed to them, but would be prepared to tolerate them being viewed by persons who wished to view them. Some pictures would not be acceptable by Canadian community standards in a children's bed-time story-book or primer but would be in a magazine for general distribution. Canadian community might be prepared to tolerate the exhibition of a motion picture to an adult audience, but would consider the exhibition of the same motion picture to a general audience, which included children, to be an undue exploitation of sex. Similarly, the general distribution of certain magazines in a neighbourhood store accessible to all ages would not be tolerable, whereas the distribution of such magazines to "adult" bookstores to which children under a certain age were not admitted might not be objectionable. The packaging and pricing of a publication may also be relevant in considering whether Canadian community standards have been exceeded. . . .

The manner and circumstances of distribution have been considered by the Courts in a number of cases in applying the test whether Canadian community standards have been exceeded.

At page 437, Howland C.J.O. continued this line of reasoning.

In my opinion, the manner and circumstances of distribution are relevant in determining whether the standards of tolerance by the Canadian community have been exceeded. Here the distribution was to ordinary confectionery stores who made their merchandise available to the general public. In my opinion, the Canadian community would be less tolerant in the case of such distribution than they would be in the case of distribution to stores who only made sales to persons 18 years of age and over, or who confine their sales to publications of legitimate interest to particular segments of the Canadian community, such as, for example, writers and artists.

In the recent decision of the court of appeal in *Regina v. Penthouse International Limited and 358071 Ontario Ltd.*, carrying on business as Inter City News Company (leased on January 17, 1979), the court dealt with an appeal from the decision of Misener C.C.J. . . . In that case, a warrant had been issued pursuant to section 160 of the Code and certain copies of the September 1977 issue of *Penthouse* magazine were seized. On the return of the Show Cause summons, Judge Misener found that the publication was obscene and made an order that the copies be seized under the warrant.

At page 4, Weatherston J.A. was not prepared to accept that the standard of tolerance was synonymous with the moral standards of the community or that the exclusive theme of the offending portions of the publications were such as to strike at the values that, "in the view of the ordinary right-thinking citizen, form an essential part of the foundation of our society."

> The question, in any event, is not whether the content of the publication goes beyond what the contemporary Canadian community thinks is right, but rather whether it goes beyond what the contemporary Canadian community is prepared to tolerate.

Thus, there is a distinction between what may be personally offensive for the private taste of the individual on the one hand and the standard of tolerance. In *Benjamin News (Montreal) Reg'd, Penthouse International Limited v. The Queen*, October 11, 1978 (unreported) as quoted at page 5 by Weatherston J.A.:

> He [the Judge] must determine whether by contemporary Canadian community standards, the book is tolerable in the sense that the general average of community thinking would have no objection to the book being read and seen by those members of the community who wished to do so. The question is not whether personal standards are affronted but whether community standards would tolerate the publication being seen and read by others.

Much argument was directed to the question whether *Gallery* magazine and *Penthouse* magazine were magazines whose dominant characteristic was the exploitation of sex. The argument was made that there were articles of fiction and that magazines of this kind were almost the sole avenue for publication by serious fiction writers. In addition, it was said that there were articles of general historical, political or current-affairs interest. Comparison was made with novels and some of the explicit sex description found in them. These two arguments were reviewed by Weatherston J.A. who made the following observation at page 8 which I find appropriate to the fact situation here:

> Emphasis was placed by counsel for the appellant on the fact that this magazine contained some serious articles, and he argued that notwith-standing his concession that a dominant characteristic of the magazine was the exploitation of sex, those articles saved the exploitation of sex from being undue. He argued that a publication must be examined and an assessment made of it in its entirety. It must be taken as a whole, and it is not appropriate to isolate for analysis those parts which seem offensive. This, of course, is true, but a magazine is to be judged in a somewhat different way than a novel. In the latter case, passages which deal in explicit terms with sex must be judged against the entire work, and in the context of its theme. They may be found to be insignificant in relation to the entire work, or to merely emphasize and give colour to its theme. This cannot be said about a magazine which has no theme. Each page must be looked at more or less in isolation from the others, for it is but rarely that a reader of a magazine will start at the beginning

and read through to the end. Offensive passages or pictorial presenta-
tions in a magazine cannot be saved merely by surrounding them with
profound articles on foreign policy.

On the question whether these magazines are obscene, I have reviewed the evidence
taken at the original hearing and perused the exhibits filed. On the evidence called
by the defence itself (Professor Mullins and Professor Layton), I would be prepared
to find that these magazines have no literary or artistic merit.

The sex-related stories in these magazines and the photographs have as their sole
purpose the undue exploitation of sex and I am prepared to find that they go beyond
what the Canadian community was prepared to tolerate in 1976 when these books
were offered for sale. In coming to this conclusion, I have taken into consideration
the stores in which these magazines were bought. The publications, by reason of
this sex-related content, had as their dominant characteristic the undue exploitation
of sex. These magazines were intended for distribution and were in fact distributed
to confectionery stores to which residents of this area of all ages had access. Though
proprietors of the stores had the last word on the display, the accused knew or
ought to have known that these neighbourhood confectionery or variety stores
would include among its customers children of tender years who would have access
to these book displays.

Accordingly, the appeal will be dismissed and the conviction and sentence confirmed.

Limits of Criminal Law

[From Working Paper 10]

The Law Reform Commission of Canada

The Aims of Criminal Law

Obscenity, then, is in our view socially and indirectly harmful by conflicting with
and threatening values essential or important for society. It runs counter to our
values on violence, freedom, and human dignity. In particular, public obscenity and
the exposure of children to obscenity, conflict with individual freedom.

Does this warrant calling in the criminal law? Does it make obscenity the business
of the criminal law? And what would calling in the criminal law achieve?

First, when is any conduct the business of the criminal law? Some would say
"when that conduct is wrong or immoral, quite apart from whether it harms or
affects others." To them the job of the criminal law is seeing to it that wrongdoing
reaps its own reward—in a word, *retributivism*.

From Working Paper 10, Sec. 9. Courtesy the Law Reform Commission of Canada.

Retributivism

The retributivist view, however, raises difficulties. One is this. Retributivism supposes some sort of supernatural or metaphysical accounts sheet, which crime or sin puts out of balance and which accordingly its punishment sets straight again. But how are we to understand this claim? How is it to be established? And how does the punishment set the balance straight?

But even if we could answer such questions, the claim presents a further difficulty. Making sin reap its own reward may well be an appropriate enterprise for a deity, but—though there is something resembling it which we can properly do and which we consider later—not for mere human beings. If *you* do something wrong, does this give *me* a right to punish you for it? "Vengeance is mine; I will repay, saith the Lord," wrote St. Paul and we respectfully agree.

Enforcing Morality

Another alternative claim is that the job of the criminal law is to see that people behave themselves—*to enforce morality*. This is like the retributivist claim in one respect: both views consider the repression of wrongful behaviour as an end in itself. But what concerns retributivism is the punishment of wrong, whereas what concerns morality enforcement is its *prevention*. The morality-enforcement claim is that it is desirable and justifiable to use the criminal law against wrongful conduct, in order to prevent the wrongful conduct.

The morality-enforcement claim not only differs from retributivism. It is also more attractive than it. For one thing, the morality-enforcement claim avoids the problems involved in the retributivist notion of a heavenly balance sheet. For another, it focuses on something we do and have to do: we often have to punish in order to prevent wrongdoing simply because it is wrong—we do so with our children.

But how our children behave is obviously our business. Is it equally obviously our business how adults behave? Is it our business at all unless their acts affect us? Is it any concern of ours what Robinson Crusoe does to Man Friday when both are living isolated on a desert island? The answer you give to this theoretical question depends on whether you think you are your brother's keeper. In the real world, however, systems of criminal law are intimately connected with the question of state jurisdiction. Most systems of criminal law, like ours in Canada, apply primarily to acts occurring in the territory of the relevant state and only in limited fashion to those occurring outside it. But this is how things stand today—no one can say it always will be so. Even in our own century we have seen changes as our world has rapidly assumed the characteristics of the "global village." We have seen the acceptance of the notion of "crimes against humanity," acts which are criminal in international law, wherever and whenever committed.

So if Crusoe murders and tortures Friday, many would say this is our business even though we are thousands of miles away—unless some other state which is more connected with the event claims jurisdiction. But what if he merely picks Man Friday's pocket and steals something inessential? Do we still feel this is our concern? And what if he is merely parading in the nude and offending Friday's sensibilities? It may be wrong of him to do this but does that mean it's up to us to stop him doing it?

Does his act in any way affect us here or do us any harm? In Molière's words: "The thing that gives offence is public scandal; to sin in silence is no sin at all."

Obscenity in Canada, however, does affect us. Some think it causes harm. It certainly offends. It also threatens some of our most important values.

Protection from Harm

So are we to use the criminal law to protect ourselves from harm? If we were sure obscenity did cause harm, would this entitle us to use the criminal law against it?

The basis of criminal law intervention on this ground is social self-defence. People in a society, runs the argument, must and may protect themselves against harm and against those who do them harm. Punishing wrongdoers provides this protection in various ways: by incapacitating wrongdoers, by making examples of them and by turning them into better citizens—the techniques of prevention, deterrence and reform.

The attraction of this view is that it bases the justification of criminal law and punishment on aims and goals which are obviously proper for human beings. If murders are happening in our midst, we clearly have a right to try and stop them. No metaphysical claims are here involved, nor any undue interference with others. How people behave is our business if their behaviour causes us harm. No doubt at all that if Robinson Crusoe killed Man Friday in Halifax, Saskatoon or Vancouver, Canadians would rightly feel themselves affected and entitled to so something about it.

Small wonder then that the harm-protection view has proved a popular one. Unfortunately it too has its difficulties. First, the goal of self-defence against harm would be a clearer justification for the criminal law if it were more certain that deterrence and rehabilitation worked. As it is, research on deterrence indicates that it by no means works as simply or as well as is suggested by a naive Benthamite view of human behaviour. And research on rehabilitation indicates that how a convicted person is dealt with makes little difference to the likelihood of his recidivism. Meanwhile the volume of crime continues to increase. So how much protection does our tax dollar buy in terms of criminal law and punishment?

To this, in fairness, one could answer: these difficulties aren't necessarily insuperable—maybe we shall devise better techniques of rehabilitation and hit on ways of making deterrence more effective. We could also point out that there remains prevention— neutralising the harm by incarcerating the dangerous person or by destroying the noxious article. All the same, people musn't think that criminal law enforcement really solves the problem of crime. Nor should they be misled by the harm-prevention theory, with its emphasis on deterrence and reform, to concentrate unduly on offenders and potential offenders and to forget the rest of society. And this is why we are increasingly attracted to the "underlining of values" view of criminal law.

Underlining Values

As we saw earlier, certain values are essential to any society. And there are others which, though not essential to any society, are necessary for our society—they help to make it the sort of society it is. So when such values are contravened and threatened we call into play the use of the criminal law.

When values are threatened, the criminal law serves various purposes: it provides a response, articulates the values threatened, helps to inculcate those values, and provides the rest of us with reassurance.

First, criminal law is a *response*. To take an analogy, when someone—a friend or colleague—dies, we feel called upon to make some response. We behave gravely, stand in silent recollection, attend a burial service, and so on. All this because death is a serious event in human affairs and one we feel a need to solemnise. It would be less than human to ignore it, as did the three bridge-players who, when the fourth fell dead at the bridge table, simply said: "We'll just have to play three-handed bridge." Likewise with crime. Once a serious crime is committed in our midst, we can't just ignore it, we must do something. And criminal law is a means of doing something.

But more than this. Criminal law is more than a mere response to breach of values. After all, what does it mean to really hold a certain value? It means various things: it means we act in certain ways, conform our conduct to that value, commend those who despite temptation to the contrary stick to the value, and condemn those who contravene the value. So if we really hold that murder is "out," then when one member of our society murders another the one thing we can't do is nothing, because we have to *articulate* the fact that we really hold it. Prosecuting, trying, convicting, and punishing the murderer does just this. Just as medals for bravery, prizes for achievement, and canonization for sanctity officially articulate our respect for exceptionally meritorious behaviour, criminal law officially articulates our condemnation of behaviour that it is exceptionally bad.

There is another purpose, though. These values which we hold are values which we have to learn and go on learning—values we have to be taught. For this we need various teaching and socialising agencies. Such agents hopefully might be our families, schools, and churches. But one such agent, and one all the more important as those others gradually abdicate their teaching role, is the criminal law. As Morton wisely said, the criminal trial is a morality play which reiterates the lesson that murder, rape, robbery, and so on are "out of bounds." Such lessons help to *inculcate* the value threatened by the criminal.

They also serve a further purpose: they provide the rest of us with *reassurance*. They reassure us first by letting us see justice done. Suppose that while most of us refrain from violence and dishonesty, one or two resort to murder and robbery and nothing is done about it. The rest of us will feel that life is unjust. Of course life is never absolutely fair. In the words of the poem,

> The rain it raineth every day
> Upon the just and unjust fellow,
> But more upon the just because
> The unjust hath the just's umbrella.

All the same, we want to minimize injustice. We want a society as just as it can be. Criminal law is one way of trying to satisfy that want: by bringing wrongdoers to justice it tries to see to it that justice is done. And this is the activity we properly engage in that closely resembles dealing out retribution.

But quite apart from the question of justice, there is another need for reassurance. If most of us refrain from violence and dishonesty even when it would suit us not to, and if one or two resort to murdering and stealing and get away with it, then the rest of us will grow cynical and disillusioned: we'll feel we are being "taken for a ride." Chances are, too, we'll take the law into our own hands and resort to lynch law. Out of the window then goes peace, order, and good government. Hence our need for criminal law.

So our conclusion on the aims of criminal law is this. The criminal law serves partly to protect against harm but more importantly to support and bolster social values. Protection against harm it seeks to achieve through deterrence, rehabilitation, and—most successfully—prevention. Support of social values it manages through the "morality play" technique—by reassuring, by educating, and above all by furnishing a necessary response when values are threatened or infringed. And this on the face of it suggests using criminal law only against conduct causing harm or threatening values.

The Limits of Criminal Law

In practical terms, however, how far does it make sense to use the criminal law against any act causing harm or running counter to our values? Take, for example, our test case of obscenity. How far should we use criminal law against obscenity? Even if obscenity offends, results in harm, and threatens some of our values, do we really need to bring in the whole machinery of the criminal law?

The use of criminal law, we pointed out, imposes a cost. The convicted offender who is punished and the citizen who is forbidden to do the act prohibited both suffer a cost. One cost is a reduction of their freedom. Of course if the act in question is quite obviously a serious wrong, like murder, we are not worried by this loss of liberty. With Justice Holmes we reply: "your freedom to shake your fist ends where my chin begins." On the other hand, the less serious the act, the more concern for freedom—one reason among others why acts in no way wrong shouldn't be prohibited by criminal law and perhaps why even some immoral acts aren't in fact prohibited by it.

After all, in Canada as in many countries, an act can be wrong without being criminal. Here attention always focuses on fornication, homosexuality, and lesbianism. But these are poor examples. We don't all agree that such things are wrong. Besides, we can find much better examples of non-criminal wrongful acts. Two spring to mind: *lying and breaking promises*.

To tell a serious lie is clearly wrong. By this we mean a serious lie where there are no justifying or excusing circumstances. It is wrong because it militates against the truth-telling value, a value which we saw was necessary to society. Why hasn't lying, then, been made a crime? It has been, but only in certain circumstances: (1) Where the lie amounts to fraud and (2) where it amounts to perjury. Short of cases where there is a danger of pecuniary loss or miscarriage of justice, liars are left to the informal sanctions of social intercourse.

The same with breaking promises. Again, breaking one's promise is clearly wrong. And here again by this we mean breaking a serious promise where there are no justifying or excusing factors. It is wrong because it militates against the highly useful social practice of promising. All the same, it hasn't generally been made a crime. At most the promise-breaker may be liable for breach of contract. And where he isn't even liable in contract, he too is left to the more informal sanctions of society.

One reason for not invoking criminal law in both these cases is the loss of liberty involved. This might well be too high a price to pay. All the more so, because of two extra factors. One is that lies and breaking promises range from very serious conduct down to relatively trivial behaviour and we wouldn't want every item of such trivial behaviour to set in motion the whole panoply of police, prosecutors, courts, and prison officers. The other factor is that criminal law isn't the only way of bolstering truth and promising—there are other informal and possibly more effective social sanctions in reserve.

Another reason for not involving criminal law in such matters is the financial cost. We simply can't afford to take the criminal-justice sledgehammer to every nut. Criminal law is a blunt and costly instrument best reserved for large targets—for targets constituting "clear and present danger"—which justify the monetary expense involved. Prosecute every simple lie or breach of promise and the game isn't worth the candle. How does this apply to obscenity?

Is it worth using criminal law against obscenity? Quite obviously obscenity itself won't ever be as significant a target for the criminal law as murder, say, or rape or robbery. Equally obviously, however, it isn't utterly without significance. Public obscenity clearly has significance—it annoys, disgusts, offends. As such it merits just as much and just as little place within the criminal law as other species of nuisance. Loud noises, nauseating smells and so on aren't anything like as serious as murder. But still they do make life less tolerable and so we use the criminal law against them to a limited degree. Society thinks the cost is worth it. So may it be with public, or involuntary, obscenity.

But what about private, or voluntary, obscenity? "A problem left to itself," said the playwright N.F. Simpson, "dries up or goes wrong. Fertilize it with a solution and you'll hatch dozens." What problems might we hatch by trying to fertilize voluntary obscenity with a criminal-law solution?

First, in order to prevent a person's private voluntary enjoyment of obscenity, we should be calling in law enforcement agents to invade his privacy and freedom. By this we should ourselves be contravening some of those very values which we are trying to protect by preventing obscenity. In order to foster freedom, privacy, and human dignity, we should in fact be invading the offender's own privacy, dignity, and freedom—his freedom of speech, of expression, and of living his life in his own way, as well as his freedom to be secure in his own home from the interventions of the authorities.

Of course there's nothing self-contradictory about this. It could be argued that the threat obscenity poses to these values and to the value regarding violence is such as to justify this invasion. Some indeed will say that the danger that voluntary consumption of obscenity will lead to Manson murders is sufficient justification. But is it? How clear and obvious is the danger? Obvious enough for us to want to deal with it by risking another danger—the danger of all our homes being open to entry, search and seizure on mere suspicion of obscenity? Obvious enough for us to want to divert law enforcement resources on to this potential harm and away from actual harms such as murder, rape, and robbery? Is that the sort of society we want?

The art of politics, however—and law is ultimately a branch of politics—is the art of the possible, the art of the practical. And is it really practical to use the criminal law against voluntary obscenity simply on account of the conflict between obscenity and our taboo on violence? Not that there may not be other and better reasons for using the law against voluntary obscenity. After all, mightn't it be in the voluntary consumer's own interest to use the law against him? Mightn't we be justified in using the law to protect him from himself?

But is it ever right to save a person from himself? Of course it is. A person might harm himself through ignorance, error, or mistake: to stop him drinking something which, unknown to him, is poison is obviously justifiable—he would want us to. Or again, a person might harm himself through weakness of will or loss of self-control: to stop him drinking himself blind on wood alcohol is clearly justifiable—he'd surely thank us afterwards. In both these cases the person we protect against himself will in general—though not at the moment of being protected—put his long-term welfare before his short-term preference.

But what if he prefers a moment of bliss to a lifetime's welfare? Of course he might not fully appreciate what is involved: he may have got his priorities wrong just now, but later come to see things as we do. But suppose, despite maturity, he just orders his priorities a different way. Suppose he really sets more store on a moment's ecstasy than on a long and healthy life. He's merely out of step with us, that's all. "If a man doesn't keep pace with his companions," said Thoreau, "perhaps it is because he hears a different drummer: let him step to the music which he hears, however measured or far away." Different people, different preferences. In the ultimate analysis each man must choose his own priorities: no one can choose them for him.

This isn't so with children. Children are a special case. We rightly stop toddlers playing with fire for their own good. Why can't we say the same about obscenity? For even though ultimately people should choose their own priorities and make their own commitments, they need maturity to do so. Children don't yet have this maturity, and exposure to obscenity could possibly prevent them reaching it. Free choice requires protection against influences militating against it: early brain-washing into some creed could rule out a full and free religious commitment later; early exposure to addictive drugs could preclude a freer choice of life-style in maturity; and early exposure to obscenity could possibly foreclose a person's options afterwards. So a limited paternalism is not at odds with liberty; in fact it serves to buttress it.

Unlimited paternalism is a different matter. Treating children as children is one thing, treating adults as children quite another. On this point we agree with John Stuart Mill that a man's own good, either physical or moral, is not a sufficient warrant for exercising power over him against his will. With Montesquieu we hold that "changing people's manners and morals mustn't be done by changing the law."

But may there not still be a reason for using the criminal law against voluntary obscenity? May it not be justifiable in order to prevent overall decline in values?

As we saw earlier, it isn't impossible that widespread obscenity could cause decline in general values. This helps to make it justifiable to use the law to prohibit involuntary public obscenity and exposure of children to obscenity. Would it also make it justifiable to go further and outlaw private, voluntary obscenity?

This brings us back to the notion of shared values and morality as the cement that binds society together. So important are these values that they have to be protected. Indeed Devlin once suggested that acts contravening and therefore threatening such values are acts akin to treason.

At the root of the analogy is the claim that a society is entitled to protect itself against change and dissolution. Yet is a society entitled to use the criminal law to resist change? If it's entitled to use it to combat treason, why shouldn't it be similarly entitled to use it to combat change due to declining values?

But why is society entitled to use the force of criminal law against treason? A paradigm case of treason is the use of force to overthrow the government or constitution. Why is this a crime? After all the new government or constitution might be an improvement. Even in Canada the constitution can't be perfect, otherwise why hold conferences to try and alter it? On the other hand, the new one might be worse. Or lots of people might consider it worse. And they of course would never have been consulted.

There is an obvious moral difference, then, between forcibly changing the government or constitution and doing this by peaceful means—by persuading society itself to change its institutions. Violent attack on these institutions, then, is rightly a crime, while non-violent attempts to bring about political changes are not. "Like may be repelled with like," says common law principle. Violent attacks can justifiably be met with force—the force of the criminal law. Non-violent advocacy of change can justifiably be met only with counter-argument in favour of the status quo.* Society can justifiably use the criminal law to stop itself *being changed* but not to stop itself *changing.*

What light does this throw on society's right to use the criminal law to stop decline in moral values? If obscenity brings about decline by changing moral values, are society and its values simply changing or are they being changed? In one sense neither, in another both. Our moral values aren't being changed by force—indeed it is hard to imagine how they could be. And yet we're not just being asked to change them. Public obscenity, after all, tramples on values many hold and forces us, unless we yield our right to frequent public places, to see and become used to seeing obscenity; and this may lessen our sensitivity and may undermine our present values. To this extent society is entitled to use the criminal law against obscenity. But if the spectator has an option and consumes it willingly, society has less right to use the criminal law, for here the victim of obscenity is changing his values himself—another aspect of the argument that adults should be free to choose obscenity if they want.

But what if their voluntary consumption of obscenity weakens the values of society as a whole? Now is society entitled to use the criminal law against this risk? It depends how great the risk is to essential values. Suppose we could prove indubitably that individual consumption of pornography would thoroughly undermine the

---

*Our law sometimes resists mere words with legal force: incitement to crime and hate propaganda are criminal offences, but neither of them advocate mere peaceful change.

principle against violence. In that event it would be time to use the criminal law against such individual consumption. But that time hasn't arrived. The threat to the antiviolence principle—and we don't deny that there may be one—is uncertain, hard to assess, and still a matter for speculation. A wholly clear and present danger hasn't been proved.

A further objection to using criminal law against private consumption of obscenity by adults is the risk of increasing its profitability. Forbidden fruit, if not sweeter, is always dearer. Illegalising it adds an extra cost. It could be that those with most to lose from the legalising of obscenity may be the dealers who supply it. Certainly there is some evidence of this from Denmark.

Lastly, one final snag. Use criminal law against obscenity and perhaps we obscure the real problem. To take an analogy, our criminal law has concerned itself with non-medical use of drugs, but may not the real problem be the overall use of drugs in the modern "chemical" society? So with obscenity. The law concerns itself with "undue exploitation of sex," but may not the real problem be something else—our society's reluctance to be open and direct in dealing with sexual matters? Sex is a basic human drive but also something calling for maturity.

Obscenity, however, is immaturity. Obscenity is at odds with personal growth. At best, as in a dirty joke or filthy postcard, it is as Orwell pointed out, a sort of mental rebellion against a conspiracy to pretend that human nature has no baser side. At worst, it is, as D.H. Lawrence said, an attempt "to insult sex, to do dirt on sex." Neither obscenity nor the law relating to it helps toward a maturer view of sex.

The True Role of Criminal Law

So should obscenity be against the criminal law? In our view, yes and no. Public obscenity—like other nuisances that give offence—can rightly be the subject of the criminal law. Private obscenity—which causes little, if any, harm and which doesn't threaten significantly—on the whole cannot. That's not to say that it can't be the subject of other types of law.

Criminal law, after all, is only one weapon in the arsenal of the law. Others are administrative regulation, custom laws, planning laws, and finally tax laws. What may and what may not be published might best be dealt with by administrative control—a technique that is particularly appropriate perhaps to television and radio. Again, in so far as the pornography industry isn't home-grown, customs regulations is an obvious method of dealing with the problem. Or, if we accept that some obscenity is here to stay, mightn't a sensible approach be to use city planning to make out certain areas for obscenity and to keep the rest obscenity-free? Or finally, if obscenity, like alcohol, is going to be always with us, why not use our tax laws to do two things—to siphon off some of the excess profit from the industry and at the same time to apply a measure of discouragement to the trade?

These questions, however, are outside the scope of this Working Paper. How far our objectives are best achieved by criminal- or civil-law techniques, how far criminal law enforcement against obscenity should allow for local varying standards, how far the present legal definition of obscenity should remain or be replaced by something else, and where precisely the line between public and private should be drawn—all these are matters calling for more detailed legal and empirical research than is called for by this inquiry which, though focusing on obscenity, does so primarily as a test case to illuminate the general question of the proper scope and ambit of the criminal law. Such an inquiry rather serves to indicate the proper goals or objectives of criminal law in connection with the specific problem of obscenity, and so to indicate in general the reaches and the limits of the criminal law.

What, therefore, are our justified objectives with obscenity? As we have said, public obscenity can rightly be a crime. Public obscenity then should remain an offence. In practical terms this means continued prohibition against lurid posters, advertisements, magazines, and so on being shown in public. It also means restricting what can be broadcast and televised.

Private obscenity too can rightly be a crime, as we have said, when it comes to children. In practice this means that things like the Ottawa peep-show discussed earlier remain against the law. It doesn't mean of course that children won't ever get obscenity. They will—just as they get cigarettes and alcohol and other things we try to guard them from. But retaining the criminal law may still have effect. In effect it will serve at least to keep obscenity out of the classroom and restrict it to the playground—and this can have two results: it may help to limit the amount of obscenity that children are exposed to, and it will give underlining support to the general view that obscenity is not for public consumption.

Apart from this, however, private obscenity in our view should no longer be a crime. In this context the criminal law can't properly be used either to save the individual or society from itself. Individuals should be free to choose their own life-style and society should be free to change. In practical terms this would mean considerable change. It would mean decriminalizing much obscenity. In detail it would mean that pornography stores, pictures, and so on carefully restricted to "adults only" would be allowed.

On the other hand decriminalizing—"legalizing," as it is sometimes called—would not imply condoning. Chamfort spoke truly when he said: "It is easier to make things legal than legitimate." In any case, voluntary consumption of obscenity could still be wrong in the civil law: contracts, for instance, to put on obscene displays for private consumption could still be contrary to public policy and so illegal. Besides, voluntary obscenity could still be dealt with, and surely better dealt with, by less formal sanctions, which after all are cheaper, and not only in monetary terms. The formal sanctions of the criminal law are in many ways too expensive.

In short, we must always bear in mind the price we pay for using criminal law. That price—in terms of suffering, loss of liberty, and financial cost—sets limits to the proper use of criminal law. Acts of violence, acts of terror, and acts causing serious distress can justifiably fall within that law. So, too, occasionally, can obscenity when it gives serious offence and causes real annoyance by threatening fundamental values. This after all is what the criminal law is for—dealing with acts that threaten or infringe essential or important values.

Restrict the criminal law to these kinds of acts and we may hope that even in a world where we get nothing for nothing, at least we won't get nothing for our penny too.

Questions

1. How would you decide whether pornography is a "clear and present danger"? If it could be shown that it is a "clear and present danger" to values judged by a majority to be important, would this be enough to justify censorship?
2. Does the Commission report allow for distinctions to be made with regard to types of pornography—hard-core as opposed to soft-core pornography, for example?
3. What are the steps through which the argument in this selection move in maintaining that although pornography is a threat to social values, only public displays of it should be prohibited? Is the argument consistent? Is it convincing?
4. Do you agree that "a man's own good, either physical or moral, is not a sufficient warrant for exercising power over him against his will"? What would the application of this principle imply for decisions concerning institutionalizing persons against their will who appear to be suffering from mental disorders?
5. Do you agree that changing people's manners and morals must not be done by changing the law?

Pornography

L.W. Conolly

I have, I suppose, been reading pornography (on and off) for a number of years, although a decade ago as a student in a smallish town in South Wales (where even the pubs couldn't open on Sundays) it was difficult enough to get hold of *Playboy*, let alone raunchy paperbacks with titillating covers. Nowadays it is rather easier to acquire pornography, but in most Canadian cities the combined forces of police and customs officials, supported by Sections 159 and 160 of the Criminal Code, do their best to keep pornography out of the bookstores and even private collections. Nevertheless, despite these handicaps, the range of my reading of pornography is modestly broad and in addition to the pornographic classics (*Fanny Hill, My Secret Life*, de Sade, and so on) I can boast of some close acquaintance with such delightfully named novels as *John Krugge: the Autobiography of an Old Man in Search of an Orgasm; Venus School-Mistress; A Handbook of Good Manners for Little Girls; Without a Stitch; The Beautiful Flagellants of New York; The Horn Book, or Modern Studies in the Science of Stroking;* and *The Altar of Venus, Wherein a Late Member of the House of Lords Has Given the True History of His Erotic Life* (all published by Grove Press).

From *The Dalhousie Review*, Volume 54, 1974–1975. Reprinted with permission of The Dalhousie Review and the author.

Over the years I have also read a number of books *about* pornography, and one reason for my writing this paper is that I have found the arguments about pornography to be bewilderingly contradictory. In a debate in which passion seems so often to dominate reason, and speculation to take the place of evidence, it has become a challenge to establish and maintain an intelligent attitude toward pornography. . . .

There are at least three good reasons why pornography should be taken seriously. First, statistics produced by the Commission on Obscenity and Pornography,[1] as well as one's own personal observations, show that pornography in many forms is now widely available and has become a marked feature of popular literature, and as such deserves and demands study. Secondly, the relationship between pornography and its readers—particularly the *effect* that pornography has on individual readers and society as a whole—raises interesting and important questions regarding the influence of literature in general and how we assess such influence. And thirdly, since governments have always, and still do, concern themselves with the control of pornography, we should carefully examine their reasons for doing so, since obviously no government should be permitted to deprive people of the right to read what they choose to read unless on very substantial grounds.

Pornography today remains pretty much what it was when it first began to attract government attention in England in the seventeenth century. Strictly speaking pornography is the description of the life of prostitutes and their patrons. D.H. Lawrence's well-known and more useful definition, to which I will return, is that pornography "is the attempt to insult sex, to do dirt on it," which he took to be an "unpardonable" offense deserving of rigorous censorship.[2] A fair account of the novels I listed earlier would be that they present an interminable and ultimately boring repetition of variations of the sexual act. "the copulation of clichés" as Nabokov has described pornography. The pornographer's sole intention is to arouse sexual excitement in his reader—usually, I might add, a male reader. This is not, I think, necessarily an undesirable or reprehensible objective; but like melodrama and sentimentality pornography arouses our emotions quickly and superficially. This is one objection to pornography (which I will develop later): it is shallow and cheap literature. But governments have never to my knowledge suppressed pornography solely on literary grounds. Their arguments and assumptions have always been that the reading of pornography has harmful effects on individuals and societies.

Historically, the reasons for government suppression of pornography have varied. David Foxon, in his study of early English pornography, *Libertine Literature in England 1660–1745* (University Books, 1965), links the suppression of pornography in the seventeenth and eighteenth centuries with the suppression of religiously heretical or politically revolutionary literature. "It seems," he writes, "that the revolt against authority first took the form of heresy, then politics, and finally sexual licence; clearly pornography is closely related to this revolt" (p. 50). The suppression of pornography in the nineteenth century was at least partly related to the threat it posed, or appeared to pose, to a social structure based on rigid sexual morality, but in recent years the emphasis has shifted to the relationship between pornography and criminal behaviour.

The Commission on Obscenity and Pornography reports that "The belief that reading or viewing explicit sexual materials causes sex crimes is widespread among the American public" (p. 269). It seems that 47% of American men and 51% of American women believe that "sexual materials lead people to commit rape." David Holbrook, a vigorous compaigner against pornography, has linked performances of *Oh! Calcutta!* (a dreary sex show devised by Kenneth Tynan and others) with increases in crimes of violence;[3] and Pamela Hansford Johnson (C.P. Snow's wife) in her analysis of the brutally sadistic murders of some children in Yorkshire some years ago suggested the likelihood of a connection between the sado-masochistic reading matter of the murderers and their crimes.[4] But this kind of causal relationship between pornography and behaviour has long been questioned. Those indefatigable sexual researchers, Eberhard and Phyllis Kronhausen, recognized some years before the Commission on Obscenity and Pornography began its work the widely accepted notion that the reading of pornography "leads to delinquency and criminal acts, especially those involving violence, for instance, rape, sexual assault, the molestation and abuse of children by adult sex deviates, and a variety of similar offences" (*Pornography and the Law*, revised ed., Ballantine Books, 1964, p. 330). The Kronhausens, while admitting the absence of conclusive evidence one way or the other, doubted the validity of the cause and effect argument; the majority opinion of the Commission on Obscenity and Pornography, albeit expressed in clumsy committee prose, was firmer: "Research to date . . . provides no substantial basis for the belief that erotic materials . . . operate as a significant determinative factor in causing crime and delinquency" (pp. 286–287).

So if there is no firm evidence that pornography harms anyone, do governments have any case for suppressing it? I think not. A British Arts Council committee succinctly summed up the case against government censorship of pornographic or any other kind of imaginative literature in a report published in 1969:

> It is not for the State to prohibit private citizens from choosing what they may or may not enjoy in literature or art unless there were incontrovertible evidence that the result would be injurious to society. There is no such evidence.[5]

Apart from the principle involved here—the principle, that is, of the individual's right to be free from government control of what he chooses to read—there is the important consideration of the consequences of government censorship so far as serious creative literature is concerned. That any kind of literature is banned or burned or bashed into pulp by government edict is bad enough; but the history of literary censorship (I recommend Donald Thomas's *A Long Time Burning*, Routledge, 1969) shows that many major authors have at one time or another been on a censor's blacklist—the Roman Catholic Church has always had a long one, of course. Courts and customs officials, especially customs officials, have never been very adept at separating literary wheat from the chaff, and important works of literature together with the rubbishy ones have been suppressed or impounded under the very same laws—*Ulysses* and *The Rainbow* are two obvious examples from the present century.

So the case against government censorship of pornography is a convincing one: such censorship abrogates a central principle of democratic society; it does so for no demonstrably sound reason; and it hinders and sometimes prevents the free circulation of the works of serious creative writers. The case, I would have thought, is a strong enough one to dismay the exponents of censorship. Yet they still speak, albeit with little authority. Here is a Professor of Urban Values at New York University: "If you think pornography and/or obscenity is a serious problem, you have to be for censorship. I'll go even further and say that if you want to prevent pornography and/or obscenity from becoming a problem, you have to be for censorship. And lest there be any misunderstanding as to what I am saying, I'll put it as bluntly as possible: if you care for the quality of life in our American democracy, then you have to be for censorship" (Holbrook, p. 193). As pretty a series of non-sequiturs as you will find anywhere. All cats must die. Socrates is dead. Therefore Socrates was a cat.

I do not see how one can argue against the unimpeded circulation of pornography among adult readers. And there was a time when I was also convinced that not only should the free circulation of pornography be defended, but that widespread circulation of pornography should positively be welcomed and even encouraged. Many still hold this view—wrongly, I am now inclined to think. Storm Jameson, the novelist, puts it this way: pornography's "wholehearted admirers see it as a great gesture of moral and intellectual liberation: the mind has been set free to explore unhindered an area of sensual experience, vitally, overwhelmingly important, hitherto repressed and degraded by taboos and hypocrisies" (Holbrook, p. 215). Twenty years ago when, in Britain at least, the freedom of writers to describe sexual behaviour as a normal part of the human condition was only just being established (in 1960 a jury found *Lady Chatterley's Lover* to be not obscene), the argument outlined by Jameson was a persuasive one. The end of Victorian prudery and hypocrisy was finally at hand. I could sit on Thomas Bowdler's tombstone in the Swansea churchyard near where I lived, and read of the sexual antics of Mellors and Lady Chatterley with the smug satisfaction that the influence exercised even from the grave below me by the reverend Mr. Bowdler was coming to an end. The age of sexual enlightenment was nigh.

But after several years' experience of reading accounts of sexual gymnastics and minutely detailed descriptions of organs and orgasms I doubt that my understanding of human sexuality has increased one iota. We have witnessed (if I may put it this way) a severe anti-climax. To be sure, the publishers of Joyce and Lawrence and other serious writers are no longer threatened with prosecution, and those non-creative writers who want to disseminate knowledge about sexual behaviour are free to do so, as Havelock Ellis once was not. That these are immensely important benefits cannot be denied—although David Holbrook (with some justification) sees Kinsey and other "scientific sexologists" as dangerous pornographers (Holbrook, p. 11). But the most obvious and perhaps the most influential product of the new freedom in sexual writings has been pornography, and in so far as pornography has falsified and will continue to falsify human sexual behaviour it has been a positive obstacle in our attempts to understand it.

But there is another argument in favour of the widespread circulation of pornography. Just as pornography's opponents turn to statistics for their evidence (the increase in sexual assaults and so on) so do its supporters. They go to Denmark to get them. Since the abolition of legal restraints on pornography in that country

(1967 on written, 1969 on pictorial pornography) crimes of a sexual nature have apparently diminished. The argument which links the easy availability of pornography with a reduction in sexual offences runs something like this: the reading of pornography by would-be sexual offenders has a therapeutic effect in that their aggressive sexual urges are satisfied by the pornography, so obviating the need for direct action, as it were. An American psychotherapist puts it this way: "Contrary to popular misconception, people who read salacious literature are less likely to become sexual offenders than those who do not, for the reason that such reading often neutralizes what abberant sexual interest they may have" (*Pornography and the Law*, p. 338). If we accept this argument then we must conclude that the writers and distributors of pornography are providing a valuable social service, perhaps even deserving of a special category of government awards to encourage them: more porn less rape might be their motto.

I am no more convinced that pornography will rid the world of sexual offenders than I am that it will populate the world with sexual offenders. The evidence, such as it is, is conflicting. Then perhaps the only attitude we can reasonably adopt is that pornography has established itself as part of the popular culture of western civilization and, like other features of popular culture—television, for example—we really cannot be certain about what it is doing or is likely to do to that culture. We are in no position to damn it or to praise it. An editorial article in the *Times Literary Supplement* of 25 February 1972 outlined what it took to be a sensible attitude toward pornography: "But it is surely reasonable to stop short of the missionary belief that pornography is an instrument of social welfare, and to stick instead with the view that it does neither harm nor good." But it is not reasonable to conclude that pornography "does neither harm nor good" simply because we cannot resolve conflicting evidence about its influence. Nor do I accept that imaginative literature of any kind is entirely neutral in effect. The *TLS* writer recognized that his attitude toward pornography was a pessimistic one, for "it implies the impotence of literature in general to influence the way we live."

The difficulty of reaching a satisfactory conclusion arises, I think, out of the terms in which the discussion of pornography has customarily been conducted. We have been engaged in a Ping-Pong game of statistics, the players puffing and blowing facts and figures, the spectators getting dizzier all the time waiting anxiously for a winner so that they can hiss or cheer according to their inclinations. But the game will never end. The attempt to answer questions about the influence or effect of literature in statistical terms is a futile one. I strongly believe that literature influences human behaviour; but such influence is not measurable, nor even can be measurable. We may be able to establish that a performance of a play caused an audience to riot; we may link a Dickens novel, say, with some area of nineteenth-century social reform; we may claim that the Bible has played an important role in the shaping of western civilization. But the precise cause-and-effect relationship between literature and life will always be unknown to us. And if we insist on trying to determine how many rapes or child molestations have been caused (or prevented) by the writings of the Marquis de Sade then we are simply wasting our time. (The absurdity to which this kind of statistical game can lead is well illustrated by a table reproduced in *The Report of the Commission on Obscenity and Pornography* [p. 204]. Some enterprising researchers showed two pornographic films to 194 male and 183 female under-graduates. Data was then gathered on "physiological responses in the genital region." The results reveal, for example, that 152 of the men managed to achieve only a "partial erection" while watching the films; 37 managed a full erection for over three minutes, while a heroic 8 men had a full erection for over six minutes. Of the women, one achieved an orgasm, 174 didn't, and six poor souls were uncertain whether they had or not.)

An article published in *The Human World* in May 1971 and a shorter piece in *TLS* on 4 February 1972 shifted the pornography debate onto new and more fertile ground.[6] The authors of these articles, Ian Robinson and Masud Khan, remind us of what we should have been doing all along: look at pornography not from the point of view of what it *does*, but from the point of view of what it *is*. Look at it not in sociological terms, but in literary terms. Khan puts it this way: "The whole issue has been side-tracked. The real issue is not that pornography is immoral but that it is pathetically bad literature. An ironic and absurd situation has arisen vis-à-vis por-nography in contemporary European cultures. While pornographic writers will engage in endless debate with the cultural moralists . . . they are dogmatically intolerant of any suggestion that pornography retails poor literature and sick psychology . . ." (Holbook, p. 131).

I am not competent to talk about psychology, but that pornography is poor literature is not difficult to demonstrate. Here is a typical passage from *The Beautiful Flagellants of New York* (vol. 2, p. 76). The scene is set in a brothel specializing in flagellation. A young man, having been tied to a couch, is being whipped by two sisters. One sister has just "exchanged her miniature rod for one that was long and supple, evidently a terrible stinger."

> The boy, starting violently at this fresh attack, let incoherent words escape his lips; and he moaned while beaten firmly with the new, stiff birch. The ladies in the audience rose to their feet, to get a better view of the young fellow's bottom as it became covered with large red weals. He bounded and wriggled in contortions of despair, and then, as a conclusion, a few blows dealt on his mangled bum with frenzied violence made him lift the trembling tender cheeks as high as the ropes would let him. His red stern fell down again, and a long, low groan of voluptuous enjoyment burst from the entranced boy.

The kind of slipshod writing that tells us something is "supple" in one sentence and "stiff" in the very next sentence is not uncommon in pornographic writing. The inappropriate language and imagery used by the writer when referring to the young man's bottom is typical too: "bum" is a word that belongs in the nursery, not the brothel, and "stern," red or otherwise, is what we see when the QE II sails. And anyone familiar with pornographic writing will recognize the usual moans and groans, the frenzy, the "voluptuous enjoyment" and the "incoherent words" that we find on virtually every cliché-ridden page of novels of this kind. The language of pornog-raphy is marked by its inability to explore and explain the meaning of the subject on which it dwells perpetually.

Of course, another feature of this passage common to all pornography is the equating of sexual fulfillment with violence. Flagellation is in itself necessarily violent, but in all pornography we find imagery of violence—"assault," "ram," "explode," "battle," "lunge," "bore," "empty the barrel of his gun," "weapon," and so on. Pornography is the literature of aggressive sexual success, of unfailing sexual achievement, of uncomplicated sexual relationships; pornography therefore lies about sex; it cheapens sex; it reduces human relationships to the level of animal sexual relationships, perhaps lower. (*Le Monde* has reported that a young woman has made a fortune out of performing sexually with stallions and dogs; and it appears that the Danish Society for the Prevention of Cruelty to Animals has felt obliged to ask the courts to outlaw the use of animals in sexual exhibitions [Holbrook, p. 8].)

Pornographers—and here I return to Lawrence—make the human sexual act "ugly and degraded . . . trivial and cheap and nasty" (Lawrence, p. 67). The danger of pornography is that it not only fails to promote understanding of human behaviour, but also that it positively retards such understanding. It destroys, or attempts to destroy, whatever sense we have made of the complexities of sex. This is why we are justified in condemning it, as Khan does, as bad literature. "Pornography," Khan concludes, "negates imagination, style and the tradition of man's struggle to use language to know and enhance himself" (Holbrook, p. 132).

Ian Robinson is also interested in the language of pornography, and although he holds no brief for the sociological cause-and-effect arguments, he does recognize (as Khan does, implicitly at least) an important, although neither immediate nor measurable, relationship between pornography and human behaviour. The individual, Robinson says, "recreates the value of sex from the language of sex of those around him . . . the language of sex spoken and written in a society expresses the commonly understood significance of sex there, and a change in the language of sex *is* a change in the experience and evaluation of sex in the lives of the speakers of the language" (Holbrook, pp. 174–175). That is, we can only understand sexual behaviour through the language we use to discuss it. If the language of sex becomes dominated by the language of pornography then we will understand sex only in pornographic terms. Pornography impoverishes the language of sex; it therefore impoverishes our understanding of sex. The language of pornography is crude, ugly, uncomplicated, and often violent (it is interesting that "fuck," a popular term for sexual intercourse, is also a common expletive). Pornography restricts and simplifies the ways in which we may talk and ultimately think about sex.

Robinson's arguments are, of course, similar to those used by Orwell in his essay on "Politics and the English Language"—and no less convincing. The quality of our political thought, and ultimately our political behaviour, depends on the kind of political language we use. The quality and nature of human sexual relationships depend on the language we use to define those relationships.

Now if it is true that the widespread reading and influence of pornography will corrupt the language of sex and thereby corrupt sexual behaviour itself, there may well be unattractive social consequences. There are those who associate pornography with fascism, for example, and it is easy to understand why. The mechanical nature of human relationships depicted by the pornographer is perhaps one aspect of the dehumanizing process which can lead to the brutality practised by fascist regimes in this century. A social philosopher has argued that if pornography is allowed to flourish "our society at best will become ever more coarse, brutal, anxious, indifferent, de-individualized, hedonistic; at worst its ethos will disintegrate altogether" (Holbrook, p. 168). This leads us back to the unsatisfactory cause-and-effect hypothesis (although not on the simplistic statistical level), but if only a small part of the dire and exaggerated prediction is true it still makes the question of what to *do* about pornography an important one.

Well, don't encourage the pornographers for a start, as the Danes have; don't line the pockets of purveyors of rubbish. On the other hand, don't prosecute them either; don't censor what they write and sell. Censorship is repugnant and unworkable, and governments have no business practising it. Ignore pornography and hope that it is only a passing fad which will soon fade away? Perhaps; but that which is cheap, ugly, and second-rate has a habit of staying around: witness our television programs or popular music, as corrupting in their own way as pornography. Ultimately, all we can do, I think, is take Ian Robinson's advice—although I am less optimistic than he appears to be:

> If the question then arises: what to do about pornography and how to prevent the corruption of our language of sex, we would say that the main answer is: recognize pornography. The recognition is the best thing that could happen. Perhaps when recognized it will slink away—pornography ought to die of contempt—but that is not the reason for recognizing it. The recognition is itself the maintenance of language of sex, and that is what we ought to hope for (Holbrook, p. 184).

Notes

1. *The Report of the Commission on Obscenity and Pornography.* Introduction by Clive Barnes (Bantam, 1970).
2. D.H. Lawrence, *A Propos of Lady Chatterley's Lover and Other Essays* (Penguin, 1961), p. 67.
3. David Holbrook, ed., *The Case Against Pornography* (Tom Stacey, 1972), p. 2.
4. Pamela Hanford Johnson, *On Iniquity* (Macmillan, 1967).
5. *The Obscenity Laws. A Report by the Working Party Set Up by a Conference Convened by the Chairman of the Arts Council of Great Britain.* Foreword by John Montgomerie (Andre Deutsch, 1969), p. 35.
6. Both articles are reprinted in Holbrook's book, from which I take my quotations.

Questions

1. Is Conolly's argument consistent with regard to the view that pornography is not harmful?
2. Is Conolly right in thinking that the kind of harm caused by pornography does not warrant censorship?

Pornography

Margaret Atwood

When I was in Finland a few years ago for an international writers' conference, I had occasion to say a few paragraphs in public on the subject of pornography. The context was a discussion of political repression, and I was suggesting the possibility of a link between the two. The immediate result was that a male journalist took several large bites out of me. Prudery and pornography are two halves of the same coin, said he, and I was clearly a prude. What could you expect from an Anglo-Canadian? Afterward, a couple of pleasant Scandinavian men asked me what I had been so worked up about. All "pornography" means, they said, is graphic depictions of whores, and what was the harm in that?

Not until then did it strike me that the male journalist and I had two entirely different things in mind. By "pornography," he meant naked bodies and sex. I, on the other hand, had recently been doing the research for my novel *Bodily Harm*, and was still in a state of shock from some of the material I had seen, including the Ontario Board of Film Censors' "outtakes." By "pornography," I meant women getting their nipples snipped off with garden shears, having meat hooks stuck into their vaginas, being disemboweled; little girls being raped; men (yes, there are some men) being smashed to a pulp and forcibly sodomized. The cutting edge of pornography, as far as I could see, was no longer simple old copulation, hanging from the chandelier or otherwise: it was death, messy, explicit and highly sadistic. I explained this to the nice Scandinavian men. "Oh, but that's just the United States," they said. "Everyone knows they're sick." In their country, they said, violent "pornography" of that kind was not permitted on television or in movies; indeed, excessive violence of any kind was not permitted. They had drawn a clear line between erotica, which earlier studies had shown did not incite men to more aggressive and brutal behavior toward women, and violence, which later studies indicated did.

Some time after that I was in Saskatchewan, where, because of some of the scenes on *Bodily Harm*, I found myself on an open-line radio show answering questions about "pornography." Almost no one who phoned in was in favor of it, but again they weren't talking about the same stuff I was, because they hadn't seen it. Some of them were all set to stamp out bathing suits and negligees, and, if possible, any depictions of the female body whatsoever. God, it was implied, did not approve of female bodies, and sex of any kind, including that practised by bumblebees, should be shoved back into the dark, where it belonged. I had more than a suspicion that *Lady Chatterley's Lover*, Margaret Laurence's *The Diviners*, and indeed most books by most serious modern authors would have ended up as confetti if left in the hands of these callers.

For me, these two experiences illustrate the two poles of the emotionally heated debate that is now thundering around this issue. They also underline the desirability

From *Chatelaine*, September 1983.

and even the necessity of defining the terms. "Pornography" is now one of those catchalls, like "Marxism" and "feminism," that have become so broad they can mean almost anything, ranging from certain verses in the Bible, ads for skin lotion and sex texts for children to the contents of *Penthouse*, Naughty '90s postcards and films with titles containing the word *Nazi* that show vicious scenes of torture and killing. It's easy to say that sensible people can tell the difference. Unfortunately, opinions on what constitutes a sensible person vary.

But even sensible people tend to lose their cool when they start talking about this subject. They soon stop talking and start yelling, and the name-calling begins. Those in favor of censorship (which may include groups not noticeably in agreement on other issues, such as some feminists and religious fundamentalists) accuse the others of exploiting women through the use of degrading images, contributing to the corruption of children, and adding to the general climate of violence and threat in which both women and children live in this society; or, though they may not give much of a hoot about actual women and children, they invoke moral standards and God's supposed aversion to "filth," "smut" and deviated *preversion*, which may mean ankles.

The camp in favor of total "freedom of expression" often comes out howling as loud as the Romans would have if told they could no longer have innocent fun watching the lions eat up Christians. It too may include segments of the population who are not natural bedfellows: those who proclaim their God-given right to freedom, including the freedom to tote guns, drive when drunk, drool over chicken porn and get off on videotapes of women being raped and beaten, may be waving the same anticensorship banner as responsible liberals who fear the return of Mrs. Grundy, or gay groups for whom sexual emancipation involves the concept of "sexual theatre." *Whatever turns you on* is a handy motto, as is *A man's home is his castle* (and if it includes a dungeon with beautiful maidens strung up in chains and bleeding from every pore, that's his business).

Meanwhile, theoreticians theorize and speculators speculate. Is today's pornography yet another indication of the hatred of the body, the deep mind-body split, which is supposed to pervade Western Christian society? Is it a backlash against the women's movement by men who are threatened by uppity female behavior in real life, so like to fantasize about women done up like outsize parcels, being turned into hamburger, kneeling at their feet in slavelike adoration or sucking off guns? Is it a sign of collective impotence, of a generation of men who can't relate to real women at all but have to make do with bits of celluloid and paper? Is the current flood just a result of smart marketing and aggressive promotion by the money men in what has now become a multibillion-dollar industry? If they were selling movies about men getting their testicles stuck full of knitting needles by women with swastikas on their sleeves, would they do as well, or is this penchant somehow peculiarly male? If so, why? Is pornography a power trip rather than a sex one? Some say that those ropes, chains, muzzles and other restraining devices are an argument for the immense power female sexuality still wields in the male imagination: you don't put these things on dogs unless you're afraid of them. Others, more literary, wonder about the shift from the 19th-century Magic Woman or Femme Fatale image to the lollipop-licker, airhead or turkey-carcass treatment of women in porn today. The proporners don't care much about theory: they merely demand product. The antiporners don't care about it in the final analysis either: there's dirt on the street, and they want it cleaned up, now.

It seems to me that this conversation, with its *You're-a-prude! You're-a-pervert* dialectic, will never get anywhere as long as we continue to think of this material as just "entertainment." Possibly we're deluded by the packaging, the format: magazine, book, movie, theatrical presentation. We're used to thinking of these things as part of the "entertainment industry," and we're used to thinking of ourselves as free adult people who ought to be able to see any kind of "entertainment" we want to. That was what the First Choice pay-TV debate was all about. After all, it's only entertainment, right? Entertainment means fun, and only a killjoy would be antifun. What's the harm?

This is obviously the central question: *What's the harm?* If there isn't any real harm to any real people, then the antiporners can tsk-tsk and/or throw up as much as they like, but they can't rightfully expect more legal controls or sanctions. However, the no-harm position is far from being proven.

(For instance, there's a clear-cut case for banning—as the federal government has proposed—movies, photos and videos that depict children engaging in sex with adults: real children are used to make the movies, and hardly anybody thinks this is ethical. The possibilities for coercion are too great.)

To shift the viewpoint, I'd like to suggest three other models for looking at "pornography"—and here I mean the violent kind.

Hate Literature

Those who find the idea of regulating pornographic materials repugnant because they think it's Fascist or Communist or otherwise not in accordance with the principles of an open democratic society should consider that Canada has made it illegal to disseminate material that may lead to hatred toward any group because of race or religion. I suggest that if pornography of the violent kind depicted these acts being done predominantly to Chinese, to blacks, to Catholics, it would be off the market immediately, under the present laws. Why is hate literature illegal? Because whoever made the law thought that such material might incite real people to do real awful things to other real people. The human brain is to a certain extent a computer: garbage in, garbage out. We only hear about the extreme cases (like that of American multimurderer Ted Bundy) in which pornography has contributed to the death and/or mutilation of women and/or men. Although pornography is not the only factor involved in the creation of such deviance, it certainly has upped the ante by suggesting both a variety of techniques and the social acceptability of such actions. Nobody knows yet what effect this stuff is having on the less psychotic.

Sex Education

Studies have shown that a large part of the market for all kinds of porn, soft and hard, is drawn from the 16-to-21-year-old population of young men. Boys used to learn about sex on the street, or (in Italy, according to Fellini movies) from friendly whores, or, in more genteel surroundings, from girls, their parents, or, once upon a time, in school, more or less. Now porn has been added, and sex education in the schools is rapidly being phased out. The buck has been passed, the boys are being taught that all women secretly like to be raped and that real men get high on scooping out women's digestive tracts.

Boys learn their concept of masculinity from other men: is this what most men want them to be learning? If word gets around that rapists are "normal" and even admirable men, will boys feel that in order to be normal, admirable and masculine they will have to be rapists? Human beings are enormously flexible, and how they turn out depends a lot on how they're educated, by the society in which they're immersed as well as by their teachers. In a society that advertises and glorifies rape or even implicitly condones it, more women get raped. It becomes socially acceptable. And at a time when men and the traditional male role have taken a lot of flak and men are confused and casting around for an acceptable way of being male (and, in some cases, not getting much comfort from when on that score), this must be at times a pleasing thought.

It would be naïve to think of violent pornography as just harmless entertainment. It's also an educational tool and a powerful propaganda device. What happens when boy educated on porn meets girl brought up on Harlequin romances? The clash of expectations can be heard around the block. She wants him to get down on his knees with a ring, he wants her to get down on all fours with a ring in her nose. Can this marriage be saved?

Addiction

Pornography has certain things in common with such addictive substances as alcohol and drugs: for some, though by no means for all, it induces chemical changes in the body, which the user finds exciting and pleasurable. It also appears to attract a "hard core" of habitual users and a penumbra of those who use it occasionally but aren't dependent on it in any way. There are also significant numbers of men who aren't much interested in it, not because they're undersexed but because real life is satisfying their needs, which may not require as many appliances as those of users.

For the "hard core," pornography may function as alcohol does for the alcoholic: tolerance develops, and a little is no longer enough. This may account for the short viewing time and fast turnover in porn theatres. Mary Brown, chairwoman of the Ontario Board of Film Censors, estimates that for every one mainstream movie requesting entrance to Ontario, there is one porno flick. Not only the quantity consumed but the quality of explicitness must escalate, which may account for the growing violence: once the big deal was breasts, then it was genitals, then copulation, then that was no longer enough and the hard users had to have more. The ultimate kick is death, and after that, as the Marquis de Sade so boringly demonstrated, multiple death.

The existence of alcoholism has not led us to ban social drinking. On the other hand, we do have laws about drinking and driving, excessive drunkenness and other abuses of alcohol that may result in injury or death to others.

This leads us back to the key question: what's the harm? Nobody knows, but this society should find out fast, before the saturation point is reached. The Scandinavian studies that showed a connection between depictions of sexual violence and increased impulse toward it on the part of male viewers would be a starting point, but many more questions remain to be raised as well as answered. What, for instance, is the crucial difference between men who are users and men who are not? Does using affect a man's relationship with actual women, and, if so, adversely? Is there a clear line between erotica and violent pornography, or are they on an escalating continuum? Is this a "men versus women" issue, with all men secretly siding with the proporners and all women secretly siding against? (I think not; there *are* lots of men who don't think that running their true love through the Cuisinart is the best way they can think of to spend a Saturday night, and they're just as nauseated by films of someone else doing it as women are.) Is pornography merely an expression of the sexual confusion of this age or an active contributor to it?

Nobody wants to go back to the age of official repression, when even piano legs were referred to as "limbs" and had to wear pantaloons to be decent. Neither do we want to end up in George Orwell's *1984*, in which pornography is turned out by the State to keep the proles in a state of torpor, sex itself is considered dirty and the approved practise it only for reproduction. But Rome under the emperors isn't such a good model either.

If all men and women respected each other, if sex were considered joyful and life-enhancing instead of a wallow in germ-filled glop, if everyone were in love all the time, if, in other words, many people's lives were more satisfactory for them than they appear to be now, pornography might just go away on its own. But since this is obviously not happening, we as a society are going to have to make some informed and responsible decisions about how to deal with it.

Questions

1. Can a clear distinction be made, either in theory or in practice, between pornography and erotica?
2. Is pornography a species of hate literature? If it is, does it follow that it should be banned?
3. Does Atwood provide convincing reasons for thinking pornography harmful?
4. How would Atwood evaluate the Loukidelis judgement included in this chapter?

Sexual Equality and the Problem of an Adequate Moral Theory: The Poverty of Liberalism

Lorenne Clark

We know that the problems of sex and class oppression developed more or less simultaneously and that this is to be expected because they developed from the same cause. It was the emergence of private property from a surplus in production which accounts for both. That, I take it, is a premise which we now accept: certainly I do and I will assume its truth throughout the remainder of my paper.[1] However, one of the reasons why it is now so widely accepted is that we are also beginning to realize that it is a statement which requires interpretation. Careful explanation and analysis of the key concepts it uses is now seen to be needed.

At the very least, however, acceptance of it as true in some important sense commits us to approaching problems about the privatization of child-rearing and the sexual division of labour from the perspective that these are based not on natural but on social relations.[2] The obvious truth that there is in it commits us at least to continuing to "look at *property relations* as the basic determinant of the sexual division of labour and of the sexual order."[3] According to Joan Kelly-Gadol, this minimum commitment to its truth is consistent with cross-cultural variations in what counts as "domestic" or "public" because an analysis of what is common cross-culturally is that "sexual inequalities are bound to the control of property."[4]

It is also consistent with the views of eminent, but certainly not feminist theorists such as Lévis-Strauss, who identifies the central feature of all kinship systems as regulation of the exchange of women between men.[5] As Gayle Rubin points out, Lévi-Strauss has thus constructed an implicit theory of sex oppression.[6] It is a theory of sex oppression which links the oppression of women with property because the theory entails that it is men who have rights over women and that women do not, consequently, have rights over themselves. It is the women who are exchanged and the men who do the exchanging. Thus we can conclude as Rubin does that kinship systems require a division of the sexes because they "rest on a radical difference between the rights of men and women."[7] And I want to add that they also require a division of labour between the sexes, a distinction, again social and not natural, between "productive" and "reproductive" labour, because it is rights to the exchange of *all* forms of property, including women, which is the most important right which is differentially distributed between men and women. Wherever there is property available for exchange, men have more rights than women to its ownership and, hence, to its disposition through exchange, and this increases directly with the amount of property available for exchange. Within all such systems women are also themselves a medium of exchange.

This is a shortened version of a paper originally published in *In Search of the Feminist Perspective: The Changing Potency of Women*, Mary Kathryn Shirley and Rachel Emma Vigier, eds. Toronto: Resources for Feminist Research, Special Publication No. 5, Spring 1979.

Thus, while there is considerable variation in the extent to which there is a division of labour, separation of the public and the private spheres, and inequality in the social status of men and women, what is clear is that there is a consistent pattern such that the greater the integration of the spheres, the more equal the status of men and women, and the greater the separation, the greater the oppression of women: it is also the case that integration is greatest in those cultures in which there is little production for exchange.[8] This certainly appears to provide strong evidence for the claim that there is indeed a close link between property and sex oppression, and hence, to justify our taking Engels' position to be true in some important sense.

But there remain problems in sorting out just what the sense is in which it is important and true, and what else is implied by the view once that sense is made clear. There are at least two important things that need to be said. First, "property," and the related concepts of "possession" and "ownership," are not natural objects, facts, or states of affairs, but are, as any lawyer knows, legal conventions designed to regulate our actions in certain specific ways. Thus, when we say that "private property emerged," it is certain that we cannot interpret this sensibly to mean anything but that *legal and/or social conventions* had developed such that there were enforceable rules prescribing the conduct of individuals in very specific ways. This is, of course, why Lévi-Strauss' view of kinship systems is important. He implicitly recognizes that it is the presence of a *system*, an articulated and enforceable set of rules, which brings about the situation in which women are forms of private property with an exchange value. It is also, of course, part of what must be involved in explicating the notion that the relation of the sexes is social and not natural. The development of this view as a central insight of feminism requires recognizing that it is structures of rules which create the relations, and not that these emerge from naturally occurring behaviours. Thus, what is of central importance is changing the rules in order to bring about a change in those relations. This is implicitly recognized by Rubin who says that what "feminism must call for [is] a revolution of kinship," namely, changing the system of sexual property in such a way that men no longer have "overriding rights in women."[9]

It is long past time that feminists realized that demands for changes in the enforceable rules which shape social relations are not simply demands for "reform," as opposed, for example, to "revolutionary" demands for something vaguely referred to as "fundamental change." The only route to fundamental change is through change of the rules, because it is the rules which create and reinforce the relations that presently exist between the sexes. A recognition that these relations are constructed out of enforceable rules is absolutely fundamental in coming to understand our past historical position and in developing a strategy to bring about fundamental change in that position. This is a point which cannot be emphasized enough, and which must be developed and seen to be absolutely central to feminist theory if any real change in our position, and in the fundamentally unequal relations of the sexes, is ever to be brought about. The days of trying to change attitudes and behaviours before or without changing the rules are over, because the most this can accomplish is creating a few more round pegs to fit into square holes. It is not, and cannot be, a method of effecting fundamentally new and different relations between the sexes because the nature of present and past relationships would not have been what they are except for the creation and maintenance of a specific set of rules designed to ensure very specific outcomes of the relations between men and women, and, subsequently, between men and men, and women and women.

This is made even clearer by coming to recognize that there is a social and conventional basis for the other key concepts used to describe allegedly natural divisions and roles which have been identified as at the root of both sex and class oppression. Chief among these are the concepts of "surplus" and of "productive" and "reproductive" labour, and of course the more general one of "a natural division of labour." A "surplus" doesn't mean anything without the concept (and probably the actuality) of having more than you *need*. And a surplus of "production" doesn't mean anything without the prior assumption that there is a division of labour, and that "productive" and "reproductive" are different *kinds* of labour, for of course these are concepts which are essential in generating the view that those who do what is labelled "reproductive" labour ought not to share in the profits made through the labour of those who do what is labelled "productive" labour.[10] We must conclude that it was the *legal institutionalization* of the concepts of private property, and those related and necessary to it, and of the concepts of productive and reproductive labour which created both sex and class oppression. Neither emerged simply as a consequence of some naturally occurring state of affairs. Some natural state did not occur *and then become* institutionalized *as* that of private property, because no natural state *could* become a state of affairs properly describable as that of "private property" *unless it was institutionalized*. It was, and could only be, a state of affairs characterized by a system of enforceable rules because "ownership" is impossible without such a structure.

A system of private property requires rules which specify what is to count as "property," how it is to be legitimately acquired, and what "ownership" entails by way of rights of disposition, sale, and exchange. The system which developed into the system with which we are intimately familiar specified that what was to be properly considered to be "property" was that which emerged from the labour of "production," and "production" was defined as the expenditure of labour power in the creation of a "commodity" with an "exchange" value. Thus, "production" bears no relation to what is in fact done, but only to what is in fact produced, and then only marginally to that. What matters is that the thing produced should be capable of being offered as a medium or item of exchange. And of course if something is available for exchange, it isn't itself needed, and is then "surplus." Thus, all of these concepts, "surplus," "production," "reproduction," are, like "private property" itself, constructs which arise from social conventions. They are created from setting up a specific system of enforceable rules which will regulate conduct in accordance with implementing and perpetuating the goals that the system has. In this case, the goals were regulation of the exchange of items within a system in which exchangeable items are owned by individuals.

The second thing, however, is that it wasn't simply private property, that is, a system of individual ownership of exchangeable items, which had emerged, but private property under (usually but not necessarily exclusively) *male* ownership, which had emerged. Within the specific system described by Engels, only individual males could own any form of private property.[11] Among the set of rules characterizing this particular state of affairs there were rules that gave rights of ownership only to males. Thus, the first class oppression was identical to the first sex oppression. It was by denying women equal rights of ownership (and usually no rights of ownership at all) that all women were first oppressed. Thus it also follows that "class oppression," as Marx and Engels used it, developed out of sexual oppression; and not the reverse. Both, however, are rooted in the emergence of a system of enforceable and enforced property relations.

Further, that it would be assured that that system of property distribution characterized both by differential sexual attribution of rights of ownership and by the attribution of unequal rights of ownership between individual males would be continued, the system of rules also contained a subset of rules which made women and children *forms* of the private property value for the ownership of males. This particular subset of rules had several important consequences. First it guaranteed to males a mechanism whereby they could determine future owners of the property under their control. The method utilized for the purpose was, of course, biological reproduction. This was harnessed to the needs of the system by giving males legal rights to the (usually but not necessarily) exclusive use of one or more females. And it was rights to the use of female sexuality and reproductivity which were centrally important in this subset. By controlling the means and products of reproduction, males solved the problem of transferring property across generations and of ensuring that the system preserved its central features, *individual* ownership. Thus, it was that males also came to have rights to determine the nature and value of women's labour. This is clearly understood by Lévi-Strauss who remarks that "the sexual division of labour is nothing else than a device to institute a reciprocal state of dependency between the sexes."[12] And as Rubin comments on Lévi-Strauss, he also accepts and incorporates this view into his theory of kinship, for his "is a book in which kinship is explicitly conceived of as an imposition of cultural organization upon the facts of biological procreation,"[13] and, I maintain, what is meant by "cultural organization" is the imposition of a structure of enforceable rules. Thus, biological procreation was turned into "reproduction." The act of *bearing* children, which is woman's unique role in the procreative process, was transformed into the process of child-*rearing*, in which women were more often than not, though not universally, held to be uniquely equipped, and hence uniquely responsible, for the process not merely of birth, but of the process beginning with birth and ending with a developed human personality capable of independent life. Maternity, along with paternity, is a social construct developed to meet the needs of the particular system under discussion.[14] Women became defined as essentially wives and mothers at exactly that point at which rules were established giving men rights to determine the nature of women's labour through giving them rights to dispose of *women* by means of exchange. By thus converting women into forms of sexual and reproductive property, women had an exchange value, and were available as the medium through which other forms of property could pass. This ensured both that a system of property transfer existed and that property would pass only or primarily between males, including property in the form of women. It also ensured quite accidentally that necessary reproductive labour was in fact performed, and that it would be performed as exploited, cheap labour. And it is that fact which must now centrally engage our attention as feminists.

But you may now be wondering what this has to do with morality, and, in particular, with the ethics of liberalism. The connections are these: the rules that are essential to preserving such a system must be legally enforceable rules, rules whose breach we are collectively prepared to punish. That is why it is instructive to look at legal rules historically and so necessary to change them. But this also throws a different light on morality. Where and/or what is the morality which one might expect to find in this system? And what is the relation of morality and law within such a system? The point is, the system is clearly an unjust one. What then has been the perspective of morality on this system, and how has this affected the kinds of legal rules enacted? Either it was a morality, or moralities, which were, to coin a phrase from labour law, "sweetheart" moralities, which did only and everything they were told, or they were, at the other extreme, organized recalcitrant, systematic alternatives in opposition to the system. While I would hardly want to rule out the logical possibility of their being the latter, it seems to be far more likely that they were the former. And in adopting this position, I have at least two solid intellectual companions on my side, men noted for their abilities to spot at least one, if not all, forms of ideology, namely Marx and Freud. As is well known, Marx considered all morality to be superstructural, reflecting and serving the needs of the dominant class. Freud believed that it reflected and served the needs of the dominant system of sexuality, a sexuality based on the equation of power = penis = phallus, which is, of course, defined within the system as *male* sexuality. His words on the subject are worth repeating:

> We cannot avoid observing with critical eyes, and we have found that it is impossible to give our support to conventional sexual morality or to approve highly of the means by which society attempts to arrange the practical problems of sexuality in life. We can demonstrate with ease that what the world calls its code of morals demands more sacrifices than it is worth, and that its behaviour is neither dictated by honesty nor instituted with wisdom.[15]

As a feminist, I want to argue that morality reflects and serves the needs of the dominant sex, as well as those of the dominant class in the Marxist sense, and the dominant system of sexuality. Indeed that it should do the latter would be expected within this system, which is why Freud is right in holding the view that he did. Within cultures characterized by differential sexual attribution of rights of ownership, male sexuality is indeed dominant because males are the dominant sex-class, and what becomes defined as "male sexuality" is that deployment by males of their sexuality in the way which serves to reinforce and support the system of which they are the primary beneficiaries. Sexuality, like everything else, is used *coercively* within this system to maintain the *status quo*. Thus, morality functions as one among several methods of social control, either through the creation of moral rules, or through setting up ideals of human character, and advocating the methods of inculcating those traits and values appropriate to life under the system. Morality reinforces and is itself a means of socialization into the system. Thus, as feminists, we should hardly expect to find a morality which reflected the ideals of sexually egalitarian relations between the sexes among those which have gained prominence within this system of property relations.

We must prove this, however, by looking at the succession of moralities which have come down to us as this basic system changed and developed historically, both infraculturally and cross-culturally. Particular moralities will have to be discussed and evaluated in terms of their specific historicity and in relation to the actual operations of the system at the times at which these moralities were dominant. My discussion of problems with the ethics of liberalism from the perspective of sexual equality is thus a particular case study within the general hypothesis.

But before moving to that, there is one further important consequence of this view which is important in this context, and that is that the relation of morality and law is also historical. It is historical in the sense that there have been periods in which the rules prescribed within a morality have been more effective methods of social control than have legally enforceable ones; and there have been other periods in which laws have been the more effective check on behaviour. We are, I believe, and have for some time been, in a period of the latter type. If we feel sufficiently justified in doing or forbearing something, we want that reflected in our legal system because we believe, and I believe rightly, that those are the most effective methods of social control. If you want someone to have to do something, you do not want it left to the *discretion* of the individual either to do it or not. We do not want it discretionary because as members of the oppressed sex-class, we know from past experience that the discretionary powers each of the members of the dominant sex-class has on an individual basis are more often exercised against us than for us, and we know too that there are all too few areas even for such potentially beneficial exercise of discretion; *the system takes care of itself*, individuals' wishes to the contrary notwithstanding, be they male or female.[16] The way *not* to have something accomplished is to have it relegated to the authority of the individual conscience.[17] The contemporary debate between law and morality is really a misnomer. The debate is between competing systems of rules; those who advance theirs in the name of "morality" are just the ones who are out of power. The point is, the views we have are the ones we would like to see implemented in law. Therefore, we should at this particular historical moment be critical of both moral systems, and legal and moral theories of the relation of law and morality, which preach a *separation* of the two.

Because the second sense in which the relationship of law and morality is historical is that one or the other of the two expands and decreases, becomes more or less important, in accordance with the degree to which the private or the public sphere is dominant and/or expanding. Morality reflects primarily the values of the private sphere—that is why so much of it is concerned with sex: indeed, morality in the popular mind is virtually indistinguishable from *sexual* morality; law, on the other hand reflects primarily the values of the public sphere. Thus, the very split between law and morality presupposes a distinction between private and public, just as it presupposes a split between owners and non-owners, male and female sexuality. The fight then is and has been over which sphere does or should predominate. That is why I think now is a time of the ascendancy of legal rules. The private has for some time been losing ground.

But this means that those who are dedicated to an obliteration of these dichotomies have no morality, among other things, to fall back on.[18] In rejecting the dichotomy between these spheres, we must develop both a new morality and a new legal system which does not presuppose a dichotomy between them. What then are or can be the relative domains of each? If there are not distinctions between spheres, each must operate in one and the same domain. What then is to be their respective content? And what consequences follow from its being one or the other type of rule which is in issue? If all moral rules become legal rules, what is there left for morality to do?

I suggest that what we must develop is a comprehensive theory of social relations which is at once a theory of the relations of production, the relations of reproduction, and the relations between the theories of production and reproduction, which is simultaneously a political, a moral, and a legal theory. Morality should go back to what it has long since ceased to do and that is to provide a set of precepts for the development of individuals. Morality has itself become corrupted by legality, and has lost most of the best of itself by becoming parasitically dependent on legal systems, a derivative framework of rule-governed behaviour without any teeth. It is time to develop a morality which raises significant and important questions about virtues and vices, habits and dispositions, and the formation of character. It should be a morality of aspiration, which presupposes that the people we are concerned to create are sexually equal and are to carry on their relations within the structure of a sexually egalitarian society. This is, of course, no short-term project, but it must be recognized as a project in order to get going at all.

At least part of that project is supplying a critique of different moralities from this perspective. My comments in what follows are, then, undertaken as a contribution to that part of the project. I want to examine the ethics of liberalism within this frame of reference. One of the reasons I have been concerned about liberalism in particular is that it is unusual in that it presents itself as both an ethical and a political theory. Thus it appears to disavow the traditional dichotomy between morality and politics or law. For that reason alone it seems worthy of our attention. But it is also closer to our own time, and perhaps for that reason can be understood somewhat more easily than those of the distant past. For the same reason, however, it is also more important than older moralities because it still has a significant hold, and is harder to refute than, say, the morality of the Ten Commandments. It is because I have found myself more and more out of sympathy with liberalism on several issues I believe to be crucial for feminism that I feel the need to provide a defence of my position through an analysis of what is wrong with it from within the feminist perspective I have developed.

Since at least the mid-nineteenth century, the fight for women's rights has largely been fought under the banner of liberalism. The ethical principles of people like John Stuart Mill formed the moral justification for these struggles, and many of these individuals were themselves committed to the cause of women's equality.[19] As such, the cause of women's liberation has much thanks to give both to the theory and to its proponents. But it is, I believe, time to take another look at the moral underpinnings we have until now accepted, though I am by no means suggesting that utilitarianism, or more popular versions of liberal, or libertarian ethics, have been the only moral touchstones upon which the demand for sexual equality has rested. This has been fed by other moralities as well, notably that deriving from the works of Marx and Engels. But at least in so far as both of these moral systems acknowledged that the historical position of women had been an oppressed and exploited one, it was possible to present a united front on many issues, particularly those most clearly related to the achievement of legal and social reform. Most of these fights were publicly defended on liberal principles, and the most famous one, the fight for the right to vote, certainly was.

The reason for this is clear. The central value of liberalism is the freedom, or liberty, of the individual. Thus, demands by women for greater participation in public life were straightforward demands for greater liberty. The demands made in the name of sexual equality were, first, to establish that women ought to be entitled to the same rights as men, and, second, to ensure that these rights could actually be practically and effectively exercised. But there is a central difficulty with liberalism in this respect. In so far as the central value of liberalism is freedom, or what has been termed more specifically "negative liberty,"[20] it is seen to consist merely in the *absence of restraint*. Thus, while liberals could accept that it was wrong to prevent women from voting they have more difficulty accepting that effective exercise of the right to reproductive autonomy necessitates providing publicly financed clinics for the provision of safe, cheap abortion. Achieving the right to vote was a good case for liberal support because all that it required was the removal of a legal impediment which promoted greater liberty. But fights which necessitate not the removal of legal restraints, but the creation of legal duties, are not good causes on which to seek liberal support, because these necessarily involve a reduction in negative liberty. Since a central tenet of liberalism is that one can be said to be free, or to have the right to something merely from the fact that there is no statute or other legal limitation which prohibits the doing to the thing in question, the absence of a prohibition is, then, itself enough to generate the idea that one has a right. Legally speaking, the right that one has is what is properly termed a "privilege" or "liberty" right,[21] and does not entail that anything or anyone has a correlative duty to do anything, or provide anything, which would facilitate one in actually getting that to which the right entitled one.

As is obvious, there are more impediments to human endeavour than legal impediments, and there is more to having rights than simply not being prohibited from doing something, at least if the having of rights is to mean anything to those who do not have the other means needed to get what they want. In the face of pre-existing social inequality, the effective exercise of rights can be assured only by creating a legal *claim*-right which *does* entail obligations on the part of someone or something else to provide the thing, or the means to the thing, guaranteed by the right. Thus, mere privilege rights must be *converted into claim rights* if those who have the rights are to be ensured the effective exercise of their rights. They can only get what the right gives them if someone else has an obligation to provide them with it, independent of the recipient's ability to pay and things of that sort. But the conversion of privileges into claims involves creating obligations on others. And the creation of legal obligations on others is one of the most important ways of limiting a person's ability to do what he or she wants. Thus, the establishment of claim rights is itself an *infringement* of liberty, or negative freedom, since it makes it mandatory to do what it was before permissible either to do or not to do. The history of social reform is largely the history of first establishing that some previously disenfranchised group ought to have rights that have already been accorded to others, then removing legal or other social and institutional impediments to their getting what they want, and then fighting further to have these privileges converted into claims. But this involves liberalism in a fundamental contradiction, because it means that, during the third stage, the libertarian has to argue for the *limitation* of the freedom of some in the name of promoting greater equality among all those nominally said to be in possession of the right. On the face of it, utilitarianism has no difficulty with this since its principle is that it is best to do whatever promotes the greatest happiness of the greatest number, where each individual counts as one. But utilitarianism thus parts company with the central tenet of liberalism in those cases in which the greater positive liberty of all demands diminished negative liberty for some. Worse, it is powerless as a moral tool in just those cases in which the loss to some is evenly balanced by the gains to others, because it does not have a principle of justice independent of the principle of utility which would justify such a redistribution even in cases where the original distribution occurs within a domain characterized by inequality. While the promoters of utilitarianism, and many of their followers, have been dedicated social reformers, there are some aspects of our continuing historical reality which they either take for granted, or about which they are at any rate unaware or unaffected by the fact that the application of their principles within these contexts perpetuates, and indeed reinforces, fundamental inequalities.

Nowhere is this clearer, I believe, than in some issues which arise out of the demand for sexual equality, though I intend here to discuss this in depth only in relation to two issues, privacy and pornography. The fundamental question we have to ask is: Is the moral theory of liberalism consistent with equality? If it is, then we must be able to show how the mistakes it has made can be explained without throwing out the theory, and hence, how it must be revised in order to prevent similar errors from occurring in future. And if it isn't, then it is time we turned our attention to looking for or developing moral alternatives which are.

One of the fundamental principles endorsed by a liberal ethic is that there must be some areas of one's life in which one has the freedom to do what one wants, free from interference by others. It has been argued that there simply are some areas of life which are none of the law's business. For those familiar with the Wolfenden Report on Homosexuality in England, and the subsequent debate that this started both within and outside academic circles, this phrase, "none of the law's business," will have an all too familiar ring. Philosophically, this is reflected in debates about which areas of one's life should be essentially characterized by negative freedom, the ability to act free of restraints and scrutiny of others. Legally, it is reflected in debates about privacy, about the areas on one's life into which others should be legally prohibited from interfering.[22] There is virtually no one who would want to say that we should have no negative liberty or no privacy, but the debate still rages as to which areas of one's life should be guaranteed as areas of negative liberty through the creation of a legal right to privacy.

The difficulty is that no one has found a satisfactory method of drawing the boundaries between the private and other areas of life. In the past, the boundary was thought to be a *natural* one, based on the traditional distinction between the public and the private. The private just *was* "the private," and, as such should be guaranteed as an area of negative liberty and fully protected by means of a legally enforceable right to privacy. This was the basis of the argument in the Wolfenden Report. Here it was alleged that sexual relations between consenting adults simply are none of the law's business and the underlying rationale was that such behaviour should justifiably be left to the absolute discretion of individuals because it has effects on no one other than the participants. This was the rationale provided by John Stuart Mill in "On Liberty," and which was reiterated and defended by Herbert Hart in *Law, Liberty, and Morality*.[23] The best defence of this liberal tenet is the view developed by Mill that the law is justified in prohibiting actions if and only if doing them results in the inability of others to exercise rights of a similar kind. The underlying view is that rights should be distributed equally, which entails that no one can have rights the exercise of which would prevent others from exercising similar rights. The difficulty with the position is that it is virtually impossible to say with certainty of any action or pattern of behaviour that it has in principle no potential effects on others, either in terms of causing harm, or in terms of limiting the effective exercise of rights. Thus it is impossible *in principle* to draw a defensible boundary between the public and the private.

And certainly it has been indefensible to draw the legal boundary on the basis of the historical division between public and private. As is now abundantly clear, privacy functioned historically to protect those who were privileged to begin with. Privacy was a consequence of the ownership of private property, and, hence, was a commodity purchased with property. It has been a privilege accorded those of wealth and high social status. But more importantly from a feminist perspective, it protected not only the dominant class in the Marxist sense, but the dominant sex-class as well. The traditionally "private" was the sphere of the personal, home and hearth. And that area was the area within which women and children were forms of private property under the exclusive ownership and control of males. As the person in whom the absolute personality of the family rested, male heads of households had virtually absolute rights over their wives and children. The family, clearly, was not and is not a partnership of equals. There is no mutuality in the marital relations and the rights and duties are decidedly one-sided.

Of course it is not the concept of privacy which is responsible for this state of affairs. But in drawing a boundary between the historically private and public, for the purpose of entrenching a legal right to privacy in the area of the traditionally private, it certainly functioned to condone and encourage the abusive and unjustified practices which were possible within this unequal relation. As is now clear, the family has been characterized by a great deal of physical violence. The legitimate basis of authority in the family is physical coercion, and it is and has been regularly relied on to secure to the male head of the house the attitudes and behaviours he wants. Women, much less children, had no right to protest such behaviour but were expected to suffer it, willingly, or otherwise. Thus, the last place feminists want to see a right to privacy is in the family. What possible sense can be made of the notion of being a consenting adult when one is in a relation in which one has no right to say no? Clearly, if we want privacy at all, where we do not want it is in the home.

The area of life most in need of regulation and control in the interest of creating more liberty and equality for women is the area of the traditionally private and personal. But greater liberty and equality for women can be purchased only at the cost of less liberty, and a loss of status, for men. To the extent that women are given more rights within marriage, men are less able to do as they please; what was before permissible would now be either mandatory, as, for example, in making it a duty for men to share the housework and childcare, or prohibited, as for example in allowing a charge of rape between spouses. Within terms of the basic principle, such changes are justified. The past operation of the law has permitted many forms of behaviour which in fact caused physical and other direct and tangible harms to others, and which certainly prevented the effective exercise of like rights on the part of others. On the principle of like liberties for all, marriage must be turned into a relation of mutuality, and the relationships within it must be subject to regulation and control.

Why, then, has the demand for privacy centred so exclusively on preserving the traditional domain of male privilege? And why do the staunchest defenders of that view fail to see that in invoking these principles within a domain characterized by fundamental sexual inequality they are in fact both reinforcing that inequality and sanctioning its worst abuses? Thus, at the very least, adherents of the liberal ethic must acknowledge that there is no *natural* basis for deciding on what is private and what is public for the purpose of entrenching a legal right to privacy, and that the traditional area of the private is the area most in need of loss of privacy, in the name of promoting greater positive liberty and greater equality. How this fares on a purely utilitarian principle is of course problematic, for since men and women each make up roughly half the population, we cannot be sure that the benefits to women will in fact outweigh the losses to men.

In my view, the whole debate about privacy has been totally miscast because it has relied on the historical division between public and private. Thus, its liberal adherents continue to stress the need for privacy in just the area where it is least defensible. Where we need the most protection, the legally enforceable right to prevent others from gaining access to information about us, and from disseminating that information to others without either our knowledge or our consent, is in the public world, the world of computers and charge-cards, credit ratings, and security forces. But this will mean much more regulation and control of the people and institutions which determine the structure and organization of the economic and social order. It will mean confronting the dominant class and the dominant sex in the public as well as the private sphere, and we should hardly be surprised to find that we are forced to part company with radical adherents of the liberal ethic. Equality cannot flourish without limiting the privileges some already have in both the private and the public spheres because the inequalities of the present system were a product of the unequal attribution of rights in the first instance; thus greater equality and liberty for those least advantaged under the present system necessitates placing restrictions on the privileged rights of those who are presently most advantaged. And since this must be done by creating obligations either to do or to forbear actions previously permitted, it can be accomplished only at the expense of negative liberty.

While the principles of the liberal ethic itself do not require the historical division between public and private, it has certainly been presupposed in liberal thinking about these issues. Recognition of the extent to which this has played a role must lead to a reappraisal of what it is that people should be at liberty to do, and it must find a basis for this which does not rest on traditional views of the different spheres of life, and the different roles of the sexes.

What is needed, at base, is a reappraisal of what is *harmful*. That, too, has historically been defined in terms of what the dominant sex and the dominant economic class find "harmful." An analysis of rape law demonstrates that point as well as anything could. Physically coerced sexual intercourse has been regarded as constituting a redressable harm if and only if the female victim was a dependent female living under either parental or matrimonial control, and in possession of those qualities which made her desirable as a piece of sexual and reproductive property available for the exclusive use of a present or future husband.[24] I dare say that when we start pressing for legal reform which will prohibit sexual harassment on the job we will find few adherents of liberalism rallying to our cause. It remains to be seen whether or not liberalism can survive and transcend the limitations of its own historical perspective, but in so far as it must renounce much of its accepted thinking about what sorts of actions individuals ought to be free to do, and must recognize that negative liberty must at least temporarily take a back seat to the promotion of equality, I cannot say I am hopeful about the outcome. But the ethics of liberalism will not do as the moral framework for the achievement of sexual equality unless it can meet this challenge.

But it is clear from a consideration of the issue of pornography that so far at least the ethics of liberalism has been unable to rethink its concept of harm in a way which is consistent with sexual equality. Feminists and civil libertarians are now at complete loggerheads over the issue. The trend among feminists is clear. More and more of them are coming to see that pornography is a species of hate literature.[25] To achieve its impact, it relies on depicting women in humiliating, degrading, and violently abusive situations. To make matters worse, it frequently depicts them willingly, even avidly, suffering and inviting such treatment. As is obvious to even the naivest of eyes, such recreations of heterosexual behaviour and relationships feed traditional male fantasies about both themselves and women.

Pornography is a method of socialization; it is the tangible, palpable embodiment of the imposition of the dominant sexual system which is a part of the dominant sex-class system. It is a vivid depiction of how to deploy male sexuality in just the way that will achieve maximum effect in maintaining the *status quo*. Pornography would be neither desired nor tolerated within any system other than one which sprang from the differential attribution of rights of ownership in which women and children are forms of sexual property, and in which they must either like it or quite literally lump it. It is the obverse of a morality which stresses female passivity and submissiveness, and it encourages the actualization of such states through active aggression and violence. Pornography has very little to do with sex, certainly with any conception of egalitarian sexual relations between the sexes, but it has everything to do with showing how to use sexuality as an instrument of active oppression, and that is why it is wrong. Some allege that it also feeds female fantasies about themselves and men, but that is certainly being questioned, at least in so far as it can be said that there is any hard empirical data to support it.[26]

That there should be no laws prohibiting the manufacture, sale, and distribution of pornography has traditionally and increasingly been defended as a freedom of speech, and freedom of press, issue. It is alleged that the reading or viewing of such material does not cause any harm, or that if it does, it is harm only to those who willingly consent to it. The premise that it doesn't cause harm is defended by arguing that it relates only to the fantasy level and does not translate itself into interpersonal behaviour. And it goes further than this to argue that, indeed, it provides a healthy outlet, a cathartic effect, for those who might otherwise be tempted to act out their fantasies. Those who oppose pornography, particularly those who advocate its prohibition, are treated as Victorian prudes with sexual hang-ups. Women who object to it are seen as uptight, unliberated, and just not "with it" sexually speaking.

The general principle underlying the liberal view is of course that expressed by Mill in "On Liberty," who argued against any form of censorship on the ground that it was only through the free flow of information that the true and false could be separated. Prohibitions against the dissemination of any form of information functions to preserve the *status quo* and to prevent the development of a critically reflective morality which is itself necessary to pave the way for needed social change. The principle has much to be said for it. But that cannot change the fact that when it is uncritically made to apply within a domain characterized by inequality and by frankly abusive behaviour, a domain which is fundamentally shaped by a framework of social relations and institutions which makes all sexual relationships between men and women fundamentally coercive in nature,[27] it is bound to produce results which will be unacceptable because harmful to those who are in the pre-existing inferior position and who stand to be most affected by the attitudes and beliefs, as well as the practices, of those who use it.

The liberal argument has been that such material isn't harmful at all, and certainly cannot be seen as harmful to anyone other than the user, if harmful even to him. It isn't harmful because it functions merely to inflame male sexual desire. What is the harm if all it does is give a guy a bit of a rush? And it is right here that we must begin our critique. Surely we must acknowledge at least two things. First, it is not "normal" to get one's rushes from just anything. Secondly, if one gets desirable reactions from things which create a clear and substantial risk to others, then one can justifiably be prohibited from getting them that way. Persons who get their sexual stimulation from watching the atrocities perpetrated against the Jews during the holocaust are not regarded as "normal," and rightly so. Furthermore, we do not feel that we are infringing any legitimate rights of others in preventing them access to material designed to provide sexual stimulation by this means. And the reasons for that are at least two-fold. First, as history has made all too clear, actions of this particular species do not remain at the level of mere fantasy. They have been acted out on the grand scale, so grand as to make any rational and reflective person aware that the possibility of a correlation between thought and action is at least strong enough to justify the imposition of prohibitions against material of this sort. Second, it stems from recognizing that even if the actual actions themselves are not acted out, the attitudes and beliefs or the persons enjoying it reflect attitudes toward the objects of the actions which are in themselves intrinsically bad and which are bound to produce practical effects in real life, if only to be expressed in bigoted and racist attitudes. All of the same arguments apply to material which depicts black people in degrading, humiliating, and abusive circumstances. Such material is, in itself, an affront to the dignity of the objects depicted, not least because they *are* being depicted purely as objects, dehumanized and depersonalized instruments for the satisfaction of someone else's perverted tastes.

The same case can be made with respect to heterosexual pornography.[28] As Camille Le Grand puts it, "pornography teaches society to view women as less than human. It is this view which keeps women as victims."[29] The typical way in which women are depicted in pornography certainly reflects a view of them as inferior to men, as inherently masochistic, and as primarily of value as instrument for the satisfaction of male lust. That is, in itself, intrinsically offensive to women, and is a straightforward objective affront to their dignity as equal persons. So on that ground alone, pornography ought to be prohibited just as we prohibit material depicting other social groups in such a fashion.

Of course, we could hardly argue within the parameters of our present culture that it is abnormal for males to react as they do to pornography. It is, unfortunately, all too normal, at least where we have any notion of statistical normality in mind. But neither is it unusual for rape victims to feel shamed, humiliated, and degraded by being raped; this is "normal" in the culture, but from any more rational perspective, it certainly is not "normal" in any normative sense. Much of recent efforts around the issue of rape have been designed specifically to change the perspective which rape victims have on that experience. Rape victims can come to see the assaultive behaviour perpetrated against them as legitimizing the anger which is appropriate to the nature of the attack. In short, it is possible both to identify the specific effects of socialization within a male supremacist and sexually coercive society, and to offset those effects with appropriate reconceptualization of the event. Women can come to identify the masochism and victimization into which they have been socialized, and can then act both to counteract it, and to be sublimely angry at a culture which socialized them into that mode. So, too, it should be possible for men to identify the sadism and attitudes of sexual aggressivity into which they are socialized and so act both to counteract them, and to be angry at a social system that produced that response. In short, *it is not a mark of personal depravity or immorality to be aroused by such material.* Given the cultural pattern of which it is a manifestation that is not at all surprising. Indeed, it is just what we would expect. But what must be recognized is that it *is* a socialized response, and that it is a response about which men should be both concerned and angry. And certainly, once its cultural roots are exposed, it is a response which should not be seen as needing or justifying the sale and distribution of the material which elicited it. Women must object to pornography because it both reflects and reinforces the patterns of socialization appropriate to a system based on the unequal status of the sexes, in which women are consistently regarded and treated as the inferiors, and the sexual property, of men. The socialization it brings about is *in itself* a limitation of the autonomy of women. Men ought to object to it for the same reason, and they ought to recognize that the socialization it brings about in terms of their self-images and internalized standards of conduct is also intrinsically undesirable given any commitment to the notion of sexual equality. To the extent that men are able to internalize the conviction that women and men are equal persons, they must recognize that the pleasurable responses they get from pornography are inappropriate to that conviction and are destructive to their ability to form self-images consistent with it. But that does not entail that they are in any sense to blame for those responses: they had as little choice about that as they did about their names. But we have, then, given strong arguments in support of the view that the eliciting of a pleasurable response is not in itself any reason to condone the sale and distribution of pornography, and that a proper understanding of the nature and causes of that response gives men as well as women solid grounds for objecting to the material which occasioned it. I believe that many more men would be able to understand and accept the feminist perspective on pornography if they could come to realize that they are not responsible for their sexual responses to it given the patterns of socialization which exist to mould us all into a set of social relations which institutionalizes male aggression and female passivity.

Thus, pornography is intrinsically harmful, both to women and to men. However, that does not end the argument with defenders of liberalism because their argument then moves on to the assertion that the harm to women is not direct enough to justify the legal prohibition of pornography. Frankly, I think that the argument that pornography is intrinsically offensive to the dignity of women ought to carry the day, but in the interests of completeness I want to go on to consider the other arguments that are brought to pornography's defence. Apart from this notion of an intrinsic harm and infringement of the rights of women, it will be argued that even if pornography is harmful to the user, it does not lead to direct harm to women, because the fantasies it supports remain fantasies, and it in fact prevents direct harm to women through its cathartic effect. I may say at the outset that I'm not at all impressed with either of these arguments. So far as the first is concerned, there is plenty of hard evidence available which supports the contention that modeling has a powerful effect on human behaviour. Studies of wife and child abuse consistently attest to the fact that there is a strong correlation between those who are abusers and those who come from family situations which were themselves abusive. The battered child becomes the battering parent; the son who witnessed his father battering his mother, and who was himself battered, becomes a battering husband.[30] Also, the evidence about the effect of violence depicted on television on the behaviour of children also points strongly in this direction.[31] People tend to act out and operationalize the behaviour that they see typically acted out around them. And surely that is hardly surprising. It is what has kept civilization going. If we weren't able to perpetuate the patterns of behaviour developed through cultural organization we wouldn't have come very far. So far as I know, however, there is no hard data to support the catharsis theory. It is a theory espoused by those who are looking for a rationale, though doubtless it has its roots in their awareness that they read pornography but don't rape and brutalize women. But raping and brutalizing women isn't the only harm that can be perpetrated against women. But so far there is little empirical support offered for the view that pornography feeds only the fantasy. Most psychiatric literature dealing with the "perversions" asserts that some people remain content with the fantasy while others do not.[32] But no one knows what differentiates the one who does actualize it from the one who doesn't. If this argument is going to be effective, it must be empirically demonstrated that this is so, and surely we cannot predict until the data are in that those who don't so outnumber those who do that we should, in the interests of an open society, tolerate the risk that some will. And since we are all imprisoned by the cultural stereotypes and the patterns of socialization appropriate to a society based on sexual coercion, how can those who do read it assert with certainty that they do not cause harm to women? They are hardly the best judges! As rape makes clear again, there is nowhere greater differences in perception than there is in the confusion surrounding rape and seduction. The men believe they are merely seducing, but the women perceive it as rape! And who is to judge? Certainly it is intrinsically unfair to permit only those who are the perpetrators of such behaviour to have a say in its interpretation.

While the liberal principle behind opposition to censorship is based on a recognition that desirable social change requires public access to information which challenges the beliefs and practices of the *status quo*, what it does not acknowledge is that information which supports the *status quo* through providing role models which advocate the use or threat of coercion as a technique of social control directed at a clearly identifiable group depicted as inferior, subordinate, and subhuman, works against the interest both of desirable social change and of the members of the subgroup so identified. This has been clearly acknowledged in the case of violently anti-semitic and other forms of racist literature. The same principles apply with respect to violently anti-female literature, and the same conclusion should follow. But this cannot come about until it is recognized and acknowledged that the dissemination of such material is itself a harm to the members of the group involved. It remains to be seen whether liberalism can accomplish this, but until they do, we cannot hope for their support on this issue.

In refusing to count as "harms" actions and practices which serve the interest of the dominant sex by reinforcing the patterns and effects of modes of socialization which support the sexist system, it renders itself incapable of changing that system and of promoting greater equality and positive liberty for women. Liberalism serves the interest of the dominant sex and the dominant class, though it contains within itself the potential for promoting greater equality and greater positive liberty for all. It can realize this potential however, only by reconceptualizing harm in a way consistent with sex and class equality, and by recognizing that negative liberty must take second place to the promotion of equality at least until we have achieved a framework of enforceable rules which guarantees equality within both the public and the private spheres. When no one is allowed to do what is harmful to others, and/or what prevents them from effectively exercising liberty rights to autonomy and equality consistent with the equal attribution and effective exercise of like rights on the part of others, then we will have achieved a state in which liberty is concrete, and not a chimera which upholds the liberty of some at the expense of inequality to the rest. As women we are members of the disadvantaged sex. We are thus acting contrary to the interests of our sex in accepting any position which does not place the achievement of legally enforceable sexual equality at the forefront of its program.

That entails that we have to challenge traditional concepts of harm, and of liberty as the absence of restraint. We have been successful in removing most of the legal restraints which made both equality and liberty impossible, and that was the stage at which the ethics of liberalism served our purpose. But it has now outlived its usefulness to us. The achievement of *real*, rather than merely *possible*, equality and liberty now depends on placing effective, enforceable restraints on others; we can expect little support from liberalism as we move into this stage of our liberation.

Notes

1. It is, of course, the view developed by Engels in *Origin of the Family, Private Property, and the State*.
2. Kelly-Gadol, Joan, "The Social Relation of the Sexes: Methodological Implications of Women's History," *Signs*, Vol. 1, No. 4, Summer, 1976, pp. 809–823, is an excellent discussion of the centrality of the idea that the relation of the sexes is social and not natural to feminist approaches to the study of history and to feminist theory generally.
3. *Ibid.*, p. 819.
4. *Ibid.*
5. Lévi-Strauss, Claude, *The Elementary Structures of Kinship*, Boston, Beacon Press, 1969.
6. Rubin, Gayle, "The Traffic in Women: Notes on the 'Political Economy' of Sex," *Toward an Anthropology of Women*, (Ed.) Rayna R. Reiter, Monthly Review Press, N.Y. and London, 1975, p. 171.
7. *Ibid.*, p. 198.
8. Kelly-Gadol, op. cit., pp. 818–819.
9. Rubin, op. cit., p. 199.
10. This is exactly what is wrong with Engels' account of the origin of sexual inequality. It rests on an unexamined assumption that there is a natural division of labour in the family based on sex, such that it naturally occurred, because men looked after the herds and harvests, that they controlled the surplus of production, which was the first form of private property. But this does not explain at all why women were not seen to deserve an equal share of the exchange value this surplus made possible even if there was a division of labour, nor does it explain what this division of labour amounted to. As is clear from the anthropological evidence, systems characterized by private property have always and everywhere a division of labour, but there is immense variation in what work is assigned to which side of that sexual division of labour. Engels never realized that "production" is an artificial and ideological construct and not some natural activity which is clearly and naturally different from the work performed by women. "Production" is simply a fancy label for "men's work," which is paid labour done as part of the relations of exchange. This is discussed at length in Clark, Lorenne M.G., "A Marxist-Feminist Critique of Marx and Engels; or the Consequences of Seizing the Reins in the Household," *Towards a Feminist Political Theory*, University of Toronto Press, forthcoming, currently unpublished.
11. And it is this particular feature of the system of private property to which Marx and Engels attributed the beginnings of class oppression that they failed to recognize as laying the basis for sex oppression. At best Engels can be said to have explained how men came to be in *possession* of items which could be made available for exchange, but

does not account for their exclusive *ownership* of it, and does not see that it is as characteristic and as central to the system of private property which laid the basis for capitalism that it was a system in which rights of ownership were exclusively attributed to males as well as that it was a system in which rights of ownership were unequally distributed between males. The consequences of this are discussed *ibid.*

12. Lévi-Strauss, Claude, "The Family," *Man, Culture, and Society*, (Ed.) H. Shapiro, O.U.P., London, 1971, pp. 347–348.

13. Rubin, op. cit., pp. 170–171.

14. O'Brien, Mary, "The Politics of Impotence," *Contemporary Issues in Political Philosophy*, (Eds.) J. King-Farlow and W. Shea, Science History Publications, N.Y., 1976, develops the notion of the ideological basis of "paternity" through arguing that it is the issue of certainty of paternity which gives rise to the oppression of women. It is, I believe, rather less well understood that "maternity" is at least as ideological as "paternity" and for the same reasons, though with different effects.

15. Freud, S., *A General Introduction to Psychoanalysis*, Garden City Publishing Co., Garden City, N.Y., 1943, pp. 376–377.

16. This is, I believe, an immensely significant point. If men can come to understand that it is not them, as individuals, who are being held to be responsible for the present inequality between the sexes, but the system which predetermines them to an advantaged position, *whether they want it or not*, then I think they can approach questions about sexual equality without feeling defensive or hostile. This is discussed particularly in relation to the pervasiveness of sexual coercion as a characteristic of this system in Clark, Lorenne M.G., and Lewis, Debra J., *Rape: The Price of Coercive Sexuality*, Canadian Women's Educational Press, Toronto, 1977, pp. 175–177.

17. Sometimes we are better off, however, having it left to individual conscience rather than having the wrong rules brought into legal existence. This seems to be true in the abortion issue at the present time. We would like to see legal provision for abortion on demand, but it may be better at this historical moment simply to argue for its being left to private morality rather than run the risk of having it again made illegal.

18. It also entails that persons who are interested in simple role reversal also have a vested interest in maintaining the present structure and all the divisions characteristic of it. I take it that alleged feminists travelling under this banner can easily be seen to be interested in nothing more than a palace revolt. They certainly are not committed to bringing about fundamental change in the relation of the sexes or in confronting the issue of ensuring egalitarian relations of reproduction.

19. This is, of course, true of John Stuart Mill himself, as is clear from his essay, "The Subjection of Women," written in 1861 and first published in 1869.

20. After the distinction between "negative" and "positive" liberty made current by Isaiah Berlin in "Two Concepts of Liberty," in *Four Essays on Liberty*, O.U.P., London, 1969.

21. I am relying here on the distinctions first made by W.N. Hohfeld, *Fundamental Legal Conceptions*, Yale U.P., 1932.

22. A more detailed account of the relationship between the philosophical and legal debates, as well as a discussion of the complexity of the legal issue of privacy itself, is found in Clark, Lorenne M.G., "Privacy, Property, Freedom, and the Family," *Philosophical Law*, (Ed.) R. Bronaugh, Greenwood Press, Conn., forthcoming, and *Towards a Feminist Political Theory*, University of Toronto Press, Toronto, forthcoming.

23. Hart, H.L.A., *Law, Liberty, and Morality*, O.U.P., London, 1963. This was Hart's answer to the objections raised by Lord Devlin to the recommendations and theory expressed in the Wolfenden Report. Devlin's position on this and other related matters is found in Devlin, Lord Patrick, *The Enforcement of Morals*, O.U.P., London, 1965.

24. For a discussion of the way in which the historical evolution and conception of rape law functioned to maintain the sexual *status quo*, and indeed continues to produce just the results we should expect to find with respect to the treatment and handling of rape cases

within the criminal justice system, see Clark, Lorenne M.G., and Lewis, Debra J., *Rape: The Price of Coercive Sexuality.*

25. Among the articles that spring readily to mind are Morgan, Robin, "Theory and Practice: Pornography and Rape," *Going Too Far*, Random House, N.Y., 1977, Ch. IV, pp. 163–169; Russell, Diana, "Pornography: A Feminist Perspective," unpublished paper; Brownmiller, Susan, *Against Our Will*, Simon & Schuster, N.Y., 1975, pp. 394–396; and Shear, Marie, "Free Meat Talks Back," *J. of Communication*, Vol. 26, No. 1, Winter, 1976, pp. 38–39.

26. For an excellent discussion of the way in which the empirical research that has been done on obscenity reflects a decidedly male bias, see McCormack, Thelma, "Machismo in Media Research: A Critical Review of Research on Violence and Pornography," *Women and Power*, (Ed.) Naomi Black, publisher and publication date unknown.

27. Clark and Lewis, *Rape: The Price of Coercive Sexuality*, Chs. 7 and 8 in particular.

28. Indeed, it is true of male homosexual pornography as well. But in the interest of not legislating in the interest of others, I am not advocating that we should prohibit this species of pornography. If men object to it, as in my view they should, whether homo- or heterosexual, it is up to them to express their opposition. Certainly I do not wish to infringe the rights homosexuals have to look at what they like, even though I cannot say with certainty that I am not adversely affected by it.

29. Quoted in Russell, Diana, "Pornography: A Feminist Perspective," op. cit., p. 7, no reference given.

30. See, for example, Martin, Del, *Battered Wives*, Glide Publications, San Francisco, 1976, pp. 22–23; Pizzey, Erin, *Scream Quietly or the Neighbours Will Hear*, Penguin Books, England, 1974, Ch. 4; Van Stolk, Mary, *The Battered Child in Canada*, McClelland & Stewart, Toronto, 1972, pp. 23–27.

31. Bandura, A., Ross, D., and Ross, S.A., "Transmission of Aggression through Imitation of Aggressive Models," *J. Abnormal and Social Psychology*, 63, No. 3, 575–582.

32. Kraft-Ebbing, Richard von, *Psychopathia Sexualis*, 11th ed. rev. and enlarged, Stuttgard, 1901, pp. 94–95; Freud, S., *Introductory Lectures on Psycho-Analysis*, Standard Edition, 16:306.

Questions

1. Is Clark right in thinking that the separation of law and morality is not sound?

2. Both Clark and Heintzman are critical of liberalism. To what extent are the reasons for rejecting liberalism similar? To what extent are they different?

3. Is the idea of harm used by those opposing the censorship of pornography adequate? Or is it in need of revision as Clark suggests?

4. To what extent does the idea of harm suggested by Clark differ from that suggested by the authors of the previous three contributions?

5. Is pornography a species of hate literature?

6. Does pornography reinforce a sexist view of women? If so, does this fact provide adequate grounds for censorship?

The Moral Right of the Majority to Restrict Obscenity and Pornography through Law

Raymond D. Gastil

Obscenity and pornography may be defined as the use of language or images relating to the body, violence, or sex that exceed the bounds of propriety that a significant part of the public finds appropriate for the context and requirements of the situation in which they are used. Efforts to limit obscenity and pornography either legally or informally are frustrated by the lack of an acceptable intellectual basis in liberal societies for such limitations. Appeals to community standards or lack of redeeming social value are weakened by a widespread feeling, especially in academic circles and the media, that the majority has no right to impose its standards on individuals or to decide on social values unless clear physical harm is involved. Moreover, attempts to regulate obscenity are frequently criticized on the ground that the regulators are enforcing standards that neither they nor the majority observe in their own lives.

The recent controversy that has focused on the works of H.L.A. Hart and Lord Devlin on the one hand, and the reports of government commissions to look into the regulation of obscenity on the other, has summarized but not greatly advanced the argument.[1] In his defense of controls, Lord Devlin fails to accept the intellectual weakness and thus ultimate unsatisfactoriness of controls defended largely by populism and conservatism, nor is he sufficiently aware of the dangers of an open-ended appeal to the popular will. On the other hand, in the Mill tradition, Hart fails to stake out the rights of the majority as firmly as he does those of the minority. He promotes a form of libertarian elitism that should be rejected because it represents an undue infringement on the freedom of potential majorities that they will not freely accept. Devlin's intuition that law and morality should reinforce one another cannot simply be ignored. Since inadequacies in the Hart position lead to an unacceptable libertarianism and those in Devlin's may lead to a purely instrumental view of freedom, both may lay the groundwork for a new "escape from freedom."[2]

In order to avoid this danger, I suggest that we build a case for the control of obscenity by establishing the following: (1) a distinction of private from public rights to expression, (2) a distinction of political from non-political rights to expression, and (3) a plausible case that the majority can claim harm from public obscenity.

The Private/Public Distinction

In a free society, the majority is responsible for establishing the laws of the community, while at the same time this responsibility is limited by certain absolute privileges granted to minorities and individuals because of attachment to a concept of basic rights or freedoms. Aside from those rational political and civil freedoms that are necessary to guarantee a democratic structure, these include rights to that degree

From *Ethics*, Vol. 86, No. 3 (April 1976), pp. 231–240. By permission of the publisher, The University of Chicago Press.

of freedom that is consonant with the freedom of others. Yet what are the rules for this consonance? For example, surely one freedom of those in the majority is to have the kind of social and aesthetic environment that they desire in the moral mode. It is with this in mind that nudists are asked to disrobe only in private or in camps segregated for that purpose. If the clash between the majority and minority over nudism meant that nudists could appear anywhere in public, then in this case majority rights would be nugatory while the minority rights would be guaranteed. To expect majorities to long accede to such situations is to imagine that people will give up being interested in determining many aspects of their social environment that have formerly been considered of importance.

The problem for the liberal, therefore, is to define basic civil rights in such a way that they preserve a meaningful area of freedom both to individuals who can form majorities capable of determining a way of life for themselves and to individuals who have not or cannot form a majority. The right to try to form new majorities is the basic right given to individuals in both the majority and the minority that makes meaningful the right of either. Adding to this an absolute right to a private sphere of life guarantees the development of that degree of individuality that would seem consonant with human dignity in the liberal view. Once he has staked out a private realm for minority rights beyond the public political sphere, the liberal may go on to make the utilitarian case that the majority will also benefit from eschewing regulation of most social behaviour. But this is an area appropriate for continual readjustment of interests and not for basic guarantees.

David Conway has recently argued in regard to pornography that there is little sense to the private/public distinction that H.L.A. Hart and the *Wolfenden Report* have affirmed as a basis for distinguishing between what may or may not be prohibited.[3] He suggest that it is not the public nature of acts that prohibitionists wish to control but the acts themselves. He believes that public and private acts lie along a continuum that cannot be arbitrarily demarcated without a clear moral boundary. Finally, Conway suggests that since many personal actions, such as marriage, are necessarily public, the public/private distinction does not adequately preserve an arena of personal freedom.

Conway's last point is an unavoidable weakness of the distinction, but the first two objections are unconvincing. First, the public or private value of an action may be an integral part of its "rightness" or "wrongness," for, physically, and biologically, actions are generally neutral and their morality or immorality is in most cases judged with reference to the context of their occurrence. Opposition to sexual obscenity might be founded upon a desire to control the tone of sexual behaviour by reinforcing one set of meanings associated with it rather than another. If so, the place and the participants in expression determine its relative desirability. Second, there are many continuums upon which we wish to start and do not desire to finish but where nevertheless the exact stopping point must be arbitrary and conventional. For example, everyone should have equal political and civil rights, but how we define "everyone" is necessarily conventional. It would be foolish to give one-year-olds voting rights, but whether the age at which one receives this right should be twelve, eighteen, twenty-one, or twenty-five can be discussed as a matter of reasoned argument. Therefore, as a basis of compromise between majority and minority rights, the private/public distinction remains the most salient available—a view supported by its acceptance in both of the reports cited above.

The Political/Nonpolitical Distinction

In the United States, the argument against controls on obscenity is frequently made in the context of the right of free speech under the First Amendment to the Constitution. Yet as Alexander Meiklejohn has pointed out: ". . . the principle of freedom of speech is derived . . . from the necessities of self-government by universal suffrage . . . The guarantee by the First Amendment is . . . assured only to speech which bears, directly or indirectly, upon issues with which voters have to deal—only, therefore, to a consideration of matters of public interest. Private speech, or private interest in speech . . . has no claim whatever to the protection of the First Amendment."[4] Therefore, it is wrong for the authors of the *Report of the Commission on Obscenity and Pornography* to assert that controls should not be imposed because of the American tradition of free speech.[5] American history has not been remarkable for libertarianism, except in regard to politically related speech and behaviour. This is even more true of a democracy such as Switzerland.

There are borderline cases. Profanity and nudity are sometimes regarded as political expression, or random violence may carry a political message. However, if the courts were not confused by the claim that the First Amendment gave an unlimited right to all expression, they might plausibly determine what is an authentic political message.

But they have been so confused.[6] Although in the Roth case (1957) the Supreme Court exempted obscenity from coverage by the First Amendment, the stipulation that any redeeming social value would lift a work of art or literature into legality was based more on J.S. Mill than the writers of the Constitution. A more recent (1973) Supreme Court decision that work must have serious literary, artistic, political, or scientific value to escape potential condemnation as obscene gives more recognition to the fact that the majority has a right to intervene when it feels there is more social disvalue than value in a particular unit of expression. Yet the court signally fails to distinguish politically and nonpolitically relevant rights and by adding "scientific" appears to rest its justification on utilitarian arguments for freedom that may unfortunately wilt when calculations change. In a majoritarian state, freedom of speech must, instead, be protected by a more absolute but less all-inclusive principle that refers to rational political discourse as an ineluctable requirement of political democracy.

A Plausible Case That the Majority Can Claim Harm from Public Obscenity

Since regulation of obscenity and pornography limits freedom, and since they bring pleasure to many, their legal restriction in a liberal society cannot be advocated unless a plausible case can be made that lack of restriction does substantial harm to potential majority interests.

Both Mill and Hart assert that only harm to individuals can be a basis of regulation, and primarily harm to individuals other than the actors. But this is hardly a confining limit if the concept of harm may be extended through psychic to social and spiritual harm to individuals or to the society of which they are a part. Three broad extensions of the principle of harm have been proposed.[7] The first is the conservative hypothesis that since received moral and legal codes are the tested results of trial and error, they are likely to meet social needs better than untested alternatives. The second is the disintegration hypothesis that lack of regulation of conduct offensive to the majority will result in the loss of a unified moral consensus in the community and thus undercut its whole moral structure, washing away finally even the limitations that the libertarian would hate to lose. In Lord Devlin's hands, the disintegration hypothesis is often defended by an additional consequentialist appeal to what would happen if we were to lose present restraints. It is, then, both a claim that any code is better than none and a claim that the code on which we have built our civilization is apt to be more supportive of social goods common even to libertarians than would be a truly libertarian world. By easy stages, this brings us to the third or majoritarian hypothesis[9] that the people of any community have a right to legislate their way of life. If wearing clothes, for example, is a part of their way of life, they have a right to enforce this custom irrespective of lack of proof as to the harm of individual nudity to others.

These arguments are supportive of control, yet they are not enough for a plausible case. As to the majoritarian hypothesis, in a democracy, of course, a majority can force its will eventually, but this fact does not help us decide whether majorities or their leaders should be taught that they have a right to exert force in a particular sphere of life. Majorities are often wrong and frivolous, and this is one reason for constitutions and basic civil rights. The disintegration hypothesis may be correct—clashing views do lead to instability—but this is a weak case for enforcing old standards. It is true that attitudes about decency in the arts and on the streets have been changing rapidly, and the wide dissemination of pornography is speeding up the change. One result of any social change is instability, and instability has losses. Yet it might be possible in the future to achieve consensus that "anything goes" in obscene expression, and in these terms stability could be restructured. Conservatively, I would argue that those who launch confusion have the heavier burden of proof. Yet this does not alter the fact that the defender of the old assumptions of a society has the responsibility to give a rational case for those assumptions or to suggest revisions in those assumptions that accord with a rational case. A living conservative tradition must be a changing tradition, or else it will fail to preserve social integration, community identity, and cherished values.

In a recent review of the relevant theoretical and empirical evidence for potential harm that has been developed by the social sciences, James Q. Wilson compared two attempts to summarize such evidence for policy purposes in the United States.[10] He found that in both cases the supporting evidence for the conclusions was weak and often only tangentially related to real-world concerns. Nevertheless, the National Commission on the Causes and Prevention of Violence recommended that violence in the media should be controlled, or further investigated with an eye to control, because of the probability that fictional violence may make individuals behave violently. On the other hand, the Commission on Obscenity and Pornography recommended widespread decontrol of sexually explicit materials because no negative results of their general dissemination could be demonstrated. Wilson reasonably surmises that the reason for the disparity between the treatment of the relation between evidence and conclusion in the two reports is due to the bias of their authors against violence and in favor in sex.

Wilson, however, goes on to point out that almost all recent major American studies testing hypothesis that major long-term behavior changes result from particular social policy or educational inputs have provided inconclusive or negative findings. Thus, studies have in recent years shown that the type of school or educational method makes no difference (Coleman report), that Head Start accomplishes little, that prison correction systems produce little gain, and that psychiatry does little for the patient. He suggests, and it is probably true, that in real-life situations there is too much going on, too many cycles of reinforcement stretched over too many years, for particular interventions to get up out of the noise. Still this does not mean that there is not a great deal of change over time[11] and that the arts, the schools, and the media do not participate in positive or negative feedback relationships that eventuate in these changes. Because Head Start did not work very well does not mean early education is not important. As the violence commission report suggests, since advertisers feel that exposure to certain symbols and fictional experiences will influence buying behaviour, it is reasonable to suppose that an increasing flow of violent pornography will influence other social behavior. The "no harmful effects" of sexual pornography reported by the pornography commission included an observation that exposure led to a more open attitude toward sex and, after initial increase in sexual interest, a general adaptation to pornography.[12]

But what is behavior? One of the curious aspects of the claim that obscenity and pornography are not significant influences on behavior is that both their production and consumption (direct and indirect) are forms of behavior. In this sense, there are then two significant but not unrelated results of uncontrolled pornography and obscenity. First, we are granted only so much time in our lives, and our minds have only so much capacity for attention at any one time. Therefore, if there is more of X there will be less of Y in our attention. And so if there is more obscenity there is less of something else. Our lives are changed (of course, some not at all, many to a degree, and few greatly changed). Second, the parts of our lives are unlikely to be either watertight compartments or tightly interconnected. The verbal and artistic forms and images we use are just that, and yet at the same time they carry meanings that habituate us to different attitudes and eventually to different qualities of behavior. With the generalization of violent and sexual pornography, our bodies become depersonalized emotive machines with many buttons to push. As Walter Berns writes:

> Consider the case of the parent who wants to convince his children of the impropriety of the use of the four-letter verb meaning to copulate. At the present time the task confronting him is only slightly less formidable than that faced by the parent who would teach his children that the world is flat. Until recently propriety required the use of the verb "to make love," and this delicacy was not without purpose. It was meant to remind us—to teach us, or at least to allow us to be taught—that whereas human copulation can be physically indistinguishable

from animal copulation generally, it ought to be marked by the presence of a passion of which other animals are incapable. Now, to a quickly increasing extent, the four-letter verb—more "honest" in the opinion of its devotees—is being used openly and therefore without impropriety. The parent will fail in his effort to educate because he will be on his own, trying to teach a lesson his society no longer wants taught—by the law, by the language, or by the schools.[13]

As an analogy, let us imagine an attractive but small square in a large city surrounded by medium-sized apartments. Among those who used the square, 25 percent were inclined to be disorderly and kept trash lying around their apartments for days, while 75 percent were neat. However, the square was always neat, for few people dropped trash in the square and a weekly cleaning by the city was quite enough for even its neatest users.

One year, however, 5 percent of the users began to drop their trash in the square. Those disturbed by the change in its appearance asked for the enforcement of antilittering laws, but the courts held that no one was being injured, for there was no danger to health because of the weekly municipal cleanup. Yet, toward the end of each week trash grew so thick that users who had not previously dropped their trash began to become less careful, and so the percentage of litterers grew to at least equal the percentage who were also disorderly inside their own apartments. By now many of those who had formerly enjoyed the square partially because of its appearance stayed away, so that finally more than 50 percent of the users were also litterers, and in the end dropping trash casually about became the social custom. For health reasons cleanup was now three times a week, but with the heavy population it was a rather trashy park most of the time. By now, many of those who formerly had kept clean apartments but had become litterers in public also kept littered apartments.

This is the course of events which those disturbed with pornography and obscenity believe they are witnessing today. I do not know if any court has ruled against littering laws in the way they have against blue laws. But if the question of the extra cost of cleanup were kept out of the legal calculation, I see no reason why in the name of individual freedom the courts should not equally do away with such laws. Why is the filling of the public arena with pornography and obscenity to be regarded as different from the delict of littering? When the movie marquee, newsstands, and popular songs all blare out *Deep Throat* and its equivalents, the city becomes a different place to walk in just as it does when everyone carelessly drops his lunch sack, candy wrapper, or pop bottle. Since everyone's likes and dislikes cannot be accommodated in the same square, the obvious basis of decision as to regulation becomes the desire of the majority of its users.

Let me, then, somewhat formalize the case for restriction of obscenity in perfectionist terms such as those of Rashdall, Moore, or de Jouvenal.

First, I define the moral-action mode as one in which a person assumes that one of his interests will be to act in ways that accord with his highest image of how a man should act. He knows he will have other interests at other times and from other vantage points, but in the moral mode he wants to act in terms of this image, and he wants to advocate that others act in these terms. If we view all actions as basically self-interested, we will assume that the actor believes that his moral actions will improve the esteem in which he is held and thus his status, and that this gain is better than other possible gains. If we assume that an actor can internalize desires to achieve the good of others or of society, then he may act morally or support such action when projected gain to self-esteem outbalances other possible gains by other means.

Since the moral code is only one of several, there is no obvious hypocrisy in a society prohibiting obscenity or pornography that most of its members in fact enjoy. One may believe that it would be better for him to eat less ice cream; he will avoid ice-cream shops, but when faced with an ice-cream counter he will always order two scoops.

Let us, then, define morality as action that is guided in the moral-action mode by a reasoned balancing of the claims to consideration of a variety of ultimate goods for man or society, limited by a set of basic moral rules placed outside immediate consideration. A moral society is one that forms it customs and laws in terms of trade-offs within limits among the ultimate goods accepted by its members. The ultimate goods are many, and no two people will have the same list. But moral persons will, in fact, develop lists that have a great deal of overlap.

For the purposes of this discussion I will classify ultimate goods under three headings. First are the goods of pleasure in all of the manifold forms in which they occur. Second are the goods of creativity, the making and doing of something beyond the self. Creativity may be intellectual, technical, organizational, or artistic. Third are the goods of significance. Most people are concerned with their place in time, with their dignity as men and women, with their specialness. It is true of course that heroic generalization would allow us to reduce all goods to those of pleasure. Yet ancient Athens was not as remarkable for the pleasures of its inhabitants as for Athenian creativity and the significance that Athenian high culture gave to man as separate from nature. For many, satisfaction with life does not come from a quantum of fun but from the significance that they find in it. The rights and dignities afforded by policies that guarantee individual freedom offer one basis of individual significance, but not the only one.

In the moral society, limits are placed on the balancing of ultimate goods both because of a mistrust of rationalization and because of the hierarchical relation of ultimate goods. For example, if an analyst hypothesizes basic social rights such as those to food, respect, and life and basic civil rights such as those to freedoms that do not infringe on the freedom of others, he in effect sets limits that he will not recommend infringing except in such extreme circumstances as a danger of imminent destruction of the human race. On the other hand, less basic ultimate goods may in ordinary circumstances be traded off against other personal and social interests in deciding upon moral action.

In order to go beyond conservative, disintegration, and majoritarian hypotheses to build a case for limiting pornography and obscenity, it is necessary to show that it is not irrational for men to value the ultimate goods of creativity and significance equally with those of pleasure. For those who evaluate in these terms, actions that move society away from a balanced mix of the ultimate goods do moral harm to individuals both separately and collectively.

As I have pointed out, moral harm may come in a variety of forms. The *Brave New World* could offer most people manifold pleasures yet fall short in offering what the reader might consider sufficient significance to the average human life. Therefore, the controls of this society would harm its members. Similarly, lack of sufficient discipline may result in a person who is so unable to put off immediate gratification that he falls short of what others consider true humanity. Lack of discipline has harmed this person as surely as dropping a rock on his foot.

In perfectionist terms, the case against obscenity is either that it diminishes man or reduces his creativity. Since the second case depends on an analysis of extensive empirical evidence that I do not have, I shall limit the argument largely to the first. Historically, one way to achieve human significance has been to emphasize the specialness of man either as an individual or as a human group. This may be because many feel that there can be no meaning to a life except to itself if it is a replaceable part in a process that could do without it. And to have meaning only to oneself is ultimately to seem to have no meaning at all.

An obvious way to establish meaning is to sharply distinguish human from animal life. No civilization has placed human and prehuman life on a plane, even when, as in Hinduism and Buddhism, animal life is highly respected. Only in recent years has man come, by means of science, to concentrate on the similarities among existences—to flatten all differences, including those between animate and inanimate matter. This is one reason why the naive reaction to Darwin was so strong. If man is only part of a process and probably not a final stage, then his consciousness, ideals, and creativity are only epiphenomena. Since what is really important is his biology, beyond eugenics the reformer's goal can only be to make the progress of individuals through the stages of life as painless as possible for all. For a person to believe that he should really live up to a set of symbolic standards or should not try to get away with whatever he can seems to be to allow oneself to be brainwashed by a social machine justified as oiling the succession of the generations. Self-fulfillment becomes letting everything happen to oneself that can, enjoying all the possibilities before it is too late. From this perspective, even self-actualization is a mocking game.

Maintaining a system of symbolic restraints on language and the arts has historically been a means of underscoring the difference between man and the process from which he emerged. Let me pose as a critical difference between man and animal the development of symbolic systems that allow us to disvalue public viewing of biological processes such as defecation, urination, or sexual intercourse. Why? There is nothing "wrong" with these actions. I suggest that what is wrong, just as what is "wrong" with the naked body, is that they remind us of our biology, of our presymbolic connections. This is why Duncan Williams attacks modern literature as the depiction of the "trousered ape,"[14] and this is why he sees pornography as both violent and sexual—the realm of the forbidden and animal in the popular mythology.

The spread of obscenity through the popular arts and up and down the streets can be interpreted as a reflection of the victory of science over religious belief. The Marquis de Sade reasoned that since man was determined and essentially a machine, anything that he might do that he found pleasurable he should do. As Francis Shaeffer has pointed out, as this view of man has come to be popularly accepted, it has been accompanied by an overriding mood of despair in the arts.[15] But literary and artistic critics have gone further to note the resulting shattering of a sense of purpose and order and standards in the arts, with dependence on sex and violence as the most universal and easiest to understand common denominator.[16] It may be plausibly argued, then, that once casual sex and violence fill our viewing and creating lives, this feeds back to further reinforce and popularize a diminished view of man.

The case, then, is that the presentation or acting out of sex or violence in public, or advertising such activities in public, will tend to popularize and familiarize a view of man and an attitude toward the self that will diminish the view that people have of the significance through specialness of human life and also divert creative artists from creative activity through the diversion of the time and money of the public toward an art world whose standards have been undermined, both directly (through taking up the space and time of the audience) and indirectly (through its feedback support of nihilism) by pornography. In the account of some people, the losses in significance and creativity are not made up for by gains in creativity and significance (freedom) released by the decontrol of pornography, or by the gains in sensual pleasure. These judgments are contingent upon a time and place in which nihilism is already far advanced and in which culture as "adversary culture" is the accepted stance.[17] The relative gains and losses in a Victorian age such as that which Freud encountered might well be different.

Concluding Note

In making these arguments, it is well to note that I have not tried to prove the contentions of those who would regulate obscenity but only to establish the extent of their moral right. The majority has a moral right to legislate, outside of the political realm, their not unreasonable conclusions as to what should be permitted in public in a moral society. In the case of pornography and obscenity, their representatives can make a plausible case for regulation. Beyond this, for any particular legislation or mode of enforcement, advocates must establish more detailed consequentialist arguments for particular definitions of public and private, political and nonpolitical, and obscenity and pornography before a framework for effective control can be preserved or constructed.

Notes

1. See Patrick Devlin, *The Enforcement of Morals* (London: Oxford University Press, 1965); H.L.A. Hart, *Law, Liberty and Morality* (Stanford, Calif.: Stanford University Press, 1963); Basil Mitchell, *Law, Morality and Religion in a Secular Society* (London: Oxford University Press, 1967); the *Wolfenden Report: Report of the Committee on Homosexual Offenses and Prostitution* (New York: Stein & Day, 1963); and *Report of the Commission on Obscenity and Pornography* (Washington, D.C., 1970), esp. p. 53.
2. On the undermining of freedom by liberalism see Thomas Molnar, "Zur Gesellschaft der Zukunft, "*Schweizer Monatshefte* 54, no. 2 (1974): 97–104.
3. David Conway, "Law, Liberty and Indecency," *Philosophy* 49, no. 188 (1974): 135–148.
4. Alexander Meiklejohn, *Free Speech and Its Relation to Self-Government* (New York: Harper & Row, 1948), pp. 93–94.
5. *Report of the Commission on Obscenity and Pornography*, pp. 53–54.
6. See ibid., pp. 295–370.

7. *New York Times* (January 24, 1973).
8. In addition to Hart and Devlin, see C.L. Ten, "Enforcing a Shared Morality," *Ethics* 82, no. 4 (1972): 321–329; and Basil Mitchell, pp. 45–47.
9. Mislabeled "conservative" by Ten, ibid.
10. James Q. Wilson, "Violence, Pornography, and Social Science," *Public Interest* 22 (Winter 1971): 45–61. Even a strong defender of the report of the pornography commission agrees with this analysis. See Weldon Johnson, "The Pornography Report," *Duquesne Law Review* 10 (Winter 1971): 190–219 (note. p. 219).
11. For example, a Gallup poll shows a 20 percent drop in the percent opposing premarital sexual relations over the four years 1969–1973 (*New York Times* [August 12, 1973]).
12. *Report of the Commission on Obscenity and Pornography*, pp. 139–264.
13. Walter Berns, "Pornography vs. Democracy: The Case for Censorship," *Public Interest* 22 (Winter 1971): 19–20.
14. Duncan Williams, *Trousered Apes: A Study in the Influence of Literature on Modern Society* (London: Churchill Press, 1971).
15. Francis A. Schaeffer, *Escape from Reason* (Downer's Grove, Ill.: Intervarsity Press, 1968).
16. In addition to Williams, see Paul Horgan, "The Abdication of the Artist," *Proceedings of the American Philosophical Society* 109, no. 5 (1965): 267–271; Katherine Ann Porter, "A Country and Some People I Love," *Harper's Magazine* 231 (September 1965): 58–68.
17. See Daniel Bell and Irving Kristol, *Capitalism Today* (New York: Basic Books, 1971), p. 22; and Irving Howe, *Decline of the New* (New York: Harcourt, Brace & World, 1963).

Questions

1. In what respects does Gastil's critique of the public-private distinction differ from the critique offered by Lorenne Clark?
2. Gastil argues that lack of restriction in the circulation of pornography does substantial harm to "potential majority interests." Does he provide good reasons for his argument?
3. Gastil argues that pornography affects creative activity; Conolly argues that pornography is harmful. Do the two arguments reinforce one another? If they do reinforce each other, why do Gastil and Conolly disagree on the question of censorship?
4. In deciding the question of censorship, where should the burden of proof lie?

Suggestions for Further Reading

Canadian Government Reports

- Law Reform Commission of Canada, *Limits of Criminal Law — Obscenity: A Test Case* (Working Paper 10). The second selection in this chapter is drawn from this report. It is available in public document sections of university libraries and from the Commission.
- *Obscenity, A Study Paper,* prepared by Richard G. Fox for the Law Reform Commission of Canada and published in 1973, provides much of

the background material used by the Commission in the development of Working Paper 10.

Other Reports

Because of the proliferation of pornography since the Second World War, and because of public agitation on the subject in various countries in North America and Western Europe, a number of thorough studies have been done by government commissions. Two are well worth examination:

- *The Report of the Commission on Obscenity and Pornography* (New York: Bantam Books, 1970).
- David Copp and Susan Wendell, eds., ''Offensive Pornography and Art,'' a report of the British Committee on Obscenity and Film Censorship, in *Pornography and Censorship* (Prometheus Books, 1983).

Both reports recommend that censorship of pornography be reduced or eliminated.

A Recent Book

- David Copp and Susan Wendell, eds., *Pornography and Censorship: Scientific, Philosophical and Legal Studies* (Prometheus Books, 1983). This book comprises a variety of material of interest, including some very influential studies on the effects of pornography on its audience by Berl Kutchinsky.

Accessibility to Canadian Materials

Although the fact is not widely known, there has been active concern with and discussion of the topic of censorship and pornography in Canada since before the Second World War. Unfortunately, that discussion is contained in limited-circulation journals and in minutes and reports of government committees. With the help of a small research grant, I have been able to accumulate many of the available documents. A table of contents for this collection is available from me on request.

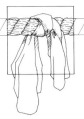

Aboriginal Rights

Introduction

Moral issues can arise out of situations involving individuals. For example, should a person who has decided to commit suicide be dissuaded or, if necessary, stopped? Moral issues can also arise in situations in which individuals come into conflict with groups — for example, where discrimination occurs. However, society comprises groups which interact as groups. Group interaction, too, can give rise to moral problems, as the issue of aboriginal rights demonstrates.

    The purpose of this chapter is to examine the claims of Canada's native peoples, the conflicts with the non-native majority which those claims have generated, and the possibility for solutions founded on principles of justice.

Background Considerations

There are many areas in which conflict between native groups and the dominant Canadian majority has become severe. One problem is land. The first settlers discovered a land which, from their point of view, was unsettled. They felt no inhibitions about sharing and then establishing ownership over the land they felt they had discovered.

    The native people have a quite different attitude toward the land and toward the question of ownership. In their view the land cannot be owned. People can use it and they can claim areas of traditional use, but ownership is out of the question. One result of these differing attitudes is that the treaties signed by the native peoples with the British and the Canadian governments are subject to quite different and incompatible interpretations. Thus, some native lawyers have argued that all the treaties are invalid — the Indians never could have agreed to surrender what, in their view, they did not own. Where no treaties exist, there is continuing dispute over the lands traditionally used by the native peoples, and disagreement about what that traditional use implies for future development of those lands.

A second problem is self-government. The European settlers encountered peoples with well-developed and effective, though largely informal, political and legal systems. With the onslaught of European civilization, the ability of the indigenous peoples to govern their own affairs was progressively undermined. Even on reservations the Canadian government insisted on the right to oversee and overrule native councils. One significant demand which has been voiced, particularly by those in the northern areas of Canada — areas not yet covered by treaties — is a recognition of the right to self-government.

Because they are small in number, the aboriginal people have been largely unsuccessful in obtaining political solutions to their problems. As a result, until recently they have had to rely on the courts. This has been particularly true of land claims in areas of the country where treaties have never been signed. Consequently, serious disputes have generally been resolved in the context of legal principles of land ownership and acquisition which are essentially foreign to the native outlook.

The Current Situation

The status of Canada's native people today is very much in flux. There is general agreement that the courts are not an adequate avenue for redress of their grievances. But most important, the new Canadian charter of rights makes reference to native rights and requires that provincial and federal governments define those rights over the new few years. It would seem, then, that there is a present need to seek a basis for a fair resolution of native demands.

The Moral Dimension

Who owns a particular piece of land can sometimes be a contentious question. Nevertheless, we normally assume that legal principles, as they now exist, will suffice in the resolution of ownership questions. Disputes over native land claims are more difficult to resolve. To begin with, they originate in actions which took place many generations ago. Those who allegedly were unjustly treated are no longer alive; nor are those whose actions are said to have originated the injustice. How, then, are such problems to be resolved? Do those living today have an obligation to rectify past injustices?

There is a second aspect of the problem. Meeting the demands of native groups may seriously affect people who are not themselves the cause of the problems to be rectified, but who have come to rely on and benefit from patterns of land use and ownership that are in dispute. Is this fair? Can it be avoided? How much weight should be given to this factor in arriving at a just outcome?

Finally, as we have seen, native land claims challenge the very concept of land ownership which is so important to the non-native way of life. Are there

moral principles to which we can appeal when there is disagreement on such
fundamental concepts?

The Readings

The readings begin with selections from the Berger report of the MacKenzie
Valley Pipeline Inquiry entitled *Northern Frontier, Northern Homeland*. This
gives some background information relating to the controversy.

One way of dealing with the ownership question is to say that it cannot be
answered. We cannot right past wrongs; we can only avoid future mistakes.
This argument, which was the stance of the federal government in 1969, is
set out by Prime Minister P.E. Trudeau. The government's stance has now
changed. But the argument continues to have a certain appeal. In his contribution, Michael McDonald evaluates that argument and a number of others in
light of currently fashionable philosophical notions about what ownership
means and how it is acquired. David Gauthier enters the dialogue by proposing an alternate view.

Behind the discussion of aboriginal rights lies the demand for self-government. Prior to contact with the European settlers, the native peoples were
self-governing. Many native spokesmen claim that self-government was never
voluntarily relinquished. This view is explained and defended by Fred Plain. If
we accept that the notion of aboriginal rights is well founded, does it follow
that Canada's native peoples have a right to self-government? What does self-
government mean in this context?

In the final reading, J.T. Stevenson asks whether there is a moral principle
which has broad cultural acceptance and acceptability by reference to which
the issues in dispute can be evaluated and resolved. He argues that there is
such a principle, which he calls ''the personal security principle.'' Applying
this principle specifically to the issue of land ownership leads Stevenson to
conclude that the basic claims of Canada's native people are well founded.
Further, just resolution will require that the demand for self-government be
recognized.

Native Lands and Treaties in North America

Justice Thomas R. Berger

When the first European settlers arrived in North America, independent native
societies, diverse in culture and language, already occupied the continent. The European nations asserted dominion over the New World by right of their ''discovery.''

From *Northern Frontier, Northern Homeland* (James Lorimer and Co. Publishers in association with Canadian Government Publishing Centre, Supply and Services Canada). By permission of the Minister of Supply and Services Canada.

But what of the native peoples who inhabited North America? By what right did Europeans claim jurisdiction over them? Chief Justice John Marshall of the Supreme Court of the United States, in a series of judgments in the 1820s and 1830s, described the Europeans' claim in these words:

> America, separated from Europe by a wide ocean, was inhabited by a distinct people, divided into separate nations, independent of each other and of the rest of the world, having institutions of their own, and governing themselves by their own laws.
>
> It is difficult to comprehend the proposition that the inhabitants of either quarter of the globe could have rightful original claims of dominion over the inhabitants of the other, or over the lands they occupied; or that the discovery of either by the other should give the discoverer rights in the country discovered which annulled the existing rights of its ancient possessors.
>
> Did these adventurers, by sailing along the coast and occasionally landing on it, acquire for the several governments to whom they belonged, or by whom they were commissioned, a rightful property in the soil from the Atlantic to the Pacific; or rightful dominion over the numerous people who occupied it? Or has nature, or the great Creator of all things, conferred these rights over hunters and fishermen, on agriculturists and manufacturers?
>
> To avoid bloody conflicts, which might terminate disastrously to all, it was necessary for the nations of Europe to establish some principle which all would acknowledge and which should decide their respective rights as between themselves. This principle, suggested by the actual state of things, was "that discovery gave title to the government by whose subjects or by whose authority it was made, against all other European governments, which title might be consummated by possession."
>
> This principle, acknowledged by all Europeans, because it was the interest of all to acknowledge it, gave to the nation making the discovery, as its inevitable consequence, the sole right of acquiring the soil and making settlements upon it. (*Worcester v. Georgia* [1832] 31 U.S. 350 at 369)

The Europeans' assumption of power over the Indians was founded on a supposed moral and economic superiority of European culture and civilization over that of the native people. But it was, nevertheless, acknowledged that the native people retained certain rights. Chief Justice Marshall said:

> [the native people] were admitted to be the rightful occupants of the soil, with a legal as well as just claim to retain possession of it, and to use it according to their own discretion: but their rights to complete sovereignty, as independent nations, were necessarily diminished and their power to dispose of the soil at their own will, to whomsoever

they pleased, was denied by the original fundamental principle that discovery gave exclusive title to those who made it. (*Johnson v. McIntosh* [1823] 21 U.S. 543)

The concept of aboriginal rights has a firm basis in international law, and we subscribe to it in Canada. During the last century, the Supreme Court of Canada in the St. Catherines Milling case and this century in the Nishga case affirmed the proposition that the original peoples of our country had a legal right to the use and occupation of their ancestral lands. The courts have had to consider whether, in given cases, the native right has been taken away by competent authority, and sometimes the courts have decided it has been. But original use and occupation of the land is the legal foundation for the assertion of native claims in Northern Canada today.

From the beginning, Great Britain recognized the rights of native people to their traditional lands, and acquired by negotiation and purchase the lands the colonists required for settlement and cultivation. That recognition was based not only on international law, but also upon the realities of the times, for in those early days the native people greatly outnumbered the settlers.

The necessity to maintain good relations with the native people led the British to formulate a more clearly defined colonial policy towards Indian land rights in the mid-18th century. The westward expansion of settlers from New England during this period had given rise to discontent among the Indian tribes and during the Seven Years War (1756–1763), the British were at pains to ensure the continued friendship of the Iroquois Confederacy lest they defect to the French. When the war ended, the British controlled the whole of the Atlantic seaboard, from Newfoundland to Florida, and the government promulgated the Royal Proclamation of 1763. This document reserved to the Indians, as their hunting grounds, all the land west of the Allegheny Mountains, excluding Rupert's Land, the territory granted in 1670 to the Hudson's Bay Company. The Proclamation stated that when land was required for further settlement, it should be purchased for the Crown in a public meeting held for that purpose by the governor or commander-in-chief of the several colonies. This procedure for the purchase of Indian land was the basis for the treaties of the 19th and 20th centuries.

The Treaties

Following the Proclamation of 1763, the British made a series of treaties with the Indians living in what is now Southern Ontario. Many of these treaties were with small groups of Indians for limited areas of land, but, as settlement moved westward in the mid-19th century, there was a dramatic increase in geographical scale. The Robinson treaties, made in Ontario in 1850, and the "numbered treaties," made following Canada's acquisition from Great Britain in 1870 of Rupert's Land and the Northwestern Territory, covered much larger tracts of land.

The treaties concluded after 1870 on the prairies cleared the way for the settlement of Western Canada and the construction of the Canadian Pacific Railway. The government's instructions to the Lieutenant-Governor of the Northwest Territories in 1870, after the cession of Rupert's Land, were explicit:

You will also turn your attention promptly to the condition of the country outside the Province of Manitoba, on the North and West; and while assuring the Indians of your desire to establish friendly relations with them, you will ascertain and report to His Excellency the course you may think the most advisable to pursue, whether by Treaty or otherwise, for the removal of any obstructions that might be presented to the flow of population into the fertile lands that lie between Manitoba and the Rocky Mountains. (Canada, Sessional Papers, 1871, No. 20 p. 8)

Treaties 1 to 7, made between 1870 and 1877, covered the territory between the watershed west of Lake Superior and the Rocky Mountains. In 1899, Treaty 8 covered territory northward to Great Slave Lake. Then, in 1921, Treaty 11 dealt with the land from Great Slave Lake down the Mackenzie River to the Mackenzie Delta. Treaties 8 and 11 together cover the whole of Northern Alberta and the western part of the Northwest Territories, including the Mackenzie Valley.

The treaties conform to a distinct pattern: in exchange for the surrender of their aboriginal rights, the Indians received annual cash payments. The amount varied with the treaty: under Treaties 1 and 2, each man, woman and child received $3 a year; under Treaty 4, the chiefs received $25, headmen $15, and other members of the tribe $12. In addition, the government established reserves for the use of the Indian bands: the area in some cases was apportioned on the basis of 160 acres of land for a family of five; in other cases, it was one square mile of land for each family. The treaties also recognized the continued right of the native people to hunt and fish over all the unsettled parts of the territories they had surrendered. Beginning with Treaty 3, the government agreed to supply the Indian bands with farm and agricultural implements, as well as with ammunition and twine for use in hunting and fishing.

The spirit of these clauses, together with the guarantee of hunting and fishing rights and the establishment of reserves was, according to the understanding of the Indians, to support their traditional hunting and fishing economy and to help them to develop a new agricultural economy to supplement the traditional one when it was no longer viable.

White settlers soon occupied the non-reserve land that the Indians had surrendered, and their traditional hunting and fishing economy was undermined. Legislation and game regulations limited traditional activities yet further. The land allocated for reserves was often quite unsuitable for agriculture, and the reserves were often whittled away to provide additional land for white settlement. The government never advanced the capital necessary to develop an agricultural base for the Indians, and when the native population began to expand, the whole concept of developing agriculture on reserve lands became impractical.

These prairie treaties were negotiated in periods of near desperation for the Indian tribes. The decimation of the buffalo herds had ruined their economy, and they suffered from epidemic diseases and periodic starvation. Often they had no alternative to accepting the treaty commissioner's offers.

The recent settlement of native claims in Alaska and the James Bay Agreement follow the tradition of the treaties. The object of the earlier surrenders was to permit agricultural settlement by another race. The objects of the Alaska Native Claims Settlement Act and of the James Bay Agreement are to facilitate resource development by another race. The negotiators for the Province of Quebec stated that, if the native people refused to approve the James Bay Agreement, the project would go ahead anyway, and they would simply lose the benefits offered by the Province. This attitude parallels the position of the treaty commissioners a century ago: they said that if the Indians did not sign the treaties offered them, their lands would be colonized anyway.

Treaties in the Northwest Territories

Throughout the British Empire, the Crown, not the local legislature, was always responsible for the welfare of the aboriginal people. In 1867, therefore, the British North America Act gave the Parliament of Canada jurisdiction over Indian affairs and Indian lands throughout the new country. This jurisdiction encompasses the Inuit, and the Metis as well, at least to the extent that they are pressing claims based on their Indian ancestry. With Canada's acquisition of Rupert's Land and the Northwestern Territory, and the entry of British Columbia into Confederation, that jurisdiction extended from the Atlantic to the Pacific, from the 49th Parallel to the Arctic Ocean.

The constitutional documents that effected the transfer to Canada of Rupert's Land and the Northwestern Territory all refer to "aboriginal rights." The Imperial Order-in-Council, signed by Queen Victoria, that assigned Rupert's Land to Canada provided that:

> Any claims of Indians to compensation for lands required for purposes of settlement shall be disposed of by the Canadian Government in communication with the Imperial Government: and the [Hudson's Bay] Company shall be relieved of all responsibility in respect of them. (Exhibit F569, p. 42)

It was upon these conditions that Canada achieved sovereignty over the lands that comprise the Northwest Territories and Yukon Territory, including the lands claimed today by the Dene, Inuit and Metis. After the transfer of these territories, the federal government enacted the Dominion Lands Act of 1872, the first statute to deal with the sale and disposition of federal crown lands. It stated:

> 42. None of the provisions of this Act respecting the settlement of agricultural lands, or the lease of timber lands, or the purchase and sale of mineral lands, shall be held to apply to territory the Indian title to which shall not at the time have been extinguished. (Exhibit F569, p. 43)

All of these instruments acknowledge the rights of the native people. They illustrate that the recognition of aboriginal title was deeply embedded in both the policy and the law of the new nation.

Treaties 8 and 11, made with the Indians of Northern Alberta and the Northwest Territories, continue both the philosophy and the form of earlier treaties. These two treaties are the subject of a recent book by Father René Fumoleau, *As Long as This Land Shall Last*. I cite his text for many official and historical documents related to these treaties.

In 1888, government surveyors reported that there was oil in the Mackenzie Valley, and that the oil-bearing formations were "almost co-extensive with the [Mackenzie] valley itself." The report of a Select Committee of the Senate on the resources of the Mackenzie Basin, in March 1888, has a familiar ring today:

> . . . the petroleum area is so extensive as to justify the belief that eventually it will supply the larger part of this continent and be shipped from Churchill or some more northern Hudson's Bay port to England. . . . The evidence . . . points to the existence . . . of the most extensive petroleum field in America, if not in the World. The uses of petroleum and consequently the demand for it by all Nations are increasing at such a rapid ratio, that it is probable this great petroleum field will assume an enormous value in the near future and will rank among the chief assets comprised in the Crown Domain of the Dominion. (Cited in Fumoleau, op. cit., p. 40)

A Privy Council Report of 1891 set forth the government's intentions:

> . . . the discovery [of] immense quantities of petroleum . . . renders it advisable that a treaty or treaties should be made with the Indians who claim those regions as their hunting grounds, with a view to the extinguishment of the Indian title in such portions of the same, as it may be considered in the interest of the public to open up for settlement. (Cited in Fumoleau, op. cit., p. 41)

No treaty was made, however, until the Klondike gold rush of 1898. It was the entry of large numbers of white prospectors into the Mackenzie Valley on their way to the Yukon gold fields and the desire of the government to ensure peaceful occupation of the land that led to the making of Treaty 8. The boundaries of Treaty 8 were drawn to include the area in which geologists thought oil or gold might be found; they did not include the area inhabited by the Indians north of Great Slave Lake because, in the words of the Indian Commissioner, Amédée Forget:

> . . . their territory so far as it is at present known is of no particular value and they very rarely come into contact with Whites. (Cited in Fumoleau, op. cit., p. 59)

Treaty 8 was signed at various points including Fort Smith in 1899 and Fort Resolution in 1900. While the treaty commissioners negotiated with the Indians, a Half-Breed Commission negotiated with the Metis. Following the procedure established on the prairies, the government gave the Metis the option of coming under the treaty with the Indians or of accepting scrip, which entitled the bearer either to $240 or to 240 acres of land. Many Metis chose to come under the treaty.

Treaty 8, like the prairie treaties, provided for an annual payment of $5 per head, the recognition of hunting and fishing rights, and the allocation of reserve lands. But these lands were not allocated then, and, with the sole exception of a small reserve at Hay River in 1974, none have been allocated to this day.

The Indian people did not see Treaty 8 as a surrender of their aboriginal rights: they considered it to be a treaty of peace and friendship. Native witnesses at the Inquiry recalled the prophetic words that Chief Drygeese spoke when Treaty 8 was signed at Fort Resolution:

> If it is going to change, if you want to change our lives, then it is no use taking treaty, because without treaty we are making a living for ourselves and our families . . . I would like a written promise from you to prove you are not taking our land away from us. . . . There will be no closed season on our land. There will be nothing said about the land. . . . My people will continue to live as they were before and no White man will change that. . . . You will in the future want us to live like White man does and we do not want that. . . . The people are happy as they are. If you try to change their ways of life by treaty, you will destroy their happiness. There will be bitter struggle between your people and my people. (Cited in Fumoleau, op. cit., pp. 91ff)

In the years that followed, legislation was enacted restricting native hunting and trapping. In 1917, closed seasons were established on moose, caribou and certain other animals essential to the economy of the native people, and in 1918 the Migratory Birds Convention Act further restricted their hunting. The Indians regarded these regulations as breaches of the promise that they would be free to hunt, fish and trap, and because of them they boycotted the payment of treaty money in 1920 at Fort Resolution.

In 1907, and repeatedly thereafter, Henry Conroy, who accompanied the original treaty party in 1899 and who had charge of the annual payment of treaty money, recommended that Treaty 8 should be extended farther north. But, in 1910, the official position was still that:

> . . . at present there is no necessity for taking that action. The influx of miners and prospectors into that country is very small, and at present there [are] no settlers. (Cited in Fumoleau, op. cit., p. 136)

The official position remained unchanged until 1920, when the Imperial Oil Company struck oil on the Mackenzie River below Fort Norman. The government quickly moved to ensure that these oil-rich lands should be legally open for industrial development and free of any Indian interest. F.H. Kitto, Dominion Land Surveyor, wrote:

> The recent discoveries of oil at Norman [Wells] have been made on lands virtually belonging to those tribes [of non-treaty Indians]. Until treaty has been made with them, the right of the Mining Lands and Yukon Branch [of the federal government] to dispose of these oil resources is open to debate. (Cited in Fumoleau, op. cit., p. 159)

Treaty 11 was soon signed. During the summer of 1921, the Treaty Commission travelled down the Mackenzie River from Fort Providence to Fort McPherson, then returned to visit Fort Rae. In 1922, the treaty was made with the Dene at Fort Liard. As with Treaty 8, the Metis were given the option of taking treaty or accepting scrip. However, the parliamentary approval necessary to pay the scrip was delayed, and the Metis were not paid until 1924, when 172 Metis took scrip. The payments of $240 to each Metis represent the only settlement made with the Metis of the Northwest Territories who did not take treaty. Rick Hardy, President of the Metis Association, told the Inquiry that the Metis do not consider that these payments extinguished their aboriginal rights.

The Dene do not regard Treaty 11, which followed the pattern of Treaty 8, as a surrender of their land, but consider it to be a treaty of peace and friendship. Father Fumoleau writes of Treaty 11:

> A few basic facts emerge from the evidence of documents and testimonies. These are: treaty negotiations were brief, initial opposition was overcome, specific demands were made by the Indians, promises were given, and agreement was reached. . . .
> They saw the white man's treaty as his way of offering them his help and friendship. They were willing to share their land with him in the manner prescribed by their tradition and culture. The two races would live side by side in the North, embarking on a common future. (Cited in Fumoleau, op. cit., pp. 210ff)

In 1921, as in 1899, the Dene wanted to retain their traditional way of life and to obtain guarantees against the encroachment of white settlers on their land. In fact Commissioner Conroy did guarantee the Dene full freedom to hunt, trap and fish, because many Dene negotiators were adamant that, unless the guarantee was given, they would not sign the treaty. To the Dene, this guarantee that the government would not interfere with their traditional life on the land was an affirmation, not an extinguishment, of their rights to their homeland.

It is important to understand the Dene's view of the treaty, because it explains the vehemence with which native witnesses told the Inquiry that the land is still theirs, that they have never sold it, and that it is not for sale.

Father Fumoleau has written an account of the Treaty negotiations at Fort Norman, based on the evidence of witnesses to the event:

Commissioner Conroy promised the people that this was their land.
"You can do whatever you want," he said. "We are not going to stop
you. . . ." This was the promise he made to the people . . . that we could
go hunting and fishing. . . .

    Then the Treaty party, Commissioner Conroy . . . said, "As long as
the Mackenzie River flows, and as long as the sun always comes around
the same direction every day, we will never break our promise." The
people and the Bishop said the same thing, so the people thought that
it was impossible that this would happen—the river would never reverse
and go back up-river, and the sun would never go reverse. This was
impossible, so they must be true. That is why we took the Treaty.
(Cited in Fumoleau, op. cit., pp. 180ff)

Joe Naedzo told the Inquiry at Fort Franklin that, according to the native people's
interpretation of the treaty, the government made "a law for themselves that as long
as the Mackenzie River flows in one direction, the sun rises and sets, we will not
bother you about your land or the animals." (C606)

    When the treaty commissioners reached Fort Rae in 1921, the Dogrib people
there were well aware that the promises the government had made to the Dogribs
and Chipewyans, who had signed the treaty at Fort Resolution in 1900, had not
been kept. The native people would not sign Treaty 11 unless the government
guaranteed hunting and trapping rights over the whole of their traditional territory.
This is Harry Black's account of the negotiations with the Dogribs:

Chief Monfwi stated that if his terms were met and agreed upon, then
there will be a treaty, but if his terms were not met, then "there will be
no treaty since you [Treaty Officials] are on my land." . . . The Indian
agent asked Chief Monfwi . . . what size of land he wanted for the band.
Monfwi stated . . . "The size of land has to be large enough for all of my
people." . . . Chief Monfwi asked for a land boundary starting from
Fort Providence, all along the Mackenzie River, right up to Great Bear
Lake, then across the Contwoyto Lake . . . Snowdrift, along the Great
Slave Lake, back to Fort Providence.

    The next day we crowded into the meeting tent again and began the
big discussion about the land boundary again. Finally they came to an
agreement and a land boundary was drawn up. Chief Monfwi said that
within this land boundary there will be no closed season on game so
long as the sun rises and the great river flows and only upon these
terms I will accept the treaty money. (Cited in Fumoleau, op. cit., pp.
192ff)

The Government of the Northwest Territories had, by this time, begun to take
shape. The first territorial government headquarters opened in Fort Smith in 1921,
and its first session was the same year, with oil the main item on the agenda. The
duties of the new administration included inspection of the oil well and of the country
to see if it was suitable for a pipeline.

The Dene had signed Treaties 8 and 11 on the understanding that they would be free to hunt and fish over their traditional territory, and that the government would protect them from the competition and intrusion of white trappers. Yet, contrary to treaty promises, an influx of white trappers and traders into the country was permitted to exploit the game resources almost at will, and soon strict game laws were necessary to save certain animal populations from extinction. The enforcement of these game laws caused hardship to the native people who depended on the animals for survival.

The encroachment of white trappers on lands that the native people regarded as their own led them to demand the establishment of game preserves in which only they would be permitted to hunt and trap. Frank T'Seleie told of such a request made by Father Antoine Binamé on behalf of the people of Fort Good Hope in 1928:

> At the present time the Indians are in fear of too many outside trappers getting into the districts outlined . . . and should these preserves be granted. . .the Indians would be more likely to endeavour to preserve the game in their own way. They at present are afraid of leaving the beaver colonies to breed up as the white man would in all likelihood come in and hunt them. (C1773)

The request was never granted, although some game preserves were established in other areas.

Wood Buffalo National Park was established in 1922 and enlarged in 1926. Shooting buffalo was strictly forbidden, although Treaty Indians were allowed to hunt other game and to trap furbearing animals in the park. These regulations were strictly enforced, and the protection of buffalo took precedence over the protection of Indian hunting rights.

In 1928, the government imposed a three-year closed season on beaver in the Mackenzie District. This regulation came at the worst possible time for the Dene, for that year they were decimated by an influenza epidemic. Other furbearing animals were scarce, and without beaver they were short of meat. The Dene at Fort Rae protested and refused to accept treaty payment until they had been assured that they could kill beaver. Bishop Breynat had appealed to the government on their behalf, and some modifications to the closed season were made. Despite continuing protests about the activities of white trappers, they received no protection from this threat. In 1937, the Indians of Fort Resolution again refused, as they had in 1920, to accept treaty payment in protest against their treatment by the government.

Finally, in 1938, legislation was passed to regulate the activity of white trappers and to restrict hunting and trapping licences only to those white persons who already held them. But, as Father Fumoleau told us, by this time most of the white trappers had turned from trapping to mining. At the same time that the native people had been restricted in their traditional activities, oil and mineral exploration and development had proceeded apace. In 1932, the richest uranium mine in the world began operation at Port Radium on Great Bear Lake. Gold was discovered in Yellowknife in 1933. In 1938, Norman Wells produced 22,000 barrels of oil, and in 1938–1939 the value of gold mined in the Northwest Territories exceeded for the first time the total value of raw furs produced.

The Dene insist the history of broken promises continues today. Jim Sittichinli, at the very first community hearing, held in Aklavik, related the recent experience of the native people:

> Now, at the time of the treaty . . . 55 years ago . . . they said, "As long as the river runs, as long as the sun goes up and down, and as long as you see that black mountain up there, well, you are entitled to your land."
>
> The river is still running. The sun still goes up and down and the black mountain is still up there, but today it seems that, the way our people understand, the government is giving up our land. It is giving [it up] to the seismic people and the other people coming up here, selling . . . our land. The government is not keeping its word, at least as some of us see it.
>
> Now, there has been lots of damage done already to this part of the northland, and if we don't say anything, it will get worse. . . .
>
> The other day I was taking a walk in Yellowknife. . .and I passed a house there with a dog tied outside. I didn't notice it and all of a sudden this dog jumped up and gave me a big bark, and then, after I passed through there, I was saying to myself, "Well, that dog taught me a lesson." You know, so often you [don't] see the native people, they are tied down too much, I think, by the government. We never go and bark, therefore nobody takes notice of us, and it is about time that we the people of this northland should get up sometime and bark and then we would be notied. (C87ff)

So far I have been describing treaties made with the Indians and Metis. No treaties were ever made with the Inuit, although the boundaries of Treaty 11 include part of the Mackenzie Delta that was occupied and used by the Inuit. They were not asked to sign the treaty in 1921 and, when they were invited to do so in 1929, they refused.

The absence of a treaty has made little difference to the Inuit, although they have been spared the invidious legal distinctions introduced among the Dene by treaty and non-treaty status. The Inuit witnesses who spoke to the Inquiry made clear that they, no less than the Dene, regard their traditional lands as their homeland. They also demand recognition of their rights to the land and their right to self-determination as a people. At Tuktoyaktuk, Vince Steen summarized the historical experience of the Inuit:

> A lot of people seem to wonder why the Eskimos don't take the white man's word at face value any more . . . Well, from my point of view, it goes way back, right back to when the Eskimos first saw the white man.
>
> Most of them were whalers, and the whaler wasn't very nice to the Eskimo. He just took all the whales he could get and never mind the

results. Who is paying for it now? The Eskimo. There is a quota on how many whales he can kill now.

Then next, following the whalers, the white traders and the white trappers. The white traders took them for every cent they could get. You know the stories in every history book where they had a pile of fur as high as your gun. Those things were not fair. The natives lived with it—damn well had to—to get that gun, to make life easier for himself.

Then there was the white trapper. He came along and he showed the Eskimo how to use the traps, steel-jawed traps, leg-hold traps. They used them, well they're still using them today, but for the first 70 years when they were being used, there were no complaints down south about how cruel those traps are—as long as there was white trappers using them. Now for the last five years they are even thinking of cutting us off, but they haven't showed us a new way of how to catch those foxes for their wives though.

After them, after the white trappers and the fur traders, we have all the settlements, all the government people coming in and making settlements all over, and telling the people what to do, what is best for them. Live here. Live there. That place is no good for you. Right here is your school. So they did—they all moved into settlements, and for the 1950s and 1960s they damn near starved. Most of them were on rations because they were not going out into the country any more. Their kids had to go to school.

Then came the oil companies. First the seismographic outfits, and like the Eskimo did for the last 50 or 60 years, he sat back and watched them. Couldn't do anything about it anyway, and he watched them plough up their land in the summertime, plough up their traps in the wintertime. What are you going to do about it? A cat [caterpillar tractor] is bigger than your skidoo or your dog team.

Then the oil companies. Well, the oil companies, I must say, of all of them so far that I have mentioned, seem to . . . have the most respect for the people and their ways; but it is too late. The people won't take a white man's word at face value any more because you fooled them too many times. You took everything they had and you gave them nothing. You took all the fur, took all the whales, killed all the polar bear with aircraft and everthing, and put a quota on top of that, so we can't have polar bear when we feel like it any more. All that we pay for. Same thing with the seismic outfits. . . .

Now they want to drill out there. Now they want to build a pipeline and they say they're not going to hurt the country while they do it. They're going to let the Eskimo live his way, but he can't because . . . the white man has not only gotten so that he's taken over, taken everthing out of the country . . . but he's also taken the culture, half of it anyway. . . .

For the Eskimo to believe now that the white man is not going to do any damage out there . . . is just about impossible, because he hasn't proven himself. As far as I'm concerned he hasn't proven himself worthy of being believed any more. . . .

The Eskimo is asking for a land settlement because he doesn't trust the white man any more to handle the land that he owns, and he figures he's owned for years and years. (C4199ff)

Remarks on Indian Aboriginal and Treaty Rights

[Part of a speech given August 8th, 1969 in Vancouver, British Columbia]

Prime Minister P.E. Trudeau

I think Canadians are not too proud about their past in the way in which they treated the Indian population of Canada and I don't think we have very great cause to be proud.

We have set the Indians apart as a race. We've set them apart in our laws. We've set them apart in the ways the governments will deal with them. They're not citizens of the province as the rest of us are. They are wards of the federal government. They get their services from the federal government rather than from the provincial or municipal governments. They have been set apart in law. They have been set apart in the relations with government and they've been set apart socially too.

So this year we came up with a proposal. It's a policy paper on the Indian problem. It proposes a set of solutions. It doesn't impose them on anybody. It proposes them— not only to the Indians but to all Canadians—not only to their federal representatives but to the provincial representatives too and it says we're at the crossroads. We can go on treating the Indians as having a special status. We can go on adding bricks of discrimination around the ghetto in which they live and at the same time perhaps helping them preserve certain cultural traits and certain ancestral rights. Or we can say you're at a crossroads—the time is now to decide whether the Indians will be a race apart in Canada or whether it will be Canadians of full status. And this is a difficult choice. It must be a very agonizing choice to the Indian peoples themselves because, on the one hand, they realize that if they come into the society as total citizens they will be equal under the law but they risk losing certain of their traditions, certain aspects of a culture and perhaps even certain of their basic rights and this is a very difficult choice for them to make and I don't think we want to try and force the pace on them any more than we can force it on the rest of Canadians but here again is a choice which is in our minds whether Canadians as a whole want to continue treating the Indian populations as something outside, a group of Canadians with which we have treaties, a group of Canadians who have as the Indians, many of them claim, aboriginal rights or whether we will say well forget the past and begin today and this is a tremendously difficult choice because, if—well, one of the things the Indian bands often refer to are their aboriginal rights and in our policy, the way we propose it, we say we won't recognize aboriginal rights. We will recognize treaty rights. We will recognize forms of contract which have been made with the Indian people by the Crown and we will try to bring justice in that area and this will mean that perhaps the treaties shouldn't go on forever. It's inconceivable, I think, that in a given society one section of the society have a treaty with the other section of the society. We must be all equal under the laws and we must not sign treaties amongst ourselves and many of these treaties, indeed, would have less and less significance in the future anyhow but things that in the past were covered by the treaties like things like so much twine or so much gun powder and which haven't been paid, this must be paid. But I don't think that we should encourage the Indians to feel that their treaties should last forever within Canada so that they be able to receive their twine or their gun powder. They should become Canadians as all other Canadians and if they are prosperous and wealthy they will be treated like the prosperous and wealthy and they will be paying taxes for the other Canadians who are not so prosperous and not so wealthy whether they be Indians or English Canadians or French or Maritimers and this is the only basis on which I see our society can develop as equals. But aboriginal rights, this really means saying, "We were here before you. You came and you took the land from us and perhaps you cheated us by giving us some worthless things in return for vast expanses of land and we want to re-open this question. We want you to preserve our aboriginal rights and to restore them to us." And our answer—it may not be the right one and may not be one which is accepted but it will be up to all of you people to make your minds up and to choose for or against it and to discuss with the Indians—our answer is "no."

If we think of restoring aboriginal rights to the Indians, well, what about the French who were defeated at the Plains of Abraham? Shouldn't we restore rights to them? And what about the Acadians who were deported—shouldn't we compensate for this? And what about the other Canadians, the immigrants? What about the Japanese Canadians who were so badly treated at the end of or during the last war? What can we do to redeem the past? I can only say as President Kennedy said when he was asked about what he would do to compensate for the injustices that the Negroes had received in American society. We will be just in our time. This is all we can do. We must be just today.

Questions

1. Does it matter that the native peoples were the first people in Canada?
2. If we restore rights to the native peoples, must we then restore rights to other groups in Canada who feel a grievance? Are the native peoples a special case?

Aboriginal Rights

Michael McDonald

How would you respond to the question "What sorts of treatment do the native peoples of Canada deserve?"

Since native peoples are amongst the most underprivileged Canadians, you might respond on the basis of your attitude to the poor. Thus, if you believe that Canadians should have welfare rights, then you would claim that Indians like other Canadians should not be allowed to fall below some national standard of minimum welfare. You may believe that this is best done through providing a guaranteed annual income or through the provision of various goods (such as food and housing) and various services (such as medical care and job training). You would then find yourself in agreement with Prime Minister Trudeau who in 1969 said that native people

> . . . should become Canadians as all other Canadians and if they are prosperous and wealthy they will be treated like the prosperous and wealthy and they will be paying taxes for the other Canadians who are not so prosperous and not so wealthy whether they be Indians or English Canadians or French or Maritimers and this is the only basis on which I see our society can develop as equals.

On the other hand, another person might make a libertarian response and deny that anyone has a right to welfare. He might argue that no one deserves "free passage"—that everyone should work his own way. The debate would then be joined over a whole set of familiar issues. What are the relative merits of free enterprise and planned economies? What does "equal opportunity" involve? How much may the government interfere in citizens' lives? And so the argument will wend its way over time-worn paths until one or both of you get tired and change the subject.

A very effective way of changing the subject is changing it so that you both wind up on opposite sides of the original question with you arguing against any special treatment for "the poor Indians" and your libertarian opponent demanding that they receive significant advantages from white society. I think this reversal is likely to happen if you shift the topic from welfare rights to aboriginal rights. Topic shifts of this sort, those which get the attacker and defender of a particular *status quo* to change places, very often provide interesting material for the political philosopher. Such is the case with aboriginal rights.

I. Entitlement Theory

What is the reason for this reversal in positions?

I would suggest that there is something different about the ways in which we

---

Reprinted from *Contemporary Issues in Political Philosophy*, ed. William Shea and John King-Farlow, Academic Publications Inc., New York.

ground welfare and aboriginal rights. That is, when we argue for someone's having a welfare right we usually base our arguments on quite different sorts of premises than when we argue for aboriginal rights. The initial problem is then to characterize these sorts of differences.

Fortunately, this task has been made easier by the recent publication of *Anarchy, State, and Utopia* (New York, 1974) by Robert Nozick, who defends Locke's libertarian political philosophy. He argues that neither more nor less than the minimum or night watchman state of *laissez-faire* economics can be justified. In the course of this argument, he has to explain how people may legitimately have the exclusive use of various things, i.e., how they may come to own things. It is this discussion of "justice in holdings" that sheds light on the salient differences between welfare and aboriginal rights.

According to Nozick there are two primary ways in which I can have a just holding. If the object is unowned, I may under certain conditions come to own it; this is called "justice in the original acquisition of holdings." If the object is owned, then its owner may under certain conditions transfer it to me; this is called "justice in the tansfer of holdings." Thus, for example, if you want to find out if the Atlantic salmon in my freezer is mine, you would want to know how I came to have the fish in my freezer: if I caught it, stole it, bought it, received it as a gift, etc. In short, you would ask for a history of ownership. The fish is mine if its original acquisition was just, and all subsequent transfers, if any, are also just. Insofar as you can trace this history, you can determine if I have *clear* title. To the extent that you cannot trace this history, it is not clearly mine, e.g., if all you know is that a friend gave it to me but you have no way of knowing how he got it, you can't say for certain that it really is mine.

If you get a clear history and then find that the original acquisition or one of the subsequent transfers was unjust, then you or someone else has the problem of deciding how to rectify this injustice in holdings. The rectification of injustice in holdings is the third part of Nozick's theory of just ownership. Thus, if you find out that my generous friend stole the salmon from a seafood store, you'll have to decide whether or not you should tell me to return it.

Now let us imagine that you decide to settle the question of my ownership of the salmon by using welfare principles solely. Let us assume that whatever welfare criterion you intend to use will only apply to the two of us in this case. First, you appeal to "need." You say that you are hungry and desperately short of protein, while I am not; since needs should be satisfied, you should have the fish. Say that I ignore that plea, so you try a hedonic appeal: you claim that you will enjoy eating the salmon much more than I will; hence, by the greatest happiness principle, you should have the salmon. It is not difficult in either appeal to imagine how I would have to respond to prove that I have a better title to the fish according to the criterion used. I would argue that I am needier than you or that I would really enjoy it more than you. Further it is not difficult to imagine the two criteria coming into conflict: you need the protein, but I would enjoy the dinner more. Then we would have to sort out which criterion takes precedence, e.g., that needs take precedence over wants. It is also not difficult to foresee some of the problems we might have in applying these considerations: how can I compare my need or enjoyment with yours, how can we properly take into account the effects of giving the fish to you or to me on each of our future needs or enjoyments, how do we know what counts as a "need" as opposed to what counts as a "want"? These are all problems which make up the bulk of philosophical debate about utilitarianism.

In our argument about who has the better welfare claim to the fish we proceed in a quite different way than we did earlier in trying to decide if the fish was a just holding of mine. Then we asked if the salmon had been justly acquired by me or justly transferred to me; in short, we looked backwards in time to see how the fish came into my possession. In the second case, we applied welfare criteria by looking to our present and future conditions to decide the issue according to our relative positions on the scale of need or enjoyment. Two major differences in the determination of ownership stand out in these cases: these are different attitudes to (a) the past and the future, and (b) the characteristics of the affected parties. Both (a) and (b) require some further explanation.

Regarding (a), we have seen that what mattered in determining justice in holdings were the acquisitions and transfers of the object; that is to say, the principle for the determination of ownership was *historical*. In the use of welfare criteria, we looked only at present and future considerations, viz. the relative degrees to which my or your having the fish would meet present and future needs or yield present and future enjoyment. Here we decided who owned the salmon on the basis of *end-results*. Our approach in the second case was *ahistorical*.

Regarding (b), you will recall that in the application of the welfare criteria we were concerned with the degree to which each of us had or lacked certain characteristics: if you were needier or would enjoy it more, then the fish should be yours. We were concerned in this case with the resulting *patterns* of the alternative distributions. In the first case, however, we proceeded without reference to patterns. There were no characteristics (such as need) which I might or might not have that would be determinative of the question of my ownership. It mattered not why I caught the fish (e.g., that I was trying to satisfy my hunger or pass the time of day) or even what I would do with it (e.g., eat it, throw it back in the stream, or use if for fertilizer). Nor did it matter why someone transferred it to me (e.g., because I paid for it, because I am his son, or because he simply felt like it). In fact it doesn't even matter if I have a freezer full of Atlantic salmon and you have none or even no food at all. Justice in holdings is *unpatterned* in that there is no natural dimension (what I call a "characteristic") or set of dimensions according to which the distribution of goods should take place.

II. Aboriginal Rights

We can now see how Nozick's approach to justice in holdings, which he calls "entitlement theory," ties in with the topic of aboriginal rights. Aboriginal rights are none other than original acquisition rights which haven't been transferred to anyone else. To defend the aboriginal rights of Canada's native peoples necessarily involves us in presenting a theory of original acquisition. Moreover, we must be willing to defend our theory of original acquisition against not only rival theories of original acquisition, but also against non-entitlement theories of ownership.

At the beginning of this paper, the argument about providing help to native people was carried on between a person who held a non-entitlement theory of the distribution of goods and one who held an entitlement theory. As you recall, one argued that native people should be helped on the basis of need. This, we have just seen, is an argument based on end-results and patterns. The other disputant argued that native people were not entitled to help. This argument is essentially historical and unpatterned.

Introducing aboriginal rights into the argument forced a change in the disputants' positions because it introduced a historical and unpatterned basis for the native peoples' entitlement. Now it was possible for the libertarian defender of property rights to argue that the natives had been dealt a historic injustice which stands in need of rectification. The defender of welfare rights must reject this approach, not because native people shouldn't receive significant benefits, but because in his view the only true basis for the reception of benefits is need. That is, he was arguing that benefits should be distributed in a patterned way with a view to the end-results achievable.

Now it is important to realize that we cannot simply let the disputants "agree to disagree." In practical terms, we are talking about claims to at least half of Canada. According to Peter Cumming and Neil Mickenberg in the second edition of *Native Rights in Canada* (Toronto, 1972), aboriginal claims have been superseded by treaties for less than one half of Canada. This would leave standing aboriginal claims to British Columbia, Quebec, the Maritimes, the Yukon, and parts of the Northwest Territories. Think of what this means to established settlements and to plans for Northern development. Remember, too, that "the natives are restless": they have been pressing their claims in the courts (in 1973 the Supreme Court of Canada split four to three against admitting an aboriginal claim), over the bargaining table (in Quebec native people have received a large cash and land settlement for allowing the James Bay Project to proceed in a scaled down form), at the barricades (in British Columbia), and before a royal commission (Mr. Justice Berger is carrying out an investigation of the effect of the proposed Mackenzie Valley Pipeline on native peoples). The questions of aboriginal rights is a real, not an ivory-tower, question.

In my examination of this question, I do not intend to say much more about non-entitlement theories except by way of contrast to entitlement theories. I shall instead focus on various problems that I see in the application of Nozickian and Lockean entitlement theories to the question of aboriginal rights in Canada. I will argue that some of the problems anticipated in such an application of entitlement theory can be adequately handled, but that other problems—particularly those at the core—are much more difficult and may well be insurmountable.

I shall proceed by presenting a number of objections to an entitlement defence of aboriginal rights. I shall first state the objection in the broad and general way it occurs in non-philosophical discussion. Here I have tried to draw upon statements made by politicians, lawyers, and native people, as well as from discussions I've had with students and colleagues. This response will consist, first, in sorting out various objections that have been confused and run together in the non-philosophical context. After that, I shall see what kind of reply can be made within an entitlement theory. I have tried to give each objection a name which suggests the sort of objection made and renders the arguments easier to remember. This mnemonic aid is important because the arguments are often interrelated and used together for or against aboriginal rights.

A. The Vandals Argument

This is the kind of argument that Trudeau has used:

> If we think of restoring aboriginal rights to the Indians, well, what about the French who were defeated at the Plains of Abraham? Shouldn't we restore rights to them? And what about the Acadians who were deported—shouldn't we compensate for this? And what about the other Canadians, the immigrants? What about the Japanese Canadians who were so badly treated at the end [of] or during the last war?

A similar position was taken by many Americans in response to James Forman's demand that American churches and synagogues pay $500 million as reparations for years of slavery. In his book, *The Case for Black Reparations* (New York, 1973), Yale law professor Boris Bittker cites the *New York Times* response to Forman: "There is neither wealth nor wisdom enough in the world to compensate for all the wrongs in history."

An objector might ask if the descendents of the Roman victims of the Vandals' sack of Rome in 453 A.D. should be able to sue the Vandals' descendents? Here, however, we see the need to distinguish two separate objections. The first is what I shall call "Historical Disentanglement," and the second "Arbitrariness."

A.1. Historical Disentanglement. The first objection rests on practical difficulties in sorting out historical issues. The problem is to find out who is a descendent of the victims of an injustice and who is a descendent of the perpetrators of that injustice. In the Vandals' case the problems seem well-nigh insuperable. Even if some sorting out is possible, there will probably be enough intermarriage to confuse most cases thoroughly. Intermarriage has been alleged a serious barrier to reparations to blacks in the United States.

In the case we are considering, however—that of native Canadians—we can get some powerful assistance from the facts. A quarter of a million Indians are registered under the Indian Act of 1951 as members of recognized bands. While we may have problems with the fairness of some of the provisions of that Act (e.g., Indian women who marry non-Indian males are deregistered and non-Indian females who marry Indian males are automatically registered), the fact remains that we have an accurate, though somewhat incomplete, record of many descendents of the purported victims of injustice. The cases of the unregistered Indians and of the Metis are more difficult, but we have two important facts which will help disentangle matters. First, these people have regarded themselves as native people. And secondly, they have been regarded by white Canadians as natives insofar as they have been objects of the same informal extra-legal distinctions (including racial prejudices) as those under the Indian Act. It should not prove to be too difficult to arrive at a consensus on who is or is not a native person amongst the Metis and other unregistered claimants of this status.

This, of course, leaves the question of tracing the descendents of those purported to have violated aboriginal title. Here again the facts help us—in this case it is the legal fact that only the Crown could seize land. In the case of New France, we can regard the Crown as the inheritor of whatever title France had to aboriginal lands.

It is also possible that we might in hard cases make use of a test Nozick suggests for determining the descendents of victims and perpetrators on the grounds that *persistent* inequalities are most likely a result of historical injustice. (While Nozick does not suggest "persistency" as a criterion here, I think it might make his suggestion more plausible.)

A.2. Arbitrariness.   The second distinct element in the Vandals Argument is the suggestion that the defender of aboriginal rights wants to make an arbitrary and invidious distinction between rectifying the injustices done to aboriginal peoples and the injustices done to non-aboriginal Canadians. This is, I think, what Trudeau was asking, namely, how could we defend rectifying the injustices done to the Indians and ignore the injustices done by our nation to the French, the Acadians, and Japanese?

Trudeau goes on to say that we cannot "redeem the past"; we can only be "just in our time." This seems to let us argue that if we can't wholly rectify all the injustices we have ever done, then we needn't rectify any. The most favourable interpretation that I can put on Trudeau's conclusion is that we may have to face a multiplicity of competing claims of all sorts including a number of competing claims for the rectification of past injustices. We may then not be able to do everything that we ought ideally to do; in an imperfect world we may have to pay our most morally pressing debts in full and make only token payments on the remainder. There need be no arbitrariness in the recognition of aboriginal rights, for we can still recognise other past and present injustices. We may not be able to fully satisfy all the claims for rectification, but that isn't arbitrary either—there is no obligation to do more than one can.

B. The Forefathers Argument

There is another way of taking Trudeau's conclusion that we cannot redeem the past, and that is to say that we are only responsible for our sins and not for the sins of our fathers. How can I be blamed for what my French-Canadian ancestors did to the Indians of New France? How can anyone do more than be just in his own time?

Let's sort out this argument.

B.1. Backwards Causation.   The first thing to clarify is whether saying that I ought to rectify injustice *X* involves saying that I am one of *X*'s causes. If my children ruin my neighbour's prize roses, may I not have an obligation to make reparations? If I do, it needn't be the case that in so doing I am admitting that it was I who tramped through the roses. I may not even have to admit that it was somehow my fault that my children were in the garden. I may have told my children to stay out of the garden. Moreover, I may have done the best I can to instill in them a sense of respect for others' property. Then there is nothing more that I should have done.

(After all, there are outward bounds like child abuse for determining how far a parent can go in instructing his children.) Indeed my children may not have acted deliberately, purposely, or even intentionally; it was an accident pure and simple, for which even they are not to blame. But there it is: the roses are ruined, and I am the one who should set it right.

The point is that "responsibility" can be used in a variety of ways. Sometimes it is used to indicate causality, in which case contemporaneousness or precedence in time is essential. But in the rose garden case, it was used to indicate who was *liable* for damages. The concept of liability is most highly developed within the law, but we do use it outside the law in our ordinary attributions of moral responsibility. The question then is whether anyone today has liability for the past violations (if any) of aboriginal rights.

There is a further confusion in this argument. This is to claim that backwards causation must be involved because I can only have obligations of my own making. Thus, I could have an obligation to contemporary native peoples respecting aboriginal rights only if I had undertaken to respect these rights, i.e., if I made a promise to or contract with their ancestors. It will take only a moment's reflection, however, to see that many obligations we have are not entered into voluntarily (or involuntarily either), e.g., not to kill, to express gratitude for favours received, to be kind, and to be honest.

B.2. Benefits Received.   In (B.1) I didn't really so much respond to the Forefathers Argument as clear the way for a response to it. That liability-responsibility is different from causal-responsibility is important; nevertheless, it does not tell us if Canadians today have liability-responsibility for violations of aboriginal title. Neither does knowing that all obligations are not of our own making tell us if the rectification of this putative injustice is our responsibility.

A much more telling response is an analogy with the receipt of stolen goods. If person *A* steals person *B*'s watch and then makes a present of it to *C*, do we think that *C* has an obligation to return it to *B* even though he had no idea that he was in receipt of stolen goods when he accepted the watch? Surely, the answer is "Yes!" We might go on to say that *A* owes *C* something (an apology at minimum) for inconveniencing and embarrassing him. We would, I think, give the save answer even if the thief *A* can't recompense *C* (say that *A* is now dead). It is worth noting here that no one is blaming *C* for *A*'s stealing *B*'s watch or even for unwittingly accepting stolen property. *C* needn't feel any guilt about either of these matters. He should, however, feel guilt if he doesn't return the watch to *B*. I see no reason to change our views about returning the watch if instead of talking about *B* and *C* we talk about their heirs. I would not extend this to *A*'s heirs, however, who presumably have not benefitted either from *A*'s theft, itself, or the gift of the watch to *C*.

The parallels with the case of aboriginal rights should be fairly obvious. Non-Indians have in Canada benefitted (albeit in very unequal degrees) from the non-compensated supercession of aboriginal title. This is not to say that non-Indians *today* refused to compensate native people for the loss of aboriginal rights *during* the last and preceding centuries. These non-Indians certainly can't be held responsible for being born into this society or for immigrating to it. In this respect, breast-beating over what has been done to the "poor native" is neither due nor appropriate. Guilt is appropriate only if nothing is done to remedy injustices in the treatment of native people including, in particular, the rectification of past injustices.

Of course, the case for reparations becomes more difficult if we change the analogy somewhat. For example, what, if anything, does C owe B if after C receives the watch he loses it? It would be different if C were keeping B's watch in trust for B, for then he could well be responsible for not losing it. This problem posed by lost or ruined articles seems quite likely to occur with the passage of significant periods of time. If we are talking about C's and B's great-grandchildren, the odds are that by this time the watch has been lost or no longer works.

That is, I think, the kind of thing that Bittker has in mind when he says that there would be no case for reparations to blacks if in the period since the Civil War there had been an unbroken ascent up to a present state of genuine equality. That is, the argument here is that reparations are not due if the relative advantage seized by the act of injustice gets lost or equalised in the course of history, so that it no longer makes any difference. It is *not* crucial to this argument that *both* the benefits accruing to the oppressors and their heirs and the evils suffered by the victims and their heirs no longer remain. It is enough to have the first without the second.

B.3. Inheritance.　There is a way of taking the Forefathers Argument that avoids the reply just advanced (B.2.). There I argued that if you can inherit benefits, you can inherit burdens chargeable against those benefits. This is like having to pay estate taxes and creditors before receiving an inheritance. As we have just seen, if you inherit nothing, you do not have any obligation (save, perhaps, "a debt of honour") to pay any debts chargeable against the estate. This suggests that there would be no aboriginal rights if there were no rights to make bequests; that is, aboriginal rights disappear if no one may rightfully inherit anything.

Native people could use this as an effective *ad hominem* argument in pressing their case. They could say to the rich and powerful in our society that Indians and Innuit will give up their claims to aboriginal rights if the rich and powerful will surrender all the property that they have inherited. This would not mean the end of private property but only the aspect of it—which I call "bequeathability." Other aspects of private property would remain (viz. rights of alienability, exclusive use, security, management, income, and so forth) but these "standard incidents" of property would be limited to the life of the holder. (To make this suggestion effective, we would have to set a limit to the life of corporations, for under our laws these "artificial persons" can be immortal.)

C. The Double Wrong Argument

The objection here is that to rectify one injustice another will have to be done, so that in rectifying the injustice done to the native peoples an injustice will have to be done to non-native Canadians by taking away from them land or the profits therefrom which they have in good faith purchased and improved. Moreover, the settlement of aboriginal claims will impose an enormous burden on those who in some cases are already disadvantaged.

The main response to this has already been made in the Forefathers Argument

(B.2.). No one has a right to receive and retain what is not another's to give. "Good faith" here excuses one from complicity in the original theft: one is not to blame for the theft, so one needn't feel guilty about it. It does not excuse one from returning the stolen goods or the equivalent. Remember that we are working within the context of entitlement theory; justice in holding demands, justice in acquisition, and transfers. To give weight to the claims of those who have unjust holdings is just the sort of thing end-result theorists would do.

Nevertheless, the entitlement theorist can reduce the practical force of this objection by pointing out that third party beneficiaries (here, non-Indian and non-Innuit property owners) must return what remains of that which was wrongfully transferred to them. Given the ravages of time, one may not have to surrender any of one's own goods in making this reparation because nothing of value remains. I say "may not" because among the benefits received from the stolen property is that there is less drain on one's own resources. Thus, in the watch analogy, C or his heirs may benefit from not having to purchase watches of their own because they have the use of the watch stolen from B. So if the watch breaks after a few years while in C's possession, B might ask for rent for the use of his watch over the years before it broke. If C is now bankrupt, there may be little B can get (unless it is the case that entitlement theory would demand that C work the rent off). If it is the case that in addition to bankruptcy C also dies, then B cannot demand that C's would-be heirs pay for it out of their own justly acquired resources (including working the debt off). Death without the transmission of a benefice would seem on the entitlement theory to end the case for repayment simply because the unjust holding no longer exists. Presumably, in this wealthy nation, most of the benefit has been transmitted to us.

A final remark on the plight of the small property holder. According to the principles of rectification of injustice in holdings, it surely must be the case that those who have benefitted most from unjust holdings owe more than those who have benefitted least. Keeping in mind the complications about inheritance discussed earlier, it should be the case that in a society like ours, in which most wealth—especially capital—remains concentrated in a few families, the wealthiest would have the most to lose by the recognition of aboriginal rights. Here I would think especially of those who have benefitted most from the exploitation of natural resources (like gas, oil, and minerals) in the areas in question, particularly Alberta, the North, and B.C. Of course, it has already been argued (B.3.) that these same people have the most to lose by denying aboriginal claims for they would thereby undermine their own claims to inherited wealth.

D. The Sovereignty Argument

In an article in *The Globe and Mail* (21 February 1973), Cumming has suggested that one possible reason for the Government's reluctance to recognise aboriginal rights is the fear that in so doing there would be a recognition of aboriginal sovereignty over the lands in question, to wit, Trudeau's reference to the Plains of Abraham. This is evident, too, in the same speech when Trudeau says, "It's inconceivable, I think, that in a given society one section of society have a treaty with another section of society." Trudeau is not the only politician in Canada's history to express concern about holding the country together; this is a country which has been plagued by threats of separatism—from Quebec, the West, and the Maritimes.

If it is the case that the recognition of aboriginal rights would necessarily involve a recognition of a separate aboriginal nation or nations then it is not clear what an entitlement theorist like Nozick would say. Nozick's invisible hand explanation of the emergence of a dominant protection agency as the (minimal) state never comes to grips with the fact that there is more than one nation in this complicated world. The fact of nationalism should also have some effect on Nozick's proposal for utopia—allowing diverse experiments in types of communities *within* a single nation. Are nationalists entirely wrong when they think that they must have control over the state and not just over the community? Another interesting way of putting this question is to ask what sorts of self-determination (determination particularly of a group's identity) are not possible in a libertarian society? Leaving aside these complex and difficult questions, it is possible to argue that if sovereignty is an issue here, then surely we must talk about more than justice in holdings.

The simplest way of dealing with this objection is to deny, as Cumming does, that sovereignty and property rights are connected except in an indirect way. In ordinary disputes over land ownership, neither claimant is trying to set up an independent nation. The adjudication usually follows the laws of the nation in which the property is situated. Although in a few difficult cases there can be arguments about which of two nation's laws are applicable, the dispute is primarily about ownership and only secondarily about sovereignty. It should be pointed out that no less an entitlement theorist like Locke claimed that rights to property are quite independent of rights to rule, for he maintained that property rights should survive changes in government including violent changes brought about by war.

E. The Litigation Argument

The general argument here is that claims to aboriginal title are unlike ordinary property claims. They are not amenable to the usual sorts of tests used by the courts to decide property rights. In particular many aboriginal claims are such as to deny courts the use of a most effective procedure for deciding between rival claims in cases where due to the passage of time both records are missing and memories are uncertain, namely, "prescription" which is "the operation of time as a vestitive fact." If this is correct, then how can anyone maintain that aboriginal claims can be settled in the same way as ordinary disputes about ownership? Indeed, how can anyone maintain that they are property rights at all?

This argument can be taken in part as a necessary corrective to the oversimplified reply that I just advanced against the Sovereignty Argument. There I argued that sovereignty and property where different kinds of rights. This may have left the impression that all property rights are alike and that aboriginal rights are like other property-rights. Neither of these contentions is true.

I agree with A.M. Honore that "property" is probably best thought of in terms of a list of "the standard incidents of ownership." This would be a list of the rights which a property owner has in the standard, full-blown case. It would include rights of physical possession, use, derivation of profit and capital, security, management, and so forth. One would probably also have to say something about the duties of ownership as well, in particular the prohibition of harmful use. If some of these incidents are missing in a particular case, we could still talk about "property-rights." In fact all the Indian treaties deny Indians the liberty of converting their reserves into capital, i.e., they may not alienate their lands, only the Crown may. In this sense, reserves could be seen as belonging to a particular people in perpetuity, not just to its present-day occupants; thus, future generations would have patrimonial rights. Aboriginal land claims involve the same kind of arrangement. (I should add here that if a whole people, conceived as a group extending across time into the future, can have property rights, then such a right might well play havoc with many of the positions that Nozick defends on the basis of actions in a free market.)

So part of my reply to this argument is that while aboriginal titles may lack some of the standard incidents of property it may well be possible to still think of them as property rights. To properly establish this reply would require a great deal more space than I presently have. I think more needs to be said, however, about this argument along somewhat different lines.

First, there is the issue of "prescription." In the law it is the case that the passage of time can extinguish or establish ownership. This is determined by time limits established by custom or statute. For example, in some jurisdictions if you have made use of part of someone else's land as a right-of-way for twenty years, then the courts will uphold your right to continue to do so and thus bar the landowner from preventing your passage. Thus time has given you a right you formerly did not have and extinguished a property-right that the landowner had. The point of prescription is quite straightforward: the passage of time is used as a conclusive evidence because it simplifies the work of the courts in determining ownership. Thus, the jurist Savigny said, "All property is founded in adverse possession ripened by prescription."

The problem for aboriginal claims is that in many cases the land claimed is not now and has not been occupied by the claimants at all or on an exclusive basis for many years more than the limits set by law for the extinguishment of title. Yet it seems unfair therefore to deny title even though it is fair to do so in ordinary cases. In ordinary cases the law protects the property-owner's exercise of his property-rights before the period of prescription has elapsed. That is, if he wants to prevent his title from lapsing, he need only take action. Thus, in the right-of-way case, the property-owner can put up a "no trespassing" sign before the twenty years are out; this completely extinguishes your claim to a legally guaranteed right-of-way. If it is illegal to post the sign, then using the passage of time to effect a transfer of title would be unfair. The parallel here is that native peoples have not been given an opportunity to present their aboriginal claims, either through the courts or directly to government.

Secondly, the Litigation Argument does raise important doubts about the appropriate *forum* for the determination of the value and extent of various aboriginal claims. Cummings says that "the court is by far the least appropriate forum for dealing with aboriginal rights" because "litigation is expensive, time-consuming, and abounds with technical difficulties." He proposes instead that there be direct negotiations between the government and native peoples. Thus, this is essentially a practical, not an in-principle concern.

Thirdly, the Litigation Argument hints at a problem which will concern us in the next and final section. The problem, as seen from the perspective of this Argument, concerns the relationship between particular property-rights and the existing legal system. One way of finding the general area of difficulty is to ask if there can be property without laws? If there cannot be property without laws (as has been argued by generations of contractarians, Kant among them), then is property merely a creature of law? If property-rights can only be created and destroyed by law, what must be said about the entitlement theorists' claim that we have a natural right to "estate" in addition to "life and liberty"? In the next section I will consider some of these questions.

F. The Acquisition Arguments

Thus far, in all the objections and replies, I have tried to apply entitlement theory to the question of aboriginal rights. If I am right, then a number of interesting and plausible objections to entitlement theory and its application can be answered. In neither the objections nor the replies have I asked if native people actually have a claim to these lands on the basis of just original acquisition; for the sake of argument I have assumed that they do, and then gone to ask whether such claims should be recognised. Obviously, if native people in general or in particular did *not* make a just original acquisition of the land, the whole case for aboriginal rights fails. This would not show that all the native peoples' claims to land ownership are null and void, but it would remove the most important and the largest claims.

There is more than this practical issue at stake here. The whole entitlement theory rests on original acquisition. If the justice of an original acquisition is called into question then so also, Nozick says, are all subsequent transfers. If *all* original acquisitions can be called into question, then, perhaps, all claims to property rights are challengeable. One way of calling all aboriginal acquisitions into question is to deny that sense can be made of the concept of "original acquisition." Another way would be to deny that original acquisition as imagined by entitlement theorists can be a basis for rightful ownership.

So now I will turn to the "keystone" issue. I should say that some of the sharpest criticisms of the original acquisition doctrine come from Nozick himself. He writes in an almost ironic, or shall I say, "contrapuntal" way that involves the reader and enlivens debate. I will present four objections and responses. The responses, I should indicate, are partial and do not, I think, save entitlement theory (though, curiously enough, they save aboriginal rights).

F.1. The Jus Tertii Argument.   One way of challenging aboriginal rights *within* the framework of entitlement theory is to deny that the Indians and Innuit had made original and just acquisition. This could be denied on the grounds that Indians and Innuit weren't the first human beings in Canada and that Indians and Innuit acquired the northern half of this continent by force. In any event, given the lack of records of property acquisition, it could be claimed that no one can know for certain if the native peoples' ancestors acquired the lands justly as either first possessors or as a result of just transfer. This would at the very least make aboriginal claims suspect.

The argument presented here rests on a claim like the following: if Bill's acquisition of Blackacres from Alice is unjust, then Chuck's acquisition of the land from Bill need not follow the rules of just transfer in order to get as good, or better, title than Bill has to Blackacres. The underlying contention is that if title is, so to speak, "spoiled" at any point the property is simply up for grabs. Here I am assuming that the just owner Alice is not laying claim to Blackacres and that Chuck is in no way acting on behalf of Alice. The question is not, then, one of Chuck's rectifying an injustice done to Alice by Bill. The objection rests on the contention that given Alice's not laying or transferring her claim to another, Bill's act of injustice returns Blackacres to an ownerless situation from which Chuck may claim it.

Before questioning this contention, I would note that even accepting this reasoning there still is a difference between showing that Bill's title is spoiled and raising a suspicion that it may not be clear. In some cases, it simply is impossible for a possessor to prove that he has clear title; however, this does not mean that others can prove that he does not. Surely the burden of proof rests on those who charge wrongful possession.

Now as to the argument itself, it is worth noting that the practice under common law is not to establish ownership *absolutely* but *only relatively*, i.e., to decide who has a *better* right to possess. It would, I believe, be the case that a court would hold that Bill has a better title to Blackacres than Chuck and Alice has a better title to Blackacres than Bill. Regardless of the court's decision, it is certainly more convenient for a court to decide matters in this relative way (adjudicating only between the rival claims presented to it) rather than trying to do this once and for all (which would involve ruling on every conceivable claim). In this case, the court would settle the dispute between Bill and Chuck leaving it to others such as Alice to bring suit separately.

Which approach should an entitlement theorist adopt—that unjust acquisition or transfer returns the object to an ownerless condition or that it simply "weakens" the possessor's title? I wonder if in answering this question we will have to fall back on utilitarian considerations, e.g., about which procedure would be the most orderly and least disruptive for a given society. I am not sure how this question would be decided on purely entitlement grounds. That is, I don't know what *natural* rights to the ownership of Blackacres are held by Bill as opposed to Chuck. I would suspect that this cannot be determined without a *policy* decision about the rules governing property. Entitlement theory does not say which is the appropriate way of deciding ownership in this case. If this is right then it indicates an important gap in entitlement theory, for it means that the theory of justice in holdings has to be patched up by resorting to utilitarianism.

Apropos the question of aboriginal rights, it would seem that if we proceed on the basis of who has better title rather than on the basis of who has absolute title, then native people's claims would seem to be stronger than those of successive possessors.

F.2 The Spoilage Argument In *The Second Treatise of Government*, Locke presents an objection to his view of justice in original acquisition:

> That if gathering the Acorns, or other Fruits of the Earth, &c. makes a right to them, then any one may *ingross* as much as he will.

Locke says that this is not so; one may take "as much as one can make use of to any advantage of life before it spoils . . . Whatever is beyond this, is more than his share and belongs to others." Locke grounds this limitation of original acquisition on God's will: "Nothing was made by God for Man to spoil or destroy." Yet it is clear that God's will is not capricious, for as Locke says earlier:

> God, who hath given the World to Men in common, hath also given them reason to make use of it to the best advantage of Life and convenience.

Men then have a right to self-preservation which entitles them to take the means thereto, viz. by acquiring the necessaries of life. Self-preservation grounds appropriation and sets limits to it.

Now it could be argued that the spoilage provision sets the limits too widely in that it allows me to refuse to share my bounty with my starving neighbours so long as I can use that bounty for "the best advantage of [my] Life and convenience." Matters are weighted heavily in favour of the propertied and against those without property. But let us for the sake of argument accept spoilage as an outward limit of just original acquisition. We can then ask whether native peoples violated the spoilage principle in acquiring these lands. If they did and if the Europeans who came here could make use of the wasted portions, then aboriginal claims may be defensible on the grounds of wastage.

If this question is answerable, it would have to be on the basis of historical evidence; however, it is fair for the philosopher to ask about the determination of the criteria for wastage and spoilage: by what marks do we identify something as waste? Here it is tempting to ask if the thing in question is used for anyone's benefit. But will any minute amount of incremental benefit suffice to justify ownership or must there be some standard margin of benefit for this use to count here for title? Must there also be standards of efficient use? Would there be a combined standard, e.g., "Makes the best use of X for the greatest benefit"? Any benefit or efficiency standard would seem to be hopelessly utilitarian and redistributivist. On the other hand, having no standards at all would effectively deny a right of self-preservation to those without property and the correlative duty to share for the propertied.

If we try to fix on some mid-point (i.e., having a spoilage provision which is compatible with entitlement theory), then the question is how to justify our selection of standards on an entitlement basis. This is a particularly troublesome question in the case of aboriginal rights. In many cases an advanced agricultural and industrialised economy came into contact with a hunting, fishing, and gathering economy. The patterns of resource use were bound to be different. What would appear as under-utilisation in one economy might appear as over-utilisation in the other. Clearly Canada's native peoples made ingenious use of the often harsh environment, but their uses could not support the numbers of people that present-day uses can. (In this paper I am being deliberately silent about how much longer we can continue our use-patterns.) However, if we move in the direction of giving title to the Europeans rather than the native peoples, then we would have to surrender our ownership claims to any society which could support more people here more efficiently. This seems quite obviously in direct opposition to the whole thrust of an *entitlement* theory: if I am entitled to something, if it's *mine*, then I should within the limit of non-harmfulness be able to use it as efficiently or as inefficiently as I wish for whosoever's advantage I choose. This would accord with Nozick's slogan: "From each as they choose, to each as they are chosen."

Tentatively, then, if we are willing to deny the right of self-preservation and more especially the correlative duty of sharing when necessary to provide it, then we can still hold the entitlement theory and so avoid the conceptual difficulties posed by the spoilage principle.

F.3. The "Proviso" Argument   Spoilage is not the only limit Locke sets to original acquisition; he also suggests what Nozick calls "the Lockean Proviso," namely that there be "enough and as good left in common for others." This Nozick says, "is meant to ensure that the position of others is not worsened." Thus, we can imagine a parallel argument to the Spoilage Argument being advanced against aboriginal rights on the grounds that aboriginal possession violated the enough-and-as-good proviso.

Factually, this is going to be a tricky argument to work out for not only must it be shown that the native people did not leave enough and as good to the immigrants, but also that the immigrants have take just enough to rectify this violation of the proviso. This will be very hard to prove, given the relative wealth of natives and immigrants. At present, indeed, native people could justifiably argue that the immigrants haven't left enough and as good to them.

Here, as in the Spoilage Argument, there are serious conceptual problems in determining the appropriate criteria. Nozick advances two interpretations of the Proviso:

> Someone may be made worse off by another's appropriation in two ways: first by losing the opportunity to improve his situation by a particular appropriation or any one, and second, by no longer being able to use freely (without appropriation) what he previously could.

Nozick accepts the second or "weaker requirement" and not the first or "the stringent requirement." The difference between the two seems to be between characterizing the proviso as applying to appropriation (ownership) or to use. But then it must be remembered that earlier Nozick says that "the central core of the notion of a property right in X is "the right to determine what shall be done with X." If I have have a right to use X, then would I not have a property right in X?

Be that as it may, Nozick argues that those who are unable to appropriate (because everything is now owned) are likely to be compensated for this restriction on their liberty by having their prospects increased by a system which allows (virtually unlimited) private acquisition. Nozick says the free market will make up for their loss of acquisition and/or use rights. The point is to compensate these people enough for not being able to appropriate or use what they could have had they been born earlier. Nozick suggests that the level of compensation can be determined by getting "an estimate of the general economic importance of appropriation."

But this, I suggest, won't do for several reasons. First, if this isn't forcing on someone a kind of compensation that he doesn't want, then in the case of those who really want to make acquisitions the state will have to take something away from various property-owners. Secondly, as my colleague Jan Narveson has argued, the level of compensation will probably have to be set high enough to amount to a tidy guaranteeed annual income. Thirdly, it isn't clear how much compensation is to be given to any particular propertyless person. Does he get as much as he would have been likely to get if he were in the position of the last person who acquired property or as much as if he were the first person to acquire property? In either case, the primary basis for distribution (his acquisitiveness) seems suspiciously patterned. Fourth, if the benefits of a free market economy really do provide enough compensation, then why does it seem so unlikely that anyone who has more than a little property, e.g., E.P. Taylor, would want to change places with one of these people who can't acquire any property because everything is owned?

All of which suggests that on a *pure* entitlement theory—one which is based on historical entitlement—there would be no room for the Proviso. On a pure entitlement theory if you are born after all the accessible and useful unowned objects have been taken up by your predecessors, you are simply out of luck. This denial of the Proviso would also seem to be in agreement with Nozick's criticisms of Rawls' contention that a system of natural liberties allows distribution on morally arbitrary grounds—that the distribution of natural talents is not on the basis of desert leads Rawls to design the social system to compensate for this "arbitrariness" by favouring (other things being equal) the least talented in the distribution of goods. Nozick criticises this is a "manna-from-heaven" model that totally ignores who has made these goods, i.e., Rawls ignores the crucial fact of historical entitlement. Similarly, the Proviso seems to ignore the crucial fact of appropriation.

Finally, as in the Spoilage Argument, we can ask what it is to leave "enough and as good"? If the standard is *usability*, then do we adopt the native peoples' idea of what is usable or the non-native immigrants'? If we defend the latter, then in effect we are denying native peoples their ways of life. According to the Proviso, this would seem to demand that we compensate the native peoples for that loss. Yet is that something for which adequate compensation is possible other than allowing them to maintain their standards of use and so their way of life? Would not "the base line for comparison" be very high indeed then?

F.4. The Invalid Acquisition Arguments. In both the Spoilage and Proviso Arguments, aboriginal title was challenged on the grounds that Indians and Innuit had acquired too much, i.e., more than they were entitled to acquire. It is possible to raise a different objection by claiming that they failed to acquire anything or scarcely anything at all. The heart of this contention is that native peoples did not perform the appropriate acquisitive acts. We get a variety of objections of this kind based on different views of what is an appropriate act of acquisition, that is depending on what sorts of human actions bring things out of a state of ownerlessness into a state of property. Before trying to get this argument off the ground, it is worth noting that both Nozick and Locke start with the assumption that before individual acquisition things are in an ownerless condition (the *res nullis* doctrine); there is another school of thought that assumes that before private acquisition takes place, things are held in common by all men (the *res communae* doctrine).

The major problem in raising this objection is fixing on some kind(s) of action that can be plausibly regarded as acts of original acquisition, i.e., upon the *rites* that generate property *rights*. Nozick raises very serious problems about Locke's criterion for ownership, namely that one owns that with which one has mixed one's labour. He asks about the boundaries of such an acquisition:

> If a private astronaut clears a place on Mars, has he mixed his labour with (so that he comes to own) the whole planet, the whole uninhabited universe, or just a particular plot?

Nozick also asks why mixing one's labour with something isn't simply throwing one's labour away, and if it isn't, then why should one have title to more than the value (if any) added by one's labour? If "mixing labour" is the acquisitive act, then surely these and related questions must be convincingly answered if entitlement theory is to proceed.

We have already seen that if usage is made the standard there are serious problems in determining whose standards of use should prevail. In fact, it would seem that an entitlement theorist should shy away from recognising usage as the acquisitive action, for anyone could take your title to X away from you by finding a better use for X (if you are already using it) or putting it to use for the first time (if you haven't used it yet). I would think that an entitlement theorist should say that it is solely up to X's owner whether and to what use X shall be put. Yet it is Locke who denies that the Indians of America have any ownership rights beyond what they use for food and clothing; English settlers have rights to the land itself because they till it. In short, Locke denies aboriginal rights because the Indians don't use the land in the same way as the English immigrants.

Perhaps, then, it will be suggested that acquisitive actions are *conventional*—literally consisting in the conventions (customs or laws) of a particular people. Thus in some society you own only what you actually have in hand or on your person at the moment, while in another you own whatever bears your mark, and in still another society you own only those things entered in the central ownership registry. Of course, there will be problems when societies with different ownership conventions each want to make exclusive use of the same objects. Each society (assuming no overlap in conventions) can say that the other society's people haven't really acquired the goods in question because of a failure to follow the appropriate conventions. I do not see how an entitlement theorist can say which set of conventions (in part, presumably, adopted for non-arbitrary reasons having to do with different patterns of usage) should prevail on the basis of entitlement theory; it seems to me that he must resort to patterned and, in the end, possibly redistributivist considerations. I think it is on the basis of these considerations that our society will have to deal with the contention (if it can be proven) that the Indian treaties are invalid because the whites and the Indians had totally different conceptions of ownership.

Conclusions

First, I hope to have shown in my consideration of entitlement theory that a number of plausible objections to it, (A) through (E), can be answered. These are essentially peripheral objections. Once we get to the core of the theory, however, serious and, I would maintain, insurmountable problems arise. The entitlement theory of original acquisition cannot be maintained without resort to non-entitlement considerations—patterns, end-results, and pure conventions. To cleanse entitlement theory of these additions will make it so unattractive that it cannot be accepted as a theory of justice in holdings.

Secondly, and somewhat surprisingly, I think that I have made out the case for aboriginal rights. I claim that this country ought to recognise aboriginal rights *on the basis of original acquisition.* Of course, this conclusion depends on the validity of my claim that the only rationale that is advanced and is plausible for the present system of holdings in Canada is entitlement theory. I contend that it is on basis of entitlement theory alone, that we could ever hope to justify the way in which most holdings are distributed in Canada. Just because entitlement theory won't work does not mean that our society won't proceed as if it does. The argument for aboriginal rights is provisional. But it ought to obtain until we are willing to redistribute holdings in this country on a truly just basis.

Questions

1. If we grant Canada's original peoples aboriginal rights, does it follow from McDonald's argument that we cease to have any obligations to provide welfare?
2. McDonald's arguments about property rights are based on a concept of property derived from Western European thought. Yet the native peoples reject the idea (so important to our way of thinking) that land can be owned or acquired as property. Does this affect McDonald's argument?
3. If entitlement theory won't work, should our society proceed as though it were a valid theory? Do we need to create a new theory?

Aboriginal Rights and the Problem of Ownership

David Gauthier

McDonald begins with the question, "What sorts of treatment do the native peoples of Canada deserve?" He mentions two very different answers: (i) "Canadians

---

From a review in *Dialogue* of Michael McDonald's "Aboriginal Rights."

should have welfare rights . . . [so] Indians . . . should not be allowed to fall below some national standard of minimum welfare"; (ii) "no one deserves 'free passage' . . . everyone should work his own way" (p. 27). McDonald then proposes to "shift the topic from welfare rights to aboriginal rights" (ibid.), suggesting that those who defend special welfare rights for Indians (because of their endemic poverty) will reject special aboriginal rights, whereas those who reject special welfare rights (because they reject all such rights) will find that they must defend aboriginal rights.

It is the second part of this reversal which primarily concerns McDonald. Those who reject welfare rights usually defend rights of appropriation. Everyone has a right to what he justly appropriates or justly acquires by transfer, and since this effectively exhausts rights to things, there can be no further welfare rights. But the native peoples were the original appropriators of Canada. Therefore . . . .

McDonald then considers a number of objections to this entitlement theory, which derives from the work of Nozick. His conclusion is that "The entitlement theory of original acquisition cannot be maintained without resort to non-entitlement considerations . . . [However] it is on basis [sic] of entitlement theory alone, that we could ever hope to justify the way in which most holdings are distributed in Canada. Just because entitlement theory won't work does not mean that our society won't proceed as if it does" (pp. 47–48). And so proceeding, "this country ought to recognise aboriginal rights *on the basis of original acquisition*" (p. 47).

My concern with this ingenious argument will be restricted here to McDonald's discussion of objections to the supposition that native peoples did indeed acquire Canada. In particular, referring to the Lockean basis of Nozick's theory, he discusses the *spoilage argument* and the *"proviso" argument*.

Rightful acquisition is limited by spoilage; one may not waste what one acquires. Did the natives, then, waste North America? Were Europeans entitled to appropriate the wasted portions, so that aboriginal rights were not violated by such appropriation?

McDonald argues that it is unclear how the condition of spoilage is to be specified. ". . . by what marks do we identify something as waste? Here it is tempting to ask if the thing in question is used for anyone's benefit. But will any minute amount of incremental benefit suffice to justify ownership or must there be some standard margin of benefit for this use to count here for title? Must there also be standards of efficient use? . . . Any benefit or efficiency standard would seem to be hopelessly utilitarian and redistributivist. On the other hand, having no standards at all would effectively deny a right of self-preservation to those without property and the correlative duty to share for the propertied."

This issue is particularly vexed in the sphere of aboriginal rights, where the native pattern of use differs significantly from the newcomers' pattern. "Clearly Canada's native peoples made ingenious use of the often harsh environment, but their uses could not support the numbers of people that present-day uses can . . . However, if we move in the direction of giving title to the Europeans rather than the native peoples, then we would have to surrender our ownership claims to any society which could support more people here more efficiently. This seems quite obviously in direct opposition to the whole thrust of an *entitlement* theory . . ." (pp. 43–44). Hence—despite the harsh consequence of rejecting a right of self-preservation—the native claim to aboriginal acquisition can, McDonald holds, be defended against the spoilage objection.

Against McDonald, I should urge the following form of the spoilage objection. Let us grant that, in the state of nature, a group of persons, A, is entitled to appropriate as much land as its members are able to use in any way at all. However, should another group, B, of would-be appropriators appear on the scene, and should this group possess a superior technology to A, then B would be entitled to appropriate, from A, as much as would leave A with land sufficient, using B's superior technology, to maintain at least as many persons as before, with at least as rich an assortment of material goods, and at least as wide a range of opportunities (though perhaps a different range), *provided B* makes its technology effectively available to A.

The rationale for my version of the spoilage objection brings us to the "proviso" argument. Rightful appropriation is limited by leaving, in Locke's words, "enough and as good for others"; this Nozick entitles the Lockean proviso. McDonald supposes the objector to argue that Indian appropriation violates this proviso, in not leaving enough land and as good for the Europeans. I do not think that this can be made to work (nor does McDonald). However, I do hold that the Europeans can justify their appropriation of much of North America by an appeal to the proviso. For in a state of nature, one is entitled to appropriate as much as does not worsen the situation of others, even if one takes from others what they previously, and legitimately, appropriated. In a state of nature, one's title is good *only* against actions which would worsen one's situation. Only under the conventional agreement which constitutes society can there be a stronger title.

The spoilage argument may be understood as a form of the "proviso" argument. To waste what one appropriates is to leave others worse off than if what one wasted had been left free for others to appropriate. The original inhabitants of North America did not appropriate wastefully, given their technology. But their appropriation was wasteful, or inefficient, given European technology, and so the Europeans could take most of North America from its original inhabitants without violating the Lockean proviso.

Summarily, then, my account is this. The Indians and Eskimo appropriated North America, and their appropriation did not in itself worsen the situation of anyone else. Hence it was legitimate. However, it was not indefeasible, for it could be overridden, in the state of nature, by any group which could leave the original inhabitants better off than they were under their initial appropriation. The Europeans, who were in a state of nature with respect to the Indians and Eskimo, by making available their superior technology, were in a position to make such an overriding appropriation, not of all of North America, but of so much as to leave the original inhabitants with a combination of land and technology superior to their initial combination.

This will put aboriginal rights into a manageable framework. It will not extinguish them, but will severely limit them. McDonald's position would require us to recognize aboriginal rights to all of Canada, with the exception (probably empty) of those rights which have been legitimately exchanged in an agreement not based on force or fraud. My account will instead require us to recognize only such rights as will leave the original inhabitants better off than prior to our coming. Since, of course, we did not provide the Indians and Eskimo with effective access to our technology, and since we did not ensure that they were left sufficient land so that they would be as well of as before our coming, we shall not find the recognition of aboriginal rights costless. But the cost is one that we may realistically consider ourselves able and willing to pay, and one that can be defended by a non-arbitrary application of the Lockean proviso to questions of appropriation in a state of nature.

Questions

1. Gauthier concludes that Locke's approach to property rights is sound and can be applied to problems of aboriginal rights. How does Gauthier reach this conclusion?
2. Has Gauthier found a sound set of reasons for the view that we can treat the native peoples justly without taking the radical step urged by McDonald?

A Treatise on the Rights of the Aboriginal Peoples of the Continent of North America

Fred Plain

I want to deal in this paper with our understanding of the meaning of "aboriginal rights." First of all, I want to quote from a paper produced by the Union of Ontario Indians in 1970. I was president of the union at that time, and I authorized the following statement, which was presented to a special committee dealing with the constitution of Canada.

> As Indian people we will always see our special status and our legal right as flowing from the original sovereignty of our nations. The colonial legal system to a large degree denied that sovereignty, but they never denied the existence of rights based on the aboriginal possession of tribal territories. It was the unauthorized violation of these rights that led to the unrest which prompted the Royal Proclamation of 1763.
>
> That document, the first written constitutional document for British North America, recognized the existence of Indians' territorial rights, and established legal procedures for the surrender of these rights. The lands which today comprise Ontario were Indian lands. In the words of the Proclamation, they had not been ceded to or purchased by the colonial power. The procedures established by the Royal Proclamation

From Menno Boldt *et al.*, *The Quest for Justice: Aboriginal Peoples and Aboriginal Rights* (1985). By permission of The University of Toronto Press.

for ceding Indian lands remain in force today. The last treaty signed under these procedures was in 1956, the Soto adhesion to Treaty #6.

Areas remain today in Ontario for which no valid treaty or surrender exists. Therefore, the procedures of the Royal Proclamation are still of practical consequence even in Ontario. Section 91.24 of the British North America Act of 1867 gave jurisdiction over Indians and lands reserved for the Indians to the Federal Government. This was not enacted as seems popularly believed out of a paternalistic concern for Native peoples.

It was enacted to make clear the power of the Federal Government to engage in colonial expansion in the West. The phrase "lands reserved for Indians" included lands not ceded by treaty as of 1867, which for Ontario comprised by far the greater part of the present territory of this Province. If the Indians and their lands had not been crucial to the opening of the West, it would have been more logical to place Indians under Provincial jurisdictions as somewhat different terms of Indian policy developed in each colony of 1867.

Following the surrender of the Hudson's Bay Company Charter in 1869/70, the Governor General, exercising prerogative power in compliance with the procedures established by the Royal Proclamation, began negotiating a series of treaties with the Indian nations in Ontario and the Northwest. The treaties were constitutional documents. They were seen by both sides as establishing basic patterns of interrelationship for the future. They were based on the idea of mutual consent and the understanding that the Indians had legal rights in their patrimony. To violate these documents is to compromise the integrity of the Canadian legal system. The Migratory Birds Convention Act, and the decisions in Regina vs. Sekina in 1964, and in Regina vs. George in 1966, and Daniels vs. White and the Queen in 1968, to Indian people represent violations of basic legal commitments.

The basic rights of the Indian peoples are of constitutional significance. Yet, these rights have not been uniformly safeguarded under the present constitutional structure. This should change.

What Are Aboriginal Rights?

In white society there has always been confusion as to what actually is meant by the term "aboriginal rights." In 1970, for example, Prime Minister Pierre Trudeau was reported to have said that the concept of aboriginal rights is so complicated as to be unworkable. But to us, the Nishnawbe-Aski, the concept is basic, simple, and unambiguous. Our definition of aboriginal rights can be summed up in one phrase: "the right of independence through self-government." When we say that our right to self-government, our right to self-determination, our right to nationhood must be recognized in any new Canadian constitution, we are defining aboriginal rights. This is the goal of the Nishnawbe-Aski as outlined in the Declaration of Nishnawbe-Aski of 1977.

Aboriginal rights defined in this way include the right to develop our own life-style and our own economy, and to protect and encourage the practice of our sacred traditions as we know them. We, the Nishnawbe-Aski, have the inherent right to determine what our future will be. We shall determine the destiny of our land. We want to see the continued development of our people under their own governing systems. Aboriginal rights were a mere concept of Prime Minister Trudeau's mind, but to my people they are a reality. We have the inherent right to develop and grow under our own system, and our own system will flow from our own people, who will develop our own constitution. Our Indian constitutions have every right to be recognized in any new Canadian constitution. This is the true meaning of aboriginal rights.

What Is an Aborigine?

The aborigines are the indigenous inhabitants of a country. For instance, the people that we know as the Indian nations of North and South America are the aborigines of these two continents. They were the first people to live in this part of the world.

Because we were the first people to live here we have a claim to certain rights. These rights include human rights—that is, the basic right to life claimed by all people. However, when we talk about aboriginal rights, we are also talking about the inherent right to self-determination that applies to all aborigines.

What Is Civilization?

To understand aboriginal rights we must understand the meaning of civilization. Civilization is the accumulation of the traditions and culture of a people: their ability to express themselves in a variety of ways—in dance, music, art, law, religion, the telling of stories, the writing of books, and so on. The aboriginal people of North and South America constituted a number of different civilizations.

Aboriginal rights guarantee each indigenous nation the right to develop its own traditions and culture—its own civilization. Each aboriginal nation has the inherent right to seek happiness and a comfortable way of living, and to develop itself at its own pace. This was a right of each aboriginal nation from its beginning, and it exists today. Each nation exercised aboriginal rights within its own lands and boundaries and under its own sovereignty.

To recognize that the aboriginal people were a civilization long before the white man came to North America is to acknowledge that as an aboriginal people we exercised our aboriginal right to govern ourselves. Conversely, to acknowledge that we have aboriginal rights is to recognize that these rights flow from our long-standing civilization.

Aboriginal and European Attitudes toward the Land

Nishnawbe-Aski means "the people and the land." Our links with the earth are sacred links that no man can ever sever. We are one with the earth, and the earth is one with us. The Nishnawbe-Aski Declaration states that we have the right to govern and control our own people in our own land, and the right to remedy our own situations. The efforts that are made to meet our needs must come from our own people.

As nations of people we made laws to govern ourselves. Among the laws that we made were laws governing our use of the land and its resources. But our attitude toward the land and its use was and still is very different from the European attitude. We aboriginal people believe that no individual or group owns the land, that the land was given to us collectively by the Creator to use, not to own, and that we have a sacred obligation to protect the land and use its resources wisely. For the Europeans, the idea that land can be owned by a person or persons and exploited for profit is basic to the system. The European political and legal systems have been developed to reflect this concept of the land.

Many European and Canadian laws have to do with regulating private property in one form or another and with governing relations among people with respect to private property. The sovereign government has created laws to govern the distribution of the scarce resource of property. The most basic form of property, other than one's own body, is land.

The idea that land can be bought and sold, or that you can exercise some rights but not others in the land, is absolutely foreign to the Nishnawbe-Aski way of thinking. Yet this is the basis for all legislation that has been enacted since the coming of the Europeans to North America.

Legislation Affecting Aboriginal Rights

The Royal Proclamation of 1763 was passed in the British Parliament because of the struggles between Indians and Europeans over the land. This document recognized the existence of Indians' territorial rights and established the legal procedures for the giving up of those rights.

The Constitution Act, 1867, established Canada as a nation. The act sets out the division of powers between the provinces and the federal government. Section 91(24) of the act gives jurisdiction over Indians and lands reserved for Indians to the federal government.

The act was intended to make clear the power of the federal government to engage in colonial expansion in the west. This was done because we Indians and our lands were crucial to the opening of the west, and the federal government wanted to be able to control us and our land in order to consolidate its power over the country.

After the royal proclamation, and until as recently as 1956, treaties were signed between the government and the Indian nations. These treaties were seen by both sides as establishing basic patterns of future interrelationships. They were based on the idea of mutual consent and on the understanding that the Indians had legal rights in and control of the land.

The treaties were a recognition by colonial law that we Indian people had sovereignty in our land. In fact, there was a widespread acknowledgment that the aboriginal occupants of the land had certain legal claims because of their historical sovereignty over the land. The English legal system developed a theory that those claims were limited in certain ways, but that aboriginal tribes had the legal right to possess their tribal territories. Under the English legal system if the lands passed into non-Indian hands, then the Indian claims had to be extinguished by a formal treaty and by some form of compensation.

The treaties were negotiated sometimes before white settlement, sometimes after. The effect of the treaties was to extinguish many aboriginal rights; to preserve some residual rights, such as hunting, fishing, and trapping; and to create some new rights, such as schooling, medical care, and annuity payments.

While the treaties have not been totally in our favour, the law has never denied that the aboriginal tribes have legal rights to possess their tribal territories.

What Does It Mean to Be a Nation?

Our aboriginal right allows us to determine our future as the Nishnawbe-Aski Nation. What does it mean to be a nation? In 1977, an international conference on discrimination against indigenous populations of the Americas put forward a declaration of principles aimed at gaining recognition for indigenous or aboriginal peoples as nations under international law. The criteria for recognition as a nation are: that the people have a permanent population; that they have a defined territory; that they have a government; that they have the ability to enter into relations with other states. We can assure Canada and the international community that using these criteria we can define ourselves as a nation. We have a population that is permanent; we have always existed and we are not going to die out or fade into oblivion. We have a defined territory stretching from James Bay and Hudson Bay west to the Manitoba boundary; from Hudson Bay and James Bay southward to the height of land known as the Arctic watershed and east to the borders of Quebec. We have a democratic government given to us by the Creator. The Royal Proclamation of 1763 refers to our sovereignty, and the government of Canada approached us as a nation to enter into a treaty with them. We continue to have the right to enter into relations with other states.

Under these criteria, the Nishnawbe-Aski have a solid basis for claiming our aboriginal right to determine what our future will be and to determine how we are going to attain our goals.

Do the Indian People Have a System of Government?

When the white man first came to America, there were systems of government in operation in this new land. The democratic system employed by the great Six Nations Confederacy was studied by the Europeans, and was picked up and incorporated into their governing systems. Democracy was already flourishing in North America before the white man came. The right to govern one's people, the right to govern one's destiny, the right to determine the paths that a nation will follow to reach its objectives must be recognized as sovereign and aboriginal rights.

We had a government. That government has been dormant because of the influx of federal law, particularly the Indian Act and its administrators, the Department of Indian Affairs. Our government has remained hidden in the hearts of our people, but it has never died. Our government will come forth under the careful guidance and leadership of the Nishnawbe-Aski Commission. We will be prepared to put the constitution of the Nishnawbe-Aski on paper, if that is what is required. Our government is a reality.

We must draw out from our people what they want to see developed in their community with regard to their own governing structure. Only then can we begin to educate our people in the traditional ways of living, traditional Indian government, and the traditional right to determine our future.

What Does It Mean to Be Independent?

When the Nishnawbe-Aski made their declaration in 1977, they stressed that their objective was to see the full development of cultural, economic, spiritual, and political independence. We think that we have to come to grips with the fact that cultural independence and economic independence cannot be divorced. One cannot exist without the other.

At the time the white man came here, our educational system was complete. The educational system and the political development of the various Indian nations in Canada determined the life-style of the particular tribe in whatever area of America they lived in. For instance, the economy of the Ojibway and the Cree living in this part of North America was based on the presence of animal, fish, bird, and plant life destined to give sustenance to the people. Hunting, fishing and trapping, and gathering were not separate issues to be dealt with at a political level by certain components of government; they were part of the socio-economic system of our people, and they are included in the overall definition of aboriginal rights. Before the white man came, all Indian nations were independent and exercised their aboriginal rights within their own lands.

The Nishnawbe-Aski and the Constitution

We did not question the statement of Prime Minister Pierre Trudeau that the people of this country have a right to their own constitution. We support the principle of patriation; Canadians have a right to determine the instrument by which government is going to make laws that apply to them.

When the constitutional negotiations became an issue, we told the British parliamentarians that we were not fighting the patriation of the constitution to Canada. We felt that the Canadian people had a right to their own constitution, but we also believed that the Nishnawbe-Aski Nation, which existed before the Europeans came to North America, have a right to their own constituion, and that they must not be deprived of the right to make their own laws and determine their own destiny through their own governing system. Because the Canadian government was unwilling to recognize our right to our own constitution, we challenged the patriation of the British North America Act.

We, the aboriginal people, must clearly spell out the true aboriginal rights that must be recognized in any Canadian constitution. These rights are non-negotiable. But we must take a united stand, or we will find it difficult to persuade Canada's first ministers to heed our claims.

What the Canadian Government Wants from the Aboriginal People

We are in the heat of a tremendous battle, a battle that is focused on jurisdiction. The premiers of the provinces and the prime minister are trying to reduce the aboriginal rights question to a series of legal issues that they can contest or disregard. At the same time, they attempt to placate the Indian people by saying, "We will look after you; we will improve your conditions; we will accommodate your needs." But ultimately they will try to consolidate their jurisdiction over our land and our resources. The first ministers have only one goal in mind in the constitutional negotiations: they hope to gain complete control over all Indian lands and resources. This is what the constitutional process is all about.

The Canadian Government's Attitude to Aboriginal Rights

The Honourable Jean Chrétien had these words to say about aboriginal and treaty rights: "We will honour our lawful obligations to the aboriginal people." Precisely what did he mean? He meant that Canada has obligations to native people only if such obligations will stand the test of the law. If the law decrees that certain obligations must be met, and if those obligations are defined in such a manner that the government can accept the definition, then they will be honoured. But what does the term "law" mean? Law, in the modern liberal state, is the creation of an autonomous and general legal system composed of: private parties; a legitimate legal sovereignty and its administrative agencies (the governor-in-council or Parliament, or the government of Canada, and its cabinet and various departments); and the independent judiciary.

When the explorers from the European nations came to America, they found a land with people and law. The Europeans had no right to come and trample that system of laws underfoot and impose a new legal system in North America. But this fact is not readily going to be recognized and acknowledged by the people who in the first instance denied the existence of the aboriginal system of law. They will fight any attempt to bring truth to bear.

Let us go back to the quotation from the Nishnawbe-Aski declaration. In the minds of our people who hunt, trap, and fish the forests, lakes, and rivers of Nishnawbe-Aski land, there is a clear concept of what our land tenure is. However, according to the government of Canada, which makes the laws, aboriginal rights are to be determined by a court interpretation. As far as the courts are concerned aboriginal rights are conceptual rights only; that is to say, they are a concept that exists only in the mind until drafted into some kind of law that makes sense in a legal system. The government makes the law defining aboriginal rights, and the government appoints judges who interpret the law dealing with aboriginal rights. If the government of Canada has it way, the white man's law and the white man's courts will determine how the concept of land tenure is defined in practice.

Who Will Decide What Our Aboriginal Rights Are?

Court cases have never solved the riddle of aboriginal rights. The *Baker Lake* case is a prime instance of what happens when the dominant governing society, through its enacted laws and its judicial system, decides what constitutes aboriginal rights. In the *Baker Lake* case, the court said that the Inuit do have aboriginal rights because they have been here from time immemorial. Because of that one basic fact, the court recognized that aboriginal rights do exist. However, the Supreme Court of Canada took it upon itself to define what the aboriginal right is not. The judgment states that the aboriginal right is not a proprietary right. In other words, the right of the aboriginal people does not relate to the land, and therefore the land is open to those exploiters who want to extract the gas and the oil, destroy the environment, and then move out. The indigenous population is then left with evil consequences that greatly outweigh any potential benefits that might come to them from the resource exploitation.

In the communities of the Nishnawbe-Aski Nation, our fishermen, our trappers, our hunters, our schoolchildren, and our women who maintain our homes understand what our aboriginal rights are. Aboriginal rights are a riddle only to those who do not want to hear or face the truth, who do not want their taking of the land interfered with by the aboriginal owners of this continent.

The aboriginal people have a clear concept of land tenure in their minds; therefore our chiefs, our elders, our people, our childen, should define our aboriginal rights—not the federal government, the provinces, or the Canadian courts. It is we who must protect our aboriginal right to self-determination as a nation and our right to develop and use the resources of the land free of interference and intimidation. We have an obligation to preserve the rights granted to us by the Creator. We have that right now. We have always had that right. We are determined to have that right in the future. We don't have to beg the prime minister of Canada and the provincial premiers to recognize that we have certain basic human and aboriginal rights.

Conclusion

I close this paper with a prayer. Great Grandfather, our hearts and our minds are jointed together. We rejoice to know that our right to live and enjoy the beauty of this great land was given to us, not by any foreign government, but by yourself. Great Grandfather, you gave us the land and its resources; you made us one with the birds, the animal life, the fish life; you made us one with nature itself. This is our aboriginal right. It is a right that no government can interpret for us.

Because you gave it to us, no man has a right to take it away from us. Many times, our hearts have been made heavy when we have seen the devastation of our land by those who seek only to mine it for its wealth and then leave it. Our hearts have been made heavy because other powers have come in and made laws that have restricted our free movement of spirit. Yet you have put it in our hearts this day to stand upon our feet once again, and boldly claim that our aboriginal right is forever.

Breathe upon us with your spirit of life, and give us greater determination to press for this right to be fully restored to us and recognized by all people. Great Grandfather, be with us in all of our deliberations, for without your leadership and guidance we are weak and helpless. Cause the sound of the drum to be loud and clear to our hearts and minds in this crucial hour.

Questions

1. Plain defines aboriginal rights to mean ''the right to independence through self-government.'' What might this mean for the native people and for Canada as it now exists?
2. The native view of land is substantially different from our own, as is pointed out in the introduction to the chapter and in this contribution. That being the case, which of the two incompatible views should prevail when land claims are under consideration? Which view would prevail our courts?

Aboriginal Land Rights in Northern Canada

J.T. Stevenson

Introduction

I believe that the usual approach to aboriginal land claims in Canada is profoundly misguided. We have imposed our political and legal system on the native peoples and have forced them to argue for their rights in terms of our current culture. In so doing, we have ignored their point of view and not addressed some fundamental issues.

Canada's Constitution Act 1982, fortunately, requires (Part IV, S. 37[2]) a constitutional conference, which is to discuss "the identification and definition of the rights" of aboriginal peoples. We thus have the opportunity, indeed the duty, to look at the whole question of land claims philosophically, in a manner broader and deeper than usual.

A Standard Approach

According to the political/legal system that developed in the course of the industrial revolution, land is treated as property, as something that can be owned, as something alien to us but over which we have dominion. In this liberal tradition, the owner of a property has, on the face of it, the sole and despotic right to do whatsoever he wills with it. Land is also treated as a commodity, as something that can be bought and sold and that has a value determined by its market price. There is an elaborate legal system for determining who owns what, for settling disputes, and for regulating the use of property. The state may, exercising its ultimate power of sovereignty, expropriate land and give as compensation other commodities (money, goods, services) equal to the market value of the land.

With the permission of the author.

Within this framework, we argue whether or not native peoples really own the land where they reside. Some say they do because of the right of first possession. They thus confer on the native peoples despotic powers over the land that the native peoples never exercised, never even conceived themselves as possessing, and do not (if they can keep their own ways) want. Others say that they do not own it because, as the Judicial Committee of the British Privy Council put it in the eighteenth century, the inhabitants were "so low on the scale of social organization that their usages and conceptions are not to be reconciled with the institutions and legal ideas of a civilized society." In similar fashion, some have recently argued that the natives may "own" the land but that we can simply take it from them because they have a technologically inferior culture—provided we offer them, whether they want it or not, our superior culture. A third position, sometimes taken by our courts, is that the natives have a limited ownership in the form of usufruct rights. This means, roughly, that ultimate ownership resides with the Crown but, because of traditional usage and custom, the natives have the right, say, to hunt and fish on certain lands. Much debate has revolved around the issue of compensation for land claims, which presupposes that the aboriginal peoples have some sort of legal entitlement to their lands but that the Crown in right of Canada, being sovereign, can expropriate land and determine an adequate form of compensation.

Why Wrong

All this, I say, is misguided. It proceeds on the assumptions of a particular culture and its political/economic legal regime, when the issue is cross-cultural and concerns that adequacy of that regime. What rarely gets a serious hearing is the native point of view[1]. The native peoples did not traditionally regard their land as something over which they had sovereign dominion, as something they owned and could do with as they pleased. The land and its other inhabitants were regarded, according to their laws, as something essential to their well-being, as something to be used with respect, care, and moderation, as something to be shared and preserved for future generations of all living things. In our terms, we might say that they regarded themselves, in a fashion, as stewards of the land with not only rights but obligations respecting it. They believed they had a very special relation with the land, which we may call religious, spiritual, or philosophical, but which, in any case, was expressed by them in myth, legend, symbol, and ceremony. Their land was not a property and commodity. It may be particularly hard for us to understand how and why the native peoples feel that their individual, personal identity is intimately connected to their relation to the land. Yet, to treat them fairly, it is vital that we make an effort to do so.

Purpose and Plan of Discussion

Because we tend to dismiss their view as primitive, mytho-poetical, or mystical rather than civilized, scientific, and rational, I shall try to explain or translate it into rational and scientific terms, the terms of philosophy, anthropology, and psychology. Some things, especially the experiential dimension, get lost in this translation, but, one hopes, the translation will provide a small bridge of understanding and sympathy.

Thus I shall present an argument designed not only to support certain conclusions, but to serve as a thread tying together a set of considerations usually overlooked in discussing aboriginal land claims. It will tie individual identity and a personal security right, on the one hand, to group rights to culture and land, on the other.

I make three background assumptions: (1) that natural justice requires that we first listen to the voices of the claimants, the native peoples, in their own terms rather than assume that we know best what is good for them; (2) that we should appeal to moral principles that are cross-cultural and find as much other common ground as possible; (3) that in tracing the consequences of our actions we should appeal to the most realistic and well-evidenced scientific theories available.

My discussion focusses on land claims in the Yukon and Northwest Territories because of the special opportunities and dangers faced by people there: on the one hand, they have not yet suffered as much disruption as native peoples in the South; on the other hand, they face severe threats because of the rush to exploit the non-renewable resources of the northern frontier and have made specific claims on us. While the experiences of the southern aboriginals will be used as evidence in the empirical steps in the argument, a solution to the problems of southern Amerindians and Metis will be particularly difficult and I say nothing directly on the question. I hope, however, that the discussion will indirectly illuminate some aspects of their problems and those of other cultural minorities.

The discussion proceeds as follows. In the second section the problem is presented as it is understood and expressed by native peoples themselves. The claims are then interpreted and summarized in terms that may be more familiar to us so that we can have a common understanding of the problem. In the third section I set out and interpret a widely accepted, cross-cultural moral principle, so that discussion can proceed on a common normative basis. The fourth section outlines a difficult empirical step in the argument: it attempts to express, in terms of theories from anthropology and psychology, the central native view that their individual identity and hence personal security is tied up with their relation to their land. It turns out, I believe, that once again we can find common ground. In the fifth section the argument is restated briefly and certain conclusions, both positive and negative, are drawn. Note that much of the basic evidence has had to be relegated to footnotes.

Native Voices

Let us listen attentively to a carefully chosen but representative selection of native voices in the North that present the problems as *they* see them.

> A.   To the Indian people our land really is our life. Without our land we cannot—we could no longer exist as people. [Note: "as people" not "as a people."] If our land is destroyed, we too are destroyed. If you people ever take our land you will be taking our life. (Richard Nerysoo)

> Every time the white people come to the North or come to our land and start tearing up the land, I feel as if they are cutting up our own flesh because that is the way we feel about our land. It is our flesh. (Georgina Tobac)

B.   Ever since they came in I couldn't make a living out of the country. This is my trouble now. There is all kinds of money made around me with the oil, and they don't give me anything. They don't think that I am a person living there. (Johnny Klondike)

C.   [They suggest] that we give up our land and resources to the richest nation [the U.S.A. which wanted a pipeline built] in the world; not the poorest. We are threatened with genocide only so the rich and powerful can become more rich and more powerful.

I suggest, in any man's view, that is immoral. If our Indian nation is being destroyed so that poor people of our world might get a chance to share this world's riches, then as Indian people, I am sure we would seriously consider giving up our resources. But do you really expect us to give up our life and our lands so that those few people who are the richest and most powerful in the world today can maintain and defend their own immoral position of privilege?

That is not our way. (Phillip Blake)

D.   For myself, I find it very hard to identify with anybody because I have nobody to turn to. My people don't accept me any more because I got an education, and the white people won't accept me because I am not the right colour. So like, a lot of people keep saying, "O.K., we've got to educate these young native people, so that they can become something." But what good is it if a person has no identity? I can't really identify with anybody and I'm lost. I'm just sort of a person hanging in the middle of two cultures and doesn't know which way to go. (Roy Fabian)

E.   The Dene have the right to recognition, self-determination, and on-going growth and development as a People and a Nation.

The Dene, as aboriginal people, have a special status under the Constitution of Canada.

The Dene, as aboriginal people, have the right to retain so much of their traditional lands, and under such terms, as to ensure their independence and self-reliance, traditionally, economically and socially.

There will, therefore, be within Confederation, a Dene Government with jurisdiction over a geographical area and over subject matters now within the jurisdiction of either the Government of Canada or the Government of the Northwest Territories. (Proposed by the Dene as an "Agreement in Principle between the Dene Nation and Her Majesty the Queen in Right of Canada.")[2]

Interpretation

Taking into account the cultural context, we can translate these statements into our terms as follows A: The people believe that they live in a complex, symbiotic relation with the land and its ecosystems; that is, their environment, culture, and personal identity are closely interwoven in a balanced system. B: They believe they are being economically marginalized and treated as non-persons. C: They believe that they are being treated unjustly, that their vital interests are being sacrificed for the less important or trivial interests of those already well-off. D: They believe the form of the enculturation process into white society that is imposed on them prevents or destroys a healthy personality integration. E: They believe they need and have the right to some forms of political and social self-determination. This, in summary but I believe fair fashion, is the native position. My argument will try to elucidate, in particular, A and D.

Let us try to find common ground, both morally and intellectually.

The Personal-Security Principle

One cross-cultural and widely accepted normative principle that is relevant is stated in the UN Charter of Human Rights (1948)—often called "the conscience of mankind"—to which Canada is a subscriber. It says (Article 3): "Everyone has the right to life, liberty and the security of person." Of course, like other abstract legal and moral principles, it must be interpreted to be applied; and its application clarifies and enriches its meaning. I shall focus on the personal-security aspect of this right— Everyone has the right to personal security—and I shall spell out what this means.[3]

Content of Right

We would agree that arbitrary, capricious killing, such as indulged in by Idi Amin in Uganda, would violate this right; as similarly would the more systematic holocaust of the Nazi regime in Germany. Hacking off a person's limbs or reducing him to slavery while keeping him alive would also be clearly prohibited. Of course the right is defeasible. That is to say, it can be overridden: we can kill in self-defence; the criminal can lose his liberty; the surgeon who mutilates a cancer patient to save his life does not violate the patient's security right. So some thought is required in applying the principle.

Such thought, I believe, will lead us to recognize that the right to the security of our person extends beyond life and limb to matters affecting basic personality structure. Many modern states, alas, practise forms of torture that leave a person alive and unmutilated but nevertheless personally destroyed. A person may, for instance, be subjected to sensory deprivation, electro-shock, and hallucinogenic drugs. As a result, he may be prey to chronic anxiety, feelings of guilt and worthlessness, and alternating passivity and rage; he may be unable to function economically and socially; he may suffer from anomie—a state in which normative standards of conduct and belief are weak or lacking, a state that is characterized by disorientation, anxiety, and isolation; he may lack purpose or meaning in his life and be unable to persevere in projects and establish normal social relations; he may lapse into alcoholism and chronic delinquency; he may be so overwhelmed by anxiety and depression that he commits suicide. In short, he may be turned into a human derelict.

Such can be the effects of torture. But, as we shall see, similar effects can be produced unintentionally by other methods and can be observed on reserves and in urban centres throughout Canada. I suggest that the personal security right protects us not only against physical death, mutilation and enslavement, but against such psychic destruction and mutilation.

Qualifications

To avoid controversy as much as possible, let us put a construction on the personal-security right. (1) The right obliges us to acts of omission rather than commission. We may not have to help or enhance a person's security, but we are required to refrain from positive acts that harm personal security. (2) These harms must be serious and substantial. In the myriad of social interactions we engage in, we daily harm other people, intentionally or otherwise: we inflict, for instance, little blows on their pride and self-esteem. But here we speak only of those major blows or the death of a thousand cuts, which strike at the core of personality, which sap our capacity to cope, which in a strong sense destroy and mutilate us. (3) The forbidden harms to be culpable or blameworthy must be foreseeable and avoidable. When we act, we sometimes "know not what we do" or "can't help what we do." We act in ignorance or unintentionally or we produce effects by accident or we couldn't have done otherwise. We speak here, however, only of what a reasonable person in the light of currently available knowledge would expect as the probable consequences of his actions where there is a genuine choice available. Of course, people who are educated or in responsible positions with special access to information and with powers to act will be less able than others to plead ignorance or unavoidability. (4) Since personal security is so important, the onus of proof should be on the agent, but the level of proof may be set conservatively at the balance of probabilities test. This means, first, that when I, as an agent, am considering an action, the burden of proof is on me to assure that I am not violating the personal security of those affected by my act. To reverse the onus would mean that the patient or potential victim would have to calculate the consequences of other people's actions and prevent or avoid consequences which would harm his, the victim's, personal security. Second, instead of setting as the level of proof required—what might be reasonable given the importance of the matter—that I refrain from acting unless it is beyond a reasonable doubt that I am harming no one's personal security, let us be conservative and impose a weaker test. I should not act unless the balance of probabilities indicates that I will not be harming someone's personal security. (5) There will be, for psychic personal security as for physical security, defeasibility conditions that prevent absurd applications of the right. Thus, for example, if I am a paeodophile whose personal-ity is integrated around my desire to sexually molest children, you do not violate my personal security right if you prevent me from acting on this desire and thereby drastically upset my personality. The personal security rights of children in those circumstances override those of paedophiles.

The problem now is to indicate how, in certain circumstances, it is possible to violate psychic personal security by disrupting a person's relationship to his environ-ment and way of life.

The Evidence of Science

Political and ethical arguments in philosophy usually rely, in part, on views about human nature and society. Often they are theories from the seventeenth and eighteenth centuries; for instance, the psychology of Thomas Hobbes or the anthropology of Jean-Jacques Rousseau. I have thought it wiser to appeal to the much better evidenced theories of the twentieth century. And from the plethora of available opinion I have made choices that I cannot here defend in the space available. I can only invite the reader to do what the writer has done: immerse himself in the literature, examine the evidence and try to make a judicious choice, one that avoids as much as possible ideological prejudices.

Systems Analysis

We have become accustomed to the idea of applying systems analysis to our environment, to regarding it as an ecosystem: a set of elements (land, air, water, plants, and animals) connected by a complex web of interdependencies and feedback loops which maintain the system in a delicate balance. For example, a lake, with its water quality, plants, fish, and aquatic animals, may form such a system. The system may absorb some shocks and regain its balance: the lake may, after over-fishing, regenerate the fish stock. But sometimes a shock will be catastrophic: the flow of nutrients into the lake may so increase (more sewage, detergents, and so on) that an algae bloom occurs, oxygen is depleted, the fish die, and we have a eutrophied lake with different forms of life in it. It is not always easy to tell which shocks will be catastrophic. For example, the human body can recover from massive bleeding and many broken bones (as in a car accident) but completely succumb to the administration of enough white powder to cover a pinhead (say the powder is strychnine). If we want to act on a system without destroying it, we need to understand its critical elements and relations, how it will respond to changed conditions and how it may adapt.

It is important to note at this point that the native belief that the natural world forms a complex, interdependent system of which the native peoples are an integral part should not be dismissed as mere primitive or magical thought. It is a view they forged in the struggle for existence and it is based on thousands of years of experience and empirical observation. Although not expressed in our theoretical terms and differing in many details, the general approach is consistent with our most advanced biological science. In their own way, the native peoples got there first.

I suggest that this common ground of a systems mode of thought can be extended from biology to our understanding of society, culture, and the development of personal identity. Two main points will be made. First, a physical and biological environment, a culture and social system in which people earn a living, and the way in which human beings grow and are nurtured into mature personalities in that culture—all three—should be regarded as one system. Second, the personal security of native peoples has been attacked by European settlers at two critical points—in their livelihood from the land and in the nurturance of their children. Let us see how.

Anthropology

The culture of a human society is an integrated pattern of behaviour that includes thought, speech, action, and artifacts, and depends on our capacity for learning and transmitting knowledge to succeeding generations. According to anthropologist

Marvin Harris, we may distinguish those broad elements of culture that interact in important ways.[4]

Harris distinguishes an infrastructure, which consists of modes of production and reproduction. The mode of production, Harris says, is "The technology and practices employed for expanding or limiting basic subsistence production, especially the production of food and other forms of energy, given the restrictions and opportunities provided by a specific technology interacting with a specific habitat." The mode of reproduction is "The technology and the practices employed for expanding, limiting and maintaining population size." Harris notes a structure of a domestic and political economy: "the organization of reproduction and basic production, exchange and consumption with camps, houses, apartments, or other domestic settings" and "the organization of reproduction, production, exchange, and consumption within and between bands, villages, chiefdoms, states, and empires." He also defines a superstructure: "the conscious and unconscious cognitive goals, categories, rules, plans, values, philosophies and beliefs" that are expressed in behaviour generally and often particularly in rituals, religion, art, music, dance, games, literature, and so on.

These interacting elements form a cultural system that can be stable or unstable, concordant or discordant, that can grow or decline, live or die. Some shocks to the system will be easily absorbed; others will produce dramatic changes and be catastrophic.

Harris has advanced a fruitful approach to anthropology, which he calls the "research program of cultural materialism." It says, very roughly: look first to infrastructural elements when attempting to explain the riddles of culture. A disruption in the infrastructure of a culture, for example, a major change in the way land is used, can have dramatic impacts on its other elements, such as its belief and value system and the way it nurtures its offspring into persons. I believe Harris has demonstrated in certain cases the fruitfulness of this approach. I have in mind, for instance, his elegant, plausible, and powerful analysis of the sacred cow taboo in India, which explains a wide range of facts (such as different sex ratios amongst adult cattle in different regions of India) but which other theories leave inexplicable and puzzling.

I am relying on his approach in stressing the importance of land use to the question of a personal-security right. A sudden and drastic disruption of the relation between a people and its environment can reverberate, through elements of its culture, to the very foundations of human personality. But to see how this can be so, we need to add a theory from psychology to the one from anthropology, in order to connect culture and personality development. My views on this are drawn largely from the work of Erik Erikson, Jean Piaget, and Bruno Bettelheim.[5] Each general point made will be followed by an illustration.

Psychology

Persons, in an important sense, are made not born.[6] We know that without some decent system of training and nurturing—the systems can vary within certain broad limits—biological human beings will not develop the cognitive, emotional, and social capacities for personhood at all or will have severe personality disorders. Our practices may be unconscious (based on habit and tradition) but even apparently trivial details can have deep effects on personality structure. A proper understanding of the phenomena requires an integrated approach to personality development.

> We are speaking of three processes, the somatic process, the ego process, and the societal process. In the history of science these three processes have belonged to three different scientific disciplines—biology, psychology, and the social sciences—each of which studied what it could isolate, count, and dissect: single organisms, individual minds, and social aggregates. . . . Unfortunately this knowledge is tied to the conditions under which it was secured: the organism undergoing dissection or examination; the mind surrendered to experiment or interrogation; social aggregates spread out on statistical tables. In all of these cases, then, a scientific discipline prejudiced the matter under observation by actively dissolving its total living situation in order to be able to make an isolated section of it amenable to a set of instruments or concepts.[7]

We now know more and can do better. We know something about how culture—the mode of reproduction, the domestic economy, and elements of the superstructure such as myths and legends—plays an important role in the development of personality. Thus anthropology is linked to psychology. We can also recognize the existence of normal pathways of development and critical stages in those paths such that an event which would be relatively harmless at most stages may have profound consequences at a critical stage. We also know something of the importance of systemic consistency and appropriateness: two methods of child-rearing, each separately successful, may, when combined, produce a severely conflicted personality; a method that produces a personality successful in one culture may not be appropriate for producing the type of personality required for success in another culture. Finally, let us note that the destruction or mutilation of personality can occur after childhood. Indeed, Erikson's work on the so-called identity-crisis of early adulthood was triggered by clinical observations of young men suffering from war-induced psychoneuroses and led to his investigations of the developmental stages and crises of the whole human life cycle.

So, in the clinical investigation of individual pathology we need to take into account differences rooted in biology (genetics), critical stages and events in personality development, and the social-cultural-historical setting in which they take place.

Let us now return to the native question. First, contrary to common European belief—which vacillated between regarding Indians as noble, untutored children of nature and regarding them as depraved, untutored savages—native peoples have elaborate child-rearing systems that have produced integrated personalities well-adapted to their culture.

> Up to recent decades child training has been an anthropological no man's land. Even anthropologists living for years among aboriginal tribes failed to see that these tribes trained their children in some systematic way. Rather, the experts tacitly assumed with the general public that savages had no child training at all and that primitives grew up "like

little animals"—an idea which in the overtrained members of our culture arouses either angry contempt or romantic elation.

The discovery of primitive child-training systems makes it clear that primitive societies are neither infantile stages of mankind nor arrested deviations from the proud progressive norms which we represent: they are a complete form of mature human living, often of a homogeneity and simple integrity which we at times might well envy.[8]

Application

Let me illustrate now the foregoing general discussion. Erikson was asked to investigate the causes of widespread behavioural and personality disorders amongst Dakota Indian children in U.S. government schools.[9] He found that in the first years of their lives they were brought up in a way which, through traditional techniques of child transport, breastfeeding, weaning, and so on, was well suited to produce personalities adapted to a culture based on the buffalo hunt. Then the children were thrust into schools well suited to produce, as personalities, the factory workers needed in an industrial society. The Indian children were deeply conflicted cognitively (e.g., in their structuring of space and time) and emotionally. Moreover, neither form of training was suited to the actual economic basis of their society. The reserves on which they were confined would support neither a hunting culture nor an industrial one. The inconsistency and inappropriateness of their upbringing left them with identity confusions, expressed in their feelings and behaviour. (Recall the statement of Roy Fabian.) Their prospects were poverty and the cycle of the welfare syndrome. The trouble started when their cultural infrastructure was destroyed—the buffalo wiped out and their lands seized—and was compounded by the efforts made to enculturate the children into white society.

Similar stories can be told about Indian bands across Canada. It was once thought that a solution could be found in residential schools, where native children would be separated from the influence of their families and thoroughly indoctrinated in the fundamentals of white society. Little was understood about the importance of critical stages of development and the effects of experiences in infancy; little regard was given to the milieu to which the children would return. The result was a catastrophe for several generations of aboriginal peoples.

If you wanted a recipe for the destruction of personality, one such would be this: destroy the material basis of a culture; force the people into an environment which provides little means for economic activity; foster the culture of poverty and dependency by means of minimal handouts; make ignorant and racist attacks on the structure and superstructure of what remains of the culture; as the adults disintegrate from these shocks, experiment blindly with their children.

I have sketched an integrated theory from anthropology and psychology which enables us to trace and understand some of the effects of our actions. Is it consistent with the native view of the matter? I believe so. When a native woman says that interfering with her land is "cutting up our own flesh," this should not be dismissed as the far-fetched, special pleading of an ignorant primitive. She may well be expressing, metaphorically, what we may express using scientific jargon. And the grounds of the belief may not be altogether different from ours: she may be expressing the native belief in the complex dependencies of the individual/social/environmental system, as well as the results of her own observations of shocks to that system.

In any case the facts must be explained. There is massive evidence of widespread personal pathology amongst Southern Canadian aboriginal peoples.[10] It can be seen with the naked eye on reserves and in urban ghettos; it is described in personal accounts by those affected; it shows up in the statistics on poverty, anomie, school failures, alcoholism, family breakdown, crime, and suicide. How are these changes in individual human lives to be explained?

Many Euro-Canadians and other whites give a racist explanation: somehow the aboriginals are genetically inferior, lacking in intelligence and adaptability. (Winnipeg magistrate Isaac Rice: "There is something in their blood. I don't know what it is but an Indian and alcohol just don't mix. . . . I have never come across a married Indian couple.")[11] The facts do not bear them out.

Even those racists who offer the evidence of IQ testing to support (however inadequately) their claims that blacks are genetically inferior have been unable to make similar claims about the aboriginal population. And it is the case that, historically, the Amerindian and Inuit peoples have shown a high degree of adaptability and cultural variation.[12]

The plain fact is that the aboriginal peoples of the Americas have been subjected to a long series of massive assaults equivalent to genocide. Sometimes it has been the genocide (in the strict sense) of politicians, generals, and settlers who conducted campaigns—still going on in the jungles of the Amazon—of slaughter and germ warfare.[13] Sometimes it has been the unexpected effect of well-intentioned efforts by politicians, economists, missionaries, and educators.

We need to be warned particularly against the latter: the politicians who, to preserve traditional life-styles, have deported Indians to reservations which cannot support that life-style or any other decent one; the economists who, under the aegis of the crude doctrines of their dismal science, turn all rights into commodities to be bought and sold at market evaluation and try to force natives into marginal positions in the wage economy; the Christians who, not understanding their meaning and spiritual significance, ban the Potlatch, the Sun-dance, the White Dog Feast as superstitious and barbarous, and replace them with a ceremony in which the body and blood of a man/god is consumed; the teachers who, to civilize and educate, transport little children hundreds of miles from their families and communities and whip them for speaking their native tongues; the philosophers who, in their ignorance, settle Indian land claims by means of *a priori* quibbles amongst themselves. As for you and me, have we ever thought to help the native peoples by offering them as a compensation for their lands the blessings of our philosophy, religion, political theory, economics, technology, and education? And to what effect?

Conclusions

Argument Summarized

So far I have argued (a) that the widely recognized personal-security right protects us against psychic destruction and mutilation; (b) that there are well attested scientific theories in anthropology and psychology that can explain how the disruption of a culture's infrastructure (particularly land use) and other key sectors can produce personal pathology; (c) that there is abundant evidence that such pathology is widespread amongst Southern native peoples who have been subjected to massive cultural assaults; and (d) that racist and genetic explanations of the facts are implausible. It follows, then, that the personal security rights of Southern native peoples have probably been violated by the political, economic and other cultural arrangements—particularly those affecting their relation to the land—that we have forced upon them. This conclusion is in general agreement with what the native peoples themselves claim. Because of ignorance, our past wrongs may not be culpable; but, since we should now know better, future ones of the same sort would be.

First Conclusions

We can draw, then, a negative conclusion concerning aboriginal land rights in Northern Canada: namely, we must not impose a settlement that would violate the personal-security rights of the peoples of those territories. This rules out certain types of proposals. For example, it rules out the radical proposals of the Liberals' 1969 White Paper, "Statement of the Government of Canada on Indian Policy."[14]

The 1969 White Paper, in the name of enlightened liberalism and perhaps in fear of Québécois separatism, proposed to abolish all forms of special status for aboriginal peoples and to force a quick-march enculturalization into industrial civilization. Those who couldn't adapt would be left to the tender mercies of provincial welfare legislation. Although the White Paper, as such, was shelved after a storm of protest, the underlying ideology and attitudes are still very much alive. They must be resisted and the implications for federalism accepted.

To be fair to the native people, we will have to give up some of our passion for symmetry and homogenization in political arrangements: a province is a province and all must be treated the same; all must have the same legal and social system; every Canadian must have exactly the same rights and must be able to move anywhere in the country without changing status. In a confederation allowing for various forms and degrees of special status for ethnic groups—whether aboriginals, Québécois or Newfoundlanders—it may seem that we are giving group rights priority over individual rights. But we are not really faced with a choice between individualism and collectivism. For as I tried to show in the case of the native peoples—and as might be shown to a lesser degree in other cases—a primary right to personal security can require, for its implementation, the recognition of certain group rights to land and culture. To violate the latter is, in certain circumstances, to violate the former.

Second Conclusion

Does this negative conclusion imply a *status quo* policy that would freeze development and prohibit change? Would it imply that Northern aboriginals be hived off in wilderness ghettos (reminiscent of the Bantustans of South Africa) and left to fend for themselves? No. The implication is only a modest conservatism which rules out certain kinds of forced change, change of the sort imposed on natives in the past.

Northern natives have already made changes from their traditional ways. They made a swift and successful adaptation from a nomadic/hunting/gathering culture to a nomadic/hunting/trading one, two or three hundred years ago. They desire further change now.

The nature and pacing of cultural change, however, must not be too drastic and swift for successful adaptation. Basic economic change should centrally and positively involve native skills and knowledge—as did the swift adaptation to the fur-trade economy—rather than something like the social and economic marginalization of natives in the later agricultural and industrial changes in the South. The changes should allow for the forms of personal and group automony required for successful adaptation and the development of healthy personalities.

These principles of successful change suggest a positive conclusion. The form of land settlement demanded by native peoples in the North is reasonable and consistent with their personal security rights. They want some form of self-determination within Confederation, perhaps through the creation of two new provinces, Denedeh and Nunavut, with their own special rules for land ownership and use. They want a mixed economy based principally on renewable resources which they can manage, with controlled and limited exploitation of non-renewable resources. They want control over educational and other cultural institutions so that these can be made amenable to their changing needs and traditions.

In short, they believe that without balanced, carefully timed changes—changes over which they have a large measure of control—in the infrastructure, structure, and superstructure of their culture, they will be destroyed, not only as a people, but as people, not only as a group but as individuals. And, as I have tried to show, they are probably right.

Notes

1. I am particularly indebted to E. Newbery and J. Dumont of the Native Studies Department of Laurentian University for providing me with reading materials used in their course, "North American Native People: Tradition and Culture." These were most useful in gaining some insight into the native perspective. A standard ethnographic work is Diamond Jenness, *The Indians of Canada*, 4th ed., Ottawa: National Museum of Canada, 1958. See also Dennis and Barbara Tedlock, *Teachings from the American Earth: Indian Religion and Philosophy*, New York: Liveright, 1975. A classic account of shamanism on the world scale is Mircea Eliade, *Shamanism: Archaic Techniques of Ecstasy*, Princeton: Princeton University Press, 1964. For a more personal attempt to understand the phenomena, see James Dumont, "Journey to Day-light Land—Through Ojibway Eyes," *Laurentian Review*, Vol. VIII, No. 2, 1976.
2. The quotation from Phillip Blake and the Dene Proposed Agreement are taken from *Dene Nation: The Colony Within*, ed. by Mel Watkins, Toronto: University of Toronto Press, 1977. The other native voices are from Mr. Justice Thomas R. Berger, *Northern Frontier, Northern Homeland: the Report of the Mackenzie Valley Pipeline Inquiry*. Vol. One, Ottawa: Ministry of Supply and Services Canada, 1977. The latter in particular is highly recommended for its comprehensiveness, insight, and compassion.
3. For a massive compendium of international work on human rights since World War II, see Louis B. Sohn and Thomas Buergenthal, *International Protection of Human Rights*, Indianapolis: The Bobbs-Merrill Co. Inc., 1973. For accounts of torture in the modern world, see the bulletins of Amnesty International. For a set of case studies and an insightful theoretical account of forms of psychological torture, see Robert Jay Lifton, *Thought*

Reform and the Psychology of Totalism: A Study of "Brainwashing" in China, New York: W.W. Norton and Company, 1969.

4. For an argumentative survey of anthropological theories, see Marvin Harris, *The Rise of Anthropological Theory: A History of Theories of Culture*, New York: Harper & Row, 1968. For a popular, accessible survey of anthropology, see Peter Farb, *Humankind*, Boston: Houghton Mifflin Co., 1978. The position in the text is drawn from Harris's *Cultural Materialism: the Struggle for a Science of Culture*, New York: Random House, 1979. For a study of the sacred cow taboo and other case studies, see the latter and the more popular works, *Cows, Pigs, Wars and Witches: The Riddles of Culture*, New York: Vintage Books, 1978 and *Cannibals and Kings: The Origins of Cultures*, New York: Vintage Books, 1978. Harris's position bears some marked similarities with and departures from orthodox Marxist accounts of culture and social change. The present writer, while relying heavily on Harris, (a) finds important technical difficulties with the epistemology of his emic/etic distinction and (b) deplores the absence of a sophisticated psychological theory—whence the emphasis on (a) the signficance of "native voices" and (b) developmental psychology in my account.

5. See Erik Erikson's seminal work, drawing upon but extending in important ways the Freudian revolution in psychology, *Childhood and Society*, 2nd ed., New York: W.W. Norton and Company, Inc., 1963, especially Part Two: "Childhood in Two American Indian Tribes." See also: *Insight and Responsibility*, New York: W.W. Norton and Company, Inc., 1964 and *Identity: Youth and Crisis*, New York: W.W. Norton and Company, Inc., 1968. An accessible survey of Piaget's theory can be found in *Piaget's Theory of Intellectual Development* by Herbet Ginsburg and Sylvia Opper, Englewood Cliffs: Prentice-Hall Inc., 1969. Some insight into the importance of myths and legends in child-nurturing among Amerindians was drawn from Hyemeyohsts Storm, *Seven Arrows*, New York: Harper & Row, 1972 and backed up by the child psychiatrist Bruno Bettelheim's *The Uses of Enchantment: The Meaning and Importance of Fairy Tales*, New York: Vintage Books, 1977. See also his *Love Is Not Enough*, New York: Avon Books, 1971 and *The Informed Heart*, New York: Avon Books, 1971.

6. I do not attempt to unravel here the complex relations amongst personhood, personal identity, and personality. But, as noted, I am drawing on the work of psychologists in personality theory. I am also assuming that certain human beings who have not developed into "full persons"—or who have declined from that state and become human derelicts—still have rights.

7. *Childhood and Society*, p. 36.

8. *Ibid.*, p. 111.

9. *Ibid.*, Part Two.

10. For a brutally frank, first-hand account of conditions on some Indian reserves, see Heather Robertson, *Reservations Are for Indians*, Toronto: James Lewis & Samuel, 1970. For statistics and an indication of the relation between personal pathology (in the form of alcoholism) and crime see Douglas A. Schmeiser *et al.*, *The Native Offender and the Law*, prepared for the Law Reform Commission of Canada, 1974. See also the Hawthorn Committee Report, *A Survey of the Contemporary Indians of Canada*, 1967. It would be grossly unfair to those whom I have described as "human derelicts" produced by culture shock to leave the impression that they are without hope. The "powerful, baffling, cunning" disease of alcoholism, the chief form of personal pathology amongst native peoples, can be successfully fought through the cross-cultural program of Alcoholics Anonymous. A multi-faceted approach is required, but key elements seem to be a rediscovery of cultural roots and a form of spiritual growth. For theoretical perspectives, see Herbert Fingarette, *The Self in Transformation*, New York: Harper & Row, 1965 and Erik Erikson's *Young Man Luther*, New York: W.W. Norton & Co., Inc., 1962, and *Gandhi's Truth*, New York: W.W. Norton & Co., Inc., 1969. For relevant personal perspectives, see Lame Deer/Richard Endoes, *Lame Deer: Seeker of Visions*, New York: Simon & Schuster, 1972, and Maria Campbell, *Halfbreed*, Toronto: McClelland and Stewart-Bantam Ltd., 1979. The creativity that can flourish amidst personal and cultural

chaos is illustrated in the life of Norval Morriseau: see his *Legends of My People: The Great Ojibway* (illustrated and told by Morriseau, ed. by Selwyn Dewdney), Toronto: McGraw-Hill Ryerson Ltd., 1965, and Lister Sinclair and Jack Pollock, *The Art of Noval Morrisseau*, Toronto: Methuen, 1979.

11. The remarks of Magistrate Rice are quoted in James Burke, *Paper Tomahawks: From Red Tape to Red Power*, Winnipeg: Queenston House Publishing Inc., 1976.

12. For an account of Amerindian adaptability and cultural evolution see Peter Farb, *Man's Rise to Civilization, as Shown by the Indians of North America from Primeval Times to the Coming of the Industrial State*, New York: Avon Books, 1971. An antidote to Hollywood glamorization of European settlements is the revisionist history, *Bury My Heart at Wounded Knee: An Indian History of the American West*, by Dee Brown, New York: Bantam Books, 1972.

13. Perhaps the first commission of deliberate germ warfare was by the British general Lord Jeffrey Amherst in 1763 when he had smallpox-infested blankets and handkerchiefs distributed to his Indian enemies. (See Farb, p. 298.)

14. For an Indian reaction to the 1969 White Paper, see Harold Cardinal, *The Unjust Society*, Edmonton: M.G. Hurtig Ltd., 1969.

Questions

1. Is there a right to personal security? Is it a universal right? How would you relate the personal-security principle to the protection-of-life or the avoidance-of-suffering principles which were introduced in earlier chapters?

2. Do Stevenson's arguments apply only to those native groups who have not signed treaties?

3. Do you think Stevenson has provided convincing reasons for rejecting the position outlined by Trudeau?

4. Does respect for the personal-security principle imply acceptance of some form of self-government on the part of Canada's native peoples?

Suggestions for Further Reading

Legal Perspectives

- Jerome E. Bickenback, ''The Baker Lake Case,'' *University of Toronto Faculty of Law Review*, Vol. 38, No. 2 (Fall, 1980). The Baker Lake case is one of the most recent native land-claim judgements. The author describes how the case was resolved and what the case means for native land claims in Canada.

- Lord Denning, ''The Queen v. The Secretary of State for Foreign and Commonwealth Affairs,'' Court of Appeal (Civil Division), England. This judgement results from a challenge made by Canada's native people in the British Court of Appeal to the request of the Canadian government for patriation of the Canadian constitution. Lord Denning outlines, in colourful fashion, the statutes and laws that have determined the legal status of Canada's native people from the time of the first explorers to the date of the judgement.

- Douglas E. Sanders, "Aboriginal Peoples and the Constitution," *Alberta Law Review*, Vol. 19, No. 3. This article traces the way in which Canadian courts have resolved issues of importance to the native peoples and relates recent demands for the entrenchment of native rights in the Canadian constitution to this treatment. In the same volume are commentaries on the Sanders article by Wallace Many Fingers, who is a member of the Indian Association of Alberta, and Gurston Dacks, a faculty member in the Department of Political Science, University of Alberta.

Non-Legal Perspectives

- Harold Cardinal, *The Rebirth of Canada's Indians*, (Edmonton: Hurtig Publishers, 1977). Cardinal, an influential spokesman for Canada's native people, explores the problems of poverty, economic development, education, the Indian Act, aboriginal rights, and treaties.
- Hugh and Karmel McCullum, *This Land Is Not For Sale* (Toronto: Anglican Book Centre, 1975). The McCullums provide in this book what they describe as "a saga of neglect, exploitation and conflict" of Canada's original people and their land.
- Martin O'Malley, *The Past and Future Land* (Toronto: Peter Martin Associates, 1976). O'Malley is a journalist who travelled with Justice Thomas Berger as he inquired into the MacKenzie Valley pipeline proposal. The book is an account of what O'Malley saw and heard and his own assessment of the issues involved.

Environmental Ethics

Introduction

In this chapter we turn to a topic that is attracting more and more attention. Perusal of the daily news will quickly make the reasons clear.

Background Considerations

Most of us are aware of the importance of the environment for our own well-being. Much of our life is spent coping with it, enjoying it, or escaping from it. Until recently, however, we have not asked about the impact of our behaviour on the environment. It seems that we have been content to assume that the environment could and would look after itself. The negative impact of our lifestyles on the world around us could therefore be safely ignored or, if not ignored, escaped by simply moving on.

The shortsighted character of this approach is now becoming inescapably obvious. Acid rain is beginning to have a devastating impact on forests, agriculture, and water resources. The Great Lakes basin has become a repository for many of the deadliest chemicals known. Our energy resources are being depleted. Nuclear power, once seen as a future source of unlimited, inexpensive energy, has become a source of serious concern on a number of counts: the threats of leaks and accidents, the as-yet-unsolved problem of storing nuclear wastes, the long-term hazards of uranium mine tailings, and so on. Our forests and soils, too, are being severely depleted. Many species of animal life are extinct or endangered, and our treatment of animals generally has come under increasing critical scrutiny. The list can be extended indefinitely.

The Current Situation

What are the ethical issues associated with the environment? This is not an easy question for a number of reasons. First, facts always play an important role in moral argument. It is true that simply assembling facts cannot in itself resolve a moral issue. We have seen this point illustrated in each of the preceding chapters. For example, neither biology nor medicine can tell us whether an unborn child is a person from the moment of conception, no matter how carefully the facts of human development are set out. A purely factual account of pornography cannot tell us whether censorship is morally justified. At the same time, in the absence of a sound factual base, moral argument is without value. If we don't know what pornography is, we cannot assess its moral character. Environmental issues pose serious problems in this respect. The relevant facts are usually assembled by scientists and are usually communicated in technical language, language that a non-scientist has a good deal of trouble understanding. Obtaining and assembling facts in a understandable way is a major task on the road to the moral evaluation of environmental issues.

There is a second problem: because we depend so heavily on scientific experts to provide the facts needed for moral evaluation, we also have a tendency to assume that environmental ethics is a field in which only experts are competent to pass judgement. This has led to the belief that the really important environmental issues are technical or scientific in nature. Ethical concerns have been shunted aside.

Faced with these complexities, moral philosophy has a difficult task. First, at least some technical expertise must be acquired. Second, a serious effort must be made to present the moral issues and to decide how they should be approached.

The situation just described makes this topic doubly important in the context of this book. First, ethical issues arising out of environmental concerns are important and worthy of attention. Second, in approaching the subject, moral philosophers have had to pay particular attention to exploring and explaining the nature of morality and the role of moral philosophy in resolving moral issues. As a result, this chapter provides a stepping stone toward an explicit and reflective evaluation by moral philosophers of how they can legitimately contribute to the resolution of moral problems.

The Moral Dimension

To arrive at a sound moral judgement in any particular situation, we must assess whose concerns and interests should be considered. It requires a sensitive and imaginative effort to understand those concerns and interests. The importance of this feature of moral evaluation was well illustrated in the introduction to the discussion of abortion, where an explicit attempt was made to identify whose concerns and interests were relevant to the debate, and the nature of those concerns and interests.

Environmental issues pose important problems in this respect. First, we must decide whether to focus our concern on human werlfare. Or should preserving the environment and its non-human inhabitants be regarded as of value for its own sake? For example, ensuring the preservation of wild fur-bearing animals is of obvious significance for those whose livelihood depends on trapping. But if no identifiable people are likely to be adversely affected by the disappearance of a species, for example, does it follow that preserving that species is of no moral significance?

Second, environmental concerns address issues of vital importance to today's world. Polluted water supplies affect our health. Destruction of the wilderness alters recreational opportunities available to people now alive. Treatment of animals on our farms and in our laboratories has immediate implications for today's world. But not all environmental issues are like this. As Andrew Brook points out, an activity like uranium mining may pose few problems for us today while posing serious problems to people not yet born. This raises questions about our obligations to future generations. First, do we have obligations to the future? Second, if we have obligations to the future, do they differ in any important way from our obligations to the present? Discussion of this second question is unavoidable in light of the fact that so much about the future is uncertain.

Finally, we need to ask: How are our obligations to the future to be balanced against our obligations to the present? The point of this question will be very real to those who gain their livelihood in industries whose continued viability may hinge on the answers arrived at and the vigour with which new environmental safeguards are imposed.

The Readings

In the discussions that follow all of the above questions are addressed. Northrop Frye sets out some of the historical and intellectual dimensions of traditional Canadian attitudes to the environment. Robert E. Goodin argues that while utilitarianism seems to offer a plausible theoretical basis for resolving environmental issues, it should be rejected for a number of identifiable reasons. He then attempts to outline the basic principles that he argues should inform morally responsible environmental decision-making. Jan Narveson takes up the question of our obligations to future generations. Adopting a contractarian perspective, he argues that we have no moral obligations to a future in which we shall have no part. Mary Midgley in "Duties concerning Islands" criticizes contractarian and other modern moral theories just because they lead to the kinds of conclusions outlined and accepted by Jan Narveson. The problem with these theories, she suggests, is their excessively individualistic view of morality. She argues that developing an adequate environmental ethic requires that we see ourselves as part of a whole in which particular individuals play a rather small part.

Andrew Brook uses the environmental problems associated with uranium mine tailings to illustrate the role that moral values ought to play in the development of public policy and why determining our obligations to future generations is a moral question that those who will benefit from nuclear energy have a moral obligation to address. Building his moral analysis on the notions of fairness, liberty, and freedom from pain, Brook suggests that we do have obligations to the future, though working out what those obligations imply for activities like uranium mining or nuclear energy can be extremely difficult. Finally, Edwin Levy and David Copp look at environmental ethics from the point of view of those now alive. Determining the moral dimensions of an activity like uranium mining, they suggest, requires careful assessment of the costs and benefits the activity in question generates. Setting out the moral character of cost/benefit analysis is the focus of their contribution to the discussion.

Canada: New World without Revolution

Northrop Frye

Canada, with four million square miles and only four centuries of documented history, has naturally been a country more preoccupied with space than with time, with environment rather than tradition. The older generation, to which I have finally become assigned, was brought up to think of Canada as a land of unlimited natural resources, an unloving but rich earth-mother bulging with endless supplies of nickel and asbestos, or, in her softer parts, with the kind of soil that would allow of huge grain and lumber surpluses. The result of such assumptions is that many of our major social problems are those of ecology, the extinction of animal species, the plundering of forests and mines, the pollution of water, as the hundreds of millions of years that nature took to build up our supplies of coal and oil are cancelled out in a generation or two. The archaeologists who explore royal tombs in Egypt and Mesopotamia find they are almost always anticipated by grave robbers, people who got there first because they had better reasons for doing so than the acquisition of knowledge. We are the grave robbers of our own resources, and posterity will not be grateful to us. There is, however, a growing understanding that our situation is not simply one of people against planes, or whatever the current issue may be, but of soil and trees and water against concrete and tarmac.

These spatial and environmental problems have a temporal dimension as well. Our history began in the seventeenth century, the age of Baroque expansion in Europe, where the countries advancing most rapidly into the future were those on the Atlantic seaboard. Rapid advance is usually followed either by rapid decline or by a rapid change in some other direction: even by then Spain and Portugal had passed their meridian of growth, and France soon turned back to its European preoccupations. If the French had held Canada they might well have sold it, as they did Louisiana. What is important is not nationality but cultural assumptions. The Baroque

From Northrop Frye, "Canada: New World without Revolution," *Divisions on a Ground: Essays on Canadian Culture* (Toronto: House of Anansi Press, 1982). By permission.

age was an age of intense belief in the supremacy of human consciousness over nature. It had discovered something of the technological potential of mathematics, once mathematics had become attached to a powerful social organization. It was not an age of individualism, as is often said, but an age of relatively enlightened despotism, and in some ways very like the dawn of civilization in the Near East, when the pyramids of Egypt and the ziggurats of Babylon emerged as dramatic witness to what men could do when united under a sufficiently strong social will. Both then and in the Baroque period mathematics, and the appearance of geometrical patterns in the human environment, was a symbol of agressiveness, of imperialistic domination. We can see the results all over our country, in the grid patterns of our cities, the concession lines that divide up the farmland into squares, the railways and highways that emphasize direction through landscape rather than accommodation to it. Improvement in such communications always means a wider and straighter path through nature, and a corresponding decline of interest in it. With the coming of the aeroplane, even the sense of passing through a natural environment disappears. Our attitude to nature is reflected in our social environment, the kind we build ourselves. Washington was a city designed for automobiles rather than pedestrians long before there were any automobiles: Los Angeles, a city never designed at all, seems to have broken through the control even of the automobile. It was, after all, named after angels, who traditionally do not travel through space but simply manifest themselves elsewhere.

The religion that the British and French brought to the New World was not a natural monotheism, like the Algonquin worship of a Great Spirit, nor an imperial monotheism like that of the Stoics, but a revolutionary monotheism, with a God who took an active and partisan role in history; and like all revolutionary movements, including Marxism in our time, it equipped itself with a canon of sacred books and a dialectical habit of mind, a mental attitude in which the neighboring heresy is much more bitterly hated than the total rejection of the faith. The dialectical habit of mind produced the conception of the false god, a conception hardly intelligible to an educated pagan. All false gods, in the Christian view, were idols, and all idolatry came ultimately from the belief that there was something numinous in nature. The Christian teaching was that there were no gods in nature; that nature was a fellow-creature of man, and that all the gods that had been discovered in it were devils. We have derived many benefits from this attitude, but it had a more sinister side: it tended to assume that nature, not being inhabited or protected by gods or potentially dangerous spirits, was simply something available for human exploitation. Everywhere we look today, we see the conquest of nature by an intelligence that does not love it, that feels no part of it, that splits its own consciousness off from it and looks at it as an object. The sense of the absolute and unquestionable rightness of man's conquest over nature extended to other cultures regarded as being in a "state of nature." The primary principle of white settlement in this country, in practice if not always in theory, was that the indigenous cultures should be destroyed, not preserved or continued or even set apart.

The spokesman for the Baroque phase of this attitude is Descartes, whose fundamental axiom, "I think, therefore I am," rested on a desire to derive human existence from human consciousness, and to see that consciousness as being in a different world from the nature which for Descartes was pure extension in space. This attitude, in itself a logical development from the traditional Christian view of nature, got so far away from idolatry that it became a kind of idolatry in reverse, the idol this time being human consciousness itself, separated from nature. We live today in a social environment which is a triumph of Cartesian consciousness; an abstract and autonomous world of interlocking co-ordinates, in which most of our imagination is focussed not on nature but on the geometrical shapes that we have imposed on nature. My own few childhood memories of big cities are full of a kind of genial clutter: crowds of people on streets, shops with their doors open, theatres with glittering lights; and certainly the exhilaration of this had much to do with the attractiveness of cities for those in smaller centres a generation or two ago. Much of it of course remains, but it is becoming clearer that each advance of technology is accompanied by an advance in introversion, and less sense of public use. Many of the streets now in these same cities, with their deserted sidewalks and cars whizzing up and down the road past scowling fortress-like buildings, show us the kind of anti-community symbolized for me by University Avenue in Toronto and by the areas in Los Angeles where pedestrians are regarded as vagrants. The amount of mental distress caused by living in an environment which expresses indifference or contempt for the perspectives of the human body is very little studied: one might call it proportion pollution.

My own university is in the middle of a big industrial city: this means great masses of box-lunch students, who commute in and out from distant suburbs and take their courses with little experience of a real university community, of the kind that Cardinal Newman regarded as the ''idea'' of the university. The surrounding streets keep steadily turning into anonymous masses of buildings that look eyeless in spite of being practically all windows. Many of them seem to have had no architect, but appear to have sprung out of their excavations like vast toadstools. City planners speak of the law of conserving the plan, meaning that Bloor Street in Toronto or Sherbrooke Street in Montreal are still where those streets originally were even though there has been a total metamorphosis of the buildings on them. But even this law, which seems at first sight like a concession to a sense of tradition, is really a means of confining change to the inorganic. And as we shuttle from a pigeon-hole in a high-rise apartment to another pigeon-hole in an office, a sense of futility and humiliation takes possession of us that we can now perhaps see in its historical dimension.

As civilization has ''progressed'' from axe to bulldozer, the growing withdrawal from nature paralyzes something natural in ourselves. A friend of my wife's, an interior decorator, remarked that she had a group of neurotic clients whom it seemed impossible either to please or to get rid of, and she suddenly realized that they had something in common: they all lived in high-rise apartments at a level above the trees. A withdrawal from nature extends into a growing withdrawal from human society itself. I mentioned the increasing introversion that technology brings with it: the aeroplane is more introverted than the train; the super-highway, where there is a danger of falling asleep, more introverted than the most unfrequented country road. The international airport, completely insulated even from the country it is in, is perhaps the most eloquent symbol of this, and is parodied in Stanley Kubrick's movie *2001*, where the hero lands on the moon, dependent on human processing even for the air he breathes, and finds nothing to do there except to phone his wife back on earth, who is out.

A revolutionary habit of mind, being founded on the sense of a crucial break in time at some point, the Exodus from Egypt, the Incarnation of Christ, the flight of Mohammed, the October Revolution in Russia, has a hostility to continuous tradition built into it. In Moslem countries everything that happened before Mohammed's time is part of the age of ignorance. Guides in developing countries, especially Marxist ones, want to show tourists the achievements of their own regime, and often get angry or contemptuous when the tourists want to see the cultural products of the old exploiting days. Similarly with our own culture. The Puritans in Massachusetts were in communion with the Puritans in Norwich who petitioned the Cromwellian government to pull down a useless and cumbersome cathedral which was a mere relic of superstition. Even the Jesuit missionaries, for all their zeal and devotion, still assumed that the Indians, so long as they were heathen, were a part of subconscious nature, and that only Christianity could incorporate them into a fully human society. A cultural sense thus got started which was still operative until quite recently. My late friend Charles Currelly, the founder of the Archaeological Museum in Toronto, was horrified by the indifference with which the authorities of his day regarded the British Columbia totem poles, and by the eagerness with which they were ready to sell them off to anyone whom they thought would be fool enough to want them. What we are now beginning to see is that an original belief in the rightness of destroying or ignoring a so-called "savage" culture develops toward a contempt for our own. In Margaret Atwood's very ironic novel *Surfacing*, the heroine, trying to get back to an original identity represented by the Quebec forest, finds that she has to destroy everything cultural that she possesses, or, as she says: "everything from history must be eliminated."

The revolutionary aspect of white settlement extended from religion into economics, as entrepreneur capitalism developed. Every technological change brought with it a large-scale shift in population centres. The skyline of Toronto sixty years ago was dominated by the spires of the great churches: now the churches are points of depression within the skyline. My moral is not the shift of interest from spiritual to financial administration: my moral is rather that the churches themselves are now largely without parishes, the population, at least the church-going part of it, having moved elsewhere. Similarly Canada is a land of ruins to an extent that the less spacious countries of Europe would not dare to be: ghost towns at exhausted mines or the divisional points of old railways remind us how quickly our economy can scrap not merely a building but an entire city. As Earle Birney remarks, the country is haunted by its lack of ghosts, for a ghost town has no ghosts: it is only one of the rubbish heaps that spring up in an economy of waste. We may remember Sam Slick on the beauties of Niagara Falls:

> "It would be a grand speck to get up a jint stock company for factory purposes, for such another place for mills ain't to be found atween the poles. Oh dear!" said I, "only think of the cardin' mills, fullin' mills, cotton mills, grain mills, saw mills, plaster mills, and gracious knows what sort o' mills might be put up there . . . and yet them goneys the British let all run away to waste."

For Sam Slick the ideal thriving mill town of this sort was Lowell in Massachusetts, where my father started in business, and it was a sad day for both us when I took him there as an old man, after all the mills had been moved to the south, and he saw only the empty shell of the town he once knew. One question that such events raise is obviously: what can or should be preserved of what is no longer functional, and has little interest in itself apart from being a part of our past?

Whatever the answer, our social environment is a revolutionary one in which the main forces are indiscriminately destructive. This has to some extent always been true. Once there was a great city called Nineveh, so great that, according to the Book of Jonah, it took three days to journey across it. Then, quite suddenly, Nineveh disappeared under the sand, where it remained for nearly three thousand years. This kind of destruction from enemy action without, is a greater danger now, as hydrogen bombs would leave nothing for the sand to preserve; but along with it is the even more insidious sense of destruction from within, destruction that proceeds from the very nature of technology itself, not impossibly inspired by some deathwish in ourselves. The only possible economic alternative to capitalism, we feel, is social-ism, but if capitalism is a destroyer, socialism is even more of one, because more committed to technology. In ancient Egypt one of the first things a new Pharaoh often did was to deface his predecessor's monuments: this is still our rhythm of life, but it is largely an unconscious one, except when rationalized as progress.

The violence of our almost unmanageable cities is bringing about another great population shift, as people move out of them and back to smaller centres. We are beginning to see a very large cycle of history turning here, and with this is slowly growing another social vision. Ecology, the sense of the need for conserving natural resources, is not a matter of letting the environment go back to the wilderness, but of finding some kind of working balance between man and nature founded on a respect for nature and its inner economies. As part of natural ecology, we are also developing some sense of the need for a kind of human ecology, of conserving not only our natural but our cultural and imaginative resources. Again, this is not sim-ply a matter of leaving alone everything that is old: it is a way of life that grows out of a sense of balance between our present and our past. In relation to the natural environment, there are two kinds of people: those who think that nature is simply there to be used by man, and those who realize that man is himself a part of nature, and will destroy himself if he destroys it. In relation to time and human history, there are also two kinds of people: those who think that the past is dead, and those who realize that the past is still alive in us. A dead past left to bury its dead ends in a dead present, a society of sleepwalkers, and a society without a memory is as senile as an individual in the same plight.

Questions

1. Frye suggests that "our attitude toward nature is reflected in our social environment." What evidence does he provide in support of this view? Is it convincing? Can you find evidence in your social environment that would support this claim?

2. Frye sees a relationship between natural ecology (conserving natural resources) and "human ecology" (conserving cultural and imaginative resources). Do you think that a good case can be made for the existence of such a relationship?

Ethical Principles for Environmental Protection

Robert E. Goodin

For purposes of public policy making, subtle ethical doctrines are invariably translated into simple-minded principles. There are many reasons for this. Some seem to be inherent in the nature of public bureaucracies. Others derive from the nature of moral principles themselves.[1] But whatever its source, this tendency does exist and it powerfully constrains moral analysts of public issues: if their ethical advice is ever to be implemented, it must ultimately be reducible to some such rules of thumb, which can be stated simply yet applied widely. Ethical analysts of public policy, just as more ordinary policy analysts, must conduct and report their research in such ways that policy makers find it "usable."[2]

Here I shall canvass several such simple principles that might be applied in environmental, natural resource and, most especially, energy policy making. One of the great advantages of focusing on specific policy issues in this way lies in the possibility of discovering important limits of and alternatives to rules of thumb, which look compellingly attractive in the general case. After surveying the orthodox "utilitarian/cost-benefit" rule and its shortcomings as a principle for environmental policy making, I shall survey six alternatives to that principle which might be better suited to this particular context.

I. Maximizing Expected Utility

The orthodox rule used in making public decisions generally and environmental ones especially is an updated version of utilitariansim. Each alternative course of action is evaluated according to the ratio of its costs to its benefits, rendered commensurable most commonly through monetary equivalents. The option which "maximizes happiness' in the modern sense of having the highest cost-benefit ratio is recommended. Where costs and benefits of each option are probable rather than certain, their expected values (or certainty equivalents) are calculated by discounting each possible cost or benefit by the probability associated with its occurrence. Those who are indifferent to running risks decide strictly on the basis of these expected values, while those who either like or loathe risks adjust these figures upwards or

Condensed version of "No Moral Nukes," *Ethics* 90 (April 1980): 417–449. Published by The University of Chicago Press.

downwards, depending on the size of the risks and the intensity of their feelings about them. Such techniques are now widely used in deciding whether and where to pollute the air and water, build cities and dams and airports and power stations. The techniques are familiar, as are the objections to them.[3] Hence my own discussion of them can be rather perfunctory.

The first objection to "utilitarian/cost-benefit/expected-utility" rules is that they are based on individual preferences, which may provide infirm foundations for policy making in various ways. When stating their preferences, people always act at least partially in ignorance. Even if they "knew" all the relevant facts intellectually, they would often be psychologically incapable of conjuring up the sort of vivid image of what it would be like to *experience* that state of affairs which is necessary in order to form a proper preference for it, one way or the other. Furthermore, people's preferences do not predate experience but rather grow out of it. We do not have a very clear idea of our preferences for things lying very far outside either our past experiences or our present possibilities. Hare's proposal for a "trial-design" method of environmental planning—asking people to choose between alternative plans rather than just to state their preferences in the abstract—might go some way towards expanding people's vision, but it cannot go far enough to meet the real objection. The point remains that desires are powerfully adaptive, tailoring themselves to people's histories and possibilities; and if what people want is largely determined by what they get, then it is ludicrously circular and irrational to decide what they should get by asking what they want. My own view is that preferences and goods do come bundled together, but that we can still sensibly determine which bundle leaves people most satisfied. We can argue in that way, however, only if we accept "cardinal" notions of utility, which are an anathema to most economists.[4]

A second objection centres around the commensurability of values which this utilitarian principle presupposes. In one aspect, this is the famous problem of comparing the preferences, desires and utilities of different individuals. Even if we had no qualms about basing policy on people's preferences, we would still need to aggregate their conflicting demands into a single social decision; although there are various ingenious techniques for such interpersonal comparisons, I am persuaded that none can provide an objective basis, and such comparisons must rest instead on ethical postulates.[5]

Another aspect of the commensurability problem, which is more central to the practice of cost-benefit/expected-utility analysis, is that not all goods are tradable for one another or able to be converted into monetary equivalents. The problem is partly with the instruments used to establish equivalence. It is, for example, absurd to suppose that the amount of insurance coverage carried on a life or a historic church represents its full value to society.[6] More fundamentally, the problem is that some things may not be tradable for one another. The stock philosophical example asks how many sweets it would take to induce you to kill your grandmother: the answer, presumably, is that you would not be willing to kill her, no matter how many sweets you were offered; and the reason is not just that you would be satiated before you ate them all but is, rather, that granny ranks lexicographically prior to sweets in your value system.[7] Similarly in environmentalist debates, old-line conservationists often argue that preserving a threatened species or wilderness should rank absolutely prior to economic growth. If there are any such commodities that are not cashable in terms of a common metric, then the summing up implicit in utilitarian/ cost-benefit/expected-utility procedures is strictly impossible. It would be like adding apples and oranges.

The third and most common objection to utilitarianism, which also applies to its modern embodiments, is that it is impervious to distributions of happiness. Suppose utility could be maximized by giving everything to one person (a "super-efficient pleasure machine"), while leaving everyone else to starve. Then utilitarianism and its heirs recommend doing so, whereas our very strong moral intuitions dictate otherwise. Cost-benefit analysis has equally distressing implications: it would be better to dam up a river so as to displace a thousand families living in £20,000 houses rather than inconvenience one family living on a £21,000,000 estate.[8] That, of course, assumes crucially that all we care about is the value of the property flooded. We may, however, care not only how high the costs are but also who has to pay them. There is nothing in the logic of expected-utility calculations that forces us to take distributions into account, but neither is there anything that precludes us from doing so. If decision makers care about the distributive impact of their policies, they can—and there is some evidence that they do—build "distributive weights" into their assessments of policy options, boosting the expected utility of policies that allocate benefits to certain favoured groups (e.g., the least advantaged).[9] Still, I take it to be a serious criticism of expected-utility procedures that they treat distributive adjustments merely as an option, whereas on most other principles they are morally obligatory.

This discussion is little more than a sketchy reminder of familiar problems associated with utilitariansim and, *pari passu*, with its modern instantiations, cost-benefit/ expected-utility analysis. While these objections are perfectly general, they apply with particular force, given some of the peculiar features of environmental decisions. Taken together, they should suffice to motivate the search for alternative principles which can be used to guide decision making on environmental and analogous issues.

II. Keeping the Options Open (Reversibility)

Some of the most poignant pleas for environmental protection are couched in "forever more" terms. We are urged to prevent the *extinction* of certain species, or to prevent the destruction of *irreplaceable* historical landmarks or natural vistas. Many factors might contribute to the power of these appeals, but surely one of the more important is that they violate Arthur C. Clarke's rule, "Do no commit the irrevocable." The Study Group on Critical Environmental Problems explicitly defined its goal as being "to prevent irreversible global damage" and, along these lines, defined as among the most critical pollutants heavy metals such as mercury, which is "a nearly permanent poison once introduced into the environment."[10]

Similar "keep-the-options-open" rules are used in more mundane ways in energy policy making. Many analysts recommend "open-ended planning" in the sense that "any choice made now must be made in such a way that . . . a later generation, or the same generation at a later date, can reverse the choice and return to the original situation."[11] This is a principle endorsed even by the United Kingdom's Department of Energy, whose *Energy Policy* review argued that choices "should not prematurely close options" and whose deputy secretary testified at the Windscale Inquiry of the need to "establish a wide range of energy options and maintain a flexible energy strategy which can be reviewed and adjusted if necessary in light of subsequent developments."[12] Such suggestions parallel Barry's analysis of the demands of intergenerational justice "that the overall range of opportunities open to successor generations should not be narrowed."[13]

Keeping options open does not, of course, entail refusing to make any choices at all. Having chosen one path, it will always be costly to shift over to some other; but, while costly, the shift is at least possible. This is all that keeping the options open requires. Thus we may, consistent with that rule, pursue certain options provided our policy is *reversible*—provided we can backtrack if necessary. Such considerations must be superimposed on ordinary decision rules, since expected value calculations overproduce irreversible outcomes even among risk-neutral decision makers.[14]

For an example of the reversibility criterion explicitly at work in policy debates, consider the issue of nuclear power. As regards implementation of the nuclear option, Rochlin recommends "reversibility" as one of two "social criteria" to be used in selecting sites and techniques for disposing of radioactive wastes.[15] It is better, he argues, to place radioactive wastes in deep rock deposits, where we can recover them if something goes wrong and they begin leaking, than it would be to put them where we cannot get them back (letting them melt their way into the polar ice or slide between continental plates in the deep seabed or shooting them off into deep space).

The same sort of reversibility criterion can be used to guide our choice between nuclear and non-nuclear energy options. Elster supposes that such considerations make fossil fuels preferable to nuclear ones.[16] Both entail risks of catastrophic consequences: carbon dioxide discharges from coal- and oil-fired plants might alter the global climate; proliferation of nuclear weapons built with plutonium from nuclear power plants might hasten Armageddon. The difference is that the "hothouse" effect could be reversed. If it really does happen—which is far from certain—then by ceasing to burn fossil fuels we can gradually reverse the damage to the climate. It is a slow process and less certain of success than Elster supposes, perhaps; but at least reversibility looks possible here. Nuclear proliferation, in contrast, seems truly irreversible. Once nations have the technical capacity to build nuclear weapons, they have it forever. Nuclear reactors and their radioactive by-products themselves impose irreversible obligations. As the Oak Ridge team concedes, "One cannot simply abandon a nuclear reactor the way one can abandon a coal-fired plant." It is instead an "unforgiving" technology which, as Kneese worries, "will impose a burden of continuous monitoring and sophisticated management of dangerous material, essentially forever. The penalty of not bearing this burden may be unparalleled disaster. This irreversible burden would be imposed even if nuclear fission were used only for a few decades, a mere instant in the pertinent time scales."[17]

Although the expected-utility rule must obviously be modified to take better account of irreversibilities, it would be inadvisable and, indeed, impossible to make decisions strictly on the basis of the reversibility/keep-the-options-open rule. Usually some options can be kept open only by closing off some others. This, many argue, is the case with energy policy choices. Lovins maintains that "hard" and "soft" energy paths "are mutually exclusive. . . . Commitments to the first may foreclose the second." Other interveners at the Windscale Inquiry claimed that, although reprocessing was justified in terms of keeping the options open, it would actually foreclose them: given the immense capital investment, we will inevitably be stuck with using such plants once we have built them.[18] If some options can be kept open only by closing off others, we must look closely at the likely costs and benefits of each. It would be foolhardy to keep the second, third and fourth options open if the price is foreclosing the first. On the other side, there are surely some options that should be closed forever. One obvious example is the option to initiate a nuclear war. Some, such as Farley, defend the expansion of "peaceful" nuclear programmes on the grounds that "they constitute a hedge against failure of nonproliferation efforts, an assurance that countries which try the nonproliferation option will not be permanently disadvantaged if it fails."[19] But here reversibility looks singularly unattractive. Keeping the option of acquiring and using nuclear weapons open in this way would be clearly indefensible if we ever could find a way to close it irrevocably for everyone. Irreversibility in this case would be a virtue. Similarly, suppose we find a guaranteed way to dispose of radioactive wastes once and for all. Provided we can be absolutely sure of the technique, it would be far better to dispose of these wastes permanently and irreversibly instead of keeping them where we (along with saboteurs, thieves and careless miners) can get at them.[20]

III. Comparing the Alternatives

If forced to make irreversible choices, we should at least do so on the basis of a full survey of all advantages and disadvantages of all available alternatives. Cost-benefit/expected-utility analysis is one way of doing so, but not the only way. This "compare-the-alternatives" principle is enshrined in the economic notion of opportunity costs and was recently brought to the attention of political theorists by Fishkin's discussion of "tyrannical-decision" rules, defined as those which impose gratuitous suffering.[21] This principle of comparing the alternatives is clearly practised in energy debates when various authors routinely compare costs, benefits and risks arising from alternative strategies. And it clearly underlies their criticisms, each of the others, for failing to make *comprehensive* comparisons between *all* the alternatives which are available.[22]

Alongside these very ordinary applications of the compare-the-alternatives principle, we also find a rather more novel one. This assesses the riskiness of a policy in terms of the *increment* of risk it adds to those pre-existing in the status quo, rather than in terms of the absolute value of the risk associated with the policy. Follesdal's paper on recombinant DNA research, for example, argues that we need not fear a "mad scientist" using these new techniques to unleash a deadly virus on the world, not because that could not happen but rather because there are already enough devastatingly lethal viral and chemical agents available to any given "mad scientist" to do the job. The "added risk" entailed in offering one more way to destroy all life on earth is effectively zero, although of course the absolute risk of that person doing so is frighteningly high.[23]

This principle emerges at various points in the nuclear-energy debate. In Cochran and Rotow's standards for an acceptable system for disposing of nuclear wastes, for example, the radiation hazard to future generations need not be eliminated altogether but only reduced to where it is "comparable to the cumulative risk to all future generations from the original uranium resources from which the radioactive wastes were derived, assuming these uranium resources were unmined."[24] Risk-added reasoning may also underlie our failure to protect future generations adequately from even rather larger risks of leaks of radioactive wastes. The present generation may be willing to forgo nuclear energy in light of such risks to successors "if that action would protect future societies forever. But it would be in no position to control the choices of future societies." And, as long as someone will contaminate their environment anyway, it might as well be us.[25] The risk-added argument is also used by the Oak Ridge team to brush aside concern with the proliferation of nuclear weapons: "We believe that the effect of a moratorium [on civilian uses of nuclear power] adopted only by the United States would be marginal . . . because reactors would be available from other countries," and these could supply plutonium for bomb building even if American-built reactors did not.[26]

Wohlstetter aptly replies that "to argue . . . that such restrictions would be irrelevant because there are other ways to get a bomb is like opposing inoculation for smallpox because one might also die of bubonic plague. Better to suggest protection against the plague."[27] That the status quo contains other ways for nuclear weapons to spread or for people to be poisoned or irradiated is a criticism of the status quo rather than a defence of policies only moderately increasing those risks. The general flaw of the risk-added approach is that it adopts the status quo as a baseline. Truly comprehensive risk-benefit analysis acknowledges no baseline. We must compare the profiles of *all* the alternatives, the status quo being just one option among many. The fact that an option is no worse than the status quo is irrelevant if there are options available that are significantly better than the status quo.

Finally, we can question the moral relevance of how bad one's alternative opportunities might be. Would we really feel comfortable buying up a bankrupt farmer's land at bargain-basement prices just because we know that there are no other bidders; would we not have a moral duty to pay a "fair market price," even if the market did not force us to do so?

The recent United States Supreme Court decision on the drug Laetrile, thought by some to cure cancer, offers a case in point. Those taking the drug are dying of cancer anyway—their alternatives are grim indeed. Still, we object to other people taking advantage of their sadly restricted opportunity set to peddle drugs which have never been shown safe and effective. The fact that cancer victims have little to lose is beside the point. The court held that the law's protection extends even to the terminally ill.[28] Judging from this case, we do seem to feel that certain things should or should not be done, whatever the competing alternatives look like. The injunction to "compare alternatives" or "inspect opportunity costs" might have distinctly limited applicability if many cases fit into this category.

IV. Protecting the Vulnerable

A further rule, suggested by the last objection to the compare-the-alternatives rule, might require that we give special protection to those who are particularly vulnerable. Someone may be vulnerable to another's actions if he is strongly and directly affected by them; or he may, like the cancer victim or the bankrupt farmer, simply be vulnerable *tout court*, in that he has so restricted an opportunity set as to put him at the mercy of others in general.

Protecting the vulnerable might mean many things. Some environmentalists seem to play on this principle when pointing out that, given modern technology, seals and whales are utterly at our mercy and are enormously vulnerable to our choices. This principle also underlies the practice of judging the acceptability of pollution and radiation hazards by reference to the dose risked by the most exposed group. The most striking application, however, seems to be to future generations, who are peculiarly vulnerable to the effects of our choices, especially in the environmental or energy fields. They would, for example, be strongly and directly affected by our decision to leave them with the radioactive wastes from our nuclear power plants; and, once we have made that decision, they have very little choice but to live with it.

Intergenerational transactions are singularly one-way affairs. Later generations are extraordinarily vulnerable to the choices of earlier ones, but forebears are largely immune to the choices of their successors. This absence of reciprocal relations would, on Hobbesian or Humean accounts, imply that we have no moral obligations toward future generations.[29] But, on other understandings, such asymmetrical power relations are the very stuff of moral obligations: those in a position of dominance have a special obligation to protect those dependent upon them. Such codes clearly underlie the patronal arrangements of peasant societies. Similarly, in our own cultures special vulnerabilities underlie codes of professional ethics and form the basis of loving relationships.[30] Or, again, within the family, the very fact that children are dependent upon their parents gives them rights against the parents. Were we to extend such a principle to policy decisions more generally, we would have to cease discounting the interests of vulnerable future generations. Instead, we would have to count their suffering (from, e.g., our leaky nuclear-waste dumps) at least on a par with our own pains and pleasures.

V. Maximizing the Minimum Payoff

Protecting the vulnerable is recommended on ethical grounds alone. A related principle—maximin, or "maximize the minimum payoff"—is recommended on epistemic ones as well. This rule compares the "worst possible outcomes" of all alternative policies, selecting that policy with the least unbearable consequence should worse come to worst.[31] This decision rule, or something very much like it, is forced upon us whenever any of the three crucial steps in the expected-utility calculus is impossible. That procedure requires that we (a) list all the possible outcomes, and that we then set (b) values and (c) probabilities for each. One or more of these steps is often not feasible. It is often impossible to list all the possible scenarios and outcomes, especially where the "human factor" might be involved (as in the operation or sabotage of a nuclear reactor).[32] Furthermore, it is typically difficult to get reliable probability estimates: objective statistics are unavailable; theories are either too few or too numerous and contradictory; and subjective estimates are unreliable. Finally, it might even be difficult to get a good indicator of the value (or cost) of each of the consequences. Such problems might motivate our reluctance to let a smoker take any risks he wants—we just do not believe he fully appreciates the pains of lung cancer.

Where any of these steps cannot be performed, the expected-utility/cost-benefit/ benefit-risk calculations cannot be performed. Instead we must rely upon other types of decision rule capable of functioning without those inputs. Two alternative rules are widely discussed. Follesdal suggests that "in such cases we estimate the probability of the worst consequence to be 1, and act accordingly," which is the maximin (maximize the minimum payoff) rule. Closely related to this is Savage's "minimax regret rule," requiring us to choose the course of action which minimizes the maximum regret we might suffer.[33] Alternatively, we might follow the suggestion of Arrow and Hurwicz, adopted by the Swedish Energy Commission for assessing nuclear reactors, to choose policies upon the basis of a weighted combination of the best possible and worst possible outcomes which might result from each alternative policy option.[34] If, as Elster argues is the case with alternative energy strategies, all options have roughly the same best possible outcomes, then the Arrow-Hurwicz rule reduces to the maximin rule, and we need only worry about maximizing the minimum possible payoffs.[35] Either of these rules would go far towards avoiding the stringent preconditions for applying the expected-utility rule: while both do require that we know enough about the range of possible outcomes to pick out the worst (or best and worst, or most regrettable), none requires any more information about intermediate possibilities, their costs or benefits; and, most especially, none requires us to know anything whatsoever about probabilities.

Popular resistance to untried technologies with the potential for causing large-scale catastrophes—usually dismissed as a rational risk aversion—might therefore be a wholly rational response to irresolvable uncertainties. It is, I think, clear enough that such uncertainties plague energy choices and render expected-utility calculations impossible. What this may mean for the choice is, however, unclear. The British Department of Energy argued in favour of the nuclear option, saying that "our energy strategy should be robust, producing minimum regret whatever course future events take."[36] Apparently the most regrettable outcome they could imagine is running short of energy. Others draw attention to plausible scenarios with still more regrettable outcomes, ranging from altering the world climate (a possible result of burning oil and coal) to genetic mutations or proliferation of nuclear weapons (a possible result of nuclear power). On balance, it would seem that both nuclear and conventional fossil-fuel power plants are disqualified on this maximin criterion in favour of energy conservation combined with a range of "alternative" strategies relying on solar, wind, wave, geothermal, etc., power.

VI. Maximizing Sustainable Benefits

Another rule directs us to opt for the policy producing the highest level of net benefits which can be *sustained* indefinitely. This contrasts with the directive of ordinary expected-utility maximization to go for the highest total payoff without regard to its distribution interpersonally or intertemporally. Utility maximization looks only to the sum total of benefits and is indifferent to whether they come in a steady stream or all bunched in one period. Considerations of intergenerational equity would demand instead that each generation be guaranteed roughly equal benefits and insist that one generation may justly enjoy certain benefits only if those advantages can be sustained for subsequent generations as well.[37] Following the "maximize-sustainable-benefits" rule would strongly encourage current decision makers to think in *maximin* terms also, since the lowest possible payoff is one that the initial generation must suffer along with everyone else.

The rule of maximizing sustainable benefits has clear and important applications to certain aspects of environmental policy, such as setting permissible levels of fish catches.[38] But it also has significant implications beyond these obvious applications. In the case of energy policy, for example, it decisively favours renewable sources (solar, geothermal, wind, wave, etc.) over utilization of scarce natural resources (such as oil and coal). Uranium falls into the category of scarce resources: "The amount of uranium available to the United States at costs that can be afforded in a LWR [light water reactor] is usually estimated to be 3×10^6 tons. Thus, prima facie, we have enough uranium to support about 25,000 reactor-years of LWRs—say 800 reactors for 30 years."[39] With the "fast breeder," of course, the supply of fissionable plutonium could be rendered virtually inexhaustible, transforming nuclear energy into a sustainable benefit. Then the question is simply which strategy, among those yielding sustainable benefits, yields maximal ones. But there is, more fundamentally, a question of whether the benefits of nuclear energy really are sustainable. The benefits must, remember, be net of costs, which will be increasing throughout time on the most plausible accounts.[40] Even if the energy flow remains constant, the benefits of nuclear power net of these constantly increasing costs will be steadily diminishing.

VII. Avoiding Harm

In all the previous principles, harms and benefits are treated as symmetrical. To avoid a harm is to produce a benefit. We are indifferent between two plans, one generating positive benefits valued at £x and the other avoiding costs of £x which we would otherwise have had to suffer. Avoiding a harm of a certain magnitude is just as desirable (and, indeed, arguably equivalent to) producing a benefit of that same size. The "harm-avoidance" principle denies this symmetry, arguing instead that it is much worse to create costs than it is just to fail to produce equally large benefits.

Initially we might be inclined to run this together with the more familiar "acts/omissions" doctrine.[41] But, in truth, the harm-avoidance principle is not only distinct from that doctrine but is also part of what really underlies its appeal. People who are victims of an immoral *act*—of fraud or criminal assault, for example—are generally worse off than they would have been in the absence of such an act. Where someone merely *omits* to perform a morally desirable act, others are usually no worse off than they were before the omission—they have just lost out on some further benefits they might have enjoyed had the action been performed. Psychological studies show that individuals, when making decisions, generally do weigh losses more heavily than corresponding gains.[42] And ethically it does seem worse actually to harm someone than merely to fail to help him. This sentiment underlies "negative utilitarianism" and the distinction Foot draws between weaker "positive duties" to help people and stronger "negative duties" not to harm them.[43]

Harm avoidance is one of the more important components in environmentalist arguments against reckless interventions into natural processes. Consider, for example, the problem of seeding hurricanes. The hope is that they will thereby lose force before hitting land, and there is every reason to believe that such an action will save many lives and reduce property damage. But there is also a slight chance that seeding the hurricane will make it worse and increase the costs. Some decision-theoretical treatments of the problem, sensitive to the harm-avoidance principle, weight such potential costs more heavily than the costs resulting from just letting the hurricane take its natural course: the government bears more responsibility for causing such damage than for letting similar damage occur naturally.[44]

Applying this principle to the problem of energy choices would, I think, argue decisively in favour of alternative and renewable sources (solar, geothermal, wind, wave, etc.), combined with strenuous efforts at energy conservation, in preference to nuclear or fossil-fuel generation of power. The worst that can be said against alternative, renewable sources is that they may yield less energy—that they produce fewer benefits. Both nuclear and oil- or coal-fired plants, in contrast, run real risks of causing considerable harm. If we weight the harms much more heavily than the benefits forgone, as the harm-avoidance principle directs, both nuclear and conventional power plants will appear much less advantageous than reliance upon solar, geothermal, wind or wave power combined with energy-conservation programmes.

VIII. Conclusion

The upshot of this discussion is that the standard maximize-expected-utility decision rule has very serious limitations. It is at best a partial response to the range of considerations that should be taken into account by policy makers, especially (but not exclusively) when environmental, natural resource or energy decisions are at issue. At the very least, we would want to modify the maximize-expected-utility rule to take these neglected considerations into account. We might, for example, want to weight outcomes in the expected utility calculus in such a way as:

1. to bias decisions against *irreversible* choices (which may sometimes be permissible, but only after much more careful scrutiny than they receive in the ordinary expected-utility calculus);
2. to bias decisions in favour of offering special protection to those who are especially *vulnerable* to our actions and choices;
3. to bias decisions in favour of *sustainable* rather than on-off benefits; and
4. to bias decisions against *causing harm*, as distinct from merely forgoing benefits.

Even after the expected-utility calculus has been modfied to meet these further ethical demands, epistemological ones remain. When the logical preconditions for applying that rule are absent, we are logically compelled to fall back on other principles (such as "maximize the minimum payoff") that build on weaker premises altogether. Obviously it would be folly to suppose that all these new rules always converge in their recommendations on particular cases. But as a general rule they would all tend to strengthen the ethical case for environmental protection.

Notes

1. Robert E. Goodin, "Loose Laws," *Philosophica* 23 (1979): 79–96. For another application, see Marshall Cohen, Thomas Nagel and Thomas Scanlon, eds., *War and Moral Responsibility* (Princeton: Princeton University Press, 1974).
2. See Charles E. Lindblom and David K. Cohen, *Usable Knowledge* (New Haven: Yale University Press, 1979); Carol H. Weiss, ed., *Using Social Research for Public Policy Making* (Lexington, Mass.: D.C. Heath, 1977).
3. On cost-benefit analysis generally, see: I.M.D. Little and J.A. Mirrlees, *Project Appraisal and Planning for Developing Countries* (New York: Basic, 1974); A.K. Dasgupta and D.W. Pearce, *Cost-Benefit Analysis* (London: Macmillan, 1972); and Richard Layard, ed., *Cost-Benefit Analysis* (Harmondsworth: Penguin, 1972). For environmental policy applications see: A.M. Freeman III, R.H. Haveman and A.V. Kneese, *The Economics of Environmental Policy* (New York: Wiley, 1973); Lincoln Allison, *Environmental Planning: A Political and Philosophical Analysis* (London: Allen & Unwin, 1975); and Robert E. Goodin, *The Politics of Rational Man* (London: Wiley, 1976), pt. 4. For critiques, see: Peter Self, *Econocrats and the Policy Process* (London: Macmillan, 1975); Alan Coddington, " 'Cost-Benefit' as the New Utilitarianism," *Political Quarterly* 42 (1971): 320–325; and Laurence Tribe, "Policy Science: Analysis or Ideology?" *Philosophy and Public Affairs* 2 (1972): 66–110.
4. R.M. Hare, "Contrasting Methods of Environmental Planning" and Jonathan Glover, "How Should We Decide What Sort of World Is Best?" in *Ethics and Problems of the 21st Century*, ed. K.E. Goodpaster and K.M. Sayre (Notre Dame, Ind.: University of Notre Dame Press, 1979), pp. 63–78 and 79–92 respectively. Jon Elster, "Sour Grapes: Utilitarianism and the Genesis of Wants," *Beyond Utilitarianism*, ed. A.K. Sen and B. Williams (Cambridge: Cambridge University Press, 1982). Robert E. Goodin, "Retrospective Rationality," *Social Science Information* 18 (1979): 967–990.
5. Robert E. Goodin, "How to Determine Who Should Get What," *Ethics* 85 (1975): 310–321.
6. Richard Zeckhauser, "Procedures for Valuing Lives," *Public Policy* 23 (1975): 454, concludes that "it would be quite rational" for a woman contemplating the threat of breast cancer "to insure no more than the medical expenses" of a mastectomy, since the insurance payment would not restore her breast should it have to be removed.
7. Cf. James Griffin, "Are There Incommensurable Values?" *Philosophy and Public Affairs* 7 (1977): 39–59.
8. Coddington, "New Utilitarianism"; Goodin, *Politics of Rational Man*, 16; Aaron Wildavsky, "The Political Economy of Efficiency," *Public Administration Review* 26 (1966): 292–310. This example further assumes that people will not be compensated for the loss of their homes, or that they cannot be fully compensated by monetary payments for moving from where they grew up.
9. Burton A. Weisbrod, "Deriving an Implicit Set of Governmental Weights for Income Classes," in *Cost-Benefit Analysis*, ed. Layard, pp. 395–428.
10. For further discussion of the reversibility rule, see (a) M.P. and N.H. Golding, "Why Preserve Landmarks? A Preliminary Inquiry," *Ethics and Problems of the 21st Century*, ed. Goodpaster and Sayre, pp. 175–190, (b) Clarke's maxim is quoted in Lynton Keith Caldwell, *Environment: A Challenge for Modern Society* (Garden City, N Y: Natural History Press, 1970), p. 214, (c) Carroll L. Wilson et al., *Man's Impact on the Global Environment*, Report of the Study of Critical Environmental Problems, vol. 4, sec. 138 (Cambridge: MIT Press, 1970), pp. 259–263.

11. David W. Pearce, Lynn Edwards and Geoff Beuret, *Decision Making for Energy Futures* (London: Macmillan, 1979), p. 26.
12. Ian Breach, *Windscale Fallout* (Harmondsworth: Penguin, 1978), pp. 27–28.
13. Brian Barry, "Circumstances of Justice and Future Generations," in *Obligations to Future Generations*, ed. Richard Sikora and Brian Barry (Philadelphia: Temple University Press, 1978), p. 243. See also Barry, "Justice between Generations," in *Law, Morality and Society*, ed. P.M.S. Hacker and J. Raz (Oxford: Clarendon Press, 1977), p. 275.
14. Kenneth J. Arrow and Anthony C. Fisher, "Environmental Preservation, Uncertainty and Irreversibility," *Quarterly Journal of Economics* 88 (1974): 312–319; Claude Henry, "Investment Decisions under Uncertainty: The 'Irreversibility' Effect," *American Economic Review* 64 (1974): 1006–1012.
15. Gene I. Rochlin, "Nuclear Waste Disposal: Two Social Criteria," *Science* 195 (1978): 23–31.
16. Jon Elster, "Risk, Uncertainty and Nuclear Power," *Social Science Information* 18 (1979): 371–400.
17. Alvin M. Weinberg et al., *Economic and Environmental Impacts of a U.S. Nuclear Moratorium, 1985–2010*, 2nd ed. (Cambridge: MIT Press, 1979): 79. Allen V. Kneese, "The Faustian Bargain," *Resources* 44 (1973).
18. Amory B. Lovins, *Soft Energy Paths* (Harmondsworth: Penguin, 1977), pp. 26, 59–60; Breach, *Windscale Fallout*.
19. Philip J. Farley, "Nuclear Proliferation," *Setting National Priorities: The Next Ten Years*, ed. H. Owen and C. Schultze (Washington, D.C.: Brookings Institution, 1976), p. 160.
20. Robert E. Goodin and Ilmar Waldner, "Thinking Big, Thinking Small and Not Thinking At All," *Public Policy* 27 (1979): 1–24.
21. James Fishkin, "Tyranny and Democratic Theory," in *Philosophy, Politics and Society*, 5th series, ed. P. Laslett and J. Fishkin (Oxford: Blackwell, 1979), pp. 197–226.
22. Lovins, *Energy Paths*; Weinberg et al., *Economic & Environmental Impacts*; Herbert Inhaber, "Risk with Energy from Conventional and Nonconventional Sources," *Science* 203 (1979): 718–23.
23. Dagfinn Follesdal, "Some Ethical Aspects of Recombinant DNA Research," *Social Science Information* 18 (1979): 401–419.
24. Thomas B. Cochran and Dimitri Rotow, "Radioactive Waste Management Criteria," mimeographed (Washington, D.C.: Natural Resources Defense Council 1979); Weinberg et al., *Economic and Environmental Impacts*, p. 94.
25. Zeckhauser, "Procedures," p. 439.
26. Weinberg et al., *Economic & Environmental Impacts*, p. 56.
27. Quoted by Czech Conroy, *What Choice Windscale?* (London: Friends of the Earth, 1978), p. 57. See further Albert Wohlstetter, "Spreading the Bomb without Quite Breaking the Rules," *Foreign Policy* 25 (1976–1977): 145–179.
28. *United States v. Rutherford* 442 U.S. 544, 551, 555, 558 (1979) came to the U.S. Supreme Court on appeal from the Tenth Circuit Court of Appeals, which "held that the safety and effectiveness terms used in the statute have no reasonable application to terminally ill cancer patients." Since those patients, by definition, would "die of cancer regardless of what may be done," the court concluded that there were no realistic standards against which to measure the safety and effectiveness of a drug for that class of individuals. The Court of Appeals therefore approved the District Court's injunction permitting use of Laetrile by cancer patients certified as terminally ill. The U.S. Supreme Court unanimously overturned this ruling. Mr. Justice Marshall, for the Court, writes, "Only when a literal construction of a statute yields results so manifestly unreasonable that they could not fairly be attributed to congressional design will an exception to statutory language be judicially implied. Here, however, we have no license to depart from the plain language of the Act, for Congress could reasonably have intended to shield terminal patients from ineffectual or unsafe drugs . . . . Since the turn of the century, resourceful entrepreneurs have advertised a wide variety of purportedly simple and painless cures for cancer, including lineaments of turpentine, mustard, oil, eggs, and ammonia; peatmoss;

arrangements of colored floodlamps; pastes made from glycerin and limburger cheese; mineral tablets; and "Fountain of Youth" mixtures of spices, oil, and suet . . . . This historical experience does suggest why Congress could reasonably have determined to protect the terminally ill, no less than other patients, from the vast range of self-styled panaceas that inventive minds can devise."

29. Barry, "Justice between Generations," idem, "Circumstances of Justice."

30. James C. Scott, *The Moral Economy of the Peasant* (New Haven: Yale University Press, 1976); Bernard Williams, "Politics and Moral Character," in *Public and Private Morality*, ed. S. Hampshire (Cambridge: Cambridge University Press, 1978), p. 56; John R.S. Wilson, "In One Another's Power," *Ethics* 88 (1978): 299–315.

31. Maximin implies avoiding the worst state of the world all round, whereas protecting the vulnerable implies avoiding the worst consequences possible for certain target groups. It is, of course, possible to build a similar distributive focus into maximin (as does Rawls, for example): but it is important to realize that we *are* building something more into the rule when we do that.

32. Robert E. Goodin, "Uncertainty as an Excuse for Cheating Our Children," *Policy Sciences* 10 (1978): 25–43.

33. Follesdal, "Ethical Aspects," p. 406; L.J. Savage, *The Foundations of Statistics* (New York: Wiley, 1954).

34. Kenneth J. Arrow and Leonid Hurwicz, "An Optimality Criterion for Decision-Making under Ignorance," in *Uncertainty and Expectations in Economics*, ed. C.F. Carter and J.L. Ford (Oxford: Blackwell, 1972), pp. 1–11; Swedish Energy Commission, *Mijoeffekter och risker vid utnyttjande av energie* (Stockholm: Liber Förlag, 1978).

35. Elster, "Risk, Uncertainty and Nuclear Power."

36. Breach, *Windscale Fallout*, p. 28.

37. Talbot Page, *Conservation and Economic Efficiency* (Baltimore: Johns Hopkins University Press for Resources for the Future, 1977). Even the goal of maximizing (undiscounted) utility usually—although not always—prohibits destruction of "interest-bearing resources . . . like crop species, fish species, draft animal species, topsoil, genetic variation, etc. . . . which are such that their capacity to supply energy for future consumption is not decreased by the utilization of some of the energy they supply . . . . Interest-bearing resources renew themselves and provide a bonus for us," and total utility derived from them is usually maximized by skimming off the interest and leaving the capital intact. This, once again, amounts to extracting the maximum sustainable yield from the resources, as argued in Mary B. Williams, "Discounting versus Maximum Sustainable Yield," in *Obligations to Future Generations*, ed. Sikora and Barry, p. 170.

38. Arild Underdal, *The Politics of International Fisheries Management* (Oslo: Universitetsforlaget, 1980).

39. Weinberg et al., *Economic and Environmental Impacts*, p. 82.

40. For a survey of these arguments, see Robert E. Goodin, "No Moral Nukes," *Ethics* 90 (1980): 417–449.

41. G.E.M. Anscombe, "War and Murder," in *War & Morality*, ed. R.A. Wasserstrom (Belmont, Calif.: Wadsworth, 1970), pp. 42–53; Jonathan Glover, *Causing Deaths and Saving Lives* (Harmondsworth: Penguin, 1977), pp. 86–112.

42. Frederick Mosteller and Philip Nogee, "An Experimental Measurement of Utility," *Journal of Political Economy* 59 (1951): 371–404, Anatol Rapaport and T.S. Wallsten, "Individual Decision Behavior," *Annual Review of Psychology* 23 (1972): 131–176.

43. Philippa Foot, *Virtues and Vices* (Oxford: Blackwell, 1978), pp. 28–30. Much the same distinction is drawn by Charles Fried, *Right and Wrong* (Cambridge: Harvard University Press, 1978), Ch. 2, although he justifies it in terms of "intentions." On negative utilitarianism, see H.B. Acton, "Negative Utilitarianism," *Proceedings of the Aristotelian Society (Supplement)* 37 (1963): 83–94; and Barrington Moore, Jr., *Reflections on the Causes of Human Misery* (Boston: Beacon Press, 1970).

44. R.A. Howard, J.E. Matheson and D.W. North, "The Decision to Seed Hurricanes," *Science* 176 (1972): 1191–1202.

Questions

1. What is the utilitarian cost/benefit rule? How serious are what Goodin describes as its shortcomings as a principle of environmental policymaking?
2. Do the six alternative principles set forth by Goodin provide a sound basis for environmental policymaking? Why or why not? Are all six principles necessary? Does the list need to be supplemented or strengthened in any way?
3. Is the approach to environmental ethics offered by Goodin superior to its utilitarian rival? Why or why not?

Moral Philosophy—What It Is and Why It Matters!

Jan Narveson

Introduction

Since ancient times people have pondered the questions of Ethics, or Moral Philosophy. And, to a degree that some find embarrassing, they keep coming up with similar answers, and they fail to reach agreement on those answers. Nor is there entire agreement about the questions, for that matter. What you will get in this short talk is undoubtedly somewhat one-sided. Even if there were time to explore more sides than we actually have, it would no doubt be one-sided, since I hope to persuade you that although there is room for reasonable people to differ about some of the most important questions, the room is by no means unlimited; some options can be rejected, and others seen to be at least plausible.

Let's begin by making a few essential distinctions. Ethics or Moral Philosophy is a department of what we may call practical thinking, broadly speaking. Practical thinking is thinking about what to do: we are active beings, we have decisions to make, and we devote some thought to making those decisions (including thought on the subject of how much more thought we should bother to devote to making them). But not all questions of the form "what am I going to do" are ethical, or at least interestingly so. If we want to know how to get to Elmira, our request is for a pretty straightforward piece of factual information; and though questions of fact are unquestionably critical in innumerable practical decisions, they are not, so far as they go, questions of Ethics. Now, the question of *why* you are thinking of going to Elmira in the first place could well turn out to involve ethics: perhaps your aim when you get there is to poison the water system or swindle some of the inhabitants out of their property. We can distinguish, then, between the questions: (a) which

---

Paper presented at "Moral and Ethical Issues Relating to Nuclear Energy Generation," a seminar organized by the Canadian Nuclear Association in March 1980.

course of action will work, will bring about what I'm trying to bring about, and (b) *should* I be trying to bring this about in the first place? The former is about Means, the latter about Ends. Moral philosophy is often thought not to be concerned about Means at all, but that would be misleading. What is true, though, is that many questions of means lie well outside the concern of the Moral Philosopher: in particular, purely technical ones of the sort that belong in the special sciences. Technical developments, as the present conference demonstrates, often raise questions of ethics, but the ethical questions are not identical with the technical ones.

And on the other hand, not all questions of Ends are within the province of Moral Philosophy either, I think, and here we need to make a more controversial distinction. We may criticize our aims as well as the actions by means of which we hope to achieve them; but we may criticize them in more than one way. (1) We may be concerned about the meaning, the purpose, the ultimate worth or value of our lives; but (2) we may also be concerned about whether it is morally permissible, whether it is right, to live the sort of life we might want to lead. This, I think, is a different matter, though obviously not totally unrelated. It is different in that one might be living a life which is perfectly legitimate, perfectly okay, from the moral point of view, but nevertheless unsatisfying, pointless, unworthy of someone such as oneself. Let us refer to the latter issue as the Meaning-of-Life question. My point is, then, that that is a different issue from the issue of Morality, and it is the issue of morality which we are concerned with here.

Two Theories Rejected

Well, which issue is the issue of Morality, then? What makes an issue a moral issue? There have been many answers to this question. I want to begin by considering two, both of which have had, and still have, a certain following in some quarters, and both of which are, I think, wrong: but wrong in reasonably interesting ways.

1.   One such wrong theory is that moral questions are simply questions about what one's society wants one to do. Every society has a number of rules, customs, requirements (we don't here count the official laws of society as among these for this purpose); and those rules are all there is to morality. Morality, then, is Relative; that is, a given person's morality is the morality of the society he lives in, and it may well be quite different from the morality of any other society. What makes a given moral judgment, in a given situation, correct or incorrect is simply the factor of its conformity or non-conformity with the morality of the society in which the question has arisen. And what makes the whole issue a moral issue is simply the fact that what is in question is that conformity.

This kind of view has some merits, but it can be attacked on several levels. The merit of it, I think, is mainly this. When we are trying to decide what to do and we feel that there is a moral question involved, we tend to represent the moral factor in the issue as a sort of demand, perhaps even a voice (the Voice of Conscience), telling us to do this or that. Moral relativism has the merit that it answers the question whose voice that is in an intelligible way: it is, as it were, the Voice of Society. Moreover, I think it is clear that society does come into the matter in some important way. But which way? That's where relativism doesn't fare so well. In the first place, relativism gets into a real embarrassment in those interesting and by no means unheard of cases in which we feel that society is in the *wrong*. Society may insist that we participate in some cruel and meaningless ritual, and we may feel that it has no business doing any such thing. But obviously we cannot thereby be feeling that society has a rule against doing what society is telling us to do! And there is another point. Suppose we are dealing with somebody from *another* society, whose rules conflict with those of our society. Whose, now, do we go by? Or is it meaningless to try to decide which society's rules are the better, or whether some further rule could not be devised to enable us to deal with the conflict? It seems to me pretty clear that the question is not meaningless, but only difficult. And in a world which is increasingly characterized by interactions among the most diverse people (Americans, and Afghans and Russians, for instance) the question of some sort of world morality is surely one to be dealt with seriously instead of dismissed as meaningless.

2. Let us now turn to the other interesting but wrong theory, which we shall call the God Theory. According to this theory, the rules of morality are not what our society tells us to do, but what God tells us to do. Again, it is a theory which has something to recommend it; but it is also fatally flawed.

One thing it has to recommend it is that there is no problem of relativism, here, since God could presumably want everybody in the world to behave the same way in certain crucial respects; and at any rate, he could certainly think rather ill of a certain society's moral codes. On the God theory, those codes are wrong: wrong because they disagree with the One True code, namely God's. Another point in favour of the theory is that God has some excellent credentials in moral matters. For one thing, he knows everything. This helps, for surely one of the main defects in moral judgment is lack of knowledge. And of course he would be superduper intelligent, so there would also be no errors in reasoning, another source of defect in moral judgment. What's more, God is supposed to be Good. Indeed, not just good, but super-excellent—in fact, Perfect. And surely it's plausible to suppose that we ought to do whatever a being who was both perfectly knowledgeable and rational *and* morally perfect wanted us to do, isn't it?

But the theory again has some crucial defects. To start with a not insignificant one, at least from the practical point of view, we must soberly appreciate that the supposed cure for relativism offered by the God theory turns out to be worth very little when we observe how different are different people's views about God. Indeed, a lot of them don't believe that there is a god at all! Now, it would, for one thing, be pretty absurd to think that what *those* people believe is that the commands of morality are the commands of God. And as to the rest, whose God's commands are we to accept? The commands of the God of the Ayatollah Khomeini? Or the God of St. Paul? Or perhaps the gods of Carlos Castenada?

That defect is serious enough—and has, as we know, led to many wars between followers of rival Gods. But from the theoretical point of view, there is worse yet to come. For openers, let us ask ourselves just *which* commands of God would be moral commands—a loaded question, as we shall see. Suppose God suddenly tells you to move to Yellowknife, no reason given. Would that make it morally obligatory to do so? Why? Actually, we may suspect, anyone who thought that God had told him to do that would probably believe the God did have some reasons for asking him to do so, but for some further unknown reason wasn't letting him in on what those reasons are. But the point is, we can't suppose that God's commands could literally be moral ones if they were just *arbitrary*. What if God tells you to go and assassinate Joe Clark? Again, no reason given. Or what if you *were* given a reason, and it turned out to be that God just didn't like the color of Joe Clark's ties? But of course this isn't what the believer expects to happen. Why not? Well, because of the goodness, the moral perfection of God. But now an insuperable obstacle arises. For the God theory has it that the existence of God is the *source* of moral distinctions, the foundation of morality. Yet now we are saying that we know that God wouldn't tell us to do certain things, and wouldn't give us certain explanations for his commands, *because* he is too good to do a thing like that. Well, what *makes* him too good? Apparently his acceptance and conformity to certain principles of morality! But if we need to know what those are before we can be sure what God would or would not tell us to do, evidently it must be possible to find out what those are whether or not God exists; and so, he is *not* the foundation of morality. Indeed, we must conclude that to posit the existence of God is only to posit the existence of somebody who would presumably be in a very good position to determine the answers to the questions of morality, but not somebody without whom there simply couldn't be any such answers, somebody in the absence of whom the questions simply wouldn't make any sense.

A Theory Accepted: What Morality Is

Although there are lots of other possible wrong theories to explore, time doesn't permit, and so instead I shall simply move to what I believe to be the correct one. The question before us is: what is morality? The answer, I think, is this: morality is the set of principles which society *has the best reason* to ask us to conform to. Not the principles which society *does* ask us to conform to, for it may be wrong; not the principles which God asks us to conform to, unless he happens to want us to conform to the right ones for society; but rather, the ones which it would be most reasonable for society to ask us to conform to.

The reference to "society" in this formulation is perhaps a trifle grandiose. In fact, a group consisting of only two persons affords quite interesting material for reflection. But the limiting case of a group is the one containing simply everybody. That is too big a group to be of much interest to us, though. Better to consider simply all whose actions have any appreciable effect on each other: the world's population, for instance, comes nicely under that description by now.

This proposed analysis of morality is meant to tell us the questions, not the answers. Before we can get answers to the question of just what the principles of morality are, we would need to know what is reasonable for people to want and expect from each other; and to do that, we must know something about reasonable activity, rational behavior. (And we need to bear in mind people's potentiality for unreasonable activity, too. We must ask what it is reasonable to expect, in view of, among other things, the fact that people are not always reasonable.) The very fact that we seek rational answers to questions about conduct might be regarded as a kind of bias by some. Certainly there have been, and are, irrational moralities. But if this be a

bias, it is an inevitable one: for when we are attempting to *think* about these matters, what sense does it make to settle for silly answers when better may be at hand?
Armed with this analysis, let us return to the main question: what *are* the fundamental principles of morality? And how do we find out?

How we find out is, in principle, as follows. First, we must have an idea of what it
is rational for people to want generally. Second, we need to see whether our answer
to that generates any rational interest in having certain general patterns of behavior
obtain in society, and therefore of having those patterns instilled into people by the
methods of criticism, praise and blame, and so forth. Third, we try to find some
suitably simple ways of expressing these requirements, in the form of general statements about what people ought and ought not to do. We eliminate those which are
really just deductions from one of the others, or alternative ways of stating them;
and the resulting set, as simple and elegant as we can make it, is the Fundamental
Principles of Morals. A few brief notes about each of these, but *very* brief on the
third.

Rationality

On the first matter, what we mainly need to concern ourselves about is the possibility that there just isn't anything at all which it must be rational to want. Luckily we
don't have to concern ourselves about it too much. There may be an odd few, for
instance, who literally don't care whether they live or die. We should surely sympa-
thize with such people, and we might have to worry about them too, since that is a
notoriously dangerous condition. But we do not have to worry about their effect
on our project, for if our question is "what ought society at large to do about such
people?" the answer will simply be to defend ourselves against them if need be, and
otherwise to ignore them. If a person has nothing to lose which morality might help
to protect him from, then he also has no complaint when it fails to protect him
from it.

This implies, as will not have escaped the keen-eyed reader, that there is a rational
interest in life, for instance. The sense in which this is true is important to spell out.
The point is not that to remain alive must be the supreme wish of every rational
person. It is, rather, that no matter what our other interests may be, we must be
alive in order to pursue or fulfill them. In lesser degree, the same sort of consideration supports a rational interest in the maintenance of one's health and bodily
integrity, and indeed in one's mental health and integrity as well, though those are
notoriously more difficult to nail down. And it is also true that any one of these
interests can be outweighed by something to which an individual attaches still greater
value. All of which also implies a further point: that the rational person is one who
has values, even though the values may differ enormously from one person to another,
and that it is in the light of those values that he acts. He attempts to achieve the
greatest possible realization of the states of affairs which he values. This latter implies an
interest in personal *liberty*, which is the condition that others do not prevent one
from doing the things which one's values require to be done. The interest in this is
so evidently great that there is room to argue that it overrides all else; a point to
which we will return.

Philosophers have invented an expression which may be brought in at this point: "utility." The idea of this term is that it represents that which an individual values *whatever* it is: the more of what he values comes about, the more utility he (by definition) gets. A measure of a person's utility is a measure of the degree to which his valued states of affairs are realized, or brought about. It is so intended, then, to be true merely by definition, that each person rationally wants to maximize his utility. What he wants to do about other people's utility is another matter; nothing on this score can be assumed right off.

Now, the status of these two notions, of Liberty and Utility, is of extreme importance to moral theory. It would be a confusion to ask: "Which is the greater value to an individual—his liberty or his utility?" For by definition, utility is simply the measure of what he values, *whatever* it is. He cannot value something *else* more than it. But it is quite another matter what an individual might rationally want regarding the values to be incorporated into a *social* system. He might want society to be concerned only about liberty, for instance. The goal of society's institutions, on that view of the matter, is simply to prevent mutual interference among individuals. On a very different view, however, it might be argued that society ought to be concerned about the *general* utility, or general happiness. It should arrange its various institutions, including its moral rules, in such a way that if we add up the utility-scores of each person, we get the highest possible total, counting each person's utility as equal in value to each other person's. Or, finally, it might be held that some mix of these two views is possible. For example, many have held that society should be concerned to maximize the utility of those who are worst off among its members, or that it should be strongly concerned with equality in the distribution of goods. How are we going to answer these questions? They are, I believe, the basic ones in moral theory today. My intention here is not to answer them, certainly, but it is to fill in the questions a bit more and to show how they have significance for the kind of practical problems we are here to consider.

From Individual to Social Values

If we accept the view that an individual acts rationally when he attempts to "maximize his Utility," and we allow that what has utility for one person might have none for another, and that a person might conceivably take little basic interest in others, is there any hope of coming up with an answer to the question which I have suggested is the basic question of moral theory: namely, what general principles, intended for the informal regulation of everyone's behavior, any rational person will want just by being a rational person? The problem is set by the fact that just because we value our own utility and our own liberty, it does not follow that we value the utility or the liberty of others. And indeed, one of the classic positions in moral theory is that morality has no foundations, that it is purely a matter of sentiment or convention, and that the search for rational principles of morals is hopeless. Do we have an effective reply to that challenge?

That there is some reason to think the answer is in the affirmative may be seen by contemplating an extremely interesting class of situations, situations which crop up frequently in all societies. Indeed, we shall choose as our sample such a situation, one for a "society" containing, in effect, only two people. The situations have come to be called Prisoner's Dilemmas, and are illustrated by the following tale. Once upon a time, it seems, there were two prisoners: Al and Bob, we shall call them. And it seems that the local Crown Attorney has apprehended these two characters, and caused them to be installed at opposite ends of the local prison. The Attorney knows, and they know that he knows, that they have committed a major crime. And he and they know that he can't convict them of it, unless at least one of them Spills the Beans. But they also know that he *can* convict either or both of them of a lesser crime, without any confessions. To each he then says the following: "If you squeal, then if the other fellow doesn't squeal, he'll get ten years in prison and you get off scot free. If you both squeal, you both get credit for it: you both are in prison for five years. If neither of you squeals, you both get convicted of the lesser crime, and you're both in for one year. What do you say?"

The situation is vastly intriguing. For consider Al's situation. If Bob squeals, then if he, Al, also squeals, he gets five years, whereas if he, Al, doesn't squeal, he gets ten. So, consulting his interest (and we suppose he has no love for Bob), he should squeal. And suppose that Bob doesn't squeal? Then if he, Al, squeals, he gets zero years in prison, whereas if he does not, he gets one year. Clearly he should squeal. And indeed, since Bob's only two alternatives are to squeal or not to squeal, it seems Al should squeal no matter what Bob does. And the same for Bob, for the situation is identical for the two. No matter what Al does, Bob should squeal. Yet if they do both squeal, they are *both worse off* (5 years in prison) than if they neither of them squeal (1 year)! Note that they are worse off in terms of their *own* values. We do not have to assume that they are nice guys.

What should they do? Well, in some respects this is debatable, but one thing is clear. If each could somehow be *sure* that the other would not squeal, it would be better for them than if both just did the best he could according to his own individual lights. If there were some kind of device—a black box, for instance—which each could actuate and which would bind both of them to silence, then each should actuate it. Is there such a device? One famous philosopher, Thomas Hobbes (1588–1676) thought that the Government could be such a device. I am pretty sure that he was wrong about that. And even if a Government will work to do this kind of job, it can only work because enough people support it, and why do they do that? I think that the answer is Morality. Morality is a set of socially reinforced psychological internalizations which can get us to do things which aren't obviously in our immediate interest—things like rescuing people from fires at considerable risk of life and limb, telling the truth even when it would pay to lie, and so forth. And my claim is that rational persons have an interest in supporting a Morality, if, of course, it has the right sort of principles, namely principles which it is advantageous for everyone to have reinforced in that way.

It might not be amiss to mention a few concrete social examples at this point. Consider, then, the case with Pollution. Suppose you are an individual firm which manufactures certain goods by methods which produce pollution. Pollution is bad for you as well as everyone else: you need clear air and water just as they do. But suppose that producing the goods by non-polluting methods costs quite a bit. And suppose you nicely choose to produce your goods by those methods: what will your competitors do? The answer is that they will probably underprice you by producing their goods by the cheaper methods, and so you will get the worst of both worlds: you get their pollution anyway, *and* your sales suffer. And similarly with all the other producers in that field. If you all agreed not to pollute, and the agreement could be enforced, then nobody would have to worry about the other guy underpricing him, and you'd all have clean air or water or whatever. A rational morality says: Don't pollute, as long as the others don't either. But it also says that *if* they do, you can too. A rational morality cannot ask anyone to sacrifice himself pointlessly.

It will not have escaped notice that this very example may have relevance to our purposes at this conference. Of course, nuclear generation of electricity is usually not done by private firms competing with each other. But it is done by nations, and although these nations may not be competing with each other in any significant way, there are plenty of possibilities for prisoners' dilemmas to arise here as well. Suppose that nation A, for instance, can dispose of its wastes in such a way as to affect the safety of people in nation B. In that event, the Bs may conclude that they may as well use nuclear generation, too, since they'll get the disadvantages of atomic waste pollution anyway. And then the Cs, and eventually, of course, the As will be affected anyway. Even though it might be in everyone's interest to rule out nuclear generation of electricity altogether, it may be in each party's interest, individually considered, to generate it that way anyway.

The general point of view on morality which I have just been developing is known as Contractarianism, since it views morality as a sort of hypothetical contract or agreement, an agreement which it would be rational for everyone to make and try to get generally adhered to in society. Since the contractarian position strikes me as perhaps the most powerful and challenging fundamental view about morality, it will be worth pausing briefly to consider what the fundamental moral principles will be on this view. It seems to me clear that there will be two major ones. *First*, there will obviously be a general requirement that we keep our agreements. The reason is clear enough: if morality is basically a sort of agreement, a general, rational, mutual understanding that we will do certain things and refrain from others, then the requirement that we keep our various particular, detailed agreements cannot fail to be endorsed. For if there were no obligation generated when we have a definite and explicit agreement, how can there be any when we have a rather indefinite and implicit, indeed hypothetical one? And *second*, there will be a general directive not to inflict harms on others merely because it is convenient or advantageous for one to do so. It is a basic fact about human life that we are *able* to inflict damage on others; and this general and basic ability has, of course, been greatly multiplied in recent times by the progress of science. This non-harm principle is, I think, virtually equivalent to a principle to respect the freedom of others: to harm is, I think, to disenable a person from doing what he wants to do. And if the foundation of morality is a rational agreement among distinct individuals with their many diverse interests and values, it is clear that that agreement must have as a leading component that we are to keep off each other's backs in general.

How much more there would be in the fundamental portion of morality on this view is hard to say. I speculate that there would be only one further principle with anything like the status of the first two. This might be called the Minimal Help principle: it calls upon us not merely to refrain from harming others, but also to be helpful to them generally when the cost to ourselves in doing so is trivial and the gain to others substantial. The non-harm principle tells us not to tie people up; the Minimal Help principle tells us to untie them if we can do so without danger or substantial inconvenience. The reason is broadly the same: what it costs us to conform to this principle is (by definition) very small, while what we stand to gain by it if others conform to it as well is potentially enormous—having our lives saved, for instance.

Some Knotty Problems

Having said this much about the contractarian view of morality, we may now note an important feature of it for our present concerns. An agreement, made in mutual interest, is, of course, *mutual*. Fundamental in this view is that we cannot be asked to sacrifice ourselves for others if we have nothing to gain thereby, even in the long run. Now, this means that nobody can, on that view, have any really fundamental obligations towards anyone who cannot in principle benefit *him*. But obviously people in the distant future are in precisely that position. By the time they are on the scene, we shall be off it. We cannot be imagined to be parties to any agreements with them, therefore—or rather, since that would be purely imaginary, there is no point in imagining it. The question therefore arises why we should worry, for instance, about using methods of electricity generation which will affect only people in the distant future. An example, of course, is generation from non-renewable fuel, such as oil. If we keep at it, it will all be gone, and there will be none left for people in the year 2100, or perhaps even the year 2000, if some prophets are to be believed. Suppose all methods of energy production were like that: then what? Should we worry about the effects on remote generations? The view of morality I have been outlining above seems at first sight to say: not at all!

But that would be much too quick. For many of us do take an interest in future people. *We* would like to have some around, and we would like them to be in good condition. Perhaps some of us are only concerned about our own descendants—but then, that's enough of an interest to do. Others may have a curious selfish interest in future fame and renown. Still others may have an aesthetic view to the effect that the world would really be much too uninteresting if there were no people in it. So now: if there are any people who simply don't care about the continued existence of the human race, say, it remains the case that on this view of morality they have to deal with the rest of us who *do* care. Perhaps some will claim that it is *irrational* to care about anyone but oneself. But that is not obviously true, at very least. For rationality, on the view I have briefly suggested, consists in promoting one's values, *whatever* they are (or at least, whatever they are once one has thought about them in the light of what one knows); and so the values of those who care about others are not on that account any less rational than the values of those who do not. The question must therefore be: on what terms do we settle matters as between people who do care in this way about future people and people who do not?

Many people talk as though we settle it by simply ruling out of court those who do not. On their view, the existence of future generations is a matter of moral obligation; those who care nothing about future people are simply immoral and we shall be justified in bulldozing them over if they object. That some people will have this view of the matter is important, for it raises a basic question about morality. The question is, in effect: who is morality *for*, anyway? My answer is that it is for *everyone*. It is for everyone, not only in the sense that it applies to everyone—its principles are to be used to criticize the behavior of everyone and not just some or most people—but also in the sense that the values which form the basis of morality must be everyone's values. And I think that the difference of opinion between those who would like to see people around in the year 2500 (say) and those who do not care whether there are any around then or not is a difference of taste; it is *not* the difference between the righteous and the wicked.

For what reason might people think that we have obligations to see to it that future generations exist? One interesting possible reason is this: some people, I think, have a sort of uncomfortable feeling that if we were to let the human race die out, say, rather than keeping it going, then we would be, as it were, letting the team down. We would be failing in our duty to mankind if we didn't perpetuate the race.

This view involves a very baffling problem: to *whom* is this supposed to be a duty? If we don't have any people after, say, 1984, so that eventually there just aren't any more around, then who could we possibly be letting down? For if this happens, then there simply won't *be* any people in, say, the year 2100. And so, there won't be any people to let down! It is also true that nobody will be around to experience the pleasure of life at that time. But equally, we can point out, they won't notice *that!* So it is simply not true that we owe the duty of perpetuating the human race to future people. If there are future people, we would automatically have fulfilled that duty, and if there aren't, then there will be nobody to be damaged, disadvantaged, or even inconvenienced by the supposed failure.

I may seem to have taken a slight excursion from the main issue here, since the main question is not so much whether there are to be future people, but rather what sort of claims on us they will have if there are any. And I have pointed out that if the contractarian approach to morality is correct, then this is a matter which must be decided by reference to the interests of us currently existing people. Is there another approach to morality on which the claims of future persons are more solidly accounted for?

Of course there are lots of "approaches to morality," if you don't care whether they have any rational appeal. What we surely want to know is whether there are any *rational* approaches, any views of morality which appeal to all of us as reasonable beings. On one different approach, we do not need to make an indirect argument based on the interests and tastes of currently existing people; on this approach, future people automatically count, just by being people. According to this view, all persons are inherently entitled to equal consideration, no matter where or when they may exist. Future people are still people: so they count. Their satisfactions are to count equally with ours, their unhappiness to have the same weight as ours. It all sounds very elevated and inspiring; it is also very ambiguous and obscure, especially in its implications for the present issue, as I shall explain in a moment. But even before we get to that, it has to be asked *why* we should think this, and what the status of these values is. It is, to begin with, fairly obvious that most people simply do not believe what this general view claims: they don't *really* believe it, that is. To cite just one example: most of us spend quite a lot of money on our own children, giving them fancy toys when infants, good clothing rather than rags, perhaps nice cars if we can afford them. We do this despite the fact, which we all know perfectly well, that the world is simply crammed with people who are far worse off than our own children, and for whom similar amounts of money, if carefully spent, would do far more good—such as preventing them from starving to death. We don't treat our own children just equally with other people. (Nor do Canadians treat non-Canadians equally with other people, as will be quickly found out if you try to hire a foreigner for your company, or even to come and play a concert for you!) Now, this difference in status between our own children and other people is not, we should point out, a matter of desert. Our children are no *better* than anybody else: on no conceivable criterion of merit could any rational parent maintain that his child *deserves* better treatment than all of those millions of other people in the world who undoubtedly need whatever we might have to offer more than our children do. Still, there it is. And as a matter of fact, nearly anybody would accept that other parents have a perfect right to be just as selfish as we are in this matter.

One could cite other ways in which it is clear that hardly any of us actually believes what this interesting hypothesis of Equality tells us to. This doesn't show that the hypothesis is wrong; but it brings into question whether it is obviously right, at least. And since morality is a practical matter, it suggests that some argument is needed to show why we should accept it. And that will be no easy matter. Meanwhile, however, let us just for a minute longer explore the question of how the adoption of the hypothesis of equality would affect such questions as whether we are within our moral rights to use up valuable resources at the expense of future generations. And here we run into another exceedingly interesting little difficulty. The difficulty comes about because of the fact that the population of the world, as times goes on, has *no inherent upper limit*. Time stretches out ahead of us forever, so far as we can see. And this means that if there are even just a handful of people at any given time, there could still be an *infinite* number of people in the history of the universe throughout time. Meanwhile, however, our question is how to distribute certain natural resources which are, by hypothesis, *finite*. Well, if you divide a finite quantity among an infinite number of applicants, each person's share is infinitesimal, that is, Zero. And so if we insist on dividing these resources equally, we may as well all quit using them altogether. If, on the other hand, we wish to justify supplying some definite amount of them to each person, then we will have to limit the number of people there are going to be. And so the question of whether we have an obligation to future people and the question of what we owe them if we have any cannot be kept completely apart. And then we see that we have to make another decision: where to set the level each person is to have. It can, in principle, be anywhere we like: all we have to do is see to it that only as many people come to exist as can each enjoy that much of those resources.

But that's interesting. If we are indeed free to set the level where we like, so long as we fix the number of people accordingly, it is hard to see how we can have any kind of basic obligation to put it at one place rather than another. And what might it be? We might say, for example, that each person should have *enough*. But enough for what? To stay alive at all? Or to live well—and if so, how well? How much *is* enough?

Meanwhile, let us go back to our hypothetical persons who do not care about future generations. The rest of us do care. We are willing to make some sacrifices to see to it that people in the future can have a tolerably good life, by whatever standards we see fit to apply. But those who don't care are not willing to do anything of the sort. What, if anything, may we permissibly impose on *them* in the way of restrictions on their use of resources which could be valuable to future people?

The answer to that question may well be: none. They are, after all, in no way responsible for the fact that there are going to be lots of people around in the future to make demands on these resources. On the other hand, of course they have obligations toward us. They can't go putting radioactive crud in our Wheaties, and they can't leave dangerous things lying around for us to stumble over; nor can they use up our oil, or whatever, without our say-so. They are entitled to compete with the rest of us for the biggest share of whatever good things life has to offer, and if they don't want to leave any for their children because they don't want to have any children to leave them for, okay. The point is that we cannot say to *them* that they are taking more than their share and not leaving enough for future people, for if they had their way about it, that would simply be false, since there wouldn't be any future people to divide it with!

Concluding Remarks

In this sketch of moral theory, with an application to a couple of relevant issues for this conference, I have not done justice to many historically interesting views of morality; indeed, I haven't even laid out at much length the main options which seem to me to be of interest currently, apart from the one which seems to me of most interest. Even if we operate within that framework, we have, as will be evident from the preceding deliberations, plenty to puzzle us. But this should not surprise us. Moral philosophy can hardly be easy, when we consider what complicated beings we are. Those complications have always been with us; but when we add to this how enormously the developments in technology over the past couple of centuries—indeed, the past couple of decades—have increased the stakes and the range of options which confront us, there is still less room for astonishment. Nevertheless, there are some main principles which continue to make sense despite all this, and that is because their rationale is precisely that they are the principles which very different and very complicated people require for the satisfactory adjustment of their interactions. The problem is to make these leading principles fit with the new difficulties thrust upon us by technology, and this problem, I think, is soluble even though very difficult.

Questions

1. Are Narveson's reasons for rejecting the theory of relativism and the "God theory" adequate?

2. In the introduction to earlier chapters three principles were introduced: the protection-of-life principle, the avoidance-of-harm principle, and the personal-autonomy principle. What would Narveson have to say about the role of these three principles in the construction of a rational morality?

3. Why does Narveson think society does not have good reason for asking those alive today to protect the interests of future generations? Does Andrew Brook provide such a reason or set of reasons? If not, what are the central differences of the two approaches?

4. Do we have obligations to future generations? If so, what are they?

5. Does the discussion of our obligations to future generations have any implications for the abortion debate? Does the discussion of the status of conceived but unborn children have any implications for the debate in this chapter concerning our obligations to future generations?

Duties Concerning Islands

Mary Midgley

Had Robinson Crusoe any duties?

When I was a philosophy student, this used to be a familiar conundrum, which was supposed to pose a very simple question; namely, can you have duties to yourself? Mill, they correctly told us, said no. "The term duty to oneself, when it means anything more than prudence, means self-respect or self-development, and for none of these is anyone accountable to his fellow-creatures."[1] Kant, on the other hand, said yes. "Duties to ourselves are of primary importance and should have pride of place . . . nothing can be expected of a man who dishonours his own person."[2] There is a serious disagreement here, not to be sneezed away just by saying, "it depends on what you mean by duty." Much bigger issues are involved—quite how big has, I think, not yet been fully realized. To grasp this, I suggest that we rewrite a part of Crusoe's story, in order to bring in sight a different range of concerns.

> 19 Sept. 1685. This day I set aside to devastate my island. My pinnance being now ready on the shore, and all things prepared for my departure, Friday's people also expecting me, and the wind blowing fresh away from my little harbour, I had a mind to see how all would burn. So then, setting sparks and powder craftily among certain dry spinneys which I had chosen, I soon had it ablaze, nor was there left, by the next dawn, any green stick among the ruins. . . .

From *Environmental Philosophy*, eds. Robert Elliot and Arran Gare (University Park, Penn.: Pennsylvania State University Press, 1983).

Now, work on the style how you will, you cannot make that into a convincing paragraph. Crusoe was not the most scrupulous of men, but he would have felt an invincible objection to this senseless destruction. So would the rest of us. Yet the language of our moral tradition has tended strongly, ever since the Enlightenment, to make that objection unstateable. All the terms which express that an obligation is serious or binding—duty, right, law, morality, obligation, justice—have been deliberately narrowed in their use so as to apply only in the framework of contract, to describe only relations holding between free and rational agents. Since it has been decided *a priori* that rationality admits of no degrees and that cetaceans are not rational, it follows that, unless you take either religion or science fiction seriously, we can only have duties to humans, and sane, adult, responsible humans at that. Now the morality we live by certainly does not accept this restriction. In common life we recognize many other duties as serious and binding, though of course not necessarily overriding. If philosophers want to call these something else instead of duties, they must justify their move.

We have here one of those clashes between the language of common morality (which is of course always to some extent confused and inarticulate) and an intellectual scheme which arose in the first place from a part of that morality, but has now taken off on its own claims of authority to correct other parts of its source. There are always real difficulties here. As ordinary citizens, we have to guard against dismissing such intellectual schemes too casually; we have to do justice to the point of them. But, as philosophers, we have to resist the opposite temptation of taking the intellectual scheme as decisive, just because it is elegant and satisfying, or because the moral insight which is its starting point is specially familiar to us. Today, this intellectualist bias is often expressed by calling the insights of common morality mere "intuitions." This is quite misleading, since it gives the impression that they have been reached without thought, and that there is, by contrast, a scientific solution somewhere else to which they ought to bow—as there might be if we were contrasting commonsense "intuitions" about the physical world with physics or astronomy. Even without that word, philosophers often manage to give the impression that whenever our moral views clash with any simple, convenient scheme, it is our *duty* to abandon them. Thus, Grice states:

> It is an inescapable consequence of the thesis presented in these pages
> that certain classes cannot have natural rights: animals, the human
> embryo, future generations, lunatics and children under the age of,
> say, ten. In the case of young children at least, my experience is that
> this consequence is found hard to accept. But it is a consequence of the
> theory; it is, I believe, true; and I think we should be willing to accept
> it. At first sight it seems a harsh conclusion, but it is not nearly so harsh
> as it appears. [3]

But it is in fact extremely harsh, since what he is saying is that the treatment of children ought not to be determined by their interests but by the interests of the surrounding adults capable of contract, which, of course, can easily conflict with them. In our society, he explains, this does not actually make much difference, because parents here are so benevolent that they positively want to benefit their children, and accordingly here "the interests of children are reflected in the interests of their parents." But this, he adds, is just a contingent fact about us. "It is easy to imagine a society where this is not so," where, that is, parents are entirely exploitative. "In this circumstance, the morally correct treatment of children would no doubt be harsher than it is in our society. But the conclusion has to be accepted." Grice demands that we withdraw our objections to harshness, in deference to theoretical consistency. But "harsh" here does not mean just "brisk and bracing," like cold baths and a plain diet. (There might well be more of those where parents do feel bound to consider their children's interests.) It means "unjust." Our objection to unbridled parental selfishness is not a mere matter of tone or taste; it is a moral one. It therefore requires a moral answer, an explanation of the contrary *value* which the contrary theory expresses. Grice, and those who argue like him, take the ascetic, disapproving tone of those who have already displayed such a value, and who are met by a slovenly reluctance to rise to it. But they have not displayed that value. The ascetic tone cannot be justified merely by an appeal to consistency. An ethical theory which, when consistently followed through, has iniquitous consequences, is a bad theory and must be changed. Certainly we can ask whether these consequences really are iniquitous, but this question must be handled seriously. We cannot directly conclude that the consequences cease to stink the moment they are seen to follow from our theory.

The theoretical model which has spread blight in this area is, of course, that of social contract, and, to suit it, that whole cluster of essential moral terms—right, duty, justice and the rest—has been progressively narrowed. This model shows human society as a spread of standard social atoms, originally distinct and independent, each of which combines with others only at its own choice and in its own private interest. This model is drawn from physics, and from seventeenth-century physics, at that, where the ultimate particles of matter were conceived as hard, impenetrable, homogeneous little billiard balls, with no hooks or internal structure. To see how such atoms could combine at all was very hard. Physics, accordingly, moved on from this notion to one which treats atoms and other particles as complex items, describable mainly in terms of forces, and those the same kind of forces which operate outside them. It has abandoned the notion of ultimate, solitary, independent individuals. Social-contract theory, however, retains it.

On this physical—or archaeo-physical—model, all significant moral relations between individuals are the symmetrical ones expressed by contract. If, on the other hand, we use a biological or "organic" model, we can talk also of a variety of asymmetrical relations found within a whole. Leaves relate not only to other leaves, but to fruit, twigs, branches and the whole tree. People appear not only as individuals, but as members of their groups, families, tribes, species, ecosystems and biosphere, and have moral relations as parts to these wholes. The choice between these two ways of thinking is not, of course, a simple once-and-for-all affair. Different models are useful for different purposes. We can, however, reasonably point out, firstly, that the old physical pattern does make all attempts to explain combination extremely difficult; and, secondly, that since human beings actually are living creatures, not crystals or galaxies, it is reasonable to expect that biological ways of thinking will be useful in understanding them.

In its own sphere, the social contract model has of course been of enormous value. Where we deal with clashes of interest between free and rational agents already in existence, and particularly where we want to disentangle some of them from some larger group that really does not suit them, it is indispensable. And for certain political purposes during the last three centuries these clashes have been vitally important. An obsession with contractual thinking, and a conviction that it is a cure-all, are therefore understandable. But the trouble with such obsessions is that they distort the whole shape of thought and language in a way which makes them self-perpetuating, and constantly extends their empire. Terms come to be defined in a way which leaves only certain moral views expressible. This can happen without any clear intention on the part of those propagating them, and even contrary to their occasional declarations, simply from mental inertia. Thus, John Rawls, having devoted most of his long book to his very subtle and exhaustive contractual view of justice, remarks without any special emphasis near the end that "we should recall here the limits of a theory of justice. Not only are many aspects of morality left aside, but no account can be given of right conduct in regard to animals and the rest of nature."[4] He concedes that these are serious matters. "Certainly it is wrong to be cruel to animals and the destruction of a whole species can be a great evil. The capacity for feelings of pleasure and pain and for the forms of life of which animals are capable clearly impose duties of compassion and humanity in their case." All this is important, he says, and it calls for a wider metaphysical enquiry, but it is not his subject. Earlier in the same passage he touches on the question of permanently irrational human beings, and remarks that it "may present a difficulty. I cannot examine this problem here, but I assume that the account of equality would not be materially affected."[5] Won't it though? It is a strange project to examine a single virtue—justice—without at least sketching in one's view of the vast background of general morality which determines its shape and meaning, including, of course, such awkward and noncontractual virtues as "compassion and humanity." It isolates the duties which people owe each other *merely as thinkers* from those deeper and more general ones which they owe each other as beings who feel. It cannot, therefore, fail both to split a man's nature and to isolate him from the rest of the creation to which he belongs.

Such an account may not be *Hamlet* without the prince, but it is *Hamlet* with half the cast missing, and without the state of Denmark. More exactly, it is like a history of Poland which regards Russia, Germany, Europe and the Roman Church as not part of its subject. I am not attacking Rawls' account on its own ground. I am simply pointing out what the history of ethics shows all too clearly—how much our thinking is shaped by what our sages *omit* to mention. The Greek philosophers never really raised the problem of slavery till towards the end of their speech, and then few of them did so with conviction. This happened even though it lay right in the path of their enquiries into political justice and the value of the individual soul. Christianity did raise that problem, because its class background was different and because the world in the Christian era was already in turmoil, so that men were not presented with the narcotic of a happy stability. But Christianity itself did not, until quite recently, raise the problem of the morality of punishment, and particularly of eternal punishment. This failure to raise central questions was not, in either case, complete. One can find very intelligent and penetrating criticisms of slavery occurring from time to time in Greek writings—even in Aristotle's defence of that institution.[6] But they are mostly like Rawls' remark here. They conclude that "this should be investigated some day." The same thing happens with Christian writings concerning punishment, except that the consideration, "this is a great mystery," acts as an even more powerful paralytic to thought. Not much more powerful, however. Natural inertia, when it coincides with vested interest or the illusion of vested interest, is as strong as gravitation.

It is important that Rawls does not, like Grice, demand that we toe a line which would make certain important moral views impossible. Like Hume, who similarly excluded animals from justice, he simply leaves them out of his discussion. This move ought in principle to be harmless. But when it is combined with an intense concentration of discussion on contractual justice, and a corresponding neglect of compassion and humanity, it inevitably suggests that the excluded problems are relatively unimportant. This suggestion is still more strongly conveyed by rulings which exclude the nonhuman world from rights, duties and morality. Words like "rights" and "duties" are awkward because they do indeed have narrow senses approximating to the legal, but they also have much wider ones in which they cover the whole moral sphere. To say "they do not have rights," or "you do not have duties to them" conveys to any ordinary hearer a very simple message; namely, "they do not matter." This is an absolution, a removal of blame for ill-treatment of "them," whoever they may be.

To see how strong this informal, moral usage of "rights" is, we need only look at the history of that powerful notion, the "rights of man." These rights were not supposed to be ones conferred by law, since the whole point of appealing to them was to change laws so as to embody them. They were vague, but vast. They did not arise, as rights are often said to do, only within a community, since they were taken to apply in principle everywhere. The immense, and on the whole coherent, use which has been made of this idea by reform movements shows plainly that the tension between the formal and the informal idea of "right" is part of the word's meaning, a fruitful connection of thought, not just a mistake. It is therefore hard to adopt effectively the compromise which some philosophers now favour, of saying that it is indeed wrong to treat animals in certain ways, but that we have no duties to them or that they have no rights.[7] "Animal rights" may be hard to formulate, as indeed are the rights of humans. But "no rights" will not do. The word may need to be dropped entirely. The compromise is still harder with the word "duty," which is rather more informal, and is more closely wedded to a private rather than political use.

Where the realm of right and duty stops, there, to ordinary thinking, begins the realm of the optional. What is not a duty may be a matter of taste, style or feeling, of aesthetic sensibility, of habit and nostalgia, of etiquette and local custom, but it cannot be something which demands our attention whether we like it or not. When claims get into this area, they can scarcely be taken seriously. This becomes clear when Kant tries to straddle the border. He says that we have no direct duties to animals, because they are not rational, but that we should treat them properly all the same because of "indirect" duties which are really duties to our own humanity.[8] This means that ill-treating them (a) might lead us to ill-treat humans, and (b) is a sign of a bad or inhumane disposition. The whole issue thus becomes a contingent one of spiritual style or training, like contemplative exercises, intellectual practice or, indeed, refined manners.[9] Some might need practice of this kind to make them kind to people, others might not, and, indeed, might get on better without it. (Working off one's ill-temper on animals might make one treat people *better*.) But the question of cruelty to animals cannot be like this, because it is of the essence to such training exercises that they are internal. Anything that affects some other being is not just practice, it is real action. Anyone who refrained from cruelty *merely* from a wish not to sully his own character, without any direct consideration for the possible victims, would be frivolous and narcissistic.

A similar trivialization follows where theorists admit duties of compassion and humanity to noncontractors, but deny duties of justice. Hume and Rawls, in making this move, do not explicitly subordinate these other duties, or say that they are less binding. But because they make the contract element so central to morality, this effect appears to follow. The priority of justice is expressed in such everyday proverbs as "be just before you're generous." We are therefore rather easily persuaded to think that compassion, humanity and so forth are perhaps emotional luxuries, to be indulged only after all debts are paid. A moment's thought will show that this is wrong. Someone who receives simultaneously a request to pay a debt and another to comfort somebody bereaved or on their death bed is not as a matter of course under obligation to treat the debt as the more urgent. He has to look at circumstances on both sides, but in general we should probably expect the other duties to have priority. This is still more true if, on his way to pay the debt, he encounters a stranger in real straits, drowning or lying on the road. To give the debt priority, we probably need to think of his creditor as also being in serious trouble—which brings compassion and humanity in on both sides of the case.

What makes it so hard to give justice a different clientele from the other virtues, as Hume and Rawls do, is simply the fact that justice is such a pervading virtue. In general, all serious cases of cruelty, meanness, inhumanity and the like are also cases of injustice. If we are told that a certain set of these cases does not involve injustice, our natural thought is that these cases must be *trivial*. Officially, Hume's and Rawls' restriction is not supposed to mean this. What, however, is it supposed to mean? It is forty years since I first read Hume's text, and I find his thought as obscure now as I did then. I well remember double-taking then, going back over the paragraph for a point which, I took it, I must have missed. Can anyone see it?

> Were there a species of creatures intermingled with men, which, though rational, were possessed of such inferior strength, both of body and mind, that they were incapable of all resistance, and could never, upon the highest provocation, make us feel the effects of their resentment; the necessary consequence, I think, is that we should be bound by the laws of humanity to give gentle usage to these creatures, but should not, properly speaking, lie under any restraint of justice with regard to them, nor could they possess any right or property, exclusive of such arbitrary lords. Our intercourse with them could not be called society, which supposes a degree of equality, but absolute command on one side and servile obedience on the other. . . . This is plainly the situation of men with regard to animals.[10]

I still think that the word "justice," so defined, has lost its normal meaning. In ordinary life we think that duties of justice become *more* pressing, not less so, when we are dealing with the weak and inarticulate, who cannot argue back. It is the boundaries of prudence which depend on power, not those of justice. Historically, Hume's position becomes more understandable when one sees its place in the development of social-contract thinking. The doubtful credit for confining justice to the human species seems to belong to Grotius, who finally managed to ditch the Roman notion of *jus naturale*, natural right or law, common to all species. I cannot here discuss his remarkably unimpressive arguments for this.[11] The point I want to make here is simply in reference to the effect of these restrictive definitions of terms like "justice" on people's view of the sheer size of the problems raised by what falls outside them.

Writers who treat morality as primarily contractual tend to discuss noncontractual cases briefly, casually and parenthetically, as though they were rather rare. Rawls' comments on the problem of mental defectives are entirely typical here. We have succeeded, they say, in laying most of the carpet; why are you making this fuss about those little wrinkles behind the sofa? This treatment confirms a view, already suggested by certain aspects of current politics in the United States, that those who fail to clock in as normal rational agents and make their contracts are just occasional exceptions, constituting one more "minority" group—worrying, no doubt, to the scrupulous, but not a central concern of any society. Let us, then, glance briefly at their scope, by roughly listing some cases which seem to involve us in noncontractual duties. (The order is purely provisional and the numbers are added just for convenience.)

Human Sector	1. The dead
	2. Posterity
	3. Children
	4. The senile
	5. The temporarily insane
	6. The permanently insane
	7. Defectives, ranging down to "human vegetables"
	8. Embryos, human and otherwise
Animal Sector	9. Sentient animals
	10. Nonsentient animals
Inanimate Sector	11. Plants of all kinds
	12. Artefacts, including works of art
	13. Inanimate but structured objects—crystals, rivers, rocks, etc.
Comprehensive	14. Unchosen groups of all kinds, including families and species
	15. Ecosystems, landscapes, villages, warrens, cities, etc.
	16. Countries
	17. The Biosphere
Miscellaneous	18. Oneself
	19. God

No doubt I have missed a few, but that will do to go on with. The point is this; if we look only at a few of these groupings, and without giving them full attention, it is easy to think that we can include one or two as honorary contracting members by a slight stretch of our conceptual scheme, and find arguments for excluding the others from serious concern entirely. But if we keep our eye on the size of the range, this stops being plausible. As far as sheer numbers go, this is no minority of the beings with whom we have to deal. We are a small minority of them. As far as importance goes, it is certainly possible to argue that some of these sorts of beings should concern us more and others less: we need a priority system. But, to build it, *moral* arguments are required. The various kinds of claims have to be understood and compared, not written off in advance. We cannot rule that those who, in our own and other cultures, suppose that there is a direct objection to injuring or destroying some of them, are always just confused, and mean only, in fact, that this item will be needed for rational human consumption.[12]

The blank antithesis which Kant made between rational persons (having value) and mere things (having none) will not serve us to map out this vast continuum. And the idea that, starting at some given point on this list, we have a general licence for destruction, is itself a moral view which would have to be justified. Western culture differs from most others in the breadth of destructive licence which it allows itself, and, since the seventeenth century, that licence has been greatly extended. Scruples about rapine have been continually dismissed as irrational, but it is not always clear with what rational principles they are supposed to conflict. Western destructiveness has not in fact developed in response to a new set of disinterested intellectual principles demonstrating the need for more people and less redwoods, but mainly as a by-product of greed and increasing commercial confidence. Humanistic hostility to superstition has played some part in the process, because respect for the nonhuman items on our list is often taken to be religious. It does not have to be. Many scientists who are card-carrying atheists can still see the point of preserving the biosphere. So can the rest of us, religious or otherwise. It is the whole of which we are parts, and its other parts concern us for that reason.

But the language of rights is rather ill-suited to expressing this, because it has been developed mainly for the protection of people who, though perhaps oppressed, are in principle articulate. This makes it quite reasonable for theorists to say that rights belong only to those who understand them and can claim them. When confronted with the "human sector" of our list, these theorists can either dig themselves in, like Grice, and exclude the lot, or stretch the scheme, like Rawls, by including the hypothetical rational choices which these honorary members *would* make if they were not unfortunately prevented. Since many of these people seem less rational than many animals, zoophiles have, then, a good case for calling this second device arbitrary or specious, and extending rights to the border of sentience. Here, however, the meaning of the term "rights" does become thin, and when we reach the inanimate area, usage will scarcely cover it. (It is worth noticing that long before this, when dealing merely with the "rights of man," the term often seems obscure, because to list and specify these rights is so much harder than to shout for them. The word is probably of more use as a slogan, indicating a general direction, than as a detailed conceptual tool.) There may be a point in campaigning to extend usage. But to me it seems wiser on the whole not to waste energy on this verbal point, but instead to insist on the immense variety of kinds of beings with which we have to deal. Once we grasp this, we ought not to be surprised that we are involved in many different kinds of claim or duty. The dictum that "rights and duties are correlative" is misleading, because the two words keep rather different company, and one may be narrowed without affecting the other.

What, then, about duties? I believe that this term can properly be used over the whole range. We have quite simply got many kinds of duties to animals,[13] to plants and to the biosphere. But to speak in this way we must free the term once and for all from its restrictive contractual use, or irrelevant doubts will still haunt us. If we cannot do this, we shall have to exclude the word "duty," along with "rights" from all detailed discussion, using wider words like "wrong," "right" and "ought" instead. This gymnastic would be possible but inconvenient. The issue about duty becomes clear as soon as we look at the controversy from which I started, between Kant's and Mill's views on duties to oneself. What do we think about this? Are there duties of integrity, autonomy, self-knowledge, self-respect? It seems that there are. Mill is right, of course, to point out that they are not duties *to* someone in the ordinary sense. The divided self is a metaphor. It is as natural and necessary a metaphor here as it is over, say, self-deception or self-control, but it certainly is not literal truth. The form of the requirement is different. Rights, for instance, certainly do not seem to come in here as they often would with duties to other persons; we would scarcely say, "I have a right to my own respect." And the *kind* of things which we can owe ourselves are distinctive. It is not just chance who they are owed to. You cannot owe it to somebody else, as you can to yourself, to force him to act freely or with integrity. He owes that to himself; the rest of us can only remove outside difficulties. As Kant justly said, our business is to promote our own perfection and the happiness of others; the perfection of others is an aim which belongs to them.[14] Respect, indeed, we owe both to ourselves and to others, but Kant may well be right to say that self-respect is really a different and deeper requirement, something without which all outward duties would become meaningless. (This may explain the paralyzing effect of depression.)

Duties to oneself, in fact, are duties with a different *form*. They are far less close than outward duties to the literal model of debt, especially monetary debt. Money is a thing which can be owed in principle to anybody, it is the same whoever you owe it to, and if by chance you come to owe it to yourself, the debt vanishes. Not many of our duties are really of this impersonal kind; the attempt to commute other sorts of duties into money is a notorious form of evasion. Utilitarianism however wants to make all duties as homogeneous as possible. And that is the point of Mill's position. He views all our self-concerning motives as parts of the desire for happiness. Therefore he places all duty, indeed all morality, on the outside world, as socially required restrictions of that desire—an expression, that is, of other people's desire for happiness.

> We do not call anything wrong, unless we mean that a person ought to be punished in some way or another for doing it; if not by law, by the opinion of his fellow-creatures; if not by opinion, by the reproaches of

his own conscience. This seems the real turning point of the distinction between morality and simple expediency. It is a part of the notion of Duty in every one of its forms, that a person may rightly be compelled to fulfil it. Duty is a thing which may be *exacted* from a person, as one exacts a debt.[15]

To make the notion of wrongness depend on punishment and public opinion in this way instead of the other way round is a bold step. Mill did not mind falling flat on his face from time to time in trying out a new notion for the public good. He did it for us, and we should, I think, take proper advantage of his generosity, and accept the impossibility which he demonstrates. The concepts cannot be connected this way round. Unless you think of certain acts as wrong, it makes no sense to talk of punishment. "Punishing" alcoholics with aversion therapy or experimental rats with electric shocks is not really punishing at all; it is just deterrence. This "punishment" will not make their previous actions wrong, nor has it anything to do with morality. The real point of morality returns to Mill's scheme in the Trojan horse of "the reproaches of his own conscience." Why do *they* matter? Unless the conscience is talking sense—that is, on Utilitarian principles, unless it is delivering the judgment of society—it should surely be silenced. Mill, himself a man of enormous integrity, deeply concerned about autonomy, would never have agreed to silence it. But, unless we do so, we shall have to complicate his scheme. It may well be true that, in the last resort and at the deepest level, conscience and the desire for happiness converge. But in ordinary life and at the everyday level they can diverge amazingly. We do want to be honest but we do not want to be put out. What we know we ought to do is often most unwelcome to us, which is why we call it duty. And whole sections of that duty do not concern other people directly at all. A good example is the situation in Huxley's *Brave New World*, where a few dissident citizens have grasped the possibility of a fuller and freer life. Nobody else wants this. Happiness is already assured. The primary duty of change here seems to be that of each to himself. True, they may feel bound also to help others to change, but hardly in a way which those others would *exact*. In fact, we may do better here by dropping the awkward second party altogether and saying that they have a duty *of* living differently—one which will affect both themselves and others, but which does not require, as a debt does, a named person or people *to* whom it must be paid. Wider models like "the whole duty of man" may be more relevant.

This one example from my list will, I hope, be enough to explain the point. I cannot go through all of them, nor ought it to be necessary. Duties need *not* be quasi-contractual relations between symmetrical pairs of rational human agents. There are all kinds of other obligations holding between assymmetrical pairs, or involving, as in this case, no outside beings at all. To speak of duties *to* things in the inanimate and comprehensive sectors of my list is not necessarily to personify them superstitiously, or to indulge in chatter about the "secret life of plants."[16] It expresses merely that there are suitable and unsuitable ways of behaving in given situations. People have duties *as* farmers, parents, consumers, forest dwellers, colonists, species members, shipwrecked mariners, tourists, potential ancestors and actual descendants, etc. As such, it is the business of each not to forget his transitory and dependent position, the rich gifts which he has received, and the tiny part he plays in a vast, irreplaceable and fragile whole.

It is remarkable that we now have to state this obvious truth as if it were new, and invent the word "ecological" to describe a whole vast class of duties. Most peoples are used to the idea. In stating it, and getting back into the centre of our moral stage, we meet various difficulties, of which the most insidious is possibly the temptation to feed this issue as fuel to long-standing controversies about religion. Is concern for the nonhuman aspects of our biosphere necessarily superstitious and therefore to be resisted tooth and nail? I have pointed out that it need not be religious. Certified rejectors of all known religions can share it. No doubt, however, there is a wider sense in which any deep and impersonal concern can be called religious—one in which Marxism is a religion. No doubt, too, all such deep concerns have their dangers, but certainly the complete absence of them has worse dangers. Moreover, anyone wishing above all to avoid the religious dimension should consider that the intense individualism which has focused our attention exclusively on the social-contract model is itself thoroughly mystical. It has glorified the individual human soul as an object having infinite and transcendent value; has hailed it as the only real creator; and bestowed on it much of the panoply of God. Nietzsche, who was responsible for much of this new theology,[17] took over from the old theology (which he plundered extensively) the assumption that all the rest of creation mattered only as a frame for humankind. This is not an impression which any disinterested observer would get from looking round at it, nor do we need it in order to take our destiny sufficiently seriously.

Crusoe then, I conclude, did have duties concerning this island, and with the caution just given we can reasonably call them duties *to* it. They were not very exacting, and were mostly negative. They differed, of course, from those which a long-standing inhabitant of a country has. Here the language of *fatherland* and *motherland*, which is so widely employed, indicates rightly a duty of care and responsibility which can go very deep, and which long-settled people commonly feel strongly. To insist that it is really only a duty to the exploiting human beings is not consistent with the emphasis often given to reverence for the actual trees, mountains, lakes, rivers and the like which are found there. A decision to inhibit all this rich area of human love is a special manoeuvre for which reasons would need to be given, not a dispassionate analysis of existing duties and feelings. What happens, however, when you are shipwrecked on an entirely strange island? As the history of colonization shows, there is a tendency for people so placed to drop any reverence and become more exploitative. But it is not irresistible. Raiders who settle down can quite soon begin to feel at home, as the Vikings did in East Anglia, and can, after a while, become as possessive, proud and protective towards their new land as the old inhabitants. Crusoe himself does, from time to time, show this pride rather touchingly, and it would, I think, certainly have inhibited any moderate temptation, such as that which I mentioned, to have a good bonfire. What keeps him sane through his stay is in fact his duty to God. If that had been absent, I should rather suppose that sanity would depend on a stronger and more positive attachment to the island itself and its creatures. It is interesting, however, that Crusoe's story played its part in developing that same icy individualism which has gone so far towards making both sorts of attachment seem corrupt or impossible. Rousseau delighted in *Robinson Crusoe*, and praised it as the only book fit to be given to a child, *not* because it showed a man in his true relation to animal and vegetable life, but because it was the bible of individualism. "The surest way to raise him [the child] above prejudice and to base his judgments on the true relations of things, is to put him the place of a solitary man, and to judge all things as they would be judged by such a man in relation to their own utility. . . . So long as only bodily needs are recognized, man is self-sufficing . . . the child knows no other happiness but food and freedom."[18] That false atomic notion of human psychology—a prejudice above which nobody ever raised Rousseau—is the flaw in all social-contract thinking. If he were right, every member of the human race would need a separate island—and what, then, would our ecological problems be? Perhaps, after all, we had better count our blessings.

Notes

1. John Stuart Mill, *Essay on Liberty* (London: Dent, Everyman's Library, 1910), chap. 4, p. 135.
2. Immanuel Kant, "Duties to Oneself," in *Lectures on Ethics*, trans. Louis Infield (London: Methuen, 1930), p. 118.
3. G.R. Grice, *Grounds for Moral Sentiments* (Cambridge: Cambridge University Press, 1967), pp. 147–149.
4. John Rawls, *A Theory of Justice* (Oxford: Oxford University Press, 1972), p. 512.
5. Ibid., p. 510.
6. Aristotle *Politics* 1. 3–8; cf., idem, *Nichomachian Ethics* 7, 2.
7. For example, John Passmore, *Man's Responsibility for Nature* (London: Duckworth, 1974), pp. 116–117; H.J. McCloskey, "Rights," *Philosophical Quarterly* 15 (1965).
8. Nor will it help for philosophers to say "it is not the case that they have rights." Such pompous locutions have either no meaning at all, or the obvious one.
9. Immanual Kant, "Duties towards Animals and Spirits," in *Lectures on Ethics*, p. 240.
10. David Hume, "An Enquiry concerning the Principles of Morals, in *Hume's Moral and Political Philosophy*, ed. H.E. Aiben (New York: Hafner, 1949), app. 3, pp. 190–191.
11. A point well discussed by Stephen R.L. Clark, *The Moral Status of Animals* (Oxford: Clarendon Press, 1977), pp. 12–13.
12. For details, see John Rodman, "Animal Justice: The Counter-Revolution in Natural Right and Law," *Inquiry* 22, nos. 1–2 (Summer 1979).
13. A case first made by Jeremy Bentham, *An Introduction of the Principles of Morals and Legislation*, chap. 17, and well worked out by Peter Singer, *Animal Liberation* (New York: Avon, 1975), Chaps. 1, 5 and 6.
14. Immanuel Kant, *Preface to the Metaphysical Elements of Ethics*, section "Introduction to Ethics," 4 and 5.
15. John Stuart Mill, *Utilitarianism* (London: Dent, Everyman's Library, 1910), chap. 5, p. 45.
16. P. Tompkins and C. Bird, *The Secret Life of Plants* (New York: Harper and Row, 1973), claimed to show, by various experiments involving electrical apparatus, that plants can feel. Attempts to duplicate their experiments have, however, totally failed to produce any similar results. (See A.W. Galston and C.L. Slayman, "The Secret Life of Plants," *American Scientist* 67 [1973]: 337. It seems possible that the original results were due to a fault in the electrical apparatus. The attempt shows, I think, one of the confusions which continually arise from insisting that all duties must be of the same form. We do not need to prove that plants are animals in order to have reason to spare them. The point is well discussed by Marian Dawkins in her book *Animal Suffering* (London: Chapman and Hall, 1981), pp. 117–119.

17. See particularly, Friedrich Nietzsche, *Thus Spake Zarathurstra* 3, section "Of Old and New Tables"; and *The Joyful Wisdom* (otherwise called *The Gay Science*), p. 125 (the Madman's Speech). I have discussed this rather mysterious appointment of man to succeed God in a paper called "Creation and Originality," to be published in a volume of my essays forthcoming from the Harvester Press.
18. Barbara Foxley, trans., *Emile* (London: Dent, Everyman's Library, 1966), pp. 147–148.

Questions

1. In the light of her critique of contractarianism, what aspects of Jan Narveson's view of morality would Midgley be likely to criticize?
2. What is it about social contract theory that leads Midgley to say that it is excessively individualistic in orientation? Is she right to suggest that one indication social contract theory is not sound is that it is based on a physical rather than a biological model of the ways in which individuals relate?
3. If my friend has no right to ask for me help, does it follow that I have no duty or obligation to offer it?
4. What do you think of Hume's claim about the nature of justice? (See pp. 439–440.) What would such a view imply for issues like abortion, euthanasia, or the use of nuclear weapons? Does Midgley offer convincing reasons for thinking that Hume was mistaken?
5. How would Midgley respond to the arguments advanced by Tooley in Chapter 1 in support of abortion and infanticide?
6. Did Crusoe have a duty not to destroy his island once it was of no further use to him? Would the situation change if it could be shown to be of no further use to anyone?

Obligations to Future Generations: A Case Study

Andrew Brook

Policy questions have at their heart moral questions. Those posed by nuclear energy are often sufficiently complex to tax the full resources of modern moral philosophy. As Arthur Porter has put it,

> . . . an assessment of the value of nuclear power . . . ultimately requires an examination of the acceptability to society of the risk and benefits of the technology, relative to other options. This process is, by definition,

Presented to a seminar, "Moral and Ethical Issues Relating to Nuclear Energy Generation," organized by the Canadian Nuclear Association in March 1980. By permission of the author.

extremely difficult since value judgments of a particularly complex kind, transcending nuclear power per se, are clearly involved. Indeed, whose values are to be judged worthy and how this assessment is to be accomplished with justice and pertinent questions.[1]

Indeed they are. A method for determining which values are worthy would be a large step in the right direction. I shall attempt to sketch one, at least in the context of one type of value, namely obligations to future generations.*

Any consideration of our obligations with respect to nuclear energy operates in a vaccum unless at minimum it begins from some of the policy-influencing facts peculiar to the industry. The environmental problems found at the "front end" of the fuel cycle, the mine/mill operation, are an important case in point. Since they are often neglected, we will single them out for special attention, as an interesting test case for our method of determining our obligations. More general applications will then be explored.[2]

Mine/Mill Wastes

A great deal has been written recently about high-level reactor wastes and some other reactor questions such as the risk of radioactive contamination from meltdowns. Curiously, remarkably little is heard about a radioactive waste problem which in terms of radioactivity becomes comparable within 300 to 800 years[3] and which may prove a great deal more intractable to manage effectively over the long term, namely low-level wastes. The low-level wastes from the fuel refinery or the reactor site (contaminated clothing and so on) may not be a serious problem. The low-level wastes from the mine/mill operation, because of their enormous volume, unquestionably are. Yet relatively little attention is being paid to them, even with respect to such basic questions as what real social cost they will impose in the long term, or what technology is required for their long-term safe management. The AECB, which formed an Advisory Panel on the Long-Term Management of Uranium Mine Tailings in November of 1976, is an exception, and a significant one. The question has received more attention in the United States than it has in Canada.[4] But overall, it has received relatively little attention.

Mine/mill wastes are not an insignificant problem. As a detailed study for the American Physical Society reports,

> The parts of the fuel cycle that contribute the most to public radiation exposure are fuel processing, uranium mining and milling.[5]

---

* The case studied in this paper is that of the long-term management of uranium mining and milling wastes, usually called tailings. I have chosen this case partly because it has been relatively neglected, but mainly because at the time of writing I was doing some work for the Atomic Energy Control Board on the issue. The paper itself was first presented to a seminar, "Moral and Ethical Issues Relating to Nuclear Energy Generation," organized by the Canadian Nuclear Association in March 1980. However—and this is important—the ethical analysis can be applied to a great many other social and environmental issues, an issue which is addressed under "Postscript" at the end of this paper.

This surprising statement refers, of course, to the United States. Canada has no reprocessing facilities and environmental release rates from the mills are much lower here. Most American mining sites are in areas of negative precipitation balance (less rain than evaporation and runoff) so they tend to be very dry and susceptible to wind erosion. In Canada, all sites have a positive moisture balance and so tend to be covered with snow or to be moist from rain most of the time. Even so, the statement is probably not far from the truth even here.

Evidence of the comparative neglect of mine/mill wastes in the public policy arena is not hard to find. The terms of reference of the Hare Committee explicitly excluded low-level front-end wastes (though the Committee in its report indicated that they needed to be studied).[6] The Porter Commission tended to follow the same trend. Although *A Race against Time* contains one brief discussion of the question and recommends a panel of internationally recognized ecologists be put to work on the problems involved, in general throughout the remainder of the report the issue is invisible. Nowhere does it receive anything like the detailed attention devoted to other waste-management problems.

When the problem *is* taken up, the time-frame is usually short. The Porter Commission's discussion, though it considers post-shutdown problems, does so only very briefly and inside a time-frame much shorter than the effective radioactive life of the wastes (at least 100,000 years). The Cluff Lake (Bayda) Inquiry could hardly avoid the tailings issue, and in fact recommended containment in concrete. (Because the ore is so rich—up to 60% uranium oxide in spots—the tailings from Cluff Lake will often be richer than the initial ore at other sites where commercial ore can run as low as 0.15% to 0.05% uranium oxide.) However, even such containment is short-term. A senior official of the Bayda Inquiry allowed in private conversation that the proposed concrete containers have a life of 100 to 200 years, and that almost no consideration was given to the question of what would—or should—happen then.

In the uranium mining and milling process, only about 15% of the radioactivity is removed (mostly in the form of uranium oxide). The other 85% (including radium, the mineral of greatest concern, and thorium, of which radium is a decay product) leaves the mill mixed in with the wastes. Since each kilogram of uranium removed leaves from one-third to two tonnes of waste ore, all of which is very finely ground, and twice as much waste water, these radioactive minerals are dispersed throughout an enormous quantity of inert wastes. In Canada in 1978 about 100 million tonnes of these wastes were in existence; the vast proportion is stored on the surface behind retaining structures, with secondary structures to capture and allow treatment of waste water. After treatment, the waste water is released into natural watercourses.

The radioactivity in these wastes can enter the environment through wind transmission, ground-water seepage and direct irradiation of any living things which happen to find themselves in the vicinity of the tailings-storage area. The transmission mechanism of greatest concern, however, is water transmission. Some of the radioactive material enters waste water in the mill; some more is leached out of the solid wastes in the tailings pile by either the waste water or normal precipitation and runoff.

The dosages to which any living being would be exposed as a result of transmission from tailings would, of course, be very low. And the long-term effects of continual exposure to low levels of radioactivity are not by any means well understood. Since there is some radioactivity in virtually all soil, we clearly have some degree of tolerance to it. However, there is some evidence to suggest that with respect to the carcinogenic capacity of radioactivity there is no lower limit or threshold below which no damage will occur, and that the effects of exposure in terms of numbers of deaths or injuries is roughly constant for a given amount or radioactive material, so that the same damage will occur whether a few people are exposed to high dosage or a great many people are exposed to a very low dosage. There is also a possibility of genetic damage.

Management of tailings piles and waste liquids in the short term is currently fairly effective. Release rates for most active sites most of the year are within federal standards. However, these management techniques involve continuous, active treatment of the wastes, which may well not continue after the mine/mill operations shut down, and rely on containment structures with an effective life of at most a few hundred years.

Because of the effectiveness in the short run of the current practices, so that real risk of damage from mine/mill wastes will occur at least tens and maybe a few hundreds of years from now, and because of the relative isolation of most tailings piles, these low-level wastes have been assigned a low priority in waste-management policy. Nevertheless, the water route from these tailings piles has the potential of transporting radioactivity (principally in the form of radium) over *very* wide areas (e.g., all of the Great Lakes from Lake Huron down), and no measures are in place or even at present required to prevent this from happening.

In fact, there is no general agreement on what measures should be taken. The material cannot be returned to the mines because it doubles in volume in the milling process. Sealing the piles effectively seems unpromising. At some sites, deep lakes exist, into which the tailings might be put. But this solution is obviously site-specific. One promising technology involves removing most of the radioactive materials in the mill, thereby generating a much smaller volume of higher-level wastes, which perhaps could be returned to the mine. However, no machinery for doing so has been proven effective even on a laboratory scale.

Nevertheless, a suitable solution, one which would render tailings safe and remove the need for further intervention in the future, can probably be found if sufficient resources are devoted to the task. As a portion of the total costs of nuclear energy, any such costs would inevitably be very small, amounting perhaps to at most 1% of the final cost of the electricity generated. And that brings us to the central moral question: are we obliged to assume these costs, or is it permissible for us to pass the costs of tailings management on to future generations?

Values for the Facts

Three kinds of policy question now need to be distinguished: what, from the point of view of policy and its implementation, is being done at present; what is likely to be done; and, what should be done? The third (which sometimes gets mixed up with the second) raises the moral issues (as well as economic, technical, sociological, managerial and even legal ones); for example, questions about the level of risk which a society is morally permitted to impose in order to realize some advantage, about whether some risks are unacceptable no matter what the gains, about how much we may, from the moral point of view, consume and how much we are obliged to leave for later generations, about human liberty and social and capital concentration and so on. We will focus on one such question: what costs of energy production are we obliged to assume (given that we are reaping a lot of the benefits) and what costs is it permissible for us to pass on to future generations? The costs (either for management or in pollution, probable suffering, etc.) of mine/mill wastes will be the test case.

It has sometimes been argued that moral views cannot at bottom be argued. They are matters of taste or feeling or whatever. A good counterexample, an argument for a moral view which is as compelling as technical or economic arguments at their best, would greatly undermine such relativism. What follows will hopefully be a step in that direction.

Mine/mill wastes have two useful features as a test case for views about obligations to future generations. Because their handling seems unlikely to yield direct benefits, they raise primarily cost questions: costs to us *vs.* costs to future people. Thus we can avoid the questions of distributive justice which arise whenever consumption of benefits is in question. Secondly, because harm from the mismanagement of tailings is not apt to appear for at least a few generations, the commands of (even enlightened) self-interest are well in the background, and the genuinely moral issues stand out by comparison.[7]

Obligations and Possible Persons

One argument that we have no obligations to future generations has enjoyed some currency, and should be disposed of. It runs as follows:

1. We have obligations only where someone has rights.
2. Only actual, not possible, persons can have rights.
3. No future person is alive (actual) now.
4. Hence no future person can have rights now.
5. Hence we have no obligations now to future persons.

Even if we accept 1 to 3, however, 4 does not seem to follow. A person's rights may well exist for more than the period of time in which he does. Thus any actual person, no matter at what time in the future he is actual, may well have rights now. At most, only possible persons *never* actualized would enjoy no rights.

The question of whether there will, at some distant point in time, *be* persons may, of course, have an influence on our obligations. It is a separate issue, to which we will return.

Principles and Obligations

Is there reason to think that we *do* have an obligation not to pass on the costs of our energy-producing activities? Three basic moral principles, to do with fairness, liberty and freedom from pain, imply that we do:

a. *Fairness*: He who benefits should bear the costs.[8]
b. *Liberty*: Our actions must not result in a preventable and foreseeable restriction

of others' opportunities (which disease, pain, mutation or the costs of avoiding these would do).

c. *Freedom from pain*: Our actions must not result in preventable and foreseeable pain (or discomfort or diminution of ability) in others.

Items (b) and (c) are, of course, closely connected. In addition to these three, there is another basic moral principle, the right to a minimally decent life, which, though not so widely accepted, also points in the same direction.

Perhaps many people would be content to stop here. But an unbridled moral skeptic (or someone who greatly desires some contrary course of action) might claim to have been given no reason to bind himself to such principles. Before we could claim that they are rationally and/or morally compelling, we would have to be able to answer him.

To refuse to accept these as reasons *at all* would be pretty much to get out of the business of *justifying* courses of action, finding good and sufficient *reasons* for courses of action, altogether. To consider them, instead, reasons but poor ones would create an onus to find better ones; and it is not clear that there could be stronger reasons than these. Moreover, we do care about these principles—they are deeply embedded in our view of how interpersonal relations ought to be governed, and therefore in our notions of self-respect and sense of decency. Not to consider them reasons and good reasons, or to suspend judgment until we find something deeper, would be to turn our backs on the convictions which are a main component of our moral personalities.[9]

But these two arguments are not decisive either. Fortunately, there is a deeper principle, for which a reasonably conclusive argument can be found, and of which the principles of fairness, liberty and freedom from pain turn out to be at least in part just more specific instances. The principle is the following:

> Prior to considerations of individual distinguishing qualities of moral relevance, each person has the same value as any other.

The argument for this principle is that it would be irrational to assign two people different moral value for no reason at all, or for reasons which could not affect their moral worth. So accepting the principle is the only rational point of view.

To be sure, some discriminatory assignments of value can be justified. Such a distinction between two people could be justified whenever it was founded on a morally relevant difference. For example, having Beethoven's powers may make Beethoven more valuable than John Smith. In general, some people have especially valuable features: genius, sensitivity, maybe even personal beauty, grace or charm. (As will become clear, the argument can be quite generous in what it allows as a morally relevant difference.) Secondly, only a few people (including myself) are within my control; special concern for or discriminating in favour of these people will increase the chances of my doing what I can to procure and distribute things of value. Similarly, special bonds of affection may justify special concern, if the loss of those bonds would seriously undermine a person's life having any point or purpose in his own eyes, seriously undercut his self-confidence, and so on—in general, reduce his chances of adding things of value to the world.

However, some differences are not morally relevant. Self-interest—maximizing (or a desire to maximize) one's own benefits and minimizing one's costs simply because the benefits and costs would accrue to *me*—is not. No difference of characteristics between me and anyone else has been invoked, and as the nineteenth-century philosopher Henry Sedgwick put it, mere numerical difference makes no moral difference. Similarly, collective self-interest by itself marks no difference of characteristics between one's own generation and future generations. In general, no one person (even if he is me) and no one generation (even if it is mine) has features so distinctive and valuable as to justify giving that person or generation preferential treatment in the distribution of costs and benefits.

What does the principle of the prima facie equal worth of each person to every other imply? It is sufficient for our argument if it implies that either amounts of costs and benefits, or at least cost-benefit ratios, cannot be assigned on any basis which discriminates in favour of some persons over others.

Since we are the ones enjoying the direct benefits of nuclear energy, any passing on of the costs of the activities involved would constitute just such a discriminatory assignment of costs and benefits—from which it can easily be concluded that we have a moral obligation to find a permanent, passive solution to the problem of uranium-mine/mill wastes. (Were we to be passing on additional benefits at least as large as the benefits we are enjoying, and yet assuming half the costs, the conclusion would change. But it seems unlikely that we are doing so at least with respect to benefits.)

Indeed, the three principles, fairness, liberty and freedom from pain, are at least in part just particularized versions of the equal-worth principle. Fairness can be seen as the principle that one may not assign costs to others without a correlative benefit and without assigning to oneself correlative costs. Now, infringement of liberty is a cost and so would require a correlative benefit. Similarly with infliction of pain. Or to be more exact, liberty and freedom from pain must go *at least* this far. They may in fact go further.

Can the Obligation to Future Generations Be Weakened?

Some are inclined to import a specifically economists'/accountants' notion of discounting into this issue, and argue that future generations, like anything else in the future, are worth less than the equivalent things right now. This principle, that a bird in the hand is worth two in the bush, can be argued for in the economists' contexts on a number of bases: uncertainties or probabilities; rates of return on present wealth; and so on. It has no relevance here. One discounts the economic value of the future on the basis of its value *for me* (now); one considers the moral worth of future generations on the basis of their *value*—for anyone, including themselves, as much as for me.

There are, however, other discounting principles. Some people might argue that far distant people, just by being so far distant, are worth less per head than people currently alive. While this does not seem a morally relevant difference, being mere location in time, two other discounting principles are perhaps somewhat stronger.

1. *Nature of future persons*: The farther we move into the future, the greater the probability that persons alive then will be different from us in one or another

of a number of relevant ways: they may be immune to radiological damage and chemical poisoning; though still at risk, such risks may not in some way affect their interests; their forms of social life may be so different from ours that their moral worth is reduced; they may be such moral monsters that they would not merit our moral concern.

Only the last of these seems to be more than a very remote possibility.

2. *Existence of future persons*: The farther we move into the future, the greater the probability that no persons will exist at all.

This claim is sound but ignores the fact (as does the first) that significant damage from radioactive tailing could occur within a few hundred years, a period sufficiently short to reduce the probability considerably.

To see the real moral force of these discounting principles, it is essential to distinguish between *epistemic possibility* ("It may, I just don't know") and *real probability* ("it may; reliable calculation reveals a chance of. . .which is more than insignificant"). If we just don't know, we can *ensure* that we have met our obligations (though we don't, of course, know that we have them either) only by acting as though there *will*, in the future, be people, and people relevantly like us. And even if we *do* know that there is some real probability that there won't be, this probability must, I think, be fairly high before our obligation to act as though there will be is significantly reduced—though this point is controversial. So long as there is any significant probability that there will be relevantly similar people, there is a probability that we have obligations. Thus any discounting principle of which I am aware seems to have only a negligible effect on our obligations to future generations.

Are There Other, Incompatible Obligations as Strong or Stronger?

Here one central issue is the question of *costs* (at some probability or risk level) and *benefits*: for a given cost, what is the greatest obtainable benefit? To meet our obligations to future generations with respect to the hazards in radioactive tailings piles would cost something. Would the benefit conferred on mankind as a whole (or, if one believes in obligations to animals or all life, on living things as a whole) from expending resources on these tailings be as great as the benefits we could confer by expending these resources in some other way? I think that if the answer is no, our obligations with respect to the tailings would be cancelled—*ought* implies *can*; we can only expend the resources once and we are obliged to expend them some other way.

Whether the answer *is* no is a complicated, partly philosophical, partly factual question: philosophical to the extent that we would need criteria for comparing costs and ranking benefits; factual for reasons which are perfectly obvious.

One example of a possible alternative expenditure of the relevant resources may serve to highlight not only the complexity but also the practical reality of both the philosophical and the factual issue. There is increasing evidence that one unhappy by-product of modern medicine is what one might call pollution of the human gene pool. The exponential increase and spread of diabetes is one example. Certainly passing on a sound gene pool would be a great benefit to future generations. Would the benefit be as great as the benefit of freedom from the dangers of radioactive poisoning from uranium tailings? And could it be secured for a similar expenditure of resources? I doubt that anyone knows the answer to either question—and rational public policy requires answers to them, and to thousands of similar questions.

In fact, two such questions are worth mentioning. What would the balance be if the comparison were with renewable energy?[10] And what would it be if the comparison were with heavy-metal contamination? (Heavy metals have no half-life, but retain their toxicity forever.)

These hypothetical questions have been framed in an artificial isolation. The real cost-benefit questions (and hence the real moral questions) are much more complicated. They must also consider the benefits side, and thus such issues as expanding or contracting benefit levels to ourselves or to others, the utilization of benefits for more or for less wealth-expanding and development purposes, and so on and so forth, almost without limit. Rationally based public policy from the cost-benefit point of view (and therefore public policy which meets even the necessary conditions of moral soundness) turns out to be extraordinarily complicated—something which will come as no surprise to those familiar with the deep and unavoidable information vacuum in which policy decisions are often actually taken.

Some Other Cost-Benefit Considerations

In some contexts, at least three further cost-benefit questions would have to be addressed—thereby adding to the complexity just mentioned. Fortunately, they do not affect our obligations with respect to uranium tailings. (i) Are total benefits of an activity greater than minimum total costs? With respect to tailings, the answer is almost certainly yes. (ii) Are sufficient total resources available to all? The answer is again yes, though the real question here is whether sufficient resources can *reasonably* be made available; and were the answer not so obviously yes, we would have to go into that very difficult question in a serious way. (iii) Will future generations be able to secure the same benefits for themselves much more cheaply than we can? Although the answer is probably no, the whole question can be rejected, if my earlier argument is sound, because it is we who are reaping the benefits of uranium mining and so there is no sound moral reason in general that future generations should be made to assume *any* of the costs.

It is perhaps worth noting, before we leave this topic, that cost-benefit issues may also be relevant to our previous discussion of probability and its effect on our obligations. There I argued that the probability of there not being relevantly similar people, or people at all, must be fairly high and determinable before our obligations are significantly reduced. This argument may have to be modified in the following way. If the costs of meeting these obligations are fairly high, or if great benefits could otherwise be achieved for these costs, our obligations relative to the probability of there being relevantly similar people may fall faster than would otherwise be the case.

Principles, Criteria, Facts

Now to broaden the focus. Since it would be impossible to broaden the moral *analysis* into all the areas relevant to nuclear policy, or even nuclear policy in the context of environment, the *methodology* will be generalized instead. Then we will look briefly at some conceptual issues related to determining our obligations which have not come up in the specific context of mine/mill wastes.

The methodology of the last section for determining what our obligations are, what policy ought to be adopted, has, to simplify, three stages. First, moral principles, as supported by argument (in the last section argument showing the only available alternative to be irrational), determine basic principles of distribution of costs and benefits over populations and times. Then conceptual analysis lays out criteria for setting costs against costs, benefits against benefits, and each against the other. (The need for this was identified, but it was not attempted in the last section.) Probably this is philosophically the most difficult part of the task. Then, with criteria settled for ordering costs and benefits (considered very broadly, to include full social costs and benefits, including indirect and by-product ones), the job of collecting the facts to which to apply these criteria can be undertaken.

This method is hardly new. It is worth laying out so baldly, though, because the moral decisions underlying policy are often made on the basis, really, of hunches, in an analytic vacuum which we would not begin to accept for making design decisions, investment decisions and so on. Similarly, cost-benefit assessments are often carried out with somewhat myopic notions of what can properly be classed under either concept.

Principles and Cost-Benefit Issues

At the point of contact between moral principles and cost-benefit analysis lie a number of thorny issues. These include:

a. the issue of whether the equal-worth principle can be realized in equal cost-benefit *ratios*, or whether equal cost-benefit distributions (so that everyone gets the same amount of each, and not just the same ratio) are required. To some extent, this is merely an academic question. Some level of cost is unavoidable to any being who has to service a human body, so any strict adherence even to the ratio interpretation will achieve at least some measure of distributional equity.

b. spin-off, by-product and other systemic effects. For example, using energy to build the industrial infrastructure, find new pharmaceuticals or develop renewable energy techniques might yield new benefits far greater than the benefits consumed.

c. distribution questions (which are closely related to the last point). It is clear that we are permitted to consume some benefits. It is also clear that the principle of equal worth rules out as impermissible the consumption of anything which happens to take our fancy. Within these parameters, however, lies an enormous range of options, both with respect to us and others alive now, and us and future generations.

Cost and Risk

In connection with costs, three issues arise which have not been mentioned so far. The first is the question of whether there is such a thing as an absolutely unacceptable cost, whatever the benefit, from the point of view of the principle of equal worth. This (usually not in these clothes) is an ancient and still vexed question in ethical theory. Given the Doomsday aura which surrounds certain aspects of the nuclear industry, it is a question which some people have from time to time asked. Even the principles, let alone the criteria and facts, for an acceptable answer probably do not exist.

The second is tied to the first: how does diminishing level of risk work, or rather, how should it work, as a discounter of costs? It is quite clear that it does do so as a matter of fact: in connection with the nuclear industry we have been able to accept some potential costs which would be quite horrendous simply because we have been able to convince ourselves that the risk of having to pay them is extremely low. Since we cannot avoid running *some* low risks of high costs in whatever we do, it seems clear that some discount factor must be morally acceptable. But how much a cost can be discounted as the probability of risk level moves to very small figures is totally unclear. It is an important question in connection with the nuclear industry generally and in particular in connection with our relation to future generations. The principle of equal worth is unlikely to be able to help us with it.

The third starts from the idea (not a new one) that the depletion of non-renewable resources is a cost factor being imposed on future generations. Since depletion is a change in environment, it is also an environmental issue. Classical economic cost-benefit analysis seems not well suited to handling such a cost factor, the suggestion in such theory being that if the price is high enough, the benefit will be provided: a Galilean, a single-kind view of benefits, perhaps, and one not well-suited to questions of depletion. Criteria for assigning cost values to questions of depletion are needed, and might be difficult to find.

Applications

The methodology for determining obligations to future generations which we applied to mine/mill wastes could be applied to many other nuclear issues, too.

Quite clearly the environmental issues all fall into much the same mold as the tailings problem. They are all questions of the environmental costs of one part or another of the fuel cycle. Equally, they are all costs which, at certain other costs, could be avoided. And they, too, display important areas of opacity which are directly relevant to an accurate cost-benefit analysis. Criterially opaque is the question of the assessment of environmental costs against economic creature-comfort benefits. Factually opaque are many questions to do with the health physics of low-level radiation, the dissemination rates of such material in the environment and so on.

The methodology could also be applied to most of the non-environmental issues which set the broader context. Included here would be: uranium and the value of a staple-based economy; the value of nuclear high technology; the terrorism and weapons risk; safety and high-level waste disposal; consumption *vs.* conservation; and industry structure and social structure. The methodology may not be as helpful for determining how political issues such as federal-provincial relations; public-sector/private-sector relations; public and interest-group attitudes; or interdepartmental competition should affect policy. Its relation to foreign policy may be the most complicated of all. It clearly is applicable to wealth-distribution questions; but there is more to foreign policy than that.

Clearly, analyses both factual and criterial are needed before real moral conclusions can be reached about nuclear energy and the environment, present or future. Much has been done,[11] many policies adopted, a number of fairly well-founded standards enforced. But more remains to be done, and the whole remains to be brought together within a single framework such as the one advocated above (or some other), before we can be sure of what we are getting into, either factually or morally, in the large-scale expansion of the nuclear-energy industry into which we have already entered.

Postscript

The moral analysis offered above can be applied to many other social and environmental issues. From the section headed "Values for the Facts" on, the argument can be directly transferred to other issues, with only minor wording changes. I myself used it this way in a paper entitled "Land Use Policy and Obligations to Future Generations," delivered to one of Simon Fraser's *Philosophy and Public Policy Conferences*, in October 1981. The issues discussed at that conference, such as soil depletion, biomass depletion, diversion of land from agriculture to housing, transportation and industry, have essentially the same moral structure as the issue of uranium mine tailings. They are all cases in which gaining a benefit for ourselves now will impose a large cost on future generations with little by way of compensating benefit unless we ourselves do something to remove that cost. In addition, removing that cost will yield little if anything in additional benefit to us, and will cost us something—sometimes, something quite substantial. And the moral issue is the same: Are we under an obligation to remove those future costs, that is, to assume the present cost of doing so?

Issues of this sort are closely related to religious issues of stewardship, and to the issue of husbanding the environment. The analysis given above is intended to be as ideologically and doctrinally neutral as possible. No political or religious point of view is assumed, and the argument should be just as compelling for free-enterprisers as for socialists, for theists as for atheists.

Since 1978, when the paper was written, there have been many significant developments in the area of radioactive waste management, but one in particular should be mentioned: the National Uranium Tailings Programme of the Department of Energy, Mines and Resources. The mandate of the programme is to provide comprehensive information relevant to the long-term management of uranium mine tailings.

Notes

1. Royal Commission on Electric Power Planning (the Porter Commission), *A Race against Time* (Toronto: Queen's Printer, 1978), p. 153 (cited hereafter as "Porter").
2. For discussions of the nuclear-energy industry as a whole, see, for example, Walter Patterson, *Nuclear Power* (London: Penguin), F. Knelman, *Nuclear Energy—The Unforgiving Technology* (Edmonton: Hurtig, 1976) or Charles Lee and Ron Glen, *Critical Choice: Nuclear Power in Canada* (Toronto: Corpus, 1978). The Report of the Cluff Lake Inquiry and the Environmental Impact Assessment of the proposed expansion of mining activity in the Elliot Lake area are basic documents in connection with mine/mill activities. The

Hare Report, *The Management of Canada's Nuclear Wastes* (Ottawa: Department of Energy, Mines and Resources 1977) is the most accessible study on the environmental impact of reactor activity. Porter also provides a good review of the latter issue. Relatively little work seems to be available on the environmental impact of the intermediate stage, the refinery.

3. For more detailed information, see a study done in connection with the Advisory Panel on Tailings of the Atomic Energy Control Board, "An Appraisal of Current Practices for the Management of Uranium Mill Tailings" (AECB 1156).*

4. Kilborn Ltd. have prepared an extensive bibliography of relevant publications for the AECB panel referred to above. Some are referred to in AECB 1156.

5. American Physical Society, "Report to the American Physical Society by the Study Group on Nuclear Fuel Cycles and Waste Management," *Review of Modern Physics*, 50 (January 1978), pp. 1—186.

6. Hare, *op. cit.*, pp. 1 and 4.

7. Some of the background to these moral issues is discussed well in R. Gaizauskas, "A Philosophical Examination of Our Responsibility to Future Generations," Project on Behalf of the AECB (AECB: Ottawa, 1977).

8. Porter, p. 64, seems to assume that such a principle is binding, though the report does not really go into the question.

9. Thus questions of self-interest of a very general sort do enter the discussion, albeit indirectly.

10. Part of this question, the part to do with health hazards, has been studied recently, in an extremely controversial report by Herbert Inhaber, *The Risk of Energy Production* (AECB: Ottawa, 1978).

11. The Porter, Bayda, Hare, Uffen and Ham Reports are good Canadian examples. On the tailings side, large-scale studies have been done by James McLaren Ltd. on the Elliot Lake region, and by Kilborn Ltd. on the long-term questions.

Questions

1. Evaluate the argument developed by Brook designed to show that we do have obligations to future generations.

2. How do the principles of fairness, liberty, and freedom from pain relate to the protection-of-life, the avoidance-of-suffering, and the autonomy principles introduced in earlier chapters?

3. Brook argues that we have obligations to future generations. He bases his argument on the equality principle. Is the the equality principle more fundamental than the principles mentioned in question 2? Can the other principles be derived from the equality principle?

---

* *Editor's Note*: The AECB studies may be obtained by writing to: Atomic Energy Control Board, 270 Albert St., P.O. Box 1046, Ottawa K1P 5S9.

The material you wish to obtain should be identified by name and date or number as indicated above.

Risk and Responsibility: Ethical Issues in Decision-Making

Edwin Levy and David Copp

It is a truism that moral and ethical considerations bear upon decision-making in the arena of public policy. However, this claim has many ramifications that often are overlooked. We shall examine[1] some of the ethical considerations that arise in risk assessment, mainly in connection with the establishment of thresholds of acceptable risk. In the first three sections of the paper, we analyze both the framework in which decisions about the acceptability of risk take place and some of the specific assumptions and arguments that are offered. We show that attempts to base standards of risk acceptability on empirical grounds are bound to fail. In the final section, we argue that risk assessments unavoidably embody ethical and evaluative principles, many of which are supplied by risk assessors themselves. In light of this, we suggest that risk assessors, as well as those who establish standards of risk acceptability, have a special responsibility to state and to defend these principles explicitly and systematically in their work.

Although our examples are selected mainly from analyses and assessments of nuclear power projects, we are not attempting to present an overview of nuclear controversies. Rather, we are convinced that the issues raised in our examples apply to an extremely wide and diverse range of engineering projects. Moreover, the establishment of thresholds of acceptable risk is an instance of the common activity of *standard setting*, an activity in which recommendations of engineers and engineering societies often play a crucial role. We believe that Leiss's observation concerning environmental standards is correct and can be applied to many other types of standard, including standards of acceptable risk:

> The "number" selected for an envrionmental standard only appears to be derived directly from the pure disinterested inquiries of the laboratory: in fact, it usually represents a rough compromise among vested interests, balancing science, politics, and economy on the knife-edge of potential catastrophe. (1979, p. 264)

But this is an observation about the politics of standard setting.[2] Our remarks do not concern the political issue of how to get a standard *accepted* as much as they concern the issue of how a morally *acceptable* standard of risk could be supported by argument. We believe that the entanglements of value and technical considerations in risk assessment illustrate the entanglements in standard setting in general and in other areas of decision-making.

It is natural to attempt to disentangle the evaluative and technical considerations in the way that Lowrance does by making a distinction between the activities of measuring risk and of judging safety (1976, p. 75 *et passim*). Lowrance argues that

---

With permission of the authors.

ethical and other normative considerations come into play almost exclusively with respect to the latter. In his view, the measurement or estimation of risk involves only the empirical or scientific activities of measuring the probability and severity of harm. We disagree that ethical considerations can be so isolated: certainly in practice, and probably in principle, ethical or other normative considerations are intertwined with the empirical procedure used in estimating risk. For one thing, the very concepts of harm and of risk are evaluative: a harmful effect is one that is *undesirable*. Thus, decisions about the types of effect to take into account in assessments of risk are partly evaluative in nature. More important, judgements of safety may be embedded in estimations of the probability of harm. There can be cascade effects whereby some harms create the probability of other harms, and in such cases the estimation of the latter risk may require taking into account the acceptability of the former; i.e., it may require a judgement of safety. For instance, the fear that may be caused by a nuclear project usually would be regarded as one of its harms. Fear in this instance would be a psychological harm caused by the perception that the risk is excessive, or that the situation is unsafe. In order to estimate the probability that widespread fear would be caused by a nuclear project, one may need to decide how *reasonable* fear would be under the circumstances, and in order to decide this, one may need to judge the safety of the project oneself. In similar ways, other harms may have a cognitive ancestry, and estimating their probability may involve judgements of safety.[3]

For these and other reasons, Lowrance is mistaken to claim that the measurement of risk is simply an empirical matter. Nevertheless most of our remarks in what follows have to do with what Lowrance and others would call judgements of safety.

1. Thresholds of Acceptable Risk

Risk assessments can be a prelude to cost-benefit analyses. For instance, inquiries into nuclear alternatives often begin by attempting to assess the risks stemming from various alternative proposals. Only *after* the risks from a given alternative are judged acceptable, that is only after the risks are judged lower than some threshold, will cost-benefit analysis of that proposal be undertaken. A commission of inquiry into uranium mining and milling described its methodology in this way:

> . . . we have tried [a] to balance risks from the development and use of nuclear power with risks already accepted by society and with risks from other energy resources and [b] to balance costs in terms of hazards with benefits from nuclear power. . . . (Bayda *et al.*, 1978, p. 279)

In the procedure mentioned in part (a) of the quotation nuclear risks are *not* assessed against benefits. The commission is first ascertaining whether the nuclear risks fall below a certain threshold. Later, and independently of this determination, the commission engages in procedure (b), which is a form of cost-benefit analysis.

It is worth noting to begin with that arguments showing that an alternative falls within a threshold of acceptable risk are inherently asymmetric. On the one hand, a proposed project may be *rejected* if it would create an excessive risk. But, on the other hand, the project could not be shown to be morally acceptable simply on the ground that its risk is less than some threshold.

To accept that there are standards of risk that can in this way mandate the *rejection* of a project is to accept that there are constraints which limit society's pursuit of economic advantage. Let us explain. Cost-benefit analysis is a means of assessing proposals for economic efficiency. It meshes with the view that *rational* social choice is choice directed to maximizing social welfare, for one is often reasonable to assume that economic efficiency contributes to social welfare (Copp and Levy, 1982). It also meshes with utilitarian ethical theory, in particular, with maximizing versions of utilitarianism which also mandate the pursuit of maximum social welfare (MacIntyre, 1977). Cost-benefit analysis recommends projects which are more economically efficient. It is a *maximizing* approach to decision-making. However, a decision procedure which involves thresholds along some dimension immediately adopts a *non-maximizing* approach. That is, the alternative which is optimal from the point of view of cost-benefit analysis may fall below a threshold along some dimension and thus be eliminated as a candidate. For instance, establishing a threshold of acceptable risk, say in the nuclear case, may eliminate the most cost-benefit effective alternative.

The establishment of a threshold or any other limitation on the pursuit of economic advantage can be justified from at least two points of view which we shall call the "empirical" and "principled" perspectives, respectively.[4] In the first place, one might aim to set a threshold in accordance with others which empirical studies indicate are already operative in society. For society does not *aim* merely for economic advantage; it can also be seen to value justice, health, and amity. The achievement of these goals, including *ethical* ones, is as much a part of social welfare as the achievement of economic objectives. Consequently, given the welfare maximizing conception of rational social choice the achievement of ethical objectives is as rational an objective as the achievement of economic objectives. Policy analysts can take this into account by attempting to employ standards of risk which are already accepted. To do so, on this way of thinking of the matter, it would have to be determined what standards *in fact* are in accord with society's moral or ethical values.

In the second place, one might hold that regardless of society's *objectives*, there are principled *ethical* constraints on the pursuit of economic advantage. Most of us actually do believe this, for we believe that members of society have political, legal, and moral rights which constrain the maximization of economic benefits. We could all agree that if an alternative is likely to cause the deaths of a substantial number of innocent persons, that policy should not be pursued no matter how large the expected economic benefits may be. Policy analysis could take this into account by attempting to determine through moral argument and analysis which constraints on economic objectives, such as which risk thresholds, can actually be *justified*.

It is easy to overlook the difference between these two perspectives because policy analysts typically share the ethical values of their society. An analyst's own assessment of what standards of risk are ethically acceptable or justifiable may therefore be an index to the views on this matter that are in accord with society's *actual* values. However, the difference is that, on the first perspective, ethical constraints are brought into play to the degree that they are found to be an aspect of our objectives as a society. On the second perspective, they are brought into play to the degree that they are found to be justified.

Policy analysts, trained as they are to regard their pursuit as objective and value-free, and to regard economics as a "positive science," may tend to reject the second or principled perspective and to seek routes to the apparently safe empirical ground on which to base ethical constraints. In the following two sections we shall argue that two standard routes to this empirical basis are not safe.

2. "Psychic" Costs and Benefits

One route that we think is commonly taken consists in treating the moral views of members of society as giving rise to "psychic" costs and benefits that need to be taken into account in risk assessment and cost-benefit analysis. All of us realize that these procedures have problems about "intangibles." An instance of an "intangible" cost is *fear*. For example, cost-benefit analysis cannot take fear into account as a cost, in the way that it takes *fuel* into account as a cost, unless a technique can be devised for quantifying these costs using a common measure. The problem of "intangibles" is a modern version of the venerable philosophical problem raised by attempts to devise a common measure that would allow the *quant*ifying of factors which are, arguably, *qual*itatively different or non-commensurable. The route that we are considering here sees moral views as giving rise to intangible costs or benefits. It sees "psychic" costs as arising from ethical views about the alternatives under examination.

In the nuclear case boards of inquiry have held public hearings regarding nuclear and other energy alternatives. Many of us have remarked that such inquiries can easily become battlegrounds for extremists from both sides. We wish to point out that there is an important sense in which the route we are considering actually *invites*, indeed *promotes*, such polarization. Consider what is done to moral concerns about projects or proposals when the analyst attempts to take them into account as part of a mix of moral viewpoints by counting a person's moral disapproval of a proposal as a "psychic" cost, and moral approval as a "psychic" benefit. Ethically based approval and disapproval become data to be tabulated rather than substantive issues to be addressed. Although this tabulation is of some relevance, it certainly is not fully adequate because the reasons people have for their moral views are not considered. Incoherent objections are treated as on a par with cogent ones, assuming they give rise to comparable degrees of "psychic" costs and benefits. This manoeuvre is objectionable for betraying a condescending failure to treat members of the community as peers of the decision-makers, as agents with reasons as well as affects; for giving irrationalities entry into the assessment of policies; and for encouraging a politics of emotional and vocal confrontation rather than of reasoned analysis.

In summary, this first route is objectionable both on ethical grounds (it is condescending and disrespectful of citizens) and on pragmatic grounds (it promotes extremist politics).

This route also misconceives the nature of ethical values. One's ethical views are not just a set of emotional affects. They are a fairly articulated structure of beliefs, some of which are more basic than others, and some of which are derived from more basic principles. It is misguided to think that an acceptable risk threshold could be devised by tabulating people's ethical feelings in order to arrive at a measure of society's ethical values. Instead, the structure of our shared beliefs would need to be investigated in order to determine what principles we accept, if any, that could provide a *rationale* for a particular threshold.

3. Arguments by Analogy

One useful way of investigating the structure of our moral beliefs is by using arguments by analogy, or comparisons between new circumstances where we are uncertain, such as in the nuclear case and circumstances with which we are more familiar. For instance, in the case of nuclear workers, the threshold of acceptable risk is often taken to be the level of risks encountered by workers in other occupations having high standards of safety. Comparisons or analogies of this form are a *second* commonly taken route to the establishment of standards. However this route does blur the distinction between the empirical and principled perspectives on standard setting.

Is the analog in a comparison to be a circumstance in which a given risk is *accepted in fact*, or is it to be one in which a given risk is *acceptable*? Those who adopt the empirical perspective aim to avoid asking value questions and so will seek to take the first option. However, the second is the only one that is *logically* available. It is clear that if we seek to *justify* a standard by a comparison, then the analog must be a case in which a similar standard is *justified* or *acceptable*. A standard which is merely *accepted* may have been *imposed*, or may never have been *ethically* assessed, and so it may *not* accord with society's ethical values even though it is accepted. In short, there is no substitute for engaging in ethical assessment regardless of which of the two perspectives is taken. Whether one thinks that thresholds or standards are to be based on *society's* moral values as revealed by empirical research, or that they are to be grounded on moral and ethical principles, one must oneself directly ask which standards are *plausibly* thought to be ethically justifiable.

The requirements of an argument by analogy, if it is to show that a proposed standard or threshold is acceptable, are basically two-fold. First, as we have been suggesting, the risk found in the situation to which a comparison is being made must be morally and otherwise *acceptable*. For instance if a proposed standard of risk for nuclear workers is to be justified by comparison with standards used in other industries, these latter standards must be shown to be acceptable. This could perhaps be accomplished if these other industries were among the safest. Our point here is that, especially in the domain of public policy, the acceptability of exposing people to a given risk is not automatically ensured by showing that there are cases in which individuals or groups are indeed exposed to such risks.

Second, there must be "ethical parity" between the analogs, i.e., either there must be no ethically relevant differences or such differences must be properly weighted. An argument by analogy involves a comparison, but it is important to realize that there are at least two different types of comparisons employed in risk assessments. There are what can be called "legitimating" comparisons. The comparison between nuclear and other occupations is an example of this sort. A legitimating comparison is meant to be the backbone of an argument by analogy. As we have said, for the legitimating comparison to be successful it must be shown that the ethical features of the situations being compared are on a par, or differences in their features must be reflected in differences in proposed standards. For example, it must be shown that the data involved are roughly equally reliable and that the situations of those at risk are approximately the same with respect to voluntariness and involuntariness.[5] For this reason, radiation risks to the *general population* must be compared with other risks incurred *involuntarily* by the general population—for instance one compares the nuclear risk to a threshold of risk which must be met if an aircraft flight path is to be allowed to traverse an urban area.

There is, however, another type of comparison which crops up in these contexts. In the nuclear and other complex cases, the terminology, phenomena, and statistics involved are unfamiliar to the general public. For this reason technologists or assessors often "translate" the risks or data into more familiar terms—this we call a "metrestick" comparison. Clearly the conditions for valid *metrestick* comparisons are much *less* stringent than those for legitimating comparisons. In a metrestick comparison one need *not* demonstrate the ethical parity of the parties at risk. A metrestick comparison fulfills its function if the translation makes the magnitude of risk more comprehensible.

Of course the two types of comparisons can be properly used but the misuses are all too prevalent—we are tempted to say ubiquitous. There are at least two related misuses: metrestick comparisons play the rhetorical role of legitimating comparisons; and the weaknesses of the legitimating comparisons which are offered are less discernible in the muddied water.

Consider for example this claim by an inquiry commission:

> . . .the fatality risk from receiving one rem of radiation exposure per year is equivalent to the fatality risk in smoking 200 cigarettes a year, or travelling 9000 miles by automobile, or 45 000 miles by air. One rem is at least 1000 times greater than the present annual additions of radiation from the nuclear industry and about 700 times greater than that from a predicted installed capacity of one kilowatt per person. These comparisons lead us to make the ethical judgment that the risk of biological effects from the much smaller amounts of radiation due to the nuclear industry upon the general public is an insignificant part of the normal risks of cancer and is, therefore, ethically acceptable. (Bayda *et al.*, 1978, p. 279)

The commission does make a comparison of nuclear risks with generally accepted non-nuclear risks, namely with the risks from smoking and travelling. But, appearances to the contrary, these comparisons do *not have a legitimating role*; rather, the comparisons with smoking and travelling serve a metrestick function.

Although the commission's comparisons between nuclear risks and the risks of smoking and travel are metrestick comparisons, we believe that their rhetorical function in the Commission's report, and in many other arguments on the issue, is to suggest that the nuclear risks are legitimate. That is, by translating the radiation risk into a portion of a cigarette smoked, the Commission at least conveyed the impression that the risk should be regarded as acceptable. However, as we have argued, a valid legitimating comparison depends on there being ethical parity between the positions of those at risk, and while smoking and travelling are voluntary activities, the risk to the general public from uranium projets is *imposed* on the general public.

However, in the quotation above there is a comparison offered which is supposed to legitimate or justify the ethical conclusion. The risks to the general public of deleterious radiation effects are said to be acceptable because they are, allegedly, "an insignificant part of the normal risks of cancer." But why should a risk be regarded as ethically acceptable merely because it will likely cause only relatively few *additional* injuries or deaths? All the Commission has done is to *assume* that the "less-than-background" (LTB) threshold is ethically acceptable, and then claim that the nuclear risks pass the threshold test.[6] They have provided no genuine legitimating comparison or argument at all.

The LTB standard is frequently taken for granted in the literature on risk assessment. For instance, Lowrance recommends it and reports that

> Following long precedent in radiation protection, the National Research Council's panel on the biological effects of radiation stated: "Our first recommendation is that the natural background radiation be used as a standard for comparison. . . ." (Lowrance, 1976, p. 85)

Lowrance adds only one reservation: "Unless one is willing to assume that nature is perfectly benevolent, this argument should not be carried too far" (p. 85). Clearly our reservation is much stronger.

It is puzzling to us that the LTB standard has been so little questioned. We suspect that the rhetorical impact of the words "less than background" may sometimes have obscured the fact that the standard would permit exposing people to *greater than background risk*. The claim that the risk stemming from a device or substance under evaluation is "less than background" may be understood in two quite distinct ways. First, it may be taken to mean that the presence of the device or substance would create no greater risk than would exist in its absence, that there would be no greater risk than background. For example when a technician reports that the formaldehyde level inside a house insulated with urea formaldehyde foam is less than the background (external) reading, he intends his remark to be taken in this first way. Second, the claim may be taken to mean that the risk created by the device or substance has a magnitude no greater than the magnitude of the background risk, that the *increase* in risk that would be caused would be no greater than the background. It is this second understanding that is intended when the LTB threshold is proposed, as should be clear from the last two quotations. Hence, understood as it is *intended*, the LTB threshold permits an increase in risk but requires that the ratio of the additional to the background risk be (much) less than unity. That is, the new total risk permitted is to be (much) less than twice the "natural" background risk. The point is that the phrase "less than background" may be misleading. As a result, the presence of incremental risks may be disguised, and it may not be realized that the additional risks must be justified.

The need to justify such risks can be demonstrated by asking what would happen if the LTB threshold were employed so that additional risks were permitted? Because most risks are cumulative, the incremental risks would be added to the "natural" background so that in the future the background would be higher than today. In short, successive applications of the LTB threshold would result in a spiral: employing the LTB standard would lead to increased background levels in the future and thus make it all the easier for future risks to pass the LTB test.[7]

We must emphasize here that we do not claim to have demonstrated the unacceptability of the LTB threshold in nuclear or other cases. We believe, however, that we have demonstrated that the ethical justification of any *incremental* risk is not accomplished merely by showing that the incremental risk is much less than background.

In summary, comparisons of risk are beguiling. In order to *justify* a standard of risk, a comparison must be a proper legitimating comparison, not simply a metrestick comparison. A legitimating comparison is part of an argument by analogy whose conclusion is, for example, that some risk is acceptable on the ground that it is no greater than some allegedly analogous risks. Even when the analogs are ethically on a par, or adjustments are made for ethically relevant differences, it is still an open question whether the analogous risk is itself morally acceptable. Policy analysts cannot properly avoid addressing such questions.[8]

4. The Responsibility of Risk Assessors

We have been arguing that the establishment of suitable standards of acceptable risk cannot be accomplished from the empirical perspective. There is no empirical procedure that can be followed to establish an ethically acceptable standard. Someone must assess various proposed standards for acceptability, and that person or group of persons must exercise ethical judgement. The ethical beliefs of these people will be reflected in the standard that is finally established.

This thesis is reinforced by a thesis about technological activities in general: *The underspecification thesis* says that even when a scientific and technological activity is mission-oriented, and the mission is set by an overriding political institution, the tasks set for technologists are virtually always *under*specified. That is, *some* of the goals and parameters are set by overriding institutions, but a host of additional goals and parameters are provided by technologists themselves or by technologists in consultation with overriding political bodies. Consider for example an engineer whose task is to design a rapid transit system or an economist whose task is to run cost-benefit analyses of such proposals. The municipal political authority provides only an outline of these tasks. Moreover, the way in which some of the additional factors become specified is by means of a dialectical process: the technologists identify those factors which require specification—often it is only by virtue of the technologists' expertise that the additional factors are even known—and the overriding body provides guidance. Still, we believe that many decisions simply are made by the technologists employing standard practices, their own judgement, or their own values, and these become incorporated into the product.[9]

When the task is to set a threshold of acceptable risk, the underspecification thesis suggests that much will be left to the discretion or judgement of the risk assessor. In selecting comparisons by which risks are judged acceptable, and in devising ways to handle "psychic" costs and other intangibles, the values of analysts and assessors are likely to be incorporated in their recommendations.

In light of these arguments we believe that the products of policy makers, risk assessors, and cost-benefit analysts have substantial ethical content. Yet it is all too typical for them to downplay or not to acknowledge this. Consider this claim by an inquiry commission:

> We do not make ethical judgments on behalf of society, our province [state] or even individuals. Rather we have attempted to set out the bases on which our conclusions have been reached and the ways in which we have tried to balance risks from the development and use of nuclear power with risks already accepted by society and with risks from other energy sources and to balance costs in terms of hazards with benefits from nuclear power. We have tried to be as objective as we could but in the final analysis our decisions are subjective ones. (Bayda *et al.*, 1978, p. 288)

We believe this claim is extremely naive. However, it might be argued that policy analysts, such as these commissions, nevertheless only make, and ought only to make, *recommendations* to governments. We have the following criticism of this view.

Although a commission does make *recommendations* to other political institutions, there is an important sense in which it makes *ethical judgements both on behalf of society and on behalf of individuals.*

A simple illustration involving uranium mining will make the latter point. Take the case of a citizen who is contemplating becoming a uranium miner. An informed and responsible citizen in this position may, besides enquiring about his own safety on the job, ask questions such as whether his work would have a genetic effect on his as yet unconceived children. Part of the answer to this question will involve an assessment of the scientific and technological data relevant to the issue. There are very few citizens who have the training and the resources to seek out and evaluate such information directly. The individual citizen will necessarily rely on government, and government will rely on specialized technical bodies which have been delegated to amass and, more importantly, to *assess* such data. It is of course true that the individual citizen still has a decision whether to accept a commission's recommendations. But if, after a lengthy process of investigation and deliberation, the delegated government bodies have recommended that the government approve uranium mining under specific conditions, then this is extremely weighty evidence on which the government may reasonably base its decision; and if the government accepts these recommendations, then this is extremely weighty evidence on which the individual may reasonably base his decision. The government will have said, in effect, that it is scientifically and ethically sound for citizens to engage in uranium mining under such-and-such conditions. The government, in sanctioning uranium mining, will to a significant degree have *relieved* the citizens who participate in this activity of much of the responsibility of a whole range of consequences which flow from mining. Suppose for instance that radiation is released into the environment and the community as a result of uranium mining, despite its having been carried on *within officially prescribed standards*. Now if anyone is to blame in the situation, then clearly the government bodies which formulated and promulgated those standards are at least as blameworthy as are the individuals and corporations who are doing the mining. After all, these bodies permitted the mining and deemed it safe.

Finally, we must emphasize that we believe the techniques of policy analysis, such as risk assessment and cost-benefit analysis, can contribute to rational decision-making. However, wisdom in their use, and in the assessment of their results, demands that the hidden ethical assumptions of policy analysis be made explicit, and it demands that relevant factors not included in the analysis of an issue be explicitly noted. We hold that it is unavoidable, and desirable, that ethical considerations be brought into play in policy analysis. But it is essential that this be done overtly so that the role which ethical considerations play can readily be discerned.

Notes

1. This article is a version of a paper given at the 2nd National Conference on Ethics in Engineering held in Chicago, March, 1982. The Conference was organized by Vivian Weil and funded by the National Science Foundation.
2. "Standards" of course covers a vast and disparate territory. The sorts of standards we have in mind are mainly those which are reflected or embodied in governmental regulations, and which relate to the environment or to human health and safety. For an indication of the types of standard with which we are concerned, see Crandall and Lave (1980) and National Academy of Sciences (1975).
3. Structurally similar cases are easy to find. For example, nuclear inquiry commissions often consider the risk of terrorist exploitation of nuclear installations (e.g., Bayda *et al.*, 1978, p. 282). One way to lessen this risk would be to increase police powers in the community, a step which might itself be harmful, for it might lead to the limitation of freedom in the community. Estimating the probability that this step would be taken may well require judgements of safety, for the step may be likely only on condition that it would be *reasonable*, and its reasonableness may depend on how *safe* the installations would be in the face of the terrorist threat.
4. Of course, the principled perspective takes into account relevant empirical data, and the empirical perspective may involve some principles. The labels are meant to convey the main orientation of each perspective.
5. The distinction between the voluntary and the involuntary may be somewhat vague. Some instances are borderline: voluntary in some respects, involuntary in others. Moreover, other characteristics of the risks being compared should be taken into account. The following remark by MacCarthy suggests both points:

   . . .workplace risks are fundamentally different from the voluntarily assumed risks of everyday life because they. . .do not typically challenge the skills of those who must withstand them, they are rarely intrinsically enjoyable or symbolically important, and they normally involve a conflict between labor and management characterized by imbalances of power, information, and mobility (p. 814).

6. The Commission then draws the conclusion that the risks are ethically acceptable. However, as we mentioned earlier, a risk cannot be shown to be morally acceptable simply on the ground that it passes some threshold test.
7. There are other difficulties involved in interpretating the LTB standard. For example in some cases the "background" risk is a matter of calculation. Then one must be careful about what constitutes the average background risk; the calculation is sensitive to the size of the population over which the risk is assumed to be distributed.

8. We have focussed on comparisons in the context of thresholds. However, legitimating comparisons are also used in arguments designed to show that the *balance* of risks and benefits is acceptable. For these arguments, too, ethical parity must be demonstrated for the arguments to be judged successful.
9. For a longer account and defense of the underspecification thesis, see Levy, 1982.

References

Bayda, E.D., Groome, A.J., and McCallum, K.J. (1978) *The Cluff Lake Board of Inquiry: Final Report.* Government of Saskatchewan. Regina, Saskatchewan.

Copp, D. and Levy, E. (1982) "Value Neutrality in the Techniques of Policy Analysis: Risk and Uncertainty." Forthcoming in *Journal of Business Administration.*

Crandall, R.W. and Lave, L.B., editors, (1981) *The Scientific Basis of Health and Safety Regulation.* The Brookings Institution: Washington, D.C.

Leiss, W. (1979) "Political Aspects of Environmental Issues," in *Ecology versus Politics in Canada,* edited by W. Leiss. University of Toronto Press: Toronto, Ontario.

Levy, E. (1982) "The Responsibility of the Scientific and Technological Enterprise in Technology Transfers," in *Science, Politics and the Agricultural Revolution in Asia,* edited by R. Anderson, P. Brass, E. Levy, and B. Morrison. Westview Press: Boulder, Colorado.

Lowrance, W.W. (1976) *Of Acceptable Risk.* William Kaufman: Los Altos, California.

MacCarthy, M. (1981-1982) "A Review of Some Normative and Conceptual Issues in Occupational Safety and Health," *Boston College Environmental Affairs Law Review,* Vol. 9, 773-814.

MacIntyre, A. (1977) "Utilitarianism and Cost-Benefit Analysis: An Essay on the Relevance of Moral Philosophy to Bureaucratic Theory," in *Values in the Electric Power Industry,* edited by K. Sayre. Notre Dame University Press: Notre Dame, Indiana.

National Academy of Sciences (1975) *Decision Making for Regulating Chemicals in the Environment.* National Academy of Sciences: Washington, D.C.

Questions

1. Levy and Copp distinguish between the "empirical" and the "principled" perspective in establishing whether a risk is acceptable. Why do the authors make this distinction? How important is it to their argument? Do you agree that it is a meaningful distinction?

2. What are "psychic costs"? Should they be considered in determining whether a project like the development of a uranium mine should go ahead?

3. Find an example of an argument by analogy. What role can such arguments play in deciding whether the risk posed by, for example, uranium mining, is acceptable?

4. What is the distinction between "legitimating comparisons" and "metrestick comparisons"? Is the distinction sound? Is it useful?

5. Do Levy and Copp argue that the central ethical responsibility for environmental concerns lies with professionals? Or does the article imply that nonprofessionals are also responsible?

6. How can nonprofessionals meaningfully participate in setting policy in areas of scientifc or technical complexity?
7. In your view, do Levy and Copp succeed in showing that assessing risk is not mainly a scientific or technological matter but an ethical matter?

Suggestions for Further Reading

Uranium Mining

*   Canadian Nuclear Association, *Moral and Ethical Issues Relating to Nuclear Energy Generation*, 1980. This volume, available from the Association (111 Elizabeth Street, Toronto, Ontario, M5G 1P7), comprises the proceedings of a seminar which took place in 1980. Participants included industry personnel, interested lawyers, and academics from many fields. The value of this collection lies in the variety of perspectives which it reflects and in the fact that those contributing papers were required to set out their ideas in non-technical language. There is a useful bibliography.
*   Cluff Lake Board of Inquiry, ''Moral and Ethical Issues in the Development and Use of Nuclear Energy,'' Regina: Government of Saskatchewan, 1978. Chapter XI concerns the ethical dimensions of the proposed development of a uranium mine and mill in Saskatchewan. The Cluff Lake Report provided the basis for a brief written by David Copp (Simon Fraser University) and Ed Levy (University of British Columbia) and presented to the Province of British Columbia Royal Commission of Inquiry on Health and Environmental Protections with Regard to Uranium Mining. A copy of the brief can be obtained by writing to Copp and Levy.
*   Dr. Arthur Porter, *A Race Against Time* (an Ontario government Royal Commission Interim Report on Electric Power Planning) (Toronto: 1978). Chapter 10 is entitled ''Social, Ethical and Political Issues.'' As Andy Brook points out in his contribution to this chapter, the Porter report does not take up the issues of mining and milling at any length. Nevertheless, it is a useful source of information. And it does make a good case for the importance of identifying and considering the moral problems which nuclear energy poses.
*   The footnotes to the Brook and to the Copp and Levy articles are a good source of additional readings.

Environmental Ethics

*   John Passmore, *Man's Responsibility for Nature* (London: Duckworth, 1974). This book, now regarded as something of a classic in the field, evaluates a variety of views of nature found in Western literature and concludes by formulating a conservation ethic.

- Ernest Partridge, ed., *Responsibilities to Future Generations: Environmental Ethics* (Buffalo: Prometheus Books, 1981). This collection includes many of the recent influential contributions on the subject of our obligations to posterity. It is helpful because of both the variety of discussions of the issues and the way it traces the development of a variety of themes in the last decade.
- Robert Elliot and Arran Gare, eds., *Environmental Philosophy* (Queensland: University of Queensland Press, 1983). This is another recent, valuable collection on the general topic of environmental ethics. Contributors are drawn from Canada, the United States, Great Britain, and Australia.

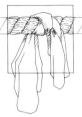

Nuclear Deterrence and Disarmament

Introduction

The potential for conflict is always present in human affairs. And all conflicts are potentially destructive for those involved in them and for those indirectly affected. Consequently, one task of moral deliberation in any society, though by no means the only one, is to provide principles designed to encourage the search for nonviolent ways of resolving disagreements and conflicts. Discussions of moral issues tend to highlight that task. Moral issues, after all, are generated by disagreements regarded as deeply important by those caught up in them; if unresolved they could lead and have led to serious conflict.

Some people are now arguing that conflict between nations constitutes the most pressing and serious moral challenge that we have ever faced as human beings. There are two reasons for this. First, individuals have a very hard time either understanding or influencing international affairs. At the same time, national loyalties generate powerful emotions that frequently discourage critical ethical evaluation of events—particularly, it seems, when those events appear to be leading to seriously destructive conflicts between nation states. In fact, some people have argued that since the focus of morality is or ought to be the behaviour of individuals, moral rules do not apply to the behaviour of nation states and can even become a serious obstacle to the nonviolent resolution of conflicts at that level. Foreign policy, they would argue, should be governed by national self-interest alone.

The second reason lies in the uniquely destructive character of modern nuclear weapons. Nuclear weapons have been used in war only once. Few people, including the scientists who had created them, knew or understood in concrete terms the destruction the two bombs dropped on Japan would unleash. In fact, the results of the bombings of Hiroshima and Nagasaki are still being felt now, more than 40 years after the end of the Second World War. It is true that no nuclear weapons have been used in war since that time. However, the size and destructive capacity of nuclear arsenals has grown beyond anything those who built the first atomic bomb could possibly have imagined. Today, a nuclear war would not only lead to the destruction of the participants; it would also, in all probability, lead to the destruction both of the world as we know it and the human race itself.

Background Considerations

In the early years of this century, those few scientists who understood the nature of developments in nuclear physics resisted the idea of using atomic physics for military purposes. However, events leading to the Second World War created conditions under which the development of the atomic bomb was a virtual certainty. The only real question was who would be the first to produce it, the Allied or the Axis powers. The victor is well known. In the European theatre of the war, the outcome was not important, since the war had drawn to a close before the bomb was ready for use. This was not true of the Pacific war, however, wherein the use of two atomic bombs to destroy two major Japanese cities played a decisive role in ending World War Two.

For a short period after the war, the United States maintained a monopoly on atomic weapons. Initial attempts to abolish "the bomb" or bring it under international control were made. But these efforts did not succeed. With the acquisition of similar weapons by the Soviet Union, the nuclear arms race had begun. Over the intervening years, the destructive power of nuclear weapons has increased, enormous stockpiles of those weapons have been created, and very sophisticated ways of getting those weapons through to their targets have been devised. Unfortunately, efforts at controlling the use and development of nuclear armaments, while not insignificant, have been less dramatic. For example, a nuclear test ban treaty has brought the atmospheric testing of nuclear devices largely to a halt. A nuclear non-proliferation treaty is in place and widely but not universally respected. In spite of these and other achievements, however, the arms race continues.

The Current Situation

Two aspects of the current situation, as seen from a Canadian perspective, are important in evaluating the moral dimensions of nuclear deterrence and disarmament. Canadians and their government find themselves today in a complex situation. Although Canada has rejected the use of nuclear weapons by its own armed forces, we are part of two alliances that rely on nuclear weapons for defence purposes. The North Atlantic Treaty Organization (NATO), accepts the use, including the possibility of first use, of nuclear weapons as an integral part of its defence strategy. That alliance deploys missiles in Europe that allow the Soviet Union less than 30 minutes' warning of a nuclear attack. Similar weapons are available to the Warsaw Pact. These developments have reduced to a vanishing point the time available to both sides to discriminate between false alarms and a real attack, something that many analysts see as potentially very destabilizing.

Canada is also party to a North American defence agreement (NORAD) that links American and Canadian air defence closely.

Both NORAD and NATO involvement has led Canada to participate in the weapons testing and development that are part of the arms race. The testing of the cruise missile over the Canadian north is just one example. Canada also faces the need to clarify its attitude toward the Strategic Defence Initiative (SDI or "Star Wars") of the United States. The purpose of SDI is to allow North American defences to identify hostile missiles after they have been launched and destroy them before they reach their North American targets. Many argue that both the cruise missile and SDI are examples of developments that have had and will continue to have a destabilizing effect on the arms race and nuclear defence.

Second, Canadian industry participates indirectly in the arms race and the production of nuclear weapons. Advanced technology developed in Canada plays a part in such things as the guidance system that will be used in the cruise and other missiles. Furthermore, our uranium and nuclear power industries, while dedicated to the peaceful use of nuclear energy, produce material that can be used for nuclear weapons. It is common knowledge, for example, that Canadian nuclear technology played a central role in the development and testing by India of a nuclear device.

Thus, Canadians are deeply involved in the nuclear weapons debate.

The Moral Dimension

Nuclear strategists see their task as directing military expenditures to the most efficient defence system possible with the resources at hand. From a strategic point of view, a nuclear arsenal is justified because it is seen as providing the best way of achieving what might seem to be a morally unchallengable goal, national defence. But if we look more carefully at the defence issue, moral questions do begin to arise. For example, are we justified in using *any* means available to us to defend Western alliance interests? The answer to this question would appear to be no. For example, our government has signed treaties banning the use of biological and chemical weapons. There seems to be wide agreement that use of these types of weapons would be immoral. Are there any limits, then, to the use of nuclear weapons? This is a question of vital importance, since one possible nuclear strategy is massive nuclear retaliation against civilian targets in the event of a serious enemy attack on either military or civilian targets, a strategy known as *Mutual Assured Destruction* (MAD).

It is worth noting here that increasing scientific evidence indicates massive nuclear exchanges would have very destructive effects on people all over the globe, even if all attacks were limited to the territories of the two superpowers involved.

If we agree, then, that massive nuclear retaliation is not a morally acceptable means of national defence, what use of nuclear weapons would be morally acceptable?

Targeting only military installations has been seen by some as a viable military option to MAD that is more defensible from a moral point of view. This is called a *counterforce* strategy. Others have suggested, however, that given the destructive power of nuclear weapons and the radiation pollution they generate, this strategy is subject to much the same type of criticism as has been directed against MAD.

This first set of questions gives rise to a second. There seems to be wide agreement that actually to unleash a nuclear war would be morally unthinkable. But nuclear arsenals are a deterrent to nuclear war only if those against whom they are directed are convinced that their opponents will use those weapons if need be. Is it morally acceptable to threaten use of nuclear weapons in order to deter a potential aggressor when the actual use of those weapons is morally unthinkable because the result would be a nuclear holocaust? That is, is it morally acceptable to threaten to do what it would be seriously immoral actually to do?

We now move to a third and final consideration. Our own government, as well as Allied governments, justify the deployment of nuclear weapons as self-defence. Yet those same governments are frequently very unclear about what exactly would warrant the use of those weapons. Normally, the discussion of nuclear weapons assumes the right of countries like our own to use military force to defend against invasion. Mutual defence treaties extend this defence doctrine to participation in the defence of Allied countries. Thus, Canada has troops stationed in Europe. At the same time, the use of nuclear weapons has been seriously considered in response to military and political developments in Korea, Vietnam, the Middle East, and Cuba.

These facts raise an important question. What interests are we justified in defending with nuclear weapons? For example, would the United States have been justified in using nuclear weapons to keep missiles capable of striking the United States out of Cuba? Would Britain have been justified in using nuclear weapons in regaining control of the Falklands? Would the United States be justified in using nuclear weapons to protect its access to Middle East oil? The contributions to this chapter deal in one way or another with all these questions.

The Readings

The chapter begins with a poem by Dr. Roger Nash and ends with one. These have been included to represent the view held by some that only if we bring our imaginations into play will we be able to understand the real horror of nuclear war. Experience cannot be our guide here because nuclear war can only happen once. The first poem is followed by a description of the medical dimensions of both nuclear war and the nuclear arms race by Howard H. Hiatt, a member of Physicians for Social Responsibility, Michael Penz, a British analyst, sets out the various strategies for the use of nuclear weapons and provides a preliminary evaluation of them. A contrary position is argued by Robert J. Art. In his view, nuclear weapons are an inescapable feature of the modern world. He offers a defence strategy that in his view would diminish significantly the dangers of a nuclear exchange in the involvement of nuclear powers in serious conflict with ideological adversaries. Conrad G. Brunk challenges many of the assumptions on which the development of nuclear strategy has relied. Trudy Govier looks at the arms race from an explicitly Canadian perspective. The final article, by Gene Sharp, evaluates the options available to countries that believe nuclear weapons to be immoral and wish to renounce their use or the threat of their use, without thereby relinquishing the right of national defence.

The World's Last Poem

The world's
last
poem
will show
what
is
left.

The world's
last
poem
will show
the world's
last
poem.

This is
the world's
last
poem.

Poem : meoP

Roger Nash

This poem and the one at the end of the chapter first appeared in *The Antigonish Review* and *Queen's Quarterly*. © Roger Nash.

Misplaced Priorities: The Human Costs of the Arms Race

Howard H. Hiatt

The bomb that exploded over Hiroshima was by today's standards a small one. It was equivalent in explosive power to 13,000 tons of TNT. That is how those bombs are measured. It is estimated to have killed something between 75,000 and 100,000 people out of a total population of 245,000, and to have gravely injured almost as many. 25% of those that died were affected by burns, 25% by radiation effects, and the rest from other injuries. The bomb destroyed two thirds of a city of 90,000 buildings; but much more devastating than these numbers are the words of those people who were eye-witnesses.

There are some that have been written, and I want to read to you the words of a colleague, a man now a Professor of Medicine at the University of Nagasaki, Professor Michito Ishimaru. He wrote: "In August 1945 I was a freshman at Nagasaki Medical College. The 9th of August was a clear, hot, beautiful summer day. I left my lodging house which was one and a half miles from the hypocentre, the point immediately under which the bomb exploded, at 8:00 in the morning as usual to catch a tram car. When I got to the tramp stop, I found that it had been derailed in an accident. I decided to return home. I was lucky, I never made it to school that day. At 11:00 a.m., I was sitting in my room with a fellow student when I heard the sound of a B-29 passing overhead. A few minutes later the air flashed a brilliant yellow. There was a huge blast of wind. We were terrified and ran downstairs to hide. Later when I came to my senses, I noticed a hole had been blown in the roof, all the glass had been shattered and I was bleeding. When I went outside, the sky had turned from blue to black and a black rain started to fall. The stone walls between the houses were reduced to rubble. After a short time I tried to go to my medical school in Urakami (Urakami is a section of Nagasaki, the section over which the bomb was exploded) which was 500 meters from the hypocentre. The air dose of radiation was more than 7000 rads at this distance." (The rad is a measure of radiation, and exposure to something of the order of 500 rads kills most people in such conditions; but here the dose was more than 7000 rads.) "I could not complete my journey because there were fires everywhere. I met many people coming back from Urakami. Their clothes were in rags, and shreds of skin hung from their bodies. They looked like ghosts with vacant stares. The next day I was able to enter Urakami on foot, and all that I knew had disappeared. Only the concrete and iron skeletons of the buildings remained. There were dead bodies everywhere. On each street corner we had tubs of water to be used for putting out fires after the air raids. In one of these small tubs, scarcely large enough for one person, was the body of a desperate man who sought cool water. There was foam coming from his mouth, but he was not alive. I cannot get rid of the sounds of crying women in the destroyed fields. As I got nearer to school, there were black, charred bodies with the white

Reprinted by permission of the B.C. Chapter of Canadian Physicians for the Prevention of Nuclear War (formerly Physicians for Social Responsibility).

edges of bone showing in the arms and legs. A dead horse with a bloated belly lay by the side of the road. Only the skeleton of the Medical Hospital remained standing. Because the school buildings were wood, they were completely destroyed. My class-mates had been in one building attending their physiology lecture. When I arrived some were still alive. They were unable to move their bodies. The strongest were so weak that they were slumped over on the ground. I talked with them, and they thought they would be okay, but all of them would eventually die within weeks." (He is of course describing what we now know to be radiation syndrome, and we know that medical intervention makes no difference.) "I cannot forget the way their eyes looked at me and their voices spoke to me forever. So many people died that disposing of the bodies was difficult. We burned the bodies of my friends in a pile of wood which we gathered in a small open space. I clearly remember the movement of the bowel in the fire. Never again should these terrible nuclear weap-ons be used, no matter what happens. Only when mankind renounces the use of these nuclear weapons will the souls of my friends rest in peace." So spoke Dr. Ishimaru. Little wonder that those people who had read his or other descriptions of Hiroshima or Nagasaki considered that ABC program, "The Day After," as an understatement.

Now, since that traumatic beginning of the nuclear age, many people have attempted to project forward what would happen in the event of a nuclear explosion. These projections take a variety of forms, and one that I will just mention is one that has been put forward by the U.S. Arms Control Agency as to what could be anticipated in the event that a nuclear device were exploded over the White House in Washington. They sneak in these projections often of what would happen with the explosion of a one megaton bomb. One megaton is 1,000,000 tons of TNT equivalent, 80 times the size of the Hiroshima bomb, and is far less destructive than the largest that have been made. The projection suggests that there would be one bomb; and yet almost everybody recognizes that at any given moment cities like Washington, Chicago, Detroit, and perhaps Vancouver, and surely Moscow, Leningrad, and Odessa are targetted by multiple bombs, and these bombs are all of very sizeable explosive potential.

Just let me digress for a moment. A one megaton bomb: I have difficulty in visualizing what is involved in 1,000,000 tons of TNT, and I asked one of my physicist friends, how do you look at that? He said, well, think of a freight train 300 miles long filled with TNT, that is one megaton explosive power of TNT. As Dean Pentz pointed out to us last night, consider a Trident D5 missile, a more recent development on the American scene, with 10 to 15 independently functioning re-entry vehicles, each bearing a warhead of something under half a megaton. That means that a freight train extending from my city, Boston, Massachusetts, to your city of Vancouver—not running from one city to the other, but extending from one city to the other—would have to exist to be filled with enough TNT to represent the potential explosive power of that one nuclear weapon. In all of World War II, it is estimated that approximately a total 3 megatons of explosive force were used by all participants, the U.S., Soviet Union, Germany, Japan, Britain, and France.

Here is a slide which indicates that at the present time there are in the nuclear arsenals of the world something of the order of 18,000 megatons, that is 18 billion tons of TNT. Three million tons was the total explosive force used in all of World War II. A single American Poseidon submarine, our soon-to-be-outdated submarine, contains enough nuclear power to destroy Moscow, Leningrad, and 200 other of the Soviet's largest cities. The most recent addition to our submarine capability, the Trident, has the power to destroy every major city in the Northern Hemisphere. And the Soviets of course have equivalent capabilities. Again, these numbers are much less impressive, as impressive as they are, than attempting to discern what would happen in the event of the use of even one of these one megaton devices.

A single one megaton device exploded over the White House, the official U.S. document tells us, would lead to more than a mile and a half of total destruction, and by total destruction, I don't talk in terms that are understandable or certainly were not by me until I had visited Hirohima and Nagasaki. Dr. Ishimaru pointed out to me in one place an impression on a wall, a shadow that is believed to have been a friend of his. That is all that is left. There would be vaporization of everything in the area of the immediate hypocentre of the explosion. For a distance of more than 10 miles, there would be fires, destruction, and death beyond belief. It is estimated that in the city of Washington, there would be 600,000 deaths, and 800,000 more injured. The long-term medical effects would be those that have been seen in Hiroshima and Nagasaki, but obviously much worse if people did survive. The long-term problem of cancer is one that one reads about a great deal, but of course there are many others. Again, I think unless one thinks in terms of what is involved in the tragedy of a single individual, it is hard to visualize these large numbers.

A delegation was asked by the Pope two years ago to call on the leaders of the nuclear powers and to offer his message urging that all steps be taken to curb the nuclear arms race. I was asked to accompany the group that called on President Reagan. I personalized my message to him, because I think that one really can better understand what happens when one talks in personal terms. I apologized for it, but I said nothing that had not been in the newspapers. His life was clearly saved after the assassination attempt on him as a result of the advances in modern medicine. I think it is fair to say that had he been wounded as gravely as he was 25 years ago, he could not have been saved. He was brought, the newspapers tell us, to the Emergency Unit of the George Washington University Hospital, where we are told he required seven units of blood transfused, and where expert teams operated on him at once to close the wounds that had been caused by the would-be assassin's bullets. Those doctors responsible for his care would quickly agree that had ten people or even five in his condition been brought simultaneously to the hospital, they could not have coped. Taking care of that terrible set of problems presented in one patient taxed the capabilities of an institution of very significant proportions.

Had three, four, or five come at the same time, they would have had to do what we call triage, a process to which I will refer later on. They would have had to decide, we are going to treat X first and Y second, or X first and Y second and Z not at all, we are going to have to send him or her elsewhere. If a bomb had exploded over the White House, there would have been 800,000 people in the President's condition and no George Washington University Hospital. The doctors having presented this kind of information to their fellow citizens, the doctors of the U.S.,

Canada, Soviet Union, and countries around the world, the doctors have said, we must look at this as we look at any epidemic for which there is no treatment and the costs of which are unacceptable. We direct all of our energy at prevention. That message has been carried widely. It has not been refuted by any group of doctors I know.

In 1981 the Board of Trustees of the American Medical Association said the following, "There is no adequate medical response to a nuclear holocaust. In targetted areas, millions would perish outright including medical and health care personnel. Additional millions would suffer severe injury, including massive burns and exposure to toxic levels of radiation, without benefit of even medical care. Medical and hospital facilities and other resources would likewise have been destroyed." It continued with the resolution of the American Medical Association, "The AMA Board of Trustees believes that it is incumbent upon the Association to inform the President and the Congress of the United States of the medical consequences of nuclear war, and that no adequate medical response is possible." Other major medical organizations throughout my country and yours, and countries around the world, have become similarly involved.

The organization that is central to the sponsorship of the conference that is going on here, "Physicians for Social Responsibility," has in the United States 30,000 members, and around the world, its international counterpart, the group called "International Physicians for the Prevention of Nuclear War," almost 100,000 members in 36 countries. To the growing number of medical professionals involved, there should be added the groups of lawyers, business persons, educators, and many other professional groups. Citizens from many regions and from many walks of life have been aided by the medical facts which physicians have disseminated, and the environmental facts that have been presented by others.

Most recently, of course, there is the work of Dr. Turco, who spoke last evening on nuclear winter, the work that demonstrates that the use of only a small amount of the nuclear explosives now in our world's arsenals might lead to extinction of life on this planet. There is discussion about some details of the work that Dr. Turco and his colleagues have put forward, and the work is being pursued in a variety of countries by a variety of organizations to explore its details. In this field, in which I am not very familiar, I have questioned colleagues who have expressed reservations about one or another detail. I have asked them whether they anticipate that anything that might emerge will ever tell us that the possibility which Dr. Turco and his colleagues have offered can be excluded. They all believe it is highly unlikely that anyone would ever be able to say that the scenario described is out of the question, or even unlikely. If it is possible, then it seems to me that the only moral position we can take is to assume that it will happen. And since we live on a planet and in a civilization that does not belong to us, which has been given to us in trust, we must behave as though it is one that we will pass on to those that follow us.

Such facts as the ones that the medical people, engineers, and physicists have brought forward, have helped to transcend the prevailing numbness and sense of helplessness that was so prevalent, and has helped people to galvanize themselves into self-education, public education, and political action groups. Some people, myself among them, just assumed that by now important steps would have been taken to control the arms race. Indeed, optimist that I am, I thought after my involvement at the outset, that in a few weeks the job would be finished.

You know, after all, at that time it was during our last presidential election campaign. There were candidates for high office who were speaking about winning a nuclear war, speaking publicly. I thought, these people can't possibly appreciate the medical realities. If they could, they would not speak this way, and therefore, it was our responsibility as physicians to point out what was obvious to us, but what was less than obvious to some others, and then just let history run what I thought would be a happy course. This view I must say was not confined to neophytes such as myself. In 1981, a distinguished physicist, W.K.H. Ponofsky said in a statement before a group of physicians, "My thesis here is to show that if the physical and medical realities of nuclear war were better understood by the people at large and the decision makers of all nations, then much of the driving force for escalation of the nuclear arms race would disappear. I am pleased that physicians have begun to publicly emphasize the medical consequences of nuclear conflict." The course of the nuclear arms race since that time indicates just how naive we were.

In 1980 it has been estimated the United States possessed approximately 9000 strategic weapons, the Soviet Union was believed to have about 6000. Now, Admiral Carroll reported last night, the U.S. is thought to have more than 11,000, and the Soviets more than 8000. The U.S. plans to build 17,000 more by 1992. More important than the numbers is the general trend for nuclear weapons and their delivery systems to become increasingly sophisticated technically, increasingly accurate, and increasingly diversified in their purposes. New missiles are being introduced by both sides in Europe, and negotiations on nuclear arms control have stopped.

What is perhaps of greatest concern is the prospect of proliferation to large numbers of countries. Now five nations acknowledge possession of nuclear weapons, and within this century, an authoritative group has estimated, 34 others will have that capability. This is particularly of grave concern since in no year since World War II have there been fewer than four wars and in some, as many as eighteen. What would happen if a leader such as the Ayatollah Khomeni or Colonel Khadafi were to have nuclear weapons and feel that that was the only recourse open to protect the integrity of what he or they considered to be what they stood for?

The costs of all of this have not been trivial, although I am told by some students in this area that nuclear devices were chosen as weapons early because they were considered to be bargains. They required fewer people, they required less in the way of maintenance, and in general would offer protection at a lesser cost, a bigger bang for the buck, it used to be called. They represent, even now some apologists say to me, 15 to 20% of the arms budget of the super powers. In our country, 15% of $280 billion this year is $42 billion, and that is probably a very conservative estimate. And nuclear weapons are getting more expensive. Admiral Carroll reported last night that the cost of 17,000 additional devices and delivery systems projected for the near future is estimated at something of the order of half a trillion dollars, five hundred billion dollars. No one will even guess at what the Star Wars folly will cost. All of this occurs at a time of escalating military budgets in general everywhere. In the United States, this year's military expenditures are up 70% from 1980, this at a time when higher education has increased by 6%, pollution control has been decreased by 19%, and conservation and land management has gone down by 73%. The estimated expenditure by my country of $2.6 trillion from 1982 to 1989 may be compared with a figure of $2.3 trillion from the end of World War II to 1981.

In the past 50 years, military expenditures worldwide have increased from less than 1% to more than 6% of the world's total population. That means that other aspects of life have decreased by the difference. Between 1960 and 1981, the U.S. spent $1.82 trillion and the Soviet Union, it is estimated, $1.3 trillion, on military programs. During this period when the annual military expenditures of all developed countries rose by more than $400 billion, their foreign economic aid rose by $25 billion. $400 in arms for every $25 in foreign aid. In 1982 their military expenditures exceeded their foreign economic aid by 17-fold. In 1983, global military expenditures amounted to $663 billion. Since 1978 these expenditures have expanded by more than 6% annually as compared with 1.7% expansion for the world economy. The implications again are that as the military goes up without a concomitant equivalent increase in the total economy, other things go down. All of this is going on in my field at a time of vast unmet needs.

I will make some generalizations concerning health, and I am sure that those in this audience and elsewhere who know fields such as education, the environment, the economy, would offer analgous comments. This spring, in my city, Boston, Massachusetts, there was great controversy about whether we should start a program in liver transplantation. It is now possible to transplant livers into those people who would die because their own livers have failed. This is a relatively new capability. For some years we have been able to do that with kidneys, and for a shorter time with hearts. It is now possible with livers, and it will surely be possible with other organs as time goes on. The reason for the debate was not as to whether our surgeons are capable, whether they are good, but rather, whether we could afford it at a time when other programs were being compromised. A decision was made to proceed on an experimental basis, and the first patient in Massachusetts received a liver transplant this spring. The cost, it was estimated, was just under $200,000 for the procedure and the follow-up care for one year. A short time later, a report was brought forward indicating that infant mortality in the population served by several inner-city, that is to say poverty-area, health clinics had increased in 1982 by 46%. This was astonishing, because infant mortality in the United States, particularly since we passed the Medicaid legislation in the mid-60s which makes it possible for all people independent of income to have access to prenatal care and care during early childhood, has been decreasing. Infant mortality is a measure of the number of babies who die in the first year after birth. That increased in Boston, and it had increased at a time when that area had been subjected to the economic recession that was nation and worldwide. But it was also at a time when the maternal and child health funds to support such activities as prenatal care and early infant care had been cut by 40%. Not a large cut in dollars, the cut was from $1.5 million to $900,000. That is a cut of only $600,000, but the calculation from the figure I have offered just a few minutes ago tells you that that cut was equivalent to the amount needed to support only three patients with liver transplants. That indicates to some extent, why the debate took place. Could we afford to move forward with a program like liver transplantation, and should we? What are the ethics of going ahead in that way to save a very small group of our population at a time when we are not meeting the needs of a much larger group?

Such triage questions are going to be confronting us more and more. Us, in the United States, you in Canada, people in every country of the world. They have confronted people in the Third World countries forever. They will be confronting us and you, in part because medical technology is becoming ever more capable of doing wonderful things, and evermore expensive. It will affect you and us because our population, like yours, is getting older. The 11% of our population now over the age of 65 consumes a third of the health dollar. That 11% will be something of the order of 20% early in the next century, demographers tell us in the United States, and I suspect the pattern in Canada will not be all that different. That is true in most industrialized countries. That 20% will require something on the order of half of the health dollar.

These tradeoffs are not tradeoffs to be made by physicians. These decisions must be made by society as a whole. Our responsibility as doctors is to lay out before the public the facts so that they can set priorities that are as rational and as equitable as possible. However, it is our responsibility and the responsibility of others to make it clear that these tradeoffs are made not only within each sector, that is to say a decision to build a new high school in one city may mean that one has to give up some other education program. These tradoffs are made within each sector, but they are made among the sectors too.

Let me give you an example: a cutback in the manufacture of one B1 bomber, that is if the United States decided it could do with 33 instead of 34 B1 bombers, would save on a prorated basis $240 million. That is almost 50% more than would be required to maintain all the maternal and child support in all of the programs in all cities in the United States in all of last year. The case for considering even more seriously such tradeoffs is perhaps sharpened when one compares the mortality rates from one country to another, the infant mortality rate. In 1981, the 3 nations with the lowest rates were Finland, Japan, and Sweden. The nuclear powers were much further down on the list. France was 10th, the United Kingdom was 13th, the U.S. was 14th, and the U.S.S.R. was 28th. Where would those four countries be if, like Japan, Finland, and Sweden, the money we are investing in nuclear weapons were devoted to maternal and child health care? I might just quickly mention to those of you who don't follow this field that there is not a necessary cause and effect relationship between that cut in maternal and child health funds. We know that such matters as housing, education of the mother, diet, and a variety of factors affect infant mortality as well. Nonetheless, improving the standard of living we know very well makes a difference.

A greater awareness of limited resources in the health area has not been without benefit. Physicians are more thoroughly evaluating the effects of medical interventions, procedures of uncertain value are being more carefully scrutinized, greater efforts are being made to avoid duplication of expensive facilities. But, even if all the waste were eliminated, the growing medical needs of our aging population and the continuing technologic advances as I mentioned will by themselves steadily widen the gap beween what we can do and what we want to do on the one hand, and what we can afford to do on the other. These needs within a country like the United States are dwarfed by what exists in Third World countries.

Most Americans are probably unaware of the devastating health picture that prevails in most of the developing countries. Eleven million babies die before their 1st birthday. Half of the world's population does not have safe drinking water, three quarters of the Third World has no sanitary facility, and most sickness and deaths in the Third World are attributable to contaminated water. Almost half a billion people suffer from hunger and malnutrition. An estimated two thirds of all couples in the Third World lack ready access to family planning services. In 1980 fewer than 10% of Third World children were immunized against the six common childhood diseases for which vaccines exist, and 5 million children die of those diseases each year. More than 2 billion people live in malarious areas, and 1 million children die of malaria each year in Africa. It is believed that 200 million people suffer from schistomiasis, a disease that does not kill nearly so much as it renders people weak, unable to work, unable to sustain families and their nations. Eleven million people round the world have leprosy.

Some of this tragedy could be averted now, and more in the near future, if resources were made available. For example, one million children can be immunized against those preventable communicable diseases for about $5 million, $5 per child. $5 million is the cost of a Pershing II missile, and probably less than the cost of one SS20. Vaccines against malaria appear to be in a late stage of development; that is a hopeful note. The total amount of money spent the year before last for all research worldwide on malaria and all other tropical diseases was less than $100 million, an amount approximating half the cost of one of the missiles in the planned MX missile system. The cost of a 20-year program to provide essential food and health needs of all Third World countries is estimated to be much less than the $100 billion that was spent last year worldwide on nuclear devices. A 4-fold increase in family planning expenditures is estimated to be what would be required to help achieve stabilization of population, and that I don't have to remind this audience is a critical need. That increase, from $920 million to $3700 million, is less than what was spent on arms in 1983 in two days.

There have been some shining examples of achievement in the area of international health. In 1967, the World Health Organization undertook to eradicate smallpox, a disease that took millions of lives over the centuries. The last naturally occurring case of that disease that the world will likely ever see occurred in 1977. The total cost of that program was $300 million dollars, less than 0.05% of the annual cost on arms. The U.S. contribution to that program was $3 million a year over that ten year period, and we now save more than $100 million a year by virtue of our having been able to discontinue vaccination surveillance and related programs that were formerly a way of life.

The urgency to commit funds to Third World health programs becomes the greater, not only on humanitarian grounds, but also to protect national security. Indeed since a significant part of the competition for health resources is from that part of the budget specifically designated for promoting national security, that is, military forces, there is reason to question how effective that effort has proven. A board inquiry into what really constitutes measures to protect security seems long overdue in our country, in yours, and in others. One might reasonably ask, for example, whether the amount that we have invested in arms for Central America, the amount that our Soviet friends have invested for arms in their activities in Afghanistan might not be better spent on health programs, and might not have promoted the interests of our two nations much more effectively. It is a pity that we do not use health, an area in which there is so much opportunity for agreement, as a basis for international dialogue and international cooperation to a greater extent.

Tradeoff decisions must of course be made in a democracy by the people and by their representatives, but as I said, they will look to professionals for the information that will help them to reach decisions that are reasonable. The process must be flexible. What is considered appropriate in one country, or even in one part of a country, will often be less so elsewhere. What is chosen by any one group in any one area may have less appeal to others. Indeed, today's choice by any single group may well change tomorrow. The problems that confront health professionals and the American people considering the use of resources in the health fields exist in every other sector of our life and exist in the lives of Canadians and the lives of every other group of people around the world. They are likely more prominent in the health area, because medical issues often attract more attention, and the decisions will occasionally and increasingly be of the life and death variety. In every nation in which aspirations will increasingly exceed resources, and that means every nation, each decision to proceed down one road is a decision to foresake others. This is true within each sector and true among the sectors. Thus, just as every commitment in my country to liver transplants may threaten new hospital beds and maternal and child health support, so every commitment to a program in education, the environment, or the military will threaten programs within that and the other sectors. The sooner this reality is laid out for and accepted by all of us, rather than our continuing to make *ad hoc* decisions without considering their overall implications, the sooner we will be able to make explicit decisions that are in accord with our value systems.

New Weapons and the Strategies for Their Use

Michael Pentz

Nuclear weapons can be "used" in only three ways: (i) as a "deterrent" or a threat; (ii) in a limited nuclear war; (iii) in an unlimited nuclear war.

I shall briefly discuss the rationality of each of these "uses."

i. Nuclear Deterrence (or "Compellance")

The claim that "the nuclear deterrent has kept the peace for 38 years" has been repeated *ad nauseam*, with little or no attempt at proof (which is not surprising, as it

Reprinted by permission of the B.C. Chapter of Canadian Physicians for the Prevention of Nuclear War (formerly Physicians for Social Responsibility).

is inherently unprovable). It is not questionable, of course, that the possession by both the USA and the USSR since the 1960s of more than enough nuclear weapons for mutually assured destruction must have been one of several factors that have induced both sides to take care not to get involved in a direct conflict with one another. "Old-fashioned deterrence" has always been beset with fundamental difficulties, however, and it has in any case been superseded for at least twenty years by counterforce strategies based on the *use* (as distinct from the non-use) of nuclear weapons. There are at least five problems with "old fashioned nuclear deterrence":

1. Morality

For the deterrent to be effective, the adversary must believe that "we" would really "push the button" if we were attacked. In terms of present NATO policy, this applies to either a conventional or a nuclear attack. The use of nuclear weapons on any appreciable scale (i.e. on a scale likely to constitute a real deterrent) would inevitably cause large numbers of civilian casualties, even in the unlikely event that escalation could be "controlled" or even prevented. This would apply particularly to Europe, where there could be millions of casualties. It would clearly be an immoral act, as has been recognized, for instance, by the National Conference of Catholic Bishops in the United States:

> We do not perceive any situation in which the deliberate initiation of nuclear war, on however restricted a scale, can be morally justified. Non-nuclear attacks by another state must be resisted by other than nuclear means. Therefore a serious moral obligation exists to develop non-nuclear defensive strategies as rapidly as possible.[1]

2. Rationality

It is possible that our posture and utterances may persuade the adversary that we are immoral enough to initiate a nuclear war. We have also to persuade them, however, that we are irrational to the point of insanity; to use nuclear weapons in response to a conventional attack or in retaliation against a (limited) nuclear attack, one must be *certain* that there will either be no counter-retaliation with nuclear weapons, or, if there is, that the ensuing nuclear war can be kept "limited." One cannot be certain of either. One would therefore be running the risk—which many would regard as bordering upon a certainty—of precipitating an unlimited nuclear war and thereby committing national suidice, all in the name of "defence." For this posture to carry conviction and hence to be an effective deterrent, the adversary must be convinced that we are mad as well as bad.

3. Stability

Implicit in the claims that "nuclear deterrence works" is the notion that it can continue to do so, for all practical purposes indefinitely. Such claims might be worthy of consideration if there were any signs that we have to do with a stable system. If nuclear deterrence were really a reliable and stable way of "keeping the peace," the numbers of warheads in the arsenals would have remained constant at the levels they had in the 1950s, which were adequate or more than adequate for mutual deterrence. Furthermore, the qualitative developments noted above, particularly in accuracy, would not have occurred. Yet the fact is that we now have at least fifty times as many nuclear warheads as would be sufficient for deterrence, and the trend towards ever-increasing accuracy is now more pronounced than ever. Moreover, the development and deployment of new weapons systems which increasingly *appear* to have first strike capabilities is manifestly destabilising. The empirical evidence overwhelmingly suggests that the system of "nuclear deterrence" is unstable and becoming more so.

Any intrinsically unstable system must have one or more positive feedback loops built into it. It is easy to discern at least one of these within the nuclear arms race (which is the objective content of "nuclear deterrence"). The process started with a clear nuclear strategic superiority on the side of the USA, which provoked strenuous efforts on the part of the USSR to "close the gap" and "achieve parity." By the simple expedient of exaggerating the success of such efforts and inventing such fictions as "the missile gap" or, more recently, the "window of vulnerability" (or "counterforce gap"), the concatenation of vested interests that Eisenhower once called the "military-industrial complex" has been able to initiate a new cycle, a new turn in the deadly spiral of escalation, and once again, in the mid-1980s, we are witnessing a repetition of the same Soviet reflex of "countermeasures to restore parity."

4. Proliferation

A Review Conference of the Non-Proliferation Treaty (NPT) is due in the near future and its prospects are viewed by arms controllers with deep gloom. The continued failure of the USA, the USSR and the UK to carry out their obligations under Article VI of the NPT has undermined its credibility and threatens to destroy it. The British government, for instance, persists in claiming that the only way for Britain to be secure in a world in which other countries have nuclear weapons is for Britain to have them too, in order to deter any real or imagined adversaries who have or may have nuclear weapons. The logical inference from this is that all countries should have nuclear weapons and then we shall have a world made secure by universal mutual deterrence. This point is evidently not overlooked by the non-signatories (and some increasingly reluctant signatories) of the NPT.

Another argument that is frequently trotted out by politicians and the military for the retention by Britain of what is quaintly described as an "independent" nuclear detterent is that if "we" did not have nuclear weapons we could be threatened or "blackmailed" by the Soviet Union, or even by some "tin-pot dictator" of a non-nuclear country. The argument invariably stops short of spelling out exactly what we might be threatened with or blackmailed into doing, or what might be the practical political purposes and consequences for the Soviet Union of making such threats. We are left to wonder why, if nuclear blackmail could be such a potent political instrument, it was not used, for instance by the Soviet Union against Yugoslavia; or why General Galtieri was not deterred by the knowledge that Britain had over a thousand nuclear warheads and was despatching a nuclear-capable task force to the South Atlantic; or why Britain did not simply threaten to launch a Polaris missile against Buenos Aires if the Argentinians did not instantly withdraw from the Falklands/Malvinas; or why the USA, faced with a humiliating defeat in Vietnam, did not try to force a Vietnamese withdrawal by threatening to drop a nuclear bomb on Hanoi. It is clear that the political penalities of nuclear blackmail would always outweigh the political advantages—a point that was clearly recognized by the US president at the time.

5. Military Schizophrenia

Another problem with "nuclear deterrence" arises out of the paradox to which I referred in my introductory remarks. Military people are trained to and expect to use the weapons with which they are provided. They naturally base their planning on the premise that weapons are there to be *used*, not merely kept in store. Now we come along and provide them with thousands of what are supposed to be the most advanced, technologically wondrous and devastating weapons ever invented and at the same time we tell them that they are not to be used, or if they are used it can only be when it is too late to serve any rational military purpose. How can we expect any self-respecting general to accept such nonsense? Is it surprising that they should join forces with the people who invent, design, develop and manufacture these weapons in a powerful political lobby to persuade governments (and the public, which has to pay the bills) that "strategies" based on the non-use of these weapons are absurd and unrealistic, and that we should be prepared and equipped to fight and win nuclear wars (which can somehow be kept "limited")? This problem is clearly linked with that of instability, for it is precisely the military (on both sides) who have been most loudly proclaiming that "national security" is threatened by the "nuclear superiority" of the other side. The absence in the USSR of any real equivalent to the military-industrial lobby in the USA has not prevented the top military there, echoed by the top political leaders, from launching (yet again!) their "counter-measures to restore parity."

"Old-fashioned deterrence" has lacked credibility for a very long time, and was abandoned overtly in the early 1970s and covertly some time before that. As a serious strategy for the "use" of nuclear weapons, it has given way to that of "counterforce," in which nuclear weapons are to be used to fight nuclear wars. To permit the necessary deception of the public, the new strategy is also publicly called "deterrence," and it is argued that a readiness to fight (limited) nuclear war strengthens such deterrence.

ii. Limited Nuclear War

If we have abandoned non-use of nuclear weapons as a "strategy for their use," we are left with the alternatives of abandoning nuclear weapons altogether on the grounds that they "serve no military purpose whatsoever" and are "totally useless," or of devising some acceptable strategy for using them. For more than a decade, that strategy, at least as far as NATO and the USA are concerned, has been "limited nuclear war."

The absurdities of limited nuclear war have been amply demonstrated elsewhere.[2] One of the most recent and convincing demolitions of limited nuclear war strategies has been that of Robert McNamara, who was one of the originators of "flexible response," which is, of course, one of the essential elements of limited nuclear war.

> It is inconceivable to me, as it has been to others who have studied the matter, that "limited' nuclear war would remain limited—any decision to use nuclear weapons would imply a high probability of the same cataclysmic consequences as a total nuclear exchange.[6]

In the simplest of logical terms, the difficulties with limited nuclear war as a strategy may be summed up in a few questions:

1. If the military and political leaders of the nuclear powers have not been clever enough to avoid starting a nuclear war, how are they going to suddenly become clever enough to perform the more difficult task of stopping it?

2. How does one stop such a war anyway? How does one *win* a limited nuclear war? One can surely not expect the other side to concede defeat and accept our terms for stopping the war while they still have thousands of perfectly serviceable nuclear weapons?

3. If it is not possible to win (or lose) a limited nuclear war, the only possible outcome has to be a "draw"—but how do the two sides agree on that, especially if "decapitation strikes" in the early stages of the war have removed the political leaderships?

4. What mechanisms exist that can be guaranteed to be capable of keeping the war under control and preventing it from escalating? In particular, even if we may assume that the political will to keep the war limited would not be undermined by the rather special circumstances, how reliable and survivable are the C3 systems?

Limited nuclear war could be accepted as a rational strategy if and only if it could be demonstrated that, beyond any reasonable doubt, it would not lead to unlimited nuclear war. This is not possible. Indeed, the balance of probabilities is very much the other way round.

iii. Unlimited Nuclear War

As an ostensible or *public* strategy, unlimited nuclear war has some obvious drawbacks. Even if the public (of the USA for instance) could be persuaded that such a war could be fought without great risk to themselves, it seems doubtful that such a strategy would be politically acceptable. Public awareness of the nuclear winter predictions will make it even more difficult to persuade people that an unlimited nuclear war could be fought and won.

In his "Star Wars" speech of 23 March 1983, President Reagan made the histrionic announcement that he was "directing a comprehensive and intensive effort . . . to achieve our ultimate goal of eliminating the threat posed by strategic nuclear missiles," and in a televised interview a few days later Secretary of Defense Weinberger made it clear that "the defensive systems the President is talking about" (as an alternative to deterrence of nuclear war by threat of retaliation) "are not designed to be partial. What we want to try to get is a system which will develop a defense that is thoroughly reliable and total, yes. And I don't see any reason why that can't be done."[3]

Leaving aside the absurdity of the idea that any Anti-Ballistic Missile (ABM) system could ever be "thoroughly reliable and total," it is worth noting that President Reagan is not proposing a joint Soviet-American effort ("in the cause of mankind and world peace") to acquire the means, on both sides, of "rendering these nuclear weapons impotent and obsolete." Were one side or the other, by some sort of magic, to acquire such means while retaining large numbers of offensive nuclear weapons, the other side would perceive an obvious first strike threat. But for the double difficulty of persuading a whole people to become accessories in the international crime of genocide and of persuading them at the same time that they could cope with the effects of a climatic catastrophe, President Reagan's talk about "assured survival" could be seen as a serious effort to make unlimited nuclear war look like a plausible strategy.

As we have seen, the only "rational" kind of unlimited nuclear war—one based upon a successful first strike—has as little credibility as nuclear deterrence or limited nuclear war, for such a first strike is now, and is likely to remain, fraught with too many intrinsic uncertainties and risks to be a viable practical strategy.

Conclusions

It is all very well to come to the conclusion, as George Kennan and others have done, that nuclear weapons are totally useless and that there are no rational strategies for their use. The fact is that we are now engaged upon the most dangerous escalation of the nuclear arms race since it began. Thousands of new nuclear weapons are being developed and deployed, and more are at the design stage, and the dangers of nuclear war whether by accident, through misperception of capability or intent, through unforeseen escalation or even through madness in high places, are rapidly increasing. This is happening in spite of the absence of any rational strategy for the use of nuclear weapons. The same applies to Anti-Satellite Weapons and to Ballistic Missile Defense systems. It is relatively easy to demonstrate the irrationality, even the absurdity, of such projects. Yet they are being pursued and millions of dollars (and roubles) are being spent upon them.

It has been apparent for some time that the *risk* of nuclear war (i.e. the combination of the chance of it occurring and the consequences for humanity if it does) is unacceptably high. Studies such as that of the Royal Swedish Academy of Sciences[4] put the estimated global fatalities in the range of one to two billion, with civilized society in the northern hemisphere almost certainly destroyed. People like Lord Louis Mountbatten or Jonathan Schell spoke of the possibility of extinction of the human species, but were accused of exaggeration. It is only within the last year that we have begun to perceive a mechanism by which such an extinction might be caused by a global nuclear war and to notice the parallels between it and the one that most probably caused the last great extinction, some 60 million years ago. Richard Turco has described this mechanism to you earlier this evening. No one is suggesting that such an extinction would be certain. It is sufficient that the possibility exists and that there are convincing scientific grounds for believing that the possibility is not negligible. As Jonathan Schell pointed out in his discussion of this contingency, extinction of the species is a consequence that would, for humanity, be infinite, and the risk would be acceptable only if the chance of it occurring were zero.

We must therefore face up to the fact that the nuclear arms race is both irrational and unacceptably risky, yet it continues and even gathers momentum. The nuclear weapons powers are evidently in the grip of irrational forces over which existing political decision-making systems seem to have lost control. The "military-industrial-bureaucratic-technological-scientific complex" which appears to be the driving force of the nuclear arms race has become self-propelled and self-perpetuating, and the individual politicians, military men, scientists and businessmen who are the component parts of the system seem to be imprisoned within it and to be incapable of either controlling it or escaping from it. We have indeed constructed a "doomsday machine" and it is out of control.

Our present peril is without parallel in our million-year history. We have created it ourselves and it threatens our continued existence. This Conference is about the Search for Solutions to our predicament. Whatever detailed practical measures might be considered as possible first steps back from the edge of the final abyss, such as a "no first use" treaty, a multilateral or unilateral freeze, a comprehensive nuclear test ban or independent nuclear disarmament initiatives, we must reckon with the fact that they will remain mere possibilities unless some completely new element, equally without precedent in our history, can be introduced, some new political force which is not imprisoned in the doomsday machine and which is strong enough to stop it and dismantle it.

I believe that such a new political force is beginning to emerge. It is the world-wide movement for nuclear disarmament and world peace. It is only just beginning to be aware of its own novelty and its own potential. The concept of massive democratic intervention in the processes of political decision-making—of no longer "leaving it to them"—is, I believe, a new one. It is true that history abounds with examples of political change brought about by popular pressures, expressed through the ballot box and through other forms of action, including armed struggle. The limited forms of democracy that exist, in both "East" and "West," were born of such popular struggles. What is needed now is more powerful and more universal. It is interventionist democracy at an altogether higher level than has ever before been achieved. If it is to succeed, in the limited time available, it will have to mobilize in effective action a majority of the peoples of at least the nuclear weapons countries, with strong support from peoples and governments worldwide. I do not believe that there is any other solution.

Carl Sagan concluded a recent article on nuclear war and climatic catastrophe with these words:

> Our talent, while imperfect, to foresee the future consequences of our present actions and to change our course appropriately is a hallmark of the human species, and one of the chief reasons for our success over the past million years. Our future depends entirely on how quickly and how broadly we can refine this talent. We should plan for and cherish our fragile world as we do our children and grandchildren: there will be no other place for them to live. It is nowhere ordained that we must remain in bondage to nuclear weapons.[5]

I would only add this—that our future depends entirely on how quickly and how broadly we can mobilize millions of people in awareness of the future consequences of our present actions and organize them in an irresistible force that will change our course before it is too late.

Notes

1. *The Challenge of Peace: God's Promise and Our Response*, A Pastoral Letter on War and Peace, 3 May 1983, National Conference of Catholic Bishops (Catholic Conference, Washington D.C., 1983); quoted in "No First Use," Blackaby, Goldblat & Lodgaard, eds., *SIPRI*, 1984 (ISBN 0-85066-260-5).
2. For instance in: Ian Clark, *Limited Nuclear War*, Martin Robertson, London, 1982
3. Richard Garwin and John Pike, "Space Weapons: History and Current Debate," *Bulletin of the Atomic Scientists*, Supplement, May 1984.
4. *AMBIO*, Vol XI, Numbers 2–3, 1982, Royal Swedish Academy of Sciences and Pergamon Press.
5. Carl Sagan, "Nuclear War and Climatic Catastrophe: Some Policy Implications," *Foreign Affairs*, Winter 1983–1984.
6. Robert S. McNamara, "The Military Role of Nuclear Weapons: Perceptions and Misperceptions," *Foreign Affairs*, Fall 1983, pp. 59–80.

Between Assured Destruction and Nuclear Victory: The Case for the "MAD-Plus" Posture*

Robert J. Art

Nuclear strategy and nuclear war are neither pleasant nor easy to contemplate. They require thinking about the possibility of a horrendous loss of life, planning for an eventuality for which we have had no experience, and confronting a sequence of events that could destroy humanity. Over the years, contemplation of such matters has led many citizens to condemn nuclear deterrence as immoral and to call for the abolition of nuclear weapons. Modern day strategists have rejected nuclear abolition as both naive and dangerous. The knowledge of how to construct nuclear weapons, they have argued, cannot be uninvented even if their physical presence could be abolished; nor do the international political conditions exist that would permit their abolition. Unilateral nuclear disarmament could too easily subject the disarming nation to the political sway of another nuclear power. And even if each nation that had them were to abolish its nuclear weapons, all would still have to worry about the ever-present possibility of a covert attempt by others to rearm with them. This continuous danger would necessitate an international institution to police a nuclear disarmament pact, but historically the nations of the world have not proved capable of devising viable international political institutions of control.

From *Ethics* 95 (April 1985): 497–516. Published by The University of Chicago Press.

* I wish to thank Robert O. Keohane, Susan Okin, and Stephen Van Evera for helpful comments on an earlier draft of this piece. But especially I thank John Mearsheimer for pushing me to think about what I really wanted to say, for forcing me to reconceptualize the first draft, and for carefully reading two subsequent drafts.

Rather than reject nuclear weapons, strategists since World War II have divided into two distinct camps in their attempts to wrestle with nuclear strategy—the finite deterrers and the flexible responders.[1] The former are commonly associated with assured destruction, countervalue or countercity targeting, and small nuclear forces; the latter, with war waging, limited nuclear options, counterforce targeting, and large nuclear forces. Finite deterrers have held to the position that what makes nuclear deterrence stable is the threat to destroy the cities of an adversary in a retaliatory blow. Because a second strike countervalue blow is sufficient, nuclear deterrence requires no counterforce capabilities and only a small number of nuclear weapons, as long as a portion of them are invulnerable to a first strike. The threat to devastate a potential attacker's cities, even only a small number of them, is all that is required to dissuade him from attacking. And when both sides have an assured destruction capability, mutual assured destruction, or MAD, obtains and makes nuclear deterrence quite stable. Flexible responders argue that the threat to destroy cities in retaliation, when the adversary can do the same to the retaliator, has lost its credibility for dealing with a wide range of political/military contingencies and, therefore, that a range of options short of countercity blows is required to strengthen deterrence.

The finite deterrent position stresses that, because a nuclear war will likely get quickly out of control and involve massive numbers of explosions, limited nuclear options are superfluous at best and dangerous at worst. They are superfluous because they will have no utility in such an all-out war. They could not prevent cities from being devastated and can, therefore, serve no useful military or political purpose. They are dangerous because they foster the belief that nuclear war can be limited and, as a consequence, could make it appear less horrendous and hence more likely. The flexible response position stresses two counterpoints: first, in the era of mutual assured destruction, threats to retaliate massively against an adversary's cities lack sufficient credibility to deter him from undertaking hostile acts against one's allies; second, the threat of a retaliatory countercity blow, if it had to be implemented, would end all hope of quickly limiting and ending such a war short of total devastation to both.

In the last few years, as both the Americans and Russians have developed highly accurate, sophisticated, and ever larger numbers of nuclear forces, the difference between the two traditional camps has widened. The advance of technology and the growth in numbers have widened the gap because the flexible responders want to exploit further the potentialities for greater flexibility, while the finite deterrers fear a lowering of the restraints on nuclear use that the additional exploitation of flexibility could bring.

As a consequence, many finite deterrers no longer argue simply that a small number of nuclear weapons delivered on cities is sufficient for the stability of deterrence. Many now take the position that the *only* utility nuclear weapons possess is to deter the use of other nuclear weapons. Former Secretary of Defense Robert McNamara has forcefully argued this position: "Having spent seven years as Secretary of Defense dealing with the problems unleashed by the initial nuclear chain reaction forty years ago, I do not believe we can avoid serious and unacceptable risk of nuclear war until we recognize—and until we base all our military plans, defense budgets, weapons deployments, and arms negotiations on the recognition—*that nuclear weapons serve*

*no military purpose whatsoever. They are totally useless—except only to deter one's oppo-
nent from using them.*"[2] Similarly, several flexible responders now argue that nuclear
wars can be successfully waged and won and that the best way to deter them and
extend the American nuclear umbrella over its allies is to convince the adversary
that one can indeed fight and win them. A prominent exponent of this view is Colin
Gray, who has stated: "In order to extend deterrence credibly on behalf of distant
allies, the United States needs both to be able to deny victory to the Soviet and—no
less important—to avoid defeat itself. These requirements add up to a requirement
for a capability to win wars."[3]

Thus, finite deterrers may be moving to the view that nuclear weapons have very
limited military, and hence almost no political, utility because their initial use makes
so little sense. Flexible responders may be turning from war wagers into war winners.
The possibilities that have developed over the last ten years for greater flexibility in
nuclear use have begun to drive both camps from their respective centers toward
the extremes inherent in each.

In my view, both these camps miss the mark. On the one hand, finite deterrers
are naive because they do not understand the effects on *statecraft* that the nuclear
revolution has produced. Nuclear deterrence dissuades an adversary from taking
actions other than simply using his nuclear weapons against another state that may
or may not have them. Nuclear deterrence produces restraining effects that are
based on the fear of nuclear war, but such effects extend far beyond simply dissuading
initial nuclear use. With or without the McNamara position, finite deterrence severely
downplays these larger political effects. On the other hand, the flexible responders,
when they become obsessed with flexibility and move toward war winning, are also
naive because they do not understand the effects on *warfare* that the nuclear revolution has produced. War waging has some specific but quite limited virtues for
deterrence, escalation control, and damage limitation. War winning, however, is
impossible precisely because of the fact that there is no defense now against all-out
nuclear use and probably not for the foreseeable future. A nuclear war could therefore be controlled and won only if one side consciously chose to lose the war, an
event as unlikely in the future as it has been rare or nonexistent in the past. It is not
necessary to win a nuclear war in order to deter it; one has only to ensure that both
are likely to lose it.

There is a reasonable position between these two extremes. It embodies elements
of both finite deterrence and flexible response. In what follows, I etch this position
out by treating in turn, first, the political effects of nuclear deterrence and, second,
the irrelevance for the stability of deterrence of symmetry in counterforce capabilities. I
thus will lay the groundwork for a position between these two extremes by analyzing the strengths and weaknesses of the finite deterrent and flexible response positions, respectively, in the next two sections.

In the last section of this article, I conclude that if we think about nuclear strategy
politically, we find that there is a viable position between the finite deterrent and
flexible response positions that, for lack of a better term, I call the "MAD-plus"
posture. It is one that relies heavily on the restraining effects of mutual assured
destruction, but that favors some limited war-waging capability for both escalation-
signaling and damage-limitation purposes. It favors some limited counterforce (what I
later term "weak" counterforce) but not a "robust" counterforce capability that

would undermine MAD. The purpose of a weak counterforce capability (which both the Americans and the Russians now have), or, better put, a targeting policy directed at soft military targets, is to avoid initial attacks on cities and thereby limit damage. The MAD-plus posture also favors some investment in command, control, communications, and intelligence (what is referred to as C^3I) to preserve control in any nuclear war that starts out limited precisely for the purpose of keeping the war limited. Some C^3I is necessary in order to maintain control over the nuclear exchanges and thereby buy enough time so that political leaders in both capitols can negotiate quickly to bring the limited war swiftly to an end. In essence, the MAD-plus posture is a hedge: it relies mainly on assured destruction but favors buying some limited options or flexibility for added insurance.

The Political Effects of Nuclear Deterrence

Nuclear weapons have political consequences that extend far beyond their military effects. Neither the assured destructors nor the flexible responders, however, accept this premise. Because the former argue that the only thing the possession of nuclear weapons does for a state is to prevent another state from using them against it, nuclear weapons dissuade only nuclear use and therefore only a small number are needed. Because the latter argue that a small number of nuclear weapons is sufficient neither to deter a nuclear attack nor to limit damage should one occur, a state needs a large number of them to deter attacks on itself and its allies and to limit damage to both should war occur. For the finite deterrers, only the civilian population of the adversary need be held hostage; for the war wagers, in addition to civilians, the adversary's nuclear weapons, other military forces, command centers, and political control structures must be subject to devastation.

Oddly enough, from the same mistaken premise, they draw opposite conclusions. While the finite deterrers call for fewer of them and the war wagers for more of them, both share a common misunderstanding about the political role of nuclear weapons. Both have grossly underestimated the powerful restraining effects that the possession of nuclear weapons have had on superpower statecraft and on that of the other states that possess them. Nuclear weapons do things other than simply prevent other states from using them. The existence of nuclear weapons not only dissuades nuclear use but also dampens down the likelihood of the use of conventional forces against an adversary that also possesses nuclear weapons or against a close non-nuclear ally of a nuclear state. Nuclear weapons have made a general war, either conventional or nuclear, between the superpowers and their associated clients less likely. Nuclear weapons make a superpower and its associated clients that are involved in a conventional war more careful than they would otherwise be about how they conduct it for fear of going beyond the permissible limits and provoking intervention by the other superpower. The threat of retaliation, the possibility of escalation, the concomitant risk that things could get out of control, and the knowledge that if they do all is lost—it is these four factors that have forced nuclear statesmen to be more cautious than their pre–World War II "conventional" predecessors.

Most wars have occurred because someone miscalculated but in a very particular way—either about what the opponent would do, what he could do, or what could be done to him. Stalin may have lost twenty million Russians in World War II, but he certainly did not expect that outcome when he made his deal with Hitler. Hitler may ultimately have been mad, but he was banking on a short war and Allied weakness. Bethmann Hollweg may have sought relief from imperial Germany's political and military encirclement by deliberately launching a Continental war, but he certainly did not seek a world war. In these cases and others, miscalculations occurred because someone was more certain about what would happen than they should have been and than events ultimately warranted.

The nuclear age does not encourage such miscalculations to arise out of such supposed certainties. The threat to both parties that matters could quickly get out of control, together with the horrendous costs that would be imposed on both if they did, has built in a bias in nuclear statecraft toward a degree of caution and restraint that, although it can never eradicate miscalculation, has, nevertheless, minimized it greatly. That is all we can expect. But that is significant. Nuclear weapons have narrowed the range of matters about which statesmen can be certain because they have widened the range of those over which uncertainty reigns. *Ironically, miscalculation has decreased because uncertainty has increased*. It is the potential for loss of control through escalation that has built into nuclear diplomacy a degree of uncertainty about the course of events that is greater than what once obtained. It is not so much the destruction that is assured, but that which *could* occur if matters got out of control, that is the basis for the MAD world in which we live today.

The existence of nuclear weapons has thus introduced a clear and pronounced restraint into the conduct of superpower diplomacy that has affected world politics generally. Wars have continued to occur, certainly; but they have not escalated into a general one between the superpowers. Clearly crises have occurred because risks have been taken by the superpowers. We do not live in a risk-free world. But when excessive risk-taking has resulted in crises, the potential for escalation has worked to defuse them. The Cuban missile crisis is a case in point. Khrushchev would clearly not have put offensive missiles into Cuba had he known that Kennedy would have reacted as forcefully as he did. He would not have knowingly and willingly put himself and his nation into the position of being humiliated, as both subsequently were. Once he saw how strong a stance Kennedy took, he backed down. But Kennedy, though insistent on getting the missiles out, also acted with restraint: he started with the least bellicose action to get the missiles out (the blockade) and did all that he could to help Khrushchev save some semblance of face, both done from his awareness of what a single misstep could bring.

The Cuban missile crisis must therefore be seen as the exception that proves the rule. Superpower statesmen have to calculate carefully because the costs of miscalculation are potentially so horrendous. Sometimes they make mistakes. But the last forty years of American-Russian relations have seen only one grevious one. And when one occurs, both nations have acted quickly to rectify it because each has a shared interest in avoiding an all-out confrontation. Each superpower will not cease testing the other, to see what it can get away with. But it will calculate as carefully as it can before it probes because it has to. Thus, nuclear deterrence can work to produce more probing actions but quick retreat if the probe hits steel. Since 1945, the "stability-instability paradox," well known to nuclear strategists, has worked more to dampen down undue risk taking by the superpowers with respect to whether they provoke crises and how they manage them than it has to embolden either to careless adventurism.[4]

Thus, because significant political effects flow from the possession of nuclear weapons, it is wrongheaded to argue either that the only function of nuclear weapons is to deter their use by another, *or* to assert that the capability to wage and win a nuclear war is necessary to deter it. Therefore, Robert McNamara is clearly wrong when he argues that nuclear weapons are "totally useless" except to deter another state from using them. The dampening down of risk-taking behavior in general, not simply nuclear use, flows from existence of nuclear deterrence. So, too, is Colin Gray wrong when he argues that a denial of a Russian victory requires an American one. It is sufficient to demonstrate simply that the Soviet Union could not win a war and could suffer terribly if it persisted, even if the United States also lost it, to deter the Soviet Union. In the nuclear era, one nation does not have to win for the other to lose. Both can lose and therefore decide the risks are not worth taking. Thus, it is the generalized caution imposed on the superpowers by their mutual possession of a retaliatory capability that invalidates the claims of both the finite deterrers and the war wagers.[5]

The fear that things could quickly get out of control, together with the costs involved if they do—these are what work to dissuade nuclear statesmen from taking undue risks. If escalation could be controlled, there would be no risk in escalating. In the nuclear era, it is precisely the potential for the loss of control that is the keystone of restraint and the essence of deterrence. In his final work, *War and Politics*, Bernard Brodie put the case well when he argued:

> We have ample reason to feel now that nuclear weapons do act critically to deter wars between the major powers, and not nuclear wars alone but any wars. That is really a very great gain. We should no doubt be hesitant about relinquishing it even if we could. We should not complain too much because the guarantee is not ironclad. It is the curious paradox of our time that one of the foremost factors making deterrence really work and work well is the lurking fear that in some massive confrontation crisis it might fail. Under these circumstances one does not tempt fate. If we were absolutely certain that nuclear deterrence would be 100 per cent effective against nuclear attack, then it would cease to have much if any deterrence value against non-nuclear wars, and the arguments of the conventional buildup schools would indeed finally make sense.[6]

In short, what makes nuclear deterrence extend so far is the fear that it might not.

Finally, if nuclear weapons have these political effects, it is because of the destruction they can wreak and the way they can do it. As Thomas Schelling put it many years ago, "Victory is no longer a prerequisite for hurting the enemy."[7] One can now destroy the enemy without having first vanquished him. Nuclear weapons have therefore separated the power to hurt from the power to defeat, what Schelling called, respectively, "coercive power" and "brute force." Because each superpower has it within its power to absorb a first strike from the other and still retaliate with a large number of warheads, the incentive for striking first is low. Each, therefore, can destroy, but not disarm, the other. What is balanced in the nuclear age is the power to hurt, not the power to disarm. What has ultimately ended all wars, as Schelling reminded us, was not the military defeat of the adversary but the ability to threaten credibly to destroy him after he was defeated militarily unless he surrendered. The outcome of the brute-force exchange had to occur first before the exercise of coercive power to bring surrender could come into play. What nuclear weapons have done is to reverse permanently the traditional sequence of warfare: it is no longer necessary to vanquish the enemy in order to be in the position of threatening to destroy him. The latter can be done now without the former.

This condition, assured destruction, leads to the following three propositions:

> First, if you do not have to destroy the other fellow's nuclear forces to devastate him, why bother?
>
> Second, if you cannot destroy the other fellow's capability to devastate you, why try?
>
> Third, great disparities in offensive forces can be safely tolerated when the power to hurt, not the power to disarm, is what is being balanced. The balancing of terror, that is, is not highly sensitive to changes in the quantitative balance of forces as long as the attacker-to-target ratio is greater than one to one.[8] With populations vulnerable, force ratios have less "force" than they once did. From a military standpoint, then, force ratio disparities are not worrisome. Militarily, it is not necessary to match forces; but, I shall argue later, there are political reasons for doing so—for having a rough parity in numbers of offensive forces.

Thus, the virtue of the assured destruction or finite deterrent school is that it reminds us of the fundamental condition of the nuclear era: as long as defense of populations is impossible, matching the adversary in the number of forces he has is not necessary. Its vice is that it is far too restrictive in its view of what nuclear weapons do in fact restrain and deter.

The Irrelevance of Counterforce Symmetry

Is the flexible responder's world, with its emphasis on war waging (if not winning) and counterforce targeting better than the finite deterrer's MAD world, with its emphasis on limited forces and countervalue targeting? Is it better to be able to target only cities rather than to be able to knock out military forces? The answer is, It depends on what one means by counterforce, on what types of forces one wishes to knock out. If by a counterforce world we mean one in which any nuclear power possessed a first strike capability against any other nuclear power's nuclear forces, clearly a MAD world is preferable. A true or "fully robust" counterforce world would be one in which all nuclear powers felt that each had an effective disarming capability. In a surprise attack, one adversary could knock out the other's offensive (and potential retaliatory) forces. If we are interested in preventing the use of nuclear weapons, which we should be, the attempt to attain such a capability is insane. As Schelling once put it, "Military technology that puts a premium on haste in a crisis puts a premium on war itself."[9] A counterforce world would encourage speedy decisions, hasty actions, preemptive strategies, grandiose ambitions, aggressive foreign policies, and the like.[10] Clearly a counterforce world lessens the political restraints on the physical use of nuclear force. It is desirable, therefore, that nuclear statesmen continue to feel insecure about defense against nuclear attack and about their own first strike capabilities and secure only about their own and their adversary's retaliatory capabilities.

If a fully robust counterforce world is not desirable, is something short of it, what we might term a "weak" counterforce world, also undesirable? Is a world, that is, in which both sides possess considerable counterforce capabilities, but those still well short of a disarming capability, destabilizing? The answer to this question should be no simply because, no matter how extensive their counterforce capabilities are and no matter how great the asymmetry between them may be in this regard, neither side would be emboldened to strike first when the other would retain the capability to retaliate on its cities. Weak counterforce capabilites can and do exist in a MAD world. But that does not alter the fundamental condition of mutual vulnerability to which both superpowers are subject.

In order to develop this argument more fully, I will attack the position, first developed by Paul Nitze in 1976, that asserts that a perceived asymmetry in counterforce capability (in Russia's favor) both weakens deterrence and puts the United States at a disadvantage in crises and intense bargaining situations. His argument received wide currency in the United States and was reflected in the Carter administration's PD-59 and "countervailing strategy" pronouncements.[11] As explained by then Secretary of Defense Harold Brown, the countervailing strategy held to the view that, although the United States did not believe that either nation could prevail militarily in a nuclear war, nevertheless, for the stability of deterrence and the advantageous resolution of crises, the United States had to strengthen significantly its own war-waging posture and thus "countervail" against the Soviet Union.[12]

I begin with Nitze's argument because he stated the asymmetry position in the most extreme form. In his influential article, he argued:

> In sum, the ability of U.S. nuclear power to destroy without question the bulk of Soviet industry and a large proportion of the Soviet population is by no means as clear as it once was, even if one assumes most of U.S. striking power to be available and directed to this end.
>
> A more crucial test, however, is to consider the possible results of a large-scale nuclear exchange in which one side sought to destroy as much of the other side's striking power as possible, in order to leave itself in the strongest possible position after the exchange.[13]

Nitze was concerned about the potential postattack position of the United States vis-à-vis the Soviet Union. If the Russians could wipe out most of American's land-based missile forces in a first strike and if the Americans did not have the same capability to wipe out most of Russia's land-based missiles in a first strike, then the Soviet leaders might be tempted to launch an attack on America's land forces, but they would more likely be emboldened to take risks that they otherwise would not because they would be acting from a supposedly superior position. In short, argued Nitze, asymmetries in counterforce capabilities, even if MAD still obtained, could be destabilizing and produce a more dangerous world for the United States. The countervailing strategy picked up this line of reasoning when it argued:

> The Soviet Union should entertain no illusion that by attacking our strategic nuclear forces, it could significantly reduce the damage it would suffer. Nonetheless, the state of the strategic balance after an initial exchange—measured both in absolute terms and in relation to the balance prior to the exchange—could be an important factor in the decision by one side to initiate a nuclear exchange. Thus, it is important—for the sake of deterrence—to be able to deny to the potential aggressor a fundamental and favorable shift in the strategic balance as a result of a nuclear exchange.[14]

Why, however, would asymmetries in counterforce capabilities be destablizing if neither side had a robust or truly disarming counterforce capability? Why would the Russians attack land-based missiles when they could not get at the sea-based ones? Did the fact that the latter were invulnerable to a disarming attack not make the former, in effect, invulnerable also? The crux of Nitze's and presumably Brown's worry was this: the United States would be "self-deterred" from retaliating against Russian cities once it had suffered a massive strike against its land-based forces. It would not hit back at Russian cities because that would cause a retaliatory Russian strike against American cities. The United States would be left in the same position many argued it once was in the fifties with its policy of massive retaliation: shoot off everything or do nothing. After its disarming blow against the land-based forces then, the Soviet Union would be in a position to intimidate the United States. In order to remedy this potential for "self-deterrence," the United States had to develop counterforce capabilities symmetrical to what the Soviet Union already had. America had, in short, to develop more of a war-waging capability in order to bolster deterrence.

The Nitze scenario and variants on it—and especially his call for the United States to develop a more formidable war-waging capability—received firm support from President Reagan's Commission on Strategic Forces in its April 1983 report:

> In order to deter such Soviet threats we must be able to put at risk those types of Soviet targets—including hardened ones such as military command bunkers and facilities, missile silos, nuclear weapons and other storage, and the rest—which the Soviet leaders have given every indication by their actions they value most, and which constitute their tools of control and power.
>
> Effective deterrence of any Soviet temptation to threaten or launch a massive conventional or limited nuclear war thus requires us to have a

comparable ability to destroy Soviet military targets, hardened and otherwise. . . . A one-sided strategic condition in which the Soviet Union
could effectively destroy the whole range of strategic targets in the United
States, but we could not effectively destroy a similar range of targets in
the Soviet Union, would be extremely unstable over the long run.

. . . We must have a credible capability for controlled, prompt, limited
attacks on hard targets ourselves. This capability casts a shadow over
the calculus of Soviet risk-taking at any level of confrontation with the
West.[15]

Early in the Reagan administration, Secretary of Defense Weinberger's call for
the United States to be able to wage a "protracted" nuclear war through to a successful conclusion signified the final step in this line of reasoning. Under the early
Reagan, America's policy shifted from countervailing to prevailing, from war waging to
war winning. The later Regan administration backed off from war winning in its
subsequent pronouncements, but it continued to invest considerable sums to procure a
formidable war-waging capability. But whether it be for war waging or war winning,
the rationale has been that because they (the Russians) have it, we need it. Is this the
case? Why should symmetry in counterforce capabilities be necessary? Why must
we be able to wage a nuclear war as effectively as some argue the Russians can
and/or intend in order to deter it or in order to limit damage in it if it should occur?
Is symmetry in war-fighting capabilities between the Russians and the Americans
necessary for nuclear stability?

My judgment is no. I should like to offer seven reasons why I think the Nitze
counterforce scenario, its many variants, and the entire symmetry-in-war-waging
argument makes little military, and even less political, sense.

1. If the war wagers and counterforces can argue that the United States would
be deterred from attacking Russian cities in retaliation for a Russian first strike
counterforce blow against America's Minuteman force, why can the "MAD men"
not argue that, similarly, they would likely be deterred from attacking the Minuteman missiles in the first place because they cannot be certain that we would not
retaliate against any, a few, or all of their cities? If self-deterrence works to prevent
us from retaliating, would not self-deterrence also work to prevent them from attacking? Why does self-deterrence work only for us and not for them?

2. If neither the United States nor the Soviet Union is prepared to threaten to
attack cities, *even if neither would ever want to execute that threat*, then each cannot
deter the other, no matter how effective their war-fighting capabilities are. To repeat,
what provides restraint is the fear that things will get out of control and that all
could be lost—both sides' cities, that is—if caution is abandoned. The war wagers,
however, argue that the Soviet leaders value their machinery and their mechanisms
of political control more than they do their populace. They do not accept the MAD
world logic. The conclusion, they assert, is that our threat to devastate their population carries little weight with them.

How, however, in reality, can that conclusion make any military or political sense?
First, a significant percentage of Russian hard targets are located in or near cities so
that extensive counterforce attacks would produce civilian casualities that would

likely be indistinguishable from purely countervalue attacks.[16] Colin Gray, for example, admits as much when he states: "Not only would one be assaulting the highest of Soviet values by counter-military targeting, and thereby minimizing if not removing entirely any Soviet incentives to exercise restraint, also one would be licensing a campaign that—if it were to be waged efficiently on both sides—would have to produce a vast amount of civilian damage. Both superpowers have very many military assets co-located with civilian society."[17] If extensive counterforce attacks would have much the same results for civilians as would pure population attacks, why do we need to fine-tune our forces for hard target kills when we cannot avoid extensive civilian damage in the process? And would that be the best way for the United States to limit damage to its civilians when the Russians know that American leaders value their populace highly? Second, would it not be extremely difficult to convince the Soviet leaders that limited counterforce strikes against military targets so colocated were aimed, not at their populace, but at them (or vice versa)? Is an attack on Moscow (or Washington) meant to be "only" decapitating, the precursor to a rolling or tit-for-tat exchange, or merely a one-time shot to show that we (or they) mean business? How could they (or we) know which was the case?

Third, finally either extensive countervalue attacks or extensive counterforce attacks against the Soviet political mechanisms would kill so many Russian civilians that there would be little left to control! Political leaders do not value political control mechanisms per se; they value the power over others that such mechanisms yield. If there is no one left (or very few) to control, what, precisely, can be the point of the machinery for control? Surely mechanisms for control, apart from the objects of control, have little political meaning to those who possess them. Either type of attack, therefore, will eradicate the civilians. And since the leaders need the civilians to control, why go after them the hard way (counterforce) rather than the easy way (countervalue)? If there is logic to this argument, then the Soviet leaders must value their populace as much as American leaders do, even if they do so for different reasons. Thus, even the war wagers' emphasis on control mechanisms leads one inexorably back to populations and to the logic of MAD.

3.   Third, what will end the nuclear war as well as prevent it is the threat of wiping out cities. Who has more weapons left over after an extensive brute-force exchange or after a series of small exchanges is irrelevant to the conclusion of the war as long as each party can still devastate the other. Postattack calculations about throw weight ratios, warhead ratios, missile ratios, and the like, make little sense. What has always brought a war to a successful conclusion for one party or a draw for both is the need to settle in order to avoid further or extensive civilian deaths. It is hard to see how disparities in force sizes, however measured, will make any difference to war termination when both will surely retain enough forces to threaten however many cities each still retains intact.

4.   The Nitze scenario of an extensive Russian first strike against America's Minuteman force, although theoretically possible, glosses over the real and intractable operational difficulties the Soviet Union would have in executing such an attack. The fratricide problem alone makes the timing of such an attack inordinately complicated.[18] Although no one would advocate such a posture unless there were no choice, the United States could always resort to a launch-on-warning or -on-attack

posture. It is difficult to imagine a Communist Party chairman of the Soviet Union imagining that an American president would simply watch the Russian missiles rain down on the United States. Would he not have to calculate that, if he shot at all of America's land-based silos, he might in effect be shooting at empty ones?

5.   A massive disarming strike against America's Minuteman force would require something approaching 2,000 separate explosions. Would that be a truly limited and containable strike? Would a decision by the Soviet leaders to launch an attack of such magnitude not be equivalent to a declaration of World War III? Why would they go after America's land-based forces when America's sea-based forces remained intact? Are not land-based systems invulnerable because the sea-based ones are? Given the civilian casualties that an attack of such magnitude would have for the United States, could the Russian leaders seriously think that an American president would leave Russian cities intact? Why would they take such a risk? Why would they feel more emboldened in a crisis when such presumed capability carries such a high risk of an American counterresponse?

6.   The United States today already possesses considerable counterforce capabilities and will, shortly, have even more. If these are to be used intelligently, that is, for deterrent purposes, they should be directed in our declaratory posture toward soft, not hard, military targets. If we ever need actually show that we are serious about escalation and if we want to hold our cities and theirs in hostage in the early phases of a nuclear war, surely limited counterforce attacks against credible, but containable, soft military targets is the least destabilizing counterforce posture available. If they ever were to occur, counterforce attacks should be limited and undertaken, not to disarm or to sever political control, but to demonstrate resolve in a way that still manages to limit the damage done.

7.   Most of the above points have been directed to prewar deterrence. Should such a war occur, the best way to limit damage is not to institute extensive and wide-ranging counterforce attacks but, rather, to negotiate to stop the war immediately. The next best way is to limit any exchanges that may occur. The worst way to attempt to stop the war is to engage in massive counterforce exchanges that will heighten the incentives to preempt and that will, in any case, bring horrendous civilian deaths. And the deliberate, extensive targeting of Russian command, communications, control, and intelligence facilities is absurd. We (and they) need someone who is in control and with whom we can negotiate. We and they both require that someone remain in charge to limit the exchanges. In short, damage limitation does not require an extensive counterforce targeting capability. The execution of such a strategy on a large scale would likely produce the very results that it is intended to prevent—namely, extensive damage.

Beyond all these points lies a final one that renders the attempt to acquire a war-winning posture illusory. If a full-scale nuclear war is inherently uncontrollable, it is wasteful, if not absurd, to try to develop fully the means to control it. Selectivity, protractedness, fine tuning, discrimination—all these are entities not likely to exist or persevere in a protracted nuclear war of any size. Desmond Ball has persuasively shown that command, control, and communications systems are inherently more vulnerable than the strategic forces themselves, for both the Americans and the Russians, and will likely remain so for the foreseeable future. The consequence of this fact is that "the capability to exercise strict control and co-ordination would inevitably be lost relatively early in a nuclear exchange."[19] Any nuclear war, then, once it begins and if it continues, is likely to get out of hand. As long as that condition obtains, the pursuit of the ability to conduct a fully controlled and sizeable nuclear war is a fool's chase. It is not that we should not take precautions to preserve some options for selectivity and controllability. These are prudent measures. But to believe that matters can, in fact, be controlled and to operate under that assumption is wrong. The probability that things will get quickly out of control remains uncertain enough that gambling it will not is foolhardy. Because that is so, we are driven back to the MAD world of deterrence, almost, that is, but not quite.

The Case for the "MAD-Plus" Posture

Is there, then, nothing at all to be said for war waging, even after we have thrown out both war winning and symmetry in counterforce capabilities? Is finite deterrence, with its emphasis on small nuclear forces and countervalue targeting, the only sensible posture to take? Are there valid reasons why it is sensible not to have a nuclear force that is dramatically smaller in size than one's adversary's? Are there valid reasons to have some limited war-waging capabilities? I believe there are valid reasons both to match roughly one's adversary in numbers and to have a limited war-waging capability, though I stress the word "limited." I offer three reasons.

First, what makes military sense in the nuclear age—the absence of a compelling need to match exactly the adversary in the number of nuclear forces he possesses—makes little political sense for the two superpowers because their nuclear forces are used to protect territories other than merely their own. The logic of finite deterrence is impeccable for the restricted case of an attack on a superpower's homeland. (This is often referred to as type 1 deterrence, deterrence of an attack only on one's own territory.) For as long as a percentage of one's forces is invulnerable to a first strike, the adversary's cities can be held hostage to retaliation by a relatively small number of weapons. To deter one superpower from attacking only it directly, therefore, the other superpower needs to have a force merely some fractional size of the former's.

What works for type 1 deterrence, however, has not proved politically feasible for type 2 deterrence. The latter encompasses the difficult problem of "extended deterrence," that is, extending the protection of each superpower's nuclear umbrella over its nonnuclear and small nuclear allies. The political imperatives that are rooted in these type 2 deterrent uses of their nuclear forces have pushed the superpowers to maintain a rough equivalence in the sizes of their forces and sometimes to strive for a superiority, that is, for a disarming or robust counterforce capability. For extended deterrent purposes, like it or not, if one superpower has a force dramatically smaller than the other, it looks weaker to the allies over whom the superpower's nuclear umbrella is being extended. Simply put, America's allies, especially the NATO allies, would feel better with an American superiority, bad with an American inferiority, and can tolerate an American equality with the Soviet Union. For the superpowers who have extended deterrent uses for their nuclear forces, the military logic of finite deterrence for the type 1 case is not sufficient for the political logic of alliance management inherent in the type 2 case, no matter how "illogical" the logic of the extended deterrent world may seem. Political concerns, therefore, dictate that having a small nuclear force when one's superpower adversary has a large one is politically disadvantageous and hence untenable. One of the underpinnings of finite deterrence—that large disparities in force sizes do not matter—does not hold.[20]

Second, finite deterrence has difficulties handling escalation scenarios that involve competitions in risk taking. Although it is true that, strictly speaking, what happens on the battlefield is not central to the outcome of any nuclear war that may begin, it is not totally irrelevant. To see the force of this argument, we must distinguish between how nuclear weapons are initially used and what subsequently happens on the battlefield.

In the nuclear era, it is the case that defeat on the battlefield cannot easily, if at all, be translated into victory in the war simply because the side that has suffered a temporary battlefield loss can always up the ante and go to a higher level of violence if he deems what he is fighting for worth the escalation. Battlefield victories have little meaning if the adversary can still destroy you after suffering them. In the nuclear era, "escalation dominance"—the ability to contain or defeat an adversary at all levels of violence except at the highest (all-out nuclear war)—is not feasible simply because the adversary can suffer defeat at one level and go to the next higher one.[21] It is not the military outcomes of battles that will determine how intensely the war is waged and when it will stop. Rather, it is how much each adversary values what he is fighting for that will determine the scope, scale, and intensity of the conflict. Resolve, not battlefield victory, is the crucial element in any competitive risk-taking situation. Each party has a shared interest in avoiding an escalation to all-out war where they both would be destroyed. Each will be forced to weigh how much he and his adversary value what both are fighting for in order to determine how firm to stand. As has been pointed out many times before, this is the proverbial game of chicken. Ultimately, one side is likely to give way to avoid devastation. It is true, therefore, that when defense of populations is not possible, escalation dominance loses its utility.

What happens on the battlefield, however, can have meaning for structuring the dynamics of competitive risk-taking situations. Battlefield actions are important for what they signal about resolve, not whether they defeat the adversary. How battles are started can affect both the perceptions of resolve and the subsequent dynamics of a competitive risk-taking situation. It is not sufficient to argue, therefore, that escalation involves a competition in risk taking and simply leave matters at that. How, exactly, does one demonstrate resolve if one has to fire one or several nuclear weapons? Are demonstration shots—those that involve explosions in remote areas where there are no military forces and civilians—demonstrations of one's resolve to use nuclear weapons or of one's fear of using them? Is it sufficient simply to fire one off to a place where its military effects are harmless? Or does one need to make a siginificant military statement by the initial use of one's nuclear forces, *knowing full well that any military gain thereby achieved is only temporary if the adversary decides to reciprocate?* Does it make sense to use such forces initially against the adversary's cities, even if only one small city is destroyed? That may demonstrate resolve all right, but will it not overly provoke the adversary and cause him to return the blow, when in fact the point of one's initial use was to cause him to stop his military action?

These questions are perplexing. The initial use of nuclear weapons in small numbers involves what Schelling once called "threats that leave something to chance."[22] The line between deliberate escalation in order to stop a war and escalation that gets out of control is a fine one, indeed. By definition, escalatory actions that are taken to manipulate risk involve the chance that they will get out of control. If they could not, there would be no risk, escalation could be controlled, and escalation to manipulate risk would turn into escalation dominance. In competitions in risk taking, the effectiveness of escalatory threats lies precisely in the fact that they can get out of control. Because that is the case, one must worry about how to walk the fine line, how to signal the adversary politically, how to get him to stop, and how to avoid provoking him into his own escalation.

There can be no definitive answers to the questions asked above. But surely common sense dictates that soft counterforce targets—divisions, transportation nodes, and the like—make more sense to threaten initially than countervalue ones if one is trying both to signal resolve and yet not overly to provoke one's adversary. And if that be the case, escalatory threats designed to signal politically must have *some* military effect if they are to have a chance of succeeding. Hence, hitting military targets can make great political sense. Thus, a second underpinning of finite deterrence, an exclusive reliance on countervalue targeting, no longer holds.

Third, finally, surely some war-waging capability is desirable for rapid war termination. Finite deterrers provide a partial answer when they argue that the best way to limit damage in any nuclear war that begins small is to stop it as quickly as possible. But, again, it is not sufficient to leave matters there. We must ask what is required of one's forces and command and control facilities for this to happen. In order to limit damage, two requirements have to be met: first, someone must be in command who has the will and desire to terminate the war; second, he must have control over his forces to limit their use. If a nuclear war begins (and ends) as an all-out spasm response by both sides, the matter of control is academic. But if it begins with a severely limited use of nuclear weapons, we must take some precautions to do what we can to maintain control in order to keep use severely limited. This requires soft counterforce targeting and sufficient investment in command, control, and intelligence capabilities such that we can have reasonable confidence that the national command authority can survive for a few limited exchanges of blows.

What is required for damage limitation in the event a limited nuclear war begins, therefore, is some prudent investment in controllability. What is not required, however, is an investment to endure a protracted and extensive nuclear war. That is beyond the pale of feasibility. Nor is it desirable to engage in extensive counterforce exchanges against hardened targets—the adversary's command and control centers and his nuclear forces—for the reasons outlined earlier. What we should procure are war-waging capabilities that are designed to end the war quickly with severely limited nuclear use. What we must avoid are war-waging capabilities that are designed for long endurance and extensive use. If this be so, that some very limited war-waging flexibility is desired, then the third tenet of the assured destruction school—an opposition to flexibility—also is no longer tenable.

There is a final point that needs to be made. In the mid-eighties, we may be on the verge of a race to build effective population defenses. The MAD-plus position clearly does not call for this type of insurance and in fact finds it dangerous. Is a world in which both superpowers have an assured defense of populations preferable to the one in which they do not? Is the BAD world (Both Assured of Defense) better than the MAD-plus world?

There can be no definitive answer to this question, but informed speculation is in order.[23] A MAD-plus world is one in which the leaders of both superpowers know that, if they do not calculate correctly and tread carefully, events could get out of control. In a MAD world, escalation and loss of control are ever-present contingencies, even if they are almost never ever-present occurrences. As argued above, it is this knowledge that makes MAD nuclear statesmen cautious, restrained, and careful calculators. In a BAD world, however, the restraint would be relaxed. If their populations were thought defendable or invulnerable to retaliatory strikes, BAD statesmen would be more likely to take greater risks. As then Secretary of Defense Harold Brown put it in 1979: "I have always been concerned about massive ABM systems because I have always felt there was some possibility that some clever briefer could delude a political decision maker into thinking that they were going to work."[24] The costs of guessing wrong would presumably be less than in a MAD world if the safety net of population defense worked. A MAD world discourages unwarranted risk taking; a BAD world would not. A MAD world balances terror; a BAD world does not. A MAD world has little or no safety net for bad judgment; a BAD world presumably does.

If, however, a BAD world turns out to be one in which a credible population defense is not really feasible and one in which risk taking is not restrained, then the costs would be horrendous. Historically, for every offensive innovation, there developed a defensive response. But in the past, no weapon possessed the speed and destructive power of nuclear weapons. Population defenses require a degree of perfection to be effective that offensive forces do not. They must be held to a higher standard of workability. There is therefore a gross asymmetry between how well nuclear offenses and defenses have to work in order to be effective that tips the balance toward the offense. Even if the population defense is nearly perfect, it is still not perfect and enough missiles will get through to assure population devastation. For the foreseeable future, therefore, the offense will always get through, either ballistically or in some other fashion.[25]

A 100 percent population defense would be nice to have but so, too, would immortality. If a credible population defense is not presently and foreseeably feasible and if neither superpower would, anyway, sit still and permit its offensive forces to be so stymied, is it not better to live in a world in which the risks of using nuclear weapons are thought to be great, not small? Is the best restraint on nuclear weapons use not fear of the uncertainties surrounding their use? And in this "MAD" world of ours, is it not better to purchase a little bit of extra insurance along the lines of the MAD-plus posture described above?

Notes

1. The best treatment of this distinction is by Robert Jervis, "Why Nuclear Superiority Doesn't Matter," *Political Science Quarterly* 4 (1979–1980): 617–633.
2. Robert McNamara, "The Military Role of Nuclear Weapons: Perceptions and Misperceptions," *Foreign Affairs* 62 (1983): 59–81, p. 79.

3. See Colin Gray, "War Fighting for Deterrence," *Journal of Strategic Studies* 7 (1984): 5–29, p. 11.

4. The term was first introduced by Glenn H. Snyder, "The Balance of Power and the Balance of Terror," in *The Balance of Power*, ed. Paul Seabury (San Francisco: Chandler Publishing Co., 1965). It refers to the fact that stability at the level of all-out nuclear war can produce instability at lower levels of violence.

5. For more on these points, see Robert J. Art, "To What Ends Military Power?" *International Security* (1980): 3–35; Kenneth N. Waltz, *The Spread of Nuclear Weapons: More May Be Better*, Adelphi Paper 171 (London: International Institute of Strategic Studies, 1981).

6. Bernard Brodie, *War and Politics* (New York: Macmillan Publishing Co., 1973), pp. 430–431.

7. Thomas C. Schelling, *Arms and Influence* (New Haven, Conn.: Yale University Press, 1966), p. 22.

8. Bernard Brodie implicitly pointed this out in his *The Absolute Weapon: Atomic Power and World Order* (New York: Harcourt, Brace & Co., 1946), when he stated that "superiority in numbers of bombs is not in itself a guarantee of strategic superiority in atomic bomb warfare; (p. 46). But the first person in the public literature to develop the point fully was Glenn H. Snyder, *Deterrence and Defense: Toward a Theory of National Security* (Princeton, N.J.: Princeton University Press, 1961), pp. 42–46, 104–10.

9. Schelling, p. 225.

10. Steven Van Evera has persuasively argued this case for Europe on the eve of war in 1914. He nicely shows how a belief in the disarming power of the offensive lessened the restraints on statecraft and helped bring on the war. See his "The Cult of the Offensive and the Origins of the First World War," *International Security* 9 (1984): 58–108.

11. For an excellent critique of America's countervailing strategy, see Robert Jervis, *The Illogic of American Nuclear Strategy* (Ithaca, N.Y.: Cornell University Press, 1984).

12. The best short description of the countervailing strategy appears in Harold Brown's fiscal year 1982 posture statement. See *The Report of the Secretary of Defense to the Congress on the FY 1982 Budget* (Washington, D.C.: Government Printing Office, January 19, 1981), pp. 38–43.

13. See Paul Nitze, "Assuring Strategic Stability in an Era of Detente," *Foreign Affairs* 54 (1976): 207–233, p. 223.

14. Brown, p. 40.

15. "Report of the President's Commission on Strategic Forces" (April 1983, mimeographed), pp. 6, 16, 17.

16. See Desmond Ball, "Research Note: Soviet ICBM Deployment," *Survival* (July/August 1980), pp. 167–170.

17. Gray, p. 23.

18. On this point, see John Steinbrunner and Thomas Garwin, "Between Deterrence and Strategic Paranoia," *International Security* 1 (Summer 1976): 138–81.

19. Desmond Ball, *Can Nuclear War Be Controlled?* Adelphi Paper 169 (London: International Institute of Strategic Studies, Autumn 1981), p. 37. See also U.S. Congress, *Strategic Command, Control, and Communications: Alternative Approaches for Modernization*, a Congressional Budget Office study (October 1981); and Paul Bracken, *The Command and Control of Nuclear Forces* (New Haven, Conn.: Yale University Press, 1983).

20. I do not accept the converse, however: that an American nuclear superiority—a robust or disarming counterforce capability—would "solve" the problems inherent in extended deterrence. First of all, neither superpower would allow the other to acquire such a capability, which makes the issue academic. Second of all, for the NATO alliance at least, even when the United States was perceived by its allies to be ahead, in the fifties and sixties, still they were not satisfied. The United States in its era of nuclear advantage had to take many additional actions *in the theater* (within Western Europe) to assuage its allies, such as permanently stationing 300,000 American troops there. For lack of space, I simply assert this proposition: extended deterrent problems cannot be solved by seeking

superiority or advantageous positions with central strategic systems; they must be handled with in-theater solutions. The way to extend deterrence, that is, is to make the territory being protected look sufficiently important to the United States such that its extension of its nuclear umbrella over it looks credible. See my forthcoming *NATO in the Era of Parity: Extended Deterrence and Alliance Politics* (Washington, D.C.: Brookings Institution, 1985) for a full treatment of this issue.

21. The best recent, if not the best, discussion of the difference between escalation dominance and the competition in risk taking, is to be found in Jervis, *The Illogic of American Nuclear Strategy*, chap. 5. I have benefited enormously from this chapter and book.

22. See Thomas C. Schelling, *The Strategy of Conflict* (Cambridge, Mass.: Harvard University Press, 1960), chap. 8.

23. For more on the likely instabilities of a BAD world, see Robert J. Art, "The Role of Military Power in International Relations," in *National Security Affairs: Theoretical Perspectives and Contemporary Issues*, ed. Thomas B. Trout and James E. Harf (New Brunswick, N.J.: Transaction Books, 1982), pp. 13–27; and Charles S. Glaser, "Why Even Good Defenses May Be Bad," *International Security* 9 (1984): 92–123.

24. Harold Brown, quoted in the *Wall Street Journal* (September 28, 1984), p. 10.

25. For the technical details of why this is so, see Ashton B. Carter, *Directed Energy Missile Defense in Space*, Office of Technology Assessment (Washington, D.C.: Government Printing Office, April 1984); and *Space-based Missile Defense*, A Report by the Union of Concerned Scientists (Cambridge, Mass.: March 1984).

Questions

1. Art suggests that the position of what he calls the "finite deterrers" and that of what he calls the "flexible responders" rest on a mistaken premise. What is that mistaken premise? What evidence is available that would tend to either confirm or refute his view on this matter?

2. What implication does Howard H. Hiatt's descriptions of the conditions that would prevail following a nuclear exchange have for the kind of argument that Art examines in his discussion "The Irrelevance of Counterforce Symmetry," and in particular the position he ascribes to Paul Nitze?

3. How would Art respond to the criticisms of nuclear armaments raised by Michael Penz in his contribution to this chapter? How convincing a response would it be?

4. Is Art's argument that symmetry in war-fighting capabilities is necessary for nuclear stability convincing? How relevant to this question are the considerations suggested by Trudy Govier in "Thoughts from Under the Nuclear Umbrella" in this chapter.

Realism, Deterrence, and the Nuclear Arms Race*

Conrad G. Brunk

I

While the competition in nuclear arms and the risks of nuclear war have been a matter of intense political debate for over 30 years, only recently have they caught the serious attention of the philosophical community. This relative inattention to what the public considers a paramount social and moral issue is especially anomalous in view of the revival in the last decade of philosophical interest in normative and "applied" ethics, and in view of the fact that the modern nuclear arsenals and the strategic doctrines behind their deployment pose a host of fundamental philosophical issues.[1] The major exception to this lack of philosophical interest in the nuclear issue has been the discussion of the morality of the possession of, the use of, or the threat to use, nuclear weapons that has taken place for the most part within the context of the traditional doctrine of the so-called "just war."[2]

Perhaps this philosophical silence has been due in some degree to the fact that nuclear weapons and the prospect of their use are in an important sense beyond the pale of moral discourse. Given the enormity of the devastation threatened by the existence of these weapons, especially the unprecedented spectre of the self-immolation of the human race itself—what Jonathan Schell has termed "the second death"[3]—these weapons are thought by many to stand outside the boundaries of all moral norms, and hence beyond all possible moral justification. This is the judgement of Michael Walzer, for whom nuclear weapons can be "justified," not by morality, but only by what he calls "the standard of necessity"; this comes into play only under conditions of the "supreme emergency," in which the only moral course of action is "to seize upon opportunities of escape, even to take risks for the sake of such opportunities."[4] Only a modern *realpolitik*, it seems, which employs weapons and warfare in the sheer egoistic interests of the nation-state, without regard to morally defined ends or limits, can comfortably rationalize the deployment of nuclear weapons as instruments of national strategy.

Traditional "just war" approaches to the nuclear question find it difficult, if not impossible, to countenance the *use* of nuclear weapons, since such use conflicts with

From *Nuclear War: Philosophical Perspectives*, ed. Michael Allen Fox and Leo Groarke (New York, 1985). By permission of Peter Lang Publishing.

* This paper is an expanded version of an article originally published in *Nuclear War: Philosophical Perspectives*, Michael Fox and Leo Groarke, eds., New York: Peter Lang, 1985. The author would like to acknowledge the very valuable comments and editorial work on portions of this paper provided by Professors Fox and Groarke. Early versions of the paper were read at the 1983 Canadian Philosophical Association meetings in Montreal and at the 1984 Faculty Colloquium at Conrad Grebel College. Many helpful suggestions were received and incorporated into the paper.

the principles of proportionality and immunity of non-combatants, among other basic tenets of this doctrine. Nevertheless, several proponents of the doctrine have found it possible to justify, not the *use* of, but the *threat* to use, nuclear weapons as part of an overall strategy of deterrence. Assuming that one can justify threatening to do that which it would be immoral actually to do, if the threat can be plausibly relied upon to deter the greater evil of actual nuclear use, the "just war" doctrine might, it seems, permit a national strategy of nuclear deterrence.[5]

Most contemporary philosophical discussions of the ethics of nuclear strategy pick up this focus upon the alleged deterrent function of nuclear weapons, assuming then that the central question is not whether the use of these weapons in war can be justified, but whether the possession of them and the implicit or explicit threat of their use can be. Nearly all of these arguments, whether utilitarian or non-utilitarian, formulate the issue simply as a matter of whether the probable benefits of the possession of nuclear weapons (e.g., deterring nuclear or conventional aggression by an adversary) can justify the risks one takes of actually using, or inducing others to use, these weapons. The differences of opinion about the justifiability of deterrence emerging in this discussion turn not so much on strictly normative or philosophical differences but on different assessments of empirical matters such as the probabilities of deterrence failing and nuclear war occurring, the chances of such nuclear exchanges escalating to higher levels, the probable consequences of nuclear exchanges at these levels, the probabilities of adversaries engaging in aggression if the other side disarms itself of nuclear weapons, the probable political consequences of this aggression, etc.[6] Of course, such empirical matters are crucially important to the moral questions involved here, whether one decides them by a purely utilitarian calculus or by appeal to additional non-consequentialist considerations. But very little new philosophical ground is being turned in debates over these matters; and even though they are in some respects empirical matters, they are notoriously difficult to settle (e.g., determining the probabilities of a failure of a deterrence system and the magnitude and consequences of the resulting nuclear war).

A fundamental assumption of philosophical interest in these debates concerns deterrence itself. Most commentators assume that the whole point of nuclear armament (on "our" side, at least) is to deter the other side(s) from using nuclear weapons, and hence to prevent nuclear war or reduce the probabilities of its occurrence to acceptable levels. To a certain degree this assumption is valid. A primary aim of nuclear strategy on both sides since the ending of the American nuclear monopoly by the Soviet Union has been the prevention of nuclear war. In the 1950s and early 1960s the strategy by which this end was pursued was that of Mutual Assured Destruction (or Mutual Assured Vulnerability, as the strategic *avant-garde* now prefer), i.e., the ability of both sides to deliver a massive retaliatory blow to the other if he should dare to strike first. Nearly all philosophical discussions of the ethics of deterrence assume this model of the strategic nuclear situation. The moral logic of this model is starkly simple: Is the threat of massive nuclear retaliation against the society of the adversary in response to a nuclear first strike, even though suicidal for the retaliator, justified by the benefit of a vastly decreased probability of an initial nuclear strike by either side?

Given the widely accepted and well-substantiated assumption that the effects of a nuclear war would be globally catastrophic, it is not surprising that most utilitarian calculations come down in support of any strategy that would appear to reduce substantially the prospects of such an eventuality.[7] Any alternative will be preferable to the almost limitless evil of even a "low-level" nuclear war, even if that alternative is itself the threat, and the preparations to carry out the threat, of that limitless evil. This calculus succeeds in justifying nuclear armament by allowing only the evil of the *threat* to use nuclear weapons to be weighed against the evil of the adversary's actual nuclear attack, thus sidestepping the question of the morality of actually carrying out the threat of retaliation should the threat fail to deter. The moral enormity of *using* nuclear weapons is neatly excluded from the moral calculus altogether.[8]

This model of deterrence, which is paradigmatic in nearly all discussions of the ethics of nuclear strategy, seriously distorts the nature of the actual strategic doctrines of the nuclear powers and the way in which the concept of deterrence informs these doctrines. In particular, it assumes the naive view that deterrence functions primarily to deter the use of nuclear weapons by one's adversary—so-called "simple deterrence." But, as anyone knows who has followed the developments in strategic doctrine since the late 1950s, the nuclear arsenals of the superpowers greatly expanded the role of deterrence to include the deterrence of aggression by conventional means—so-called "general deterrence"—and even more broadly, the deterrence of unfavourable policies potentially adopted by the adversary. In this last function, the threat of nuclear weapons becomes an integral part of the violent struggle for political advantage that is a normal aspect of modern superpower diplomacy. It is commonly referred to as "extended deterrence."[9]

Under these expanded doctrines of deterrence the moral equations look vastly different from those utilized in the typical ethical discussions. For here, the evil of the risks of nuclear war posed by the deterrent threat must be weighed against the evil of a non-nuclear military action by one's adversary, or, under extended deterrence, against the evil of a non-aggressive or non-military, but yet undesirable, policy. Here the balance of utilities is far less likely to fall on the side of the deterrence policy. Anyone who doubts the political reality of these expanded notions of deterrence need reflect only for a moment upon the instances in recent history when the United States overtly appealed to its nuclear threat to deter Soviet action. In the Cuban missile crisis, for example, President Kennedy brought the world to the edge of the nuclear abyss, not in order to deter an imminent nuclear or conventional attack by the Soviets, by to deter their stationing of missiles in close proximity to the U.S. border in response to American missiles on their border in Turkey. U.S. presidents have appealed at least implicitly to the nuclear option to deter the cutting off of the flow of oil in the Middle East. Indeed, the official policy of the Western alliance (NATO) is to deter any kind of conventional attack upon its members by the forces of the Warsaw Pact with a threat of immediate nuclear response. This doctrine of "Flexible Response" and "Immediate Escalation" is bedrock NATO policy. These are the utilities that realistically ought to appear in the moral equations assessing nuclear deterrence, yet they rarely do so.

Of course it could be argued that it is only the simple deterrence of nuclear war that can stand up under ethical scrutiny, and so much the worse for the extended versions actually practised by the superpowers today. This would certainly be an advance in the debate. Yet there is a further, more fundamental, difficulty with the concept of deterrence as it actually functions in modern nuclear strategy, and it is this difficulty I wish to elucidate. My concern will be not so much with the *justifiability* of deterrence itself as with the dynamics of a deterrent strategy practised under other assumptions about international diplomacy. The assumptions in question here are those of the modern American school of so-called "political realism." This school is of special interest to philosophers because of its firm grounding in a philosophy of society and political order that is widely accepted.

My thesis is that some of the most significant aspects of the nuclear arms race, commonly ignored in the typical ethical analyses of deterrence, cannot be understood apart from the operation of these philosophical assumptions. There is within the logic of deterrence itself, at least deterrence practised according to the tenets of modern *realpolitik*, a kind of practical *reductio ad absurdum* in which deterrence refutes itself. In the very attempt to deter nuclear war "rational" strategies are adopted that make nuclear war more likely. Debates about the ethics of nuclear deterrence that fail to take into account this deadly logic are simply out of touch with the "real world" of nuclear strategy. In this "real world," the product of deterrence strategies is not the creation of the relatively stable system of what Churchill called "mutual terror" at some assumed level of force parity. Rather it is an accelerating escalation in the numbers and technical sophistication of nuclear weapons, which pushes each side into the adoption of hair-trigger launch strategies and first-strike or nuclear-war-fighting strategies, and which pushes the whole world onto the increasingly precarious edge of the nuclear precipice.

Nearly everyone agrees that sooner or later (and probably *sooner*) the world must move into substantial, if not complete, nuclear disarmament. Even the idealized "simple" deterrence defended by the ethicists is justified only as a stopgap measure on the way to ultimate disarmament. The question to which no one seems to have an answer is how to reach that goal from where we now find ourselves.

The difficulty is that the combined logics of deterrence and political realism prevent even this minimal step from being taken. For together they demand that the deterrent threat be made as effective and as credible as possible, so as to minimize the vulnerability to any possible attack by the other side and to maximize strategic advantage. Political realism, strictly adhered to, can never be content with simple minimum deterrence because it is maintained only by an acquiescence in mutual vulnerability by both sides. *Realpolitik* allows neither the acceptance of vulnerability to one's adversary nor the failure to exploit the adversary's vulnerability. It requires *maximum* deterrence through *maximum* threat. Consequently, it militates against both arms control and disarmament measures. I shall devote the remainder of my discussion to an elaboration of this point.

II

It may strike many readers as a kind of philosophical hubris to suggest that an important dynamic in the nuclear arms race could be a philosophical conception of the world and the prevailing social order. We are well accustomed to explaining events of this social magnitude in terms of hardnosed political and economic power struggles, and to minimize the role of ideas and ideologies. But, as important as economic, political, and technological factors may be in fuelling this race to oblivion, they are reinforced and legitimated by an ideology which also serves to discredit any voice of dissent or social pressures that might blunt or redirect these other forces.

All human activities, especially institutional activities, take place within a "symbolic environment" of abstract symbols and systems of symbols. This "environment" creates a reality all its own which can be far more significant in determining human behaviour than the "real" biological and physical determinants in the non-symbolic environment.[10] No human activity is more conditioned by purely symbolic determinants than nuclear strategy, which has been formulated and reformulated over the past 40 years in the virtual absence (thankfully) of any empirical experience of nuclear utilization. Strategies are formulated, not on the basis of experience, but on the basis of highly theoretical prognostications, game-theoretical models, speculations about the probable actions of national leaders, and the probable accuracy, survivability, and destructiveness of the weapons systems. Deterrent strategy depends upon how each side *thinks* its own and its adversary's weapons are likely to perform or be utilized under varying conditions, knowing all the while that no one has a clue as to how they would *actually* perform or be utilized should they be called upon. Nor is it clear what possible political objectives might be served, or thought to be served, by the use of these weapons. Nuclear strategy tends to develop in a highly insular, abstract world, determined by the internal dynamics of that world itself rather than by real disputes over substantive political issues. Hence, the nuclear arms race tends to be motivated by the weapons themselves, each side at every step merely "fulfilling a theorem in deterrence theory," as British historian E.P. Thompson observes in his argument that it is the weapons that will most likely be the cause of nuclear war.[11]

It is for this reason that the philosophical and political dogmas behind the strategic theorems directing the arms race are extremely significant and require careful scrutiny if a full accounting of that phenomenon is to be given. The philosophical dogma involved here is primarily that of the American "political realist" school, associated with such well-known figures as Herman Kahn, Thomas Schelling, Hans Morgenthal, Raymond Aron, and Henry Kissinger.[12] The "political realism" of these writers has become a virtual orthodoxy in American foreign policy since the end of World War II. It establishes the ideological context in which the American and NATO buildup of nuclear arms has taken place in this period, and its axioms have not remained unlearned or unappreciated by the Warsaw Pact countries, whose behaviour has become a virtual mirror image of their Western realist adversaries.

In order to understand the realist school of thought and its strategic implications, it is necessary to go back to its philosophical beginnings, which, at least in the modern period, find their most comprehensive expression in the thought of Thomas Hobbes. Political realism holds basically that the international system is fundamentally a Hobbesian "state of nature" in which mutual reliance upon the respect and forbearance of others is impossible, in which adherence to moral or legal norms is self-defeating and pointless, and in which, therefore, each party can act only out of sheer self-interest. The conditions essential to the establishment of a social, and therefore moral, order do not exist in the international system; hence international diplomacy must be conducted in an amoral atmosphere of absolute mistrust of one's adversaries.

Hobbes argued that adherence to moral principles of any sort requiring the sub-ordination of self-interest to a larger good is impossible in the "state of nature." The latter he defined as that state in which there are no guarantees that other persons will act in other than completely egoistic ways, and hence no reason for anyone to expect the reciprocity of others. The "state of nature," therefore, is a state of "war of every one against every one,"[13] in which no person, no matter how strong, can guarantee his own security. Moral relations can be established among persons only where there exists a centralized coercive force which can guarantee the security and the reciprocity of all. Nations, being defined by Hobbes as social entities in which there exists just such a coercive power—a government with a monopoly on the use of force—have the power to create the conditions for moral action, hence, persons within states can be subject to moral obligations. But nations find themselves as actors in relation to other nations in a situation in which no central coercive guarantee of state action exists. They remain, in other words, in the "state of nature," and, says Hobbes, "Where there is no commonwealth, there is nothing unjust."[14]

According to this dogma, several conclusions follow from the situation in which nations find themselves. First, while the internal morality of states is binding upon the citizens in their dealings with each other, it is not binding upon the state itself nor upon those who conduct the affairs of state in relation to other states. Here the only imperative is to maximize the national self-interest.

Second, international trust and cooperation are made impossible in situations of potential conflict of interest, for one nation can never be certain that its cooperation will not be taken advantage of by others. In Rousseau's well-known example, the five men who might cooperate to trap a stag and divide it among themselves each find it to their own individual advantage to sabotage the cooperative project if doing so permits them to grab the hapless hare which happens across their path. Since no one's cooperation can be counted on, it is to no one's advantage to cooperate.

Third, in the absence of any monopolized coercive power at the international level there is no arbiter of disputes between nations other than the recourse to coercion on their behalf and ultimately to war. As Rousseau pointed out, within a situation of international anarchy, war becomes a *necessary* occurrence. It is up to each state, then, to maximize its advantage in every way, including the threat and use of its military power. This systemic account of the place of war in international relations was merely elaborated by the nineteenth-century military theorist Carl von Clausewitz, with his oft-cited dictum that war is merely "the continuation of policy by other means"[15]—a normal aspect of the relations among states. Clausewitz viewed the international system as Hobbes's state of nature writ large, with no "Super-Leviathan" available to prevent the "war of every one against every one."

Of course, just as the Leviathan—the sovereign ruler holding a monopoly on the use of force—is the Hobbesian solution to civil anarchy, so also is a "Super-Leviathan"—a world government with a similar monopoly—the obvious Hobbesian solution to international anarchy. The problem is that such a solution has never actualized itself in the international arena, nor does it appear likely to do so in the near future. Further, no one has yet come up with a persuasive formula for bringing such a creature into being, and for many people the prospect of such a monster suggests a cure that might be worse than the ailment. Nations are so tightly wedded to their own sovereign rights of self-defence and self-determination that there is little willingness to accede to even the barest minimum of international law and order.

In the absence of Super-Leviathan, the most attractive Hobbesian solution to emerge thus far to the problem of constant war in the system of international anarchy is the modern "balance of power" theory of international diplomacy. This theory holds that while war between states can never be eliminated, its frequency and perhaps even its intensity can be reduced and controlled by each nation's pursuing a policy of deterrence through maintenance of military alliances in rough parity of military strength. A "balance of power" reduces the advantage gained by any one party initiating military hostilities, and hence reduces its attractiveness to all parties. Within this school of diplomatic thought the worst mistake a nation can make is to permit another nation or alliance to gain clear military superiority. To do so is to invite war.

Contemporary diplomatic-military strategy, and its application to nuclear strategy in particular, can be understood only against the background of these Hobbesian assumptions about the "state of nature." Anatol Rapoport aptly calls contemporary political realists "neo-Clausewitzians" because they embrace Clausewitz's understanding of the political nature of war.[16] They might also be called "neo-Hobbesians" in view of their commitment to the Hobbesian principles just outlined. The axioms of political realism that most significantly influence the dynamics of strategic nuclear deterrence can be summarized as follows.

First, in the international arena, nation-states cannot afford to govern their behaviour by moral means, for, where there are no guarantees that other nations will so govern their own behaviour, to act morally is merely to place one's own nation at serious disadvantage.

Second, as a consequence of the amorality of international diplomacy, national policy must be guided by the principle of self-interest alone, though, of course, of the "enlightened" variety. Failure to maximize one's own advantage over others in the system only creates a weakness that will surely be exploited by others. Subordinating national interest to a larger international interest will likely produce the same result. Or what is worse, national policy in the pursuit of some moral ideal (e.g., "liberty," "equality," "a world safe for democracy") will only upset the relatively stable balances of power and make everyone worse off.[17]

Third, in the international "state of nature" the war of all against all is a natural and normal state of affairs. War, and the threat of war, are normal instruments of national diplomatic strategy, not the consequence of breakdowns in diplomacy. War is best controlled by the stability of a system of alliances in rough balance of power where the *threat* of war rather than war itself becomes the major diplomatic tool. The greater the "power to hurt," as Schelling calls it,[18] the greater the deterrent power of the threat of war.

Fourth, in the international state of nature it is irrational to trust other actors not to exploit one's vulnerability. There can be no covenants of mutual trust in the state of nature,[19] except where the parties can mutually extort compliance with the covenant. No nation, therefore, can afford to base its strategy and military preparedness upon an assessment of what adversary nations are *likely* to do, given what is known of their national aims and preferences, and certainly not upon what they might promise to do. Rather, one's own defence must be based upon what the adversary *could* do if he in fact had the very worst, and even irrational, intentions.

It is the realist adoption of this fourth Hobbesian axiom that is most important for our discussion. In contemporary strategic parlance, the principle is known as the "worst case hypothesis," under which one prepares to defend oneself, not from any *likely* attack, but any *possible* one. It constitutes the banishment of even minimal trust from international affairs, and demands that one assume the worst of one's potential adversaries. This "worst case" thinking, implicit in the Hobbesian model, constitutes one of the most serious obstacles to meaningful arms control and disarmament measures, especially with respect to the contemporary race in nuclear arms.

III

When nuclear weapons first appeared on the scene and it became clear that their possessors were not about to place them under the control of any international agency, early nuclear strategists began to hope that the very threat to human survival posed by them might be turned to an advantage. Nuclear weapons held out the promise of an unprecedented solution to the Hobbesian dilemma of security in the system of international anarchy. In the Hobbesian view, the state of nature can be transcended only through the interposition of a monopolized coercive force. On the international level this translates into a world government or Super-Leviathan. This was what some of the early atomic scientists, notably Albert Einstein, saw as the only feasible solution to the threat of nuclear weapons. But the idea of world government continued to be viewed by most political theorists and policy-makers as either politically unfeasible in the short term (and a rapid solution was required) or highly undesirable. Some form of "balance of power" seemed to be the only workable policy, even if it had proven in the recent wars to be a notoriously fallible one.

Early nuclear theorists like Bernard Brodie hit upon the idea that nuclear weapons could in fact enhance the balance-of-power concept, because their awesome power could virtually guarantee the devastation of any state who chose to break the international order, regardless of its military strength. Here was the next best thing to the Super-Leviathan. It was a single deterrent force that could coerce peaceful behaviour, even though it remained under the unilateral control of the sovereign nation-states who could thereby police each other. Out of this concept of deterrence— the concept that the primary function of weapons was not to fight wars, but to prevent them—arose an optimism about nuclear weapons that spanned the first two decades of the nuclear era. The early nuclear strategists assured us of a peaceful future through the deterrence provided by the ability of the nuclear powers to assure each other's destruction. Henry Kissinger even argued that the superpowers would be able, under the protection of this "nuclear umbrella," to carry on their diplomacy of violence, even to the point of medium-scale conventional war, without fear of escalation to total war.[20]

The promising aspect of nuclear weapons as deterrents to war lay in their unambiguous threat of retaliation. Unlike the old balance of power through conventional military strength, under which the misperception by one side or the other that the balance had swung in its favour constantly drew them into war, the new nuclear balance was far less likely to be mistakenly perceived. Even if one side perceived itself in a position of advantage, the risks of acting on the perception were far too high.

This vision of international stability under the new Nuclear Leviathan which guarantees assured destruction of those who break the nuclear peace as well as those who retaliate for the breach is the vision underlying most philosophical discussions of the ethics of nuclear deterrence. It holds out the promise of minimizing the potential violence and destruction of the system of international anarchy—the best that can be hoped for in a mean and unforgiving world. Though born of a tough-minded realism about the world, in the strategic context of the 1980s it has the appearance of an idealistic hope. To suppose today that the probabilities of nuclear cataclysm are so acceptably low as to stay the present course of nuclear competition, itself requires a leap of faith in the face of evidence to the contrary. The actual evolution of nuclear strategy and technology under the doctrine of deterrence has, ironically, turned Hobbesian realism into its opposite. It has placed the human community upon a path of almost inevitable destruction, from which it seems powerless to extricate itself. The nuclear world in which we live today is far from the simple state of stable deterrence envisioned by the early nuclear optimists. It is a world where there are a hundred times more warheads in the nuclear arsenals than are needed for the "mutual assured destruction" of simple deterrence; where delivery systems have the accuracy to destroy the yet-unlaunched weapons of the adversary, thus tempting their possessors to mount the first strike and gain the strategic advantage; where the reaction time for the decision to launch an irreversible counterstrike has been reduced from the hours it took in the 50s to fly bombers across the pole, to the five or six minutes it takes the European-based Pershing IIs or SS-20s to reach their targets after initial detection. It is a strategic world where the threshold of nuclear war is lowered to increasingly tenuous levels by the deployment of "tactial" nuclear weapons among conventional forces, who would be forced early on in a difficult battle to take recourse to their "nuclear option"; where the first nuclear explosion could so seriously disrupt the system of Command, Control, Communications, and Intelligence ("C^3I") that the entire weapons network would be cut loose from all central control and unleash its furor indiscriminately on the world. All these factors work to weaken seriously the stability of the ideal deterrence system by creating an increasingly sensitive "hair trigger" to a nuclear war that would be ever more destructive.

But there is a dynamic within the logic of the deterrence system itself that generates these destabilizing and perilous aspects of the nuclear arms race and illustrates the self-defeating or contradictory nature of deterrence, at least as it is practised under

Hobbesian assumptions. This dynamic is also of most interest philosophically, for it has to do with the concept of deterrence itself and the concept of rational choice within a system of deterrence. Simple deterrence through mutual assured destruction has always been plagued with the internal contradiction that if you limit your nuclear options to massive retaliation for a first strike, your adversary knows that you have little to gain by launching it, because you only bring greater destruction upon everyone, including yourself. Indeed, given the likely suicidal consequences of carrying out the retaliatory strike, it has all the deterrent credibility of a double-barrelled gun with one barrel pointed back at the gun-holder. As Jonathan Schell observes, it might make sense to threaten a burglar wanting to enter your house with this gun, but it could never make sense to fire it.[21] Of course, the burglar knows as well as you that it doesn't make sense. More importantly, the burglar knows that a single-barrelled gun pointed only at him would be a far more credible deterrent.

Herein lies the dilemma of nuclear deterrence. The threat of mutual suicide at least allows for the theoretical possibility of an agreed-upon level of nuclear weapons sufficient to guarantee a retaliatory strike without massive overkill, first-strike, or "prevailing" capacities. It therefore has the theoretical possibility of relative stability in the system: low incentive for first strike and high incentive for arms limitation and disarmament to minimum levels necessary for deterrence. This is part of its attraction for the ethicists who defend nuclear deterrence.[22] But because its retaliatory threat is suicidal, it has low credibility, at least lower credibility than the threat to launch a "successful" preemptive, or damage-limiting, strike. Any strategic theorist who takes seriously the Hobbesian-realist dogma that rational action in the state of nature requires minimizing one's own vulnerability and maximizing one's own strategic advantage is thus driven to strive for the stronger deterrent threat. The stronger, more credible, deterrent threat is not that of massive retaliation, but rather some threat of a preemptive, counterforce (targeting weapons before they can be fired, not population centres) strike that would limit the damage inflicted by the other side. In short, if I can convince the burglar that I can make him worse off than he can make me should he try to enter my house, I am more credible than if I threaten to kill us both.

This is precisely the reasoning that has informed the strategies on both sides of the present nuclear arms race. It is clearly articulated in the strategic literature on the Western side. Colin Gray, an advisor to the Reagan administration and apologist for its nuclear policies, clearly exemplifies this reasoning in a recent book on nuclear strategy.[23] Gray shows how American nuclear deterrence doctrine has moved through various stages. The first is the "Societal Punishment" doctrine of massive (and suicidal) retaliation, which Gray thinks was rightly abandoned because of its low deterrent credibility. The second stage was that of "Countervailing Strategy" or "Flexible Response" developed in the Kennedy administration, which involved developing the added capability to strike at Soviet war-waging structures, denying them victory and limiting the collateral damage. The third stage, adopted by the Reagan administration, is a "Prevailing Strategy." It is a natural extension of the second stage to the development of the capability of imposing a military—and hence political—defeat on the Soviet Union, "to secure the achievement of Western political purposes at a military, economic, and social cost commensurate with the stakes of the conflict."[24] A credible American deterrence, says Gray, "would flow from Soviet belief, or strong suspicion, that the United States could fight and win the military conflict and hold down its societal damage to a tolerable level."[25]

It is clear that the recent developments in nuclear strategy toward war-fighting rather than retaliation capability, and toward first-strike, counterforce technology, are in no way departures from the concept of deterrence, as they are commonly believed to be by the peace movement generally and deterrence ethicists in particular. They are "enhanced" or "extended" versions of deterrence. Again to quote Gray, "There is widespread agreement that a perceived ability to wage a nuclear counterforce . . . war is probably critically important for the credibility of nuclear threats and hence for the stability of prewar [sic!] deterrence."[26] Deterrence through the ability to "prevail" in an actual nuclear war answers the old difficulty of simple deterrence: What do you do if deterrence fails? Its answer is that you carry out those threats, not just because it is part of your threat policy but because it will actually serve your interests to fight the nuclear war. You will limit your own damage while maximizing your adversary's. The obvious question of what "damage limitation" actually means under these cataclysmic conditions is rarely addressed in any detail in these doctrines.

Enhanced deterrence by capability to "prevail" in an actual nuclear war also lends credibility to the "extended deterrence" doctrines mentioned earlier. Once deterrence is maintained by what the strategists want us to believe is a non-suicidal war-fighting strategy, it becomes more credible as an instrument of coercive diplomacy. Thus Gray argues in favour of a nuclear strategy he calls "Damage Limitation for Deterrence and Coercion." Under this strategy, "the fundamental purpose of the strategic forces is to deter, or help deter, hostile acts against vital U.S. interests."[27] Gray also holds that this is the present policy of the Reagan administration he advises. Anyone who still believes that the sole purpose of nuclear weapons is to deter only nuclear war, as most deterrence ethicists do, is simply out of touch with strategic reality.

David Gauthier's recent argument about the rationality of deterrence is an all-too-common example of philosophical discussion out of touch with strategic reality.[28] Gauthier argues that if deterrence by threat of massive nuclear retaliation is a rational policy, then it could be rational to carry out a suicidal retaliatory strike if the deterrent failed. Gauthier argues, incredibly, that the carrying out of such a strike is rational (and therefore moral) no matter how monstrous the consequences of doing so. Even were Gauthier able to make this claim credible, it quite misses a more important point, which is implicit in his own game-theoretical approach to the question, just as it is in the Hobbesian-realist dogma. This point is that from the game-theoretical point of view, with its definition of rationality as the maximization of expected utility (for the actor), as for Hobbesian realism, the policy of deterrence by retaliation is itself judged irrational. This is because a threat to "prevail" over an enemy, should he behave aggressively, is itself more rational than a threat to commit suicide, which, of course, on its own terms is completely pointless and irrational. Rationality conceived in terms of "expected utility maximization" thus should lead one to reject a policy of deterrence through mutual destruction in favour of extended deterrence through the threat of fighting and prevailing in a nuclear war. Gauthier, however, fails to follow the logic of his own theory of rationality, unlike the strategic theorists who design the "real-world" strategies.

The problem, of course, is that both sides, having read the same strategic text-books and used the same game theory, reason and act according to the same logic. This produces the irrational result that both sides develop nuclear arsenals designed to prevent nuclear war by being able to fight and win it. It is the classic "Prisoner's Dilemma" situation in which the apparent rational strategy, when adopted by both players in a two-person game, leads to an irrational outcome for both. More accurately, in the nuclear case, it is a game of "Chicken," because the payoff from adhering to the rational strategy is mutually disastrous. The irrational outcome here is the fact that the "rational" strategy locks both sides into a continuous race for nuclear superiority in which they each design more and more weapons, designed more and more to be *used*, not merely threatened. In this deadly "game" there is no even theoretical equilibrium point where both parties can agree to freeze their deployment of new weapons. The only equilibrium point is the actual fighting of the war itself. The logic of deterrence under Hobbesian assumptions of rationality thus sets both sides on a course of preparation for war-fighting that is bound to lead them into that war by the sheer inertia of the preparations themselves.

The strategy is "rational," however, only within the logic of the Hobbesian-realist dogma, and the game-theoretical models that give it an air of mathematical precision and scientific objectivity. If it is assumed that the other actors in the system will exploit every vulnerability on your side to their maximum advantage, that only your own reciprocal exploitation of advantage can counter it, and, hence, that ever *possible* strategic advantage of the other must be forestalled regardless of the probabilities of its actually being exploited (the "worst-case" assumption), then the suicidal result becomes virtually inevitable. The Hobbesian logic requires that every "window of vulnerability" be securely boarded up, no matter how small, or in how remote a part of the strategic attic, it may be. It is instructive to note that the so-called "window of vulnerability" feared by the Reagan strategists was precisely the possibility that the Soviets might develop the ability to neutralize the U.S. ability to "prevail" in a nuclear war, forcing the U.S. to resort to mutual suicide with them.

Our present precarious situation of nuclear roulette with its growing risks of nuclear holocaust is a logical and predictable consequence of the Hobbesian-realist model. If policy-makers and strategists continue to be dominated by its orthodoxy, it will in all probability fulfill its own suicidal fears. The "balance of power" strategy may well have worked a utilitarian result in the pre-nuclear world where the consequences of the inevitable periods of breakdown in the balance and the resulting wars were less destructive than the consequences likely to accrue from a more idealistic or moralistic foreign policy. But in a nuclearized world where there are virtually no limits on the power to destroy, where the power of one actor no longer serves effectively to limit an adversary's power to destroy, and where the technological developments are increasingly destabilizing, this conception of the international system generates its own refutation.

There is no reason, consequently, to place any confidence whatever in the fact that nuclear weapons seem to have deterred nuclear war for 40 years. Such confidence rests upon the fallacious assumption, among others, that the system of deterrence is not subject to the inherent dynamics of escalation toward war imposed upon it by Hobbesian realism. It assumes that the situation today is the same as in 1955 and will be the same tomorrow. It is for this reason that the assumption that nuclear weapons actually deter war could be, as one writer has aptly put it, "the most costly *post hoc* in human history."[29]

IV

If the preceding analysis is fundamentally correct, it seems reasonable to conclude either that the Hobbesian model provides the best account of the international situation and we simply must learn to live with increasingly dismal prospects of survival, or that it is not accurate and we should therefore search about for a more workable alternative. But one of the greatest problems faced by those who believe some better way than the present nuclear course is possible and necessary, is that there seems to be no alternative model of international order that holds out a promise of effective control and reduction of nuclear arms.

The model most often appealed to by the nuclear disarmament community, beginning with Einstein and his colleagues, is the model of a world government to which would be given the monopoly on nuclear and ultimately all weapons. On this view it is national sovereignty itself that has become obsolete and impossible in the nuclear world. This, of course, is itself a paradigmatically Hobbesian solution to the problem of war. Order can be created out of international anarchy only if it is maintained by threats backed up by the monopolized force of the Super-Leviathan. But this solution has had little appeal among political theorists, least of all among the Hobbesian realists themselves.

There are some good reasons for skepticism about the world-government solution—some of them having to do with the weaknesses of the Hobbesian view itself. One important reason is that there seems to be no way under Hobbesian assumptions to implement the solution. It is not "rational" for any nation to give up its sovereign right of self-defence when it cannot rely upon others to do so as well or not to take some advantage of its vulnerability. The Hobbesian solution is a Catch-22 from which Hobbes himself and all Hobbesians have difficulty extricating themselves. It is a fundamental flaw in Hobbes's entire view of the social contract. While he holds on the one hand in the "Second Law of Nature" that "all men seek to abandon the state of nature by laying down their right of self-defence," and as a law of reason "To endeavour peace, as far as he has hope of obtaining it,"[30] nevertheless he recognizes that this cannot be done unilaterally. And in the absence of the Leviathan to guarantee the performance of all others in the laying down of their right, there is no possibility of multilateral action either. Hobbesianism can find no way consistent with its own axioms to transcend the state of nature.

This is precisely the dilemma of the nuclear arms race so long as it is guided by Hobbesian principles. Nearly everyone recognizes that before this competition pushes both sides, perhaps unintentionally, into the nuclear holocaust, there must be some kind of bilateral agreement to freeze the weapons development, to reduce the numbers of the weapons through disarmament procedures, to eradicate the hair-trigger launch-on-warning policies that threaten accidental war, and to reach some at least provisional agreement to live with a parity of deterrent force. But even these minimal steps to preserve the security of the world require cooperative, non-guaranteeable initiatives. Even if, on the way to meaningful de-nuclearization of the world, we need to step back to the "good old days" of mutual assured vulnerability, we can do it only if we are willing to live with vulnerability and give up the Hobbesian urge to maximize our security and our advantage.

In the long run, of course, we must rid the world of nuclear weapons. But given that the extremity of the present situation requires a short-term solution, perhaps we shall have to live for a time with some form of deterrence at lower and more stable levels of nuclear weapons systems. This means that the immediate, urgent need[31] is not only for a freeze in the development of new weapons, but also disarmament to the minimum levels required for simple deterrence. Ultimately deterrence, if it functions at all, will have to be essentially non-nuclear.

But there is no way to achieve even these limited goals if we do not break the grasp of the Hobbesian-realist dogma that demands continued escalation to inevitable war. The first tenet of Hobbesian orthodoxy to be thrown off must be the assumption that there can be no even minimal reliance upon the nuclear adversary not to break through every tiny "window of vulnerability." Arms control, disarmament, even a stable system of deterrence, requires a degree of cooperation based upon a certain reliance upon others not to exploit that cooperation to their own maximum advantage. This, it seems to me, merely reflects a simple fact about the necessary conditions for human social life and community that the strict Hobbesian model fails to recognize. There is no way to transcend the "state of nature" without the willingness to take unilateral initiatives that rely upon a certain faith in the reciprocal action of others. It is perhaps a symptom of the massive self-deception of our life in the nuclear shadow that overwhelming evidence from the study of conflict management demonstrating the necessity of unilateral gestures in reversing conflict escalation is universally rejected in strategic theory. It is rejected in favour of the thesis that one's adversary can be deterred from escalating a conflict only by a threat of superior force. One must always "negotiate from strength." No thesis has been more thoroughly discredited by empirical studies of conflict management than this one. It almost always guarantees escalation of a conflict. This should not surprise anyone of common sense. A person need only reflect upon what he himself would do, following Hobbesian principles, if the other party to a conflict with him decided to "negotiate from strength."

It should be pointed out that the strict Hobbesian dogma against the possibility of non-enforced cooperation and in favour of maximizing strategic advantage is rejected, not only in the theory of interpersonal conflict, but in the theory of non-military international diplomacy as well. Few nations today, and certainly not the superpowers, conduct themselves on the assumption that non-enforceable treaties or canons of international law carry no weight whatever in international affairs. The international system of commerce and non-military diplomacy simply is not a "state of nature," nor do most nations act as if it were. Trust in the reciprocal action of others is essential to the functioning of the system, and it is not maintained solely by threat of force. It is only in matters of strategic military doctrine that the Hobbesian dogma is involved as religious orthodoxy.

We are here at the heart of a fundamental philosophical question about the nature of human society. It puzzled not only Hobbes, but Rousseau, Hume, Kant, and others as well. It is the question of the rationality of acting in accord with ideals or principles that put one at serious disadvantage *vis-à-vis* others if they cannot be counted on to act reciprocally. Hobbes believed that it was not rational except where the performance of others could be guaranteed by coercive sanctions. Hence, as we have seen, he finds himself trapped in the state of nature where the "laws" of reason and nature show him the rationality of everyone's getting out but not the rationality of any *one* person doing what is necessary to get there. David Gauthier has argued that those moral philosophers who disagree with Hobbes's view of the matter must necessarily invoke, as did Locke and Kant, a religious faith in a God whom one hopes will turn one's own unilateral performance of one's duty to ultimate good even if others do not perform likewise.[32] Gauthier complains that many contemporary moral philosophers have abandoned the faith in this deity yet cling to a morality of unilateral performance of duty. But once the faith is gone, one has to accept the Hobbesian conclusion, as Gauthier himself does.

It may be for this reason that the nuclear disarmament movement in North America and Europe has been most strongly supported by religious institutions and persons. But the strategists who are responsible for the interests and security of their nations have never felt it responsible to rely entirely upon Providence without at least providing God a sufficient military backup. At the level of military strategy nearly everyone becomes Hobbesian about vulnerability by unilateral initiative. To the strategist the peace movement's call for cooperative disarmament measures initiated by non-maximizing policies of restraint appear naively idealistic, resting upon the all-too-tenuous faith that God might bring them to fruition.

Annette Baier has argued persuasively in response to Gauthier that indeed some faith in the reciprocation of others to one's own moral actions is absolutely essential to the building and maintaining of a moral community.[33] Where there is no belief in God to sustain this faith, then it must, and can be, a "secular faith." Moral community is not possible unless there is some faith—not necessarily faith that others are essentially good, but only that they are not absolutely and unconditionally evil, ready to take full advantage of every vulnerability of their peers. Indeed, as Baier quite rightly points out, even Hobbes himself could not escape this reality. For while he accepted it as a "rule of reason" that "every man ought to endeavour peace . . .," and hence end the state of nature, he found it necessary to place upon this law the qualification ". . . as far as he has hope of obtaining it."[34] Only *hope* for a reciprocation that cannot be absolutely guaranteed, Baier observes, can get even Hobbes out of the state of nature.[35]

Nothing ought to illustrate more graphically and inescapably than the suicidal course of the nuclear arms race the inherent fallaciousness of the Hobbesian view of human society. There simply cannot be progress in the control and reduction of nuclear arms, and the development of some more stable structure of international security, unless nations are willing to renounce the desire to maintain maximum advantage through unilateral escalation. They must be willing to take unilateral steps that forego advantage or the need to maximize every vulnerability. Applying Baier's analysis, what is required today is not naive faith that the Soviets (or the Americans) will be good if the other side completely renounces its right of defence, but simply the recognition that we can step back from the nuclear abyss only if we find ways of relying on each other's interest in that goal while renouncing the need to guarantee absolutely the other's reciprocity. Moral community, and in this case survival, requires mutual reliance and cooperation even when reciprocation cannot be absolutely guaranteed. We must learn to accept this fact or else resign ourselves to the fate which Hobbes himself saw to be intrinsic to the "state of nature." Under the conditions of a nuclear "state of nature" our life as a species on this planet will indeed be "poor, nasty, brutish, and short."

Notes

1. Trudy Govier has outlined some of the most significant philosophical questions posed by nuclear weapons and the threat of war, and rightly calls for more serious philosophical attention to them. See her "Nuclear Illusion and Individual Obligations," *The Canadian Journal of Philosophy* 13 (4) (December 1983), p. 471.

2. See, for example, the discussion by Paul Ramsey in *The Just War: Force and Responsibility* (New York: Scribner, 1968), pp. 177ff.; Michael Walzer, *Just and Unjust Wars* (New York: Basic Books, 1977); National Conference of Catholic Bishops, "The Challenge of Peace: God's Promise and Our Response," *Origins* (National Conference Documentary Service) 13, (1) (May 19, 1983).

3. Jonathan Schell, *The Fate of the Earth* (New York: Alfred A. Knopf, 1982).

4. Walzer, *op. cit.*, p. 283.

5. This position founders always on the question of whether it is possible to make a credible nuclear threat without actually *intending* to carry out that threat, and if not, whether it is morally justifiable to intend to do what it would be immoral to do. This is especially a problem given the fact, usually ignored, that the corporate intentions of a government or nation entail a kind of institutional commitment to carry out threats that is virtually irreversible when the threat fails to deter the unwanted action of the adversary. In institutional behaviour there is such a strong link between the issuing of a threat and the carrying out of the threat, that any moral distinction in theory between the two is immaterial in practice. For a contrary view of this matter, see William H. Shaw, "Nuclear Deterrence and Deontology," *Ethics* 94 (2)(January 1984): 248–260.

6. A good example of this kind of debate can be seen in the recent exchange between Douglas Lackey, "Missiles and Morals: A Utilitarian Look at Nuclear Deterrence," *Philosophy and Public Affairs* 11(3)(Summer 1982): 189–231 and Gregory S. Kavka, "Doubts about Unilateral Nuclear Disarmament," *Philosophy and Public Affairs* 12 (3)(Summer 1983): 256. The former's argument for the utility of unilateral nuclear disarmament, and the latter's argument against it, tell us more about their respective views of the Soviet Union and their fears about the risks of nuclear deterrence failure than about any genuinely philosophical difference of opinion.

7. Douglas Lackey is one of the few to have argued the utilitarian case to the opposite conclusion. See Lackey, *op. cit.*

8. A recent and notable exception to this approach to the discussion is David Gauthier's "Deterrence, Maximization, and Rationality," *Ethics* 94 (3)(April 1984): 474–495. Gauthier argues that if it is rational to threaten a retaliatory nuclear strike as a deterrent, it would be rational to carry out that strike should deterrence fail, even though the worst possible consequences (including, presumably, destruction of the species) resulted. It is rational because it is part of a rational policy. This radical conclusion at least takes seriously the fact that in national behaviour, the making of a threat is usually a commitment to carry it out if it fails, and that hence the morality of the threat cannot easily be

isolated from the morality of carrying it out. One would expect this to lead Gauthier to question the morality of making the threat in the first place rather than justify unleashing the nuclear holocaust because the threat itself appears justified when viewed in isolation from the holocaust. Gauthier argues that the decision at time T_1 to follow a deterrence policy commits one (rationally and morally) not to revise that policy at Time T_2 after deterrence failure, when one is faced with a wholly new set of circumstances in which following the policy (i.e., retaliating) entails wholly different (incalculably evil) consequences. This incredible move makes normative the fact that in policy to make a threat is to make it difficult not to carry it out if it fails. But this fact about policy, from a moral point of view, can only justify the likely consequential act; it cannot disqualify the antecedent act (i.e., the threat itself).

9. For one informed account of this development in the function of deterrence doctrine, see Colin S. Gray, *Nuclear Strategy and Strategic Planning* (Philadelphia: Foreign Policy Research Institute, 1984).

10. For an excellent analysis of this idea, see Anatol Rapoport, *Conflict in a Man-Made Environment* (Harmondsworth: Penguin Books, 1974).

11. E.P. Thompson, *Beyond the Cold War* (New York: Pantheon Books, 1982), p. 22.

12. See, for example, Henry A. Kissinger, *Nuclear Weapons and Foreign Policy* (New York: Harper & Row, 1957); Thomas C. Schelling, *Arms and Influence* (New Haven: Yale Univ. Press, 1966); Raymond Aron, *Peace and War: A Theory of International Relations* (Garden City: Doubleday, 1966); Herman Kahn, *On Thermonuclear War* (Princeton: Princeton University Press, 1960) and *Thinking about the Unthinkable* (New York: Horizon Press, 1962); Robert Osgood, *Limited War: The Challenge to American Strategy* (Chicago: University of Chicago Press, 1957).

13. Thomas Hobbes, *Leviathan* (London, 1651), Ch. 14.

14. *Ibid.*, Chap. 13, 15.

15. Carl von Clausewitz, *On War* (Baltimore: Penguin Books, 1968), p. 119.

16. Anatol Rapoport, "Introduction," in Clausewitz, *ibid.*

17. See Henry Kissinger's discussion of the immorality of being moral in international diplomacy in *A World Restored* (Boston: Houghton Mifflin Co., 1957), pp. 108ff and Cheryl Noble's discussion of his view in "Political Realism, International Morality, and Just War," *The Monist* 57(4)(October, 1973): 595–606.

18. Schelling, *op. cit.*, pp. 1–34.

19. Hobbes, Ch. 14.

20. Kissinger, *Nuclear Weapons and Foreign Policy*.

21. See Jonathan Schell, "The Abolition," *The New Yorker*, January 2, 1984, p. 60.

22. Assuming one dispenses with the morally unpleasant fact that it involves holding populations of innocent people hostage by threatening them with nuclear annihilation.

23. Colin S. Gray, *op. cit.*

24. *Ibid.*, p. 2.

25. *Ibid.*, p. 3.

26. *Ibid.*, p. 7. The President's Commission on Strategic Forces (The Scowcroft Commission) embraced the same concept, that the best deterrent is a war-fighting capability. *Report of the President's Commission on Strategic Forces*, April 1983, p. 7.

27. Gray, *op. cit.*, p. 79.

28. Gauthier, *op. cit.*

29. Trudy Govier, *op. cit.*, p. 480.

30. Hobbes, Ch. 14.

31. In Jonathan Schell's recent series in *The New Yorker* (see note 21), he puts forward a novel scenario for nuclear disarmament which does not rely on a Hobbesian world government to guarantee compliance. Schell argues for a

form of deterrence through a combined system of *conventional* defences against nuclear weapons and complete nuclear disarmament to the level of maintaining the industrial-technical capacity to build nuclear weapons. Deterrence would then consist in the threat to build up nuclear arsenals in "retaliation" for the adversary's buildup. In Schell's view, this would be a much safer deterrence system because it would increase the time for diplomatic initiatives to head off the hostile actions before nuclear war could be fought. This is a form of deterrence that could be maintained only on non-Hobbesian principles.

32.   David Gauthier, "Why One Ought to Obey God: Reflections on Hobbes and Locke," *The Canadian Journal of Philosophy* 7(1977): 425–446.

33.   Annette Baier, "Secular Faith," *The Canadian Journal of Philosophy* 10(March, 1980): 131–148.

34.   *Leviathan*, Ch. 14.

35.   Baier, *op. cit.*, p. 134.

Questions

1.   Both Brunk and Art use the Cuban missile crisis to support their position. Yet the two positions are incompatible. Who is right about the significance of that event for an understanding of the ethics of nuclear deterrence and disarmament?

2.   Would it be correct to describe Art's position as an endorsement of "simple deterrence" as that phrase is defined by Brunk? How do Brunk's arguments apply to Art's position? What counterarguments would Art offer? Whose position is more convincing?

3.   Why does Brunk feel that some form of faith is an essential ingredient if nuclear disarmament is to begin and progress? Is he right about this?

Thoughts from Under the Nuclear Umbrella

Trudy Govier

Every month I read about something new and interesting about the universe that some scientist has discovered, such as what it was that caused the extinction of the dinosaurs sixty-four million years ago. It is really wonderful, the world, and one wonderful part about it is that there are sentient beings here who are able to appreciate the wonders of the world, to understand them! So I feel we have a duty to try and prevent the nuclear war, to reverse this situation. I believe that it can be done.

> Linus Pauling, in a speech given at the Hotel Vancouver, October 1982; quoted in Perry

Philosophers examining issues of nuclear weapons and nuclear war have been fascinated by the problem of nuclear deterrence. Whether it can ever be morally

From *Nuclear War: Philosophical Perspectives*, ed. Michael Allen Fox and Leo Groarke (New York, 1985). By permission of Peter Lang Publishing.

right to threaten to do something which it would not be morally right to do is a vexing question which underlies the ethical appraisal of nuclear deterrence. But while this issue is profound and important, it has been explored by many other philosphers. I propose, therefore, to take a different direction in this paper. I shall discuss an argument which has been popular in the political debate about cruise missile testing in Canada and use that argument to raise some issues about the risks of nuclear deterrence and the role that allies have in seeking change in the pace and direction of the arms race.

The argument I have in mind may sound small and insignificant, but I believe it carries considerable weight with many Canadian citizens. I suspect that appropriately adapted versions of it are found compelling in Britain and Europe as well. For American readers, I hope that the discussion will be useful in showing how nuclear issues appear to those outside superpower countries. The argument I refer to maintains that those who shelter under a "nuclear umbrella" should not criticize the manufacturer. Rather, they should help him with his business, when requested, and refrain from skeptical comments. To criticize is presumptuous, ungrateful, and exploitative; if we get protection from the American nuclear umbrella, that benefit gives us an obligation to assist American defense programs when we are asked to do so. As minor players and beneficiaries, we cannot do otherwise.

Prime Minister Trudeau gave a brief statement of this argument in his open letter to Canadians on the cruise testing issue, published on May 9, 1983: "It is hardly fair to rely on the Americans to protect the West, but to refuse to lend them a hand when the going gets rough. In that sense, the anti-Americanism of some Canadians verges on hypocrisy. They're eager to take refuge under the US umbrella, but don't want to help hold it."[1] This response was, in particular, aimed at cruise missile protesters who had urged that the cruise was a destabilizing war-fighting weapon which would not contribute to nuclear deterrence. In essence, Trudeau maintained that as beneficiaries of American nuclear policies, Canadians must toe the line and do what Americans ask us to do or be hypocritical freeriders, failing to hold up our end of the sheltering umbrella provided by our beneficent allies. He assumed, in effect, that criticism of nuclear policy was inappropriate for Canadian citizens. As minor players in the nuclear arms race, our proper role is to be loyal allies and do as we are told, hoping against hope that things will turn out in the final analysis.

One aspect of such reasoning is effectively satirized by W.B. Gallie in a recent essay entitled "Three Main Fallacies in Discussions of Nuclear Weapons."[2] Gallie questions the common belief that only the superpowers who control the present nuclear arms race can have a constructive role in ending that race and resolving its problems. The view, apparently realistic and commonsensical, rests, he says, on assumptions whose enormity is difficult to appreciate. It is necessary to expose "the innocent hugeness and naivety of the habit of thought which they disclose." To expose the assumptions, Gallie offers a fable about giants and cave-dwellers. A derelict remnant of the human race, surviving in caves after a nuclear holocaust, is divided between two rival giants who each have a cache of highly explosive devices which are most effective when released in a cave. The cave-dwellers are constantly at risk of being devastated by these super-rivals.

What, then, should the cave-dwellers do? Wait in hope for the rival giants to see the light, forego their rivalry, and bury their grenades in a "place of safety"? Or should they humbly petition the giants to do so? Or, judging the giants to be irreconcilable, should they take their pick between them, and put their relatively slight strength behind the one whom they think more likely to win out and more likely to befriend them if he proves victorious? Or should they look around for more—even if probably dud—grenades to increase their usefulness as allies of the giant of their choice? What these suggestions have in common is this: they all present the problem of the cave-dwellers' survival as primarily dependent upon what the giants will do. And, on the face of it, the giants, who rely upon their grenades, have already decided to settle the issue between them by means which threaten the very existence of the group, the giants themselves included.[3]

Gallie argues that we need not assume that superpowers must find the way out and that minor powers, such as Britain and Canada, must act as the cave-dwellers in the fable. Minor players can seek to influence the superpowers. If they fail, they can withdraw their cooperation from a system which will involve their own ultimate destruction. "In fine, because one party has the power to destroy the other, it by no means follows that the former is wholly immune to effective pressure from the latter."

We have no evidence that Trudeau read Gallie's essay, but his overall position on the role of allied powers in determining nuclear policy underwent change. In the fall of 1983, only a few months after the publication of his open letter, he had undertaken a "peace initiative" and had made public criticisms of NATO's first use policy and of the American invasion of Grenada. Nevertheless, his original argument is a popular one, used by many people, and merits exploration. Gallie did not extend his fable to cover the circumstance that exists when a cave-dweller has willingly accepted the protection of one giant for a period of time and is hesitating about the details of further alliance. The essence of the pro-cruise argument used by Trudeau and other defense establishment people is that the recipients of a benefit have obligations to their benefactor; that Canadians benefit from the American nuclear umbrella; and that Canadians have, accordingly, obligations to participate in, and assist, American defense activities. I propose to use this common argument as a take-off point for examining various dimensions of the nuclear debate as it occurs in the political realm. There are moral aspects to this debate, certainly, but they do not primarily concern the morality of nuclear deterrence.

The point of the argument Trudeau used is not that there is a legal obligation, in the NATO treaty, or in a specific treaty between the United States and Canada, to do some specific thing such as testing cruise missiles or manufacturing parts for the MX missile. Nor is it that Canada has no choice but to accommodate American requests, due to her economic and political powerlessness in comparison to the United States. Those are different arguments, and they are not moral arguments. It is possible that in some contexts, the moral argument is a cloak for the coercion argument, which people are embarrassed to express.[4]

If Canada has no choice but to accede to American requests, because the United States would bankrupt the country, or invade, or take over the Arctic, there would indeed be no decision for Canadians to make. There are significant strands of this thinking in Canada—and no doubt in other allied countries as well. In "Canada and the US Nuclear Arsenal," Ernie Regehr quotes a 1945 Canadian policy document which allowed that "The pressure which would be brought to bear on Canada by the United States in the event of Canada seeming reluctant or refusing to cooperate with [the United States] in continental defence would be very substantial and might be difficult to resist."[5] These considerations, taken very seriously, might make any moral argument otiose. But whatever the impact of the strictly moral argument on real political decision-making in the highest circles, it is significant in public debate. It does influence many people and affects policy decisions.

Some nevertheless question the meaningfulness of moral analysis and reflection in the domain of international politics. For a variety of reasons, people have seen such analysis as misplaced, naive, and inappropriate. A prominent line of thought is that international relations occur in a Hobbesian world—a set of states in a state of nature so to speak—where there is no operative moral order. Because this is the case, there is no morality in international relations, and any moral analysis of foreign policy is misplaced. This account ignores the extensive cooperation, trust, and orderliness that do exist in international affairs: in trade, communications, shipping, weather prediction, development activities through the United Nations, and many other areas. It also ignores the practical use of moral argument to defend national actions. There are constant appeals, in the rhetoric of international affairs, to abuses of human rights, the failure of systems to attain economic equality, unwarranted invasions, illegitimate regimes, and so forth. Moral discourse on international affairs is appropriate to expose and assess such comments, if for no other reason.

Another line of reasoning tells us that actions such as those of political leaders are necessary—inevitable—and beyond meaningful moral analysis. It is in this vein that we may be told that there was no real alternative to using the first atomic weapon at Hiroshima, given the investment in the Manhattan Project, the enormous bureaucratic momentum built up during the Project, and the previous conventional bombings of Dresden and Tokyo.[6] In *Just and Unjust Wars*, Michael Walzer effectively criticizes this necessitarian line of thought. He points out that even when it has retrospective plausibility, it ignores the fact that decisions were made by moral agents. Even in crises, there were alternatives, though they may not have seemed feasible or advantageous, or politically popular when critical choices were made.[7] To choose to do what is popular rather than unpopular, what has short-term rather than long-term advantages, what has a lower rather than a higher economic cost, is still to make a choice. The fact that the choice seems, in retrospect, natural or inevitable does not show that it was not a choice. Agents do make choices when they act in the international area, just as they do in other contexts.

A third view is that the dogmatic intervention of moralizing people only serves to make international relations worse than they need to be.[8] Moral analysis is presumptuous in its assumption of an objective viewpoint from which things can correctly be appraised. It is just this kind of presumptuous thinking which leads to hostility, aggression, war, and destruction. Behind this criticism are important reminders. We cannot be sure our own ethical stance is the correct one. In international affairs, people have been too ready to defend a "morally correct" stance with horrifying means and disastrous results. Ultimately, though, the idea that the moral analysis of international relations will only make things worse and should not be pursued is itself an expression of a moral position. The moral position is admirable in its advocacy of non-dogmatism, lack of presumption, and restraint in pursuit of our ends. It is, however, within morality and not outside it. As the expression of advice to remove moral talk from the international area, the position is a moral one which is self-defeating.

There are moral arguments used in the discussion of foreign and defense policy, in Canada, as elsewhere, and these arguments are not beside the point. One prominent view in Canada seeks to derive obligations from benefits received—the obligation to test the cruise missile from the protection Canadians receive as they shelter under the American nuclear umbrella.

A first stage in reflecting on this argument is to examine the concept of the "nuclear umbrella." Obviously, this is highly metaphorical. It is also misleading and euphemistic—a comfortable, familiar word disguising an awesome and dangerous reality. A number of writers have commented on the bland, euphemistic nature of so much of the language of nuclear strategy and the nuclear debate.[9] To appreciate the general problem, think about the expression, "nuclear exchange." This sounds as though what is going on is something essentially civilized and polite, like an exchange of gifts. The term disguises the fact that millions would be vaporized, more millions cruelly burned, landscapes torn apart, and that thousands would die in agony without medical aid in such an "eventuality."

The expression "nuclear umbrella" sounds innocuous and familiar, sheltering, unthreatening, and comfortable. We have to stare at it, think about it, and force ourselves to think about what it means. It means that we owe our survival to the existence of 30,000 nuclear weapons in the American nuclear arsenal. Any single one of these weapons, if detonated on any targeted area, would cause hundreds of thousands of deaths and devastation of the environment. According to standard deterrence doctrine, we owe our survival in the nuclear age to our readiness to detonate those weapons on human beings in Russia—on innocent Russian men, women, and children. The umbrella which is said to protect us and our way of life, is a war machine of awesome potential, a war machine which could destroy our species if used. It is a war machine which human beings threaten to use and are prepared to use. To keep the nuclear umbrella in existence, thousands of human beings are trained to be prepared to kill millions of other human beings with a single push of a button. All around the world, such people combine an "ordinary life" with a job that involves continual preparedness to launch the apocalypse.

Having brought the euphemistic aspects of the term "umbrella" to the surface, we should explore the assumptions underlying its use. These are common wisdom within the nuclear establishment and too often escape analysis. These assumptions have to do with the protective nature of the umbrella. An umbrella, after all, keeps something from falling down upon us. That is why it is a protective, sheltering umbrella. With it, we don't have Russian bombs exploding on our country, and without it we would—or could. The term "umbrella" encapsulates establishment thinking about nuclear deterrence. That is:

1. Nuclear weapons have as their primary function the prevention of nuclear and major conventional war.[10]
2. Nuclear weapons have performed this primary function, historically. Because we have had nuclear weapons since 1945, we have not had nuclear (or major conventional) war in that period.
3. Nuclear weapons will continue to perform this function in the future. We will go on developing and maintaing nuclear weapons, and they will never be used in a nuclear war.[11]
4. Maintaining a nuclear arsenal which we implicitly or explicitly threaten to use is the only way of preventing a nuclear war, and it is the best way of preventing a major conventional war.[12]

These assumptions are all a part of the metaphor of the nuclear umbrella. The first assumption spells out the common belief that the purpose of the American nuclear arsenal is entirely, or at least primarily, to serve a deterrent (protective) function. It exists to prevent a nuclear war, not to launch or fight one, and not to make nuclear threats against non-nuclear countries. The second stipulates that the arsenal has sheltered us in the past. This is the benefit which we have received from American defense activity, and the benefit which produces present obligations. The third assumption is that the umbrella is a safe, accident-proof device, which can be maintained forever without risk of misuse. The fourth is that there is no alternative to nuclear deterrence. We have "enemies" with nuclear weapons, they will always be there with their nuclear weapons, and the only way for us to prevent them from attacking us is to have nuclear weapons of our own. We might wish the world were otherwise, but wish is not reality.

All four assumptions are open to cricitism. The first is historically false; the second is unverifiable, though it might be true; the third is unreasonably optimistic, unverifiable, and most likely not true. The fourth is the product of uncreative thinking about alternative arrangements and a failure to appreciate the very real disincentive to the use of nuclear weaponry which would continue to exist even if only one superpower possessed these weapons.[13] Casual use of the umbrella metaphor tends to inhibit us from reflecting on the assumptions, because we make them without even being aware that we are doing so.

The first assumption is undermined by a number of careful analyses of the nuclear age. From 1942 President Roosevelt regarded the atomic bomb as something with enormous "diplomatic potential" in the postwar world. (Note the euphemistic phrase.) He thought that with this ultimate weapon the United States would be able to dominate the postwar world. Clearly, this line of thinking embraced the use of tacit or explicit nuclear threats for limited strategic purposes. Nuclear threats have been made against non-nuclear countires (Russia in 1946; North Vietnam in 1969; China in

1958). Current policy embraces the use of tactical nuclear weapons in the context of disputes in the Third World. The idea that nuclear superiority is relevant to political "clout" around the world is pervasive. Nuclear weapons are part of an arsenal designed to protect American interests and have not been viewed solely as a means to preventing nuclear attacks.[14] Daniel Ellsberg, formerly an insider in American defense planning circles, has emphasized this point and, in a recent paper, points out that evidence for it that was not made public in previous decades is now availble in diaries and memoirs of Eisenhower and other leaders.

> Almost no one seems to be aware of this, but the fact is that every President in his term of office (except possibly Ford) has had occasion to consider the imminent use of nuclear weapons against, in almost every case, an opponent that did not have nuclear weapons. This was probably less dangerous than doing it against the Soviet Union. However, each of those opponents–the Koreans, the Indochinese, the Chinese– were allies or clients of the Soviet Union, so the problem remained one of preventing Soviet retaliation.[15]

The second assumption encompassed by the notion of a nuclear umbrella is unverifiable. To know that it is true, we would have to know that without nuclear weapons, there would have been a major conventional war involving Russia, the United States, Europe, and Canada after 1945. We would, that is, have to know something about an alternative world, a world missing a feature which is pervasive and deeply significant in our actual world. Nuclear weapons probably have served to make leaders more cautious but they have probably also served to make relations more hostile. Certainly Russian suspicions of the United States were greatly increased by the secretiveness of the Manhattan Project and the sudden use of atomic weapons on Hiroshima and Nagasaki. Many Russian analysts believe that the primary reason for the bombings was not, as American officialdom has it, to end the war with Japan quickly but rather to terrify the Russians and bring them "in line."[16]

It is the third assumption, however, which is most crucial to the nuclear umbrella argument. If we are to benefit from the umbrella, it cannot explode into a fireball or a radioactive cloud. Even granting the first two assumptions, there is little benefit to the "nuclear umbrella" unless we assume that it will continue to ward off the attack. We are protected by the umbrella only insofar as it continues its "sheltering" function. The umbrella metaphor encourages us to ignore that many risks involved in nuclear deterrence. In a renewed Cold War atmosphere, with 50,000 nuclear weapons in the possession of the two superpowers, with a launch-to-detonation period of less than seven minutes for Pershing II missiles recently deployed in Europe, there are substantial risks in nuclear deterrence. Ever-more-accurate weapons are aimed at opponents' weapons, increasing the risk of preemptive first strikes. The development of "smaller,"more flexible nuclear weapons makes it more likely that they will be used in a battlefield context, perhaps in a Third World dispute. With nuclear proliferation, and client states of the superpowers, such as Israel, having nuclear weapons,[17] disputes involving them could "go nuclear." There have been a number of close calls, and accidents continue to be possible, with the weapons' velocity making the detection of false alarms before response time all the more difficult.

For Canadians especially, a sober consideration of these risks will make the umbrella metaphor appear extremely inappropriate. Placed between the superpowers, Canadians would be devastated by a nuclear exchange between them. Missiles would be flying over our country; our airports and cities would in all likelihood be targeted due to our role in American defense systems and proximity to the United States. Analysts of the likely fate of Canada have said:

> Any significant margin of survival after an exchange of nuclear weapons could easily constitute "victory," however hollow and short-lived such survival might be.
>
> In these circumstances it is difficult to believe that military planners in the Soviet Union would try their utmost to destroy the United States while leaving on its northern border an intact ribbon of land that is rich in natural resources, energy (already being exported to the United States in large quantities), agriculture and industrial development which could give the American survivors a margin that could make the difference between such a "victory" and total annihilation.[18]

If, in some less-than-total scenario, Canadian cities and airports were not directly targeted, damage from fallout and other global effects of nuclear detonations would be considerable. The same may be said for other allied countries and, indeed, for all the nations of the earth.

There is, of course, some possibility that the nuclear arms race will be unlike all other arms races and will not end in a war. We must earnestly hope that this is the case. Nuclear weapons are unique in their potential to destroy our globe. If leaders continue to perceive this uniqueness, it just might be that they can continue stockpiling these weapons indefinitely without ever again using them in war. However, it does not seem wise to stake our future on this hope. That the nuclear umbrella will continue to protect us from nuclear war is less likely than that it will explode in such a war—a war which its very existence has helped to bring about.

The fourth assumption, that the only way to prevent nuclear war is to continue our reliance on nuclear weapons, is just the kind of claim to which skepticism should be applied. There is very rarely only one way of doing something. Arrangements for joint security without nuclear weapons as a deterrent against war have not been seriously pursued by the superpowers since 1946.[19] It is premature to say in advance that no such arrangements would be possible. The possession of nuclear weapons by one superpower increases insecurity and hostility within the other, and propels the arms race leading in many cases to destablizing technological developments. There would be very little incentive for one superpower to use weapons on another which had none, for global effects of fallout and damage to the earth's climate and the ozone layer would hurt the aggressor as well as the defender. In addition, world opinion would be overwhelmingly against the aggressor. The superpower contest is as much a contest for global influence as for control over territory. There would be no point in burning and radiating a territory one wished to control, in any case. Bilateral disarmament has never been seriously pursued as an approach to national security, and even unilateral disarmament probably brings with it less risk of nuclear war than the current situation. It is absolutely presumptuous to assume that our current system of nuclear deterrence based on a continuing arms race is the only way to prevent nuclear war.

If we return now to the argument that we benefit from the American nuclear umbrella and are therefore obligated to do our part in upholding American defense systems, we see that the opening premise is disputable in the extreme. Even if we agree that there have been some benefits in the past, it is very unlikely that the indefinite continuation of the system of nuclear deterrence will benefit us. If obligations to our allies come because we stand in a relationship in which we are receiving benefits, then perhaps we have no obligations after all.

There are however, several complicating factors here. One is that there is some case for claiming past benefits, even though that would be hard to demonstrate. Another, more important point is that Canadian and other allied leaders have obviously believed that there is a benefit in the nuclear umbrella. They have not seen the risks of nuclear deterrence as sufficient to warrant changing their defense system and have entered into alliances (in the case of Canada, NATO and NORAD) on the assumption that nuclear deterrence is the route to national security in the nuclear age. Perhaps perceived benefits generate obligations just as much as real benefits do, especially if agents enter into voluntary agreements pertinent to those perceived benefits. Perhaps for this reason, Canadians and other allies are obligated to participate in upholding the American defense establishment.

If an agent voluntarily accepts from another agent what he believes to be a good thing, then does he thereby acquire an obligation to assist that other agent, when called upon? There is a sense in which he does and a sense in which he does not, as we can see by exploring a simple parallel case. Suppose that Sam offers to protect Johnny against Ivan's dogs because he wants to keep the dogs out of their neighbourhood. Johnny is happy enough to have Sam help him. So they build a massive fence, and for forty years, neither Sam nor Johnny encounters any of Ivan's dogs. Johnny has, so far as he knows, benefitted from Sam's help. (Neither Sam nor Johnny knows that any of Ivan's dogs were headed in their direction in the first place, but they do know that they haven't had any dogs around, and they assume that their fence kept the dogs away.) Now Sam thinks the fence needs strengthening and he asks Johnny to help him with some of the costs. But in the meantime, Johnny has started to worry about their situation. It seems that the material used for the fence is dangerous. It turns out that the construction materials contain a harmful substance, found to cause a debilitating disease which will show up after a long period. Eventually, everyone is likely to succumb to this disease unless the materials are removed from the neighborhood. Johnny hesitates about supplying the materials to Sam. Sam is furious. He tells Johnny that he has benefitted from Sam's help in the past and is therefore obliged to do something to assist him now. He accuses Johnny of hypocrisy and freeriding. He isn't asking much of Johnny—just a few materials—and now, after all he has done for Johnny, Johnny won't do anything for him.

Now Johnny does have some obligation to Sam in this case, clearly. He has had amicable relations with Sam in the past, and they have cooperated in an endeavor which both thought was beneficial, with Sam doing most of the work and supplying most of the money. Johnny should not simply turn his back on Sam and ignore the request. But is it his obligation to accede uncritically to Sam's request? Given what he believes about the construction materials, he should tell Sam the risks involved and try to establish a discussion in which they consider other means of protecting their property. In fact, for Johnny to accede uncritically to the request and supply material which he knows is dangerous is for him to ignore his benefactor's welfare as well as his own. He should communicate his concerns and try to bring about a change. If this fails, and Johnny remains convinced that their protective strategy is a dangerous one, he may withdraw from their arrangement. His obligation is to cooperate with his "benefactor" for their mutual good, as he best understands this. It is not to meet any and every request, regardless of whether he believes that his cooperation would endanger them both.

The benefit-obligation argument can be used to show that Canadians and other allies have obligations to the Americans. It cannot be used to show that they should unthinkingly meet every American request, nor that they should meet requests when they believe that the activity in question will increase their mutual danger. Those citizens of allied countries who sincerely believe that nuclear deterrence is an ever-more-risky system of national security have an obligation to consider the well-being of American citizens as well as their own. Their governments have voluntarily allied themselves with the American government and have perceived that alliance to be beneficial. Even if the system established were no longer beneficial, the previous cooperation and perceived benefits would establish a relationship in which future cooperation should be sought. Canadians and other allies should first try to work with Americans when they seek to lessen dependence on nuclear weapons and bring the dangerous arms race to a halt. Cooperating does not mean that they can only accede to American requests and must do what they are told without working for constructive change. Cooperation is not domination. It is not taking orders. Rather, it is working together, with all members thinking for themselves about what would be best for the group as a whole.

Whatever the morality of nuclear deterrence, it is a dangerous system in the long run. We have had nuclear weapons since 1945 without having had another nuclear war. This is no guarantee that nuclear war will never occur. The umbrella metaphor connotes safety in an unsafe situation. Our obligation is not to give whatever "aid" is requested, but to participate as thinking and concerned members of an alliance to work for global security. Contrary to the received wisdom in defense and foreign policy circles, nuclear deterrence is not, in the long run, the only route to global or national security. Nor is it even one such route. The obligation of citizens around the globe is to try to determine the best political strategy for departing from this risky situation and to work to make that strategy a political reality.

Notes

1. *Calgary Herald*, May 9, 1983. The open letter was reprinted in the *Bulletin of the Atomic Scientists* (October 1983, 2).
2. In Blake and Pole, pp. 157–178.

3. P. 176.
4. This is likely to be true in many circumstances; however it has been my experience that the moral argument does substantially affect the thinking of ordinary conscientious citizens, even though it is possible that astute politicians such as former Canadian Prime Minister Pierre Trudeau really use it as a cover-up for something else.
5. Cited by Ernie Regehr in "Canada and the US Nuclear Arsenal," in Regehr and Rosenblum, eds., pp. 10–12.
6. This view has been effectively argued by Bernstein in *The Atomic Bomb* and in a lecture presented to the Stanford University Alumni Society in August 1983 ("The Use of the Atomic Bomb: Politics, Ethics, and Impact on Western Culture," available on tape from the Stanford University Alumni Society).
7. Walzer.
8. Put to me in correspondence by Prof. S. Kounosu, Department of Physics, University of Lethbridge, Alberta. *In Just and Unjust Wars*, Walzer reports that a similar view was urged under the name of "realism" by people who thought wars regarded as moral crusades were likely to be even more ferocious and horrifying than those fought under nonmoral banners such as that of national interest.
9. See, for example, Hilgartner, Bell, and O'Connor; also Fox, "The Nuclear Mindset," this collection.
10. This presumption is relevant to the particular issue of cruise testing. Public officials defended the testing by discussing NATO and the role of the American nuclear arsenal, and the cruise as part of that arsenal, in defending Europe. In fact, the missile to be tested in Canada is the air-launched cruise, which plays a part not in Europe, but in American strategy in defending its interests around the globe—primarily in potential areas of conflict in the Third World.
11. Powers reports that the many military people he interviewed were unanimous in believing that nuclear weapons would always be necessary and would never be used.
12. This assumption is clearly at work in many circles. For just one example, see Morris.
13. See, for example, Lackey, "Missiles and Morals" and the subsequent discussion of his views by Hardin and Kavka.
14. I have argued this point in "Nuclear Illusion and Individual Obligations." Extensive historical documentation may be found in Sherwin, chap. 9; Herken, chap. 1; Jungk; and Ellsberg, "Nuclear Weapons." See also Ellsberg, "Confronting the Rising Risk of World War III," in Perry, ed.
15. Ellsberg, "Confronting," p. 257.
16. See Roy and Zhores Medvedev. The authors, prominent Soviet dissident scholars, say, "Soviet analysts—corroborated by not a few eminent Western historians—have generally viewed the American decision to destroy Hiroshima and Nagasaki with atomic bombs in August 1945, at a moment when the surrender of Japan was already imminent, as a demonstration of force primarily designed to intimidate the USSR at this juncture."
17. According to Pringle and Spigelman, who present considerable documented evidence, Israel already possesses nuclear weapons. See chaps. 17 and 18.
18. Bates et al., "What Would Happen to Canada in a Nuclear War?" in Regehr and Rosenblum, eds.
19. I give this date because 1946 was the year in which both the United States and the Soviet Union presented to the United Nations plans for the international control of atomic energy. Neither plan was approved by both powers, due largely to the US belief that its atomic monopoly was good for at least twenty years and to the developing Cold War atmosphere of the time.

Questions

1. Is the umbrella analogy a good one to describe Canada's position as a defence partner of the United States in NORAD and NATO?
2. Govier lists four assumptions that are part of what she describes as the nuclear umbrella argument. Does Robert Art's position on the need for nuclear parity depend on any of those assumptions? Does Art provide a defence of any of those assumptions that Govier fails to take into account in her critique? Is Govier's assessment of each of these four assumptions sound?
3. How does Govier's account of the implications of being under a nuclear umbrella compare with the account offered by Art?
4. If nuclear deterrence is not the only route to global or national security, what are the alternatives?

Making the Abolition of War a Realistic Goal

Gene Sharp

The destructiveness of modern war is widely understood. Yet most governments, backed by their populations, amass the largest array of military weaponry and forces of which they are capable. Clearly, none of the past proposals and movements to abolish war and to bring in an era of world peace has succeeded. Indeed, in significant respects the achievement of those goals now seems less likely than it did in earlier decades.

This is, of course, not the only grave political problem we have failed to solve. Others include dictatorship, genocide, systems of social oppression, and popular powerlessness. They must be considered as we seek a solution to the problem of war.

Most people respond to the continuation of wars and war preparations with a sense of resignation, hopelessness, or powerlessness. "War is inevitable," it is thought; we blame "human nature" or our favorite "evil forces." Other persons faithfully persist in plodding the old paths to the now tarnished dreams—without reexamining

---

This essay, which won the Wallach Awards Competition 1979–1980 sponsored by the Institute for World Order, first appeared in *Midwest Newsletter* (World without War Issues Center), December 1980. © Gene Sharp. By the same author: (1) *The Politics of Nonviolent Action*, 3 Vols.: I, *Power and Struggle*, 144 pp., paperbound $3.95; II, *The Methods of Nonviolent Action*, 368 pp., paperbound $4.95; III, *The Dynamics of Nonviolent Action*, 480 pp., paperbound $5.95. (Porter Sargent Publishers, 11 Beacon Street, Boston, MA 02108.) (2) *Social Power and Political Freedom*, 456 pp., cloth $15.95, paperbound $8.95. (Porter Sargent Publishers [address above].) (3) *Making Europe Unconquerable: The Potential of Civilian-based Deterrence and Defense*, 2nd ed., with foreword by George Kennan, 190 pp., paperbound $14.95. (Ballinger Publishing Co., Order Dept. Harper & Row, 2350 Virginia Ave., Hagerstown, MD 21740.)

whether they are heading in the right direction. Still others try to run faster to their goal, or seek shortcuts, or carry out acts of desperation—without a basis for confidence that their efforts can succeed either, or even certainty that they will not make matters worse.

All this is not good enough. More creative responses are possible. Indeed, it is our responsibility to seek to develop them. If soundly based and realistically developed and applied, they might offer new hope.

If new responses to the problem of war are to be soundly based they must take into consideration some hard facts which most peace workers rarely face. These include the following:

- Conflicts of some type will always exist within societies and between societies, requiring use of some type of power;
- "Human nature" need not, and most likely will not, be changed;
- People and governments will not sacrifice freedom or justice for the sake of peace;
- Mass conversions to pacifism are not going to occur;
- There is no break in the spiral of military technology within the context of military technology and military assumptions;
- Brutal dictatorships and oppressive systems exist, will continue, may become more serious, and may seek to expand;
- The abolition of capitalism does not produce the abolition of war;
- Negotiations are no substitute for the capacity to struggle and apply sanctions;
- Unilateral "disarmament"—abandonment of defense capacity—is no alternative to the war system and is not possible;
- Major multilateral disarmament is nearly as unlikely;
- National independence is not the origin of war;
- World government is either unrealizable, or if achieved would itself be likely to produce a world civil war, become tyrannical, and be used to impose or perpetuate injustice.

Our search for a solution to the problem of war must not be based on utopian illusions, or naiveté the political intentions of protagonists in international conflicts.

War as an Alternative to Impotence

Without understanding the nature of a problem well, it is exceptionally difficult to find or develop a solution to it. It is possible that we have not understood the problem of war adequately. It is necessary to look beyond the proposals and doctrines of the past if we are to deal with this problem. It is often difficult to begin to explore fresh approaches, for we may be emotionally attached to a favorite remedy, and we are sometimes intellectually unprepared for thinking about the problem in unfamiliar ways.

War, and military preparations to threaten or to wage it, are obviously complex in their causes and consequences. They have also changed significantly in recorded history. Despite this complexity and variability it is possible to look again at these phenomena and gain new insights into their nature and the reasons for their perpetuation.

War and military capacity have served various functions, including to attack and oppress the people of another society, or even of one's own society. Those ignoble uses of war and military means should not, however, lead us to ignore the more noble purposes for which they have been used (or in some cases claimed to be used thereby gaining popular support which would have been uncertain for the real objectives).

Important issues of lasting importance are often at stake in major internal and international conflicts. The world is politically a dangerous place. Dictatorships arise, perpetuate themselves, and often expand. Countries are attacked. Oppression exists in a variety of forms. Minority cliques, military and political, overthrow legitimated governments, and establish new oppression. Genocide is perpetrated. Whole peoples are exploited and dominated by domestic and foreign masters.

Effective means of struggle are therefore needed to meet a variety of conflict situations. Counterviolence has been used in such conflicts to control, restrain, limit, or defeat opponents using violence to serve their own ends. Thus, violent struggle including war has very often been used to advance or defend humanitarian goals and societies against hostile forces.

Violent conflict has served as a technique of struggle, as the ultimate sanction, to be applied in times of severe danger to advance or defend the way of life, beliefs, independence, or chosen social system against oppressors and attackers. Whatever the disadvantages of such violence, people in many societies and historical periods have believed it to be the only alternative to impotence and passive submission in face of threats to that which they have cherished.

In the case of foreign invasions, the answer was defensive war. War has thus relieved people of a sense of impotence in times of danger, and has given them a powerful technique to pursue the conflict in defense and furtherance of their principles, objectives, and society. The mass of humanity has believed—and still believes—that no other technique could be adequate in such crises.

War may have been brutal and immoral, but—whatever its demerits and results—it provided an ultimate sanction and means of struggle which could be held in reserve to support one's arguments in international negotiations and to deter attack, and which could be used in open struggle when people believed that foreign military action threatened their principles and liberty. The justifications of war and military preparations offered by both governments and ordinary men and women boil down to that.

Even in an age of missiles and hydrogen bombs, which—people know—could lead to widespread extermination rather than genuine defense, people still cling to war. They do this because they see the present weapons as simply an extension of the earlier forms of war. If they know that such weapons cannot be used in a rational conflict, they believe that their existence will prevent the conflict from turning into war, and thus prevent their way of life being taken from them. The weapons thereby help to keep people from feeling entirely helpless in the face of international dangers.

As long as there is a felt need for such a means of struggle, and as long as people see no adequate substitute to take the place of war, there is no chance of war being renounced or abandoned. People and whole societies will not choose to be defenseless.

A Substitute Defense Policy?

Since war is threatened against and used to attack other countries which need to be strong enough to deter attack and to defend themselves, no break in the cycle of war is possible as long as people and governments do not perceive the existence and effectiveness of alternative nonmilitary means of defense.

Peace proposals and movements of the past have failed to offer a credible alternative defense policy in place of war. Therefore, whether they instead offered as solutions to the problem of war negotiations, compromises, conciliation, international conferences, supranational leagues, or anti-war resistance, their common failure could have been predicted.

On the other hand, the stubborn persistence of advocates of strong defense in considering only military means and failing to investigate nonmilitary possibilities has led to the present dangerous situation and to the lack of development of possible options.

If we want to reduce drastically, or remove, reliance on war and other types of violent conflict it is necessary to substitute a nonviolent counterpart of war, "war without violence," by which people can defend liberty, their way of life, humanitarian principles, their institutions and society, at least as effectively against military attack as can military means.

Such a substitute defense policy would need to be one which can be (1) held in reserve to encourage settlements without resort to open struggle (as by facilitating settlements, reducing misperceptions, and deterring aggression) by effective defense capacity as such, and (2) used effectively in an open defense struggle against attack. ("Defense" here must be understood literally, as protection, warding off of danger, preservation, and the like. Defense is therefore *not* necessarily tied to military means, and has been provided by nonmilitary forms of struggle.)

Power Sources for a New Policy

In 1939 Albert Einstein signed a now famous letter to President Roosevelt expressing the view that it was possible that new weapons of a completely different type could be based on nuclear fission. Although atomic nuclei themselves could not be seen by ordinary human beings, and although no such atomic weapons, even primitive prototypes of them, had ever existed, the Manhattan Project was launched. With sufficient scientists and resources a whole new weapons system was created.

More evidence exists today that we could develop a new type of defense system not requiring military means than existed in 1939 that nuclear bombs were possible. In this case we have primitive prototypes of the new policy, in cases of improvised predominantly nonviolent revolutions against tyrants and defense struggles against coups d'état and foreign occupations.

We also have an insight into the nature of political power, which may be in politics as significant as has been in military weaponry the theory of the workings of the atom. The power of all rulers and governments is vulnerable, impermanent, and dependent on sources in the society. Those sources can be identified: acceptance of the ruler's right to rule ("authority"), economic resources, manpower, military capacity, knowledge, skills, administration, police, prisons, courts, and the like. Each of these sources is in turn closely related to, or directly dependent upon, the degree of cooperation, submission, obedience, and assistance that the ruler is able to obtain from his subjects. These include both the general population and his paid "helpers" and agents. That dependence makes it possible, under certain circumstances, for the subjects to restrict or sever these sources of power, by reducing or withdrawing their necessary cooperation and obedience.

If the withdrawal of acceptance, submission, and help can be maintained in face of the ruler's punishments, then the end of the regime is in sight. Thus, all rulers are dependent for their positions and political power upon the obedience, submission, and cooperation of their subjects. This not only applies internally, but also, with variations, in cases of attempted foreign invasion and occupation. The theory that power derives from violence, and that victory goes to the side with the greater capacity for violence, is false.

Resisting the Weaknesses of Dictatorships

Instead, the will to defy and resist becomes extremely important. Hitler admitted that the problem of "ruling the people in the conquered regions" was "psychological":

> One cannot rule by force alone. True, force is decisive, but it is equally important to have this psychological something which the animal trainer also needs to be master of his beast. They must be convinced that we are the victors.

The civilian population can refuse to be convinced.

A vast history exists of people who, refusing to be convinced that the apparent "powers that be" were omnipotent, defied and resisted powerful rulers, foreign conquerers, domestic tyrants, oppressive systems, internal usurpers, and economic masters. Contrary to usual perceptions, these means of struggle by protest, noncooperation, and disruptive intervention have played major historical roles in all parts of the world, even in cases in which attention is usually concentrated on parallel or later political violence.

These unrefined forms of nonviolent struggle have been used as major or the predominant means of defense against foreign invaders or internal usurpers, or both— mostly improvised, without preparations, training, or planning—in various instances and countries. These include: German strikes and political noncooperation to the 1920 Kapp *Putsch* against the Weimar Republic; German government-sponsored noncooperation in the Ruhr in 1923 to the French and Belgian occupation; major aspects of the Dutch anti-Nazi resistance, including several large strikes, 1940–1945; major aspects of the Danish resistance to the German occupation, including the 1944 Copenhagen general strike, 1940–1945; major parts of the Norwegian resistance to the Quisling regime and the occupation, 1940–1945; and the Czechoslovak resistance to the Soviet invasion and occupation, 1968–1969.

The nature and accomplishments of the Czechoslovak defense are already forgotten by many and are being distorted when reference is made to it. The resistance ultimately failed, but it held off full Soviet control for *eight months*—from August to April—

something which would have been utterly impossible by military means. It also, it is reported, caused such morale problems among Russian troops that the first units had to be rotated out of the country in a few days, and shipped, not to European U.S.S.R. where they could report what was happening, but to Siberia. All this was done without preparations and training, much less contingency planning. This suggests even in final defeat (as a result of capitulation by Czechoslovak officials, not defeated resistance) a power potential even greater than military means.

In addition to such cases as these, other resistance movements and revolutions against internal oppression and dictatorships are relevant. These include major aspects of these cases: the 1980–1981 Polish workers' movement for an independent trade union and democratization; the 1944 revolutions in El Salvador and Guatemala against established military dictatorships; the 1978–1979 revolution against the Shah in Iran; the 1905–1906 and February 1917 revolutions in Imperial Russia; the 1953 East German Rising; the Polish movements of 1956, 1970–1971, and 1976; the 1956–1957 Hungarian Revolution; the 1963 Buddhist campaign against the Ngo Dinh Diem regime in South Vietnam; the 1953 strike movement at Vorkuta and other prison camps in the Soviet Union; and diverse other cases.

This type of resistance and defense is possible against dictatorships because even extreme forms of them are unable to free themselves from dependence upon the population and society they would rule. Dictatorships, contrary to the usual assumption, are not as strong and omnipotent as they would have us believe, but contain inherent weaknesses of various types which contribute to their inefficiency and reduce the thoroughness of their controls, and limit their longevity. Those weaknesses can be located and resistance can be concentrated at those cracks in the monolith. Nonviolent resistance is much more suited to that task than is violence.

Civilian-Based Defense

The experiences of the above and other cases of improvised resistance against internal usurpers, foreign invaders, and domestic dictatorships do not offer a ready-made substitute defense policy which can be simply applied as a substitute for war. However, that experience does provide primitive prototypes which could by research and analysis, and by careful evaluation, refinement, preparations, planning, and training become the basis of a new defense policy—one based not on military weapons and forces, but on the civilian population and the society's institutions, on societal strength. An alternative to military defense is possible.

This alternative policy of deterrence and defense is called "civilian-based defense." That is a defense policy which utilizes prepared civilian struggle—nonviolent action—to preserve the society's freedom, sovereignty, and constitutional system against internal usurpations and external invasions and occupations. The aim is to deter to defeat such attacks. This to be done not simply by efforts to alter the will of the attacker, but by the capacity to make effective domination and control impossible by both massive and selective nonviolent noncooperation and defiance by the population and its institutions. The aim is to make the populace unrulable by the attackers and to deny them their objectives. A genuine capacity to do that, if accurately perceived, could deter both internal takeovers and foreign invasions.

It is possible to exert extreme pressure and even to coerce by nonviolent means. Rather than converting the opponent, civilian struggle has more often been waged by disrupting, paralyzing, or coercing the opponent by denying the cooperation he needed, and upsetting the normal operation of the system. This is a foundation for civilian-based strategies.

An attack for ideological and indoctrination purposes, for example, would likely involve noncooperation and defiance by schools, newspapers, radio, television, churches, all levels of government, and the general population, to reject the indoctrination attempts, and reassertion of democratic principles.

An attack aimed at economic exploitation would be met with economic resistance—boycotts, strikes, noncooperation by experts, management, transport workers, and officials—aimed at reducing, dissolving, or reversing any economic gains to the attackers.

Coups d'état and executive usurpations would be met with noncooperation of civil servants, bureaucrats, government agencies, state and local government, police departments, and virtually all the social institutions and general population as a whole, to deny legitimacy, and to prevent consolidation of effective control by usurpers over the government and society.

Defense Responsibilities

Various population groups and institutions would have responsibility for particular defense tasks, depending on the exact issues at stake.

For example, police would refuse to locate and arrest patriotic resisters against the attacker. Journalists and editors refusing to submit to censorship would publish newspapers illegally in large editions or many small editions—as happened in the Russian 1905 Revolution and in several Nazi-occupied countries. Free radio programs would continue from hidden transmitters—as happened in Czechoslovakia in 1968.

Clergymen would preach the duty to refuse help to the invader—as happened in the Netherlands under the Nazis.

Politicians, civil servants, judges, and the like by ignoring or defying the enemy's illegal orders, would keep the normal machinery of government, the courts, etc., out of his control—as happened in the German resistance to the Kapp *Putsch* in 1920.

The judges would declare the invader's officials an illegal and unconstitutional body, continue to operate on the basis of pre-invasion laws and constitutions, and refuse to give moral support to the invader, even if they had to close the courts.

Teachers would refuse to introduce propaganda into the schools—as happened in Norway under the Nazis. Attempts to control schools could be met with refusal to change the school curriculum or to introduce the invader's propaganda, explanations to the pupils of the issues at stake, continuation of regular education as long as possible, and, if necessary, closing the schools and holding private classes in the children's homes.

Workers and managers would impede exploitation of the country by selective strikes, delays, and obstructionism—as happened in the Ruhr in 1923.

Attempts to control professional groups and trade unions could be met by persistence in abiding by their pre-invasion constitutions and procedures, refusal to recognize new organizations set up by the invader, refusal to pay dues or attend meetings of any new pro-invader organizations, and the wielding of disruptive strikes, managerial defiance and obstruction, and economic and political boycotts.

These defense tasks are only illustrative of a multitude of specific forms of defense action which would be possible. Civilian-based defense operates not only on the principle that the price of liberty is eternal vigilance, but that defense of independence and freedom is the responsibility of every citizen.

This is a more total type of defense than the military system, since it involves the whole population and all its institutions in defense struggle. Because such participation must be voluntary in order to be reliable in crises, and because of reliance on nonviolent means, however, civilian-based defense is intrinsically democratic.

As in military warfare, this type of struggle is applied in face of violent enemy action. Casualties are—as in military struggle—to be expected. In this case, however, they are utilized to advance the cause of the defenders (as by increasing their resistance) and to undermine the opponent's power (as by alienating his own supporters). There is no more reason to be dismayed by casualties, or to capitulate when they occur, than there is when they occur in military conflict. In fact, it appears that casualties in civilian struggles are far lower than in military conflicts.

Other Theaters of Operation

Civilian-based defense also has an attack capacity against usurpers and invaders—which one United States Army general has called "the sword of CBD." The basic dynamics of nonviolent struggle—particularly the process of "political *jiu-jitsu*"—and deliberate efforts would be aimed to undermine the will, loyalty, and obedience of the attacker's troops, functionaries, and administrators. The result could be to make them unreliable, inefficient, less brutal in repression, and at times mutinous on a large scale. This could, in extreme cases, dissolve the machinery of repression and administration.

Similar undermining efforts would be aimed at the enemy's usual supporters and home population, with the objective of producing dissent, disruption, and opposition in his own camp. This would, if achieved, be highly important, but prime reliance should not be shifted from the home front.

Under some conditions, significant international opposition to the attack and support for the civilian defenders may be aroused. Occasionally this would involve international economic and political sanctions against the invader or internal usurper. These sanctions may be significant at times—witness the Arab oil embargo—although the defenders must primarily rely on their own actions.

Of the three broad theaters of defense—denial of the enemy's objectives, provocation of morale problems and unrest in the opponent's camp, and arousal of international support for the defenders and sanctions against the attacker—the direct blockage by the civilian defenders of the attacker's objectives is by far the most important.

Nuclear Weapons

Major attention is required in consideration of this policy to its possible relevance or limitations in relation to nuclear weapons. This field has not yet been adequately examined. It is possible, on the one hand, that civilian-based defense may be developed to be an adequate substitute for conventional military defense, but be irrelevant to the nuclear question. In that case, nuclear weapons would need to be dealt with by other means, such as arms control treaties, other international controls, unilateral initiatives to reduce reliance on nuclear weapons, or even unilateral dismantling of them as sources of greater danger than safety.

On the other hand, civilian-based defense may be relevant to the problem of nuclear weapons in several indirect ways. For example, a country with a civilian-based defense policy and without nuclear weapons is far less likely to be targeted by nuclear powers than are countries with nuclear armed rockets aimed at other nuclear powers.

In a different context, the massive buildup of so-called "tactical" nuclear weapons in Western Europe to be used in case of a Soviet *Blitzkrieg* westward is premised on the incapacity of NATO forces to defend Western Europe successfully by conventional military means. Thoroughly prepared civilian-based defense policies in Western European countries by their capacity to ensure a massive and continuing defense struggle capable of maintaining the autonomy of the attacked societies, denying the Soviets their objectives, and undermining the morale and reliability of the Soviet troops—evidence for that exists—would constitute a more powerful deterrent and defense policy than can conventional military means. Therefore, the reliance on nuclear weapons to deter and defend against a Soviet attack on Western Europe would not be required. Much careful work on such questions is needed.

Transarmament

Since civilian-based defense once fully developed and prepared to be a powerful defense policy would only be adopted if it is judged to be effective, it would be possible for only one or a few countries initially to adopt the policy, even without treaties with other countries pledged to do so, and while most countries remain militarily armed. Later, when convinced of the effectiveness and advantages of the policy, other countries might also transarm.

The first countries to adopt civilian-based defense are likely to be those which most want self-reliance in defense but which lack the ability to achieve this by military means. Governmental studies and public discussion on this policy have proceeded further in Sweden and the Netherlands than elsewhere, but the policy potentially suits the strategic needs of Austria and Finland more obviously. At this point, smaller Western European countries seem the most likely to be the first both to add a civilian-based defense component to their overall defense posture, and also, at a significantly later date, to transarm fully to the new policy.

It is extremely difficult to make accurate predictions, but it is quite possible that one or even several Western European countries might add a civilian-based defense component to their predominantly military policies—with or without alliances—by 1990 and that the first full case of transarmament to the new policy could occur by 2005.

There would inevitably be strongholds of resistance to adoption of the policy, and large military powers are unlikely, and probably unable, to transarm in a short span of time. Even they, however, might add a civilian-based defense component, if its effectiveness and utility for given purposes could be convincingly demonstrated.

Any country which begins to move toward adoption of this policy must, almost inevitably, begin by making such an addition of a civilian-based defense component alongside the predominantly military policy. As preparations and training proceeded, and as justifiable confidence in the ability of the new policy to deter attack and defend successfully against it grew, it would become possible to expand this component. The military component might then be seen as progressively less needed, and even as harmful to the full effectiveness of civilian-based defense. The military component could then be gradually reduced and phased out.

Dictatorial regimes and unstable governments would probably cling hardest to military capacity for both domestic and international purposes. Dictatorships could, of course, still be influenced, both by removal of fear of foreign military attack (contributing to internal relaxation), and by nonviolent pressures for liberalization and democratization from their own populations.

Consequences of Civilian-Based Defense

Assuming that civilian-based defense is developed into a viable policy, it would have several highly important consequences. In some cases it would reduce international tensions by separating the defense capacity from the attack capacity of a country, which in military means are largely the same. The policy would restore to small and medium-sized countries self-reliance in defense.

Although not without costs and needs for resources and personnel, civilian-based defense would be significantly less voracious in its consumption of the society's raw materials, industrial capacity, financial resources, and energy supplies than is military defense.

Civilian-based defense would free the foreign policy of a country, and its policies toward United Nations activities, from the controls based on the needs of its military policies. On the other hand, civilian-based defense would be conducive to development of foreign and international policies to assist the resolution of outstanding world problems, meet human needs more adequately, and promote understanding and friendship for the country which had adopted this nonmilitary policy.

The consideration of the possible merits of civilian-based defense, and the planning, preparations, and training for it, are likely to stimulate a reevaluation of the principles and institutions of the society deemed worthy of defense, social improvements to make the society and polity more just and free, and increased popular participation in the operation of the society in peacetime as well as during defense struggles.

In some cases, despite the development of civilian-based defense into a viable policy for deterring and defending against internal usurpations and foreign invasions and occupations, powerful elites and governments may persist in maintaining instead strong military capacities and rejecting civilian-based defense. In that case, those elites and regimes will not—as has long been the practice—be able to "justify" the military preparations on the plea of national defense, when the real purpose is less noble. People will then become able to perceive that the motive for holding to the military capacity is not what they have been told, and to make their judgements and determine their actions accordingly.

Creating a Choice

Civilian-based defense could break the technological weaponry spiral, and bypass the major problems of negotiated disarmament and arms control agreements. With full recognition of international and domestic dangers, whole countries could mobilize effective capacities to prevent, deter, and defend against attacks—while at the same time reducing, and finally abandoning, reliance on military means.

For the first time, therefore, it becomes possible in advance of crises to choose between reliance on military capacity to deter and defend against attack and reliance on an alternative to war for the same puproses. Without such a choice between two or more policies to deter attacks and defend against them, overwhelmingly, with only the possibility of rare exceptions, most people and governments will cling to war. They do not really have a choice.

With the development of a choice, the future course of events hinges to a significant degree on the extent to which the civilian-based defense option is in fact adequate to the defense tasks and also on the perception of its adequacy. Therefore, the advance basic research, problem-solving research, policy studies, feasibility studies, preparations, contingency planning, and training are of extreme importance. So also are the population's defense will, the resilience of the society's non-State institutions in resistance, and the skill of the civilian defenders in formulating and implementing wise strategies. Advance identification of possible objectives of potential internal usurpers and foreign attackers and of vulnerable points in such groups and regimes will also be important.

In all probability, the initial instances of full transarmament to civilian-based defense would not be followed quickly by a rush of many other countries also to transarm, especially in cases in which they felt relatively safe with their military policies and alliances. When civilian-based defense has been put to the test in crises, and has in a few cases demonstrably deterred a possible internal usurpation or foreign invasion, and successfully defended the society against those attacks, the consequences are likely to be profound.

Such evidence of the effectiveness of civilian-based defense could lead to increasing numbers of societies beginning the process of transarmament. Although some countries might never abandon military means entirely, demonstrations that aggression does not pay and can be defeated could limit the harm they could do. Other countries, however, could increasingly move, by adoption of a substitute for military defense, to abandon war as an instrument of national policy. This could lead progressively toward the removal of military power and war as a major factor in international relations.

Questions

1. Is the idea of a ''non-violent substitute for war'' meaningful?
2. Sharp lists a number of historical events of this century wherein nonviolent defence has been successful. Can you add events of the

1980s to the list? Is Sharp correct in thinking that events of the sort he lists provide relevant evidence for evaluating the efficacy of non-military defence strategies? If the evidence is relevant, is it convincing?

3. Is relying on nuclear weapons for defence purposes morally acceptable? Is unilateral disarmament the only alternative? Is unilateral disarmament morally acceptable?

Message Transmitted from a Distant Constellation

Our world is a world
of great winds ranging over continents
in herds, rogue ears held
aloft, straddling fig trees
impetuously, mating moistly with mountains,
yet side-stepping cobwebs out of ancient respect.

This world is a world
where shafts of sunlight smoke into the oceans,
where ceaseless tongues stir up a cloud
of dust, where bent pillars of sulphur
lean above our cities, though a lingering scent
on the sheets at dawn still smells of grass.

This world, our world,
brings reprieves to the just executed,
inheritances to the yet unconceived, rebirth
to dawns and small stones, but extraditions
to whole continents. The lips of our youngest
children taste continually of storms.

This world, as a world,
was always too large or too
small to know how to live on; its sunsets
too sudden to distribute fairly.
We frequently fought for a share of the clouds
and soft blouses for our women in summer.

Our world is a world
where youth always, suprisingly, ended.
Morning mist faded indiscernibly
for centuries. It was stored at the backs of our ancestors'
eyes. Each world has songs that won't ever
be sung, and its haze of vaporized pianos.

On our one world,
we are wearing our best for this special transmission.
Shoes no longer quite fit. We kiss you
across time on whatever you count as your lips.
Please don't bother to answer this. Disinfect
our words by rinsing them twice in your music.

Roger Nash

This poem and the one at the beginning of the chapter first appeared in *The Antigonish Review* and *Queen's Quarterly*. © Roger Nash.

Suggestions for Further Reading

Background Material

- National Conference of Catholic Bishops, ''The Challenge to Peace: God's Promise and Our Response'' (a pastoral letter), *The Chicago Catholic*, June 24–July 1, 1983. Probably the most important recent contribution to the just war debate. It surveys the traditional views of the use of military force by the Roman Catholic Church and applies those views to an assessment and a moral critique of American nuclear defence policies and armaments.
- Franklyn Griffiths and John Polanyi, eds., *The Dangers of Nuclear War* (Toronto: University of Toronto Press, 1979). This book comprises the proceedings of the 30th Pugwash Symposium held in Toronto in 1978. Though some of the articles are now somewhat dated, the section ''The Avoidance of Nuclear War up to the Present'' is of substantial and continuing interest. The contributors include W. McGeorge Bundy, John Steinbruner, Vice-Admiral Miller (Ret.), and George Ignatieff.
- Thomas L. Perry, M.D. and Dianne DeMille, eds., *Nuclear War: The Search for Solutions* (Vancouver: Physicians for Social Responsibility, B.C. Chapter, P.O. Box 35426, Station E; 1985). This collection results from a symposium held in October 1984 at the University of British Columbia. It includes a wide variety of articles contributed by former military personnel, politicians, Soviet Union representatives, strategists, and academics. Two of the contributions to this chapter are drawn from this collection. Of particular interest are ''Nuclear Winter: Global Effects of Nuclear War'' by Richard Turco and ''Contributions of Game Theory to Peace Education'' by Anatol Rapoport. The latter paper explores and develops a number of themes introduced in a less technical way by Conrad Brunk in his contribution to this chapter.
- Ernie Reghr and Simon Rosenblum, eds., *Canada and the Nuclear Arms Race* (Toronto: James Lorimer, 1983). This book is a compendium of

articles drawn together by two well-known Canadian crusaders against the nuclear arms race. Contributors examine nuclear armaments from social, economic, ethical, religious, and military perspectives.

- *Canadian Spectrum* (R.R. 2, Lyden, Ontario) is published by The Inter-Professional Centre for Arms Control, an educational and research organization concerned solely with nuclear arms control issues. *Canadian Spectrum* is a newcomer to Canadian journalism that attempts to present both sides of the controversial issues surrounding nuclear armaments, using direct quotations from well-known magazines and national newspapers. The early editions describe it as an excellent source of concrete discussions of nuclear weapons, the arms race, disarmament issues, and the merits of contemporary defence strategies such as Star Wars. At the time of this writing, it is not certain whether this journal will survive.
- *Disarmament: A Comprehensive Study on Nuclear Weapons* (New York: United Nations Centre for Disarmament, 1981). Commissioned by the UN, this study provides information on present nuclear arsenals (now somewhat dated but still significant) and addresses such topics as the effects of the use of nuclear weapons, doctrines of deterrence, and disarmament issues.

Philosophical Anthologies

- Volume 95 of *Ethics* (April 1985) is devoted to a discussion of the ethics of nuclear deterrence. The volume contains excellent assessments of the central justifications and criticisms of nuclear deterrence by strategists and philosophers. The contribution by Robert Art in this chapter is drawn from this issue of *Ethics*.
- Michael Allen Fox and Leo Groarke, eds., *Nuclear War: Philosophical Perspectives* (New York: Peter Lang, 1985). This anthology results from a conference held at the University of Waterloo in 1984. Articles and commentaries are organized under the following heads: ''Nuclear Delusions,'' ''The Individual and the State,'' ''The Environment,'' ''Conceptual and Psychological Dilemmas,'' and ''The Pursuit of Peace.'' Two of the contributions in this chapter are drawn from the Fox and Groarke anthology.
- Richard A. Wasserstrom, *War and Morality* (Belmont, California: Wadsworth Publishing Co., 1970). This book does not focus on nuclear deterrence; however, it does introduce and discuss some of the classic justifications of the use of military force. Included is an article on pacifism referred to below.

Disarmament and Pacifism

- Jan Narveson, ''Pacifism: A Philosophical Analysis,'' in *War and Morality*, cited above. This is a widely cited attack on pacifist responses to aggression in which the author argues that the only philosophically interesting version of pacifism is logically untenable.

- Cheney C. Ryan, ''Self-Defense, Pacifism and the Possibility of Killing,'' *Ethics*, April, 1983. This article evaluates the various justifications of the use of violence in self-defence and concludes that all are faulty. In the course of his argument, Ryan evaluates and rejects Narveson's criticisms of pacifism.

- Conrad Brunk, ''Pacifism: A Philosophical Defence.'' In this as-yet-unpublished paper, Brunk undertakes a systematic analysis of Narveson's arguments. He concludes that pacifism, as it has been traditionally defended by religious communities like the Mennonites, is indeed a coherent and defensible response to military aggression. The paper is available from the author.

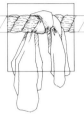

Philosophy and the Resolution of Moral Issues

Introduction

Any human activity can be approached at two levels. We might call the first the level of participation and the second the level of reflection. Thus, for example, we can participate in a game like hockey or chess. Or we can stand back and reflect on the nature of the game and how it is played.

Resolving moral issues can be thought of as an activity. And, as with any human activity, we can, if we wish, participate by becoming involved in discussions aimed at resolving particular issues. Or we can stand back and reflect on the nature of morality and how moral problems are solved. As with most activities, of course, serious reflection presupposes some direct experience with the activity itself. That is one of the reasons the approach to moral issues that has dominated this book has been that of participant in the activity of resolving concrete moral issues. However, participation in the resolution of concrete moral issues raises questions which are genuinely interesting in their own right, questions which can be approached only by reflecting on our own attempts, as well as the attempts of others, to resolve particular moral problems.

What kinds of questions are suggested by discussion and argument in previous chapters? I shall highlight just two. First, one of the striking features of the readings collected in this anthology is the extent to which those who have made serious efforts to develop and support positions on particular issues disagree. What are we to conclude from this fact? One possible response is simply to throw up one's hands in frustration and go on to some more ''productive'' activity. But this response has serious implications. The issues we have been examining are important and virtually unavoidable. If we cannot resolve them through rational discussion, how are they going to be resolved? Through the use of force? By subterfuge? Some would argue (as for example in the capital-punishment debate) that the position of the majority should prevail. But this, too, has worrisome implications, which require careful exploration. It would seem, on reflection, that there is no ''easy'' way to escape the fact that well-intentioned people do disagree on moral questions. Why is this so? Does it tell us something of importance about the nature of morality?

Consideration of these questions has given rise to a number of positions, many of which are reflected in readings in previous chapters. Faced with disagreement on moral questions, some have opted for a position of moral relativism, a view of morality which the values-clarification approach (see Chapter 8) would seem to imply. Others, for example Jan Narveson in ''Moral Philiosphy—What It Is and Why It Matters!'' (Chapter 7), reject this view. An alternative position might be that not all moral disputes are alike. In some cases agreement can be achieved and in some cases it cannot. This view may be implied by Grant Cosby in the reading ''Abortion, An Unresolved Issue'' (Chapter 1). Cosby appears to argue that while agreement on how we ought or ought not to treat persons is possible at least in some cases (where murder is involved, for example), it may not be possible to reach agreement based on rational argument in other cases—for example, whether an unborn child is a person.

Finally, some have argued that there are basic principles which no agent could rationally reject. If moral argument is built on those principles, agreement should be possible. This view would seem to be implied by Andrew Brook in his discussion of our obligations to future generations (Chapter 7) and by J.T. Stevenson in his discussion of aboriginal rights (Chapter 6).

Asking whether moral issues can be resolved would seem to lead to further questions: Is the resolution of moral issues a general responsibility? Or is it a task which can be or ought to be assigned to experts? If so, do moral philosophers have the requisite expertise?

There is one sense in which responsibility for resolving moral problems clearly cannot be assigned to others. If I am faced with a request by an ill person that he be helped in terminating his life, then I must respond to the request. No one else can do it for me. In this sense no one can assign responsibility for his own behaviour to someone else. But it is always possible to seek advice in deciding what to do. We might, then, rephrase our question by asking whether moral philosophers are a good source of advice for those who are faced with difficult moral problems.

We can now see how this question is related to the first. By participating in the discussion of moral issues, philosophers imply that moral issues can, at least on occasion, be resolved. They also imply that as philosophers they have something to contribute in that regard. As we have seen, moral philosophers are also prone to reflect on the nature of morality and the features of moral argument. And frequently what is said at the level of reflection is designed to guide the first-order activity of the participant. So we can ask whether philosophers—as philosophers rather than simply as interested participants—have a special contribution to make to the resolution of moral issues. If so, what is the nature of that contribution? It is this set of questions which provides the focus for the readings that follow.

The Readings

Terence Penelhum introduces the discussion by asking whether as a society we have the moral resources to deal with the moral issues with which we are confronted today. He argues in that there is a sense in which philosophers can be said to have moral expertise. They are trained to work with concepts or ideas, they are experts in detecting errors of reasoning, and they have the time to search out the relevant facts and to reflect on them. Béla Szabados takes issue with Singer. He argues that there are moral experts but that the study of philosophy is unlikely to impart the skills which expertise demands. And there are some aspects of the moral life where the notion of expertise has no place. Kai Nielsen continues the dialogue by arguing that Szabados has neglected an important aspect of moral argument, namely that aspect that deals not simply with the individual faced with moral dilemmas but with "the design of a well-ordered society." Central to the discussion are the development and evaluation of philosophical theories about the nature of man and the nature of society. Finally, Michael McDonald argues that much of the contribution of contemporary moral philosophy to the resolution of current moral issues is based on ideological and philosophical presuppositions which are inevitably inadequate to the task of elucidating and developing some of our most important moral values. If moral philosophers are to make a genuine contribution to the resolution of moral issues, the atomistic or excessively individualistic interpretation of the idea of moral autonomy will have to be replaced with a philosophical theory which provides a greater understanding of the social dimensions of human existence.

This chapter is designed to draw your attention to an aspect of moral philosophy which many have regarded as essential to the resolution of moral issues, namely the development and evaluation of moral theories. Theories have played an important role in much of the argument in preceding chapters. A possible next step in the exploration of moral philosophy and its role in the resolution of moral issues, then, would be the study of moral theory. The suggested readings with which this chapter concludes are designed to provide some guidance for such study.

Our Technology and Our Moral Resources

Terence Penelhum

I think I can best introduce the range of problems I want to address by referring to a recent newspaper item and the way it affected me. Some weeks ago, I noticed a report, with photograph, of an event that took place at the Science Expo in Tsukuba, Japan.[1] A couple were shown, according to the caption, being married by a robot "priest," which conducted the wedding ceremony before about 70 witnesses. The couple were wearing "metallic silver wedding garb," although the intended significance of this fact was not indicated. Perhaps it was to reduce the visual differences between the all-metal robot and the wedding couple, but there were no quotation marks around the words "couple" or "wedding."

As my tone may have indicated, I was very negative in my response to this report. But the initial negativity was followed by two other reactions, which I would like to use to introduce my arguments. First of all, I tried to get a little clearer about what it was about this story that offended me. As a philosopher, and as an aging technopeasant, I have learned to ask myself this question when confronted with novelties that do not appeal to me. I decided that what I found offensive was the fact that a machine was being enlisted to perform a role that properly belonged only to a human being, and indeed only to a human being of special status and authority: namely, the role of approving, and perhaps sanctifying, one of the key rites of passage in two human lives; and that the two human lives were being in some way cheapened by the fact that the subjects of them consented to this.

But identifying the object of my distaste set up a further train of thought. Perhaps my negative response to this story was only a rationalization of my refusal, as a privileged citizen of a less technologically advanced era, to acknowledge the benefits of recent inventions. Was I not just one more of those academics who rush round the world in jet planes to foregather with colleagues whom they would never otherwise set eyes on, in order to bewail the dehumanizing effects of technology? Was what this couple were doing so very bad? Aren't a number of real flesh and blood clergy and magistrates less responsive, less articulate, and more mechanical than a well-programmed robot? Could a robot not, at least, be guaranteed to follow the prescribed form of ceremony without forgetting its lines? If their participation in this new ritual indicated a less solemn view of marriage than mine, was that not, perhaps, a more accurate reflection of what the institution of marriage has become? And ought I not, as a citizen of our multicultural world, to accept benignly whatever view of personal relationships two other persons choose to follow together, even if it is not the same as mine?

In other words, my initial reaction was followed by a counterreaction, in which I contended with a complex form of self-doubt, which made me wonder how far to trust my own moral judgement.

Reprinted with slight alterations from *Transactions of The Royal Society of Canada* 4 (1985) (23): 33–44. By permission of the author and of the Royal Society of Canada.

I think my ambivalence is not unique. Indeed, I think a similar ambivalence is typical of the response of a large class of people, of varying moral persuasions, when confronted repeatedly with new applications of contemporary technology. And I do not think we can understand what that technology is doing to us unless the elements in our ambivalence are explored further.

I

I said that my episode of self-doubt was a complex one. People have a multitude of different reasons for worrying about their own moral judgements. I want to concentrate on two.

In the first place, I was concerned at having responded only to one of the moral aspects of the situation, and not to others. I was anxious, in other words, to avoid being morally bigoted—a moral bigot being someone who confines his or her attention to one such aspect exclusively. One of our culture's great positive achievements is its fear of moral bigotry, this fear being an expression of its determination to be tolerant of moral differences. As a product of this culture, I had recoiled instinctively from the temptation to see the situation as a morally simple one, and had instead viewed it as a possible source of moral conflict or dilemma.

But this was not the whole of it. I was reflecting my culture in another way, which is often confused with the first, and which is not commendable at all. In addition to being troubled by the moral complexities of the situations we are placed in, most of us are troubled by the fact that it is *we* who are called upon to make these moral decisions; we feel we are *unqualified* to make them. In an era unique in history for the number of new moral problems that must be decided upon, we who have to decide upon them are afflicted with a failure of nerve about our capacity to do it. We doubt whether we have the *moral resources*. I think we do. But I want to look at the reasons for the very common view that we have not; and then to go back to the nature of the dilemmas that technology forces us to face, and enquire how our moral resources can be drawn upon to help us resolve them. I shall be talking throughout about our ability to make the right judgements, and not about our power to see to it that these judgements can be carried out. I shall be dealing, in other words, with our moral resources, not our political or economic or military resources.

II

We have all heard it said repeatedly that in modern society our scientific and technical knowledge has advanced dramatically, but that our moral knowledge has not kept pace. I think this view is quite false, but I will approach that conclusion slowly, because I think it should be said, first of all, that it is not too clear what it means.[2] It might mean that while we can tell a very impressive story of progress, in the sciences, beginning with the ancient Greeks, or the ancient Egyptians, or the medieval alchemists, and proceeding through Archimedes, Roger Bacon, Galileo, Newton, and Darwin, to Einstein, we cannot tell a parallel story of *moral* growth and success. But we can. We can start with Socrates, and go on through Plato and Aristotle, divert through Moses and the prophets, consider the preaching of Jesus, and then tell a continuous story of moral development incorporating such names as those of

Augustine, St. Francis, Thomas Aquinas, Butler, Kant, Wilberforce, John Stuart Mill, Gandhi, and Martin Luther King. If someone says that this list is not a success story in the way that the other one was, why is it not? Is it because in the one case there is an increasing body of knowledge and understanding, but not in the other? Not at all: each of these great moral figures built upon the achievements of his predecessors, and said so, each produced new insights, and each was articulate and effective in spreading the insights he had acquired, just as all the great scientific figures I named were able to do. Is it because the scientists have all left us unassailable truths which have been passed on to everyone and become part of the universal fund of common-sense knowledge, whereas the moralists have not? No, because we have a substantial fund of common ethical knowledge, which has in many cases come to us largely through the teachings and insights of the people on my list. I doubt, for example, whether many of our acquaintances would admit to *not knowing* that one should not return evil for evil; but human beings used not to know that, and they learned it from Socrates and from Jesus, primarily. I doubt whether many would admit to *not knowing* that slavery is morally evil; but people a few centuries ago had not learned that, even from Socrates and Jesus, and they had to learn it from Wilberforce and his friends, but they did. And I doubt whether many would admit to *not knowing* that freedom of speech is a moral right; but people used not to realize it was, and had to learn it from thinkers like John Stuart Mill—and some have not grasped it properly even now.

No doubt some would say that I have missed the point. Even if there is a real body of developing moral knowledge, there is also a great deal of moral disagreement; and the knowledge I have been pointing to is only found in *our* society and some other societies like it, and so it must be, as they say, "culture-relative." Now if these things really show that there is not a real body of developing moral knowledge, then it is just as easy to produce an argument that would show there is no real body of developing scientific knowledge. For there is lots of scientific disagreement, and always has been; and there are plenty of societies in which the truths *we* have learned from Newton, Darwin, and Einstein are not recognized. I agree that such an argument would look absurd; but that shows that the parallel argument against moral knowledge probably has no merit either. The existence of primitives and ignoramuses does not show there is no knowledge to be had, only that there are lots of people who have not acquired it, and this goes for the one body of knowledge as much as the other.

Another thing that might be meant when it is said that our moral knowledge has not kept pace with our science is that although most of us are better able to *do* things requiring technology than our ancestors were, our actions are not *morally* better than the actions of our ancestors. I do not propose to argue about this claim, except to say that it, too, is hard to assess. This is because it is hard to decide what would confirm or refute it, and it is not as open-and-shut as it looks when you consider the evidence. Undoubtedly most of us can drive cars and mend fuses and run vacuum cleaners and dial our friends on the telephone; and our ancestors did not know how to do any of these things. But if these things show that developing technical knowledge has been put to use, then it can be noticed that slavery has been formally abolished virtually everywhere, that we increasingly follow the principle that wrongdoers should be rehabilitated rather than visited with retribution, and that the right of free speech is far more widely honoured than it used to be and is nominally respected even in many places where it is denied in practice. Undoubtedly these are all very partial successes, and there are vast tracts of moral failure and evil; but even in our sophisticated age, people have automobile crashes, and electrocute themselves, and get wrong telephone numbers. But having said all that, I have to agree that in some sense which is obvious, even though hard to state, there is a more unambiguous increase in the application of our scientific and technological knowledge than in the application of our deepening moral understanding—if only because the morally *bad* applications of technology, like nuclear weapons, count on the credit side in the one case, but not in the other.

But even though this is true, it is irrelevant. For what I have been examining up to now is the common belief that our moral knowledge has not kept pace with our scientific knowledge, not the quite different belief that we have not *applied* our moral knowledge as effectively as we have applied our scientific knowledge. There is a fundamental difference between saying that we are able to see what we ought to do with our new technical powers, but are too morally weak, or too self-interested, or too lacking in political will, to do what we see we should; and saying that we are not capable even of seeing what we should do with these powers. To say the first is to bewail our moral character. To say the second is to say we lack moral understanding. I am not suggesting we have all the moral character we need. But I am suggesting that we are not as badly placed as we like to think we are when it comes to moral understanding. I will go even further. I suggest we have a strong inclination, in our culture, to tell ourselves we cannot make moral judgements in order to avoid confronting our character-defects: to pretend we are mixed up when in fact we are morally weak.

III

I have been trying to enter a protest against the popular view that we are blessed with ever-greater scientific knowledge but cursed with incorrigible moral ignorance. I have tried to do this by listing some very familiar facts that we all know. Many will be impatient with an argument like this. Haven't I heard that whereas science is international, objective, and value-free, moral judgements are reflections of culture-specific wants and habits, are irreducibly subjective, and redolent of emotion? Yes, I have; and the lack of confidence about our moral resources that I have been criticizing is usually expressed in terms of these contrasts. I cannot explore them in detail here, and the literature on them is a vast one. Instead I want to emphasize that when claims like this are made we are in the realm of philosophical *theory*, not that of moral judgement itself. And the reason why there are such widespread doubts in our culture about our ability to arrive at viable moral judgements in the face of rapid technological change, is that our popular culture has become deeply imbued with certain philosophical theories, just as it has also been deeply imbued with psychoanalytic theories and used to be deeply imbued with religious doctrines. A number of second-order philosophical theories about the nature of moral thought have come to be widely accepted by the public at large. These theories are of a *skeptical* character, and have a very long history usually unknown to those whose assumptions have been affected by them. Skeptical moral theory is ethically enervating. A theory, of course, can be enervating and still true, just as it can be invigorating and still false. I want to argue, briefly, not only that skeptical theories about our moral judgements are ethically enervating but that there are some strong reasons against them.

The skeptical tradition in Western philosophy goes back at least to the fifth century B.C., when Socrates reacted against it.[3] For many centuries it consisted of a body of arguments which questioned our confidence *both* in our power to learn how the world is *and* in our power to determine how we should live in it. Skeptical arguments cast doubt on the real possibility of both science and moral knowledge. And just as the Skeptics attacked both together, so their opponents, like Socrates, Plato, and Aristotle, defended the credentials of both together without denying the differences between them. Broadly speaking, Skeptic arguments were based upon the fact that in both these spheres of thought the conditions under which human beings come to make their judgements affect the judgements they make. For example, our perceptual judgements about the objects around us are affected by the light in which we see them, the distortions of perspective, or the state of the perceiver's health; and the judgements we make about what is good or evil are coloured by the interests and prejudices of the particular city or country or class we belong to. Since *all* our judgements are made under *some* such conditions, we can never be sure, the Skeptics argued, that we have an undistorted opinion of how reality is. We have to be content with the way it appears to us in the time or place where we find ourselves.

Historically, this line of thought was both debilitating and inevitably conservative, and scientific and moral progress has always taken place because it has been disregarded. The literature of Skepticism exhibits great intellectual ingenuity and dialectical skill; but it is all expended on the task of showing, or trying to show, that this or that alleged criterion of truth is a failure. Instead of looking for ultimate truths, it is said, we had best give up and recognize that our opinions are the results of the environment that has produced us and that there are no good reasons to suppose we can better them. A realization of this will lead to inner peace, because it will stop us from contending with those whose opinions have come to be different, and will reconcile us to the received teachings and practices of our own society. It is easy to see that the commonplace relativism and subjectivism of our popular culture are contained in outline in this ancient tradition.

But in modern times skepticism has taken a new turn. Although there have been more modern skeptics than is generally realized, on the whole skepticism about *science* has almost no supporters. But skepticism about *morals* is a cornerstone of popular wisdom. I think the main historical reason for this is that since the seventeenth century it has been a high cultural and economic priority to permit scientific research and technological application to go forward without political, and (above all) without theological, interference. One has only to remember Galileo to see why. This determination to protect scientific advances from intrusion has been given every possible theoretical and cultural support, and from this we inherit all those standard dualisms and contrasts which have been designed to prove that science is an autonomous, objective, value-free enterprise into which clerics and politicians have no right to poke their noses. Matters of value, on the other hand, could not be exempted from such scrutiny, since *they* had to be offered to the spiritual authorities as the price of peace. The need for this sort of cultural compromise is long gone, but the intellectual effects of it are still with all of us. All first-year students reject skepticism about scientific truth with instant contempt if it is put to them; but they embrace skepticism about morals with passionate conviction whether it is put to them or not.

I said that skepticism about moral judgements is ethically enervating, and that there are some strong reasons against it. There is no need to separate these two very sharply. For the primary difficulty facing the various kinds of moral skepticism is the fact that in our actual moral discourse we make use of notions that moral skepticism implies we have no right to use. We could not, for example, try to decide in court whether the defendant knew right from wrong at the time he committed the act for which he is being tried, if we believed that no one is ever *really* able to know right from wrong. Similarly, we cannot, without a similar inconsistency, say that the Nazis were morally wrong to commit the outrages of the Holocaust, while admitting that their culture encouraged such acts, if we do not think that our moral judgements express moral realities as opposed to cultural appearances; the most we can say is that *our* culture disposes *us* to consider they were morally wrong. It is just as true in ethics as it is in science that actual moral discernments occur because skeptical theories are disregarded. But it is only too clear, in my view, that skeptical moral theories have not been disregarded enough, and have made us hesitant to pass moral judgements when we need to do so. I now regard my own hesitations about the wedding couple and the robot as an example of such improper reluctance.

Hume said that while the errors in religion are dangerous, those in philosophy are only ridiculous.[4] I think the prevalence of moral skepticism shows him to have been mistaken about this.

I do not claim to have refuted skepticism. This is notoriously hard to do. What I have argued is merely this: that in our day we seem happy to live with one form of skepticism (about morals), while being unwilling even to consider another (about science), when the case for one is as good, or as bad, as the case for the other. I have been remarking on what a strange geological fault in our mentality this is.

IV

I have attacked this fault in our mentality because I think it has led to a failure of nerve in many of us when we confront the need to make moral decisions in the face of technical innovations. The reason we need to recover our nerve is that the moral problems we have to face are real, deep, and difficult, so that we need to take proper measure of our powers to deal with them.

What sorts of moral problems are they? Many of them are what I have called moral *dilemmas*.[5] In most moral dilemmas, two or more moral principles, each of which applies to our situation, yield conflicting obligations. We are all familiar with occasions when our moral principles conflict, in the sense that we cannot follow one of them without violating another. There is a moral cost to pay even if we make the right choice between them, for even though we will then have decided to do the right thing, there will still be some thing that we ought to do that we will not do. There is a simple example in Plato's *Republic*: if a friend entrusts a weapon to me, and then he goes crazy, most of us would agree that we should not return it to him when he asks for it, even though we do have an obligation to return property that is entrusted to us. This dilemma is easy to resolve, but some are very hard. Think of trying to advise a friend whether to stay in an unhappy marriage for the sake of the children, or of trying to decide whether to yield to the claims of openness or those of secrecy in the law relating to adoptions. It is also common to find that what one person thinks it hard to resolve, another thinks easy—because they have different estimates of the importance of the principles which clash.

Our present technological world is presenting us with a large number of *hard* dilemmas. And one vocal segment of the population thinks the resolution of each dilemma should go one way, and another thinks it should go the opposite way, and the rest of us are torn, wishing we could indulge in the luxury of not deciding. The respect for persons that is characteristic of our moral culture leads us to seek their fullest development and satisfaction by relieving them of drudgery, perfecting their performance in intellectual tasks, and facilitating their access to information; but in the very act of doing these things we render them vulnerable to displacement, emptiness, and intrusion. Which of these evils are we going to allow our society to perpetrate? If we have to put up with some of each, how much of one is equal morally to how much of the other? How are the ecological costs of increased cultivation and food production to be weighed against the more familiar catastrophes of hunger and disease? How are we to weigh the relative demerits of security bought with the threat of mutual destruction, and insecurity brought on by reliance on conventional defences? In each of these cases, our choice entails our accepting a major evil we would not, by itself, wish even to contemplate.

These are all moral dilemmas of great gravity; but although our age is uniquely productive of such dilemmas, they are not problems of a new form. Some recent technical advances, however, seem to present us with dilemmas of a genuinely new kind. Many would argue that the nuclear threat does this, for, they say, in the past the most dramatic dilemmas, though they may well have involved facing the deaths of many individuals, have never entailed the possible death of *all* the morally relevant individuals; this is an outcome that is not commensurate with any other evils that could be weighed against it in our moral scales. Whatever the merits of this view, I would like to draw attention to perplexities that are more obviously new in their form, however we assess their relative gravity. These surface as a result of the recent explosion in biological knowledge, which I think has to take pride of place currently as a source of moral perplexities. Some of these are conventional in their form though new in their detail. For example, the nearly universal recognition that humans are animals, and that there is a mutual ecological dependence with other species, has prompted a new sensitivity to the needs of other species so that we no longer look with total indifference on the fact that developing food resources for ourselves involves destroying the habitat of other creatures. But the very same increase in the understanding of our biological natures has also led to greater technological control over the mechanisms of human reproduction, which has stimulated renewed emphasis on the *distinctive* character of human procreation. So biological advances have led to developments in moral thinking which stress our likeness to the beasts on the one hand, and our differences from them on the other, and these emphases are likely to lead to opposed moral demands.

But let me come to a more genuinely new form of dilemma. One of the most famous of the Greek myths is the story of Sisyphus, who was condemned to roll a heavy stone uphill, only to have to see it roll down again as it reached the top, on and on, forever. This is the classical paradigm of the meaningless life.

Suppose someone suggests that the gods could turn Sisyphus' hell into heaven, by the simple expedient of changing his nature, so that he is forever dominated by a craving to push heavy stones up hills;[6] then the fact that they roll back again when he gets to the top will be a good thing, because it will ensure that he will have unending opportunity to do the thing he wants most of all to do. I think we would feel that something had gone wrong somewhere; that this would *not* give adequate meaning to the life of Sisyphus, even though he might now be quite happy at his work. It is probably impossible to articulate what is wrong with this proposed solution to his plight without invoking the idea of human *nature*—a concept which all red-blooded moral philosophers would love to do without. I think we would all want to say that Sisyphus would still lack real happiness, because some basic need of his nature would still be violated. It is a world of beings violated in this way, who are happy in the constant satisfaction of desires that have been programmed into them, that Huxley depicts for us in *Brave New World*. Now the theoretical possibilities of genetic manipulation seem to me to go beyond even this concern. For it is now easy enough to imagine someone suggesting that whatever feature of human nature would render that implantation inadequate as a solution could itself be corrected, and our anxieties forestalled. For generations thinkers have argued about what forms of life and society are desirable by asking which forms best meet the needs of our natures, and they have all assumed that there is a common human nature, while differing a great deal about what it is. But speculations about genetic engineering do not just raise questions about what sort of life best fits our natures. They raise questions about *what sort of nature* it is a good thing to have. This looks like a question of a totally new order.[7] How is one to decide what human nature should best be? This question is deeply perplexing because it places a question mark against all the standard supports of our moral principles, which we tend to see as ways of living that best fit our nature as it is. If it does not have to *be* the way it is, such justifications are inevitably much weakened.

V

So I do not suggest that the moral problems our modern technology presents to us are simple to solve. But I have emphasized that we are not without moral resources in approaching them. For we do have a substantial body of moral principles which are not just simple rules learned from schoolbooks, but represent the accumulated moral perceptions of generations, and have been tested, over the generations, both by the experience of those who have followed them and by that of those who have not. We also have available to us a wide range of reflection and reasoning devoted to the criticism of moral principles and the resolution of conflicts between them. It would be very surprising if all of this were irrelevant now, even though it is true that our circumstances are changing more rapidly than ever before, and we are in constant danger of major moral decisions being made by default because we have not had time enough to ponder them. I think we even have some preparation for the radical rethinking of moral priorities that I last mentioned, for decisions about how human beings might best change can be illuminated if we understand how different attempts to satisfy their present natures have succeeded or failed.

Now all this may show, certainly, that none of us can escape taking part in the resolution of the dilemmas that our growth in technological knowledge keeps creating. But to some, this will point up yet another contrast between the realms of science and morals; namely the alleged absence of *experts* in morality, when there are experts galore in the sciences. I will finish by addressing this issue.

There are, of course, a group of people who have for centuries addressed problems about the justification of our moral principles, the relationship between them, and the kinds of change they should undergo. They are moral philosophers. Moral philosophy began with Socrates and Plato, who believed that philosophers, rightly trained, could become moral experts of such quality that the reins of society should be put in their hands. There have not been many philosophers in recent years who have proclaimed this, even though our Western tradition of liberal education owes more to Plato's programme of training than to any other single influence. It is not so long ago, either, that the majority of moral philosophers insisted that they had no moral expertise to offer at all, and could only propound theoretical analyses of the nature of moral reasoning and the meaning of moral terms. We are at present in a period where moral philosophers are again addressing actual moral problems, including some of those ethical dilemmas of which I have been speaking, and the competence of some of them seems to have gained a certain amount of social acceptance:—for example with the inclusion of philosophers on the ethical committees of many hospitals.[8]

It would be very dreary for me to use this occasion to urge the claims of my own discipline, and I am not about to do so—partly because I am not a moral philosopher in any case. But it is wise to look at the claims of the philosophical expert to be a source of specialist assistance in our common quest for the resolution of our contemporary dilemmas. Since I have maintained we have a fund of moral knowledge to draw upon in tackling these dilemmas, it would be surprising if I did not also think that some people have more of this moral knowledge than others have. In fact I gave a list of some of those people whose moral insights we have all learned from. Now some of them were moral *philosophers*, but others were persons of moral genius who were not philosophers. The skills that philosophers cultivate are, of course, those of perceiving consequences, performing conceptual analyses, discerning clashes of principle, detecting non sequiturs, and the like, and the ability to exercise these essentially logical skills on moral subjects, is, I think, one vitally important *part* of moral expertise. And it is one we all need to draw on when reflecting on moral dilemmas. So there is a clear sense in which everyone is called upon, from time to time, to do *some* moral philosophy.

Monsieur Jourdain was delighted when he was told that he had been talking prose all his life without knowing it. Experience teaches me, however, that my acquaintances are likely to respond with hostility or boredom when told that the discussion they have just been engaged in was philosophy. So I hasten to add once more that the insights we all need to draw upon do not come exclusively from philosophers, but from expert persons in many fields: cultural historians, who know about the way in which changes in moral principle have affected human societies; anthropologists, who know about how differing conceptions of kin relationships affect social structures; economists, who know about the interrelation between economic interest and social ideals; and psychologists, who can tell us about developmental factors in the formation of moral commitments. Not all the practitioners of these disciplines have moral expertise, but some do—namely those who enlist their insights in the service of our moral needs. I need hardly say that great imaginative literature is a well-known vehicle for the expression of moral expertise and the exploration of moral conflict. We are not short of moral experts; if anything, we have too many of them. What we need in any generation is people who can sift the moral resources such persons have made available to the culture, relate it to present moral dilemmas, and help resolve *our* moral conflicts. I make no apology for suggesting that this sort of analysis and synthesis is a particularly philosophical task.

It is sometimes said that you have to be a morally good person to be a moral expert. Aristotle, for example, seemed to believe this.[9] My own view is that moral goodness is not a necessary condition for moral expertise, but that it helps. Some of the names I have listed were persons of conspicuous moral goodness; others were not. But then, some medical experts smoke.

VI

I conclude by returning to the couple who were married by the robot, and the morals to be drawn from our reactions to such things. We should not be troubled by the fact that we have moral responses like these, for they show that these new phenomena come within the range of the principles which our moral heritage has instilled into us. We are right, nevertheless, always to review and to question such responses, since the very newness of these phenomena makes it likely that they will be within the range of several principles at once, and may require us to reflect on how to develop new ones. Only reflection and experience can help us decide whether it is the principle that first comes to mind, or the countervailing ones that come to mind later, that should win.

As these conflicts proliferate and disagreements abound, we need to draw upon that special combination of logical skill, imagination, and sympathy that I have called moral expertise. The real recipe for calamity is to use the very skills it involves in the service of some form of moral skepticism which undermines our will to resolve them. For skepticism in all its forms is a self-deceiving tradition that enables intellectuals to indulge in the professional pleasures of destructive intellectual activity at a safe distance from the quandaries which they have the training to resolve, but not the will. There are signs that what has hitherto been a form of indulgence for a small number of philosophers like Carneades or Montaigne or Hume, is being used as an escape mechanism by much larger numbers of anxious moral agents confronted with changes they do not know whether to fear or to welcome. We should face these changes with a confidence that may never match that of the scientists and technicians who generate them, but at least reflects a realistic awareness that we can meet our responsibilities.

Notes

1. The report was an Associated Press item in *The Calgary Herald*, Sunday, April 21, 1985.

2. I am much indebted in what follows to Renford Bambrough, *Moral Scepticism and Moral Knowledge* (London: Routledge and Kegan Paul, 1979).

3. Scholarly awareness of the extent and complexity of the skeptical tradition has recently increased. See, for example, Myles Burnyeat, ed., *The Skeptical Tradition* (Berkeley: University of California Press, 1983). The most important classical text is Sextus Empiricus' *Outlines of Pyrrhonism*, available in Vol. 1 of the Loeb Classical Library edition of Sextus, trans. J.B. Bury (London: Heinemann, 1967).

4. See "Conclusion" in Book I of *A Treatise of Human Nature*, p. 272 in the Clarendon edition, L.A. Selby-Bigge, ed., rpt. 1968.

5. A classic article on this theme is E.J. Lemmon, "Moral Dilemmas," *Philosophical Review*, Vol. LXXI (1962), pp. 139–158.

6. This suggestion is made by Richard Taylor in *Good and Evil* (New York: Macmillan, 1970), Ch. 18. It is discussed at some length in David Wiggins's "Truth, Invention, and the Meaning of Life," *Proceedings of The British Academy*, Vol. LXII (1976), pp. 331–378.

7. I am indebted here to some comments in a public lecture by Professor Stephen Stich.

8. For a valuable collection of papers assessing the recent philosophical work in "applied ethics" see the special issue of *The Monist*, Vol. 67 (1984), No. 4. For good analyses of the concept of moral expertise, see Béla Szabados, "On 'Moral Expertise,' " *Canadian Journal of Philosophy*, Vol. VIII (1978), pp. 117–130 and Terrance C. McConnell, "Objectivity and Moral Expertise," *Canadian Journal of Philosophy*, Vol. XIV (1984), pp. 193–216.

9. "It is clear, then, from what has been said, that it is not possible to be good in the strict sense without practical wisdom, nor practically wise without moral virtue." *Nicomachean Ethics*, 1144b, 30.

Moral Experts

Peter Singer

The following position has been influential in recent moral philosophy: there is no such thing as moral expertise; in particular, moral philosophers are not moral experts. Leading philosophers have tended to say things like this:

> It is silly, as well as presumptuous, for any one type of philosopher to pose as the champion of virtue. And it is also one reason why many people find moral philosophy an unsatisfactory subject. For they

From *Analysis*, Vol. 32, No. 4 (March 1972), pp. 115–117.

mistakenly look to the moral philosopher for guidance. (A.J. Ayer, "The Analysis of Moral Judgments," in *Philosophical Essays*.)

or like this:

> It is no part of the professional business of moral philosophers to tell people what they ought or ought not to do. . . . Moral philosophers, as such, have no special information not available to the general public, about what is right and what is wrong; nor have they any call to undertake those hortatory functions which are so adequately performed by clergymen, politicians, leader-writers. . . . (C.D. Broad, *Ethics and the History of Philosophy*.)

Assertions like these are common; arguments in support of them less so. The role of the moral philosopher is not the role of the preacher, we are told. But why not? The reason surely cannot be, as Broad seems to suggest, that the preacher is doing the job "so adequately." It is because those people who are regarded by the public as "moral leaders of the community" have done so badly that "morality," in the public mind, has come to mean a system of prohibitions against certain forms of sexual enjoyment.

Another possible reason for insisting that moral philosophers are not moral experts is the idea that moral judgments are purely emotive, and that reason has no part to play in their formation. Historically, this theory may have been important in shaping the conception of moral philosophy that we have today. Obviously, if anyone's moral views are as good as anyone else's, there can be no moral experts. Such a crude version of emotivism, however, is held by few philosophers now, if indeed it was ever widely held. Even the views of C.L. Stevenson do not imply that anyone's moral views are as good as anyone else's.

A more plausible argument against the possibility of moral expertise is to be found in Ryle's essay "On Forgetting the Difference between Right and Wrong," which appeared in *Essays in Moral Philosophy*, edited by A. Melden. Ryle's point is that knowing the difference between right and wrong involves caring about it, so that it is not, in fact, really a case of knowing. One cannot, for instance, forget the difference between right and wrong. One can only cease to care about it. Therefore, according to Ryle, the honest man is not "even a bit of an expert at anything" (p. 157).

It is significant that Ryle says that "the honest man" is not an expert, and later he says the same of "the charitable man." His conclusion would have had less initial plausibility if he had said "the morally good man." Being honest and being charitable are often—though perhaps not as often as Ryle seems to think—comparatively simple matters, which we all can do, if we care about them. It is when, say, honesty clashes with charity (if a wealthy man overpays me, should I tell him, or give the money to famine relief?) that there is need for thought and argument. The morally good man must know how to resolve these conflicts of values. Caring about doing what is right is, of course, essential, but it is not enough, as the numerous historical examples of well-meaning but misguided men indicate.

Only if the moral code of one's society were perfect and undisputed, both in general principles and in their application to particular cases, would there be no need for the morally good man to be a thinking man. Then he could just live by the code, unreflectively. If, however, there is reason to believe that one's society does not have perfect norms, or if there are no agreed norms on a whole range of issues, the morally good man must try to think out for himself the question of what he ought to do. This "thinking out" is a difficult task. It requires, first, information. I may, for instance, be wondering whether it is right to eat meat. I would have a better chance of reaching the right decisions, or at least, a soundly based decision, if I knew a number of facts about the capacities of animals for suffering, and about the methods of rearing and slaughtering animals now being used. I might also want to know about the effect of a vegetarian diet on human health, and, considering the world food shortage, whether more or less food would be produced by giving up meat production. Once I have got evidence on these questions, I must assess it and bring it together with whatever moral views I hold. Depending on what method of moral reasoning I use, this may involve a calculation of which course of action produces greater happiness and less suffering; or it may mean an attempt to place myself in the positions of those affected by my decision; or it may lead me to attempt to "weigh up" conflicting duties and interests. Whatever method I employ, I must be aware of the possibility that my own desire to eat meat may lead to bias in my deliberations.

None of this procedure is easy—neither the gathering of information, nor the selection of what information is relevant, nor its combination with a basic moral position, nor the elimination of bias. Someone familiar with moral concepts and with moral arguments, who has ample time to gather information and think about it, may reasonably be expected to reach a soundly based conclusion more often than someone who is unfamiliar with moral concepts and moral arguments and has little time. So moral expertise would seem to be possible. The problem is not so much to know "the difference between right and wrong" as to decide what is right and what wrong.

If moral expertise is possible, have moral philosophers been right to disclaim it? Is the ordinary man just as likely to be expert in moral matters as the moral philosopher? On the basis of what has just been said, it would seem that the moral philosopher does have some important advantages over the ordinary man. First, his general training as a philosopher should make him more than ordinarily competent in argument and in the detection of invalid inferences. Next, his specific experience in moral philosophy gives him an understanding of moral concepts and of the logic of moral argument. The possibility of serious confusion arising if one engages in moral argument without a clear understanding of the concepts employed has been sufficiently emphasized in recent moral philosophy and does not need to be demonstrated here. Clarity is not an end in itself, but it is an aid to sound argument, and the need for clarity is something which moral philosophers have recognised. Finally, there is the simple fact that the moral philosopher can, if he wants, think full-time about moral issues, while most other people have some occupation to pursue which interferes with such reflection. It may sound silly to place much weight on this, but it is, I think very important. If we are to make moral judgments on some basis other than our unreflective intuitions, we need time, both for collecting facts and for thinking about them.

Moral philosophers have, then, certain advantages which could make them, relative to those who lack these advantages, experts in matters of morals. Of course, to be moral experts, it would be necessary for moral philosophers to do some fact-finding on whatever issue they were considering. Given a readiness to tackle normative issues, and to look at the relevant facts, it would be surprising if moral philosophers were not, in general, better suited to arrive at the right, or soundly based, moral conclusions than non-philosophers. Indeed, if this were not the case, one might wonder whether moral philosophy was worthwhile.

Questions

1. Do you think that the moral philosopher does have "some important advantages over the ordinary man" when it comes to knowing "the difference between right and wrong"? Can you find evidence in this or preceding chapters to support your view?
2. Do you agree with Singer's suggestion that there would be little or no point in doing or reading moral philosophy if moral philosophers were not "better suited to arrive at the right, or soundly based, moral conclusions" than non-philosophers?
3. Does it follow from Singer's position that *only* moral philosophers have the skills required to become moral experts?

On "Moral Expertise"

Béla Szabados

Not so long ago it was fashionable to claim that it is not the moral philosopher's business to say what things are good or what actions we should perform. This view is succinctly stated by A.J. Ayer:

> There is a distinction, which is not always sufficiently marked, between the activity of a moralist, who sets out to elaborate a moral code, or to encourage its observance, and that of a moral philosopher, whose concern is not primarily to make moral judgments but to analyse their nature.[1]

On the other hand, in direct opposition to this, recently many philosophers actively moralize, in the sense that they argue for substantive normative ethical positions.[2] In doing this they tend to assume but not to explore seriously two views: (1) that

From *Canadian Journal of Philosophy*, Vol. 8, No. 1 (March 1978), pp. 117–129.

the notion of moral expertise is unproblematic, and (2) that moral philosophers in particular are moral experts. My aim in this paper is to promote the exploration of these questions. (1) is logically prior to (2). Nevertheless I begin with discussing (2); for puzzles about expertise in morals naturally emerge when one examines the credentials of candidates for the job.

1. Moral Philosophers as Moral Experts

It has been said that perhaps no one is properly equipped to give moral advice to anyone else, but if anyone is it is the philosopher, who at least may be supposed to be able to tell bad reasoning from good.[3] It would seem however that the ability to produce valid arguments and to detect invalid ones is not sufficient for a good moral adviser. For to solve moral problems it is also essential to gather the relevant facts and to be "acquainted" with moral concepts. As Peter Singer argues in a stimulating recent contribution:

> Someone familiar with moral concepts and with moral arguments, who has ample time to gather information and think about it, may reasonably be expected to reach a soundly based conclusion more often than someone who is unfamiliar with moral concepts and moral arguments and has little time.[4]

Singer's position is that moral philosophers are tailor-made for moral expertise. For they are "familiar with" and "understand" moral concepts and moral arguments, have ample time to search out the relevant facts and to think about them.

The idea that moral philosophers have important advantages in moral matters over ordinary men seems plausible. Difficulties arise however as soon as the ambiguity of expressions like "familiarity with," and "understanding of," moral concepts and argument is noticed. Singer (and like-minded philosophers) speak as if the non-philosopher is not familiar with, does not understand moral concepts, arguments and issues. This is misleading. It is plain that a distinction is to be drawn between (1) someone who understands moral concepts in the sense that he knows how to use them—he makes moral judgements and puts forth moral arguments, and (2) someone who understands them in the sense that he can give an account of moral concepts and arguments. Once this distinction is taken seriously it becomes implausible to claim that philosophers have special competence in understanding moral concepts in sense (1). In fact one is often impressed with the deep moral insight of some ordinary men of wide experience and of writers of imaginative literature. Occasionally it may even be that it is the non-philosopher who has an advantage over the philosopher. For philosophical reflection is a double-edged sword: it may obscure as well as enlighten. Being in the grip of false theories about morals may blind one and one's hearers to certain moral issues and phenomena. For example, a philosopher whose analysis renders "self-deception" incoherent will have (ceteris paribus) a less adequate picture of "insincerity" than the rest of humanity. Naturally, this is likely to have implications for his first order moral attitudes and judgements. These remarks are not meant to deny that philosophical thinking can deepen one's appreciation of moral matters. They are meant to remind us that intellectual skills are also subject to various kinds of misuse and breakdown.

Singer's final reason for claiming expertise at morals for moral philosophers is that they have ample time to gather information and think about it. This is odd. For lots of people have time and some philosophers are always busy—think of the pedagogic, administrative, social and family obligations that they are likely to have. In any event, saying that one did not have enough time to think on it is hardly a good excuse for wrong-doing; in fact it is a common tactic for evasion.

I believe that there are two main reasons for the failure of Singer's account. First, he falsely assumes that being moral is just a matter of having (and successfully using) certain skills. This results in the neglect of such essential features as love of the good and moral regard. For the latter are typically exhibited in good deeds—deeds done out of concern for the good. If morality were merely having certain skills, we could not distinguish between the truly moral man and the merely prudent man—the man who does the right thing just because he wants to get on in the world. Secondly, Singer's construal of the range of skills involved in morality is too narrow. He restricts them to the cognitive skills required by complex cases of moral reasoning and fact-finding. While such skills are essential for expertise in doing and teaching moral philosophy, an exclusive focus on them leads to an insufficient recognition of the multifarious practical skills required by living a morally good life. These are often distinct from the cognitive skills required by philosophical analysis and argument.[5] Simple good folk are not walking anomalies but one of our sources of moral inspiration.[6] Plainly, being highly moral is not the same thing as being clever or very well informed. This is not meant to deny that the cleverer and better informed a person is, he is, to that extent, good and his potentialities for good works are greater than those of the mediocre or the stupid. However, it is important to remind ourselves that intellectually taxing moral problems and dilemmas do not exhaust the range of the moral life, although they can constitute a significant part of it.

The upshot of these remarks is that the notion of moral expertise is radically ambiguous. The distinction between being a perceptive user of the moral vocabulary and being an expert at the second order task of giving an analysis of moral discourse was already noted. Further distinctions to be noticed are (1) expertise at advising, (2) at teaching, (3) at living, (4) at clarifying debate, (5) at adding perspective. (Naturally this list is not exhaustive.) Now the special cognitive skills that philosophers have do make them likely experts at theorizing about morals, at teaching moral philosophy, at clarifying, and adding perspective to, moral controversy. But none of this implies that philosophers are likely experts at living a morally good life. For who is not acquainted with the gap between moral knowledge and action that St. Augustine's prayer reminds us of: "Oh Lord, give me chastity but not yet."[7] One does not become morally good by learning a set of true ethical propositions but by making moral considerations operative in one's life. The latter is a mark both of the simple good man as well as of moral exemplars and reformers.

Do moral philosophers have special skills at advising? There are at least two kinds of situation in which people seek moral advice: first, an advisee may be perplexed about what moral considerations are relevant to his problem, second, he knows what such moral considerations are, yet still needs assistance in resolving the problem.

In the former case the adviser would make clear the moral considerations that bear on the problem. By adding perspective, he would "sharpen" the problem. In the latter, the adviser would try to deepen and, if need be, correct the advisee's understanding of the relevant moral factors. One way of doing this is to draw needed distinctions, say, between the killing of the innocent and the killing of those who have caused the death of others. Plainly, moral philosophers are trained to be especially skilled at these tasks.

On the other hand, there are other essential requirements for advising that philosophers do not have qua philosophers. Consider what we mean when we say that a person does not have a broad enough experience of life. This means at least that he does not have the knowledge that is "not the knowledge of formulas, or form of words, but of people, places, actions—a knowledge not gained by words but by touch, sight, sound, victories, failures, sleeplessness, devotion, love—the human experiences and emotions of this earth and of oneself and other men."[8] It is this kind of knowledge that J.S. Mill must have had in mind when he has described his competent judges in morality: those who have had experience of the different kinds of pleasure and pain.[9]

Now such a person may still be deficient in that he may be caught up in experiences of his own that helped to shape him and ignore the diversity of human needs, wants and aspirations. Indeed the claim that one really understands human needs is fertile soil for self-deception and a likely source of tyranny.[10] But our candidate for moral expertise may acknowledge the diversity of human needs, yet have extra insight into life concerning those fundamental goods needed by everyone and those evils which are harmful to everyone. For example, a certain measure of affection, friendship, security, work are perhaps needed by everyone. It seems to me that these requirements for moral advisers are more likely to be found among priests, psychiatrists, social workers, those with age, breadth of experience, experience of oppression, than among philosophers. To sum up the argument so far: the range of skills and abilities involved in being moral is much broader than it is thought by some philosophers.[11] These skills and abilities include not merely cognitive ones, but also ones requiring moral imaginativeness ("imagine how he must feel"), insight into basic human needs and wants, an ability to predict the consequences of actions and their effects on the agent, and so on. The moral life is a range; moral philosophers are trained to have skills which equip them to have, ceteris paribus, a better grasp of some parts of the range than non-philosophers; other parts of the range require skills and abilities to which philosophers cannot lay claim, but perhaps priests, novelists, psychiatrists, social workers, people with experience of oppression can.

Clearly there are skills, tasks and abilities involved in being moral at which some people are better than others. It is also plain that these skills can be taught and the relevant abilities can be more or less developed. It is these features that lend credibility to the idea of moral expertise. However, there are other, no less important features which should remind us of the disanalogies between morality and having skills, and therefore, of the fact that the idea of expertise is in need of qualifications when applied in morality. It is on these disanalogies that arguments purporting to show that moral expertise is an absurdity feed.

2. Is Moral Expertise an Absurdity?

A. The first important difficulty arises when one starts thinking about "expertise" in general. It is natural to speak of expertise in situations where we seek means to achieve agreed-upon ends. For example, an engineer may have the problem of how to reinforce the shaky foundations of a building. He works out the ways and means for doing this. Once the method is successfully devised, his problem is solved. Here it makes sense to talk of expertise and we know what would count as a standard of expertise for we can judge success and efficiency by well-defined criteria. Now some philosophers speak as if all moral problems were technical problems like that of the engineer. This is implausible. For the moral problems that philosophers seem most interested in have to do with conflicts of values. And such problems are unlike technical problems in a crucial respect. Here we are not concerned merely with working out ways and means to achieve well-agreed on purposes. Here there is no agreement about the ends themselves. For example, there is a tendency among writers to treat the problem of capital punishment as if it were a technical problem only. They speak as if the only or the only important problem about capital punishment lies in the calculation of the social consequences such as the deterrent effects of the practice. Now the problem of devising efficient procedures for protecting society at large is clearly important. Nevertheless, a narrow consequentialist emphasis seems unfortunate if only because it is apt to distort and oversimplify the problem and its moral significance. By drawing attention only to one way in which the problem may start and be resolved, it draws attention away from other ways in which the differences may have come about. To spell this out: first, people may disagree about capital punishment simply because they disagree about the relevant facts such as its effects as a deterrent; second, they may agree about its force as a deterrent, yet still disagree as to their moral positions, for these are the natural outcome of the conflicting moral perspectives they hold on the issue. In the latter case what we have is a dispute as to which end should have primacy: (alleged) regard for life or (alleged) just desert. Cases like these where moral argument breaks down in a disagreement that reason seems unable to resolve point to an important difference between morality and fields (like science) where the notion of expertise has a straightforward application. For although expert scientists sometimes disagree, they at least agree on the methods by which their disputes could be settled.

Considerations like these perhaps led H.O. Mounce and D.Z. Phillips to reject the notion of moral expertise as an absurdity.[12] They argue thus:

> If the expert's answer is to be relevant then it will have to be a moral answer. But if it is a moral answer then it will be just another competing view.[13]

It seems to me that this argument fails to show that "expertise" can have no useful role in matters of morals. It relies on the false assumption that every decision in any morally dilemmatic situation is essentially arbitrary and contestable and ergo it is necessarily just another competing view. Take this variation on Plato's simple example as a counterexample to this: A friend leaves his gun at my home, saying he will be back for it this evening. He arrives and declares that he is going to shoot his wife because she has been unfaithful. Now here is a simple moral dilemma involving a need for a decision. This is evidently best resolved by not returning the gun. I do not mean that this decision cannot be challenged. However, anyone who challenges it must have an absurdly high stake in keeping one's word or an absurdly low regard for human life—and these are either marks of moral primitiveness or moral blindness. Although we have no clear blueprint for the criteria whereby such issues are to be decided, this does not show that some people are not better at making such decisions than others. One would be surprised if well-informed, clear-headed, imaginative, sympathetic persons would not be better equipped to arrive at correct decisions than those who lack these qualities. This shows that an attempt to appeal to ethical experts for advice does not necessarily reduce to a dispute about who are the ethical experts.[14] For the criteria for expertise need not involve the answer to the problem at issue.

B. The second objection to moral expertise is that it conflicts with the principle of moral autonomy.[15] In science the authority of the expert involves the notion of someone qualified to speak. It presumes standards by which expertise is assessed and recognized, for example, training and professional reputation. Evidence of this sort serves as reasons why laymen should take the expert's word without understanding his reasons, even without asking for them. For to accept someone as authoritative is to accept the judgement that one ought to obey that person. But it is widely thought that in morals the authority of each man's conscience is ultimate and unchallengeable. This poses the following problem. Suppose that an expert tells one that one (morally) ought to do A. One's conscience on the other hand tells one to do B. Now insofar as one agrees that the person is a moral expert, one must agree that one ought to do A. And insofar as one acknowledges the authority of conscience, one must agree that one ought to do B. But the situation is such that one cannot do both A and B.

The two concepts that are most in need of discussion are those of conscience and authority. It is a commonplace that conscience can be conceived either as the faculty of moral judgement itself or as a psychological phenomenon whose status and credentials may present a problem to one's moral judgement.[16] I do not believe that either of these ways of understanding "conscience" excludes the possibility of moral expertise. Consider the following story. Suppose that in the past Smith has made his difficult moral decisions by following the dictates of his conscience. With the passage of time he comes to realize that many of these decisions were mistaken. He also notices that there are others, in particular Jones, who are much wiser than he is. And there is considerable evidence for this. Jones is thoughtful, clear-headed, experienced, sensitive to moral considerations and can "put himself in another's shoes." In the past Jones gave Smith advice which Smith at the time ignored, but now he sees that he was wrong to do so. So Smith chooses Jones as his moral adviser. And occasionally Smith follows Jones's advice even when they disagree over a certain moral matter. He justifies this by saying: "I believe that B is the right thing to do but since Jones (who is very wise) thinks it is not, I am likely to be wrong. So I follow his advice and do A."

Now suppose that one thinks that the authority of conscience is ultimate and unchallengeable. This may be argued by pointing out that one can challenge an authority only by appeal to some other authority, so that one must rest somewhere with a decision to accept some ruling as final; and this decision will be a moral decision and conscience the final authority.[17] Now since Smith's decision to take Jones's advice is a final moral decision, it follows that it is approved by Smith's conscience, if "conscience" is understood in the above sense. Alternatively, suppose that one thinks of "conscience" as one's super-ego—the retention of the character of the father. This picture presents no special difficulties concerning moral expertise; for in this sense any deliverance of conscience is challengeable and subject to moral scrutiny.

I do not wish to suggest that the story I told about Smith and his "guru" could become a pervasive feature of the moral life. All I claim is that in cases of complex moral dilemmas a decision to take the advice of someone whom one deems to be morally wiser is both intelligible and intelligent and does not necessarily conflict with one's autonomy. The crucial point is that in such matters what advice one accepts and what adviser one picks one has to judge for oneself and thus ultimately depends on one's own moral judgement.

C. This brings us to an important difference between expertise in science and in morals. In science an expert is a man who can be appealed to by the ignorant layman. We are wise to take his word even if we do not understand his reasons. In general there is no blame attached to lack of scientific knowledge. On the other hand, moral ignorance (as exhibited in the expression "He does not know right from wrong") is either blameworthy or a diagnosis of a certain form of mental illness recently referred to as psychopathic personality and traditionally as moral imbecility.[18] Now the ways children learn morals are in many ways analogous to the ways laymen learn science. Here ignorance is replaced by knowledge. But this picture does not do justice to the fully grown, mature, responsible moral agent. For it depicts him as a child or as someone deficient in basic capacities. The way an autonomous agent learns from a Jesus or a Nietzsche is much like the way a competent mathematician learns from someone who is creative and original in mathematics—viz., by listening to arguments and by recognizing how one step follows from another and so on. When Jesus said,

> Ye have heard that it was said by them of old time, "Thou shalt not commit adultery." But I say unto you, that whoever looketh on a women to lust after her hath committed adultery with her already in his heart,

he taught us the importance of purity of heart. But this was possible only because we already thought of, say, good intentions as a morally relevant consideration. When Nietzsche appears to disparage honesty by saying:

> It is so convenient to be frank and honest. This confidingness, this complaisance, this showing-the-cards of German honesty, is probably the most dangerous and most successful disguise,[19]

he is reminding of us people who are honest only because this is a successful tactic for getting on in the world. At the same time he gives us a more adequate picture of hypocrisy by pointing out that men can deceive not only others but themselves. Nietzsche can do this only because we already think of sincerity as a moral value.

There are perhaps cases where a good piece of moral advice is so startling that one cannot right there and then grasp it or agree with it. Even in such cases it must be possible to appreciate it in retrospect. Thus we may come to regret for not having taken the advice or for not pondering on it more carefully.

The upshot of these remarks is that we are all morally required to try to become moral experts while there is no such requirement for scientific expertise. Why is this so? The idea of expertise involves the idea that one should (prudential "should") obey another person on all matters belonging to his field of expertise. However in morals this is itself a momentous moral decision. And a person who deems himself shaky in making individual moral decisions because of occasional criticisms of these in the past should certainly deem himself shaky in making such a large moral decision. So perhaps he ought to let the expert decide this. Such a decision, I suggest, deprives a human being of the status of moral agent—for he could no longer be said to be the source and originator of his actions. This is why reliance on others cannot be a pervasive feature of the moral life.

D. To be an expert at something is to have acquired special skills and knowledge. It is, however, argued by Gilbert Ryle that the moral man is not an expert at anything. He says:

> But knowlege of the difference between right and wrong is common knowledge, and it is not mastery of a technique. There is nothing in particular that the honest man knows, ex officio, how to do. He is not, ex officio, even a bit of an expert at anything.[20]

Von Wright opts for a similar stance:

> But there is no specific activity at which the courageous man must be good—as the skilled chess-player must be good at playing chess. . . . There is no art of "couraging," in which the brave man must excel.[21]

I believe that these arguments are wrong-headed. Ryle's argument feeds on a one-sided diet of moral situations. "Honesty is fine. I know I ought to be honest, but I am tempted by the gains that will accrue to me if I tell a lie." I do not wish to deny the reality or even the frequency of these situations. However, this simple picture of the moral life ignores the importance of moral dilemmas and perplexities. It is when moral values clash that the moral man needs special knowledge, the skills of clear thought and long experience to decide what is right and what is wrong. It is when honesty clashes with clarity or when the obligation to care for one's widowed mother conflicts with one's duty to fight for one's country that knowledge of what is right and what is wrong is neither a simple matter, nor "common knowledge," nor merely a matter of being well-intentioned.

While Ryle and von Wright are perhaps right in saying that there is no specific know-how involved in being honest, courageous or charitable, it does not follow that diverse skills and knowledge (their kind and species being contingent on the demands of the particular moral situation) are not required by these virtues. On the contrary! For a person who indiscriminately throws his money at crowds is not really charitable but wasteful and foolish. So-called brave ignoramuses are better described as foolhardy.

On the other hand, Ryle is right when he says that

> To have been taught the difference (between right and wrong) is to have been brought to appreciate the difference, and this appreciation is not just a competence to label correctly or just a capacity to do things efficiently. It includes an inculcated caring, a habit of taking certain sorts of things seriously.[22]

Plainly, this leaves open the possibility of expertise in morals.

That morality is partly a concern and respect for persons points to yet another difference between expertise in fields like science and morals. Philosophers who stress the roles that skills and knowledge play in moral matters tend to overlook that while it is possible to be an expert physicist, carpenter or cook and go on vacation and thus not practice one's special skills, the idea of a virtuous man who does not practice virtue is surely absurd. Although love of cookery is likely to make one into a better cook, the idea of a first-rate chef who hates or is indifferent to cooking is neither strange nor uncommon. However, the idea of a truly moral man who hates or is indifferent to moral considerations is incoherent.

To conclude then: I have argued that the moral life is profitably viewed as a range. Parts of this range require skills and abilities that render the notion of competence and expertise in morals intelligible and useful. This expertise is diverse and multi-faceted corresponding to the diverse roles and parts of morality: living a morally good life, resolving one's own moral problems, giving moral counsel and advice, the teaching of morals to children, teaching moral philosophy, bringing about moral change and so on. No one person is likely to have a monopoly on all these skills. On the other hand, there are other no less important parts of the range of morality where the notion of expertise can have no application. Here qualities like love of the good and respect for persons are paramount. It is these essential features of what it is to be moral that require us to qualify any use of "expertise" in matters of morals.

Notes

1. A.J. Ayer in his editorial foreword to P.H. Nowell-Smith's *Ethics* (London: Penguin Books, 1954), p. 7.
2. Many philosophical journals but especially *Philosophy and Public Affairs* contain many examples of such arguments.
3. E.J. Lemmon, "Moral Dilemmas," *The Philosophical Review* 71 (1962), 156.
4. Peter Singer, "Moral Experts," *Analysis* 32 (1972), 115–117.
5. In this connection the work of psychologists like Kohlberg may mislead, for they also

tend to see moral maturity merely in terms of skills of moral reasoning. See L. Kohlberg, "Stage and Sequence: The Cognitive-Developmental Approach to Socialization," *Handbook of Socialization Theory and Research* (Chicago: Rand-McNally Co., 1969).

6. This has been deeply felt by many, including Rousseau, Kant and Tolstoy.

7. Saint Augustine, *Confessions* (London: Penguin Books, 1961), p. 169.

8. Adlai E. Stevenson, *What I Think* (New York: Harper and Row, 1956), p. 174.

9. J.S. Mill, *Utilitarianism* (The Library of Liberal Arts, 1957), p. 15.

10. See Solzhenitsyn's brief "portrait" of Stalin in *The First Circle* (Bantam Books, 1968), p. 130: "Only he Stalin, knew the path by which to lead humanity to happiness, how to shove its face into happiness like a blind puppy's into a bowl of milk—'There drink up!' "

11. E.g., Singer, op. cit.; Russell Grice, *The Grounds of Moral Judgement* (Cambridge University Press, 1967), pp. 201–203; Benjamin Gibbs in "Virtue and Reason," *The Proceedings of the Aristotelian Society*, Supplementary Volume for 1974, pp. 23–41.

12. D.Z. Phillips and H.O. Mounce, *Moral Practices* (London: Routledge and Kegan Paul, 1969). For a similar view, see R.W. Beardsmore, *Moral Reasoning* (London: Routledge and Kegan Paul, 1969), pp. 88–89.

13. Phillips and Mounce, op. cit., p. 108.

14. Contrary to Renford Bambrough's view that "an attempt to appeal to experts simply transforms an ethical or political dispute into an equally unsettleable dispute about who are the ethical or political experts." See Bambrough's "Plato's Political Analogies," in Peter Laslett's *Philosophy, Politics and Society* (Oxford: Basil Blackwell, 1956), vol. I, p. 10.

15. Kant seems to have thought this. He says: "Mere analysis of the concepts of morality," would show us that the "principle of autonomy is the sole principle of ethics." (*Groundwork*, p. 108, Paton translation.)

16. Bishop Butler, for example, held that conscience is the faculty of moral judgement and thus it has supreme moral authority. Vide Joseph Butler, *Fifteen Sermons*, ed. W.R. Mathews (London: Bell and Sons, 1969), p. 53. For a further discussion of Butler's views and the paradox of errant conscience, see my paper "Butler on Corrupt Conscience," in *The Journal of the History of Philosophy*, October 1976. On the other hand, Freud's account of conscience as super-ego allows one to speak of challenging a dictate of one's conscience.

17. Bernard Mayo argues thus in his *Ethics and the Moral Life*, p. 171. His view of conscience is reminiscent of Butler's.

18. Here not knowing the difference between right and wrong amounts to lack of moral concern. There seem to be individuals who appear to be unable (and not merely unwilling) to care about others. See Hervey Cleckley, *The Mask of Sanity* (Saint Louis: 1964).

19. F. Nietzsche, *Beyond Good and Evil*, trans. Walter Kaufmann (New York: Vintage Books, 1966), p. 180.

20. Gilbert Ryle, "On Forgetting the Difference between Right and Wrong," in *Essays in Moral Philosophy*, ed. A.I. Melden (Seattle: University of Washington Press, 1958), p. 157.

21. Georg Hendrik von Wright, *The Varieties of Goodness* (London: Routledge and Kegan Paul, 1963), p. 139.

22. Ryle, op. cit., p. 156.

Questions

1. How does the account of moral expertise offered by Szabados differ from that offered by Peter Singer?

2. The idea of moral expertise appears to conflict with the principle of autonomy. How does Szabados resolve this apparent conflict? Is his solution sound?

3. In a passage quoted by Szabados, Ryle suggests that the difference between right and wrong is something we all know. Is Ryle correct? If so, why is there so much disagreement?

4. Can disagreement on moral issues be resolved? Is the role of moral philosophers in the resolution of moral issues important?

Moral Expertise—A Reply

Kai Nielsen

Szabados rightly refuses to dismiss the notion of "moral expertise" as an absurdity or conceptual anomaly. He argues convincingly both that there are parts of "morality where the notion of expertise can have no application" and that there are elements in the moral life which "require skills and abilities that render the notion of competence and expertise in morals intelligible and useful."[1] My principal quarrel with him is over an omission. It seems to me that he leaves entirely out of consideration a crucial part of moral philosophy where a conception of moral expertise is most important. Szabados views morality and moral philosophy and the putative role of moral experts in too personal a way in effect failing to acknowledge, as Rawls has in our time, and as Bentham, Mill and Sidgwick did earlier, that moral philosophy is also, and centrally, concerned with the design of a well-ordered society or, to put it even more broadly, as Marx did, with the design of a truly human society.[2]

The idea of expertise is much less fanciful when we seriously ask fundamental questions about social justice and about the sort of society in which meaningful work and unexploitative, unmanipulative and nonoppressive human relations would be possible, so that a genuine human flourishing could become a reality. There is, of course, room for expertise in the evident way in which a philosopher can bring his conceptual skills to bear in sharpening our understanding of what we are asking when we ask such questions about the design of a good society and about human flourishing. Even more obviously, there is as well the expertise involved in answering the causal questions, evidently involved in such moral issues, about the conditions under which certain social arrangements arise and about what sustains them and would alter them. Concerning such causal questions it is clear enough what at least in principle it would be like to have such expertise. And it is plainly something that the complete moral philosopher ought to acquire. Beyond the above, where the

The third section of a paper written in reply to "On 'Moral Expertise' " by Béla Szabados. Originally published in longer form in *Midwestern Journal of Philosophy*, Vol. 6, No. 1 (Spring 1978).

idea of expertise is evidently not a Holmesless Watson, there is in addition perhaps room for expertise in affording us an enhanced understanding of what we want to know about the fundamental goods needed by everyone and the evils which are harmful to everyone. In Rawls's terminology, we want to know what are the primary social and natural goods and we want, if we can, to see if reflection, analysis and investigation (including, of course, empirical investigation) can give us grounds for setting up priority rules where the primary goods are not in any extensive measure available to everyone or where in attempting their realization the different primary goods conflict. We want such priority rules to give us grounds for a fair distribution of these primary goods and an understanding of what conditions would lead to their just realization. In probing such matters, questions of expertise surely enter. In the argument between Rawls and Barry about the Aristotelian principle and between Rawls and Macpherson about the nature and inevitability of classes and the difference principle, there is plenty of scope for expertise, as well as its being the case that large issues about social justice and a good society turn on what are the more reasonable answers to such relatively technical questions.[3] Only if the very idea of one answer here being more reasonable than another is utterly and essentially contested, do we have good grounds for turfing out the idea of moral expertise.

We should also not forget that there is an attempt, on the part of philosophers such as Rawls and Richards, to elaborate systems of normative ethics, to consider their rationale and to compare them in detail not only with our considered judgements (where it is not clear that there is any place for talk of expertise) but also in thinking about them to consider what we know about society and human nature. This can hardly be done without some reasonable knowledge of the history of ethical theory, for we need to understand, and understand in detail, the different elaborations of a good society that human thought has devised and we need to understand clearly their rationale and implications. But we also, and plainly, need, in making such comparisons, knowledge of economics, political sociology, the theory of classes, history and psychology.

In such contexts there can be no reasonable ruling out of the very idea of expertise, though there is plenty of room for scepticism about whether anyone at present has it and there should be, as well, the recognition that often ideology, sometimes disguised as expertise, enters here. But that is an occasion for hard work and a broadening of methodological perspectives and not for, à la Phillips and Mounce, a closing in and regarding of the very idea of moral expertise as an absurdity rooted in a blend of conceptual confusion, *hubris* and moral insensitivity.

The extended scope for moral philosophy, exemplified most powerfully in the work of Rawls, but also found in Gert, Richards and Nozick, avoid the methodological rigidities of the philosophical work in the analytical tradition during the interwar period and first two decades after the war, typified by the work of Stevenson, Hare and Foot. Its utilization of empirical claims in its theorizing makes for a healthy impurity in philosophy, leaving added scope for expertise. We should, however, be reluctant to call it *philosophical* expertise, while at the same time refusing to get very exercised about how it is labelled.[4]

I think this tendency should be pushed still further. The specific direction in which it should be pushed can, I believe, be discerned, if we attend to some perceptive criticisms made by Bernard Williams of some basic methodological commitments in Rawls and Nozick.[5] Both, Williams reminds us, approach large scale theorizing about a good society and just institutions "from moral perceptions recovered in intuition," though they appeal to and perhaps have a different range of intuitions. These moral sentiments—Rawls standardly calls them intuitions or considered judgements—play a role in such accounts similar to the role played by the linguistic intuitions of the native speaker for the linguist.[6] We finally check out the correctness of our theoretical accounts against the firmest of these intuitions. However, Rawls does not face, as Williams point out, and as Steven Lukes has as well, the fairly evident problems of relativism which emerge here.[7] Rawls, and Nozick as well, are, as Williams puts it, "utterly untouched . . . by the kind of relativist anxieties which haunt all social philosophy which grows out of sociology and social anthropology, anxieties which surely express, however confusedly, some proper reflexive doubt whether our current moral priorities can be universally applied."[8] Rawls and Nozick give this very great scope to intuitions (moral sentiments), yet they ignore history, anthropology, political sociology and the myriad problems emerging (often confusedly) out of the sociology of knowledge. "They," Williams continues, "both regard the enterprise of thinking philosophically about society in abstraction from history or concrete social conditions; and, connectedly, the social sciences they use, Nozick even more than Rawls, are economics and decision theory, both of which can be pursued at a high level of abstraction."[9] But such abstract bits of social science, among other things, tend to serve as a distraction from facing questions about who are the "our" in "our considered judgements" and about how we can (if we can) possibly, given the great diversity of human cultures and subcultures, reasonably place such weight in moral theorizing on *our* considered judgements.[10]

Williams challenges the assumption in Rawls and Nozick that one can rightly fall back on the moral intuitions one has and, starting from there, elaborate social principles which afford an Archimedean point for assessing society. We cannot justifiably short-circuit such historical and sociological considerations, for too much is known about the origins of our moral sentiments and about the origins of our moral conflicts to make such an individualistic approach viable. We cannot so start from historical scratch and individual morality. What we need instead, Williams argues, is a moral-cum-social philosophy which starts "rather more determinately from the highly elaborated, and very densely occupied, social and political scene we actually have."[11] This, of course, is more demanding of moral philosophers. We would have to know a lot more; and this knowledge would not only have to be quantitatively greater, it would also have to be about many more different things than we are accustomed to thinking we need to know about in order properly to do moral philosophy. It is surely natural, in certain moods anyway, to feel such requirements are so demanding that such a conception of moral philosophy becomes "larger than life"—that operating in accordance with it is just too much to task of a moral philosopher—but even where such scepticism is generated about our ability to accomplish anything like this, still a recognition of the importance of such factors should make us more cautious about trying to do moral philosophy *sub specie aeternitatis*. Yet, it is also the case that the very source of our scepticism is also the source of our awareness of the importance of and the place for expertise concerning such matters.[12]

This drive for greater impurity in philosophy, this drive away from scientistic assumptions and from a certain abstract way of doing things, should direct the attention of moral philosophers to the human sciences (particularly political economy, political sociology and social anthropology). They should develop an intimate and extensive knowledge here and this knowledge will surely carry with it an expertise. They should, however, in doing this, do as well systematic normative ethics. But it should be work much more historically and sociologically oriented than it has been in the past, so that in future good moral philosophy will be intimately linked with the developing of a critical theory of society. But this is a place where there is no even getting to first base without a lot of expertise.

Notes

1. Béla Szabados (see "On 'Moral Expertise,' " pp. 583–593). I am here citing an earlier version.
2. *Ibid.* This is partially rectified in the later version of his paper presented in the *Canadian Journal of Philosophy*.
3. Brian Barry, *The Liberal Theory of Justice* (Oxford: Clarendon Press, 1973), pp. 27–33 and 84; C.B. Macpherson, *Democratic Theory* (Oxford: Clarendon Press, 1973), Chapter IV; "Rawls's Models of Man and Society," *Philosophy of the Social Sciences*, Vol. 3, No. 4 (December, 1973).
4. Kai Nielsen, "For Impurity in Philosophy," *University of Toronto Quarterly* (January, 1974). Some distinctions useful in this context are drawn in my "Speaking of Morals" in *The Centennial Review*, Vol. II (Fall, 1958).
5. Bernard Williams, "The Moral View of Politics," *The Listener* (June 3, 1976). The quotations are taken from this publication of his radio broadcast.
6. John Rawls, *A Theory of Justice* (Cambridge, Massachusetts: Harvard University Press, 1971), p. 49. Thomas Nagel decisively and succinctly makes the essential point here. "[The] intuitions of native speakers are decisive as regards grammar. Whatever native speakers agree on is English, but whatever ordinary men agree in condemning is not necessarily wrong. Therefore the intrinsic plausibility of an ethical theory can impel a change in our moral intuitions. Nothing corresponds to this in linguistics . . . where the final test of a theory is its ability to explain the data." Thomas Nagel, "Rawls on Justice," *Reading Rawls* (New York: Basic Books, Inc., 1975), p. 2.
7. Bernard Williams, *op. cit.* and Steven Lukes, "An Archimedean Point," *The Observer* (June 4, 1972) and "Relativism: Cognitive and Moral," *Aristotelian Society*, Supplementary Vol. XLVIII (1974), pp. 179–188.
8. Bernard Williams, *op. cit.*
9. *Ibid.*
10. *Ibid.* See also my "On Philosophic Method," *International Philosophical Quarterly*, Vol. XVI, No. 3 (September, 1976), pp. 358–68.
11. Bernard Williams, *op. cit.*
12. We should not forget that there was a time, not so very long ago, when this was done. The author of *Utilitarianism* is also the author of *Principles of Political Economy* and the author of *The Wealth of Nations* is also the author of the *Theory of Moral Sentiments*.

Questions

1. In the light of your readings in previous chapters, how important is a theoretical framework of the sort to which Nielsen is referring in the resolution of moral issues?

2. Does Nielsen provide convincing reasons for rejecting moral relativism?
3. What does Nielsen mean when he calls for "greater impurity" in moral philosophy? Evaluate his proposals for greater impurity in light of previous readings.
4. How important is Nielsen's criticism of Szabados's position?

Ideology and Morality in Hard Times[1]

Michael McDonald

These are hard times ideologically: not just for those whose lives feel the effects of ideology—inflation paired with unemployment, increased taxes yet diminished social services, rising arms expenditures along with growing international tension—but also for the ideologies themselves—both (welfare-) liberalism and (neo-) conservatism.[2] Liberals perceive a growing meanness and nastiness in our attitudes to the poor, minority groups, and in general to the powerless, while conservatives feel hamstrung by decades of liberal legislation and by a sense that the public is not willing to pay the costs conservatives see as necessary for recovery. On the public's part there is a general sense that neither ideology really works: liberals are "too soft" on welfare cheats, criminals, and so on, while conservatives are "too hard" on the environment, the middle class, etc.

Now this debate between "softs" and "hards" has been a feature of our moral, political, and legal lives for the past several decades. Until recently this debate would have seemed to many Canadians highly productive and beneficial, providing a nice balance between those who wanted to go "too fast" and those who were "too slow." But no more, we've "soured" on this debate. Even the leading "hard" and "soft" spokesmen seem less confident of their views than they did a decade ago.

At this point, you may be well nodding agreement with these observations but be wondering what a philosopher could contribute to your understanding of our current malaise. Let me try to make these worries about a philosophical contribution more precise and at the same time respond to them. One concern might be that a philosopher is likely to look "too deeply" for an explanation of our current plight and that it is really to economists, sociologists, and other "experts" we should look for answers to what is basically a short-term economic crisis.

But this masks both what experts do and the extent of our current malaise. Experts, after all, are often ideologically motivated; in any case the "solutions" they urge on us have profound ideological implications. Their solutions would not only affect our economic lives but also our very conception of ourselves as moral and social

---

With permission of Michael McDonald, University of Waterloo.

beings. For example, if we decide to use the Canadian Shield as a dumping ground for the world's nuclear wastes, we have made an important decision about the environment, native peoples, future generations, and perhaps even our very existence. In any case, the malaise that is the subject of this paper is not just economic and political; it appears throughout our moral and social lives in attitudes to pornography, abortion, euthanasia, and in fact for all the issues considered in this volume. For on all these, we can to some extent find a debate between small "l" liberals and small "c" conservatives.

But you might object that people are often inconsistent. For example, someone who demands that government get out of the nation's bedrooms might have no compunctions about demanding that there be a governmental presence in each of the nation's boardrooms. What dominates discussion, you might go on to argue, are questions about the facts and how to get things done most efficiently.

Here though you have to be careful. While factual disagreements are important (e.g., will aid to the poor *work*?), they often mask normative disputes (e.g., what is *fair* treatment of the poor?). In any case we are familiar with situations in which agreement on the facts is fairly clear but in which the parties still disagree (e.g., the deterrent effects of capital punishment) or in which factual disagreements conceal conceptual and normative problems (e.g., whether the fetus is a person, and what does the moral treatment of persons require?). This still leaves us with the question of inconsistency raised in the bedrooms/boardrooms example. Perhaps those who take the stance in question (liberals) aren't being inconsistent when they insist that bedrooms are private whereas boardrooms are public; for they may argue boardroom activity hurts nonconsenting third parties, whereas bedroom activity doesn't. Nevertheless, their consistency can only be determined by looking at possible justifications of their positions: to what underlying principles may they appeal when they make these two seemingly inconsistent judgements?

What I try to do as a philosopher in such cases is to uncover and articulate the *network of principles* that people could use to sustain their particular practical decisions. I then examine that network for consistency and unity to see how well the principles in question cohere. But one might object here that this may be a search for a will-o'-the-wisp especially in English Canada, for we pride ourselves on our pragmatism. As John Stuart Mill observed so percipiently in the last century, the English are deeply suspicious of all philosophising and *doctrines générales*. For evidence here, one might well point to the Common Law tradition with its emphasis on precedent and careful judicial discrimination and contrast it with the far more *a priori* and deductive approach of Continental Law (which in Canada obtains only in Quebec).

This pragmatic response misses on two basic counts. First, it would be highly unpragmatic to ignore principles. Life is simply not that disconnected—a solution to one problem has a bearing on other problems (this is the essence of the Common Law notion of precedent and of the moral principle that like cases be treated alike). To establish common social expectations and coordinate our various interactions we have to resort to principles. Indeed the absence of principles strikes us on reflection as at times both evil and inefficient (though in quite different ways). Secondly, taking a pragmatic, anti-philosophical stand is itself a philosophical position that requires defence. Constant resort to *ad hoc* judgements and unarticulated intuitions inevitably requires some justification, at least in terms of enunciating one's criteria for success.[4]

My conclusion, thus far, is that something significant may be learned if we take a philosophical look at these current "hard times," *viz.* by articulating the networks of values underlying the hard and soft principles that ground their characteristic value-judgements. However, this isn't all we want to do; we also want to make sound judgements on particular issues based on defensible principles. But this may occasion a further worry: if you don't know where you stand on some particular question (say, aboriginal rights) how will you be in a better position if you understand the justifications offered for the opposing views on this and other questions? Won't you simply be more deeply confused, i.e., confused not only about aboriginal rights but also about the liberal and conservative views on other issues, such as on property?

Perhaps you still will be undecided, though at least you will be aware that more than just your view of one isolated issue is at stake and that there are issues of principle involved. And this realisation of your own ignorance is, as Socrates was fond of reminding his auditors, the beginning of wisdom. Moreover, you may find that one or the other of the deeper views you discover in your philosophic search for justifications has implication you cannot accept. Thus, in my paper "Aboriginal Rights" I try to show how a conservative view of property (Locke and Nozick's libertarianism) has disturbing implications if we take it seriously, *viz.* that natives should own most of Canada. Beyond that I argue (Section F, "Acquisition Arguments") that the libertarian notion of property is itself faulty, for property is conventional and requires reference to the shared values of its users. But in the case of aborigines and European colonists there is no community of shared values. However one thinks the particular question of aboriginal rights should be resolved (and here one should take account of Gauthier's response to my argument), I want to claim that the philosophical approach I used in exploring that issue has considerable value: look for the underlying network of norms, take those principles seriously, then ask if they make sense and if your community can live with their implications.

Now this is just what I propose doing for our current "hard times for ideology." I will begin by sketching the rival "hard" and "soft" positions in such a way that their opposing basic principles are made apparent. I will argue that liberals defend, while conservatives attack, a process of "equalization" or transfers of resources and opportunities from the "haves" to the "have-nots" so that some sort of minimum is provided for everyone. I then will argue that despite this very great difference in principle the two positions in question share a common fundamental conception and ideal of rational self-sufficiency or autonomy taken as a basis for moral, social, and legal equality. In the last part of my paper, I call this notion of autonomy and equality into question and argue for a shift to a more community-centred notion of values. So my ultimate aim is to challenge at a fundamental level some of the most basic ideas on which liberalism and conservatism are founded and at least suggest something better in their place. Perhaps, this will help us find our way out of our current hard times. (Here I hasten to add a cautionary note—while philosophers can *help* resolve normative disagreements they certainly don't have *all*, let alone, the *right* answers.)

I. "Hard" and "Soft" Moralities

What divides hard-liners from soft-liners in moral, political, and legal matters?[5] The account I propose centres on the notion of the individual person or agent as the centre and subject of morality. Obviously hard-liners and soft-liners disagree about what the moral treatment of persons involves. Less obviously, they deeply disagree about the minimal conditions necessary for the "meaningful" exercise of autonomous choice. Conservatives contend that the conditions for autonomous choice are few and simple and that in our society they are generally met. Liberals deny both contentions, arguing that various people in our society find themselves in positions where they lack meaningful choices. They claim that there is a society-wide failure to respect the autonomy of various individuals (native people, women, the poor, workers, and so on). Thus, liberals go on to argue that public efforts are required to make available significant options to these people and to provide the wherewithal necessary to exercise those options. Both these contentions are denied by hard-liners: (a) that these people have been wrongfully denied anything by society; and (b) that in their present circumstances they lack meaningful options.

The conservative bases (a) and (b) on his notion of fair legal and moral requirements as being limited to "the negative service of non-interference, except so far as he (a sane adult) has voluntarily undertaken to render positive services to others."[6] The conservative claims that these essentially negative requirements fully respect individual autonomy. To go further by requiring a person to positively assist another (other than in the case of promise-keeping) is in effect to promote a kind of "slavery"; thus, to make person A pay taxes to provide out of work person B with minimum welfare assistance is in effect to enslave A to B for at least that portion of his working hours necessary to provide the welfare payment.[7] Only if moral and legal requirements are thus restricted to an essentially negative role will the individuality and autonomy of persons be adequately respected. The conservative argues for this strongly individualistic position on the grounds that each person must be free from outside interference to lead the sort of life that he or she chooses. In essence the conservative views each of us as saying to all others, "It is my life; let me lead it as I please, so that I can make of it as meaningful an existence as I desire." The "root idea" here is that a meaningful experience requires individual autonomy to be respected, and this respect can only be afforded by mutual non-interference in each others' affairs.[8]

The liberal does not deny the importance of leading one's own life and making one's own decisions. However, he does not believe that respect for individual autonomy is simply negative (non-interference); rather he sees autonomy as a positive condition in which an individual is *able* to make what use he pleases of the options available to him. Unfortunately, not everyone is able to make use of their options; they require help to be in a position to act autonomously. So the liberal claims that in these cases respecting individual autonomy requires the transfer of resources from one person (A) to another (B). Does this mean, as the conservative argues, that A is thus made a slave of B? The liberal denies that this need be so; for while A's choices are somewhat diminished by such requirements, A still could have available to him enough options of a significant kind to lead a meaningful life. But more than that, the liberal argues that in transferring resources to B, A is meeting a significant moral requirement and thus exercising his autonomy morally; thus, A reinforces his own autonomy. So there is deep disagreement between liberals and conservatives over the nature and extent of autonomy and the basic moral requirement to respect autonomy.

Economic justice provides some clear cases of this battle between conservatives and liberals. Take, for example, consumer protection legislation and labour law. Liberals argue that consumers and workers are so weak compared to producers and employers that they need to have the government on their side to make available meaningful choices of products and jobs. So the liberal pushes for strong consumer-protection legislation, placing high standards of product-liability on producers, and strong labour laws protecting job security and safety by making the employer bear such costs. Conservatives reject these demands on the grounds of (a) and (b), arguing essentially that in the market-place the consumer and worker have meaningful choices to make and if they lack such choices it is their own fault; for they are free to start their own businesses, buy a different product, change jobs, and so on.

We can see this division in other areas of life as well. Consider attitudes towards crime. Some people seem to "tilt" towards the protection of the accused and even the convicted in our criminal justice process tending to see them as the victims of various social processes (stigmatization, inadequate acculturation, etc.) which robbed them of autonomy. To restore that autonomy various special protections for the accused and for criminals have to be provided, ranging from legal aid to half-way houses. Others "tilt" the other way—arguing for quicker and harsher "justice" with more thought to the actual victims of criminal wrongdoing and less to the wrongdoers. The conservative believes these people are responsible for their wrong doings, whereas, liberals call into question a crucial component of that claim, viz., that those "wrongdoers" are fully autonomous.

Even on the pornography issue, recent feminist arguments for censorship present what I claim is a typically "liberal" approach. For the feminists argue that pornography degrades women and treats them merely as objects; hence, pornography encourages an attitude and practices that deny women autonomy. Censorship is then a way of respecting women as persons. A "conservative" (and here I use them in a sense more stipulative than descriptive) argues for the market-place of ideas— even for a "pornotopia."[9] While a conservative would argue for the protection of all citizens from the threat of physical violence, he would not (I think) see in censorship the enhancement of autonomy but rather its restriction. On the broader issues of feminine emancipation, the conservative would tend to rely on the market-place and its intellectual and cultural analogues.[10]

So what I want to claim is basic to liberal and conservative disputes on a wide variety of moral questions is the issue of "equalization"—a term which I borrow from federal-provincial relations. Remember that "equalization" does not mean "making equal," rather it involves a transfer from the "have" provinces to the "have not" provinces. The intention of these transfer payments is to provide a level of government services to Canadians in all provinces to ensure *full* or *meaningful* participation in Confederation. Thus, there is the notion of a minimum level of various government services (e.g., health and education) that must be ensured in all parts of the country. So what I am claiming is that equalization divides liberals from conservatives or softs from hards. The equalization in question needn't take the form of money; it might involve protective legislation or the sanction of popular morality (e.g., against sexual stereotyping). In any case, it involves the transfer of a benefit from the better to the worse off on the grounds that the latter lack the wherewithal (e.g., education, income, self-confidence, information) to exercise significant options.

II. Morality and Rational Self-Sufficiency

So while liberals argue that conservatives see people generally as more self-sufficient than they really are, conservatives argue that liberals are too tender-hearted (and minded) because the capacity for independent, self-sustaining activity is more fully developed than liberals realise. Now this of course makes certain "factual" disputes particularly significant, e.g., do income supplements work, what are the genetic determinants of intelligence, does pornography cause sexual assaults? But the basic issues here are normative: are the relative differences in people's positions with respect to wealth, social status, and occupation unfair or fair?

Given the history of debate over this basic question, it may well seem that the normative (and factual) controversies are intractable and undecidable. But this is too pessimistic a view, for it ignores the important commonalities in the liberal and conservative positions. Both are grounded on a conception of morality in which the idea of persons as autonomous plays the leading role. I want to argue this even though it is clear that philosophically the concept of morality has been formulated in quite different ways, for example as natural rights in Locke, Nozick, and others, as artificial rights founded on human rationality in Hobbes and now Gauthier and Narveson, and as rights constructed to account for certain moral intuitions in Kant, Rawls, and Dworkin. And, of course, there are views that do not fit easily into the above pigeon-holes—such as the views of Feinberg, Vlastos, Hart, and Williams. I will now try to at least outline the core of agreement.

However expressed, moral requirements are seen as being either explicitly or implicitly the solution of a specific problem; call this "the moral problem." The problem is roughly this. While people (the potential subjects of morality) have diverse plans, projects, and aims, they lack *both* intrinsic concern for the plans, projects, and aims of others *and* any common impersonal or objective scale by which to assess the value of these diverse goals. The former means that in the absence of moral roles people come into conflict with each other. And the latter implies that they have no person-independent way of assessing these goals according to their worth. The only solution is then that the worth of a given end be taken to consist solely in the fact that people happen to want that end. What morality does is provide an inter-subjective (but not objective) way of resolving conflicts that arise in the pursuit of these conflicting and diverse ends.[11]

David Gauthier put this nicely when he described justice as "the virtue that curbs the self-interest of those who are not also self-sufficient." This lack of self-sufficiency is also apparent in the different states-of-nature described by Nozick and Rawls. Rawls (and Dworkin) go somewhat beyond the description of this insufficiency as solely self-interested conflict (but not in any way to which either Nozick or Gauthier would object) by describing it as a competition between diverse conceptions of the good life as it ought to be lived; thus, as Rawls says in his Dewey Lectures, there are different ideas of "the Rational" or "highest-order interests."[12] In any case, there is implicit general agreement with Rawls that *pluralism* is basic to the problem morality is meant to solve.

The solution to this problem is to find "fair terms of cooperation," which Rawls labels as "the Reasonable"; such terms must embody "reciprocity and mutuality." But this as Gauthier tells us means that each must restrict his pursuit of his own self-interest; reciprocity here requires a shift from unconstrained to constrained maximisation.[13] Now there is, as is often remarked, an element of paradox at this point—at least an apparent antinomy: namely that we each to some extent eschew the pursuit of our objectives to better advance those objectives, or to use Rousseauian language, we bind ourselves in order to free ourselves.

Whether or not self-interest and reciprocity can thus peacefully coexist, or whether the former leads to the latter, the outlines of justice are clear. Each is to be granted by all the rest a meaningful guarantee of a kind of moral space (Nozick) over which he is sovereign (Feinberg); under normal circumstances, either strictly and conservatively (no equalization) or broadly and liberally construed (some equalization), "no trespass" or the Principle of Liberty is the rule. There must be here both agreement about what constitutes each person's sovereign territory (whether founded on natural or conventional rights or through Kantian constructivism) and a pooling of individual resources to enforce (conservative) or provide (liberal) territorial integrity. This finds its expression in the creation of effective rights and remedies.

Because these rights and remedies belong to each and every person, morality requires the creation of a classless society (Vlastos) or what we might want to call "a moral peerage" (Wolgast), in which all have the same fundamental rights and privileges.[14] To that extent, in contrast to other views like Plato's, Aristotle's, or for that matter Nietzsche's, morality requires full and equal citizenship for all. Whether each person or group is actually capable in the real life situations of immediately exercising the rights of that citizenship fully is, as I said in Part I, a matter of dispute beween liberals and conservatives; but what is not a matter of dispute is the right to full and equal citizenship.

Now basic to this picture of morality and the "problem" that gives rise to it is the notion of rational self-sufficiency or autonomy which is exercised when confronted with "meaningful" choices.[15] If justice makes us sovereigns over our own moral territories then we must be thought of as at least minimally capable of not unwisely exercising that sovereignty. To conceive morality as a kind of bargain between those with diverse and conflicting aims, it is essential to think of the bargainers as at least potentially capable of exercising a meaningful choice amongst the alternatives before them on the basis of their highest interests (as they conceive them). That is, at least three conditions must be met for rational self-sufficiency or autonomy: (i) individualism must have a rational (consistent) and realistic set of objectives or preferences; (ii) they must be capable of assessing and revising that set in the face of changed conditions in themselves and in the world; and (iii) given appropriate external circumstances they must be capable of acting on that set of preferences.[16] If these three conditions are met, then the basic requirements of morality are plausible, *viz.*, that each is to respect the autonomy of all others. Otherwise, justice would appear to be *un jeu de folie*.

III. Autonomy and Atomism

I now want to return to our current ideological malaise—our deep disenchantment with both liberalism and conservatism. I think there is a very good reason for this disenchantment, *viz.*, that the picture of rational self-sufficiency or autonomy common to both views so inadequately represents the human moral situation that both liberalism and conservatism are self-frustrating enterprises.

This can be partially illustrated by the conservative complaint that the equalization process favoured by liberals seems inherently endless—if education doesn't equalize then try social workers and welfare, if that doesn't work then job creation, and so on. Yet liberals have a strong point when they accuse conservatives of myopically ignoring the facts of racial, social, and economic inequality of the deepest sorts. Conservative nostrums of self-help here seem lamentably out of touch and even gratuitously insulting.

Neither liberals nor conservatives can realise their ideals of morality because each would destroy (though in different ways—liberals through over-watering and conservatives through under-watering) the social institutions and values on which they rest. For we are not born rationally self-sufficient; we only become so over time and in relationships that cannot be that of equal to equal and certainly not that of rationality self-sufficient to rationally self-sufficient. And this is true not only of the more individualized relationship of child to parents, but also of the more social-ized relationship of individuals to their culture, heritage, and language. In neither case can we picture the relationships involved as the transfer of high or low quality goods to those who are or should be treated as equals. We are not dealing here with individuals who have fixed and determinate interests on the basis of which they can judge and determine the acceptability of the merchandise we as parents, educators, and elders in society offer them. We are involved in a process of shaping or creating (within broad and ill-defined limits) would-be autonomous agents.[17] It does not help to insist that what these consumers need is more equalization to set them on a par with us. The liberal insistence on autonomy for all parodies itself here (e.g., in the assertion of equal rights for children and the ideal of a sexless society) just as the conservative portrayal of the self-made individual as the examplar of liberty and initiative parodies itself. And what is true here of the relationship of the older to the younger is also true in many circumstances of the interrelations of adults, e.g., in doctor-patient, lawyer-client, teacher-student. In these and a multitude of informal relationships rational self-sufficiency is obtained (if at all) as a kind of group or relational activity and not as the achievement of solitary individuals. If this is so, then we should picture morality as designed to solve a different problem than that considered above in Part II, *viz.* as I have suggested elsewhere the problem of achieving through a variety of public and private means the collective interest.[18]

Consider, for example, the demand native people (or for that matter francophones or anglophones) make for control over the education of their children. We would seriously misunderstand such demands if we construed them simply as demands for the recognition of *individual* rights (*viz.*, the right of parents to determine the nature and extent of their children's education). Rather we have to see here a call for *community* rights—the right of a distinct people to preserve their own community without the interference of the majority and, perhaps, even with their assistance. That is, the demand is for a collective (negative and positive) right to the re-creation of the community in the next generation. And here we have to face squarely the possibility that the sorts of communities that natives want do not fit either the conservative or liberal models simply because they do not share a commitment to the central common value of both models, *viz.*, atomistic autonomy. They may not then accept our view that education prepares the child to compete on a more or less equal footing for a share in the world's scarce resources. It is then myopic of us (the white majority) to view natives either conservatively as ne'er-do-wells who have failed to optimise their opportunities and so deserve their lowly status in Canadian society or liberally as poor unfortunates who stand in need of more of our education and know-how so that they can then compete on an equal basis with us. What we fail to see then is an alternative conception of the relationship between the individual and the community—one that takes autonomy as more of a community possession than an individual one.

This should lead us to a more general point—one that can be applied to native and non-native communities alike. In an important sense, morality is common, not individual, property; for having an effective morality involves having shared attitudes and practices at the most fundamental levels. To treat morality as a bargain between the unequalized or the equalized (cf. Section II) misses the way in which morality is common property and in which it involves an effort across generations to maintain certain valued ways of living. As my colleague Jan Narveson blithely (but revealingly) admits in his article, individualists don't have any intrinsic concern for future generations; their concern is simply with those people who already exist (and whomever, if anyone, they may care about). The perspective I am urging is clearly at odds with that dismissal of the future. In fact it seems to me that one of the major tests to which we should submit any proposed morality is whether or not it can ensure its own continuance or is in the long term self-destructive. And here I would suggest, though I have not the space to argue, that the morality espoused by Narveson simply fails that test. As should be patently obvious, I am not much more sanguine about the real target of Narveson's article, *viz.*, the liberal alternative. For I do not think the major issue is equalization. To think it is requires a belief that individual autonomy is the overriding moral value. And that I have rejected by insisting on the importance of the community in shaping and securing individual interests.

Now I do not want to deny that the problem of morality discussed in Narveson's paper and above in Section II is not a real problem for us and even for the sort of society at which I have just hinted (in terms of avoiding exploitation and stupidity). My claim is that it is not our only major moral problem. If we act as if it is our only moral problem of any size, then I suggest we have only ourselves to blame for perpetuating our current malaise: for we will create through our narrowness of vision subsequent generations that think that this is the sole problem of any size. An inaccurate and misleading picture of our situation is not less powerful because of its misrepresentation, rather it threatens to perpetuate its hold on us by creating the very conditions it was meant to remedy.

And finally I would suggest that in treating the problem of the accommodation of the interests of the rationally self-sufficient as the central problem of moral and political philosophy we cut ourselves off from both our own past and from a good deal of the world today—for while most of the world may envy us our wealth they do find our atomistic individualism corrosive and destructive of all they hold dear.[19]

Notes

1. A shorter version of this paper appears under the title "Justice in Hard Times" in *Social Justice* which is a volume in the *Bowling Green Studies in Applied Philosophy* scheduled to appear in 1982. The impetus and opportunity for this revised and extended version of my paper came from Wes Cragg, for whose suggestions and hospitality I am most grateful.
2. In talking about "liberals" and "conservatives," I am not exclusively referring to members of the Liberal Party or the Progressive Conservative Party. In fact, as will be seen subsequently, I am not even limiting my concerns to exclusively political issues.
3. See *Mill's Ethical Writings* (New York, 1965) edited by J.B. Schneewind, especially the Introduction, pp. 13–17.
4. Here I am not, of course, referring to American Pragmatists (Peirce, James, Dewey, and so on).
5. See Ronald Dworkin's "Liberalism" in *Public and Private Morality*, Stuart Hampshire, ed. (Cambridge, 1978) pp. 113–143. My main difference with Dworkin is over who are the "conservatives." Dworkin describes Burkean conservatives (e.g., Canadian Red Tories) when he argues that conservatives base justice on a theory of "the good for man or good of life because treating a person as an equal means treating him as a good or truly wise person should wish to be treated" (p. 127). This does not really capture conservatives of the Reagan-Thatcher type or contemporary libertarians. So I am concerned with the quarrel between welfare-liberals and contemporary conservatives who would both satisfy Dworkin's description of liberalism as not espousing in their theories of justice particular views of the good life.
6. Henry Sidgwick, *The Elements of Politics* (London, 1902), p. 42. The classic expression of liberalism is John Stuart Mill's *On Liberty* (1859) in particular the one very simple principle, *viz.*, "that the sole end for which mankind are warranted, either individually, or collectively, in interfering with the liberty of action of any of their number, is self-protection."
7. Cf. Robert Nozick, *Anarchy, State, and Utopia* (New York, 1974), pp. 290-292.
8. Nozick, pp. 32–33 and 44–45.
9. Cf. David Richards, *The Moral Criticism of the Law* (Encino, 1977), p. 71.
10. The same split can be discerned concerning "hate literature."
11. See Sections 5 and 6 of my colleague Jan Narveson's paper, "Moral Philosophy—What It Is and Why It Matters!" which appears earlier in this volume.
12. John Rawls, *J. Phil.* 77, September 1980, p. 528.
13. "Reason and Maximisation," *The Canadian Journal of Philosophy* IV, March 1975, pp. 411–435.
14. Gregory Vlastos, "Justice and Equality," in *Social Justice*, Richard Brandt ed. (Englewood Cliffs, 1962), pp. 31–72. Elizabeth Wolgast, *Equality and the Rights of Women* (Ithaca, 1980), Ch. 3. It should be noted that Vlastos and Wolgast are in radical disagreement over the nature of "equality."
15. Feinberg in *Social Philosophy* (Englewood Cliffs, 1973), pp. 88–94, speaks of respect for persons as a "groundless attitude" like love, citing Vlastos as well. This seems to me to distort the attitudes in both love and respect for persons. One cannot love or respect a cipher—these are intentional attitudes which need characteristic objects. In the case of the latter (the subject of this paper) I have suggested it is autonomy as rational self-sufficiency. Feinberg is right in worrying that since individuals vary in their rationality it

may be impossible to insist that equal respect is a human right. I have tried to remedy this on behalf of autonomy's defenders by thinking of autonomy like citizenship—if one meets the appropriate qualification one is a citizen—no more or no less than one's compatriots. I am not however sympathetic to basing morality on autonomy in this or any other form—see my paper, "Autarchy and Interest," *The Australasian Journal of Philosophy 56*, August, 1978, pp. 109–125.

16. For condition (ii) see Charles Taylor's insightful paper, "Responsibility for Self," in A.O. Rorty, *The Identities of Persons* (Berkeley, 1976), pp. 281–299. For the general conditions of autonomy see Stanley Benn's "Freedom, Autonomy, and the Concept of a Person," in *The Proceedings of the Aristotelean Society 76*, 1975–1976 pp. 109–130. I have explicitly criticised Benn's position in the above-mentioned (n. 15) "Autarchy and Interest." A recent and extremely significant discussion of rationality is contained in Richard Brandt's *A Theory of the Good and the Right* (Oxford, 1979), on which I have commented in a critical notice in *Canadian Journal of Philosophy 12*, 2 (June 1982), pp. 375–390.

    James Fishkin (Yale) and Larry Thomas (North Carolina) pointed out that my original formulation of (iii) was too strong for it implied that autonomy required the availability of one's most preferable options, e.g., for foie gras accompanied by fine wine. My only aim in (iii) was to require the absence of internal obstacles like weakness of will, phobias, or compulsions, so that if the subject is presented with the possibility of securing what he most wants at little or no cost, he seizes the opportunity. Thus, if he is in Les Eyzies in June and it is time for dinner, he will not pass up the opportunity of ordering fresh foie gras and Château Panisseau at the Centenaire.

17. Nozick's *non*-treatment of either the parent-child relation or the individual-culture relation is most revealing here. For the latter he simply treats culture and language as a kind of free good (just as air and water used to be described in classical economics). On the former he is surprisingly silent. I say "surprisingly" for like his exemplar Locke he maintains a theory in which both the following propositions are held to be true: (i) that what one makes with one's own materials is one's property; and (ii) each person is sole proprietor of himself. See also Wolgast, p. 145. An interesting alternative approach here would be to treat culture and the like as a kind of public good which à la Gauthier requires enforced contributions. Rawls seems to do this in talking about education as the development of autonomy. But this, I think, raises serious difficulties. For example, why would selfish individuals want to create autonomous rivals? And, beyond that, I seriously wonder if the paradigm of justice as a contract amongst equals can be successfully maintained, for there is a clear lack of voluntariness on the part of one of the major parties as well as a lack of clear interests—a point which I have tried to make in this section of the paper.

18. See above note 15.

19. This paper clearly owes a great deal to David Gauthier's extraordinary work; his paper, "The Social Contract as Ideology," *Philosophy and Public Affairs*, Winter 1977, pp. 130–164 makes a parallel point in its concluding sections. However, the main impetus for this particular paper comes from Elizabeth Wolgast, both from conversations with her and her most recent book (see n. 14).

Suggestions for Further Reading

There are two ways to proceed in your exploration of the ideas introduced in this chapter. The first is to go directly to the authors referred to in the notes appended to each of the contributions. An alternative approach is to look for a guide which will provide an overview of the field of moral philosophy as well as suggestions for approaching primary sources. It is with this latter approach in mind that I recommend three short books which, in my experience, have proven helpful.

- D.D. Raphael, *Moral Philosophy* (Oxford: Oxford University Press, 1981). This book is intended as an introduction to the subject and requires no previous knowledge of philosophy. Written expressly for beginners, it makes a point of showing the connections between abstract ethics and practical problems, in law and government and in the social sciences generally.
- Paul W. Taylor, *Principles of Ethics: An Introduction* (Belmont, California: Wadsworth Publishing Company, 1975). The chief merit of this book as an introduction to moral philosophy is that it discusses some of the most important perennial topics encountered in moral philosophy, topics such as relativism, egoism, and freedom of the will. The book also includes lists of suggested readings which might prove helpful.
- Mary Warnock, *Ethics since 1900* (Oxford: Oxford University Press, 1978). This, too, is an introductory text. However, its approach is quite different from that used by Taylor. Warnock surveys the development of modern moral philosophy by introducing some of the major moral philosophers and philosophical schools of the twentieth century.

Notes on the Contributors

Warren Allmand is a member of parliament from Quebec, a former member of the Cabinet, and a long-time opponent of capital punishment.

Robert J. Art is the chairman of the Department of Politics at Brandeis University.

Margaret Atwood is a well-known Canadian novelist, poet, and essayist.

Hugo Adam Bedau has contributed to a number of anthologies. He edited *The Death Penalty in America* (1967), co-edited *Capital Punishment in the United States* (1976), and is the author of *The Courts, the Constitution and Capital Punishment* (1977). He teaches philosophy at Tufts University in Medford, Massachusetts.

Rodger Beehler teaches philosophy at the University of Victoria. He is the author of *Moral Life* (1978) and his essays have appeared in legal, political, and philosophical journals.

Justice Thomas Berger led the Mackenzie Valley Pipeline Inquiry. He is author of *Fragile Freedoms* (1982), was a justice of the Supreme Court of British Columbia, and now practises law in Vancouver.

Walter Berns is the author of *For Capital Punishment* (1974) and a resident scholar with the American Enterprise Institute for Public Policy Research.

Neil Boyd teaches criminology at Simon Fraser University.

Andrew Brook was a member of the Atomic Energy Control Board Advisory Panel on the Long-Term Management of Uranium Mine Tailings. He teaches philosophy at Carleton University.

Alan Brudner teaches law at the University of Toronto.

Conrad G. Brunk teaches philosophy at the University of Waterloo, where he is also a member of the Peace and Conflict Studies Department.

C.H. Cahn teaches psychiatry at McGill University and is Director of Professional Services at the Douglas Hospital Centre, Verdun, Quebec.

Lorenne Clark is an active member of the feminist movement. A former member of the University of Toronto philosophy department, she now practises law in Digby, Nova Scotia.

L.W. Conolly is the chairman of the Department of Drama at the University of Guelph.

David Copp teaches philosophy at the University of Illinois in Chicago. He is a co-editor of *Pornography and Censorship* (1983).

Grant Cosby teaches philosophy at the University of Manitoba.

Mr. Justice Dickson practised and taught law in Manitoba before his appointment to the bench. He is currently Chief Justice of the Supreme Court of Canada.

Ezzat A. Fattah teaches criminology at Simon Fraser University. His research on the deterrent effect of capital punishment was presented by the Solicitor-General of Canada as background information for those participating in the parliamentary debates on the abolition of capital punishment in the 1970s.

Joseph Fletcher is the author of many books and articles in applied ethics, including *Situational Ethics* (1966).

Northrop Frye is a well-known Canadian academic and the author of numerous books and articles. Many of his essays on Canadian culture have been collected in *Divisions on a Ground* (1982).

Raymond D. Gastil works with the Batelle Seattle Research Centre in Seattle, Washington.

David Gauthier, formerly a member of the faculty of the University of Toronto, currently teaches philosophy at the University of Pittsburgh. He is the author of *Practical Reasoning* (1963), *Morality and Rational Self-Interest* (1970), and *Morals by Agreement* (1986), and has written on a variety of problems in the field of moral philosophy.

Ian Gentles teaches history at Glendon College (York University). He is the editor of *The Right to Birth* (1976), as well as a book on euthanasia.

Robert E. Goodin is a member of the Department of Government at the University of Essex.

Trudy Govier, formerly of Trent University, now resides in Calgary. She has contributed essays to a number of journals and anthologies.

George Grant is the author of *Lament for a Nation*, *Philosophy in a Mass Age*, and *Technology and Empire*. He currently teaches philosophy and religion at Dalhousie University.

Sheila Grant is an active member of the "Right to Life" movement.

Colin P. Harrison practises medicine in Vancouver.

Howard H. Hiatt, Dean of the Harvard University School of Public Health, is a scientist and a physician.

Edward W. Keyserlingk is the author of *Sanctity of Life and Quality of Life*, a study published by the Law Reform Commission of Canada. He is a consultant with the Law Reform Commission of Canada, a member of the McGill Centre for Health Sciences, Ethics and Law, and teaches in the faculty of medicine at McGill University.

Bora Laskin, now deceased, is a former law professor, member of the Ontario Court of Appeal, and Chief Justice of the Supreme Court of Canada.

Edwin Levy teaches philosophy at the University of British Columbia and is coordinator of Science, Technology and Society Studies.

Judge Spiro Loukidelis is a judge of the County and District Court and resides in Sudbury.

Michael McDonald teaches philosophy at the University of Waterloo and is the editor of *Dialogue*, which is published by the Canadian Philosophical Association.

Mary Midgley, formerly a member of the University of Newcastle (England), is now retired. Her latest book is entitled *Wickedness: A Philosophical Essay* (1984).

Jan Narveson is the author of *Morality and Utility* (1967). His more recent work defends a contractarian perspective on moral issues. He teaches philosophy at the University of Waterloo.

Roger Nash is a member of the Laurentian University Department of Philosophy. His poetry has been published in many periodicals and has won a number of awards.

Kai Nielsen has written extensively in the field of social and political philosophy. He is an editor of *The Canadian Journal of Philosophy* and teaches philosophy at the University of Calgary.

Patrick Nowell-Smith has contributed to a number of anthologies and journals on topics related to ethics. Author of a Pelican book entitled *Ethics*, and a former member of the Philosophy Department at York University, he is now retired and living in Wales.

Terence Penelhum, F.R.S.C., teaches in the Department of Religious Studies at the University of Calgary. He is the author of a number of books, the latest of which is *God and Skepticism* (1983).

Fred Plain is a policy analyst on intergovernmental relations for the Nishnawbe-Aski Nation. He has served as President of the Union of Ontario Indians and as Chief of the Chippewas of Sarnia.

Madam Justice Proudfoot practised law in British Columbia prior to her appointment to the bench. She is currently a Justice of the Supreme Court of British Columbia.

Gene Sharp teaches political science and sociology at Southeastern Massachusetts University. He is the author of several books, including *The Politics of Non-Violent Action* (1973) and *Social Power and Political Freedom* (1980).

Peter Singer teaches philosophy at La Trobe University, Victoria, Australia. He is the author of *Animal Liberation* (1975) and *Practical Ethics* (1980).

Jack T. Stevenson teaches philosophy at the University of Toronto.

L.W. Sumner is the author of *Abortion and Moral Theory* (1981) and teaches philosophy at the University of Toronto.

Béla Szabados teaches philosophy at the University of Regina.

Michael Tooley teaches philosophy in Australia and is the author of *Abortion and Infanticide* (1983).

Pierre Elliott Trudeau is a former Prime Minister of Canada, and currently practises law in Montreal.

James Woodward is a member of the faculty of the California Institute of Technology (Division of Humanities and Social Sciences).